CHIANG KAI SHEK

CHIANG KAI SHEK

China's Generalissimo and the Nation He Lost

JONATHAN FENBY

CARROLL & GRAF PUBLISHERS
NEW YORK

CHIANG KAI-SHEK
CHINA'S GENERALISSIMO AND THE NATION HE LOST

Carroll & Graf Publishers
An Imprint of Avalon Publishing Group Inc.
245 West 17th Street
New York, NY 10011

Copyright © 2003 by Jonathan Fenby

First Carroll & Graf edition 2004

Library of Congress Cataloging-in-Publication Data is available.

ISBN: 0-7867-1318-6

Printed in the United States of America
Distributed by Publishers Group West

To Sara and Alexander,
with love

CONTENTS

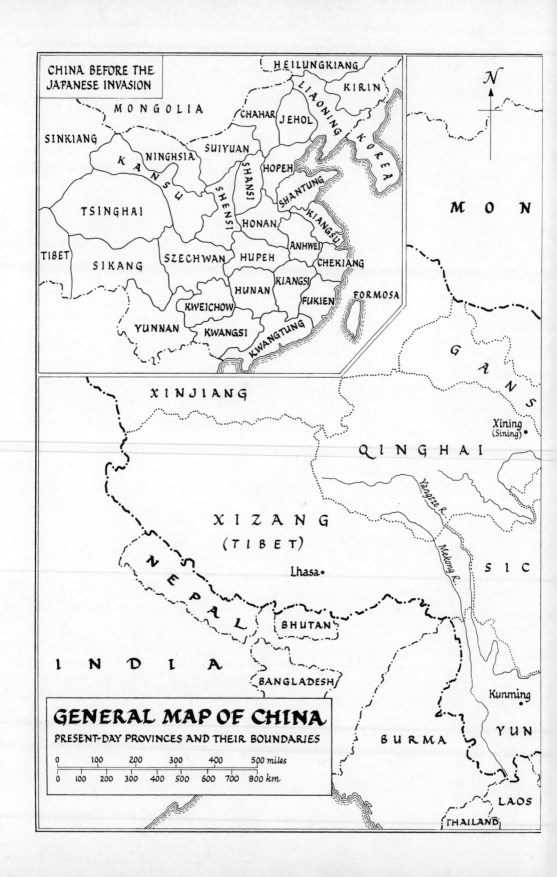

CHINA BEFORE THE
JAPANESE INVASION

MONGOLIA

HEILUNGKIANG

KIRIN

SINKIANG

CHAHAR

JEHOL

LIAONING

KOREA

NINGHSIA

SUIYUAN

HOPEH

KANSU

SHANSI

SHANTUNG

TSINGHAI

SHENSI

HONAN

KIANGSU

TIBET

SZECHWAN

HUPEH

ANHWEI

CHEKIANG

SIKANG

KIANGSI

HUNAN

FUKIEN

FORMOSA

KWEICHOW

KWANGSI

KWANGTUNG

YUNNAN

N

M O N

XINJIANG

G A N S

Xining
(Sining) •

QINGHAI

Yangtze R.

X I Z A N G
(T I B E T)

Mekong R.

S I C

Lhasa •

N E P A L

BHUTAN

I N D I A

BANGLADESH

Kunming
•

GENERAL MAP OF CHINA
PRESENT-DAY PROVINCES AND THEIR BOUNDARIES

BURMA

YUN

0   100   200   300   400   500 miles

0   100   200   300   400   500   600   700   800 km

LAOS

THAILAND

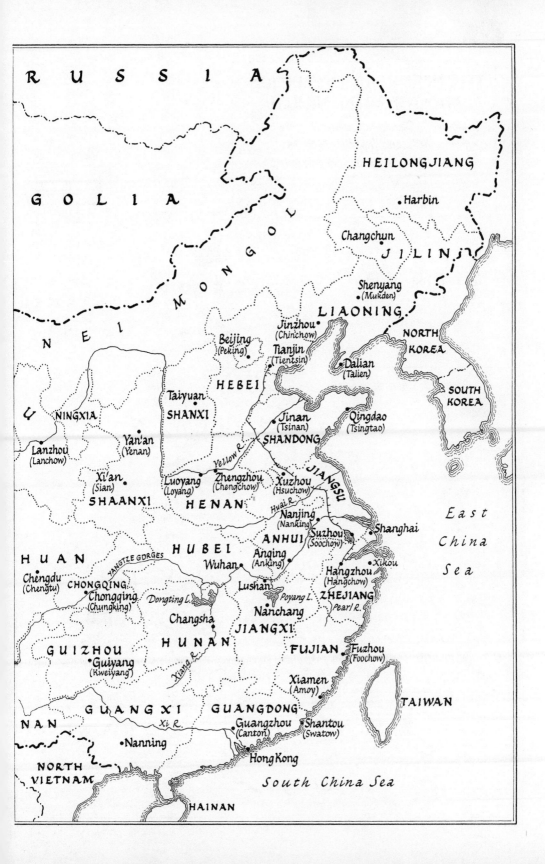

THE NORTHERN EXPEDITION
AND THE LONG MARCH

→ The Northern Expedition 1926–28
←--- The Long March 1934–35
Province boundaries are those of the present day

0   100   200   300 miles
0   100   200   300   400   500 km

QINGHAI

GANSU

SHAANXI

Lanchow
(Lanzhou)

Bao'an
Oct.1935

Yenan
(Yan'an)

Lazikou
Pass

Sian
(Xi'an)

Grassland

SICHUAN

Bailong R.

Great Snowy
Mountains

Chengtu
(Chengdu)

Luting
(Luding)

Anshunchang

Chungking
(Chongqing)

Yangtze

Sichang
(Xichang)

Tsunyi
(Zunyi)

GUIZHOU

Kweiyang
(Guiyang)

Liping
(Defeng)

Kunming

YUNNAN

GUANGXI

Si R.

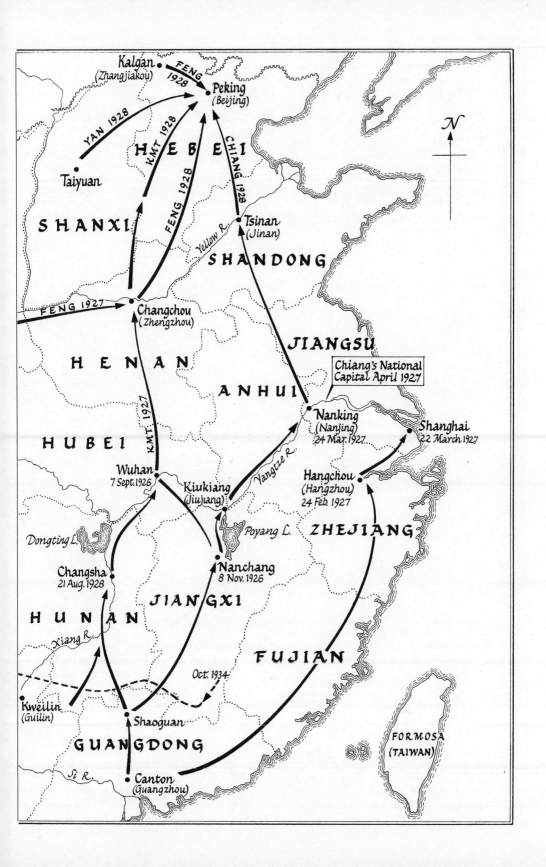

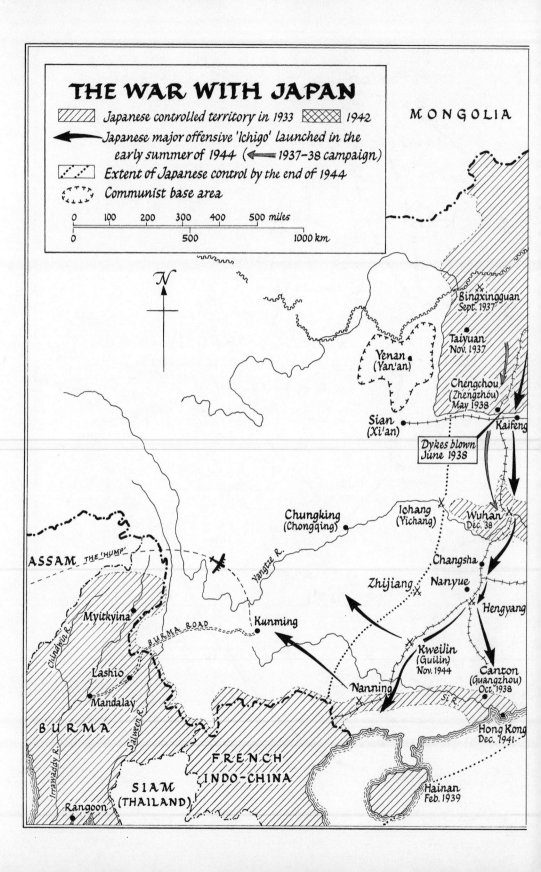

THE WAR WITH JAPAN

▨ Japanese controlled territory in 1933 ▥ 1942

← Japanese major offensive 'Ichigo' launched in the early summer of 1944 (← 1937–38 campaign)

⋯ Extent of Japanese control by the end of 1944

⊙ Communist base area

```
0    100   200   300   400   500 miles
0              500            1000 km
```

N

MONGOLIA

Bingxingguan
Sept. 1937

Taiyuan
Nov. 1937

Yenan
(Yan'an)

Chéngchou
(Zhengzhou)
May 1938

Kaifeng

Sian
(Xi'an)

Dykes blown
June 1938

Chungking
(Chongqing)

Ichang
(Yichang)

Wuhan
Dec. 38

ASSAM   THE 'HUMP'

Yangtze R.

Changsha

Zhijiang   Nanyue

Hengyang

Myitkyina

Kunming

BURMA ROAD

Kweilin
(Guilin)
Nov. 1944

Canton
(Guangzhou)
Oct. 1938

Lashio

Mandalay

Chindwin R.

Salween R.

Nanning

Si R.

BURMA

Hong Kong
Dec. 1941

Irrawaddy R.

FRENCH
INDO-CHINA

SIAM
(THAILAND)

Hainan
Feb. 1939

Rangoon

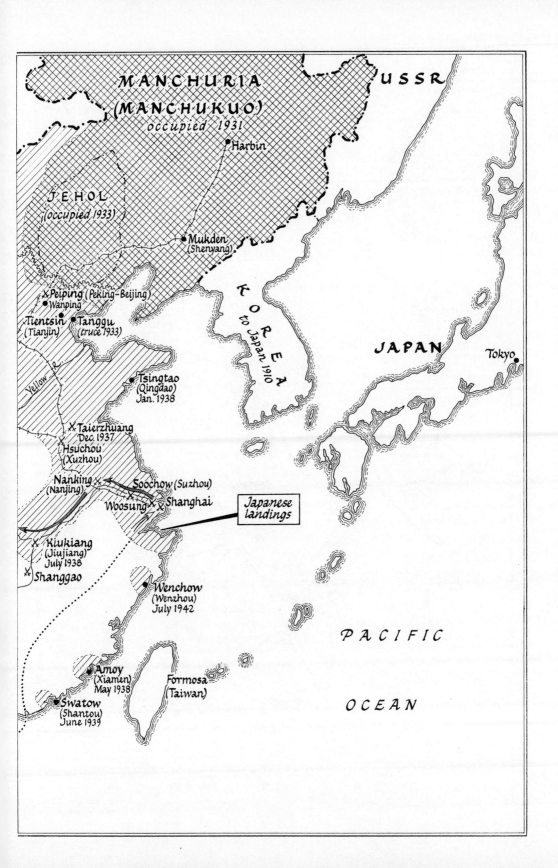

MANCHURIA
(MANCHUKUO)
occupied 1931

● Harbin

JEHOL
(occupied 1933)

USSR

● Mukden
(Shenyang)

K
O
R
E
A
to Japan 1910

JAPAN

Tokyo ●

X Peiping (Peking–Beijing)
● Wanping

Tientsin
(Tianjin)

● Tanggu
(truce 1933)

Yellow

● Tsingtao
(Qingdao)
Jan. 1938

X Taierzhuang
Dec. 1937
X Hsuchou
(Xuzhou)

Nanking
(Nanjing)

X Soochow (Suzhou)
X Shanghai
Woosung X

Japanese
landings

X Kiukiang
(Jiujiang)
July 1938
X Shanggao

● Wenchow
(Wenzhou)
July 1942

PACIFIC

● Amoy
(Xiamen)
May 1938

Formosa
(Taiwan)

OCEAN

● Swatow
(Shantou)
June 1939

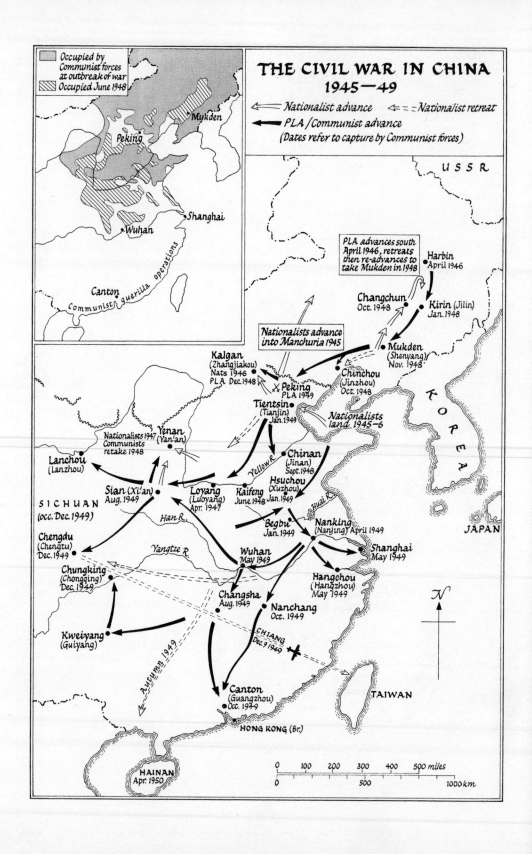

THE CIVIL WAR IN CHINA 1945—49

Occupied by Communist forces at outbreak of war

Occupied June 1948

⟵ Nationalist advance   ⇠ = Nationalist retreat

⬅ PLA/Communist advance

(Dates refer to capture by Communist forces)

Mukden

Peking

Shanghai

Wuhan

Canton

Communist guerilla operations

USSR

PLA advances south April 1946, retreats then re-advances to take Mukden in 1948

Harbin April 1946

Changchun Oct. 1948

Kirin (Jilin) Jan. 1948

Nationalists advance into Manchuria 1945

Mukden (Shenyang) Nov. 1948

Kalgan (Zhangjiakou) Nats 1946 PLA Dec.1948

Chinchou (Jinzhou) Oct. 1948

X Peking PLA 1949

Tientsin (Tianjin) Jan. 1949

Nationalists land 1945-6

KOREA

Yenan (Yan'an)

Nationalists 1947 Communists retake 1948

Chinan (Jinan) Sept. 1948

Yellow R.

Lanchou (Lanzhou)

Sian (Xi'an) Aug. 1949

Loyang (Luoyang) Apr. 1947

Kaifeng June 1948

Hsuchou (Xuzhou) Jan. 1949

SICHUAN (occ. Dec. 1949)

Han R.

Begbu Jan. 1949

Nanking (Nanjing) April 1949

Huai R.

JAPAN

Chengdu (Chengtu) Dec. 1949

Yangtze R.

Wuhan May 1949

Shanghai May 1949

Chungking (Chongqing) Dec. 1949

Hangchow (Hangzhou) May 1949

Changsha Aug. 1949

Nanchang Oct. 1949

N

Kweiyang (Guiyang)

CHIANG Dec. 9 1949

Autumn 1949

Canton (Guangzhou) Oct. 1949

TAIWAN

HONG KONG (Br.)

HAINAN Apr. 1950

0 100 200 300 400 500 miles

0   500   1000 km

ACKNOWLEDGEMENTS

This is the first full biography of Chiang Kai-shek for almost three decades. It would not have been possible without drawing on extensive research into the period up to 1949 by scholars in mainland China and Taiwan, Hong Kong, the United States, Britain, Australia, France and elsewhere. I am grateful to all those whose work is referred to in the text or appears in the source notes. I also benefited from conversations with Lu Fan-Shang, Chen Yung-Fa and Yu Mii-ling of the Academia Sinica, Professor Jiang Yung-chiang, and officials at the Government Information Office and Kuomintang Party headquarters in Taipei where K. Y. Kuo was extremely helpful, both in arranging meetings and in providing his four-hour video recordings of the Young Marshal. Also in Taiwan, Jason Blatt gave ever-cheerful help; Windsor Chen indicated contacts; and Parris Chang spurred ideas on Chiang's last year on the mainland. I am indebted to the librarians at the Academia Sinica, *Taipei Times* and the *China Post*. Since this book may not be to the taste of some in Taiwan, I would like to stress that the responsibility for what I have written is mine alone. In Hong Kong and mainland China, I am particularly grateful to Willy Lo Lap-Lam, Mark O'Neill, Jasper and Antoaneta Becker, John Gittings and Matthew Miller, to Michelle Wan in Shanghai, and for the assistance of guides on visits to key places in Chiang's life.

I owe a particular debt to two people who read the manuscript in its final stages; Keith Stevens has been a constant fund of useful suggestions and provided great linguistic help while Rana Mitter was a steady source of support and assistance, in particular in coming up with significant comments that improved the manuscript in its final stage. In Cambridge, Hans van de Ven was kind enough to let me see the manuscript of his book on the Chinese Army as well as advice on various points. Frederic Wakeman's 2003 biography of the Nationalist police chief, Dai Li, provided insights into that powerful figure. In Oxford, I had illuminating conversations with Stephen Tsang at St Anthony's and with Graham Hutchings, who also provided the lead to photographs from the Nanking archive. I also benefited from the help of Frank Dikötter and Gary Tiedemann at the School of Oriental and African Studies, and of conversations with Shu Yun, Eddie U, Ann and Don Morrison, and Jean-Philippe Béja. The late Doon Campbell was good enough to provide papers from his time as Reuters correspondent in Chungking.

The library of the SOAS in London was an invaluable resource, and I would like to thank the staff for their help, in particular the Chinese librarian, Mrs Small. As well as academic works, SOAS proved to be a trove of books and diaries by contemporary visitors to China, many of which do not appear to have been used before, and for the files of the *North China Herald* which I read from 1911. I have also drawn on reporting by correspondents in China whose work has been little used by previous writers on the period. For their descriptive scope and detail, I am in debt to Hallett Abend, Jack Belden, James Bertram, W. H. Donald, Rhodes Farmer, Peter Fleming, Henry Misselwitz, Edgar Mowrer, Robert Payne, Arthur Ransome, Harold Timperley, Seymour Topping, Teddy White, and anonymous stringers for Reuters (plus Christopher Isherwood's wonderful account of his journey to war with W. H. Auden). In Paris, the staff of the Foreign Ministry Archives helped to identify documents from the French Concession in Shanghai. In Los Angeles, Kaustuv Basu and Stella Lopez at the Annenberg School of Communications tracked down and supplied Gardner Cowles's privately printed memoir used in Chapter 22.

Andrew Gordon not only initially commissioned the book, but also understood that Chiang's story deserved to be treated in full. His editing suggestions moved the narrative through some roadblocks, and sharpened the final draft. I owe my usual debt to Christopher Sinclair-Stevenson both for his belief in a new biography of Chiang, and his encouragement along the way. Martin Bryant saw the book into production with efficiency and eminent good cheer. Gillian Kemp provided sharp-eyed copy-editing. Reg Piggott turned complex campaigns into clear map lines. Edwina Barstow produced an impressive array of photographs. Andrew Armitage provided the expertly constructed index while Caroline Ransford gave the book a final tooth-combing. Sara Fenby contributed invaluable technical assistance, and Alexander Fenby helped on various travels. Hamish McRae offered insight; Jack Altman provided illuminating leads on Japan; and David Tang was generous with the loan of volumes from the China Club in Hong Kong. For hospitality during the writing and for acting as sounding boards as I worked my way through the complexities of the Chiang saga, I am indebted to Peter Graham, Ginette Vincendeau and Simon Caulkin, Sally and John Tagholm, Lisa and André Villeneuve, Maša and Michael Unsworth, Ann and David Cripps, and Rosamund and Etienne Reuter.

My greatest debt, as always, is to my wife, Renée, both in the research, and with the innumerable improvements she brought as first and last reader. She also put up with my growing obsession with my subject, and the dislocations that a project like this inevitably involve in everyday life. Whatever this book is worth, it would have been much less without her.

AUTHOR'S NOTE

Transliteration

Transliterating from Chinese into English is a minefield in dealing with events before 1958, when the Pinyin system of transliteration was introduced to replace the Wade-Giles system. Some names are so familiar to readers outside China in the old transliteration that it would be confusing to use their Pinyin forms from Mandarin. The subject of this book, for instance, is generally known from the Cantonese version of his name as Chiang Kai-shek (according to Wade-Giles) rather than Jiang Jieshi (Mandarin). Where I judge that the general reader would be most familiar with the Wade-Giles form, I have retained it – among these are Sun Yat-sen (Sun Zhongshan in Pinyin) and the Soong (Song) family. Most place names have been given their Pinyin form, with Wade-Giles in a footnote, but I have retained the old form where it is likely to be more familiar, as for Canton (Guangzhou), Yangtze (Yangtzi), Nanking (Nanjing), Chungking (Chongqing), and Hong Kong (Xianggang). The older or newer forms are given in footnotes at first reference.

Currency

The dollar sign in the text stands for Chinese dollars except where otherwise stated. The official conversion rate to sterling and US dollars varied during the period covered by this book – and was affected in different localities by prevailing local rates. From 1937, the real rate was far below the official level. The rates given by the *North China Herald* in Shanghai were as follows in the middle of the years indicated:

	£1	US $1
1926	$9	$2
1930	$17.20	$3.40
1935	$13	$2.70
1937	$16.40	$3.40
Dec. 1940	$71	$18

Subsequent changes in parity and the vast disparity with real market rates are given in the text from 1941 on.

DRAMATIS PERSONAE

Bai Chongxi   Muslim general in Guangxi clique. Leading strategist. Commander in Shanghai in spring 1927, and in war with Japanese before fighting final battles against PLA in central China in 1949.

Borodin (Mikhail Markovich Grunzeberg)   Soviet adviser to Kuomintang. Instituted its Leninist structure and propagated united front. Leading figure in left-wing regime in Wuhan. Expelled from China in 1927. Died in Siberian camp.

Chen brothers: Lifu and Guofu   Chiang lieutenants and leaders of the CC Clique in the Kuomintang. Nephews of Chiang's early mentor, Chen Qimei. Extreme conservative anti-Communists. Lifu became Minister of Education, and tried to impose conformity on universities.

Chen Cheng   Nationalist general whom Chiang designated as his chosen successor. Commander of Y Force in Yunnan during the Second World War. As War Minister, tried to introduce army reforms. Briefly commander in Manchuria against Communists.

Chen Jieru (Jennie)   Chiang's second wife. Married in 1921. They lived together in Shanghai and Canton until Chiang dropped her in 1927 for Meiling Soong, sending her to America and denying that she was his wife.

Chen Jiongming (The Hakka General) Reforming early Republican commander in Guangdong. His troops drove out Sun Yat-sen in 1922. Constantly at odds with Chiang who defeated him in the two Eastern Expeditions.

Chen Qimei Shanghai revolutionary and mentor to Chiang. Governor of Shanghai after 1911, but then ousted. Staged unsuccessful risings with Chiang before being assassinated.

Chennault, Claire American advocate of air power. Commanded US pilots flying for Chiang. Feuded bitterly with Stilwell over strategy and supplies. After 1945, ran civilian airline which worked for Nationalists.

Chiang Ching-kuo Chiang's only child. Spent twelve years in Soviet Union, returning to hold provincial posts during war with Japan. In charge of currency reform in Shanghai before fall of Nationalist regime. Became President of Taiwan in 1978.

Dai Li Much feared Nationalist political police chief. Regarded as one of the most powerful figures in the regime. Headed secret operation with Americans, using aid to further repression. Killed in plane crash.

Donald, William Henry Australian adviser to Chiang, Sun Yat-sen and Zhang Xueliang. Helped to negotiate end of Xi'an Incident. Worked closely with Chiang's third wife, saving her life in 1937, but left China after she told him he could not criticise her family for corruption. Returned to die in Shanghai hospital after the war.

Du Yuesheng (Big-Eared Du) Shanghai Green Gang boss. Helped stage anti-Communist purge in 1927. Ran opium monopoly and branched out into business.

Feng Yuxiang (The Christian General) Allied with Nationalists on second stage of Northern Expedition, and then fought major war against Chiang.

Alternately, uneasy ally and adversary of Nanking. Died in fire on Russian ship in 1948.

Fu Zuoyi Former warlord general who commanded Nationalist forces against Communists in north China, but then surrendered Beijing at the beginning of 1949. Subsequently held posts under Communists.

Galen (Blyukher, Vasilii Konstantinovich) Soviet general who played major role in Chiang's early military successes as adviser. Left China after Wuhan regime expelled Russians in 1927. Fought subsequent campaigns against Japanese before being executed on Stalin's orders.

He Yingqin Long-time Minister of War. Chiang associate since mid-1920s. Commander of First Army on Northern Expedition. Proposed bombing Xi'an during 1936 incident. Fervent anti-Communist.

Hu Zongnan (The Eagle of the North-West) Commanded army which blockaded Communist northern area during war with Japan. Then fought last-ditch campaign in Sichuan in 1949.

Hu Hanmin Kuomintang politician and ideologue. Forced out of Canton in 1925. Subsequently allied with Chiang, heading Legislative Yuan in Nanking, but then went into opposition.

Hurley, Patrick American politician sent as presidential envoy to China in 1944, he became Ambassador and tried to arrange an agreement between Chiang and Mao. Subsequently blamed Communist sympathisers in the State Department for his failure.

Kung Hsiang-hsi (H. H.) (Kung Xiangxi in Pinyin) Banker who became Finance Minister and Prime Minister, overseeing printing money that fuelled inflation and undermined the currency. Married to Chiang's sister-in-law, Ailing Soong.

Li Jishen Commanded Fourth Army in Northern Expedition. Associated with southern movements against Chiang. Joined Communist regime after 1949.

Li Zongren   Leader of Guangxi clique who joined the Nationalists for the Northern Expedition, but later led revolts against Chiang. Commanded forces in battle of Taierzhuang in 1938. Vice-President in 1948. Acting President after Chiang's resignation in 1949. Left for New York at end of 1949, returning to mainland China in 1966.

Liao Zhongkai   Kuomintang politician, close associate of Sun Yat-sen. Minister of Finance in Guangdong. Allied with Soviet advisers. Assassinated in suspected rightist plot in 1925.

Lin Biao   Long March veteran who led campaigns against Nationalists in Manchuria and northern China. Later named as Mao's successor but lost his confidence and died in plane crash while fleeing to USSR.

Long Yun   Long-time autonomist Governor of Yunnan at the end of the supply route from India. Served under Communist regime after 1949.

Mao Fu-mei (Mao Fumei in Pinyin)   Chiang's first wife in arranged marriage in his home village. Mother of Chiang Ching-kuo. Chiang left her to live in Shanghai and Canton. Killed in Japanese air raid.

Mao Zedong   Communist leader who worked in united front in Canton in mid-1920s before establishing base area in Jiangxi. Led Long March to Yan'an. Met Chiang in Chungking talks of 1945. Proclaimed People's Republic in October 1949.

Marshall, George   American Chief of Staff in Second World War who later became Secretary of State. Sent to China in 1945 to mediate between Nationalists and Communists. Arranged truces, but mission ended in failure after a year due to intransigence on both sides.

Soong, Ailing (Song Ailing in Pinyin)   Eldest Soong sister. Married H. H. Kung. Known for her love of money, including using her husband's ministerial position for profit.

Soong, Meiling (Song Meiling in Pinyin)   American-educated youngest Soong sister. Married Chiang in 1927. Became intermediary with

Americans including successful 1943 trip to the United States.

Soong, Qingling (Song Qingling in Pinyin)   Middle Soong sister who married Sun Yat-sen. Prominent on the left of the Kuomintang. Became a vice-chairman of the Central People's Government of the People's Republic in 1949, held other posts under the Communist regime and travelled as a goodwill ambassador for Beijing.

Soong Tzu-wen (T. V.) (Song Ziwen in Pinyin)   Eldest Soong brother who became Nationalist Finance Minister before falling out with Chiang, his brother-in-law. Envoy to Washington in Second World War. Returned as Prime Minister in 1944. Banker and businessman, said at one point to be the richest man in the world.

Stilwell, Joseph (Vinegar Joe)   American general sent as Chief of Staff to Chiang in 1942. In constant disagreement with the Generalissimo whom he referred to as 'the Peanut' and a 'rattlesnake'. Proposed extensive reform of Chinese army, and pressed for offensive in Burma. Recalled by Washington in 1944.

Sun Fo   Son of Sun Yat-sen. Held series of senior positions in Nanking despite differences with Chiang.

Sun Yat-sen (Sun Zhongshan in Mandarin Pinyin)   Revolutionary and founder of the Kuomintang. Briefly first President of the Republic. Subsequently leader of Canton regime, dreaming of uniting China and proclaiming Three Principles of Nationalism, Democracy and People's Livelihood. After his death in Peking, he became the patron saint of the Nationalist regime.

Sun Zhuanfang   Eastern warlord controlling Lower Yangtze provinces. Defeated by Nationalists in 1926 and lost Shanghai the following year. Staged several unsuccessful offensives against Nanking.

Tan Yenkai   Former governor of Hunan, led Second Army on Northern Expedition and became important supporter of Chiang as head of Executive Yuan in Nanking.

Tang Enbo Nationalist general who held senior commands in central China in war with Japan. Routed by Japanese in Henan in 1944. Commander in Shanghai at end of civil war.

Tang Shengzhi Hunanese general allied with Nationalists in Northern Expedition. Became leading military figure in Wuhan but defeated by Nanking and fled to Japan before returning to work with Chiang.

Wang Jingwei Kuomintang politician and potential heir to Sun Yat-sen. Forced out of Canton by Chiang in 1926. At different times ally and opponent of Chiang before heading pro-Japanese collaborationist regime in Nanking.

Wedemeyer, Albert American general who succeeded Stilwell as Chiang's Chief of Staff in 1944 and adopted a diplomatic approach to Chiang.

Wu Peifu (The Philosopher General) Yangtze warlord, defeated by Northern Expedition in 1926.

Xue Yue Cantonese general known for his pursuit of the Communists on the Long March and defence of Changsha against the Japanese. Distrusted by Chiang as potential ally of southern rebels.

Yan Xishan (The Model Governor) Shanxi ruler, allied with Nationalists in second phase of Northern Expedition. Skilful politician who changed sides to maintain his autonomy.

Yuan Shikai Imperial general who reached accommodation with the revolutionaries after 1911. When Sun Yat-sen stepped down, he became President and briefly proclaimed himself Emperor.

Zhang Jingjiang (Zhang Renjie) (Curio Chang) Zhejiang native and Shanghai businessman who supported Sun Yat-sen and was Chiang's early patron. On right of Kuomintang, he became Governor of Zhejiang and Director of National Reconstruction Commission.

Zhang Xueliang (The Young Marshal) Inherited control of Manchuria from his father. Allied with Chiang, and commanded army in north China. Lost Manchuria with the Mukden Incident of 1931. Sacked by Chiang, but then returned as senior military figure. Kidnapped Chiang at Xi'an in 1936. Sentenced to house arrest which lasted for fifty-five years.

Zhang Zonchang (The Dogmeat General) Shandong warlord who opposed Nationalists in Lower Yangtze in 1927 and later threatened Nanking before being forced to flee.

Zhang Zuolin (The Old Marshal) Manchurian warlord involved in major civil wars in mid-1920s. Associated with the Japanese, but assassinated by them as his troops were handing over Peking to the Nationalists.

Zhou Enlai Political officer at Whampoa and then Communist organiser in Shanghai who allied himself with Mao on Long March. Helped to reach solution to Xi'an Incident. Main Communist negotiator with Nationalists.

PROLOGUE

❦

Thirteen Days in Xi'an

THE MAN WHO CLAIMED to rule over more human beings than anybody else on earth was in his nightshirt when the soldiers came for him in the winter dawn. Driving up in four trucks, they killed the sentries and burst into a complex of richly decorated pavilions with curved roofs round a hot spring where an emperor had entertained his favourite concubine. Climbing the stone steps, they advanced under the moonlight through an ornate bath house into a walled square.

It was 12 December 1936, and there was snow on the ground at the Huaqing hot springs outside Xi'an in the north of China. Capital of Shaanxi province, the city stood at the eastern end of the Silk Road that had linked China to India, the Islamic world and Europe. Its Bell and Drums Towers were celebrated Ming dynasty monuments, as was its 1,897-room pagoda and its 10-mile brick city wall reaching up 50 feet from the ground. More recently, it had been the scene of a siege in which some 30,000 people had died, many starving to death. North of Xi'an lay a major Communist base which should have been the target for liquidation the day the soldiers arrived at Huaqing.

Led by a twenty-five-year-old colonel with cropped hair and a face as broad as it was long, the 120-strong raiding party circled a lotus pool, shooting while it advanced towards a one-storey building set behind a broad, paved terrace. In the simple, white-painted room on the far left, the Generalissimo of China was doing his early morning exercises as he had done every day since boyhood. Hearing the noise outside, his chief bodyguard ran out onto the terrace from his room on the far right, and a gun battle erupted. Bullets pierced the glass panels in the doors. As the shooting raged, Chiang Kai-shek climbed through the back window. Not pausing to dress, he left behind his uniform, shoes and false teeth.[1]

Joined by two servants, the fifty-year-old leader of Nationalist China scaled a 10-foot wall, with a steep drop into a moat on the other side. He slipped and fell. 'I felt a bad pain and was unable to rise,' he recalled. 'About three minutes later I managed to stand up and walked with difficulty.'

At a small temple on the peak above the hot springs, guards helped him to climb further up through the snow. The attackers kept firing up the slope. 'Bullets whizzed by quite close to my body,' Chiang remembered. 'Some of my bodyguards were hit and dropped dead.' He tripped on brambles, injuring his back and knee. Eventually, he found refuge in a cave behind a large rock. Down at the hot springs, the raiders shot dead his particularly unpopular nephew. Then they set out to search the peak.

In Xi'an, officers of the local army huddled round telephones monitoring events. As dawn broke, their soldiers were busy grabbing Chiang's generals who were staying in the city. One jumped from a window, and was shot dead. Others were said to have been arrested in compromising night-time company. Some of the troops ran wild, looting and killing the manager of a bank. Flour worth $1.5 million was stolen from a train.[2]

Twice, searchers passed the cave without finding their prey. Then the Generalissimo heard soldiers talking outside, and decided to give himself up, trembling with cold and exhaustion. The commander of the attack, Colonel Sun Mingjiu, the round-faced man described as having 'the shy yet eager manner of a schoolboy', was summoned. In a formal tone, he addressed his captive by his rank. Chiang replied: 'If you are my comrades, shoot me now and finish it all.'[3]

The ruler of a nation of 450 million people asked for a horse: his feet were bleeding and he was blue with cold. 'There is no horse here,' said Sun, kneeling in the snow. 'But I will carry you.' Chiang hesitated, and then got on the colonel's broad back. At the bottom of the hill, a car was waiting.

When they reached the springs at Huaqing and saw the bodies strewn on the ground, it was decided to drive on to military headquarters where the commander-in-chief was greeted by a military band. 'Don't salute me,' he shouted at the officers waiting for him.

News of the kidnapping shot across China. In the capital of Nanking, the reaction was bellicose – worryingly so for the Generalissimo's wife, Soong Meiling, the sophisticated, American-educated daughter of one of China's leading families. Rumours flew that the rebels had murdered her husband. The War Minister, General He Yingqin, led a military group that pressed for an attack by bombers and troops stationed east of Xi'an. Meiling objected that this would put Chiang's life at risk. In stormy meetings, her arguments were met with disdain, as was her suggestion that she should fly north. 'Nobody is going to Xi'an,' He declared. 'We are attacking Xi'an. The Generalissimo is dead.' Meiling wondered if the generals really wanted to see her husband killed, so that they could take his place.[4]

In the caves and villages of the poverty-stricken north of Shaanxi, where they had come to rest after their 6,000-mile Long March, the Communists received the news with glee. They knew that the Generalissimo had been about to launch vastly superior forces in what he called 'the last five minutes' of his battle to eradicate them. The previous day, Mao Zedong had received a cable which contained two characters that his secretary could not work out. Seeing them, his boss smiled, and said, 'There's good news on the way.' The Communist leader usually slept till noon after working all night, but he was up early on 12 December. The field telephone rang continuously. A mass rally called for Chiang to be put on trial. The Politburo demanded his execution. The leading Communist negotiator, Zhou Enlai, set off by mule to take a plane sent to fetch him by Chiang's kidnapper.[5]

As Zhou made his way towards Xi'an, Chiang was confronting the man who had sent Colonel Sun to snatch him. Aged thirty-four, Zhang Xueliang was generally known as the Young Marshal, to distinguish him from his father, the Old Marshal of Manchuria. The younger Zhang had allied with Chiang after the Japanese had assassinated his father. Then, in 1931, Tokyo's army seized his huge territory of Manchuria, and pursued him into northern China. A drug addict with a playboy reputation, Zhang had been dismissed by the Generalissimo, after which he took a cure, made a lengthy trip to Europe and returned to assume new commands – the latest of which was to 'pacify' the Communists north of Xi'an. But, after several defeats and aware that Chiang was planning to demote him, he had come to the conclusion that the Nationalists should form a united front with the Communists to oppose the Japanese who had taken his homeland from him.

Although Zhang could decide his life or death, Chiang hit a habitual tough note. 'From now on,' he shouted, 'despite the size of the world, where will you be able to find a place for yourself? Living, there will be no place to put your feet; dead, there will be no place to bury your bones . . . If you are a brave man, kill me; if not, confess your sins and let me go.' When the Marshal asked Chiang to fight the Japanese rather than the Communists, the Nationalist leader replied, 'Get out!' Though he had set in motion secret preparations for war with Japan in due course, his policy was set – to eliminate the Communists before confronting the invaders. It was a stance he had adopted since 1931, and he was not going to alter course now.*

The room in which the Generalissimo of China was being held was small, with a wooden bed. The hangings were dirty. There were no sanitary facilities. A bucket stood in one corner; in another, some brooms. Chiang lay on the bed, pulled the blanket over his head, and turned his face to the wall. As the hours passed, he refused food and tea. An officer keeping watch outside the door offered him a fur-lined cloak. The captive waved it away.

The Generalissimo declined to eat breakfast which the guard and his colleagues bought for him with their own money. When a suggestion was made that he should move to a house with steam heating and a lawn, he replied that, if he were not released, he would die where he was. The pain in his loins and legs was such that he could hardly sit up. Soon after midnight, Colonel Sun walked into the room, a pistol in his hand. He told Chiang he had to move. The prisoner refused, and repeated, 'If you want to kill me, kill me now.' Sun stayed for ninety minutes before giving up. Zhang Xueliang came twice; once, according to Chiang, he stood at the door, tears in his eyes.

The Young Marshal had reached his moment of truth. Subsequently, he

---

* The conversation is from Chiang's diary in *China at the Crossroads* p. 161 et seq. This was written after the event, and is self-serving. But the words and attitudes are characteristic of both men.

would be portrayed as a shining nationalist hero whose only desire was to end the civil war and get the Chinese to unite against the foreign aggressor. But he had played a double game for months, conducting secret negotiations for a mutual non-aggression pact with the Communists he was meant to be fighting, including all-night talks with Zhou Enlai in a Catholic church. While patriotism was certainly a motivation, he had other reasons to act. Apart from the threat of losing his command, the impending arrival of Chiang's elite troops to join the anti-Communist campaign and the denial of supplies threatened his regional base. He had lost Manchuria and his subsequent domain round Peking; now, he risked being marginalised by the Generalissimo in his last haven. The power play of kidnapping his commander had appeared to offer a way of preserving his position, while a united front against the Japanese would water down Chiang's authority. The American ambassador, who dismissed Zhang as irresponsible and vain, was moved to describe him as acting like 'a first-class Chicago gangster'.[6]

Dubbed 'villain of the week' by the strongly pro-Chiang *Life* magazine, the Marshal was not alone. The kidnapping idea had originated with a local general, Yang Hucheng, a former bandit who was equally worried about his position. When Yang suggested holding Chiang and forcing him into line, Zhang initially rejected the notion, but his thinking changed after Chiang warned him that he was going to send in a more gung-ho general to lead the anti-Communist campaign, and excluded him from military conferences.

The Marshal was under pressure from left-wing advisers who favoured working with the Communists. A Chinese victory against Japanese puppet troops in Inner Mongolia added to the call for action. Flag-waving students staged demonstrations through the streets of Xi'an making the same demand, and calling for the release of seven patriotic figures (the 'seven gentlemen') who had been detained in Shanghai for urging resistance to Japan. The Generalissimo demanded that Zhang's leftist advisers should be punished, and branded Xi'an a 'Red city'. Police opened fire on the demonstrators, killing two. When Zhang had put the students' case, Chiang had cursed and pounded the table.[7]

On 11 December, the commander-in-chief had gone to see the Marshal in his compound of modernist brick buildings with tall windows. The two men then moved to a dinner hosted by the Generalissimo. One of his generals had warned Chiang of a plot against him and advised leaving by train. But the Nationalist leader decided to stay, driving through the snow-covered wheat fields east of the city to the hot springs. Zhang attended another social occasion before returning to his headquarters. He climbed the sixteen steps of the front building and went to the second-floor conference room with its white-covered sofas and armchairs, chandelier of brass and pink glass, and large wall maps. Thirteen officers were waiting. The Marshal told them he had decided to take Chiang prisoner. 'Unless absolutely necessary, no shot should be fired,' he instructed. 'The Generalissimo must be taken alive and unharmed at all costs. If he gets hurt, I will shoot you.'

After the kidnapping, during which Colonel Sun's men had ignored the order not to fire, Zhang followed the customary practice of setting out his position in a telegram to national and regional leaders. He called for the 'reorganisation' of the government, an end to the civil war, the release of the anti-Japanese detainees in Shanghai and other political prisoners. He wanted free speech, the end of restrictions on patriotic movements, a National Salvation Conference and the implementation of the aspirations for nationalism, democracy and the people's livelihood enunciated by the Father of the Republic, Sun Yat-sen.

After that, Zhang was at a loss as to what to do next. His captive would not speak to him. His military position was not strong. Nanking troops were moving towards Xi'an. Local soldiers refused to attack the airfield, from where twenty bombers under the control of pro-Chiang commanders made a flight over the city to underline its vulnerability. In his uncertainty, the Marshal reached out to the most extraordinary Westerner in China.

William Henry Donald was from Australia, a former journalist who had become adviser to a succession of Chinese rulers, including Zhang Xueliang, though he spoke no Chinese. The British writer, Christopher Isherwood, described the teetotal Australian as 'a red-faced, serious man with . . . a large, sensible nose'. When Isherwood said that he and his travelling companion, the poet, W. H. Auden, were going to visit a war zone, Donald warned that they might have to eat Chinese food. 'Never touch the stuff!' he added, his face contracting with disgust. 'It ruins my stomach.'[8]

'Donald of China' was now working for the Chiangs, and was particularly close to the Generalissimo's wife who called him 'Don'. But he had also kept in touch with the Young Marshal, whose cure from drug addiction he had arranged a couple of years before. When Madame Chiang and her relatives met in Shanghai to discuss the kidnapping of her husband, the former journalist was the only non-family member invited. Solicited by both parties, he flew north, bearing letters from Meiling and a volume of Chiang's diary to show that he was more anti-Japanese than was supposed.[9]

At the airfield, Donald was greeted by a young, Chinese-speaking Scot called Jimmy Elder who worked as the Marshal's treasurer. They drove to see Zhang at his office just inside the city wall. The Marshal explained why he had acted, and recounted the disputes of the past months. A photograph shows the bespectacled Donald leaning forward as his host sits in an armchair reading a sheet of paper. It could have been the letter from Meiling saying the kidnapping was disastrous for national unity, and urging a change of course before it was too late. While admitting there might be legitimate grievances which could be explored, she had not taken the demands in the Young Marshal's circular telegram seriously; with the cynicism of the age, she thought he was after a transfer to a richer region.

Donald and Zhang met other officers, including General Yang. With Elder interpreting, the Australian rebuked them for the kidnapping, and said the Generalissimo should be released. Yang, who had had a sticky meeting with Chiang, appeared unconvinced. Donald and the Marshal then drove to see Chiang. As they walked into his room, the prisoner sat up in his bed, tears in his eyes. Donald gave him a letter from Meiling. She and Chiang were Methodists, and she wrote that she would pray for him.[10]

Things grew tense when Donald said Meiling planned to fly in. 'You cannot bring her into this den of thieves,' her husband cried. Turning to face the wall, he drew the blanket over his head. 'I think you should leave this room,' Donald said. 'It is no place for you.' Chiang lowered the blanket, his face glowering. The room was uncomfortably quiet. At last, the Generalissimo said, 'I will go with you.'[11]

Donald and Zhang went outside, and the commander-in-chief got up for the first time for sixty hours. 'When he emerged in full uniform, sentries clicked to attention, saluting as the trio walked to a motorcar,' Donald's biographer wrote on the basis of information given to him by his subject. As they rode through the city, the Generalissimo gripped the Australian's hand.

Reaching the house with the lawn and steam heating, the Marshal stood to attention as the Generalissimo spoke harshly to him. Donald noted that the younger man was so tired he was hardly able to stand. As Chiang brushed aside Zhang's demands, Donald could see the depth of anger behind the incident, and marvelled at Zhang's self-control. With the Marshal interpreting, the Australian told Chiang he was surrounded by a pro-Japanese clique, and should listen to the opinion of the people as expressed in Xi'an. When Donald became too blunt, the Marshal refused to continue to translate, so Jimmy Elder stepped in. The Australian suggested Zhang go home. As the door closed, according to Donald, the Generalissimo's superb front evaporated. He turned to his adviser with a look of despair, waved his arm and exclaimed: 'Finished. It is finished.'*

The Australian went to the airport to fly to the military centre of Luoyang,† 200 miles to the east, from where he could communicate more easily and securely with Madame Chiang in Nanking. Snow was falling, the cloud was low, and the plane crept over the mountain, the wings almost touching the cliffs along the Yellow River. On arrival, Donald telephoned Meiling to tell her what was happening. She said the Nationalist generals were determined to attack, risking her husband's life.

Military aircraft had started bombing east of Xi'an, and some followed Donald's plane as it flew back, forcing it to detour along a mountain crest – it landed with only a few gallons of fuel left. When the Australian told Chiang of the bombing, the Generalissimo asked eagerly: 'Do you think they will make another try?' His adviser looked at him blankly, wondering, 'My God, will I ever know this man?' The next morning, Zhang reported that Chiang was asking why planes were not attacking Xi'an.

The reason was that snow had grounded the bombers. 'God is protecting you,' Donald remarked. 'If the planes could get in, they'd finish you off in a hurry.' Chiang shrugged. 'He wants to be a martyr,' the Marshal said. But not quite yet: at the suggestion of a Nationalist officer also being held in Xi'an, the Generalissimo wrote to Nanking ordering a three-day truce. As for Zhang, Chiang recorded him as saying that, if

---

* Since neither man spoke the other's language, this may have been more a matter of gesture than the dramatic words given by Donald's biographer, Selle (pp. 326–7), based on Donald's recollections.
† Known at the time as Loyang.

the revolt failed, he would either kill himself or become a bandit in the hills.

While Donald was flying to and from Luoyang, Zhou Enlai arrived in Xi'an. His mission had turned to embarrassment, calling for all the poise he had inherited from his mandarin family and all the subtlety which would mark him out as the Communists' prime diplomat. Stalin had deflated the initial enthusiasm for the kidnapping, which the Kremlin decided was a Japanese plot. Berlin and Tokyo had just concluded a pact against international Communism, and Moscow wanted Chiang as an Asian ally. Mao and his colleagues were told the kidnapping was 'objectively detrimental' to the anti-Japanese cause. Though Chiang had been killing their members for ten years, they kowtowed. Zhou was told to seek a settlement.

That was what the Young Marshal now desperately wanted. His feet were growing colder by the day. After reading Chiang's diary brought by Donald, he concluded that the commander-in-chief was a better patriot than previously thought. He dropped half of his demands, and arranged for another mediator to fly in – Madame Chiang's brother, T. V. Soong, a stout and enormously rich banker who had been Chiang's Finance Minister. Soong brought a note from Meiling to Chiang saying that if her brother did not return within three days, 'I will come to live and die with you.' When her husband read this, his diary records, 'my eyes were wet'.

But he still refused to bow for his freedom. He gave Soong his will, and showed him a plan for an attack on Xi'an. Evidently feeling a lot better, he slept till 11 a.m. on 21 December when his brother-in-law came to see him before returning to Nanking. Donald also left for the capital where he met Meiling who decided to accompany him back to Xi'an. She took with her a pistol and her husband's spare false teeth. As they landed, she pressed the revolver into the Australian's hand, murmuring: 'Please shoot me if any soldiers touch me.' The adviser assured her she would not be molested. 'Please,' she repeated. But when she stepped from the plane, in a long black coat with a fur collar, she looked as composed as ever.[12]

Zhang came to meet the plane – he and Meiling had known one another since 1925 when she was the smart, twenty-eight-year-old daughter of one of Shanghai's greatest clans and he was living in a modern apartment building in the city. Now, she found him 'very tired, very embarrassed, and somewhat ashamed'. She and Donald had agreed to adopt a placatory tone with the rebels, and she said she needed some tea before seeing her husband. Then, at 4 p.m., she walked past guards with machine guns into the house where Chiang was being held. As she entered his room, the Generalissimo exclaimed that he had known she would come, having read a biblical passage that morning saying, 'Jehovah will now do a good thing, and that is, He will make a woman protect a man.'

Meiling recorded her resentment when she saw her husband 'lying there injured and helpless, a shadow of his former self, with his hands, legs and feet cut by brambles and bruised by the rocks he clambered over when scrambling about the mountain'. But she kept up a moderate tone in discussions with Zhang. She and Donald stayed in the only modern hotel in the city, with central heating, a barber's shop, a white dining room with a dance floor and rose-coloured bulbs. Walking at dusk in its garden, Meiling and Donald concluded that Zhang could not make the final decision on his own. General Yang was taking a tough line, fearing he might become the fall guy. He was insisting on the withdrawal of Nationalist troops east of Xi'an and a written pledge from Chiang to implement the main rebel demands. The Generalissimo refused to do any such thing.

The situation in the isolated city was becoming increasingly difficult as food prices soared, and coal grew scarce. Fearful local inhabitants dug air-raid shelters or were forced to work on trenches outside the city. Government planes dropped thousands of copies of newspapers reporting that the rest of China was up in arms over the kidnapping. In desperation, the Marshal proposed to Meiling that the Generalissimo should be disguised and smuggled out by car. She turned this down because of its indignity, and because her husband was in no shape for such a journey.[13]

Help came from Zhou Enlai, who was staying in the Marshal's headquarters. Urged on by Zhang and Donald, Meiling agreed to meet the Communist envoy. In a two-hour talk, Zhou said her husband was the only man able to lead the country. On Christmas Eve, he went to meet the Generalissimo.

The two men's destinies crossed time and again. They had been colleagues a dozen years earlier at the military college where Chiang had begun his rise to power, and where Zhou was a political commissar. The Communist had narrowly escaped with his life when Chiang purged the left in 1927. By all accounts, the conversation in Xi'an was cordial – or high-level play-acting. The Generalissimo said there should be no more civil war. 'All the time we have been fighting, I have often thought of you,' he added. 'I hope we can work together again.' For his part, Zhou said the Communists wanted to back Chiang as the nation's leader against the Japanese.

The next morning, Donald left Christmas presents by the fireplace – a portable typewriter for Meiling and a steamer rug for her husband. Chiang laughed for the first time for thirteen days. An even better present was delivered by Zhang courtesy of Zhou. The Communist had had a second meeting with Meiling at which, employing language the Marshal or Mao might have used, she said they were all Chinese and should not be fighting each other. 'Internal problems should be solved by political means, and not by military force,' added the wife of the man who had used the army to get to the top. In keeping with Stalin's instructions, Zhou decided to take this at face value, and persuaded Yang to drop the demand for a written pledge from Chiang. It was agreed to settle for a verbal assurance of unity. The Generalissimo was free to go.

Before doing so, he had to have the last word. His 'admonition' to Zhang and Yang, published shortly afterwards, was Chiang's summing up of the situation as he would have liked to have seen it. He insisted that he had made no promises and that the two men must unreservedly obey the orders of the central government so as to 'turn a national calamity into a national blessing'. According to the official account, his sermon was taken down by his wife as the two soldiers stood to attention. Whether he actually delivered it at the time is doubtful; one of the Generalissimo's aides reported writing it after the event. But the admonition became Chiang's evidence that he had not given way. On the other hand, a local newspaper, presumably inspired by the Zhang–Yang camp, wrote that he had agreed to a united front with the Communists. Mao Zedong contended that Chiang was 'willing to accept those terms which are beneficial to the state and the nation and will keep his promise in spite of the absence of his signature'.[14]

At 4 p.m., the Chiangs arrived at Xi'an airport, the Marshal riding in the front of their car beside the chauffeur. The main actors took time to pose for a group photograph. The Young Marshal, wearing a padded jacket and plus fours, put on a set smile. General Yang, the only one in uniform, stood to attention. The Chiangs were beside one another, Meiling stylish in a black top and long pale skirt, her husband in a thick black gown and trilby hat. Zhang, who had shown neither the stomach for war with Nanking nor a readiness to commit suicide or head for the hills, asked to fly out with the Chiangs, and face whatever punishment might be considered suitable. As Meiling noted, it was the first time 'any high officer responsible for mutinous conduct has shown eagerness . . . to be tried for his misdeeds'.[15]

They went first to Luoyang. According to Donald's recollections of the flights, the Marshal appeared drawn and strained while Madame Chiang gazed out of the window with a faint smile and her husband slept. After they landed, the Generalissimo insisted the Marshal ride in his car to the military academy where they spent the night, Zhang sleeping in a room opposite his. The next day, the Chiangs flew to Nanking to be met by a crowd of tens of thousands. In recognition of his work, Chiang awarded Donald the Order of the Brilliant Jade, Grand Cordon of Blue. The Generalissimo offered his resignation for having allowed his subordinates to revolt, knowing that his gesture would be refused. Then, he went to recuperate in his home village in the eastern province of Zhejiang.[16]

The Young Marshal flew to Nanking in a separate plane. At the airport, there was only one official to accompany him to T. V. Soong's ochre-coloured villa in the city, but secret police followed them, and Zhang was quickly put on trial. At one point during the court martial, he shouted that Chiang was the only member of the ruling group worth a damn; 'None of the rest of you would be any loss to China,' he added. 'If I am freed, I'll start a revolution!' The sentence was ten years' imprisonment, later changed to detention at Chiang's pleasure.[17]

Although the Generalissimo had not put his name to any agreement in Xi'an, the incident was a crucial historical moment. The national reaction demonstrated the yearning for unity in the face of Japan's aggression. There was only one man who could meet that need, a man whose unbowed conduct at Xi'an gave him a special status. When he arrived back in Nanking, Chiang wrote that he was 'conscious of living a second life'. But the swell of popular patriotic feeling made it impossible for him to press on with final suppression of the Communists. When a close aide suggested an immediate attack on the Red Army base in Yan'an, Chiang bent his head and did not reply. The Communists obtained a vital breathing space when they were weak and vulnerable. Had the Xi'an Incident not occurred, Mao might well not have survived to become Chiang's successor as ruler of China. That is why the thirteen days in December 1936 constituted a crucial moment of the twentieth century.[18]

The man who had brought it about would spend half a century under arrest. The Young Marshal was to be kept in houses and caves all over China before being flown in 1946 to Taiwan where he was eventually released in 1991. Converted to Christianity, he married his long-time companion and they went to live in Hawaii where he died in 2001 at the age of 100 – he put his longevity down to sleeping well and not worrying. In an oral history released after his death, he said Chiang 'absolutely detested' him for having advocated fighting the Japanese rather than the Communists, and described the Generalissimo as a total egotist. 'Our friendship was like flesh and blood,' he added in a television interview. 'But our political dispute was like the relationship between two sworn enemies.' The grateful Communists hailed him as a great patriot – President Jiang Zemin called him 'a hero for eternity'.[19]

For the Marshal's first place of detention, Chiang chose the Xuedou Mountain Hostel in a picturesque area south of the eastern port of Ningbo. Tea plantations stretched below the three-room bungalow suite. There were peach blossoms in the garden. Alongside was a Laughing Buddha temple said to be 1,500 years old. Zhang planted two trees on a terrace, and set off fireworks to calm his sorrow at what had happened. After six months, a fire in the kitchen destroyed the hostel, and the Marshal moved into quarters in the temple. 'The lonely shadow of my body lies under the sky,' he wrote in a poem. 'There is a long way to go; my hair turns white from growing old; little by little my tears become bright and the wind of spring is still blowing.' Down the hill lay the village of Xikou, where Chiang had been born fifty years earlier. Of all the places in China, the Generalissimo chose one next to his first home as the prison for his most illustrious captive.

PART I

SON OF THE SALT-SELLER

Xikou, Zhejiang Province, October 1887

———

Canton, Guangdong Province, June 1926

CHAPTER 1

Cold Realities

IN LATE OCTOBER and early November of 1887, China suffered droughts, flooding of the Yellow River and cholera outbreaks in the cities of Nanking and Hangzhou. In Shanghai, a criminal was sentenced to stand in a cage without food or drink until he died. Along the Yangtze River, a magistrate conjured up the ghosts of dead men at a murder trial. Down south, a campaign to get rid of 'evil characters' led to 906 summary executions in Guangdong province. In the city of Canton, the god of plague was sighted – 'a semi-human monster with huge feet'. In Peking, there was great concern about the illnesses of two Manchu imperial princes. A physician summoned from Zhejiang province on the eastern seaboard cured one, and called for the livers of river otters to deal with the malady affecting the other.[1]

In the doctor's home province, a messenger carrying a lantern walked through the night to call a midwife to assist with the birth of a child in the village of Xikou.* On the upper floor of a two-storey house by the river running through the village, a boy was born at noon on 31 October. His paternal grandfather gave him the 'milk name' of Jui-yuan (Auspicious Beginning). His mother later called him Chung-cheng (Balanced Justice),

* Known at the time as Chikow or Hsikou.

and he finally gained the honorific name of Jieshi (Between Rocks) which would have a prophetic echo as he found himself sheltering in the cave outside Xi'an forty-nine years later. When he moved to Canton in the 1920s, its rendition in the local dialect produced the name by which he was to be generally known in the West, Chiang Kai-shek, though in the national language of Mandarin he is known as Jiang Jieshi.

Xikou was a small village with three streets lying on a crossing point of the slow-flowing Shanxi River. The Yutai Salt Store run by Chiang's family looked out at the waterway with its flat-hulled bamboo boats. Salt was a government monopoly, and the merchants who handled it enjoyed a certain standing. The house lay behind a wall topped with circular tiles, with a flagged courtyard onto which a room opened where Chiang's father and grandfather sold salt, wine, rice and sundry goods over a wooden counter. There were two other rooms on the ground level, one with a phoenix design set into the floor.

Across the river were thickly wooded hills and, beyond them, the trading harbours of the East China Sea. The big port of Ningbo was 30 miles to the north along a broad track through valleys and vegetable fields. Verdant hills with rows of tea bushes rose behind the village to the monastery where Zhang Xucliang would be held. Above it towered a ridge known as the Snow Mountain. In spring and summer, pink, purple and red blossoms dotted the slopes. From the peak, there was a commanding view of a lake and a stony path to a waterfall with a 600-foot drop. On the ridge, Chiang would later build a summer residence called Miao Terrace, writing its name in his own calligraphy to hang over the central courtyard. With its back to the mountains in the midst of pine woods and bamboo, the two-storey building was classically restrained, and reflected its owner's love of nature. The Generalissimo, who was brought up from Xikou in a sedan chair, liked to sit outside contemplating the hills. A photograph shows him dressed in a long robe, black slippers, skullcap and spectacles sitting looking into the distance from a wicker chair. The caption reads: 'Mr Chiang Kai-shek thought deeply at Miao Terrace'.

The Chiangs were the leading family in the village, being among a multitude of Chinese who claimed descent from a celebrated ancient statesman, the Duke of Zhou. They had lost much of their assets in the great Taiping rebellion which spread over China in the middle of the nineteenth century. The paternal grandfather, Yu-piao, gave the job of rebuilding the family fortunes to one of his three sons, Chiang Shu-an. Running the family shop, he was known as an honest broker in village disputes, a peace-maker who inspired confidence in his neighbours. His first wife died giving birth to their second child. He married again, but his second wife, who appeared to be barren, passed away eighteen months later. So, at the age of forty-five, he wed for the third time.

His wife was Wang Tsai-yu, the twenty-two-year-old, widowed daughter of a farmer who had retreated to a Buddhist monastery after her husband's death. An accomplished seamstress, she was sharp and ambitious. She gave birth to Chiang a year after the marriage; she had no breast milk, and a local man recalled that his grandmother fed the baby – 'from then on, Chiang's family sent us a gift of money every spring festival,' he added. One of Shu-an's cousins took over as wet nurse for the baby, living in a room at the back of the salt shop.[2]

As a child, Chiang was often in bad health. When not ill, he sought to stand out among his playmates, behaving in what he described as a haughty and lordly manner. In games of soldiers, he preferred to be the commander. A contemporary recalled that he 'liked to be at the head of the children'. Looking back, Chiang took a theatrical view of the perils of his childhood playing. 'I was frequently exposed to the risk of being drowned or burnt to death, or else severely cut or wounded,' he wrote. There were certainly times when he put himself in danger, for example by pushing chopsticks down his throat to see how far they would go, or nearly drowning in a water jar. But the habit of making himself the centre of melodramatic attention was to be a hallmark of his behaviour as a young man.

His early education was entrusted to village tutors, with whom he made slow progress in rote learning of classic texts. He showed a solitary side which would be evident throughout his life, going off on his own to bathe in mountain streams, walk in the hills and visit monasteries. He listened to roaring waterfalls and birds, and rode bamboo rafts down streams to watch the fishermen using cormorants with bands round their necks to prevent them from swallowing the catch they plucked from the water.[3]

When the boy was five, the paternal grandfather passed away, and his three sons squabbled over the inheritance. Two years later, Chiang's father died, and his widow was left to fend for herself as her in-laws and stepchildren took most of the family assets. Much later, Chiang's second wife would set down a very different version of his origins, claiming that an investigation showed he was really the son of a poor farmer in the central province of Henan who had abandoned his wife and son during a famine – she had found a job as a nurse and governess for a widowed salt merchant called Chiang whom she subsequently married. Unless contemporary inhabitants of Xikou and later historians were involved in a vast campaign of deception, the chronology of this tale makes no sense. In an inverse process to the family's claims to notable lineage, the story quoted by his second wife, whom he had abandoned, looks like a bid to take a leader down a peg by attributing humbler origins than those he proclaimed.*[4]

On the other hand, the story of the mother protecting her son against adversity does have a certain echo. Every account attests to Chiang's remoteness from his father, his closeness to his mother, and her difficulties after she was widowed. Parallels would be drawn with the Confucian sage, Mencius, whose mother brought him up with great devotion despite her poverty. Chiang would invoke Wang as a leitmotif of his writings and diaries, constituting a mantra through which he could set her up as a model whose perfection was a continual reproach to himself and his unworthy compatriots. His filial attachment acted as a resource by which he could demonstrate to himself that he possessed the humility needed by a truly superior being. In the Chinese code, a man who was aiming high had to admit – in letter if not in spirit – to his own inadequacy; how better to do this than to measure himself against an iconic mother figure to whom all possible virtues could be attributed, and who was beyond reality as a construct of her son's psychological needs?

After she was widowed, Wang left the salt store and moved into a three-room house down the street by the river. In due course, this would become Chiang's main residence in the village, greatly expanded as befitted his status with an ancestral hall, rock garden and large reception room. But, by his account, his mother struggled to make ends meet, raising her children in a spartan, authoritarian regime. No longer the wife of a prominent member of the village, she had to take in sewing and was

---

* There was an intriguing episode in the 1940s, however, when a man from Henan turned up at Chiang's headquarters claiming to be his brother, and was well treated as if he had some claim on the ruler of China. (See Introduction by Lloyd Eastman to *Chen: Chiang Kai-shek's Secret Life*.)

regarded as an outsider because she came from another district. On one occasion, tax collectors demanded money she did not have readily available. So they imprisoned Chiang until she came up with the sum. That made a deep impression on him; a memoir he wrote on his fiftieth birthday recalled: 'My family, solitary and without influence, became at once the target of . . . insults and maltreatment . . . To our regret and sorrow none of our relatives and kinsmen was stirred from apathy.'

For a few years, Chiang was outdone in his mother's affections by a younger brother who was described as having extremely good looks and whom Wang loved as her favourite child. But the boy died at the age of four. After that, Chiang recalled, 'She centred all her hopes on me, hoping anxiously that I should make a name for myself.'

'Her love was more than the love of an average mother: she was more of a disciplinarian than any strict teacher,' he wrote later. 'She taught me about the value of hard work as well as the elements of good social behaviour . . . From early morning to late at night every minute of her time was devoted to my well-being.' When he was eighteen, Chiang posed for a photograph with her, a handsome young man in a quilted jacket standing behind his mother who sits squarely on a wooden chair. Her eyes are deep-set. Unsmiling, she epitomises the harshness of her existence, what Chiang later called 'the shadow of cold realities'.[5]

From his mother, he learned to erect a protective wall between himself and his surroundings, and to tread warily while never admitting defeat. From an early age, he lived on his internal resources, and followed his own morality. Impulsive and domineering, demanding attention and regarding himself as the centre of the universe, he could become self-absorbed and introspective, withdrawing from the world. 'At play, he would regard the classroom as his stage and all his schoolmates as his toys,' a teacher recalled. 'But when he was at his desk, reading or holding his pen trying to think, then even a hundred voices around him could not distract him from his concentration. His periods of quietude and outburst sometimes occurred within a few minutes of each other: one would think he had two different personalities.'[6]

There was little or no time for relaxed family relationships. Rather, an intensity bordering on hysteria reigned. When he left his mother on a trip, a tutor recalled, Chiang wept till his eyes became red. When he was downcast, one of his teachers remembered, 'the contagion of his grief would deeply depress the neighbours and cause his mother to retire to the adjoining room, there to shed tears herself'. When the boy came home from a stay with cousins at the age of twelve, he burst into uncontrollable sobs on seeing his mother. 'From his childhood, [he] constructed a number of strong ego defence mechanisms against an experientially hostile world,' the historian Pichon Loh wrote in his study of Chiang's character in early life. 'They were to become a powerful mental wall behind which the rejected boy could withdraw in isolation, the better to preserve the stability of his personality or to re-stabilise a personality threatened with collapse.'[7]

In 1901, a marriage was arranged between Chiang and Mao Fu-mei, a robust, illiterate village girl. He was fourteen; she was five years his senior. His heart was hardly in becoming a husband. During the wedding banquet, Chiang joined boys playing outside, and had to be dragged back to the meal. Wang saw the girl as a useful helper since her feet were only partially bound, but her affection was limited: Chinese mothers-in-law are not known for their tenderness to their daughters-in-law. After meeting Mao twenty years later, Chiang's second wife recalled her saying that the first two months of the marriage had been happy as Chiang took her on walks in the hills and raft rides down the river. But his mother then blamed the teenage bride for being a disturbing influence on her son, and leading him astray as they gallivanted in the mountains. When Kai-shek and she talked or laughed in the house, Wang would tell her to be silent.

'Therefore,' Mao recalled, according to this account, 'I kept quiet and seldom spoke. More and more I avoided any direct conversation openly with him in the house. That was not easy, however, especially when he asked me questions and expected my answers. The situation went from bad to worse, and Kai-shek soon became impatient with me. I dared not say one word to defend myself, even when he scolded me, for, as you know, the villagers in their narrow-mindedness would accuse me of being an unfilial and disobedient daughter-in-law. And you know what that means in an isolated village like ours! The strain gradually caused a split between Kai-shek and me. All I could do was to weep secretly over my utter helplessness, and for a long period I suffered from melancholy.'[8]

Mao found solace in devout Buddhism while Chiang left the village to attend the Phoenix Mountain School in the district seat of Fenghua, from which he was nearly expelled for leading a protest calling for better teaching. After two years, he shifted to a private school in Ningbo where he heard a teacher extolling the importance of the army. A year later, he moved again, to the Dragon Middle School in Fenghua. The classical Chinese learning by rote, with no questions asked, formed his mindset – he was always to believe that the issuing of an instruction was enough; orders were to be obeyed just as the texts of Confucius and his disciples were to be enunciated as eternal truths.

One of Chiang's teachers, Hollington Tong, later to be his obsequious information director, recalled him as a 'serious-minded student' who grabbed the newspapers when they arrived from Shanghai and studied them in the small reading room. He had also already adopted his lifelong habit of getting up early, practising exercises and meditating while others slept. 'It was his custom to stand erect on the veranda in front of his bedroom for half an hour,' Tong wrote in a hagiographical biography. 'During this time his lips were compressed, his features were set in determination, and he stood with his arms folded. It is, of course, impossible to say with certainty what thoughts filled his mind at such times, but it was fairly obvious that he was thinking of his future.'[9]

Chiang had decided to pursue a military career, and to train in Japan, a country whose embrace of industrial and military modernity contrasted so sharply with the conservatism of China's imperial system. In August 1894, Japan had declared war on China over a dispute in Korea, which was under the protection of the Manchu Empire in Peking. Tokyo's victories marked the start of half a century of expansion into China, and confirmed Japan as the Prussia of Asia, with a military command that was a law to itself. In 1904–5, that status was confirmed when it defeated Russia in their Far Eastern war to demonstrate its power on the world stage.

Seeking to learn from the Japanese system, Chiang sailed across the East China Sea in the spring of 1905. His mother sold possessions to raise the money for the trip. By then, the adolescent from Xikou had read an incendiary book, *The Revolutionary Handbook*, which called for the killing of the Manchu Emperor, the establishment of a republic with a constitution based on that of the United States, the expulsion of all Manchus, and 'the freedom to revolt'. Before leaving China, the young man cut off his pigtail – a symbol of submission to the imperial dynasty – and sent it home. This declared him to be on the side of the revolution. His relatives were duly alarmed.[10]

In Japan, he suffered a terrible disappointment. Chinese could gain admission to military schools there only with a recommendation from the Board of War in Peking, which he did not have. Rather than turning round and returning home immediately, Chiang spent several months in Japan picking up the language before heading back to Xikou. He took out his frustrations on his wife. Later, Mao complained that he beat her, and, on one occasion, dragged her down the stairs by her hair. He would write that he could not bear 'hearing the sound of her footsteps or seeing her shadow'. Soon he was off again, to China's greatest metropolis of Shanghai, 200 miles to the north.

Before long, his mother followed him. A fortune-teller had told her that, if Mao gave birth to a son, the offspring would become a high official. So Wang travelled to the big city with the oppressed wife in tow. Chiang made it plain he was not interested in testing the prophecy. But, after his mother threatened to commit suicide if he did not sleep with his wife, he relented. Mao became pregnant and in due course gave birth to a boy.[11]

Showing the perseverance inherited from his mother, Chiang applied for a Chinese army school as a stepping stone towards getting to Japan. He secured one of fourteen places allocated to his province. The college had Japanese instructors, some of whom did not hide their contempt for the Chinese. One produced a lump of clay during a lecture on hygiene, and said it could contain as many as 400 million microbes, 'like China with 400 million people'. Enraged, Chiang walked up to the desk, picked up the clay and threw it down so that it split into pieces. The instructor complained to the director, but the young man escaped with a reprimand.[12]

When an examination was held to select cadets for Japan, Chiang was not on the list because he was not studying Japanese. He appealed on the grounds that he had already learned the language in its home country, and was allowed to sit for the test, qualifying as one of forty applicants chosen.

His destination was the Shimbu Gakkô military school, where courses for Chinese students were paid for by the Peking government. After graduating there, Chiang joined a field artillery regiment in northern Japan: he was 5.59 feet in height and weighed 130 pounds. A photograph shows a trim young man in uniform and boots. A short sword hangs from his belt, and he holds a flat cap in his right hand. He groomed horses, shined boots and learned how guns worked, but did not impress his instructors. One commented that he 'did not reveal innate ability'. Another called him 'a commonplace cadet'.[13]

Military life was tough. Even in the bitter winter, Chiang recalled, 'we never failed to get up before five o'clock every morning and to wash our faces with icy cold water which we ourselves had to bring up from the well'. Initially, he suffered from the thin diet – a bowl of rice at each meal with three slices of dried turnip and sometimes a small piece of salted fish. Bean curd, green vegetables and a tiny piece of meat were added only on Sundays. For the first three weeks, he supplemented this by buying biscuits, but then grew accustomed to the small quantities provided. Looking back, Chiang came to believe that his year as an ordinary soldier in Japan provided a foundation that stood him in good stead. It certainly gave him an appreciation of the value of discipline, hard work, political indoctrination and modern weapons, in an army largely free of external control.[14]

Though Peking banned Chinese students in Japan from such activities, Chiang formed a small political circle at the college. More important, he met a young man from his home province of Zhejiang called Chen Qimei who was in Japan as a student but whose main activity was working with the movement founded by the perennial Chinese revolutionary, Sun Yat-sen. Aged thirty, Chen was eleven years older than Chiang. The contact was to set the course of the young man's life. The two became sworn brothers, and Chen introduced Chiang to an umbrella grouping of anti-Manchu underground organisations established by Sun under the name of the Tongmenghui or United League, with Tokyo as its headquarters.

Subsequent literature is peppered with accounts of a meeting between Sun and Chiang in Japan in 1908: in some, Sun predicts that the young man will become a hero of the revolution, and even takes to consulting him before making any plans. Such stories appear to have been the product of retrospective hagiography. At the time they were supposed to have met, Sun was elsewhere, and Chiang was too junior to figure in his projects – in any case, he did not become a member of the United League until 1910.[15]

In the autumn of 1911, Chiang received a coded telegram from Chen in Shanghai telling him to return to China to join the revolution that had just broken out against the Manchus. Chiang obtained a forty-eight-hour leave permit. Before departing, he joined Japanese officers and two other Chinese at a dinner during which the cups were filled with water that was meant to symbolise the willingness of military men to die in battle. One of the other participants recalled much later that, after the two other Chinese had taken a sip, Chiang drained the cup, his face red with emotion. He then travelled to Tokyo with his two companions. There, he changed into civilian clothes, and sent his uniform and ceremonial dagger to military headquarters by registered mail to show he was not a common deserter. He took the train to Nagasaki and, on 30 October, sailed in disguise for Shanghai. 'This,' he recalled, 'was the real beginning of my revolutionary career.'[16]

CHAPTER 2

Sworn Brothers

THE FALL OF THE Manchu Empire was a tale foretold. From 1850 on, the dynasty – known as the Qing – which had ruled since 1644 was challenged by armed uprisings on a huge scale, reform movements, and a growing sense that China could not remain in splendid isolation from a world which was clearly outstripping it. The Manchus and their predecessors had always seen their rule as universal, rising far above the mere government of a nation state and based on Confucian principles. No other power could be acknowledged: though the dynasty was often flexible in practice, the principle was that there could only be vassals. But, by the second half of the nineteenth century, their hold on the mandate of heaven became increasingly shaky.

Earth-shaking as constitutional reforms were for traditionalists, they were too late. The ceding of power to provincial gentry weakened Peking's authority. The abolition of the Confucian civil service examination deprived the Manchus of a dedicated elite. The system could not handle the emergence of a public sphere among those who wanted to run their own lives and think for themselves. The imperial treasury was under constant strain; the court riven by intrigue. Corruption was rampant. The backwardness of industry and the infrastructure mocked the pretensions of the Sons of Heaven. The Empire became the single great symbol of what was wrong with China, its unpopularity heightened by nationalist resentment at a dynasty whose founders had invaded from the north and which made its subjects wear pigtails in a sign of submission. Advocates of change united round one tenet: the Manchus must go. What was to follow was less clear.

In the second half of the nineteenth century, popular rebellions broke out across the country. Much the biggest was that of the Taipings, followers of a farmer's son from the south called Hong Xiuquan who proclaimed himself the younger offspring of the Christian God. Taking their name from the Chinese characters for 'great peace', the Taipings set out to create a Heavenly Kingdom on earth in which private ownership of property would be abolished, idols cast down, men and women made equal, and opium, prostitution, slavery and foot-binding outlawed. Swelling to half a million men, the Taipings took the old capital of Nanking which they renamed the Heavenly City. By the time it lost momentum and was put down, the fourteen-year revolt had affected sixteen of China's eighteen provinces with a death toll put at 20 million.

Though defeated in 1864, the Taiping rising had important effects. Peking gave more authority to Han Chinese – the ethnic majority – particularly to a group of Confucian statesmen who offered to strengthen the regime. The battles against the rebels brought into being armies under professional commanders who came to relish their positions and whose elite troops received instruction from foreign advisers. At the turn of the century, changes in education, political administration, industry, law and the budget were proclaimed. But the reactionary Dowager Empress, Ci Xi, blocked progress with a coup which led to the arrest of the Emperor, her nephew, and his mysterious death, widely attributed to poisoning at her behest.

The accession of the three-year-old Pu Yi to the throne in 1909 further weakened the Manchus. Pressure for change mounted and the gentry increasingly took over affairs in the provinces. Imperial authority had also been shaken by defeat at the hands of the West in two opium wars, and then by Japan. The foreign military expedition to Peking to put down the Boxer rebellion in 1900 had made things even worse, leaving China saddled with indemnity payments to the powers whose property and citizens had been attacked. Sovereignty was impaired by the extraterritorial rights that gave foreigners immunity from arrest by the Chinese authorities, and by the granting of autonomous concessions to half a dozen foreign powers in coastal and river ports. The weakness of the Empire faced with these small bands of foreigners, and the ceding of treaty rights to them, compounded China's shame.

In the generation of educated Chinese pressing for modernisation through study circles, secret societies and journals, nobody was more active than Sun Yat-sen, the son of a peasant family in Guangdong province in the south. Though he had studied medicine in Hong Kong, where he was baptised by an American Congregationalist, Sun's true calling was revolution. He travelled incessantly to spread his gospel and raise funds from the overseas Chinese diaspora, evolving his anti-Manchu, nationalist creed as he did so. The dapper doctor became a hero in 1896 when he was kidnapped and held for five days in the Chinese embassy in London before a press outcry led the British government to obtain his release.*

At the head of the United League, Sun propounded three principles of Nationalism, Democracy and the People's Livelihood. The first meant uniting China, ending the privileges granted to foreigners and winning the country a proper place in the world; the second involved devolving power to the people after periods of tutelage by the doctor's party; the third could be interpreted as anything from gentle reformism to full-blown socialism. Sun was a vague thinker – his second wife would say he put together his pronouncements on the spur of the moment depending on the political context and his audience. He acted as a dictator within his movement, which was rent with factionalism. Still, he pressed on, often with only a handful of followers, plotting from havens in Japan or French-ruled Vietnam. After failed initiatives in the south-west, he engineered an abortive army mutiny in 1910 in the Guangdong capital of Canton.† The following April, he prepared another rising there, but the action began before the main body of his force arrived up the Pearl River from Hong Kong, and between seventy-two and eighty-six rebels died.[1]

In May 1911, a new Cabinet took office in Peking under an imperial prince known for his traditional views and corruption. One of its early decisions was to nationalise railway lines planned in Sichuan province. This

---

* It remains unclear whether Sun was grabbed by Chinese diplomats or went to the embassy voluntarily and was then held. See Bergère: *Sun* p. 62 et seq.
† Now known as Guangzhou.

angered the gentry there, and led to demonstrations on which imperial troops opened fire. The Sichuan unrest was localised, calling for reform rather than revolution. But more radical opposition was gaining ground in army units whose officers saw themselves in a role similar to that of the general staff in Prussia.

The decisive spark came on 9 October 1911, when a bomb exploded accidentally at the headquarters of a military revolutionary group in the Russian concession of the Yangtze River city of Hankou. Police swooped and grabbed the group's membership list. That forced the soldiers into action. The following day, troops in the neighbouring garrison city of Wuchang mutinied, and marched to the quarters of their colonel, who agreed to take command of the rising: one story is that he only did so after his men found him hiding under his bed and threatened to shoot him if he did not join them. The date – 10 October or the Double Ten – became the most sacred anniversary in the Republican calendar. Two days later, the rebels controlled Hankou and the two nearby cities of Hanyang and Wuchang, making up the tri-cities known as Wuhan. But they had no plan of what to do next, and revolutionaries elsewhere were taken by surprise, making the revolt a headless dragon.

At the time, Sun Yat-sen was in Denver, Colorado, as part of a fund-raising trip to the United States. He was told of events in China by a telegram from Huang Xing, his portly, thickset co-conspirator in the Canton revolt six months earlier who had been named as the second-ranking figure in Wuhan. One account is that Sun could not understand the cable because it was in code, and he had left his crib in Texas. Another is that he was feeling too tired to respond, and went to bed instead, only reading of the uprising in a newspaper the following morning. Then, instead of returning immediately to China, Sun travelled to London and Paris to seek declarations of neutrality from Britain and France.[2]

To defend themselves, the Manchus called back their best general, Yuan Shikai, who had led the regime's German-trained new armies at the start of the century before being banished from the capital for being too powerful. Under his direction, imperial forces partially defeated the rebels in Wuhan. But the revolt had spread to fifteen provinces, and Yuan turned his power on the throne. Though he was allowed to go on living in the Forbidden City, Emperor Pu Yi was forced to abdicate while Yuan had himself appointed Prime Minister, and formed a cabinet containing only one Manchu.

For Chiang Kai-shek, the 1911 revolution provided the apprenticeship for his rise to power. After his tough experience in Japan, he became immersed in the very different world of Shanghai with its overlapping layers of politics, plotting and violence. The city was the biggest and most modern urban centre in the country, the home of cut-throat commerce and finance with a huge labour force fuelled by migrants from poor rural regions, a brutal metropolis on the make. China's writ did not run in the British-American International Settlement and the French Concession which Peking had ceded by treaties imposed by the imperial powers in the nineteenth century. As well as housing foreigners, the concessions, with their modernity, attracted a far more numerous Chinese population. For revolutionaries and political exiles, they were a great haven.

After responding to Chen Qimei's call to join him in 1911, Chiang became well acquainted with the dark side of the city, which he would use in murderous fashion in due course. He could not have found a better training ground or a better teacher than the sworn brother he had met in Japan, for whom he had a sword made to celebrate their undying relationship.

The son of a businessman, Chen Qimei had been apprenticed to a pawnbroker and worked for a silk merchant before his brother, an army officer, paid for him to go to study in Japan. Though enrolled at military school there, his real interest lay in political activity, and he attended the meeting with Sun Yat-sen which formed the United League. Chen saw the constant use of violence as the way to revolution. Mild-looking with protruding ears and owlish spectacles, he had an almost adolescent air. But he led a successful assault by several hundred rebels on the city's arsenal, the seat of military power, on 3 November 1911, and then became military governor of Shanghai. Sun later commented that the rising in Shanghai had been the greatest contribution of any in 1911. Chen had a good relationship with businessmen, who welcomed the lifting of imperial restrictions on trade and finance. He also forged links with the city's secret societies and underworld, including the main criminal outfit, the Green Gang. One of his associates, Ying Guixin, employed criminals to conduct kidnapping, robbery and extortion missions.

Chiang Kai-shek's revolutionary blow was struck 100 miles south of Shanghai, in Hangzhou, chief city of his native province of Zhejiang. He travelled there in early November to organise a 100-strong unit, writing to his mother to ask her forgiveness for having neglected her. Her reply, as recorded by one of his admiring biographers, was that Chiang should do as his duty required. Early on 5 November, a storming party headed by two young women throwing home-made bombs moved on the governor's headquarters, and set it on fire. With reinforcements, the attackers then staged a two-pronged attack on the garrison camp by the West Lake. The demoralised defenders were quickly disarmed. Among those who took part in the attack was a 'Dare to Die' unit which, if the Shanghai precedent was anything to go by, included men from the Green Gang.

The provincial revolts which followed the October uprising raised the possibility that China might fall apart as regions went their own way. To prevent this, a conference was held in Shanghai with a representative of Yuan Shikai. On Christmas Day 1911, Sun Yat-sen landed in the city after returning from Europe via Singapore. Going to a house in the French Concession, he telephoned the leaders of the revolutionary delegation at the conference. Two of them went to see him, accompanied by the Australian who would be at Xi'an a quarter of a century later, W. H. Donald.

In a drawing room where a weak fire was burning, Sun sat to one side of the hearth. On the other side was a hunchback, dressed in a uniform with big shining buttons and medals. This was an American named Homer Lea, who had latched on to Sun as an adviser. The doctor hailed him as 'a world brilliant military talent', but his presence went down badly that afternoon: according to Donald's biography, the Chinese could not understand how the would-be leader of the revolution could have chosen such a man, and Lea was soon sidelined. On 29 December a provisional parliament met to elect the doctor as provisional president of China under a constitution which promised China's first national parliamentary election.[3]

Sun formed a government with several figures who would work for or against Chiang in the decades ahead, including the southern politician and theorist, Hu Hanmin, as secretary general of the President's office. The cabinet met round a large rectangular table in a Western-style building looking out on a neat garden at the back of the former imperial governor's headquarters. But its authority was extremely limited, and the task of turning from revolutionary theory to practical administration soon became too much for the doctor. After only forty-five days, he handed over to Yuan Shikai. Responsibility for uniting the nation and establishing the Republic was thus vested in a general who said he had no time for 'abstract ideas' like democracy.[4]

Returning to Shanghai with his first victory under his belt, Chiang was put in command of a revolutionary army brigade funded by local merchants. According to a critical account written in 1930, the men were riff-raff, and their commander soon gave up trying to train them. Chiang followed the example of Chen Qimei by forging links with secret societies, and plunged into the flamboyant Shanghai nightlife. A photograph of the time shows him as a debonair figure with his hair slicked back, wearing a shirt with a high stiff collar and a three-button striped jacket. He also got to know Zhang Jingjiang,* a prominent financier whom he added to his list of sworn brothers.

Zhang, son of a wealthy family in Chiang's home province of Zhejiang, had been bought an imperial rank by his father. He went abroad to join the Chinese legation in Paris where he established a trading company dealing in gold, tea and silk: he also ran a bean curd factory and a lucrative antiques business which gave him his nickname of 'Curio Chang' in the transliteration of the time. During the First World War, he moved across the Atlantic. His wife stayed in America when he returned to China after the armistice, but his five daughters, all with Western names, joined him.

After meeting Sun Yat-sen on a boat, Zhang became a devoted follower of the doctor, and contributed large sums to his cause. His home near the racecourse in the International Settlement was a gathering place for politicians and businessmen. Zhang suffered from creeping paralysis of the spine which led the French Concession police to dub him 'Quasimodo'. A photograph taken after the revolution shows Sun striding forward while Zhang lurches awkwardly to his left, wearing a light homburg hat and multicoloured embroidered coat. In later years, as his illness grew worse, he would be carried about on a litter, referring to himself as 'the Reclining

* Also known as Zhang Renjie.

Cicada'. With his dark glasses, Richard III-like appearance and aura of money and power, he was one of the city's distinctive figures, his influence increased by underworld and secret society contacts to whom he introduced Chiang. The young revolutionary clearly struck Zhang as a man with a future. For his part, Chiang referred to his feeling of 'fear and respect' for the businessman.[5]

Despite such useful associations, Chiang was not the most popular man in revolutionary circles. He had a nasty temper and insisted on having his own way. His fiery side was well illustrated in 1912 when he went to see a rival of Chen Qimei, who was in hospital at the time. As a quarrel developed, Chiang pulled out his pistol and shot the man dead.*

After this episode Chiang, now twenty-five, took off for Japan, where he published a military magazine, for which he wrote articles extolling the doctrine of 'blood and iron' and the centralisation of military power. China, he argued, should be ruled by an enlightened despotism which would combine 'Washington's ideals' with 'Napoleon's methods', and democratic thought with revolutionary spirit. He considered going to Germany to further his training, but returned to Shanghai instead for fresh enterprises with Chen Qimei against the growing power of Yuan Shikai.[6]

The city's revolutionary administration had lost its initial popularity as taxes rose and corruption grew. Yuan Shikai edged Chen out, and installed his own men. Sun Yat-sen had also proved malleable. In August 1912, he was lavishly received in Peking, and had thirteen meetings with the President after which he proclaimed his host to be 'just the right man'. On 25 September, the doctor was among those who put their names to an agreement that handed the stocky, bull-headed general a ten-year term in the name of stability and national reconciliation. The National Assembly backed one of his cronies as prime minister. 'The Chinese revolution is a very young baby,' Yuan told a diplomat. 'It must be nursed and kept from taking strong meat or potent medicines like those prescribed by foreign doctors.'[7]

Sun found a new enthusiasm as Director for Construction of All Railways in China, and set out for an inspection tour in a long train with two dining cars. The preference for grand schemes over practicality which marked

---

* According to the adulatory biography by Sie, Chiang acted in 'legitimate self defence' (p. 92), but others say he took the initiative.

Sun's politics also applied to his new passion. On a large map, he drew thick lines between provincial capitals with thinner lines for branch links. If a connection was crooked, Sun would wipe it out with wet cotton and draw a straight line regardless of the terrain or natural barriers. He was keen to show his map to journalists who boarded the train, but W. H. Donald, who accompanied him, prudently arranged for it to be temporarily mislaid.

Though Sun had allowed himself to be sidelined, the Nationalist Party, the Kuomintang (KMT) which was formed in August 1912 to replace earlier revolutionary groups, acquired a potent young political organiser called Song Jiaoren as it prepared for the general election promised by the constitution. Still only thirty, Song appealed to the middle class, landowners and merchants by ditching any mention of Sun's principle of the 'people's livelihood', which many equated with socialism. Equality of the sexes was also dropped. In February 1913, the results of the election gave the Kuomintang 269 of the 596 seats in the lower house of the legislature and 123 of 274 in the upper house. Its score meant that it would have no difficulty concluding alliances with smaller parties to form a majority, enabling Song to become Prime Minister at the head of a cabinet to displace Yuan Shikai's regime.

To eliminate that challenge, one of Yuan's henchmen contacted Chen Qimei's gangster former associate in Shanghai, Ying Guixin, who felt that the revolution had not treated him well enough. His relationship with Yuan's regime became so close that the Prime Minister gave him a copy of its secret code book. After receiving a telegram from the capital promising him a high award if he destroyed Song, Ying approached a young man called Wu in a teahouse and offered him a trip to Europe if he would 'lighten the labours of Yuan Shikai and smooth his path'.[8]

On 20 March, Song Jiaoren went to the Shanghai station to board the train for Peking. As he walked along the platform, Wu, dressed in black, opened fire with a Browning revolver. Song was rushed to a hospital where the doctors were told to wait for official permission from Peking to operate. By the time this came, peritonitis had set in. Song died the following morning. A Western woman doctor said he could have been saved if she had been able to act immediately. On 21 March Ying sent two telegrams to the capital. One read: 'The urgent order was executed.' The other added: 'The insurgent leader is already annihilated; none of our army was killed or wounded.'

The Yuan administration tried to blame the killing on internal Kuomintang feuds, and then conjured up an unknown organisation called the Women's Assassination Group. But Ying was an immediate suspect, and was arrested while smoking opium in a brothel. In his house, police found the exchange of telegrams with Peking, together with the murder weapon. There was also an incriminating letter from the Prime Minister who soon stepped down on the grounds that he was suffering from toothache – he died after being fed poison the following year. The assassin, Wu, was also arrested, and also died of poisoning while awaiting trial. Ying, however, escaped and went to Peking to seek support. Soon afterwards, he was stabbed to death with two swords in a railway compartment. Responsibility for his death was not established.

After Song's death, Sun Yat-sen joined the opposition in criticising Yuan Shikai for having raised a £25 million loan from an international banking consortium without consulting Parliament. The general sent troops to surround the legislature, and sacked three provincial governors who sympathised with the nationalist cause. Seven provinces declared their independence of Peking in what became known as the Second Revolution, but were defeated without much difficulty. Yuan ordered the dissolution of the Kuomintang, meaning that Parliament could not meet for lack of a quorum. A constitutional conference in the spring of 1914 confirmed him as dictator for life. Egged on by an American adviser, F. J. Goodnow, who thought empire the right form of government for China, Yuan laid plans to elevate himself to the throne, and ordered a 40,000-piece porcelain dinner service from the former imperial pottery.

As part of the Second Revolution, Chiang Kai-shek was entrusted with an attack on the Shanghai Arsenal. On his way there, he was arrested by a sentry, but escaped. The early morning attack was a fiasco. After his outnumbered force suffered heavy losses, Chiang fled to the International Settlement, gave up his arms and went with his wealthy patron, Zhang Jingjiang, to try to raise support in Nanking. When this got nowhere, Chiang and Chen Qimei, who had a price of $50,000 on his head, sailed once more to Japan.[9]

The next year, the young man was involved in plans for another rising which was aborted by the security forces of the Shanghai military governor, Admiral Cheng Ju-cheng, a graduate of the Greenwich Naval College in London. The authorities bribed a fellow revolutionary they had arrested to kill Chiang. But he sought shelter with his rich patron, Zhang Jingjiang. When police tracked him down there, Chiang walked out of the house with a young lady on his arm, gambling that the watchers would not expect him to be accompanied. As he stepped into the street, the police asked if he was their quarry. 'No,' he replied. 'We've just said goodbye to him in the drawing room.' Returning to Japan yet again, he rejoined Sun Yat-sen who was working on the establishment of a new movement, the China Revolutionary Party. With only 500 members, it was more of a secret society than a political party, described by one Kuomintang veteran as 'a small group of oddly-assorted people . . . without the slightest political training'. Chiang became its 102nd member.[10]

For all his long years of struggle, the doctor's own status was questionable at this point. His insistence on unchallenged authority over colleagues alienated potential partners. Nor was Sun's prestige enhanced by his womanising. He had abandoned his wife, whom he had wed in an arranged marriage in his home village. They had had three children, but Sun had left her in Hawaii while he went on his travels. 'Even his close associates were disturbed by the way Sun consorted with prostitutes in Southeast Asia,' a historian of the clandestine revolutionary movement has written. 'That was the trouble with the old boy,' W. H. Donald noted. 'Couldn't keep him off the women.' He pursued a liaison in Japan from which a daughter was born, and invited what the Australian described as 'a large number of beautiful Chinese women' to join his railway inspection tour in 1912.[11]

Among the party as Sun's secretary was Ailing Soong, the American-educated eldest daughter of the Shanghai tycoon, Methodist and republican supporter, Charlie Soong. According to Donald's recollection, the doctor stared at her during the train journeys without a flicker of his eyelids. He asked her father for her hand in marriage, but this was refused, if only on the grounds that the doctor was still married to his first wife and the Methodist businessman could not approve of bigamy. Ailing, who was more interested in money than in politics, soon left the doctor's employ. Her place was taken by her beautiful sister, Qingling, also a graduate from the Methodist Wesleyan College in Macon, Georgia.[12]

Charlie Soong tried to keep his daughter away from Sun, locking her in their Shanghai home. But she climbed out of a window and escaped with her man. In October 1915 they married. He was fifty; she was twenty-three.

Aware of the controversy, the doctor did not appear at public functions with his wife for more than two years.

To raise funds for the revolution, Sun sent Chen and Chiang on a trip to South-east Asia. Their boat called at Shanghai, and the lure of the city proved too much – they went ashore and stayed there when the ship travelled on. After the failures of the previous two years, Chiang pushed for action against the main symbol of Yuan's power in the city. On 10 November 1915, the revolutionaries struck.

That morning, the military governor drove in his black Delage limousine to the Japanese Consulate for a reception in honour of the Emperor. As the car slowed down to cross tram tracks onto the riverside Bund, a Chinese man on the pavement threw a bomb. It arched over the limousine and exploded in a cloud of smoke. The bomb thrower and another man, both wearing gowns, drew Mauser pistols. One jumped on the running board and pumped bullets inside; the other ran alongside, firing as he went. Bullets shattered the windscreen, and riddled the woodwork and upholstery. One of Admiral Cheng's medals was blown off. Two passing British police inspectors intervened, and overpowered the attackers. They carried ammunition belts containing 198 bullets. Hit sixteen times, the Admiral was dead on arrival at the hospital. The assassins said they had been 'very disappointed' at Yuan Shikai's plans to become emperor, and had resolved to kill Cheng as his representative.[13]

Chen Qimei and Chiang hoped the assassination would clear the way for a naval mutiny they were planning to incite by taking over the local flagship, the 2,750-ton, British-built *Chao-ho*. With the help of a Green Gang member, they spent $200,000 on bribes to the crews of two other ships to join in. In the evening of 5 December 1915, a yellow-funnelled launch carrying two dozen young men sailed alongside the *Chao-ho*. The passengers, who looked like students, asked to be allowed to visit the warship. Once aboard, they surrounded its guns, drew pistols and demanded the keys of the magazine, managing to get access to ammunition for the smaller cannons. At pistol point, the gunners were forced to shoot eighty-five three-inch shells at the city. Though they aimed high, some buildings were hit, including a hotel where a shell passed through the kitchen as the cooks prepared dinner.

Simultaneous attacks were launched on police stations, the main telephone exchange and the electricity station. Bombs were left in parcels and fruit baskets. But the revolt fizzled out, in large part because of incompetent preparations against superior forces. Fire from loyal ships hit the boiler of the *Chao-ho* and, since none of those who had boarded it knew how to move the ship, it became a sitting target. The crews of the two other ships failed to join in. The revolutionaries on land were soon dispersed.[14]

Heading out from the French Concession, Chen and Chiang found themselves alone as more and more enemy soldiers appeared. 'Luckily,' Chiang recalled, 'it was fairly dark, and they could not distinguish who we were.' The two retraced their steps to a safe house. No sooner had they arrived than police turned up with drawn pistols. Chen's nephew, Chen Guofu, banged the doors and pushed tables and chairs around to make as much noise as possible to warn his uncle and Chiang who were upstairs. 'Very softly, Chen Qimei and I climbed over the next building and from there went into hiding in my private room on the Avenue Joffre,' Chiang recounted. Though he said their spirits never wavered, he admitted that 'the days seemed dark and bleak'.[15]

Chiang joined an attempt to subvert a fortress north-west of the city, which was initially successful as local troops revolted. But the general appointed as the revolutionary commander changed sides after being bribed by Yuan Shikai. Chiang stayed on with some of his men till they were beaten by superior numbers and their chief, a former bandit, was beheaded. According to one account Chiang was left alone in the fortress at midnight when two soldiers came up and put him on the road back to Shanghai.[16]

The revolutionaries suffered other reverses and growing financial problems. But, in May 1916, Chen Qimei thought he had hit a rich vein when a man contacted him with a scheme to raise money from a Japanese financier, with a Chinese mine serving as collateral. Though Chiang advised caution, Chen told him the contact was 'one of us'. A meeting was arranged to finalise the deal. Half a dozen men in a hired, chauffeur-driven car drove up to the house where Chen was staying. There was an initial discussion, but the visitors were assassins working for Yuan Shikai, who shot Chen dead. Chiang took the body in a car to a hideout in the French Concession where he held a rite. He then arranged a funeral at which he delivered the eulogy to say that he and Chen were so close that 'we had almost forgotten we were two separate personalities'.[17]

Fearing he was next on the hit list, Chiang took shelter in a hideout in a pleasure garden, and then moved in with one of Chen's two nephews, both of whom would later play key roles in his regime. Sun then ordered him to join an expedition organised with Japanese help to try to bring revolution to the large coastal province of Shandong. It was very badly organised and poorly armed; Chiang left after two weeks as it collapsed.[18]

This low time came at a moment when the wind was moving in favour of the forces opposing Yuan Shikai. With his old-fashioned outlook, dozen concubines and traditional manners, the general could not meet China's desire for change despite some attempts at modernisation. A bid to impose a more effective system of land taxation alienated the provincial gentry. After eighty-three days on the throne, Yuan was forced to retract his imperial claims. In the spring of 1916, he received W. H. Donald in his palace in Peking. His stumpy body was bent, his hair grey, his face white and shrunken. He slouched forward in his chair, and, after a brief conversation, shuffled out of the room. In June, a month after the murder of Chen Qimei, he died of blood poisoning, ushering in the warlord era in which competing militarists, big and small, fought endless battles across China.

As revolving cliques of generals jostled for power in north and central China, the only place left for Sun Yat-sen was his native province in the south. An army from neighbouring Guangxi province, which had moved into Guangdong, was ready to let him set up in the capital of Canton. The doctor named Chiang as his military adviser, putting him in charge of a field operations section of the revolutionary army under the overall command of the chief provincial general, Chen Jiongming. The two officers quickly fell out, Chiang complaining about a lack of discipline and the difficulty of getting his views across. His Zhejiang accent and dialect also made communication difficult with the Cantonese.[19]

Sun took the title of Grand Marshal, donning a braided uniform with epaulettes and decorations. His national claims were boosted after the ruling clique in Peking sent troops to surround the parliament building there, and legislators headed south to elect him head of a government which was to mount an expedition to take power in the capital. But he had no army, and the commanders in Guangdong were more interested in regional power than in conquering China. The doctor's government was a lacklustre affair; its officials spent their time sitting around playing chess and Sun's influence stopped at the gates of the cement factory he used as his headquarters. His bluff was called when a leading southern militarist sent a message to the gentry, merchants and parliamentarians in Canton saying that the 'rather confusing title of Grand Marshal' was subject to question, and that China did not need another national government. Even the parliamentarians from Peking rejected him by now, and the Grand Marshal was forced to leave for Shanghai in the summer of 1918. Chiang followed him on another journey to the metropolis where, as it turned out, he would find a new wife.[20]

CHAPTER 3

Going to Extremes

IN HIS EARLY THIRTIES, Chiang Kai-shek was a restless, ambitious young man hanging on the coat-tails of revolution as he sought his way forward in life. Subject to impulsive moods and erratic behaviour, he was self-centred and suspicious. In his funeral eulogy for Chen Qimei, he had talked of those 'who have been trying to attack me, slander me and destroy me'. His diary records that he was 'often wary'. He suffered problems with his eyes and teeth, nervous pains and a typhoid attack. He thought of seeking new horizons abroad, and read widely on everything from military matters to astronomy and geography, with a backbone of classical Chinese literature that shaped his conservative views.

Drawing on Chiang's own thoughts, the biographer of his early years, Pichon Loh, says these stressed the importance of serenity, attentiveness, tranquillity and constancy. He set himself high-minded precepts, but found no problem in acting in a less lofty manner. A warrant appears to have been issued for his arrest in connection with an armed robbery. A list of Green Gang members includes a 'Jiang Dezheng' which seems to be a version of Chiang's name: the entry is for a man from his birthplace who gives his profession as 'politician'.[1]

For all his injunctions to apply Confucian respect for elders and superiors, Chiang's petulance and insistence on having his way had become a dominant feature of his character. Before he left Xikou, one of his tutors had written of his wild attitude. A village elder called him 'stubborn, jealous, tactless, bad-tempered and egotistical'. Chiang admitted to his patron, Zhang Jingjiang, a lack of 'cultivation, respectfulness and constancy', and to being stubborn, rude and offensive.[2]

With rare exceptions such as Sun Yat-sen and Chen Qimei, he respected nobody. 'Your hatred of mediocrity is excessive,' the doctor told him. Chiang saw himself as a man who was straightforward and acted in keeping with his conscience, but his friend and Kuomintang colleague, Dai Jitao, referred to his 'unreasonable fury' and called him 'extremely self-willed to an almost incorrigible extent'. 'Whenever you are despondent and in a state of intoxication, you let your anger go unchecked,' Dai added in a letter.

Chiang himself said the murder of Chen Qimei drove him 'into a life of debauchery'. In 1924, he acknowledged that 'everyone says that I am given to lust', but said this was 'a thing of last resort, in a state of utter depression'. His earliest biography records that, after the first revolutionary success, he went through 'a period of rather riotous living' in which 'there was much chance for moral degeneration', and the results began to tell. Other reports described him as a 'suave and knowing lover' and talked of his uncontrollable urge for alcohol and girls as he 'sowed his wild oats [and] scattered his seed all over Shanghai'.[3]

He took as his concubine a plump-cheeked sing-song girl called Yao, whom he described as 'a petite beauty and very charming'. They met at the pleasure gardens where he hid after Chen's death. She belonged to an elderly man who became jealous of her relationship with Chiang. At a dinner given by her patron, Yao brought shark's fin soup to the table. The old man asked if she would give up her new friendship. She said no. According to Chiang's account, her patron told her he had spent thousands of dollars on her, yet she made him lose face repeatedly by consorting with the younger man. Then he took the bowl of soup, and emptied it over her head, saying, 'Since you prefer this penniless revolutionary to me, wear this hat!' The boiling liquid disfigured her, and ruined her career of entertaining men in teahouses.[4]

While Chiang ran wild, Sun Yat-sen and his young wife settled into a neat, two-storey villa at number 29 Rue Molière, in the French Concession, bought with donations from Overseas Chinese. Though always certain of his own correctness, the doctor cut an isolated figure, ill at ease with the modernity adopted by the vanguard of Chinese intellectuals. For all his advocacy of nationalism, he played no part in the biggest protest of the time, arising from the way the Allies treated China which had sent shiploads of labourers to the Western front after coming out against Germany in the later stages of the First World War. In return, the Chinese expected to regain German concessions in Shandong province on the east coast. Instead, secret Allied treaties gave them to Japan. On 4 May 1919, 5,000 students protested in Peking. Mixing nationalism, anger at the Shandong decision and denunciation of the militarist government in the capital, they drew on a rising tide of opinion that China needed to free itself from old modes of thought that were preventing it from becoming a modern nation. Though it could not stop Japan moving into Shandong, 4 May became a landmark in the rise of Chinese nationalism. Later, Sun would try to weave his own mythology round the protest, but, at the time, he dismissed 'young students who prate about the new culture and espouse cosmopolitanism . . . we have no place for them.' Like most revolutionary leaders, he did not fancy any movement he did not control.

In his Shanghai exile, Sun was in regular touch with his financial benefactor and adviser, Zhang Jingjiang. One summer afternoon in 1919, he went to see the crippled businessman at his home in the fashionable western section of Nanking Road, accompanied by Chiang and Dai Jitao. Walking into the drawing room, the three men found Zhang's five daughters and a girlfriend doing a Chinese lesson. Sun delivered a brief lecture about how the young could serve China, Chiang smiling approval. The teenagers then quit the room, returning occasionally with refreshments for the men before Sun and his companions left the house in the early evening.[5]

The sixth girl, known by her 'milk name' of Ah Feng, was the daughter of a paper merchant and of a well-educated woman noted for her calligraphy. One of Ah Feng's friends, called Zhu Yimin, had married Zhang after his first wife died in America. When they came back to Shanghai after their mother's death, his daughters needed to learn Chinese, and Yimin suggested that her acquaintance, who spoke Chinese and English, should help the tutor engaged by their father. After saying goodbye to Yimin that evening, Ah Feng found Chiang standing at the front gate like a sentry. 'The man's face was flushed from the wine he had drunk, and he looked so very red,' she wrote later, describing Chiang as of average height, somewhat wiry, with shaven head, jutting jaw, prominent chin and a short, straight nose. When he spoke, he grunted, revealing unusually long teeth. His eyes were dark and penetrating, his lips sensuous, his tone lecherous as he asked her where she lived. She gave a wrong address to mislead him. He offered to walk with her. She refused. He stood in her path. She dashed past, hurrying home while he gazed after her.[6]

Four decades later, Ah Feng, who had taken the adult name of Chen Jieru and was also known as Jennie, wrote her memoirs in English with the help of a collaborator in Hong Kong. After a US firm offered to publish the book, two of Chiang's aides threatened legal action, and the offer was withdrawn. With the help of its friends in Washington, Chiang's administration in Taiwan was determined to suppress the memoirs for fear of the embarrassment it might cause. The agent handling the book in the United States was attacked and beaten up twice. His office was broken into. He was threatened with lawsuits, and investigated by the FBI. After American publication was blocked, a lawyer representing Chiang's son bought copies of the manuscript from the Hong Kong collaborator for US$170,000.

When Jennie died in 1971, it seemed that her recollections would never see the light of day. But, eighteen years later, a leading expert on Republican China, Professor Lloyd Eastman, tracked down a copy of the manuscript in the Hoover Institution in California. In 1992, the memoirs appeared in book form in Chinese, followed by the English original the next year. They are, naturally, told from the author's viewpoint and contain incidents for which she is the only source. Although there are errors in dating and some sections are gushing and melodramatic, there is no reason to doubt their overall accuracy: indeed, the book is far from the negative portrait that might have been expected given her husband's behaviour.

When Chiang first saw her, Ah Feng was, in her own words, 'tall and lanky, but well formed . . . Although I had a smooth complexion and sharp features, my mouth was large, with prominent teeth, and my jawbones were rather heavy . . . I wore thick, heavy bangs, which almost covered my eyebrows, and my hair hung in a long plait down my back.' A week after the meeting, she was sewing at home in Tibet Road in the International Settlement when Chiang walked by. Her mother had gone shopping, and had left the door open to give her daughter light to work by. Seeing her,

Chiang said he had been searching for her, but had been misled by the wrong house number she had given. She told him she had done this because she did not want him to come to her home. Ah Feng's mother then returned, and got rid of him. The next day, Yimin told Ah Feng that Chiang was madly in love with her. He kept coming to Zhang's house when she was there, and eventually talked her into lunching with him at St George's Restaurant in the International Settlement.

'Throughout lunch, he bombarded me with a stream of questions for which I had few answers,' she recalled. 'He was so excited and spoke so loudly in his Ningbo dialect that I had to tell him to lower his voice several times.' After the meal, Chiang invited her to visit his sister. Ah Feng said she had homework to do, but he brushed that aside. She insisted he walk ahead of her since she considered it improper for a young girl to be seen in the street with a strange man.

After covering several blocks of Bubbling Well Road, he stopped at the driveway of the Burlington Hotel where he said his sister lived. Ah Feng remarked that the place was for foreigners. But Chiang led her through the lobby and up the thickly carpeted staircase. A white uniformed attendant met them on the landing, and led them down the hall to a room. 'On entering . . . I was surprised to see it was a large bedroom with a wide, foreign bed at one side and a dressing table at the other,' her memoirs went on. 'The large French window had long snowy-white lace curtains. Everything looked so white and clean.' The girl walked around the room, looked into the bathroom, and asked Chiang where his sister was.

By then, he was turning the key in the door lock. 'Don't be alarmed,' he said with a smile. 'I want to talk to you and tell you a secret. Ah Feng, I'm really lonely. You are the only person who can make me happy, but your coldness makes me unhappy.'

He took her hand and kneaded her fingers, trying to embrace her. She ran to the door. 'To stop me, he showed uncontrollable temper,' she recalled. 'He seized me with both his arms in manic frenzy. Then he threw his arms around me and forcefully kissed my cheek and then my mouth. But I fought like a tigress. I kicked and lashed out with all my strength to strike at him.'

Chiang let go, and Ah Feng screamed for help. At that, he opened the door. She dashed out. Reaching home, she told her mother she had a headache, and went to bed. Stubborn as always, Chiang telephoned the next morning. 'What do you want?' Ah Feng snapped. He asked to see her again to be forgiven. She hung up, amazed at his nerve.

He kept telephoning, but she would not speak to him. In a letter, he said her refusal would diminish the 'morale and spirit' of the revolution. 'I cannot rest until I receive your reply,' he added. 'I lay my heart at the hem of your skirt. Say that you will forgive me and talk to me again very soon. Let me see you today!' Ah Feng replied with an implied promise of a reward if he left her alone: 'Your letter received. Don't annoy me by telephoning or writing, and you shall, in time, be forgiven.' He was thirty-two, she, thirteen.

In the autumn of 1920, a Guangdong general with progressive views drove out the militarists who had ejected Sun from Canton. Though his reputation would suffer in later official history, Chen Jiongming, known as the 'Hakka General' after the early inhabitants of the area, was a considerable figure, regarded by the British military attaché as one of the ablest soldiers in China. From a landowning family in eastern Guangdong, he had been provincial vice-governor after the 1911 revolution, and got opium and gambling banned; but he was driven out after the collapse of the Second Revolution in 1913. Moving to the south of neighbouring Fujian province, he built schools and roads there, and encouraged freedom of expression.[7]

After taking Canton and establishing his dominance of Guangdong province, Chen, a broad faced man with a straggling moustache, invited Sun Yat-sen to return. Installed in the city again, the doctor worked on his grand scheme to launch an expedition to the north to make himself president of all China. He called on Chiang to join him, but the younger man had fallen out with Chen on previous trips south, and took several months before moving. When he did, he insisted on going in a private capacity – Guangdong was not a suitable place for him to stay in for long, he declared.

Chen brought in a constitution which limited military spending to 30 per cent of the budget. Twenty per cent was to go to an educational reform programme headed by a noted progressive intellectual, Chen Duxiu, who championed the use of the vernacular language and would become the first leader of the Chinese Communist Party. The government paid for students to go abroad, some to an anarchist-run college in France. Soviet agents called Chen a man of 'great willpower and self control' and 'a brilliant organiser, receiving the sympathies of the masses'.[8]

Favouring the creation of a southern confederation independent of the great warlords in the rest of China, Chen had no time for Sun's schemes for a military expedition to Peking – he respected the doctor but considered him an impractical idealist. Undeterred, the doctor opened negotiations with a northern militarist for a joint attack on the capital which, given the paucity of his resources, was a pipe dream. He subsidised 225 members of the national parliament to assemble in Canton and elect him Extraordinary President of China (since there was no quorum, he could not take the full title). The assembly backed his plans for the expedition, and Sun set out with a small force for the north of Guangdong.

Even more ambitiously, Chiang presented a plan for alliances with warlords in Jiangxi and Sichuan provinces, and an attack in the north-west at a cost of $30 million. It was sheer folly, so Chen refused to put up any money. Chiang flounced out once again for his home province of Zhejiang. When Sun urged him to return, Chiang said he would not make the trip before a proper expeditionary force was mobilised. After the doctor cabled to say this was being done, he relented. Back in the south, however, he dreamed of a snow-covered landscape, and woke sensing a bad omen for his mother, white being the symbolic Chinese colour for death. On 14 June she died at the age of fifty-three. Fiercely individualist to the last, she instructed that she was not to be buried in the same tomb as her husband and his first two wives. She also exhorted her son not to forget members of the family who had helped her in difficult times, leaving a list which, by omission, told him who had not been supportive. Both the sense of standing apart and the cultivation of clan loyalties would mark her son through the coming decades.[9]

Chiang went to Xikou to mourn. He had a tomb built in the pine woods on a hill that is thought to resemble a laughing Buddha with the grave as its navel. On the way up the path, 6-foot-high inscribed tablets were erected, one provided by Sun Yat-sen. In front of the tomb, surrounded by trees and bushes, is a carved image of bamboo and a phoenix – the phoenix representing women, the bamboo the hills where Chiang's mother was born. The smoke from villages below was said to be like incense. Behind the tomb, the earth rises in a triangular form with a flower on top.

In mid-August, Chiang left for Shanghai, where he had a dream which made him fear for the safety of his mother's grave. Hurrying back to Xikou, he found the village had been flooded, but the grave was safe. Finally arriving in Canton in mid-September, Chiang called on Chen Jiongming, but the meeting went so badly that he returned immediately to Shanghai. Surveying his situation, he decided that 'the trouble with me in society is that I go to extremes. Therefore, I have lifelong, sworn, intimate friends, but no ordinary boon companions or social acquaintances. The same applies to my words and actions.'[10]

In Shanghai, Chiang learned of the death of the father of the teenager he had taken to the Burlington Hotel. He visited the family house in his mourning clothes. The body was laid out in the front room. As was the custom, the widow stayed in seclusion while Ah Feng and her brother received visitors. Chiang lit candles and incense, and knelt three times on a cushion beside the bier. Unshaven and looking forlorn, he bowed to the children. They bowed back in silence.[11]

In the following days, Chiang called frequently at Zhang Jingjiang's house to ask about Ah Feng, who was now fifteen. Her friend, Yimin, pressed his case with the girl's mother who engaged a private detective to investigate his private life. The report showed that Chiang was unemployed, and had a wife and a concubine. Ah Feng's mother said there was no question of marriage. This provoked a visit from Zhang, who proffered her assurances that Chiang was divorced from his first wife and that the concubine had signed a separation agreement. He also explained that Chiang was his very good friend, was infatuated and had asked him to act as matchmaker. 'He is most persistent and will not take no for an answer,' the businessman added.

Asked by Ah Feng's mother for a candid assessment of Chiang, Zhang replied: 'He is a man with a good heart, and as a revolutionary he has absolute devotion. I feel he will make your daughter a good husband, Mrs Chen. But, to be very honest, I must say that he is extremely impulsive, opinionated, and too often hot-headed. His only fault is that he takes risks unnecessarily. He is a junior member of our group, and we like his quality of absolute loyalty. But we do not always follow his opinions or suggestions.'

As her mother grew increasingly persuaded, Ah Feng's anger at the hotel incident was moderated by Chiang's forlorn appearance at her father's bier – she did not know that he was still mourning for his mother.

A meeting was arranged at Zhang's house. Sun Yat-sen was also visiting. As she stood in front of the doctor with her head bowed and her eyes on his tan-coloured shoes, Ah Feng heard him say: 'She is a very fine girl, but so young.' After telling the couple to get married if they were in love, he delivered a homily on the need to dedicate their lives to the revolution.

When Sun left, Chiang led the girl into Zhang's library and declared his love. She found it impossible to reply. He took her by taxi to a park in the French Concession, and recounted his arranged marriage and his relationship with the concubine. If they married, he promised, she would be 'his one and only legal wife'. Then, she recalled, he intoned a short poem:

> Oceans may evaporate,
> Mountains may crumble,
> But my love for you
> Will never change.*

When Ah Feng remained tongue-tied, Chiang took a knife from his pocket, and offered to cut off a finger to show how serious he was. She was won over. They became engaged. At a rendezvous at a cafe, he presented her with a photograph of himself in uniform, and said he had decided she should take the name Jieru, meaning 'pure and unblemished'.†

The wedding was held in the Great Eastern Hotel in the Wing On department store building. The bride wore a pale pink satin dress with silver and gold embroidery, and pearl ornaments in her hair. The groom was in a long, dark blue gown with a short black satin jacket. The marriage certificate lay on a table covered with heavy red silk. Another table bore a large pewter incense urn, two candlesticks with red candles, and plates with pagoda-like piles of fruit, sugar cane, cakes and condiments. On the wall, the characters for Double Happiness were embroidered in gold on red satin.[12]

Zhang Jingjiang, who officiated, rose with difficulty from his chair to make a short speech wishing them happiness and good fortune. Bride and

---

* This text is given by Chen Jieru: there is no way of knowing whether she recalled it through a Gershwin prism.
† Chieh-ju in the transliteration of the time – this is the name she uses on her memoirs.

groom pressed the seal into a vermilion ink pad and stamped the marriage certificate. After bowing to the guests, they walked to the other end of the room, knelt at the altar and drank from a silver wine cup while the matron of honour chanted wishes that they might enjoy long life and harmony and have many children. Firecrackers were let off outside to end the ceremony. 'Whenever I looked up to steal a glance at Kai-shek,' Chen's memoirs record, 'I could see that he had a preoccupied and uncomfortable look about him, appearing to be happy and proud, but a little impatient. I knew instinctively his main thought was to get the ceremony over with.'

A bridal suite with modern European furniture had been reserved in the hotel. The brass double bed was hung with pink silk curtains embroidered with dragons and phoenixes, a design repeated in the cover and pillows. Four satin-covered padded quilts were folded lengthwise on one side of the bed. Red scrolls hung on the walls. The trousseau was packed in four trunks.

The bride waited in the room as Chiang stayed with guests at the wedding feast. The matron of honour advised her that she should not resist when he touched her – 'in fact, you must do everything to cooperate and allow him to do what he wishes'. The matron arranged the bedclothes and laid down a small sheet, placing hand towels and lubricant near the pillows. Leaving when the groom came up, she repeated: 'Don't resist the bridegroom. Let him have his way ... Now don't be afraid. Congratulations! May you have a hundred sons and grandsons!' Turning to Chiang, she said cheerily, 'Congratulations and good night, Mr Bridegroom.'

Chiang locked the door. Then, Jennie recalled, 'he took me in his arms, and I could feel my heart thudding against my breast. I stood there like a clinging vine, defenceless with eyes half-closed, and waited ... Then he pressed himself against me passionately and held me tight. I yielded to his desire.' They spent the next day in the room. At one point, between 'gusts of passion', Chiang spoke of the ambitions he had formulated after the death of his mother – to marry Jieru, to win Sun's confidence and become his heir, and to emerge as the country's greatest military leader who would unify China and become illustrious throughout the world.

For their honeymoon, the couple went to Xikou where the bride encountered her husband's family and his first wife. They walked through the hills and floated down the river in a flat-bottomed bamboo boat. On their return to Shanghai, Jennie met Chiang's son, Ching-kuo, who was only four years younger than her. He seemed a well-behaved, quiet lad, but afraid of his father. When Jennie pleaded with her husband not to be harsh, he replied that the worst thing for a boy was to be spoiled by his parents – 'he must learn discipline'.[13]

The new bride also became aware of another member of the Chiang family, a boy whom her husband had adopted. He told her that the child, called Wei-kuo – or Wego – had been fathered during a stay in Japan by his Kuomintang associate and sworn brother, Dai Jitao. The Japanese mother had turned up with the baby one day. Dai, who was now married, did not want to acknowledge his son; so Chiang agreed to adopt him. Jennie described Wei-kuo as delicate and frail, with a long, thin face. He was obedient, intelligent and curious, and Chiang seemed to have a soft spot for him that contrasted with his harshness towards his natural son. 'Ching-kuo is teachable and Wei-kuo is lovable,' he recorded in his diary. He confided care of the child to his former concubine, Yao, and they went to live in Chiang's home village. Seventy years later, the adopted son said Chiang's first wife frequently abused them, making them inhabit a pigsty where they slept on straw.[14]

On returning to Shanghai, Jennie made another, more alarming discovery after suffering from skin irritations. She went to see a doctor who took blood samples. Three days later, she wrote in her memoirs, he told her she had gonorrhoea.

The bride rushed in a taxi to her mother's home. Chiang arrived there half an hour later. He said the complaint was mild, and could be treated. According to Jennie, he also admitted that he had contracted the disease before their marriage, and had infected her. Given the life he had led in the city, this was hardly surprising: between 10 and 15 per cent of the population of Shanghai was estimated to have suffered from syphilis, and even more had gonorrhea.

Jennie's mother gave her son-in-law a tongue-lashing, while Jennie shouted, 'You are an evil man. I will divorce you!' Chiang stood with head bowed, begging forgiveness. That afternoon, the two of them went to see the doctor. He told Chiang to leave the room. Then he injected an antidote containing arsenic into Jennie's arm. A course of ten shots would cure her, he said. But he warned that this might make her sterile.

They went into the waiting room, where, Jennie recalled, the doctor told Chiang he should have finished his own course of treatment before getting married, and revealed that the groom suffered from epididymitis, which made him sterile. Swearing remorse, Chiang pledged as a penance never to touch alcohol. 'I was too miserable to argue,' Jennie recalled. 'What could I do? What could any young wife do under these circumstances, except to forgive? So, I forgave Kai-shek. And true to his promise, he gave up liquor and all kinds of liquid except boiled water.'[15]

There is no reason to doubt Jennie's account, which is supported by the fact that Chiang had no children by either of his last two marriages. Many years later, his adopted son provided a more graphic version of his inability to procreate. At the end of his life, Wei-kuo gave an interview to a history professor in Taiwan. His story was that, as a youth in his home village, Chiang had sat on an iron handle of a wood-burning stove, severely burning his sexual organs. His mother treated the injury by rubbing lard on it. A little while later, Chiang went to defecate in a field. Attracted by the smell of the lard, a dog ran up and bit his testicles. Chiang was dead by the time the story appeared, but one of his bodyguards promptly dismissed it, adding that the Generalissimo had been sexually active into his sixties. Wei-kuo's story looked like an attempt by the adopted son to undermine the legitimacy of the natural son, branding Ching-kuo as the bastard of the first wife and a local businessman. Dynastic games are an old sport in China.*[16]

By the time they boarded the liner, the *President Taft*, for the south to join Sun Yat-sen at the beginning of 1922, Jennie appears to have forgiven Chiang. Her account of the voyage is upbeat. It was the first time she had been on a foreign ship, and everything was modern and luxurious to her. Chiang loved the expanse of the ocean, and looked forward to seeing Sun Yat-sen again. They had a first-class cabin; two servants travelled steerage. As well as his clothes, Chiang took two suitcases full of papers, maps and books, and studied the menu to try to pick up some English. Jennie read

---

* In her 1955 biography of Chiang, the American writer Emily Hahn, who lived in China in the 1930s, implies that Wei-kuo was, in fact, Chiang's son (Hahn, p. 48). But other contemporary accounts stick to the adoption account. If Chiang was his father, Wei-kuo's story of the stove and the dog makes no sense. But it must be said that Wei-kuo looked more like the Generalissimo than Ching-kuo, whose square face resembled his mother and grandmother.

books about the revolution. In Canton, they were met by one of Sun's principal lieutenants, Liao Zhongkai, who took them to a hotel on the riverside Bund. After Liao had briefed him on the latest events, Chiang discussed with his wife whether to pay a call on the Hakka General, Chen Jiongming, telling her of their intense mutual dislike.[17]

After she urged him to seek a meeting, he set out for Chen's headquarters, where he was kept waiting for twenty minutes before being granted admittance. Chen explained his reasons for opposing Sun's expedition to the north, and invited the visitor to lunch with his officers. As they ate, Chiang heard one refer to the doctor by the nickname of 'the Great Cannon' – meaning 'the big talker'. Chiang asked Chen to go with him into an adjoining room where he demanded how such an insult could be tolerated. Chen suggested he show a sense of humour. Chiang stalked out.

He and Jennie went to join Sun in the north of Guangdong province. The doctor's expedition was advancing slowly on a fleet of steam launches and wooden boats, preceded by two regiments of soldiers. Chiang grew increasingly annoyed by the Nationalist leader's praise of Chen Jiongming. When he advocated dismissing the Hakka General and launching an attack on him, Sun told him to be more trusting and tolerant. 'Seeing that Dr Sun was adamant, Kai-shek turned, broke down and wept bitterly,' Jennie recorded. The next day, glum and irritable, he told her they were returning to Shanghai. On the way, Chiang shouted orders to troops in his dreams.[18]

Despite Sun's refusal to follow Chiang's advice, Chen and the general in charge of Canton, Ye Ju, were growing fed up with the doctor. The Hakka General considered him unqualified to organise a military expedition. Worse, he added, the Kuomintang chief was listening to 'that Zhejiang rogue, Chiang, who wants me dismissed from office'. An intermediary, who went to Hong Kong to order arms for the doctor, was shot dead at the station on his return, allegedly on Chen's orders. From Shanghai, Chiang wrote 'a last appeal' to Chen to help with Sun's expedition. The letter was returned unopened. On the back of the envelope was written 'Upstart-jealous-ill-tempered-stupid-egotistical mischief maker'.[19]

Sun's hopes of a national role were temporarily boosted in his own mind by a war between major militarists in northern and central China in which he hoped to play a role. But the conflict ended before he could move his puny forces from Guangdong. He then received a second blow when a warlord in neighbouring Hunan province, with whom he had an understanding, deserted him. Alarmed by the hostility of General Ye in Canton, he returned to the city with fifty bodyguards, issuing a hysterical warning that he had 'eight-inch guns with poisonous shells capable of entirely finishing off sixty battalions in three hours'.

Ye showed what he thought of that by ordering an early-morning bombardment of Sun's residence on 16 June 1922. The doctor told his wife to dress and flee with him. Qingling urged him to go alone, and he made his way to the Whampoa Fort on an island in the Pearl River where loyal naval units awaited him. Half an hour after he had left, Ye's men opened up with rifles on Sun's bodyguards under the command of a young officer called Xue Yue who would become a leading Nationalist general. 'From eight in the morning till four that afternoon, we were literally buried in a hell of constant gunfire,' Qingling wrote. She escaped to a farm, and then made her way to join her husband on a gunboat. A fire at the house destroyed his manuscripts and notes for a book setting out his political philosophy. The next day, five of the doctor's boats steamed up the river and machine-gunned the street along the Bund. Sun sent telegrams to Chiang telling him what had happened, and adding: 'Matters critical: hope for your speedy arrival.'[20]

On receiving the news, Chiang paced up and down, shaking with fury and screaming, 'I predicted it! I predicted it!' He told his wife to pack so that they could take the first ship south. She was in the middle of putting up the curtains at their new flat, and her mother told Chiang he should leave her daughter behind – 'bringing your wife to Canton at this time is like delivering a lamb into a tiger's mouth'. But Jennie decided to go with him. Before leaving, Chiang wrote to his patron, Zhang Jingjiang, asking him to look after his family if he were killed.[21]

The Chiangs sailed to Hong Kong and then travelled up the Pearl River to Canton where they boarded a motor launch that took them to Sun's flotilla of blue-grey gunboats. When Chiang stepped onto the flagship, the *Yung-feng*, Sun looked at him with tears in his eyes. Chiang's diary records, on what evidence is unclear, that Chen Jiongming turned blue in the face when he heard of his arrival. With Chiang on the scene, he warned, there would be 'a great many devilish ideas'.

Sending his wife and Dr Sun to shelter below deck, Chiang instructed the captain to sail up the river to fire at a fort. As the boat moved forward,

Sun sat at a table writing a speech. Sweat rolled off his forehead. Jennie got him a damp face towel, and stood behind him waving a palm-leaf fan. A shell hit the boat, throwing her to the floor. 'Dr Sun held on to the table, but his chair fell on top of me,' she wrote in her memoirs. 'When I rose, I felt my drawers sticking to my legs, and I knew that I had unconsciously urinated from shock.'

Despite a barrage from shore guns, the little fleet reached a mooring near the British Concession on a sandbank in the Pearl River where it was less likely to be attacked. While Sun tried to negotiate, Chiang whiled away the time reading translations of Sherlock Holmes stories. The doctor's position grew steadily weaker and, by the beginning of August, even Chiang had had enough. 'Everything seems against us,' he wrote. The British provided a boat which was allowed through to Hong Kong. On board were the Chiangs and Sun – Qingling followed later. After the weeks cooped up on the gunboat, they sailed to Shanghai on the *Empress of Russia*, the largest liner plying in the Pacific, complete with lifts, Persian carpets and a soda fountain. As they travelled, Chen took the title of commander-in-chief in Guangdong and was recognised as governor of both that province and neighbouring Jiangxi by the major warlord of central China, Wu Peifu; there were reports that Wu had sent him $5 million.[22]

The debacle in Canton served Chiang well in establishing himself as a loyal right-hand man for Sun: the doctor contributed a preface to an account the younger man wrote of their weeks together on the Pearl River. Four decades later, Chiang spoke of the 'wordless rapport' that grew out of their time on the boat. With what veracity it is impossible to say, he also claimed that Sun had told him that, while he, himself, expected to die within the coming ten years, 'you will have at least fifty more [and] if nothing untoward happens in the future, it is not too much to expect you to carry on the struggle for fifty more years for the sake of our principles'.[23]

Sun plunged into a round of meetings with potential allies in Shanghai, and worked on the reorganisation of the Kuomintang. Three of his supporters sat briefly in the Cabinet in Peking. The French consul called his house 'a veritable ministry'. The *New York Times* described it as 'a Mecca for political leaders of all shades of opinion'. However, his attempts to enlist American support got nowhere, leading him to turn to Moscow for backing, and to form a link with the newly founded Chinese Communist

Party. At the suggestion of Hendricus Sneevliet, a Dutch agent for the international Communist organisation the Comintern, members of the Chinese movement were allowed to join the Kuomintang as individuals while retaining their own party affiliation. The Communists would have preferred to go it alone, but the overbearing Sneevliet insisted, and Moscow decreed that the Kuomintang should be seen as a revolutionary party, starting a relationship that would swing from cooperation to war during the following three decades.[24]

At the end of 1922, Moscow sent an experienced diplomat, Adolf Joffe, to China to try to gain recognition from the government in Peking. Failing to do so, Joffe met other prospective partners, including Sun. In January 1923, they issued a statement declaring the need for national unity and independence for China. At the doctor's insistence, it added that the country was not ready for Communism. The prospect of an alliance with a nation where revolutionaries had conquered power was intoxicating, but Sun knew that he needed a base if he was to build his strength. As he wrote to Chiang: 'To get that we must recapture Guangdong.'[25]

Moving between Shanghai and his home province of Zhejiang, Chiang was growing increasingly bad-tempered. His weeks on the gunboat in Canton had led him to imagine he would enter Sun's inner circle, but he was still regarded as a military operative rather than a political figure. 'For the first time in our married life he made no effort to control his temper,' his wife recalled. 'Something had to be done for his own sake to alleviate this intense hatred; otherwise he would become a mental case . . . I began to make him relax his tension and tried to humour him to the best of my ability. But at best it was terribly difficult.'[26]

Jennie's friend, Yimin, came up with a solution: Chiang should join a share broking company set up by her businessman husband, Zhang Jingjiang. Unknown to his wife, Chiang had already been involved in stock exchange speculation, and the idea appealed to him. He was certainly in the right place. Shanghai had the country's most advanced market exchanges for everything from gold and silver to soap and tinfoil. Trading was often highly speculative, with companies ramping their own shares – and plenty of dubious dealing. To become a partner in the new enterprise, Chiang bought four shares at $1,000 each which he registered under a false name. As he became absorbed in trading, his anger diminished. But he made bad punts, including one on textile shares which lost $20,000.

A brokerage career did not beckon, and Sun was soon calling him to Canton.

Rather than trying himself to dislodge Chen Jiongming, the doctor had paid mercenaries from Yunnan and Jiangxi $400,000 to invade Guangdong, forcing the Hakka General back to his heartland in the east of the province. Chiang said such alliances were justified if they helped to advance the cause. On 21 February 1923, Sun returned to Canton, naming the future Generalissimo as his chief of staff. The ever-helpful Zhang Jingjiang stumped up the money to cover his trading losses, and a Green Gang boss was also said to have chipped in. But Chiang still played hard to get, going on a trip to Zhejiang, and then pleading that he had to stay in Shanghai for eye treatment. When he finally set off, he insisted on going in a personal capacity. In a letter, he remarked that he would do best if he could 'act summarily without interference from anyone'.[27]

CHAPTER 4

꧁

The Will of Heaven

ONE EVENING AFTER GETTING TO Canton, Chiang was invited to dinner at the home of a prominent Kuomintang politician with whom his career would be entwined for twenty years. Wang Jingwei's revolutionary pedigree included an unsuccessful assassination attempt on a Manchu imperial viceroy. Handsome and a fine orator, he was now one of the three main figures below Sun Yat-sen. Wang's wife, Wang Bijun – known as Becky – a wealthy heiress with luxuriant hair, large eyes and a strong chin, greeted the guests at the door of their villa in a new residential district of the city. They were shown into a spacious drawing room where tall French windows opened onto a large terrace. The room was decorated in yellow and black, with calligraphy scrolls on the walls.

Sun Yat-sen was the guest of honour, surrounded by politicians and generals. At dinner, the women sat apart from the men and, when the food arrived, followed tradition by staring at the dishes in the centre of the table without serving themselves. As the third course came, Jennie Chiang got to her feet, and dished it out, saying that, as revolutionaries, they would be hypocritical to accept the old idea that eating was ugly.[1]

After dinner, Sun left, looking pallid and ill. Kai-shek made a point of talking to a mercenary commander, Liu Zhenhuan, whom the doctor had dubbed 'Living Angel' after he suffered stomach and shoulder wounds during the conquest of Guangdong which had enabled the Kuomintang leader to return to the south. The accolade took no notice of the far from angelic behaviour of the mercenaries camped in and around Canton. Though they received up to $35,000 a day for food and upkeep, they stole from shops, took hostages, levied charges on railways, grabbed taxes, seized boats, indulged in outright piracy, and ran gambling, prostitution and drugs – one group advertised its narcotics in the newspapers. When his men complained about not being paid, a commander replied: 'Since you have guns, why should you be short of rations?'[2]

The mercenary presence was just one symptom of the way in which Sun's revolutionary base in the south fell short of the vision he proclaimed for China. An American traveller, Harry Francke, who did not share the usual disdainful Western attitude to China, wrote that no province led 'a more miserable life than Canton under Sun Yat-sen and his lieutenants . . . [It] was probably the most mis-governed city in China.' To pay the soldiers, the administration called on merchants to 'lend' it cash, and slapped special duties on everything from pigs to what a newspaper described as 'so-called dancing halls conducted by Russian women'. The city's 800 opium dens paid so much duty that the managers held a protest meeting at a teahouse. Monopolies, public property and official jobs were auctioned. Boat owners had to buy special flags at $50 or be attacked by police as pirates. Provincial banknotes traded at 20 per cent of face value. In 1923, Sun tried to seize Canton's customs revenue which was sent to the central government in Peking – the foreigners who ran the collection brought in warships from the fleets their native countries kept in Chinese waters, and the doctor desisted.[3]

Still, with 800,000 inhabitants, Canton was rich and worldly by contemporary Chinese standards. Distance meant links with Peking were tenuous, making Guangdong virtually autonomous. Emigrés returning from abroad brought new ideas, and funds to finance their implementation. From 1729 to 1842, Canton had been the only place in China where Western merchants were allowed to operate, and in the late imperial era had become one of the early treaty ports where foreigners were granted concessions.*

---

* The other four ports were Shanghai, Xiamen (Amoy), Fuzhou (Foochow) and Ningbo (Ningpo).

There were cigarette, brick, tanning, dyeing and knitting factories, an automated match plant, and more than twenty firms making latex and rubber footwear. New streets were laid, and buses were imported, fitted with special narrow seats to maximise the number of passengers. Three hundred cars drove on the new roads, used mainly by officials and militarists who sped about with armed bodyguards on the running boards. The waterfront Bund boasted two big department stores, one with a top-floor entertainment area offering opera, acrobatics and films. Bright illuminations shone through the night, and gramophone music played from the shops.[4]

Alongside this modernity, the old ways continued in much of the city. The bulk of its 35,000 shops were small family concerns. Working conditions were often primitive. A French visitor described houses in the old areas 'compressed so closely together that they give one the feeling of being indoors, and seem like an infinite number of corridors in an immense palace'. Though benefitting from its remittances from Overseas Chinese, the surrounding province of Guangdong suffered from all the drawbacks of the epoch – poor communications, the exactions of militarists, peasant poverty, and natural disasters. Some 85 per cent of the land was held by absentee owners who rented the fields out for half to three quarters of the proceeds of the crops. Heavy rainfall regularly burst dykes causing major flooding.[5]

Canton's left-wing credentials were boosted by growing trade union activity: in 1922, the First All-China Congress of Workers met in the city, and, with Kuomintang backing, seamen won a strike against Hong Kong-based operators of Pearl River shipping. The following year, Sun Yat-sen decided to develop his links with the Soviet Union, which had promised him two million gold roubles and arms. He sent Chiang – who now had the rank of general – to Moscow to see what help the KMT could raise there.

Arriving on the Trans-Siberian Express on 2 September at the head of a four-man mission, Chiang was unable to see either Lenin or Stalin, but did meet Trotsky, who said the USSR would do its best to provide aid. As well as observing how the Red Army was trained, the thirty-five-year-old general visited model villages, an electrical light bulb factory and a power generation plant. Having bought a Chinese translation of *Das Kapital*, he found 'the first half of this work is very heavy-going, but the second half is both profound and entrancing'. He received advice from the Comintern, the Revolutionary Military Council and the army, though he resisted an attempt to co-opt him into the Communist Party.[6]

But the Comintern delivered a nasty shock at the end of November. While it was ready to recommend military aid, the international Communist organisation opposed Sun's request for help with a campaign to northern China, describing the Kuomintang as being only at the 'organisation stage' and as not having built on the overthrow of the Manchus. Any campaign outside Guangdong would be premature, adventurous and doomed to fail, it decided. First, the KMT had to develop an army and win over the masses.[7]

Chiang took the train for China the next day. In his last letter from Moscow to Jennie, he criticised the Comintern for being 'so ignorant of a friendly party' and added: 'With such a narrow outlook, how can it hope to be the centre of world revolution?' His wife's memoirs record that, when they met in Shanghai on his return, he said: 'You cannot trust a Communist.' Instead of going to Canton, he travelled home to Zhejiang province to write a report which said the Soviets were ready to send fifty military advisers, plus financial aid and matériel. But he warned that they lacked sincerity, and called their policy Tsarism by another name, seeking to annex northern territories and sovietise the country. 'The sole aim of the Russian party is to make the Chinese Communist Party its legitimate heir,' Chiang continued. 'In truth, they do not believe that our Kuomintang can cooperate with them permanently in achieving success.' In a separate letter to Sun's lieutenant, Liao Zhongkai, he stated baldly: 'My personal observations lead me to the conclusion that the Russian Communist Party cannot be wholly trusted. I told you that we could believe only 30 per cent of what the Russians had to say. That was really an understatement.' Facts, he wrote, should not be ignored simply because one might agree with Communist theories.[8]

Sun was not in a receptive mood for such views. While Chiang had been away, he had acquired a Soviet adviser who was to play a crucial role in the development of the Kuomintang, and who had already proved his worth by saving the doctor from his most persistent adversary.

Mikhail Markovich Grunzeberg was an experienced Comintern agent. Born in 1884 in western Russia, in the Pale where, under Tsarist rule, Jews were placed, he had worked underground in Mexico and Britain under the name of 'George Brown'. After six months in a Glasgow prison, he had been expelled, being described by Special Branch as a 'most dangerous man'. Returning to Russia, he was chosen to take revolution to China, adopting the name of the composer, Borodin, as his pseudonym. He knew nothing of the country, and did not speak its language. But he was used to operating in difficult places with unfamiliar collaborators, and would be able to converse with Sun in English. An impressive figure, and an excellent organiser, he was adept at working in the shadows, leaving others to take the credit, and thus ensuring their 'face'.[9]

Tall and thickset, with a heavy moustache and deep bass voice, Borodin often dressed in a tunic and high boots. A smitten American journalist, Milly Bennett, described him as 'a dreamer, an intellectual, an original [who] always managed to look like an actor. He walked into a room with that lumbering, awkward kind of grace, and presto, the situation was his.' His hair, noted the *New York Times* correspondent, Hallett Abend, 'always seemed to be in need of the attention of a barber'.[10]

Reaching China on the Trans-Siberian Express, Borodin went by boat to Canton, not stopping at Hong Kong in case the British arrested him there. The ship was caught in a typhoon which caused the death of 200 sheep on board. On his arrival on 6 October 1923, the Russian recorded, 'Sun Yat-sen welcomed me very warmly, made me sit with him and looked at me fixedly for several seconds.'[11]

The relationship was a marriage of convenience, with major internal paradoxes on both sides which would eventually lead to a bloody outcome. Communism was based on the class struggle, but Sun rejected this, insisting that the whole nation could be brought together regardless of social differences. This enabled him to draw support from merchants, landlords and overseas Chinese businessmen who had no taste for a Bolshevik revolution. But, if he was to organise his party and conduct his expedition to the north, the doctor needed the help of Russia.

For Moscow, Sun was its most promising ally in the world's most populous nation. Guangdong's trade unions offered the base of a mass labour movement, and the proximity of Hong Kong meant Canton could be used to combat British imperialism. So taken was Stalin with the opportunity Sun offered that he decreed a united front in which the Chinese Communists would play second fiddle. Naturally, they resented this. But they were few in number, and to preach the solitary pursuit of true revolution was to fall in with the heresy of Stalin's bitter enemy, Trotsky.

Thus, a pattern was set by which the Chinese party's policy would follow the dictates of the Kremlin, rather than its own interests.

Borodin had no illusions about his new partner. The Russian called Canton a 'veritable Babel'. Sun, he noted, 'is very backward. He judges very badly in political matters. He . . . often reasons in a simple way like a man on the street. He considers himself the hero and the others the mob, while . . . he is simply an enlightened little satrap.' Sun claimed 30,000 members of the KMT, but only between a fifth and a tenth were active participants. Yet the doctor was the sole centre of the Kuomintang universe and had a unique national vision that could provide a legitimacy the warlords lacked. From the other side of the spectrum, Britain's Consul General, Bertram Giles, said of Sun: 'One day, if he lives, he will rule all China. He's a fanatic, he's inconsistent, he's unpredictable and, from my point of view, he's a nuisance, but he's got the seeds of greatness in his soul.'[12]

Borodin went to work as soon as he arrived, drawing up new statutes to organise the Kuomintang on Leninist lines. Hard-core cells were to be established in Canton and Shanghai, with local structures elsewhere across the country. As the Russian was working on this, Sun's nemesis, the Hakka General, Chen Jiongming, advanced on Canton from the east. Borodin proposed a volunteer defence force, rousing peasants and workers to action by promises of land redistribution, a minimum wage, an eight-hour working day and a six-day week. The merchant and gentry members of the Kuomintang did not like the idea, and Sun prevaricated, saying he could not agree to 'sovietisation' that would lose important supporters. His letter setting this out was delivered to Borodin by his close aide, Liao Zhongkai. After handing it over, Liao told the Russian he agreed with him.

Sun remained indecisive, asking whether arrangements could be made for him to visit Moscow. But Borodin organised a volunteer unit which marched to the front. Chen withdrew. Safe, Sun expressed his complete agreement with the Russian. When supporters in the USA asked him, 'Do you know that "Borodin" is a pseudonym? Do you know his real name?' China's would-be Washington replied, 'I know, Lafayette.'

Under Borodin's guidance, a KMT reorganisation congress opened on 20 January 1924. Sun's Three Principles of nationalism, democracy and the people's livelihood were adopted as the guiding ideology. The doctor delivered eight speeches, speaking of the Russian party as the only good example for the KMT. He won a big majority in favour of allowing Communists to join the Kuomintang while remaining members of their own party, but he had a reference to the leading role of workers and peasants expunged from the manifesto. Sun was elected life president of the party. With Borodin, he picked the forty-one full and alternate members of the Central Executive Committee. The Communists got ten seats; they were entrusted with the Peasant Affairs department and the Organising Department responsible for recruitment, assignments and job supervision. The Propaganda Department was headed by Chiang's associate from his Shanghai days, Dai Jitao. When Dai went off to write and think the following year, his replacement was a young man called Mao Zedong.

The reorganisation established a double power structure, in which the party duplicated the organs of government on the Soviet model. Though Borodin proclaimed the old Kuomintang dead and buried, two thirds of party officials were non-leftists. As usual with the KMT, things were a lot less clear in practice than in theory.

Under Borodin's spell Sun did not respond to Chiang's criticisms of what he had seen in Russia. The younger man fired off a letter mixing indignation with a plaintive plea for recognition. 'Apparently you feel that I have completely failed in the mission,' he wrote. 'Or perhaps you no longer have faith in me. In either case, I feel an intense slight and that my reputation has plunged to the ground!' Sun replied with a letter asking 'Brother Kai-shek' to travel south immediately.[13]

Chiang's prime aim was to establish a military Academy to form an army that would give the Kuomintang military muscle, and free it from dependence on the mercenaries. The site was at the Whampoa Fort on an 8-square-mile island 10 miles down the Pearl River from Canton. The need for such a school was shown by the reports drawn up by Russian military advisers who came to Canton after Borodin. They reckoned that only Sun's personal bodyguard of 200 men was unquestioningly loyal. The mercenary generals owed no obedience to the revolution. The quality of officers was extremely poor. Many smoked opium. The rank-and-file, wrote the Russians, had 'neither clothing nor footwear; their pay was not given to them for years . . . everybody was stealing'.[14]

Whampoa was to be day to the mercenaries' night, producing a trained force at the service of the revolution. Its officer cadets would be properly paid and well looked after. It was to be highly politicised: orders by the chief of the school had to be countersigned by the head of the Political Department who reported to Sun. Officers were ideological messengers, proselytising among the soldiers. Most of the cash to get the Academy off the ground came from Moscow which also sent 8,000 rifles and 4 million rounds of ammunition. A revolutionary hero, Pavel A. Pavlov, arrived to head the military advisers, but he was drowned in an accident in the summer of 1924, and was succeeded by another Red Army legend, General Vasilii Blyukher.[15]

The course the cadets followed combined elements from Chiang's own training, Japanese manuals, traditional Chinese strategy and lessons he had learned during his visit to Moscow. The overall curriculum followed that of the Red Army. Linguistic difficulties led Soviet advisers to concentrate on practical matters where they could teach by example – only twenty-five students attended the course to learn Russian. Stalin's doctrine of the united front ruled. When Zhou Enlai argued for a Communist army, Borodin told him to forget it.

The combination of military training and ideological instruction created a cohesive and disciplined base of a kind known only among elite warlord troops. The cadets were told to be austere, daring and brave. Chiang insisted on decent food and health facilities, and instructed cadets not to gamble or visit brothels. The principle of collective responsibility known as *lian zuo fa* was adopted, providing for the execution of units which retreated without orders to do so. Chiang urged the young men to be ready to die for their cause, and uncompromising on principles whatever the odds. The emphasis was on performance in the front line – one favourite exercise was a 'storming party' drill in which teams of half a dozen men ran 150 yards with scaling ladders to climb walls under fire. Little attention was paid to administration, supply or logistics; this meant that, when they came to command large formations as their careers progressed, the graduates would lack expertise in handling big armies.

Even before the Academy opened, the future Generalissimo was embroiled in another of his recurrent rows. The Russians thought the course should last for eighteen months, but Chiang wanted to turn out as many graduates as possible and so proposed a shorter curriculum. Adopting his customary tactic, he left Canton for Zhejiang and Shanghai. The outcome was that the course was set at six months. Chiang also

1. Devoted son: Chiang with his mother in his home village.

2. Training for life: Chiang as a military cadet in Japan.

2

3. Man about town: Chiang in Shanghai after the 1911 revolution against the Manchu Empire.

4. Sun Yat-sen and his wife,
   Soong Qingling.

5. Sun and Chiang at the
   opening of Whampoa
   military academy.

6. The Mukden Tiger,
Zhang Zuolin.

6

7. The Philosopher
General, Wu Peifu.

7

8. Li Zongren of Guangxi.

9. Zhang Xueliang, the Young Marshal of Manchuria.

10. Chiang with Feng Yuxiang, the Christian General (left) and Yan Xishan, the Model Governor (right).

11

11. To the north: seeing Chiang off from Canton station for the Northern Expedition in 1926. Left to right: Mikhail Borodin; unidentified man; Fanny Borodin; Liao Zhongkai's widow; Jennie Chiang; General Galen; Chiang (smiling); his adopted son Wei-kuo; Dai Jitao; Zhang Jingjiang (seated).

SHOWDOWN IN SHANGHAI

12. Heads of rebels hung from lamp-posts by warlord troops, 1927.

13. Underworld boss Big Eared Du, who helped Chiang to take China's richest city, and remained a collaborator for two decades.

14. Chiang's troops arrest leftists.

15. Retribution: Nationalist executioners repress the Canton rising of 1927.

obtained a free hand in spending from Liao Zhongkai, who was running the regime's finances and became the school's political director.[16]

In a letter from his home province, Chiang told Sun that, in Canton, he had been 'as restless as if I were sitting on a mat full of nails ... absent-minded and careless, and aimless in my actions'. Then he went into his habitual complaint about suffering from the jealousy of others, and said the Kuomintang was threatened by a 'new influence', meaning the Russians. Once again, he sought reassurance, asking the doctor: 'Do you really repose deep trust in me or do you not?' But he also showed unusual independence by writing to party leaders that they should not automatically allow Sun to dominate at the expense of their integrity. When his own domain was concerned, however, Chiang brooked no opposition. In a letter about the Whampoa regulations, he instructed party colleagues: 'Do your duty and refrain from having too many opinions'. On 21 April 1924, he returned to Canton. At the beginning of May, he was appointed Principal of the Army Officers Academy, and Chief of Staff of the Guangdong Army.[17]

The opening ceremony at Whampoa was held on the second anniversary of the attack on Sun's residence in Canton, to drive home the point that such an occurrence would be impossible once the Kuomintang had its own army. The doctor spoke for two hours from an open-fronted bamboo structure decorated with party and national flags. His wife stood to his left, in a long black skirt and flowered top; to his right was Chiang Kai-shek, in uniform, knee-length boots and white gloves. Watching and holding a sun hat, was a portly, cigar-smoking London-born arms dealer called Morris 'Two-Gun' Cohen who acted as the doctor's aide and bodyguard.

Despite suffering heart trouble, Sun was in full rhetorical form as he explained the need for the school. 'After thirteen years of revolution,' he said, 'the Republic is just an empty name and, even today, the revolution is a complete failure.' The lack of an army had meant the dominance of the warlords, but now 'our aim in opening this Academy is to create the revolutionary task anew from this day, and students of this Academy ... will be the bones and trunks of the forthcoming Revolutionary Army.'

Sun and Chiang were photographed later on their own in a stone-flagged arcade. The KMT leader sat in a wicker chair. The Whampoa commander stood beside him, in dark jodhpurs and a tightly belted tunic with a sword hanging down his left leg and his right fist on his hip. Chiang's level, unsmiling gaze into the camera is that of a man who knew where he was heading. 'If I control the army, I will have the power to control the country,' his wife records him as saying. 'It is my road to leadership.'[18]

To provide cadets for the Academy, Kuomintang officials across China were asked to nominate graduates aged between eighteen and twenty-five with middle school or higher primary school education. They had to write an essay on why they wanted to serve their country. On graduation, they ranked as Second Lieutenants and would serve a minimum of three years in the army. The KMT's national presence enabled it to recruit far from its base in Guangdong, plugging into the growing sense of nationalism. The first class numbered 645. As Chiang had planned, the intake increased sharply. By 1926, 3,000 had graduated. A few came from Mongolia, Tibet, Thailand and Korea. A Vietnamese contingent was supervised by a revolutionary called Nguyen Ai Quoc, later Ho Chi Minh.[19]

The requirement for decent educational qualifications meant that the Academy was anything but a training ground for proletarian youth. A study by the American academic, Richard Landis, shows that three quarters of the cadets were sons of landlords, middle-income peasants or officials. The Shanghai recruiters were right-wingers, including Chen Qimei's nephew, Chen Guofu, and a Green Gang member. Like Chiang, the cadets might be anxious for a strong, united China, but that did not mean they stood on the left as the Russians and Kuomintang leftists had hoped. A strong anti-Communist group emerged in the Academy, and the military side of Whampoa grew ever more dominant, providing many of the members of the cliques that sprouted around Chiang in the coming decades. The new army became the equivalent of the families the cadets had left, demanding the same loyalty and obedience as Chinese parents. At the head of the family tree stood a figure whose character and ambition demanded fealty of the most classic kind as he strove to become 'illustrious throughout the world'.[20]

Kai-shek and Jennie lived on the first floor of the main Whampoa building in a flat consisting of a living room, dining room and bedroom with teak furniture. In the evenings, he practised calligraphy; his rendition of the Academy's motto, 'Affection with Sincerity', was mounted on silk on his office wall. His reading list took in European wars, psychology and geography. Next to his quarters was a large conference room with a long table and twenty-four high-backed chairs. Chinese and Kuomintang flags hung on one wall. On another was a big map of China dotted with green, red and blue flags to mark the path of the planned northern expedition. Chiang's wife did much of his secretarial work. One job was to log letters marked 'secret', and stow them in a locked file in their flat.[21]

Given Canton's conspiratorial nature, Chiang was justified in being on guard, but his suspicion bordered on paranoia. 'Those I once thought could be trusted turned out to be all the more untrustworthy today,' he wrote. 'In all things, one had only oneself to rely on.' According to Jennie, 'In his intense desire to be first in everything, he inclined to be pompous', and cultivated only friendships likely to be useful in furthering his aims.[22]

'My lowly self is replete with transgressions and evils,' his diary recorded. 'How can one not be pained by this? I will renew myself daily from now onward in order that I may nurture the divine elements in my nature.' He suffered from recurrent health problems, at one point being taken to hospital against his will for an operation to stop continuous nose bleeding. At times, eye trouble stopped him reading and doing his job normally. 'I was so vexed that several times I thought of taking my own life,' he wrote. 'But then I would comfort myself by saying, "It is the will of Heaven that I should undertake the mission of the party. How is it possible that it would destroy my eyesight? All I need is to recuperate until health is restored."'

He noted his 'meticulous self-control', which would have surprised those on the receiving end of his rants and rages. His rigidity was unwavering; he would, he wrote, rather be 'ridiculed as archaic and doltish than be regarded as wild and ungovernable'. When his wife asked what he would do if his plans proved unworkable, he replied: 'I am willing to make slight alterations, if things are unsuitable. But I emphasise having a fixed, basic plan. Once decided upon, it must not be altered at random. There may be some small points that require change, and those can be adjusted later.'[23]

Chiang adopted an equally rigid attitude towards his son. His letters, published by Ching-kuo in the 1970s, were sternly schoolmasterish, endlessly reproaching the boy for failings in his calligraphy. The nearest the general got to showing any feeling was to advise his son that if he had his teeth filled or crowned, he should make sure the dentist sterilised the instruments.

Ching-kuo visited Canton after finishing studies in Peking where he had become acquainted with left-wing ideas. The fifteen-year-old had been offered a scholarship in Moscow, and wanted his father's permission to accept. According to Jennie, he was so intimidated that he asked her to put the idea to Chiang. 'What's the use of him going away so far?' her husband replied. 'I can't afford his expenses.' His wife said he only finally agreed after she had pleaded.[24]

In Moscow, the teenager was given the Russian name of Nikolai Vladimirovich Elizarov at the university of the Toilers of the East. He learned Russian, edited the Red Wall bulletin board, and studied peasant and labour groups. When his suitcase was stolen, Ching-kuo wrote to his father asking for cash to buy new clothes. Jennie says Chiang refused on the grounds that young people should learn to be more responsible with their belongings. Jennie advanced him money from her savings, pretending it came from the general. When Ching-kuo had left Canton, she felt it was 'as if I was losing a part of myself'. To fill the emotional gap of not being able to have a child because of the treatment for the sexual disease Chiang had passed on, she adopted a baby girl.[25]

Chiang showed himself a stickler for discipline and order with the Whampoa students, too. He would call cadets over to ask why they had a loose bootlace or button. 'When the reply was unsatisfactory, he would shout for a corporal and, in a verbal blast, order the culprit to be reprimanded or even placed in the brig,' Jennie recalled. She remembered an occasion when a cadet gave a patriotic reading before an audience of 3,000 people. He had tried to memorise the speech, but forgot a line in the middle. Taking a soiled sheet of paper from his trouser pocket, the cadet unfolded it and began to read. 'Stop!' Chiang shouted. 'You should know better than to put a folded piece of paper in your trouser pocket where it would get crumpled! It should be placed in your shirt pocket! Remember that, you blockhead!'[26]

Three days after the opening of Whampoa, the French community in Canton gave a dinner for the visiting Governor of Indo-China, Martial Merlin. The meal was held in the foreign concession on Shameen, a sandbank opposite the riverside Bund. Covering 44 acres inside a wall, the enclave had broad streets and low brick and granite buildings, surrounded by lawns, flowerbeds and bougainvillaea. An American visitor described its leisurely streets as suggesting a New England village. The British occupied four fifths of the island: the French the rest. There was a single hotel, the Victoria, where the dinner for Governor Merlin was held.

As soup was served to the fifty guests, a man in white singlet and shorts threw a leather bag through an open window into the dining room. The bomb inside exploded immediately. Three of the diners were killed on the spot; two others died in hospital. The blast blew knives and forks and porcelain fragments from the plates into people's bodies. The attacker jumped into the river. Two days later, the authorities announced finding the corpse of 'an Annamite' who left a will denouncing French colonialism.

The Shameen authorities ordered all Chinese, but not other non-Westerners, to show a pass with their photographs to gain entry to the island at night – hardly the most logical reaction since the bomb thrower had been Vietnamese. The Canton government protested. Chinese workers in the enclave walked off the job, followed by watchmen who kept order for the foreigners. A picket isolated the concession from the city; foreign women and children left for Hong Kong; food was brought in on steamers from the British colony; the Victoria did a thriving business in the absence of domestic cooks and servants.

The confrontation heightened the radicalism of the Canton workers, encouraged by the Russians and the left wing of the Kuomintang. Though a compromise over Shameen was reached in October, the incident raised the reputation of the city as the heart of 'Red revolution'. To protect themselves, Chinese businessmen developed a khaki-clad militia, the Merchants' Volunteer Corps (MVC) which drilled under instructors and built fortified positions. Accounts of their numbers varied from 6,000 to double that. They bred emulators in other towns and cities: in May 1924, 100 volunteer groups from Guangdong met in Canton. To counter them, the Kuomintang set up a Labour Volunteer Corps whose members got 35 cents a day, a uniform, a dagger and a rifle.

While many of the merchants were conservatives, opposition was not just a matter of reactionaries defending their turf. Prominent modernising figures were disillusioned with the regime, calling the Kuomintang leader *Sun Dapao* – Sun the Windbag. The head of the MVC, a rich merchant and former comprador* for the Hong Kong and Shanghai Bank, Chen Lianbo, insisted the Volunteers were a self-defence force made necessary by the dislocation of trade and the depreciation of investments.[27]

---

* 'Comprador' was the term for Chinese acting as agents for foreign firms, often growing extremely rich.

In mid-August 1924, a Norwegian freighter, the *Hav*, steamed up the Pearl River with a consignment of arms ordered by the MVC: the manifest listed 4,850 rifles and as many pistols with 3.5 million rounds of ammunition. On Sun's order, the guns were seized, and taken to Chiang's stronghold at Whampoa. In protest, the merchants called a series of business strikes. The doctor left town on on a fresh bid to launch his expedition to the north, but Chiang refused to follow him, saying he was determined to defend Canton to the death.[28]

An agreement was reached for the government to hand over half the weapons to the merchants in return for payment and a tax on houses. On 10 October, as MVC members went to the riverside to get their guns, a parade of Sun loyalists, Whampoa cadets and leftists marking the anniversary of the fall of the Manchu Empire came up the road. The Volunteers refused to let them pass. Shooting broke out. Half a dozen people were killed on the spot: the final death toll may have been three times as high. The Volunteers sent out armed patrols, and closed the gates round the business district, posting men on roofs and on the towers in which pawnshops were often set.

The Kuomintang leadership, with Borodin present, formed a Revolutionary Committee. Chiang was put in charge of military operations. His force consisted of 2,000 troops, including a detachment from Whampoa. At dawn on 15 October he launched the attack on the business district. Shells rained down, demolishing its gates. Police fired machine guns from the top of a building on the riverside Bund. Donning civilian clothes, Chiang's men slipped through the lines. The Volunteers fought from the roofs, erecting improvised bridges above the narrow streets. Setting fire to buildings, the attackers shot those who fled from them.

Estimates put the death toll at anywhere from thirty to 284 for the government, fifty to 200 for the MVC, and 300 among civilians. There were follow-up murders, including one when a general invited two prominent merchants to dinner and, after discussing politics for a while, had them executed. The MVC leader, Chen Lianbo, fled to Hong Kong. Reports of the number of buildings destroyed ranged from 700 to 1,000. A journalist arriving by boat recorded: 'The air was thick with the acrid smell of smoke and smouldering wood . . . Chinese of all ages, but chiefly old men and women and little children, squatted weeping at the sight of what had once been their homes.' Still, there was high praise from the British Communist

Party which sent Sun a cable expressing its 'hearty congratulations' for his 'gallant struggle against foreign Imperialism and native capitalism'.[29]

After returning briefly to the arsenal outside Canton during the battle, Sun Yat-sen went back to northern Guangdong, hoping to intervene in a war between the Peking regime run by the main warlord of Central China, Wu Peifu, and a coalition headed by the ruler of Manchuria, Zhang Zuolin, who had subsidised Sun in the past. That this would mean allying with a reactionary, pro-Japanese militarist did not trouble Sun – nor did the paucity of his forces or the distance to be travelled to the war zone. He saw himself as a figure who might yet rally the nation; the dream was his only way to escape from Canton, which he called a place of death.

Before setting out, the doctor visited the city for a lantern-lit parade of 20,000 people to mark his fifty-eighth birthday. He gave Chiang authority over all military units, and named him head of a new Military Department. A huge crowd on the Bund saw Sun and his wife board a gunboat to sail down the river. They called at the Canton Christian College, where a faculty member recorded that the KMT leader, wearing a long grey Chinese gown, brown Western shoes and a grey fedora, 'was in a fine mood . . . laughing and talking about his trip to Peking'. The final stop was at Whampoa. Chiang took Sun round the Academy, and the doctor reviewed the cadets. The commandant recorded him as saying, 'Even if I should die, my conscience will be at peace'. Then the Father of the Revolution sailed to Hong Kong on his way to Shanghai. He was never to return.[30]

By the time he left Canton, Sun's presence in the warlord struggle had been rendered unnecessary after Wu Peifu's main ally abruptly changed sides, making the Manchurians and their associates masters of northern China. Still, Sun did not give up his quest. From Shanghai, he went to Japan where he blasted the Western powers as responsible for all his country's woes, proclaimed 'the doctrine of greater Asia' and suggested uniting with Russia and India against the West. Against all the evidence, he declared that the outcome of the war in the north meant the way was open for a 'great central revolution'. But one of the victors called the KMT policy of abrogating the unequal treaties with foreign powers 'startling', and noted that Sun would be at his wits' end if party members in Peking impeached him for his actions against the merchants in Canton.[31]

Back in China, the doctor suffered from abdominal trouble, and had a fainting spell. On 31 December he entered the American-funded Peking Union Medical College. An operation on 26 January 1925 confirmed terminal liver cancer. In mid-February, he was moved to the Peking home of a Kuomintang member.

There, Sun dictated his last will and a political testament calling for the masses to be roused to get other nations to recognise China as an equal, the holding of a national reconciliation convention, and the abrogation of the unequal treaties. Another document, drawn up under the supervision of Borodin, who had also gone to Peking, was addressed to Moscow. It expressed the 'fervent hope' that China and the Soviet Union would soon be able to advance as allies to 'victory in the great struggle for the liberation of the oppressed peoples of the world'.

Sun died on 12 March 1925. Though his memory would be hallowed by both Nationalists and Communists, his life had been, in the words of the historian C. Martin Wilbur, 'a sombre story of shattered dreams'. Its incoherence continued with a wrangle over the funeral. His second wife and son wanted a Protestant ceremony since he had died a Christian – one of his last utterances was reported to have been: 'Just as Christ was sent by God to the world, so God also sent me.' Other members of his circle thought a service of a foreign religion unsuitable for a nationalist revolutionary. So two ceremonies were held, the first in the Medical College chapel and the second in front of the old imperial palace. The Soviet ambassador ordered flags on his country's diplomatic buildings to be flown at half mast, and said he would have a glass-topped bronze coffin like Lenin's brought from Russia. Reuters reported that it was 'not new', and was a poor tin imitation with a thin bronze covering. It was not used.[32]

Sun's body lay in state for three weeks before being transferred to a temporary resting place in the Temple of the Azure Clouds in the hills west of the city. Calling the Kuomintang 'the cancer of China', the Manchurian militarist with whom the doctor had wanted to form an alliance predicted that the party would fall apart. The reactionaries appeared all-powerful. But, even as Sun was dying, a military force was stirring on the southern battlefields which would elevate its commander to a status greater than the mightiest of warlords.[33]

CHAPTER 5

꩜

The Red Protector

AS SUN YAT-SEN WAS DYING far away, Chiang Kai-shek was on his first battlefield campaign at the head of his Whampoa cadets. Known as the Eastern Expedition, it also marked the first outing in the field in China for the chief Russian military adviser, Vasilii Konstantinovich Blyukher. Born into a poor peasant family of German origin in the Volga region, he had fought in the Red Army in the Urals, Crimea and Far East where he rose to become commander in chief: Chiang first met him there on his way back from his mission to Moscow. The Russian general was the first recipient of the Order of the Red Banner, which he was to be awarded four times.

Of average height, with a shaven head, he was powerfully built with a boxer's arms, steady grey eyes, bushy eyebrows and a black moustache. An American journalist described the general, then thirty-five, as 'harsh and severe in character and fiercely energetic, a tough taskmaster . . . he was forever stomping about, filled with ideas for fresh works'. The general's dark-haired, nervous Russian wife, who had grown up in Manchuria, acted as his secretary and interpreter.[1]

Like the other advisers, Blyukher took a pseudonym, using the initials of his wife's first name and patronymic to form 'Galen'. In the hierarchy of the advisers, he came under Borodin, but he was to play a more central role in Chiang's rise. 'War as a whole, and each operation taken separately, are first of all mathematics and calculations,' he told colleagues. Trotsky denigrated him as a theatrical figure and political dilettante, but another adviser, A. I. Cherepanov, recalled that he 'had an immense military talent and the gift of foresight'.[2]

Galen got on well with the Chinese, sometimes donning a Nationalist uniform and showing enthusiasm for Cantonese food. Chiang recognised 'an outstanding Russian general as well as a reasonable man and a good friend. What was most unusual about him was that he had none of the traits associated with Bolsheviks.' The adviser focused on the military task at hand, and showed limited enthusiasm for ideology. 'Revolution is not so simple,' he warned.[3]

The first test for Chiang and the Russian came when the Hakka General, Chen Jiongming, prepared a fresh attack on Canton. Galen advised seizing the initiative by launching an offensive. In February 1925, Nationalist troops moved out on the footpaths along the East River from the city. The weather was warm. The soldiers wore blue cotton tunics, short trousers, sandals woven out of twine, puttees, oilcloth caps and large round grass hats. Some carried umbrellas of rubberised tent cloth to keep off the rain. Communications and maps were primitive, leaving the officers, as an adviser remarked, feeling 'like captains of ships sailing in a fog'.

The first encounter was at a railway station controlled by several hundred enemy troops. General He Yingqin, a senior instructor at Whampoa who had attended the same Japanese military college as Chiang, was in command of the First Infantry Regiment which was thrown into the battle. Cherepanov, who was suffering from dysentery, suggested that the short, round-faced general should climb a small hill to get a better view of the fighting. As he did so, the Russian recalled, 'something happened to him: he grew blue in the face, rolled his eyes, and his legs gave way under him. Three messengers with some difficulty dragged him up the hill, where in a machine-like manner, he repeated as orders my advice concerning deployment of the regiment in battle formation. He was apparently not aware of what he was doing. Soon his natural colouring returned and he gradually came to his senses.' Cherepanov offered He some of the cocoa he himself was taking for his ailment: the general liked it so much that he asked for it to be served regularly.

The rail line was captured, and Whampoa cadets lined up with flags on the platform, their Communist commissar shouting 'Long Live

Revolutionary China!' The next target was a town protected by a thick wall up to 20 feet high. One unit attempted two unsuccessful assaults without waiting for the main body of the army. Then the Russians placed two cannons on the nearby heights, ready to fire at the wall. When Chiang arrived, he proposed a partial encirclement of the town, reckoning the defenders would surrender in a couple of days. An adviser pointed out that this would enable them to get reinforcements, and pressed for a quick assault. After what the ever-critical Cherepanov called 'painful hesitation', the commander agreed, though delaying the attack until 6 a.m. the next day.*

A point on the wall was identified to be attacked on foot by Whampoa graduates, executing the 'storming party' tactic they had practised at the Academy. An hour late, the guns opened fire, and the troops moved up. Incomprehensibly, they had no ladders. Wearing a felt coat, Chiang walked up and down behind the guns. 'From time to time he would raise his arms with a cry like a croaking raven and the cloak's ends would rise,' Cherepanov wrote. 'He looked at the advisers with eyes filled with hatred as if one of us and not himself were to blame that the assault group had not been provided with ladders.' General He crouched behind some bushes, 'blue in the face like a drowned man'.

Cherepanov remembered a climbing technique he had learned while in the fire service. One man bends with his hands against the wall, the next climbs on his back and shoulders, the first straightens up, and the second is raised in the air. He and another Russian went down to the wall to do this. As one of them stooped, a Chinese political officer and a flag-carrier ran up, and insisted on going first. The standard-bearer got onto the wall, where he was wounded. Others followed, and opened the gates. Cherepanov said 700 enemy were captured, with 1,000 rifles and six machine guns. The Nationalists lost ten killed and forty wounded.

After a stiff battle to take the strongpoint of Mainhu, which was celebrated as a landmark in the Kuomintang's military history, Chiang's troops drove on to the port of Shantou,† their biggest target. Despite having to make their way through floods, they 'had very much a walkover. Chen's troops have suffered from paralysis,' the *North China Daily News*

---

* Cherepanov is highly critical of Chiang in his memoirs which appeared during the Cold War. His views may have been coloured by the politics of the time, but provide a rare anecdotal account of this campaign.

† Known at the time as Swatow.

wrote. In Shantou, the occupiers issued declarations pledging that there would be no looting. Meetings denounced foreign missionaries as imperialists, and pamphlets were distributed explaining Kuomintang doctrines.[4]

After Chiang's troops had chased their opponents across the border into Fujian province, the campaign ended with the reported capture of 12,000–13,000 rifles, 110 machine guns, 8 million cartridges, 1,500 shells, thirty old cannons, six modern mountain guns and three wireless sets. One third of the booty went to Whampoa. Chiang paid tribute to the political workers who accompanied the troops, and to the Russians. 'The Kuomintang and the Chinese Communist Party are cooperating and we have the support of the whole country,' he said. Though Sun Yat-sen was dead, 'there is still Adviser Borodin to lead us,' he added. An American, Earl Swisher from the Canton Christian College, recorded hearing Chiang lead chants of 'Cooperate with the Soviet Union' and 'Long Live Kuomintang–Communist Unity'. The Communist leader, Chen Duxiu, said anybody who criticised the general was a counter-revolutionary.[5]

Using propaganda techniques new to China, political commissars under Zhou Enlai enthused the peasants with the promise of land reform. The Whampoa troops showed tight discipline, and did not plunder the people or press them into service. Such behaviour won over farmers who acted as guides, messengers and spies. Battlefield performances were recorded and analysed for promotions and sanctions. Wounded men got extra pay. The dead were properly buried: Chiang attended a memorial service for them. 'With loyalty and courage, you officers and men have shown discipline and bravery,' he said in one speech. 'You have astonished everyone.'

Galen, who had nearly been killed in one encounter, expressed himself content, praising the fighting valour of the soldiers. 'General Chiang Kai-shek succeeded in bringing to the front two regiments, well supplied, disciplined, and so thoroughly trained in the political sense that they could hold firmly enough at the front, and did not loot the population,' Galen wrote. Even the hostile *North China Daily News* acknowledged the new army as 'a really fine body of troops, well armed and sternly disciplined and, in every way, superior to any who might be expected to oppose them'. According to his wife, Chiang had seen the future, jumping up from his chair one day, and exclaiming at the top of his voice, 'I've got it! My slogan will be: "To unite China, first unite Guangdong."'[6]

Without Sun's presiding presence, uniting even Canton, let alone Guangdong or the whole of China, was a major task. The regime displayed ever-increasing factionalism. Workers grew resentful as wages fell behind price rises and unemployment increased. There was a round of strikes. Almost a hundred new labour organisations were formed. The Communist-led Farmers' League claimed 200,000 members. Reuters reported that, in northern Guangdong, unemployed peasants were forming groups to take over land and practise the 'nationalisation of women'.[7]

The chronic lack of funds brought public services to a halt. Teachers' pay was up to eight months in arrears. Fresh taxes were slapped on everything from graves to aerated water. In March 1925, 400 women with babies on their backs demonstrated for the repeal of a levy on suckling pigs. Such duties brought in relatively little money because most of the proceeds went to tax farmers to whom the government sold collection rights; the *Canton Republican* newspaper said the administration would get only $5,000 a year from the suckling pig tax while the collector netted $80,000.

The murder rate rose, and some banks stopped handling cash because of the number of robberies. The mercenaries were out of control. Some burst into a wedding party, searched the guests, and tore down the decorations on the grounds that it violated the official mourning period for Sun Yat-sen. After seizing wedding gifts and other articles said to be worth more than $100,000, they fined the host $20,000.

Chiang and Liao Zhongkai officiated at a service for Sun at Whampoa, at which, one eyewitness recalled, 'Mr Chiang, unable to contain himself, wept bitterly and audibly, causing all in the assembly to shed tears.' Though his wife says the general saw himself as a man who could unify the party, nobody regarded him as much of a political leader. The Nationalists were split into three main groups – the mainly right-wing 'Old Comrades' from Sun's lengthy past, the 'Party Men' who had come to the fore in Canton, and the 'Crown Prince' faction round the late leader's son, Sun Fo. The second group was much the strongest, headed by the two succession contenders, Wang Jingwei and Hu Hanmin.

After a classical education and a scholarship in Japan, Wang had joined revolutionary and anarchist groups, and tried to assassinate the Prince Regent in 1910. Freed from prison by the 1911 revolution, he refused to become a minister under the would-be emperor, Yuan Shikai, and travelled to Europe. Returning to work with Sun in 1917, he proved himself an impressive speaker, supple negotiator and accomplished writer. A handsome, nattily dressed, somewhat stout man who suffered from diabetes, Wang was described by a Russian woman interpreter as 'a humbler of female hearts'. A photograph of the time shows a dour Chiang Kai-shek with shaven head and strict military uniform standing beside Wang in a white suit, his hair wavy and pomaded, his face full, his eyes looking cheerfully into the camera.

Now forty-one, Wang had been at Sun's bedside in his last days, taking down the leader's will. Identified with the left and on good terms with the Russians, he was Borodin's choice, becoming acting chairman of the KMT and head of its political and military councils. But he also had a record of indecisiveness. A Russian report noted: 'He is an ambitious man, capable of resolute and energetic action, when he is certain of having behind him power and support.'[8]

The tougher Hu Hanmin, four years Wang's senior, had also gone on from a classical education to study in Japan. Slim, with receding hair and large round spectacles, he fitted the traditional profile of the scholar-administrator, and had headed the Guangdong revolutionary government after the fall of the Manchus. One of the regime's leading ideologues, his cold character, temper and indifference to the corruption of his two brothers made him unpopular. Although his revolutionary regime had taken a leftist path, Hu subsequently moved rightwards, warning against 'communisation'. He also developed a low opinion of his rival, saying on one occasion that 'Wang told the truth to no man'.

Chiang backed the younger man as the most likely winner, counting on him to ensure Russian supplies and support for an attack he planned on the mercenaries. When Jennie recalled Sun's admiration for Living Angel Liu, Chiang replied, according to her memoirs: 'The past is the past. Liu has outlived his usefulness. He must be eliminated along with the others . . . I am planning to take control of all the armies in Canton. This is impossible so long as the [mercenary] leaders are in my way. The only way is to use this opportunity to oust them, once and for all.'[9]

To prepare the ground, documents said to have been found during the Eastern Expedition were circulated to show that the mercenaries had negotiated with the regime's enemies, and received 'tea money' bribes from the warlord, Wu Peifu. They reacted by grabbing taxes, and taking over the arsenal. In May 1925, as Nationalist troops from outside Canton advanced on the city, the government sacked the mercenary chiefs. They hit back by seizing telephone, telegraph and lighting services, digging in east of the city, and throwing up barricades on the Bund by the river. Following a battle plan drawn up by Galen, government troops moved up while railway workers and waterfront coolies went on strike against the mercenaries. Chiang was named Garrison Commander.[10]

Fighting began in the afternoon of 6 June 1925. There was heavy shooting along the river into the following day, interrupted only by a rainstorm. Government gunboats opened up with machine guns and cannons. The regime's flagship steamed up and down, firing at hostile craft. Nearly 1,000 Whampoa troops, wearing red scarves and with a Soviet adviser, crossed the river at night. Coordination was maintained through a wireless system suggested by Galen after the Eastern Expedition.[11]

By 12 June, the bulk of the mercenaries had surrendered or fled. That afternoon, the battle ended. The mercenary generals escaped to Hong Kong. The government took 16,600 rifles, 120 machine guns and twenty cannons. Earl Swisher from the Canton Christian College noted in his diary: 'Few dead on the Bund – beating Yunnanese [mercenaries] to death on the jetties with bamboo clubs – came home sick from the sight.'[12]

The victory boosted the status of Chiang and his cadets who had grabbed the limelight with their river crossing. But the general was also arousing jealousy. An anonymous letter in an envelope marked 'secret' warned him that politicians were discussing ways of restraining him. Another unsigned missive said: 'Your rapid rise is being watched with enmity, especially by some members of the Cantonese Naval headquarters.'[13]

The success against the mercenaries served as fresh testimony to Galen's abilities: a report by a visiting Soviet diplomat said the Chinese had such confidence in him 'that his every statement on questions pertaining to military operations was considered to be law'. Still, the Russian recognised the limits of what the advisers could achieve. In a speech, he held up both his hands and pointed to one little finger. That was all Moscow could do: the other nine were what the Chinese would have to do themselves. He aimed to build up an elite force rather than going for the huge numbers of poor troops which swelled the warlord armies. 'Quality, not quantity, must play the chief role,' he insisted. All China could be swept by three or four well-trained, well-armed and well-motivated divisions, he thought.[14]

On 1 July 1925 a National Government of the Chinese Republic was proclaimed in Canton, with a clear tilt to the left under Borodin's influence. Wang Jingwei became chairman and head of the Military and Political Councils. Liao Zhongkai took the finance portfolio while remaining party representative to Whampoa and the army. Chiang sat on the eight-man Military Council which pursued the expansion of the army and the centralisation of the command structure. Hu Hanmin was sidelined as Foreign Minister: since nobody recognised Canton, there was little foreign relating to do.

The radicalisation of the Kuomintang regime increased after what came to be known, from its date, as the 30 May Incident. This grew out of a strike by Chinese workers at a Japanese-owned weaving mill in Shanghai that set off street protests in the city's International Settlement. A junior British police inspector ordered Sikh police to open fire on demonstrators, killing eleven and wounding dozens. Anti-foreign boycotts spread across China, reviving the nationalist spirit of the 4 May movement in 1919. In the Pearl River Delta, the unions waited until the mercenaries had been defeated in Canton before joining the protest. Then they launched a strike in Hong Kong for improved working conditions, equality of treatment for Chinese, the end of child labour, the reversal of rent rises, the right of Chinese to vote for members of the legislative council and an end to racial discrimination. Tens of thousands of strikers left the colony for Canton. Remembering the events of the previous year after the killing of the French governor, foreigners in the enclave of Shameen battened down the hatches. A community kitchen was opened at the Victoria Hotel as, once again, women and children were evacuated.

On 23 June a large anti-foreign demonstration moved down the tree-lined Bund, led by mounted police and a boys' brass band. Among those marching were cadets from Whampoa. Chiang's associate from the Academy, General He Yingqin, was also present. The gates on the bridges to Shameen were closed, and the foreigners set up machine-gun nests behind sandbags and barbed wire. As the rear of the procession came abreast of the bridge, firing began. The Chinese insisted that the British and French started it; the British Consul pointed the finger at the

Whampoa cadets. At least fifty people died, twenty from the Academy. The bodies were laid out to be photographed in neat lines on a side street by a police station. One foreigner was killed at Shameen, a French merchant who was hit in the head; four others were injured.

Crowds surged through the streets calling for action. Although there was some sniping, the authorities decided to use blockade and boycott. More workers from Hong Kong flooded into Canton: estimates of the total varied from 60,000 to double that. They got a subsidy from the Russians, and the government paid for their food and housing. Official authorisation was given for the resumption of opium boiling to provide funds for the strikers. Chinese stayed away from work at foreign companies. British products were banned. Posters went up showing Indian colonial soldiers killing Chinese women and children. A local newspaper editor advised Hallett Abend of the *New York Times* not to wear shorts because they were associated with the British.[15]

Shameen came under siege again behind concrete blockhouses, sandbags, barbed wire and machine-gun emplacements. Indian soldiers were sent from Hong Kong to strengthen the defence. Eight foreign warships took up positions in the river. A three-man Council of Defence, on which Chiang Kai-shek sat, was formed. Under Communist leadership, the strikers set up their headquarters in an entertainment centre in the city's East Park, with dormitories, an armoury, schools, courts and a jail. Some became unruly, smoking opium, staging robberies and running protection rackets. Pickets at the main prison forced the release of arrested colleagues. Merchants had to buy transport permits. Strikers cut off water, light and food from missionary hospitals: at one foreign institution for the insane, they turned 300 inmates out into the streets.

Rumours of a counter-move by the right circulated, with Liao Zhongkai as the main target. As well as the political enmity he incurred, the Finance Minister had launched a house-cleaning campaign that threatened corrupt elements in the regime, including some officers in the Canton Army. Suspicions of a plot centred on Hu Hanmin, some of whose relatives were outspoken rightists and known to be heavily engaged in graft; one of his brothers, Hu Yisheng, ran a secret society and published a newspaper that suggested both Liao and Wang Jingwei should be eliminated. Handbills also advocated the assassination of Chiang. The plotters were said to be in league with Chen Jiongming and the British in Hong Kong. The Governor there did, indeed, ask for permission to fund an operation in Canton 'to suppress the Reds'. London told him to drop the idea.[16]

On 20 August, Liao and his wife, the daughter of a rich Hong Kong tea trader, left home after breakfast to drive to the Kuomintang central office. Entering the courtyard outside the building, Mrs Liao stopped to talk to the Russian adviser, Cherepanov, who was passing. As they spoke, a shot rang out from attackers hidden behind the columns at the entrance. Mrs Liao thought it was a firecracker. Then she saw her husband on the ground. Calling for help, she crouched over him, trying to find the wound. More shots were fired. Chiang, Wang Jingwei, Borodin, Hu Hanmin and the head of the Canton Army, General Xu Chongzhi, hurried from a meeting in the building. 'Wang and Chiang wept bitterly,' a 1931 biography of the former recounted. 'So did Borodin. Hu and Xu, however, did not betray any emotion.' Liao was picked up, blood dripping from him. By the time he reached hospital, he was dead.[17]

A guard fatally wounded one of the attackers in the head. According to Wang's biographer, a list of names followed by annotations of sums of money was found on the corpse. The names were those of private guards of a former air force officer who was a prominent member of the right-wing secret society set up by Hu Hanmin's brother. The former officer escaped, but a gun found at his home had bullets identical to those used by the assassins. At Borodin's suggestion, a committee with full powers was established, consisting of himself, Wang Jingwei, General Xu and Chiang. Martial law was declared. A hundred arrests were made. Chiang shot one suspect dead point-blank. Two military men picked up at a banquet in a private room of a restaurant on the Bund were taken to the Eastern Parade Ground to be executed. One had recently denounced Chiang for 'sanctimoniousness, cajolery and cunning'.[18]

Hu Hanmin initially evaded a search party, hiding in a derelict building before being found and taken to Whampoa. His brother fled town. Borodin and Chiang saw Hu as the 'ideological leader' of the assassination, and it was decided to send him to Moscow to see the virtues of Communism. On 22 September, the former Foreign Minister boarded a Russian ship leaving Canton. The following week, to consolidate its military force, the regime set up the National Revolutionary Army (NRA) with five main constituent units, headed by Chiang's First Corps from Whampoa.

That left General Xu, commander of the Canton Army and War

Minister, as Chiang's next target. The old-school, opium-smoking officer was vulnerable on a number of counts. A Russian evaluation connected him with 'comprador circles' and right-wingers. After the assassination of Liao Zhongkai, he had refused to act against a minor warlord on the grounds that, though he knew the man was an unreliable counter-revolutionary, they were old friends. His slogan of 'Canton for the Cantonese' was a threat to Whampoa graduates from other regions. There were reports that, though he was on bad terms with Hu, he had made common cause with the politician's brother, and that his officers had joined the anti-government secret society.[19]

In his earlier days in Canton, Chiang had numbered Xu among his friends. Now, he accused him of being in contact with the Hakka General. With the agreement of Wang Jingwei, Chiang sent troops to disarm the Canton Army and to surround its headquarters. He then told Xu that his men had to be reorganised, which required him to leave town. After Xu handed over his jade seal of office, Chiang accompanied him to a steamer. The official line was that the older man had brain trouble, and needed to recuperate in Shanghai.

Approaching his thirty-eighth birthday, Chiang was now the top Nationalist military figure, and one of the ruling triumvirate alongside Wang Jingwei and Borodin. 'Canton is under the absolute control of General Chiang Kai-shek, a general in the employ of the Soviet High Command,' Reuters reported. The *North China Daily News* wrote that he was called the Protector of Canton, and that he and the Russians 'have it all their own way due to their military superiority'. He had shown his ability to act with a decisiveness rare in Kuomintang politics. 'I could clearly discern a sudden change in his temperament,' his wife recalled. 'He basked in his infallibility as a budding leader. Dissatisfied with existing conditions, he issued imperious commands for new changes, even far beyond his own domain, and he became a kind of self-appointed dictator.'[20]

The absorption of Xu's Cantonese soldiers swelled the size of the army to 30,000. This threatened Galen's doctrine of quality not quantity. The new recruits, who included opium addicts, were well below the standard set at Whampoa, but there was now no danger of them backing a rightist coup, while Chiang felt he needed all the men he could get to prepare for his ambition of launching an expedition to unify China.

Before he could press ahead with realising Sun Yat-sen's dream, he had to deal with a fresh offensive by supporters of Chen Jiongming who recaptured the port of Shantou. Chiang prepared a force of 20,000 men, plus 160 political commissars headed by Zhou Enlai. Galen had left for a lengthy visit to a populist northern warlord, Feng Yuxiang, with whom Moscow wanted to forge an alliance. In his absence, Chiang dropped the flanking movements the Russian had implemented in the previous campaign, and launched an assault on a large fortress held by pro-Chen troops which was protected by a river, an artificial lake, a canal and hills. According to Jennie Chiang's memoirs, there were four lines of defence – looped wire, boards with 3-inch nails sticking out, wooden block 'horses' covered with barbed wire, and a 15-foot high wall with electrically charged wire.

As Chiang directed operations from a ridge, the attack started with an artillery and machine-gun barrage. Foot soldiers advanced, the front rank carrying ladders. On the right flank marched a standard-bearer with a blue Kuomintang banner; another on the left waved red troop colours. Cherepanov watched a 'young, well-groomed commander' drawing his Mauser pistol from its wooden holster as he led his men forward.

The first detachment was badly hit, but others ran up to try to dismantle the barbed wire loops. 'Unit after unit followed, and finally a part of the loops collapsed,' Chiang's wife wrote, presumably on the basis of what she heard later from her husband. Then the cadets charged over the nails which pierced the thin soles of their boots. Unable to extricate themselves, they became easy targets. But others climbed on their bodies to the third barrier. A new wave heaped burning straw on the electric netting.

'More and more soldiers advanced with straw,' Jennie Chiang wrote. 'Bullets and bombs showered down on them from above. With the netting finally down, many places in the city wall were blasted with dynamite.' The fighting continued into the next day as the attackers and their flag-bearers moved through a barrage of grenades, bombs, stones, quicklime and logs. Ladders were set up, and the Nationalist banner was raised on the wall. 'Grenades exploded on the battlements: rifle and machine-gun fire was heard,' Cherepanov recalled. 'The soldiers cheered, swept away with the elation of victory.'[21]

The Revolutionary Army advanced northwards, helped by railway workers who blocked enemy trains. Chiang suddenly faced personal danger when an ex-soldier from Chen's forces tried to shoot him at a station. But he was unhurt, and led his troops to retake Shantou at the beginning of November. In a cable to Canton, he reported that the campaign had resulted in the capture of 6,000 prisoners and as many rifles. Chen Jiongming would not trouble him again, remaining in exile in Hong Kong where he died of typhus in 1933.[22]

The success of the two Eastern Expeditions boosted the government's revenue as its new territory enlarged its tax base. The Nationalists had also enrolled a key figure to run their finances in the substantial shape of Sun Yat-sen's brother-in-law, Harvard-educated Soong Tzu-wen – T. V. Soong. A later American adviser described Soong, who wrote English better than Chinese, as having 'a fine mind; a very quick mind; a very practical mind'. Son of the Methodist Shanghai tycoon, Charlie Soong, T.V. was a brother of Sun Yat-sen's widow, Qingling. He had worked for three years at the International Banking Corporation in New York, before moving to Canton to bring order to the Central Bank there. 'He already had the habit of watching any caller with an intent, almost unwinking, round-eyed gaze, and in spite of [his] courtesy his attention often seemed engaged in some remote mental speculation,' Hallett Abend of the *New York Times* recalled. 'He was given to short silences when asked direct questions, and after these silences, during which his mind evidently worked with extreme rapidity, he would give his final opinion or decision in remarkably few words, always well chosen.'[23]

Soong built up a silver reserve to give the Canton currency a solidity rare in China at the time. Moving on to the finance ministry, he simplified the fiscal system, and brought in more effective methods of tax collection. The government's dependence on land duties was reduced, and property ownership reassessed. Gambling on the game of *fan tan* was legalised, with an accompanying duty. Additional income came from levies on luxury goods, petrol, hotels, opium and prostitution. As a result, the tax take doubled between 1924 and 1926, and further revenue was raised by obliging households and shopkeepers to buy government certificates backed by taxes. Private savings held in banks rose six-fold. A drive was launched against smuggling and corruption. Expenditure was examined by a budget committee. All this enabled Soong to float government securities successfully, and provided Chiang with the funds to improve the pay and conditions of his troops, buy arms, hire experts and subsidise cadets coming to Whampoa. Though he fought no battles, Soong was a vital element in giving Chiang the ability to pursue his ambitions.[24]

Several other young men with international experience and education gravitated towards the Nationalists, and contributed expertise. C. C. Wu, who became both Mayor of Canton and Foreign Minister, was another Harvard graduate who held a British law degree. Sun Yat-sen's son, Sun Fo, had studied municipal administration at Columbia University; Chen Gongbo, head of the Workers and Peasants Departments, had earned a PhD in economics there. In cities like Shanghai, the Nationalists attracted the support of progressive journalists and teachers who encouraged bright pupils to head south. For educated Chinese anxious to help the modernisation and unification of the country, the Kuomintang offered the best hope with the great advantage of having its own army to give force to the nationalist urges the country felt.[25]

At the start of 1926, Chiang's men notched up another success by taking the 13,000-square-mile island of Hainan off southern Guangdong, rich in crops and mineral deposits. As the troops of the local warlord fled, the Nationalists in their grey uniforms and red armbands put up posters saying that they were fighting the 'running dog' of imperialism. The left seemed dominant at the party's annual congress which opened soon afterwards. Delegates wore hammer and sickle banners. Planes flown in from Moscow crossed the skies. Two thirds of the Executive Committee came from the left of the Kuomintang and the Communist Party. Borodin was presented with a silver tripod inscribed 'Co-operative Struggle'. But, though some rightist dissidents were expelled, the purge was limited. Despite having been bundled off to Moscow, Hu Hanmin was among those who got the highest vote for the Executive Committee.

Chiang also scored well in the voting, and was described by a Communist leader as 'a man of extraordinary achievement' and an important military bulwark. But, while keeping in with the party's biggest faction, he was also building bridges with the right, aided by his wealthy Shanghai backer, Zhang Jingjiang. Extolling party unity, the general opposed the expulsion of old-line party members. At Whampoa, renamed the Central Military and Political Academy, active anti-Communism emerged under the banner of the Society to Study Sun Yat-senism. This had originally been a broad church organisation, but then the Communists were expelled and it became firmly anchored on the right, providing many of Chiang's later supporters. The local correspondent of the *North China Daily News* quoted a close friend of the general as saying that long acquaintance led to 'the definite conclusion that Chiang was anything but Red, and that when the time was ripe he would make evident his hatred of Bolshevism and the Bolshevists'. Without naming names, Zhou Enlai warned Borodin that some leading figures 'may not be as friendly as you think they are'.[26]

Hallett Abend recalled Chiang at the time as slender and wiry, with magnificent flashing eyes. 'His ambition was immense, but he was surrounded by enemies and by danger and was unsure of his authority,' the journalist added. 'He always acted with such abrupt directness as to catch his political and military opponents unprepared. Chiang's enemies were inevitably slow and fatally tardy, whereas the Generalissimo's mobile mind worked swiftly, and he was always on guard.' A Russian adviser's report described him as conceited, stubborn, and enjoying his prestige. It said he 'easily becomes enthusiastic and then just as easily crestfallen, not knowing how to take a middle course and lacking the necessary coolness and firmness of character'. Inevitably, he was studying the career of Napoleon, and another Russian report compared him to the Jacobins of the French revolution.

Despite Zhou's warning, the Russians had no doubt of his loyalty, noting that 'he is so connected with us that the possibility of rupture on his part can hardly be admitted.' They cannot have been aware of an occasion on which, addressing Whampoa cadets, Chiang drew a goose and a stove on a blackboard. The goose represented Russia. If it was not cooked very soon, the general said, it would get so big that it might be able to catch the cook and do the cooking itself, putting the Chinese on the fire.[27]

In keeping with his rising status, Chiang rented a house in the city, owned by the widow of the assassinated Liao Zhongkai. Small and modern, it had a dining room and sitting room with dark upholstered chairs and sofa, and two bedrooms, one with a low double bed covered by an embroidered bedspread. The bathroom was all white, with nickel-plated taps and fittings. 'Everything was new, clean and orderly,' Jennie recalled. The Chiangs were particularly pleased with the telephone link to Whampoa.[28]

At the start of 1926, the general hired a confidential secretary: Chen Lifu, a nephew of the Shanghai revolutionary leader, Chen Qimei. The young man, who would remain with him through his life, had trained as a mining engineer, but decided to throw in his lot with Chiang. He quickly won his employer's confidence by his devotion to the job, his handling of correspondence and his skill at coding and decoding secret messages. Chen moved into the Chiang house, and the two men ate most meals together, starting work on urgent matters before breakfast after Chiang had done his early morning exercises and meditated for half an hour. Chen soon noticed the general's tendency towards gloom and bad temper which could boil over into uncontrolled anger. But he understood why Chiang was so volatile. A political crisis was brewing.[29]

The commander's relationship with the left-wing Kuomintang leader, Wang Jingwei, was becoming fraught. Chiang feared that the politician was trying to undermine him. His Shanghai patron, Zhang Jingjiang, travelled to Canton in what was billed as a bid to bring the two men together, but was more likely to have consisted of encouraging Chiang to stand up to the left. The right was increasingly worried. The Kuomintang was being outpaced among political activists by the Communists. Chiang's friend Dai Jitao wrote to him that 'most of the combative youths of today are Communists while the corruption and cowardice of the KMT comrades cannot be denied.' A further drift leftwards or a pre-emptive move by the right would each destroy Chiang's attempt to find a central position for himself that would enable him to act independently and don the mantle of Sun Yat-sen without being beholden to any group.[30]

The chief Soviet military adviser, V. V. Kuibyshev, who was standing in for Galen and who went under the pseudonym of 'Kisanka' – 'Pussycat' – was also a source of concern. Not only did he back Wang Jingwei, but he also worked with another officer in Canton, and sent aid to militarists in Yunnan and Jiangxi.

Unsettled, Chiang made plans to go to Russia, apparently hoping Moscow would give him more authority. He and Chen Lifu put their papers in order, packed, and got foreign currency from Hong Kong. As they drove to the pier to leave, Chen asked Chiang why he did not stay in Canton and make a stand. At that, the general told the driver to take him back home. Then he changed his mind again, and said they should head for the pier after all. 'At which point,' Chen wrote, 'I raised the question: "If we leave, who is going to take over the post of commandant?"' Chiang reflected, and this time said firmly: 'Go back.'[31]

His fears deepened when Wang was named 'General Party Representative' to all Kuomintang forces, and decided to increase the power of political workers in the army. Matters got even worse when Borodin followed Galen north for secret meetings with Soviet delegates to discuss future policy in China. His absence meant there was no strong figure to act as a mediator between Chiang and Wang. On top of this, the general was concerned at a Soviet move to work with the northern warlord, Feng Yuxiang, which could result in his being relegated to the status of a junior military partner.

Handbills criticising Chiang circulated in Canton. According to his official biographer, there were two assassination plots against him, one to be carried out at Whampoa. The general noted in his diary that he was suffering 'extreme pain and anxiety'. He replaced two army commanders whose loyalty he doubted, and drew up a list of Communists at Whampoa. Though the main threat came from the left, there was also a growing danger that rightist generals would mount a coup and, seeing him as part of the regime, oust Chiang as well as Wang. In the year since Sun Yat-sen's death, the Canton leadership had gone through a steady winnowing process. Logic pointed to Chiang's being the next to go, so there was every incentive to strike first.

The occasion came in mid-March in an incident which remains a subject of controversy. Canton was tense. Armed police patrolled the streets. A curfew had been declared. Rumours of rightist plots were rife. In case he needed to leave town, Chiang bought a ticket on a steamer to Shantou. During the morning of 18 March, the telephone rang at Chiang's home. He was out, and Jennie answered. The caller was Wang Jingwei's wife, Becky. Saying she was speaking on behalf of her husband, who was ill with diabetes, she made enquiries about Chiang's plans for the day, particularly about when he would be taking a boat for Whampoa and which jetty he would leave from. In the next two hours, Becky Wang telephoned five times seeking the same information. 'It was well known that the haughty Becky never did anything without a purpose,' Jennie wrote, 'so the more I thought of it, the more suspicious I became.'[32]

When Chiang came home, Jennie urged him to postpone his trip to the Academy. The general put in a call to Whampoa, and was told that the Kuomintang flagship was lying off the island after sailing from Canton. This was the gunboat on which he had spent seven weeks with Sun Yat-sen in 1922, now renamed as the *Zhongshan*, the doctor's name in Mandarin. Its captain had recently been arrested for subversion by the head of the naval political department, Li Zhilong, who had taken over command of the ship. Li told the Whampoa authorities he had received an order by telephone to sail to the Academy and to load coal for a long journey. He understood the order had originated with Chiang. Knowing that he had not issued any such order, the general decided not to go to Whampoa. Li, a Communist, kept his boat off the island all night.

Shortly after midnight, a man knocked on the front door of Chiang's house, and told his secretary, Chen Lifu, he had urgent matters to report – for the general's ears only. Chiang was in bed, but had told his secretary to wake him for anything pressing; so he was roused. The visitor was Hu Gongmian, a Communist who knew Chiang from his home province. The two men talked for some time in whispers.[33]

Later in the morning of 19 March, according to Chiang, he received several telephone calls from somebody he did not name asking when he was going to Whampoa. He left the house for a while and, during his absence, the dean of the Academy, Deng Yanda, called at the door, appearing extremely uneasy. 'He did not ask Chiang's whereabouts,' Chen Lifu recalled, 'as though he knew in advance what was about to happen.' After Chiang returned, Captain Li telephoned to ask if he could bring the *Zhongshan* back to Canton, saying Deng had passed on the original order as coming from Chiang. The general replied that, since he had not issued the instruction, it was not for him to tell the boat to return. Li did sail back, but kept the steam up and arms at the ready.[34]

In the early hours of March 20, Chiang set up headquarters in the cement factory Sun Yat-sen had used as his base in 1917. Back at his home, Chen Lifu received a spate of telephone enquiries as to where his boss was. One caller was the persistent Mrs Wang. 'The third time she called, she became angry, cursed me, and slammed the telephone down,' Chen recorded.[35]

Chiang brought in trusted troops to encircle the railway station and the Central Bank. A regiment regarded as unreliable was put onto barges and kept in the river for two days. The gunboat commander, Li, was arrested, and his ship seized. Soldiers surrounded the strike committee base, disarming 1,000 pickets. Communists were rounded up: at Whampoa, Zhou Enlai was among those held. The Russians, including a delegation that had just arrived to study conditions in Canton, were placed in 'protective custody'. A letter to Chiang from the Soviet adviser, Kuibyshev, was returned with a note saying the addressee was not at home.

Calling on the sick Wang Jingwei, Chiang explained that his action was aimed only against the Communists. He said he had not given Wang notice of what he was doing since, if it went wrong, he wanted the politician to have a free hand to put things right. Two days later, when his patron, Zhang Jingjiang, arrived from Shanghai, Chiang dropped the fudge, insisting on 'settling the issue once and for all'. On 23 March he sent Wang a letter accusing him of siding with the Communists and rejecting the party faithful. The Central Executive Committee agreed to Chiang's suggestion that 'comrades of the left . . . should retire for a while'.

Diametrically opposed interpretations have been given of the 20 March coup. Chiang depicted it as self-defence against a Communist attempt to kidnap him, and the telephone calls from Becky Wang suggest something was afoot. But the left saw it as a pre-emptive strike. What seems most likely is that the political tension had made a showdown inevitable, and that the general took advantage of a confused situation to assert himself. A report written in April for the *North China Daily News*, based on information from 'persons who are very close to some of the high government officials', indicated that the leftists had hoped Chiang would join them to block threats from the right, taking his anti-imperialist rhetoric as a sign that he was on their side. 'General Chiang pretended to be enthusiastic, and promised that at four o'clock the following day he would lead his soldiers into Canton City to carry out this plan,' the story added. If Chiang did play along while mustering his forces, this would explain the visit from the dean of Whampoa who was believed to have been involved in the plot, and, above all, the midnight conversation between Chiang and the Communist visitor. It was a perfect moment to grab the initiative – Borodin was away, Wang was ill and the Russian advisers were busy with the visiting delegation from Moscow. Lulling adversaries by pretending to go along with them while preparing a counter-stroke would become a familiar Chiang modus operandi.

Having asserted himself so dramatically, Chiang moved swiftly to spread oil on the water – again, a technique he would frequently use to disarm opponents and give them 'face'. He blamed everything on a series of misunderstandings, offered an apology to the strikers, and removed the troops round their headquarters. Li was released, and the naval officer who had seized him and his boat was arrested instead as a convenient scapegoat. Sounding a nationalistic note, Chiang said he had been forced to move against the Chinese Communists because they had become the 'dogs' of the Russians. Cherepanov adds that the general told Liao Zhongkai's widow 'he had been offended: his budget had been reduced, arms passed to the other corps, and so on, that the Russians and Communists were against him, and he knew the plans of the Comintern'.[36]

Though he withdrew soldiers surrounding the Russian compound, Chiang pressed for the departure of Galen's replacement, General Kuibyshev, who had bypassed him. The Kuomintang's Political Council adopted a resolution that, while cooperation should continue, 'those Soviet comrades whose opinions . . . did not conform should immediately leave Canton'. On 24 March, Kuibyshev and two other advisers Chiang disliked sailed out with the visiting Soviet delegation – a dozen others regarded as uncooperative went three weeks later. The Kuomintang gave them a farewell banquet, but Chiang pleaded illness not to attend. His aim achieved, the general told a newspaper that reports of his being hostile to the Soviet Union or the Communists were the work of 'running dogs of imperialists'.[37]

Next, he turned to Wang Jingwei. Following the conventions for such occasions, each man blamed himself for what had happened. Wang said he had failed to control events. Going to the politician's sickbed, Chiang said he was willing to accept punishment for not having obtained authorisation for his actions. The next day, Wang told a meeting of the Political Council in his bedroom that his illness meant he should temporarily step down. Chiang repeated his readiness to accept sanctions, writing a resignation letter and leaving Canton for a fortress south of the city. The Finance Minister, T. V. Soong, caught up with him there and, playing to the script, begged him to return.

Back in Canton on 1 April, the general set out his proposals for the party and government. Wang withdrew to a village outside the city, and then came back to hand the seals of his offices to Chiang before heading off to France. As Wang was getting ready to leave, the other revolutionary veteran, Hu Hanmin, reappeared from his 'study tour' of Russia, and was greeted by some on the right as a potential government leader. Chiang had no desire to have him in town seeking to reassert his political claims. So he isolated the politician to such an extent that he decided to leave for Hong Kong. Wang and Hu took the same boat out of Canton; they stayed in their cabins to avoid meeting each other on board.[38]

The general next showed his muscle with the strikers. When the unions marched through the city on May Day, they found soldiers with fixed bayonets posted along the route or manning machine-gun and artillery emplacements. Still, showing the twin-track approach which was becoming his trademark, Chiang delivered fiery speeches extolling revolution and declaring solidarity with striking miners in Britain.[39]

Borodin had been caught completely by surprise by the events of March. Indeed, only a few days earlier he had assured a meeting with Soviet delegates in Peking that Chiang could be depended upon. The general certainly still needed Russian supplies: in May and June, 13,694 rifles, 11 million cartridges and nine planes were brought in along with financial aid. But, when Borodin returned to Canton, Chiang let him know that Hu had recommended his arrest; it was a way of bringing home to the Comintern agent how vulnerable he was if the general decided to act.

The Russian accepted a substantial diminution of the position of the Communists proposed by Chiang. Party members were removed from official jobs or reduced in rank – to balance the scales some of Chiang's right-wing rivals suffered, too. All orders from the Chinese Communist Party (CCP) had to go through a committee on which the Kuomintang was represented. Borodin agreed in the name of preserving the united front, for which Stalin was ready to sacrifice the interests of the Chinese Communists. In Moscow, the Comintern described the Nationalists as 'a revolutionary bloc of workers, peasants, intellectuals, and urban democracy'. A leading China expert, Gregory Voitinsky, called stories of a coup by Chiang 'an invention of the imperialists'. Once again, the Russians proved prime helpmates for a man out to use them for his own purpose.

On the morning of 15 May 1926, troops took up positions in the city and on the roofs of government buildings as Chiang told the Kuomintang Central Executive Committee of the new relationship with the Communists. Soldiers stood at the door of the meeting room. Leftists objected that what was happening was contrary to the sacred will of Sun Yat-sen; but, after a heated debate, they caved in. 'Many foreigners are inclined to place great confidence in General Chiang Kai-shek, believing that he has a level head,' the *North China Daily News* wrote. 'One cannot but arrive at the conclusion that his every move has been actuated by the desire for self-aggrandisement.' In similar vein, a Russian adviser, V. A. Stepanov, who had worked with him, wrote: 'We consider Chiang Kai-shek a peculiar person with peculiar characteristics, most prominent of these being his lust for glory and power and craving to be the hero of China . . . No one is allowed to argue with him over any matter or to act for him.'[40]

'His journeys are only known about in advance by his closest associates,' the French Consul reported. 'He moves surrounded by bodyguards standing on the running board of his car who are ready to shoot at anybody who makes a gesture they consider suspect'. The reason for such caution was made clear when Chiang went one afternoon to a meeting at party headquarters. As he walked down the corridor, accompanied by his wife and bodyguards, a young man in uniform approached with a bunch of newspapers held in front of him. His hand came out from behind the papers, holding a revolver. A bodyguard jumped for the attacker, but not before he had fired a shot which went wide. Chiang and Jennie ran down the corridor as a guard wrestled the attacker to the ground and another emptied his pistol into him: he turned out to be a relative of the exiled Cantonese General Xu. Jennie recalled that she and her husband 'were shaking like a leaf'.[41]

In the army, Chiang put loyalists into key positions. Generals were ordered that all recruitment was to be done through the Military Council. Chiang sent troops to the office of the right-wing police chief, Wu Tiecheng, to tell him he was being replaced on the spot. Wu, described by Chiang's secretary as 'unprincipled but smooth and tactful', was clapped in solitary confinement, accused of having diverted weapons and money from the police to an army unit he controlled, and of having grabbed $400,000 in tax revenue. The real reason for getting rid of Wu was that he represented a latent threat from the right who had to be eliminated: his successor was put under the Military Council. Another leading rightist, C. C. Wu, found it prudent to pay a protracted visit to his father's tomb in Shanghai.

Despite the moves on the two Wus, Chiang's overall tilt was clearly against the left. Communists, including Mao Zedong, were edged out. Russian contacts with officials were restricted. In a foretaste of later attempts to bind every section of society to the regime, an umbrella Alliance of Workers, Merchants, Intellectuals and Peasants was formed. In a speech to workers, Chiang denounced the 'crimes' of the Communists, and said they would never be allowed to hold posts in government or in the Kuomintang. The Sun Yat-sen Society and its left-wing rival were both disbanded – the group which replaced them, the Association of Whampoa Schoolmates, was under Chiang's control. The Academy's magazine depicted the Communist Party as a rat, and Russia as a fat imperialist with two 'running dogs' – the CCP and a warlord.[42]

In the east of Guangdong, Chiang's associate General He Yingqin ordered his troops to rein in peasant and worker groups which were putting pressure on the local gentry. Chiang called in rightists from Shanghai and his home province of Zhejiang. Among them was his secretary's elder brother, Chen Guofu, who went to work in the Organisation Department where his job was 'to comb out the real Communists'. Growing concerned, the Communists asked Wang Jingwei to return, but he preferred to stay in the Alpine spa of Evian where he had taken up residence.[43]

A new Foreign Minister was appointed, a British citizen called Chen Youren, or Eugene Chen, with the job of reaching an agreement with Hong Kong to end the strike. Born of Chinese parents in Trinidad, the voluble Chen did not read Chinese, and spoke it only partially. But his studies of the common law gave him an advantage as a negotiator. Hallett Abend of the *New York Times* described him as 'small, very thin, with a disproportionately large head, and snapping black eyes, he spoke English with an ultra-British accent, and both in conversation and in his state papers was a master of stinging invective'.

In only sixteen months since Sun's death, Chiang had established himself as the military and political master of Canton, with an army springboard the doctor had never possessed. The political system was unique in China, combining a government claiming popular support and a party organised on centralised lines with its own ideology and a powerful call on Chinese nationalism. Though Borodin remained, his influence had diminished. Chiang was his own man, owing nothing to anybody else for his rise to the top. He was still seen as a revolutionary, and there was no doubting his fervent national feeling, his desire to unify the country and undo the unequal treaties imposed by the foreigners. Nor could his dedication to the memory of Sun Yat-sen and his principles be questioned. But there was nothing intrinsically progressive about any of this.

Chiang's idea of revolution was conservative, even reactionary. Where Sun had melded nationalism and social revolution, with the promise of democracy after a period of political tutelage, Chiang intended to pursue the first without accentuating the other two, causing an endless conundrum for the Russians who saw the national and social revolutions as intimately linked. The general was, by nature, in agreement with the Kuomintang aspiration for a classless, corporatist society in which social harmony and union would reign, or, if necessary, be imposed by force. But he did not see this as involving the destruction of the classical structure of Chinese society. On the contrary, Confucian authoritarianism permeated his thinking, with a heavy emphasis on obedience to the teacher-leader – so long as it was him.

In his rise in Canton, Chiang had shown his ability to meld force with great political skill. Now, he stengthened his control by having the Kuomintang Central Committee elect his patron, Zhang Jingjiang, as Chairman of its Standing Committee to tighten party discipline. The general became head of the Organisation Bureau, controlling appointments. Sun's Three Principles were the tablets of the faith; his political will was elevated to the status of holy writ, recited at party meetings and in schools; his photograph stared down throughout Nationalist-ruled areas. If Chiang could now lead his army to Peking, he would be able to claim to be the true successor who had realised the doctor's dream. At thirty-eight, he was ready to take on the rest of China, and the mighty warlords who ruled it.

PART II

SHEDDING BLOOD

Canton, July 1926

———

Nanking, December 1927

CHAPTER 6

Lords of Misrule

THE MEN CHIANG KAI-SHEK FACED in the struggle for China had set their stamp on the nation in the years after the death of the would-be emperor, Yuan Shikai, in 1916. As central authority fragmented in the absence of anybody able to enforce his rule on a continuing basis, the warlord era saw anarchy on an immense scale as major militarists fought for dominance over great regions – at the height of his power, the Manchurian chieftain Zhang Zuolin governed a domain as big as Western Europe. Petty commanders, meanwhile, jockeyed for local authority; China's largest province of Sichuan was estimated to have seen 500 conflicts between fifty generals in twenty years.

Some warlords started life as bandits, others as water carriers or coolies. It was a time for upward mobility through force of arms and political cunning. A few rulers showed an interest in modernisation, building roads, schools and public facilities, and making use of young men who had returned from study abroad with new ideas. But, as a whole, China was held back by the essentially primitive nature of the system at a time when it needed to join the twentieth century, thus heightening the appeal of the Kuomintang as a force that preached national unity, with a trained army to use against warlord forces exhausted by years of civil war.

Superior foreign observers mocked the warlords as comic opera generals with ostrich-plumed headgear and ornate uniforms, braided epaulettes, banks of medals and ceremonial swords hanging down to the ground: the diminutive Zhang Zuolin, with delicate hands and gold-capped teeth, posed for one photograph with his two young sons beside him in child-sized identical plumed hats, medal-bedecked tunics and swords. But, far from springing out of Gilbert and Sullivan, most warlords were mercurial exponents of brute force. In their amoral world, everything was possible and permissible in pursuit of power. All that mattered was being on top, by whatever means were required, squeezing peasants, farmers and merchants for the funds needed to maintain as large an army as possible. Public power was a function of personal control of troops, territory and money.

The 'Dogmeat General' of Shandong, Zhang Zongchang, was described as having 'the physique of an elephant, the brain of a pig and the temperament of a tiger'. The contemporary writer Lin Yutang called the hard-drinking former coolie 'the most colourful, legendary, mediaeval and unashamed ruler of modern China'. The last Manchu emperor, Pu Yi, recalled him as 'a universally detested monster', his bloated face 'tinged with the livid hue induced by opium smoking'. His soldiers were known for 'opening melons' – splitting the skulls of opponents with their swords – and then hanging severed heads from telegraph poles. Zhang spoke of himself as a 'big, round-faced, long-legged overfed Shandong ruffian'; popular mythology gave him a penis as long as a pile of eighty-six silver dollars. He was said to have allocated his concubines numbers because they were so many that he could not remember their names. Among them were Chinese, Koreans, Japanese, White Russians, and two French women as well as somebody described by a visiting journalist as 'one bedraggled female who said she was an American'.[1]

Other warlords had greater depth. The amber-eyed, poetry-writing Wu Peifu, known as the Philosopher General, had passed the imperial civil service examination. Basing his power on the prosperous central Yangtze Valley region, Wu liked to identify with George Washington, whose portrait hung on his office wall. Known for his taste for alcohol, including imported brandy, he kept up his cultural claims by posing for photographs at his writing table, calligraphy brush in hand, but it was said that the quality of the texts declined noticeably when his private secretary died. His national pride was such that he refused to enter foreign concessions, even to be treated for blood poisoning from an infected tooth which eventually killed him.[2]

In Manchuria, the illiterate, heavily moustachioed Zhang Zuolin, known as the Old Marshal, had begun as a graduate of the University of the Green Forest, that is to say, a bandit. Allying himself with the Manchu Empire, he used force and guile to establish mastery over the three provinces of the far north-east, an area as big as France and Germany combined. His domain had only 3 per cent of China's population, but 90 per cent of its heavy industry, thanks to Japanese investments. Zhang's large army with its fast-charging cavalry was a constant threat to rulers south of the Great Wall, and, in time, he would make himself the greatest warlord in the land.[3]

In Shanxi province, west of Peking, the portly Marshal Yan Xishan became known as the 'Model Governor' as he introduced reforms and fashioned a creed which claimed to combine elements of militarism, nationalism, anarchism, democracy, capitalism, communism, individualism, imperialism, universalism and paternalism. Protected from outside interference by the mountainous borders of the province and his diplomatic skill, Yan ran his railways on a different gauge from the rest of China to prevent invasion by troops in trains and to safeguard Shanxi's coal and mineral resources. Another regional leader described him as 'a dark-skinned, moustached man of medium height who rarely laughed and maintained an attitude of great reserve . . . At first sight I knew him to be an artful man . . . Yan never showed his inner feelings.'[4]

The Christian General, Feng Yuxiang, whom Galen and Borodin had gone to visit as a possible second ally in China, banned foot-binding, closed brothels, had the streets cleaned, and professed admiration for Gladstone, Bismarck and Theodore Roosevelt. His troops were bombarded with slogans in favour of the frugal moral life and against smoking and drinking: he sent Wu Peifu a gift of a bottle of water as a comment on the Philosopher General's alcohol consumption. As they marched, Feng's men sang songs on the need to conserve ammunition to the tune of 'Hark the Herald Angels Sing'. The son of a poor peasant, their bulky commander often dressed in simple soldier's clothes with a big bush hat. A convert to Methodism, he was reported to have carried out mass baptisms with fire hoses, though he said his territories in northern China were too poor to have such equipment.

Feng's praise of frugality made him an exception in an age when conspicuous consumption and self-indulgence were prized as status symbols. Wu Peifu was reputed to own the biggest diamond on earth, and Zhang Zuolin to wear the world's biggest pearl in his black skullcap. In his capital of Mukden, the Old Marshal built himself a palace stocked with French wines, five wives and Confucian texts; the kitchens employed a staff of seventy. In Shandong, Zhang Zongchang ate off a forty-piece cut-glass Belgian dinner service. Visiting him, an American correspondent reported: 'He gave a dinner for me where sinful quantities of costly foods were served. There was French champagne and sound brandy.'[5]

These men were, in the words of the historian Lucian Pye, 'instinctively suspicious, quick to suspect that their interests might be threatened ... hard-headed, devoted to the short run and impervious to idealistic abstractions'. They were ruthlessly authoritarian. The Model Governor might proclaim his attachment to modernisation, but Shanxi was a police state. Wu Peifu might aspire to Washingtonian status, but his troops massacred striking railway workers, beheading their leader on a station platform. When Zhang Zuolin's soldiers raided the Russian embassy in Peking, a score of Chinese Communists sheltering inside were dragged out, tortured and strangled or shot. For all their hymns and homilies, the Christian General's men waged a campaign against Muslim rebels which cost an estimated 100,000 lives, with terrible cruelty on both sides. It was a brutal era in which human life counted for little; a British diplomat recorded seeing the fate of prisoners after a battle in Sichuan – two were cut up in the street and their hearts and livers hung in a cookshop; two others were wrapped in wadding and burned alive in front of a huge crowd; the others had slits made in their bodies into which candles were inserted and burned before they were hacked to death.[6]

The way in which the warlords used force as they wished was reflected by their subordinates and all the way down to the often undisciplined infantry. In 1921, the *North China Daily News* reported from Shaanxi province: 'Violence and robbery stalk abroad. Farmers are afraid to venture out of doors with even a donkey, lest both man and beast be pressed into the service of some warring faction.' In Henan province in 1924, a correspondent recounted: 'Unimportant cities are loaded with parasite soldiers well fed and well clad whose hardest piece of work is marching daily through the streets singing. Each general is a despot in his own sphere.'

Soldiers and bandits were often interchangeable, with local militia acting in both roles. An officer who served with a 'rabble army' in the north recalled how, after the evening meal, his colleagues got into civilian gowns, strapped on their Mauser pistols and went out to rob and extort. As a letter to a newspaper from Sichuan put it: 'Soldiers come and bandits follow them, then the bandits withdraw and the soldiers come back – and what's more, it is the armies who maintain the scourge of banditry here. All discharged soldiers become bandits; and when the army needs one more soldier, it enlists a bandit . . . soldiers and bandits are two names for the same thing.' Or, as a President of the Republic remarked, when armies disbanded, soldiers turned into bandits; when they recruited, bandits turned into soldiers.[7]

As well as murder and looting, kidnapping was a common scourge. Families were encouraged to pay the ransom by being sent a severed finger or ear of a victim. Those seized were known as 'tickets' – 'lottery tickets' for the rich, 'pawn tickets' for the poor; if the money was not forthcoming, the bandits would 'tear up the ticket' by killing their prey. In an incident which hit the headlines in 1923, outlaws attacked the luxury Blue Express train in Shandong province and grabbed 300 passengers, among them thirty 'foreign tickets' including a member of the Rockefeller family. The central authorities were so worried by the international implications that they agreed to pay the ransom and handed $300,000 in compensation to the dean of the diplomatic corps.[8]

Alongside the plain bandits were rural secret societies with a patina of playing a Robin Hood role or of protecting farmers. The anti-warlord Red Spear Society, which was strong enough to storm cities, performed elaborate ceremonies and secret rituals, including eating from a magic amulet to confer invulnerability. A Russian adviser saw naked adherents riding bareback into battle smeared in red clay with headgear like fierce temple guardian statues. The young unmarried women of the Iron Gate Society dressed in white and carried fans which they believed would deflect bullets into baskets held in their other hand. The most celebrated outlaw, Bai Lang, the White Wolf, called for revolution and established contact with Sun Yat-sen as he roamed the north at the head of a 'Citizens' Punitive Army'. After an epic march on Xi'an, he was forced back to his mountain stronghold where he died of wounds. Government troops dug up the body, cut off the head and hung it from the wall of the provincial capital.[9]

The villagers who made up over three quarters of China's population were usually defenceless against both the troops and the bandits. Men were pressed into service as porters, women abducted and raped. Food was stolen, carts seized, farm animals grabbed for slaughter or to carry supplies. In Shandong, a Japanese report recounted: 'Not only have arson, theft and rape occurred everywhere, as if wild beasts were on the prowl, but murder and kidnappings are performed in broad daylight . . . peasants in the same locale are pillaged two or three times by outsiders . . . [they] are without houses, without food and their plight has become extremely miserable.' For such peasants joining an army or becoming a bandit offered the only escape from impoverishment and oppression, and the opportunity to better themselves materially by looting and brigandage.

The peasants also had to cope with huge natural disasters. In 1918, a northern drought killed an estimated half-million people. Famines are thought to have cost from 4 to 6 million lives in 1920 and 1921. Up to a dozen provinces suffered serious flooding in 1923–25. There were earthquakes and crop pests. China's vast countryside was poor and backward. Communications were rudimentary. Most villagers never moved outside their immediate home patch, and there was no education or media to spread the idea of national government. Rivers and tracks were the main means of transport. According to one estimate, two thirds of the rural population lived at or below the subsistence level. Education was virtually non-existent. Absentee landlords owned three quarters of the fields, taking half the income or more in rent. A third of farmers were reckoned to be in debt, paying annual interest of 20 to 200 per cent.[10]

The First World War had boosted China's urban economy as the West's industry was devoted to production for the conflict, and exports to Asia dipped. This opened the way for Chinese factories to serve the domestic market, and sell to neighbouring countries. But, though there were some sizeable enterprises in warlord territories and the militarists encouraged arms production, the development of an economic base for military operations was rarely pursued except in Manchuria, thanks to the Japanese presence in mining, steel, glass and ceramics there. In the textile industry, three cities with foreign concessions – Shanghai, Tianjin and Qingdao* – accounted for 70 per cent of national capacity.

An international conference in Washington in 1922 guaranteed China's sovereignty and territorial integrity. Peking remained important for its symbolic status and as the seat of governments recognised by foreign nations where attempts were made to develop state institutions. Warlords liked either to control the capital, or to have their men there. But real power lay with their armies, and the system produced its own self-regulatory mechanism: if one general threatened to become dominant, a blocking coalition formed to halt him. The post-imperial divisions of the country were thus exacerbated, reflecting both the strength of regionalism and China's vast geographic, geological and cultural differences.

In this ever-shifting world, personal factors were of great importance. Intersecting networks of family, regional, institutional and teacher–student relationships between older and younger commanders provided multilayered links, strengthened by membership of secret societies and sworn brotherhoods. Warlords created ladders of loyalty by handing the running of provinces and counties to lieutenants. But treason was everywhere, aided by bribery, known as 'silver bullets'.

Ambitious subordinates could turn on their masters – the Old Marshal's leading general secretly allied with the Christian General to stage a revolt which only ended when his officers reverted to their original loyalty and deserted him; he and his wife were shot and their bodies displayed for three days. Calculations of self-interest might lead a warlord to switch sides for fear that an ally was becoming too powerful, a subordinate too ambitious or an enemy too strong. In one major war, the Christian General abruptly changed sides to get his hands on Peking. The man he betrayed, Wu Peifu, lamented that China was 'a country without a system; anarchy and treason prevail everywhere. Betraying one's leader has become as natural as eating one's breakfast . . . Underlings think of nothing but getting rid of their leaders in order to take their place, so disorder keeps spreading without end.'[11]

Despite all the rhetoric that preceded the fighting, and occasional murders in a Chinese garden or after banquets, the early years of the warlord period were marked by a distinct desire to avoid too much serious violence. Fighting was a dangerous undertaking. Better to practise

* Known at the time as Tientsin and Tsingtao.

'alignment politics' to sew up the best possible alliances and force opponents to retreat. Given the shifting tides of battle, it was also prudent to think of the future. On one occasion, Wu Peifu let two trains of defeated Manchurian troops steam home, knowing he might need a similar courtesy one day – sure enough, in their next war, Zhang Zuolin provided transport after beating him. As the saying had it, China's civil wars were very civil – so long as one was not a foot soldier dying from wounds without medical care or a peasant who had lost his food, wife, daughters and possessions to a locust army.

As the decade went on, however, fighting grew more intense, and more widespread. In 1916, there were estimated to be around half a million soldiers in China. The wars of 1922 and 1924 saw the number of men under warlord flags at treble that number. This cost money they did not have: in relatively rich Manchuria, Zhang Zuolin spent $51 million on his forces in 1925 on revenue of only $23 million. As a result, warlords employed the most immediate and repressive methods to fill their coffers. Everything became subservient to their need for money. In Sichuan, there were twenty-seven taxes on salt. Seventy levies in the port city of Xiamen* covered everything from night soil to firecrackers and prostitutes. Revenue due to the central government from salt and stamp duties was held back. Local duties on the movement of domestic goods – known as the *lijin* – were a major source of funds. One shipment of paper was taxed eleven times along the Yangtze to a total of 160 per cent of its value. Elsewhere, a warlord slapped a 100 per cent tax on railway freight including food, at a time of famine.

A survey found 673 different kinds of land taxes in the mid-1920s. In Manchuria, these rose twelve-fold between 1922 and 1928 to gobble up a third of the income from crops. Payment might be demanded for the future and the past: the American writer Pearl Buck recorded a case in which farmers had to stump up taxes due ten years later while others had to pay a levy on fields that had belonged to their ancestors. A warlord driven out of a region would collect taxes before going, and his successor would do the same on arrival. Defeated armies demanded 'travel payments' to leave peacefully. Victorious commanders exacted a 'welcome subsidy' not to let their troops off the leash.

* Known at the time as Amoy.

Banks were squeezed for loans. Chambers of Commerce were forced to accept warlord bonds. When Wu Peifu's eye lighted on the Chinese River Steamship Administration, he had the man in charge arrested and released him only after he agreed to hand over the company. Warlord-controlled banks set the presses rolling to provide cash; in some cases, notes were run off on duplicating machines. Hunan province printed $22 million in paper money on a reserve of under $1 million. In Shandong, notes worth $55 million were issued on a silver reserve of $1.5 million. The Christian General, Feng Yuxiang, established a bank with no capital. Zhang Zuolin called in merchants to tell them to make sure the currency remained stable despite his excessive printing of notes. To drive his point home he had five of them shot. The slide continued.[12]

Monopolies were sold off, and, in times of disaster, some generals 'borrowed' money or grain from relief bodies. On one occasion, Feng seized 27,000 sheep to feed and clothe his men. When he was military master of Peking, he sent soldiers to collect the entrance money at tourist attractions: he also opened the Honest and Clean Hotel in his northern stronghold and set up the Northwest Automobile Transportation Company as the only authorised user of motor vehicles. When Peking failed to send him money he demanded, he stole hundreds of thousands of dollars in government funds from a train.

A commander who rose to become President of China was said to have embezzled $20 million in his time as a provincial military governor. The Ministry of Communications reported in 1925 that $180 million had been taken from the railways up to the end of the previous year. Having grabbed $6 million from one line, almost half its gross annual income, Wu Peifu installed an aide as its boss, and raised mortgages on land along the track before getting a $5 million loan against the railway's property, which was used to open a bank that issued $20 million in bonds.

Given their constant need for money, how could the warlords be expected not to exploit the trade in opium which the British had introduced into the country in the previous century in the name of the freedom of commerce? The narcotic was officially outlawed, but no warlord took any notice of that. Drug monopolies were leased to the highest bidder, and revenue raised on production, distribution and use. Smoking dens and their apparatus were taxed. Farmers were ordered to plant poppies: in a southern province, those who did not grow the flowers were fined for laziness. Opium Suppression Bureaux raised yet more money through fines, or sold confiscated shipments to dealers and addicts.

The annual revenues of militarists from narcotics were put at $50 million in Yunnan, $20 million in Gansu and Fujian, anywhere between $10 and $30 million in Sichuan. Though Feng denounced drugs and forbade their use by his men, his annual income from opium taxes was reckoned at $20 million at one point. Regions which did not produce much opium but lay on transport routes imposed transit taxes: Guangxi's position on the way from the poppy fields of Yunnan to Hong Kong and world markets enabled its rulers to make almost enough to cover their military spending. Some commanders gave their troops opium in lieu of wages. Troops from Yunnan grew so rich from the traffic that common soldiers flaunted gold rings and watches, earning more in a day than ordinary people made in a month.

There were good troops in warlord ranks who took soldiering seriously. Wu Peifu's elite Third Division began daily drills at 6.30 a.m. Feng Yuxiang's men hardened themselves with gymnastics, trench-digging in frozen ground and 45-mile marches carrying 65-pound packs. The motto of his Big Sword units declared: 'When we fight, we first use bullets; when the bullets are gone, we use bayonets; when the bayonets are dull, we use the rifle barrel; when this is broken, we use our fists; when our fists are broken, we bite.' A British Brigadier General, C. D. Bruce, came away from a war of the mid-1920s with the conviction that, properly led, soldiers from the north of China were 'the finest Oriental raw material' with a physique second to none, and an iron constitution.[13]

For all Bruce's enthusiasm, most warlord soldiers were untrained peasants, unemployed urban dwellers and drifters. A survey of one garrison reported that nearly 90 per cent were illiterate. Many came from very poor families. Only a third had served for more than two years. In 1926, the future US adviser to Chiang Kai-shek, Joseph Stilwell, observed a 'scarecrow' company: 20 per cent were less than 4.5 feet tall, many were under fourteen, some were barefoot. 'The wildest stretch of the imagination could not imagine this rabble in action except running away,' he wrote in his diary.[14]

Still, when units were ordered to disband, they sometimes mutinied in protest, seeing possession of a gun as their best lifeline: one demand of the bandits who held up the Blue Express was to be integrated into an army.

Soldiers on the losing side would expect to be absorbed into the victor's army. This enabled the winner to increase the size of his forces, but brought in poor units of doubtful loyalty. When Wu Peifu fielded 200,000 men in one war, many had never fought under him before, and some of his subordinates owed him no allegiance.

As well as being of generally poor quality, most warlord armies were badly armed. Artillery was scarce. When modern weapons were bought from abroad, the men did not know how to use them. Feng's Russian advisers found Chinese officers had no idea how to deploy machine guns. On an inspection tour of Shandong, a British mercenary reported that hardly any of forty field guns on display were serviceable. Though the initial appearance of planes caused panic, their pilots flew too high for effective bombing, in order to escape ground fire. In 1924, there were 170 military aircraft in China: four years later, the total had risen to only 240. In one war, eight days of attacks by Manchurian aircraft killed five enemy, knocked down two trees and damaged a hotel, for the loss of two machines. Feng told his men they were as likely to be hit by bombs as by bird droppings.

So the warlords called in advisers and mercenaries. The Russians who helped the Kuomintang and the Christian General were there for ideological and political reasons, but most of the foreigners in China chased the spoils of war. Americans flew planes. Zhang Zuolin employed 400 Japanese soldiers, mainly gunners. He also had on his staff a one-armed old Etonian called Sutton, a Russian inventor who was working on aircraft with movable wings which would take off as soon as the motor started, and a German engineer who was locked up in a vermin-infested jail after being convicted of killing a boy who called him a Foreign Devil.

The largest foreign presence was of White Russians fleeing from the Soviet regime. Some fought in Manchuria wearing greatcoats and Tartar hats: according to one, they 'went through the Chinese troops like a knife through butter'. In Shandong, the Dogmeat General employed a unit led by General Konstantin Nechanev, formerly of the Russian Imperial Army. Kitted out in dark green uniforms and thigh-length yellow boots, his men were known for their ruthlessness and rapacity. In fighting in 1926, they drove three armoured trains machine-gunning civilians and stealing everything movable. When local inhabitants pulled up the rails, the Russians devastated the nearest town.

Railways were a key to warlord conflicts, offering the fastest way to shift large bodies of troops. Armoured trains bristling with guns acted as artillery. In 1925, 70 per cent of locomotives between Peking and the Yangtze centre of Wuhan were reported to be used by armies. On the Shanghai–Nanking line, fighting took more than half the locomotives out of service, and traffic was blocked by 300 wagons occupied by soldiers as living quarters. In another war, half the locomotives on the Peking–Mukden line were in military use. Campaigns were fought along the tracks, with major battles for railheads and junctions. Retreating generals ordered track to be ripped up to prevent pursuit. In 1924, damage to railways was estimated at $100 million. Fighting in the centre and east of the country in the next two years cut non-military traffic by a quarter, hampering transport of food and manufactured goods, causing big build-ups of cargo, raising prices and cutting towns off from the countryside.

A leading writer, Lu Xun, likened the state of China to syphilis, congenitally rotten and with 'dark and confusing elements' in its blood vessels which required total cleansing. The warlord system replaced the oppressive certainties of the imperial centuries with a world of cut-throat competition in which those who would never have risen to even the lower ranks of the civil service held sway over vast swathes of territory. Instead of standing in awe of Confucian sages, the Chinese kowtowed to men whose only claims to authority were the armies at their command. In the absence of an effective national political structure, they were the agents of power.[15]

Their era ensured that there was no imperial restoration, no turning back to a more settled age. There was economic, social and intellectual progress in places, particularly along the coast and in cities with foreign concessions. But the warlords had no system to offer, and the nation's weariness with the anarchy they embodied meant they had no well of support on which to draw. For all their braggadocio, even the greatest of the militarists lacked the power and determination to become the ruler of the country. They had broken the mould, but were unable to forge a new one. With the partial exception of the Christian General, the idea of winning hearts and minds, let alone of constructing a regime with a legitimacy beyond the force of arms, was foreign to their natures. In contrast, the Nationalists deployed Sun Yat-sen's Three Principles, backed by a trained army, an organised political party and a financial system more advanced than anything elsewhere in China. The balance of forces made the challenge launched from Canton in 1926 a highly hazardous undertaking, but a power now existed which could aspire to unify the nation and give it a structure of modernity. By the time Chiang Kai-shek established his supremacy in Canton, China was ready for the Northern Expedition.

CHAPTER 7

To the North

ON 1 JULY 1926, Chiang Kai-shek read out the mobilisation order for the Northern Expedition which was to be the world's biggest military campaign between the two world wars. 'To protect the welfare of the people we must overthrow all warlords and wipe out reactionary power so that we may implement the Three People's Principles and complete the National Revolution,' it declared. Recognising the general's power and the importance of giving him everything needed for success, the Kuomintang Central Committee voted to place in his hands 'the control of all organisations, civil and military, private as well as public' – except for the party itself.

Eight days later, Chiang swore his oath as commander-in-chief of the expedition in a ceremony at the Eastern Parade Grounds in Canton attended by tens of thousands. To underline the legacy of Sun Yat-sen, the doctor's son held up a portrait of his father. In his stentorian, high-pitched tone, Chiang said a decisive moment had been reached at which 'the country will sink if we do not shed blood'. The general was presented with a blue flag on which was written 'Down with militarism, the tool of foreign imperialism'. Mounting a white horse, his feet thrust forward in the stirrups, he saluted the troops.[1]

Three weeks later, the commander drove to Canton station where a 200-strong farewell party awaited him. Smiling broadly, he stood on the platform for photographs with a group that included Borodin, a poker-faced Galen, Jennie and his adopted son, in knee-length trousers and holding a straw hat. The general's Shanghai patron, Zhang Jingjiang, sat at the front in a bamboo chair with the look of a death's head. When his wife asked to accompany him, Chiang laughed, and recalled the episode on the gunboat with Sun Yat-sen. 'When women hear the roar of cannons, they are so scared that they urinate in their pants,' he said. Jennie recorded that as the train moved noisily away she had tears in her eyes, and that Chiang waved back until she could see him no longer.[2]

The odds ahead of the expedition were enormous. The main militarists of central and northern China could muster up to 750,000 men between them, at least five times the size of the Nationalist forces. They enjoyed overwhelming superiority in arms. Reports by Russian advisers showed that some of the Kuomintang units had no arms; others carried matchlock rifles. Watching them move out, Hallett Abend of the *New York Times* described them as 'unimpressive, straw-sandaled, mostly little men . . . clad in ill-fitting cotton uniforms of dirty grey or dusty yellow . . . Disorganization seemed complete, and the expedition appeared to be a hopeless folly.'[3]

The cost was beyond anything Canton had faced – the army took up three-quarters of the budget and produced a $20 million deficit, setting a pattern for the next two decades. While the Nationalist soldiers were paid better and more regularly than warlord troops, a third of their income was in the form of promissory notes to be redeemed in territory which the Expedition was heading for. The home base was far from stable, with street fights between labour groups and high unemployment. The anti-British boycott disrupted trade, and prevented war supplies being brought in through Hong Kong.

Despite such difficulties, Nationalist morale had been boosted by the success of the Eastern Expeditions, and the Whampoa graduates had proved themselves. The Russians had taught them to mount flanking offensives, and circle round the back of their opponents. Widespread discontent with the warlord struggles, exploitation and banditry provided a favourable climate for a party that promised to advance the people's livelihood. The major war in 1924 between Wu Peifu and the Manchurians had weakened both. The KMT was present across wide areas of China, giving it an unmatched geographical spread. The broad nature of the party Sun had founded enabled it to appeal to nationalists, democrats, modernisers, technocrats, progressives, seekers after social justice, educational reformers, entrepreneurs, and all who wanted China to play its proper part in the world. Communist work on rural reform provided a well of peasant support.

The National Revolutionary Army was split into eight corps whose heterogeneous nature reflected the prevailing conditions in the south, and whose commanders would play major roles in the coming two decades. Chiang's own First Army was the most proficient, with a large contingent from Whampoa and priority access to equipment that annoyed other generals. Twenty thousand strong, it contained veterans of the Eastern Expeditions, with Chiang's associate, He Yingqin, leading its crack units.

The Second Army, of 15,000 men, was headed by Tan Yankai, a former governor of the neighbouring province of Hunan who had joined Sun Yat-sen in Guangdong and became a Chiang confidant during the March coup, succeeding Wang Jingwei in the chair of the Political Council. The 10,000 men of the Third Army came from the wild and mountainous south-western province of Yunnan. The similarly-sized Fourth Army was under right-wing General Li Jishen, a graduate of the main imperial military academy. Given its commander's political orientation, this was considered a safe place to park leftists, including an independent regiment with a chief of staff called Ye Ting, who had secretly become a Communist while studying in Moscow. The largely autonomous Fifth Army, whose speciality was running protection rackets on the waterways round Canton, was left behind as a home guard, but the Sixth, under a Guangdong general, was regarded as loyal and reliable.[4]

The presence of the Seventh Army was the result of an alliance with the rulers of Guangxi province, to the west of Guangdong. Birthplace of the Taiping rebellion, it was full of backward villages – the leader of the ruling group, Li Zongren, was frightened almost out of his wits when he first saw a steam engine on a visit to Guangdong at the age of twenty-five. Li and his fellow militarists in what came to be known as the Guangxi Clique were politically compatible with the Nationalists as they turned temples into schools, and encouraged their troops to behave well. The historian Eugene Levich has characterised Li as 'aggressive, ambitious, intelligent, nationalistic, puritanical, efficient, honest, daring and innovative'. British intelligence described another clique member, the Muslim Bai Chongxi, as 'tall, well-built with a high intellectual forehead. A thinker and planner in the realms of both politics and strategy . . . A sense of humour . . . A Moslem who drinks wine and eats pork.'[5]

The Eighth Army came into the Nationalist fold when a general in southern Hunan who staged a revolt against Wu Peifu's provincial governor there was beaten back and looked to Canton for help. The son of an imperial mandarin, Tang Shengzhi was described by one Russian adviser as 'lively, resolute and radical in speech' and by another as a possessive, caustic character and a conceited careerist. He followed the advice of a personal Buddhist priest, taking a religious statue with him to battle. Tang forbade his men to smoke, though he was reported to have used opium. An adviser noted two fingers on his right hand 'stained as dark as smoked sausages'.[6]

The Kuomintang and the Guangxi warlords had every interest in shoring up Tang; if he was defeated, Wu Peifu's men would be on their northern borders. So Tang's forces became the Eighth Army, and Guangxi troops, accompanied by a special corps of 100 women, moved over the provincial border to assist them. Thus, as the historian Diana Lary notes, 'The Kuomintang found itself in the anomalous position of having its great revolutionary enterprise led, at the front, by a man who only a few weeks before had been an undistinguished warlord, and staffed in the main by troops of other recently converted warlords.'[7]

Chiang's initial plan had been to push north on two fronts through Hunan and Jiangxi province to the east. However, Galen persuaded him to avoid splitting his forces, and to concentrate on reaching the major Yangtze city of Wuhan, 600 miles to the north, which was a fief of Wu Peifu.

The campaign set the pattern by which Chiang would operate for the next two decades. All the major warlords would have to be confronted in due course if the Nationalists were to unite China. But the wisest course was to face them one by one, exploiting their mutual suspicions. Leaving the front-line fighting to Tang and the Guangxi generals, the commander remained behind at the town of Shaoguan in northern Guangdong to concentrate on diplomacy, political manipulation, control of finance, organisation and bribery. From the start, he was trying to negotiate with a major eastern warlord, Sun Zhuanfang, and to get senior officials in Hunan and Jiangxi provinces to change sides. By the end of July, he had induced six generals in the opposing camp to join the Nationalists, boosting the size of his forces but further undermining Galen's quest for quality over quantity. In operational matters, he counted heavily on the Russian, who wrote that Chiang's chief of staff would come to see him, get his opinion, write an order and take it to the general, who signed without alterations. 'He does not make a single decision without my approval,' the adviser added.[8]

The alliance with Tang, the Buddhist General, ensured the Nationalists a smooth passage through southern Hunan. As they moved on the provincial capital of Changsha, Wu's men abandoned the city; 'peace-maintenance corps' formed by workers seized their weapons as they went. Two warlords from Guizhou province, to the west, rallied to the cause, their troops becoming the Ninth and Tenth Armies.[9]

In Shaoguan, Chiang was joined by his wife. Jennie found him thin, but in high spirits. They went to their lodgings in a tall house with traditional blackwood furniture. As Chiang closed the door behind them in their room, she recorded, 'he grabbed me savagely to his breast and murmured endearments. I could see how much he had missed me by the way he caressed me so passionately.' That night, they went to their room early after dinner. Chiang spoke of the possibility that he would be killed: she said it was the first time he had talked to her of death.[10]

The commander and Galen crossed the mountains into Hunan in the intense summer heat, lodging in local houses, and, once, in the rooms of a Presbyterian girls' school. 'Whether the Chinese nation and race can restore their freedom and independence hangs in the balance,' Chiang told his generals. Becoming so agitated that he lost his voice, he upbraided officers for gambling and visiting prostitutes, as well as for occupying civilian homes and not treating their men properly. His irritation was sharpened by an impacted tooth which was extracted by an American dentist from a hospital in Changsha run by Yale University.

On 18 August the Nationalists advanced along the rail line into northern Hunan. Wu's troops held out for two days in their trenches before withdrawing. A Nationalist feint drew them into a trap where they were surrounded and routed. An attack was then launched on a big base at Yueyang,* on the junction of a huge lake and China's greatest river, the Yangtze. According to a report in the *North China Herald*, the assault on the fortress began with ten huge rafts crammed with soldiers sailing towards the defences, but the wind changed, and the rafts stopped. The defenders

---

* Known at the time as Yochow.

opened fire, killing hundreds of those on board. A second attack was successful; as the southerners marched in, the *Central China Post* noted that they 'quietened the city, treating the people very well, paying for everything they got'. On 26 August Chiang ordered his forces to advance across the border into Hubei province towards the biggest urban area in central China.[11]

Strategically located where the Yangtze meets its biggest tributary, the Han, Wuhan consisted of three cities housing 800,000 people. Wuchang, on the south bank of the river, was the provincial capital, with a 7-mile city wall and historic links with the kingdom of Zhou from which Chiang claimed to descend. Across the river, Hanyang housed Wu Peifu's main arsenal. Hankou, the most heavily populated of the three, was a commercial metropolis with foreign concession areas, compared with Chicago as an industrial hub and agricultural entrepôt and described by one contemporary guidebook as 'the best-groomed and best-dressed station in the Far East'.[12]

Water dominated the region. The Yangtze was a mile wide at high water. The Australian historian C. P. Fitzgerald, who worked in Wuhan in the mid-1920s, recalled the district round his office as 'a swamp crazily crossed here and there by gangplanks, or navigated by rickshaws up to their axles in mire and dirty water'. 'The mud, filth and stench are unbearable,' the *North China Daily News* reported as the Nationalists approached. Roads and railways lines were submerged. Both sides blew up bridges for tactical advantage: Wu Peifu's executioners beheaded eight students caught trying to set off explosives under one.[13]

Moving with customary speed, the Nationalist Fourth Army spearheaded the advance, its leftist independent regiment playing a key role. Farmers guided the southerners to attack a supposedly impregnable railway bridge at Tingsiqiao, 50 miles south of Wuhan, from the rear. Wu Peifu took personal charge of the defence and executed officers who retreated without orders. The bridge changed hands three times in twenty-four hours of fighting before the Nationalists emerged as victors. Two thirds of the 10,000 defenders were captured or killed. Many drowned as they fled; some were said to have been run over as Wu's train steamed out in the retreat to Wuhan. Putting calculation above solidarity, the Guangxi and Hunanese troops did not join the battle, their generals preferring to conserve their strength for the future.[14]

Wu Peifu sent a cable to Sun Zhuanfang asking for help, but the eastern militarist bided his time, waiting to step in when Wu and the Nationalists had torn one another apart. Dykes were breached to impede the attack. Wu demanded $6 million from the Wuhan Chambers of Commerce, and summoned reinforcements. But his troops were in poor condition, described by a journalist as 'shabby and dirty, showing marks of weeks in the field'. Many were ill, and had little to eat. In contrast, the southerners were 'civil and well disciplined [with] a profound contempt for both bullet and shell'.[15]

On 2 September, the Nationalists reached the lake south of Wuchang. Chiang moved to the front by train as Wu Peifu joined the exodus across the Yangtze to Hankou. An American journalist, John Powell, who travelled to see him at his headquarters, found the Philosopher General drinking heavily, and depressed by the collapse of his forces. He was carrying a frayed copy of *The Military Campaigns of the Kingdom of Wu*. 'They didn't have any machine guns or airplanes then,' he remarked nostalgically.[16]

After being addressed by Chiang, the Nationalists marched on Wuchang. Soldiers with grenades and pistols ran forward to try to scale the 28-foot-high stone and brick wall. What followed was reminiscent of an earlier debacle. The vanguard had no ladders. Heavy fire rained down. Two hundred attackers died. Again, a Guangxi unit failed to appear and the Hunan general's troops were slow to join the attack. Eight of Chiang's regiments launched a new assault but could not break through the formidable city walls, so both sides settled down for a siege.[17]

There was better news the next day from Hanyang, across the Yangtze. In return for a bribe, the defending general handed over the city and its arsenal, arranging a bolt hole for himself in the foreign concession in Hankou after insisting on being allowed to take his car with him. To make sure there was no resistance, his soldiers were paid $10 for each rifle they handed over.

With Hanyang lost and Wuchang surrounded, Hankou was defenceless. The city fell without a fight when Wu Peifu withdrew to the north. As word of the good behaviour of the Nationalists spread, they were welcomed with food and shelter by local inhabitants. 'The Cantonese effort seems so reckless and foolhardy that it is hard to believe it could have been planned, much less carried out,' wrote a correspondent of the *North China Daily News*. 'Hankow has been blinking in bewilderment at the Cantonese for many days like a grown-up brought face to face with a fairy tale come true. It is impossible to avoid the conclusion that the Cantonese have achieved amazing things.'[18]

Despite the successes of the 600-mile march from Canton, Wuchang still resisted. But food was scarce in the city, and cholera broke out. Corpses rotted outside the walls. 'Dead bodies were everywhere, and their stench permeated the air,' wrote Chiang's secretary, Chen Lifu. The corpses had black faces, but when my horse approached and its tail moved, the flies covering the dead scattered and the black faces disappeared.'[19]

No sooner had Hankou been taken than Chiang launched a fresh offensive into Jiangxi province to the south-east. For once, he did not consult Galen, preferring to act on his own initiative. At first, it seemed a master stroke. Southern Jiangxi was quickly taken, helped by the defections of three commanders, while Nationalist troops advanced from the north. The provincial capital of Nanchang was conquered after hand-to-hand fighting. But then the warlord, Sun Zhuanfang, sent reinforcements by rail and river, himself travelling in on a steamer to organise a successful counter-attack on the city. His troops executed hundreds of students, teachers and Nationalists. Short 'Russian-style' hair was cause for death. Heads dripping with blood were stuck on stakes.[20]

Nationalist coordination broke down. The Third Army from Yunnan declined to follow orders, and other units retreated before being told to do so. A Russian adviser reported that Chiang was 'confused, took wrong measures, and became a mere shadow of his former self'. A Guangxi general took over the organisation of the retreat.[21]

The death toll in the southern forces in Jiangxi was high: in some units, half the battalion commanders and up to 80 per cent of company and platoon officers were killed or wounded. For the first time, the expedition had lost the initiative, and the offensive had drawn Sun into the war. His troops caught three Nationalist spies and extracted from them the secret password to enter Chiang's headquarters. The warlord sent men in captured Nationalist uniforms on an assassination mission, but they were detected and most were killed.[22]

At this point, the third Wuhan city fell after some of the defenders in Wuchang defected and helped the Nationalists to get over the wall. Highly symbolically, this came on the fifteenth anniversary of the start of the anti-Manchu revolution in Wuhan. The same day, 10 October, also saw the end of the anti-British boycott in Canton – to placate them, the government agreed to pay the strikers $100 each from a customs surcharge. There was also a brief glimmer of hope from Chiang's home province of Zhejiang where the governor declared his independence from Sun Zhuanfang. But the warlord's soldiers saw off the attack, machine-gunning hundreds of the rebels in the moonlight. The governor was caught fleeing in his car. He was shot dead, his corpse decapitated, and the head sent to Sun. Illogically, the Communist-led trade unions in Shanghai waited until after his defeat to stage a strike which soon fizzled out.[23]

For Chiang, it was time to turn to Galen. The Russian decided to concentrate on taking Jiangxi's only rail line through the broad valley north of Nanchang to reduce the enemy's mobility and cut off the provincial capital. He made sure that the men had warm uniforms against the winter cold, that field hospitals were set up and that telegraphic communications were established. Reinforcements were brought in from Wuhan along with a few Soviet planes. There was more bribery to win over opponents. In a week of fighting, the southerners cut the railway, took a major base in the valley, and pinned the main enemy force against the waters of the vast Poyang Lake in the north of the province. Other units made their way along mountain paths round the enemy lines to capture the city of Jiujiang* on the Yangtze. With air support, armies from Hunan and Yunnan forced the surrender of Nanchang on 8 November. Forty thousand of Sun's troops were captured.

With victory achieved, leading political figures from Canton travelled north to make Wuhan their new capital. On the way, they went to confer with Chiang in a mountain resort above the Yangtze. When they left, Chiang stayed where he was in Jiangxi. His eyes were on an advance further east to Nanking and Shanghai, and he had no intention of becoming embroiled in the politics of Wuhan. As in Canton, independence and the solitary exercise of authority was his key to power. 'No one can be [his] superior; no one can be his associate,' as a saying had it. 'One can only be his subordinate.'[24]

By the start of 1927, the Nationalist flag flew from Hainan Island off the south coast of China to the Yangtze basin. After Hunan, Hubei, Jiangxi,

---

* Known at the time as Kiukiang.

Guangdong, Guizhou and Guangxi, Chiang's associate, General He Yingqin, added a seventh province to the Nationalist realm when he beat back an attack from coastal Fujian, pursued the enemy home and occupied the provincial capital of Fuzhou.* The NRA's death toll in the whole expedition was put at 25,000 – 15,000 of them in Jiangxi. The number of wounded, and of those who died subsequently, was far higher. Two dozen militarists had rallied to the cause, bringing the Nationalists' strength to 260,000 soldiers in thirty armies spread across half a million square miles with 170 million inhabitants. As always, finance was a problem. There were mutinies by troops who did not receive their wages. In January 1927, Chiang had to stop payment to the armies after a breach with T. V. Soong who must have been all too aware of the budgetary effect of the general's spending. Chiang warned the Finance Minister that, if he did not receive $1.5 million immediately, he would regard this as 'the final rupture in our relations'. After T.V. was granted control of the finances of Jiangsu and Zhejiang provinces, he came up with the funds, but the pattern was set for a long conflict between the two men over expenditure.[25]

The behaviour of the southerners was not always as exemplary as the legend has it, while Chiang's wife recorded him as dismissing the militarists who had joined the Nationalists as 'stinking opportunists' who were 'willing to ally with me or anyone else, just so they save their skins'. Even if the core Kuomintang soldiers distinguished themselves from warlord troops by paying shopkeepers and farmers, their money was often military scrip. In one incident in Nanchang, officers were shot and banks attacked by troops unhappy at the low value of their wages. Nor were their political leaders always a model of behaviour. The admittedly hostile *North China Daily News* reported how a group of politicians visiting Chiang's headquarters smoked in bed, burned the sheets, fraternised with Russian women and indulged in 'indiscriminate spitting'.[26]

Still, this was a new model army. Its best units had fought with bravery, determination, speed and skill. It even had a female 'Dare to Die' unit led by Foo Foo-wang, 'Canton's Joan of Arc', who was photographed in jodhpurs, knee boots, a belted tunic and army cap. There was no doubting the popular support the NRA enjoyed. As one of its songs proclaimed: 'Soldiers and the people are like one family, so never take advantage of them. If we sing the

---

* Known at the time as Foochow.

song of love for the people every day, heaven, earth and man will be at peace.'[27]

The political cadres built on this foundation. Harold Isaacs, whose *Tragedy of the Chinese Revolution*, published in 1938, set the template for the idea that popular revolt was the vital element in the expedition's success, wrote that 'The spontaneous rising of the people gave the Kuomintang armies little more to do, often, than occupy territory that had already been secured for them.' That verdict was nurtured in decades to come by the Communists, but puts the cart before the horse in pursuit of ideology. The initial advance through Hunan was made possible because Canton had allied with General Tang, not because of a popular rising. Though local farmers were valuable as guides and for logistical support, the soldiers did not enjoy a walkover secured by workers and peasants in their battles with the troops of Wu Peifu and Sun Zhuanfang. A contemporary poster reflected reality when it showed a soldier with fixed bayonet moving ahead of a peasant, a worker, a clerk and a student. Hanyang and Wuchang were won by treachery, not mass risings. Labour agitation in Wuhan occurred after the three cities had been taken, and the Canton strikers were a drag on the campaign. As the historian Donald Jordan concluded in his authoritative account of the campaign written nearly forty years after Isaacs, the thesis of the expedition as a victory from below 'seems highly insecure'. It was the army which opened the door to revolution, rather than the other way round, even if the subsequent career of the man who led that army made such a truth unpalatable.[28]

This is not to deny that the expedition embodied a new political awareness and militancy which gave it a unique depth and resonance. The KMT-Communist alliance drew idealistic young people like the future author Hsieh Ping-ying whose celebrated autobiography would chart the way revolutionary women broke out of the confines of traditional society. Against the background of the warlord years, it carried a message of hope for a new China and a vision of a modern nation which the political cadres could propagate when the soldiers marched on. This sowed the seeds for wider confrontation between the prophets of a new order and Chiang's more traditional vision of an authoritarian, militarily-led administration. While the general developed his links with the right of the Kuomintang in Shanghai, the party's left wing turned Wuhan into a seedbed for revolution, using its control of party organs to assert its sole legitimacy.[29]

Though, for reasons of face and politics, he left the front of the stage to members of the KMT left, Borodin played a key role in orchestrating developments. The Soviet adviser, who drove round the city in Wu Peifu's old car and occupied a flat in the former Russo-Asiatic building, saw Wuhan as the key to the success of the revolution. One of his visitors, T. V. Soong's youngest sister, Meiling, found him a commanding presence with a leonine head and slightly wavy, dark brown hair reaching down to the nape of his neck. A British cigarette dangled between the index and middle finger of his left hand while his right fist was bunched close to his tunic – Borodin let the cigarette ash grow until it almost fell and then flicked it on to an ashtray as he paced round the room. Speaking in a deep, clear, unhurried baritone of mid-Atlantic intonation without a trace of a Russian accent, he gave Meiling an impression of 'great control and personal magnetism' as he spoke of British and American history, Lenin and the Bolshevik revolution, religion and communism.

The new spirit won plaudits even from the generally hostile *North China Daily News.* 'No matter how one may dislike certain phases of the present Nationalist movement, there is one outstanding fact – the people, in general, seem to have entered into a realm of freedom and safety never before enjoyed,' its correspondent wrote. 'On every hand, there is to be seen a harmony and a clubbing together which never was dreamt of under the recent . . . regime. Shopkeepers are no longer afraid and women and girls not only venture out after dark, but go unattended.' So much so that 'husbands of emancipated women' marked Women's Day by protesting that their wives did not come home at night, but acted 'like alley cats'.[30]

Unions sprouted – there was even one for Buddhist priests and nuns. Heavy taxes were levied on merchants. Mass rallies stoked the political temperature. Students demanded the power to sack teachers. The Madame Sun Yat-sen Political Thought Training School for Women was established. Holidays were proclaimed for the anniversaries of the birth of Karl Marx, the Paris Commune and the death of Lenin. The Servants' Association called for an annual holiday of three weeks, and for employers to provide medical attention for all ailments except venereal diseases.[31]

On Women's Day, sing-song girls handed out leaflets stating: 'We, the prostitutes of Hankou, wish the public to know that despite the arrival of revolutionary forces here we are still suffering . . . owing to unsettled conditions we have only a small number of guests.' But the city's cabarets were crowded with a bizarre mixture of diplomats, merchant navy captains, foreign businessmen, lawyers, doctors, bankers and Chinese officials. 'Communists from Moscow danced side by side with the men they were seeking to force out of China,' an American journalist, Henry Misselwitz, wrote. 'Young girls, always Russians, laughed at them and danced with them all, demanding frequently, "You buy me small bottle wine, pliss?"'[32]

In the countryside, associations of small farmers and peasants blossomed, attracting more than a million members each in Hunan and Hubei. The movement, organised mainly by the Communists, combined livelihood issues and politics. Granaries were opened, and fields confiscated from absentee landlords. Revolutionary courts handed down sentences on corrupt officials, landowners, bullies and 'evil gentry'. Heading the committee for peasant affairs, Mao Zedong was developing the thesis that revolution would come from the countryside, seeing big landlords as the foundation of imperialism and the warlord system.

Such activism deeply worried the Kuomintang right, which viewed mass movements as a dangerous force to be kept under control, or eliminated entirely. Its gentry and merchant members could only be alarmed at the way the party was heading – Soong Meiling compared Wuhan to the Paris Commune. Stalin, too, grew concerned at reports of radical peasant action which was much too close for comfort to the belief in continuous, agrarian revolution promulgated for China by his rival, Trotsky.[33]

The Nationalist success was also making Western powers reconsider their attitude. Britain, previously a backer of Wu Peifu, sent its Minister in Peking to Hankou for talks, followed by a proposal to the other major powers that they should express readiness to negotiate on revision of the treaties in China and all other outstanding questions when the country had an established government. But there was trouble when the Northern Expedition spilled over into attacks on foreigners and their religious missions. In some churches, portraits of Sun Yat-sen were put up in place of crucifixes. A poster declared: 'Jesus Christ is dead. Why not worship something alive such as Nationalism?' Some of the British set up defensive strongholds in Yangtze cities into which they smuggled arms in cricket bags. In early January 1927, anti-foreign riots in the city of Jiujiang were followed by fighting in Hankou between Chinese protesters and British marines with fixed bayonets. The demonstrators rushed into the concession, and the council there handed it over temporarily to the Nationalists. Britain then opened talks that led to a permanent agreement which boosted the KMT as the first administration in China to reclaim territory from foreigners.[34]

That success emboldened the left wing in Wuhan which established a Provisional Joint Council as its supreme body, headed by Chiang's most outspoken critic, the Justice Minister, Xu Qian, a man with a small head and wrinkled forehead who, at fifty-five, was older than most of his colleagues. A fervent nationalist and admirer of Russia, he had shunned the foreign concession quarters and kept his ministry in a small block of flats in the Chinese city. A visiting British journalist, Arthur Ransome, the future author of the children's classic *Swallows and Amazons*, said Xu enjoyed high prestige among his younger colleagues, but appeared to be 'a brilliant man with something seriously wrong with his brain . . . unbalanced, incalculable, obstinate and dogmatic'.[35]

As posters in Wuhan denounced him as a despot, Chiang hit back by forming a Provisional Central Political Council in Nanchang, where he kept his military headquarters; he also made sure that as many military supplies as possible went to his First Army. After Borodin had declined an invitation to visit him, the general travelled to Wuhan with Galen. The visit was a disaster. Borodin made pointed remarks about power-seeking militarists, and there was a row about where the new capital should be. The left favoured Wuhan, pending an advance on Peking. Chiang insisted on Nanchang as a temporary choice – he planned to move from there to his homeland of the Lower Yangtze to establish himself permanently in Nanking, with its link to Sun Yat-sen's presidency in 1912.

For the first time, Chiang faced a military rival in the Nationalist ranks in the shape of the Hunanese general, Tang Shengzhi, who had emerged as the leading military figure in Wuhan. 'Chiang is fatigued,' he told a Russian adviser. 'It would be better for him to take a rest.' Tang was hardly a model revolutionary, establishing contacts with the agents of the warlord Sun Zhuanfang and conferring with the Japanese. Meeting Communist representatives, he said he wanted Galen as his adviser, and asked Moscow to send him money. The adviser V. K. Tairov compared him to 'a beautiful woman who shows off her beauty . . . and gives herself to whomever gives her the most'. For all his faults, Tang provided the regime with a military chief it thought could stand up to Chiang. As the commander headed back to Nanchang, the Justice Minister prepared a party conference to bring him to book. Significantly, Galen chose to stay in Wuhan.[36]

Another challenge emerged on the other side of the world when Wang Jingwei left France for Germany to start the journey home in answer to the call for his return by a Kuomintang congress the previous autumn. Though Chiang insisted they were the best of friends, the politician would be a serious rival. According to a report by a 'Russian spy', Chiang sent him a message hinting that he was not needed. Receiving this in Berlin, Wang showed a characteristic lack of resolve, and turned back to Paris. Then he changed his mind again, and headed for China after all.[37]

On top of all this, Chiang also faced a new enemy in eastern China when the Dogmeat General of Shandong entered the conflict as an ally of the warlord Sun Zhuanfang in an alliance of militarists known as the Anguojun, or National Peace Army. His burly, vicious troops moved south with their White Russian mercenaries in an armoured train. Wearing padded coats against the winter cold, Zhang Zongchang's men were assigned to defend the provinces of Jiangsu and Anhui north of the Yangtze, in return for a monthly payment of $600,000 from Sun. At the end of February 1927, they took over the defence of Nanking, and Zhang travelled to join them in his private railway train with his harem, sitting on an elaborately decorated, lacquered hardwood coffin, drinking and chain-smoking.

Chiang decided to go on the offensive, launching an attack by the First Army into his home province of Zhejiang, south of Shanghai. But the southerners suffered heavy losses. Despite their criticism of Chiang, the left in Wuhan could not sit back and see him defeated – victory for Sun would have threatened its position further up the Yangtze. Stalin's insistence on the united front also led Borodin to agree to a request from Chiang for Galen to return to advise him.

The Russian general organised an advance against the Anguojun forces on both banks of the river. The Nationalist army in Zhejiang also moved up under the Muslim general from Guangxi, Bai Chongxi. Soldiers sloshed through flooded fields as their opponents blew up bridges and dykes. But the provincial governor defected, and the warlord troops abandoned major cities without a fight after being paid to leave quietly by local businessmen. 'The rout of Marshal Sun's men was complete,' a reporter wrote. 'Hundreds of boats passed us.'[38]

The advances strengthened Chiang's military position, and his confidence – he sent a telegram to Moscow asking for the recall of

Borodin. But the Central Executive Committee of the Kuomintang asserted itself by withdrawing the exceptional powers granted to him at the start of the expedition. He was left with a seat on a new governing board and his post of commander-in-chief, though even that was circumscribed – his activities were to be overseen by a commission which included a Communist and his enemy, the Justice Minister.

Travelling to join her husband at Jiujiang, Jennie found him thin, seedy and feverish, though tender and affectionate towards her. He had lost his appetite, and likened himself to 'a horse with a spear stuck in its body, a tiger coming in front of me and a wolf behind'. The Chiangs stayed in the home of a leading local citizen with weeping willow trees and a red lacquered bridge and pagoda in the garden. Concerned about Chiang's health, Jennie insisted on his resting in bed, followed by a trip to the Lushan Mountains above the Yangtze where they were carried in sedan chairs, and strolled in the hills. On the first evening, after climbing the slopes till their feet ached, they sat on a large rock to watch the sunset. Each formulated silent prayers. 'Kai-shek looked at me so intently I thought there was something stuck on my face,' Jennie recalled. 'I raised my hand to wipe away whatever it was, but . . . he seized my palm in his and said "It is extraordinary how much I love you. I just asked Buddha to protect and guard you."' Then they walked silently back to their bungalow.[39]

On his return to Jiujiang, Chiang was given a telegram from Wuhan relaying the decisions taken against him. He threw it away. Then, according to his wife's memoirs, he hit his head with both fists, picked up a vase from a table and smashed it, slumped into an easy chair, bent his head, and wept. 'For an hour Kai-shek behaved like a madman,' she added. 'He banged the table, shouted to high heaven, and cursed Borodin in no uncertain terms.'*[40]

The general fired off a telegram to Wuhan asking for a representative to come to explain what was going on. The government sent the widow of the assassinated Canton leader, Liao Zhongkai. Sitting in the Chiangs' drawing room, she explained that there had been a majority vote. After that, she handed over a handbill describing the commander as a dictator, and a letter

---

* As with her other accounts of Chiang's behaviour in private, there is no way of corroborating what Chen Jieru wrote of this episode, but it accords both with events at the time and her husband's character and behaviour.

from General Xu Chongzhi of Canton whom he had sent into exile in Shanghai in 1925. 'Obey orders and confess your mistakes,' the letter said. 'Censure yourself for bad faith and keep your promise so that the country will be at peace.' Mrs Liao warned that officers in Wuhan whom Chiang had considered loyal were denouncing him as a new warlord.

Jennie recorded seeing her husband's face turn an ugly white as he fumed, clenching his hands convulsively. Fearing what he might do, she slipped up to their bedroom, took his revolver from its holster hanging on a clothes stand, and hid it in one of his riding boots. When she returned, Mrs Liao was handing Chiang a letter written by Wang Jingwei, warning of Chiang's despotic ambitions, and calling on party comrades to 'rise up in arms and wipe away this rebel'. Borodin, Mrs Liao added, had issued a proclamation saying the 'dictator and military autocrat' could not be tolerated for another day.[41]

Chiang got up as if in a trance, and went to the bedroom. For all his public inscrutability and preaching of the need for Confucian calm, he had never been one to take reverses well. 'An intense hate and fury poured out of him, shattering all sense of proportion,' Jennie wrote. 'He foamed and fumed, pulled the two suitcases off the chair and dumped their contents on the floor. But the revolver was not there. Mrs Liao and I stood at the door trembling while he raved: "Where is my revolver?"

'I could see a strange gleam in his eyes. By this time, I was weeping, and Mrs Liao tried to calm him.

'"Where is my revolver?" he repeated desperately. I could see his face was livid and his hands were shaking . . . Then he ran amok. He swept things off the table and broke the furniture.'

Putting a hand on his arm to restrain him, Mrs Liao said he was behaving like a spoiled child: she reminded him that he was not in his own home, and was destroying other people's property. 'Then, like a baby, he broke down and wept bitterly,' Jennie recalled. 'All that afternoon and evening, he refused to eat or talk. All military matters came to a standstill. He was not at home to anyone. Even the servants were kept outside our room.'

The next morning, Chiang was calmer. He admitted that he would have shot himself had he been able to find his revolver. 'He lay there and closed his eyes,' Jennie wrote. 'I brushed away the tear that trickled down his cheek. He looked so worn and weak.'[42]

If Chiang was prone to crumble at the onset of bad fortune, he had a great capacity to pull himself together and plot retaliation. Summoning loyal generals, he drew up defensive plans in case Wuhan attacked. Having restored his own morale, he addressed a rally with a fiercely anti-Communist speech, and then turned back to the war in the east. As usual, he used bribery to smooth the path for his soldiers. The Governor of Anhui declared his neutrality, reportedly in return for $600,000. Three divisional commanders led their men into the Nationalist ranks. The defections meant that the Dogmeat General would not be able to use the railway through Anhui to bring in reinforcements. In Shanghai, the naval commander joined the southern camp, and the head of the waterway police in Jiangsu province, to the north, also changed sides, giving the Nationalists control of canals and waterways there. An agent went to work on the Shanghai garrison commander who was annoyed because Sun Zhuanfang had not made him mayor.[43]

Chiang was not the only one intent on taking control of Shanghai. As the Nationalist army advanced, Communist-led unions in the city called a general strike joined by 100,000 workers, demanding the formation of a government to protect the people, elimination of warlords, an increase in wages, freedom of expression, improved factory conditions and six-week maternity leave. If they had expected the NRA to hurry to take the city, they were disappointed. Chiang was not ready, and had no desire to ally with leftists associated with his opponents in Wuhan. So the strikers were left to the mercy of Sun's squads of executioners who roamed the streets hunting down suspected subversives. Some of those caught were summarily beheaded, and their heads hung in wooden cages from lamp posts. A White Russian armoured train, the *Great Wall*, was ferried across the river, and moved up to join the defence, decorated in sky blue, primrose yellow and black – a journalist described it as 'a sinister thing of beautiful colour'.[44]

The union uprising and the advance of the Nationalists led the foreigners to beef up their forces in the metropolis. Vietnamese troops arrived to reinforce the French Concession, and 1,500 men of the Durham Light Infantry landed in the International Settlement. The Americans brought in Marines; the Japanese strengthened their defences. By mid-February, there were twenty-three foreign warships in the river.

In mid-March, Chiang left Nanchang on the 550-mile journey to Shanghai. One crucial figure was not with him. Galen had counted on

Shanghai being taken by a mixture of the military offensive and a fresh labour rising. But he had become increasingly aware that Chiang had no wish to work with the left. His hopes that the Nationalist commander would still prove himself to be a true revolutionary were being dashed by the day. So he left for Wuhan, whether entirely at his own volition or on Borodin's instructions is not clear. Three years after they had set out together on the first Eastern Expedition, the Chiang–Galen partnership was over, broken by the growing split behind the facade of the united front.[45]

Despite the Russian's absence, Chiang's troops implemented a plan typical of his tactics, trapping their opponents in a large enveloping manoeuvre along both banks of the Yangtze and up from the south. As he headed eastwards along the river, Chiang's actions fully justified Galen's decision to depart. In Jiangxi, a Communist union leader was executed. In Nanchang, the leftist Kuomintang headquarters was dissolved. In Hangzhou, troops and unionists clashed. In Jiujiang, martial law was declared and Communist-led bodies were suppressed. In the Anhui provincial capital, an attack on the left was authorised. As Chiang's secretary said, the purpose was simple: Communist influence must not spread – 'we had to stop it.' This made inevitable a bloody watershed in the history of China.[46]

CHAPTER 8

Light, Heat, Power

SHANGHAI, WROTE THE BRITISH AUTHOR, Aldous Huxley, was life itself – 'nothing more intensely living can be imagined'. The city the Nationalists were about to attack was the most vibrant and modern place in China, with its tycoons, burgeoning middle class, nationalistic students, adventurous writers, painters and film-makers, Communists, foreign concessions, refugees, and half the motor vehicles in the country. Boosted by migration, the population rose by a million each decade to 3 million by the late 1920s. On a wide tributary near the mouth of the Yangtze, Shanghai was both a great port, handling half the country's foreign commerce, and the prime industrial and financial centre. It contained half China's factories, employing 40,000 workers, and accounted for a third of all foreign investment in China. The banks in their neoclassical headquarters on the Bund along the Huangpu River in the Anglo-American International Settlement introduced Western financial practices. The shipyards were the biggest in China. The huge bulk of the electricity plant symbolised the city's power: a celebrated novel, *Ziye* (*Midnight*) by Mao Dun, opened with the image of a gigantic neon sign on its roof flashing out in flaming red and phosphorescent green the words (written in English in capitals) LIGHT, HEAT, POWER.

Multi-storey department stores were the acme of retailing, containing restaurants, cinemas, ping-pong tables, massage parlours, dance halls and hotels such as the one where Chiang and Jennie had been married. Media and advertising boomed, reinforcing the city's view of itself as the height of modernity. Smart young Chinese picked up Western fads in clothing and behaviour. Women marcelled their hair and wore flapper dresses. Tall buildings sported the latest Art Deco interiors. Among the progressive bourgeoisie, smaller, nuclear families replaced the extended Chinese clan.[1]

Bankers came from Ningbo, traders and retailers from Guangdong, pawnbrokers from Anhui. Overseas Chinese returned home with knowledge picked up abroad. Compradors amassed fortunes as go-betweens with Westerners: to them, it was said, a foreigner's fart was fragrant. Conservative businessmen found their leader in Fu Xiaoan, president of the General Chamber of Commerce, head of a steamer line and director of iron, coal and paper companies. His main rival was another shipping tycoon and former comprador, Yu Xiaqing, a celebrated merchant and entrepreneur associated with the reformist movement and the Nationalists. Yu had been among those who had helped Chiang in his short-lived career as a market investor, and he travelled up the Yangtze in early 1927 to renew his links with the commander, while Fu offered aid to the warlord regime.[2]

At a more modest level, the city was home to a mass of small traders, shopkeepers and agents who formed a myriad of associations organised by trade or street or their owners' place of origin. As their armies advanced, Kuomintang agents were active in persuading these groups that their best interests lay with the Nationalists. Then there were the Soongs. As a young man, the family patriarch, Charlie Soong, had gone to the United States where he became a Methodist. Returning to China as a preacher, he found this was not his vocation, and set up as a Bible publisher instead. Fluent in English, he built a big textbook business, acted as comprador, and managed Shanghai's largest flour mill. He backed Sun Yat-sen until the doctor's marriage to his middle daughter caused a chill between them. Though Charlie died in 1918 before the city reached its commercial apogee, his sons and daughters were to make the family the dominant dynasty of Republican China.

Shanghai was equally celebrated for its non-Chinese business magnates in their great houses and tall office blocks of the International Settlement and the French Concession. H. E. Morris, owner of the *North China Daily News*, lived in a complex in the style of the British Home Counties covering a whole city block. Victor Sassoon, whose family originated in Iraq, ran a huge trading and property empire, but was equally famous for his parties, his pursuit of women, and his passion for the turf – 'There is only one race greater than the Jews,' he said, 'and that's the Derby.' Crippled by a First World War flying accident, he had a half-timbered hunting lodge and an apartment with a 360-degree view atop Sassoon House on the Bund, which also contained the Cathay Hotel where Noël Coward wrote *Private Lives* in forty-eight hours while laid up with influenza.

Another Sephardic Jew, Elly Kadoorie, indulged his passion for the tango in a 400-square-foot ballroom lit by 3,600 bulbs at his white-painted Marble Hall mansion. Silas Hardoon, who started work as a warehouse watchman, lived with his Eurasian wife and ten adopted children in an estate with three houses, pavilions, artificial hills, lakes and bamboo groves, where the Dogmeat General stayed as he planned the defence of the city against the southerners. Even when super-rich, Hardoon liked to collect rents in person. His untidy office had no carpet, curtains or heating.*[3]

Middle Eastern Jews followed the Sassoon trail, and were joined by others fleeing from Europe to the foreign settlements which required no entry visas. Germans expelled from the British Straits settlements in the First World War travelled north. Japanese ran a third of the city's cotton mills. After the Bolshevik revolution, White Russians poured in from Vladivostok; there were 8,000 in the French Concession. Some worked in commerce; others were employed as bodyguards, dance hostesses and prostitutes. The God-fearing built an Orthodox church in the French Concession.†

The foreign areas in Shanghai and other great commercial cities like Wuhan and Tianjin were an affront to Chinese nationalism and sovereignty, run on colonialist lines, living reminders of the humiliation of the unequal treaties forced on China in the evening of the Empire. But they brought gaslight, electricity, and telephones, running water, cars,

---

* The Cathay is now part of the Peace Hotel. Coward recalled 'lots of parties, and Chinese dinners and cosmopolitan junketing . . . and three English naval officers . . . with whom we visited many of the lower and gayer haunts of the city.' The Morris estate is a guest house. Kadoorie's home is a Children's Palace. Hardoon's gardens have been built over.

† It is now a restaurant.

trams, a legal system and commercial stability for forward-looking Chinese companies. The local people who chose to live in the concessions far outnumbered the foreigners; of the half-million people in the French area, only 19,000 were non-Chinese – of those, just 1,400 were from France. Many rich Chinese preferred houses on Bubbling Well Road or the Boulevard des Deux Républiques to the native city. For all his anti-imperialism, Sun Yat-sen had settled on the Rue Molière, and it was in the French Concession that the Communist Party held its inaugural meeting.[4]

While Shanghai's elan made it much the most potent modernising force in China, prosperity was the preserve of a select few. The city, as the saying went, consisted of a narrow layer of heaven on a thick slice of hell. For those below, public hygiene was non-existent, and disease endemic. Tens of thousands lived in sampans on the filthy river. Workers crowded into tiny rooms in alleys and tenements, or slept in packed dormitories. A tribe of beggars, hawkers and boatmen camped on the river pontoons in the middle of the city. The poorest of all slept in the street. Factories offered low wages, ten to fourteen-hour shifts, six or seven-day working weeks and tyrannical overseers. The premises were cramped and unventilated, even in the oppressive summer. Doors were shut to keep staff inside. Fires were common, with escape sometimes blocked by locked doors.

Many workers were indentured labourers, illiterates who signed on with a thumbprint. Textile plants were the biggest employers. Conditions in the silk filatures were appalling as workers drew thread from cocoons over pans of boiling water into which their swollen, red hands often dipped. One visitor reported seeing a hundred or more babies lying on benches in the thick steam while their mothers worked. Another wrote: 'Tiny children stood for an eleven hour day, soaked to the skin in a steamy atmosphere, their fingers blanched to the knuckles and their bodies swaying from one tired foot to another, kept at their task by a stern overseer who did not hesitate to beat those whose attention wandered.' Strikers at a Japanese-run cotton mill protested that their employers 'look upon us as horses and cows, and treat us as pigs and dogs'.[5]

Bad as factory conditions were, life was even more precarious for the 150,000 people on the margins of society – casual workers, rickshaw pullers, coolies, street sleepers and beggars. They were prey to predators on all sides. The organisation of labour gangs gave enormous power to underworld contractors who provided workers and raked off a slice of the wages. Even beggars had to hand over part of their takings to secure places on the streets.

This encouraged mutual assistance organisations and sworn brotherhoods. Growing from secret societies of boatmen, the Green Gang provided a vast underworld network, with generational grades and connections in all areas of the city's life. The combination of toiling masses, reformers and left-wing intellectuals also made Shanghai a breeding ground for unions and radicalism. The power of the street had been seen in the anti-foreign movement of 1925 which produced the General Labour Union. The Communist Party had its headquarters in the city, and Zhou Enlai had moved from Canton to organise political and union activity. If anybody in China was ready for urban Marxist revolution, it was the Shanghai proletariat. But there were also powerful 'yellow unions' run by the underworld and the Green Gang which manipulated workers, and decided whether they would be pliant or rebellious according to how much cash employers handed over. One celebrated figure, a rotund, elegantly dressed female gang member called Mu Zhiying, built up a network of silk mill forewomen to protect owners from unrest, at a price.[6]

For the rich living lavishly and the poor seeking to forget their pain, Shanghai offered diversions of every kind. 'In the matter of mellow creature comforts, of savoury fleshpots deftly served, no Croesus of America, North or South, can ever hope to attain the comfortable heights and depths that Shanghai takes for granted,' wrote the London *Times* correspondent. One showpiece was the Great World centre in the French Concession built by a manufacturer of elixirs and tonics who plastered its walls with advertisements for his range of 500 products. As described by the visiting film director, Josef von Sternberg:

> On the first floor were gambling tables, singsong girls, magicians, pickpockets, slot machines, fireworks, birdcages, fans, stick incense, acrobats, and ginger. One flight up were the restaurants, a dozen barbers, and earwax extractors. The third floor had jugglers, herb medicines, ice cream parlours, photographers, a new bevy of girls, their high-collared gowns slit to reveal their hips . . . and, under the heading of novelty, several rows of exposed toilets, their impresarios instructing amused patrons not to squat but to assume a position more in keeping with the imported plumbing.

The fourth floor was crowded with shooting galleries, fan-tan tables, revolving wheels, massage benches, acupuncture, hot-towel counters, dried fish and intestines, and dance platforms serviced by a horde of music makers competing with each other to see who could drown out the others. The fifth floor featured girls whose dresses were slit to their armpits, a stuffed whale, story-tellers, balloons, peep shows, masks, a mirror maze, two love-letter booths with scribes who guaranteed results, rubber goods, and a temple filled with ferocious gods and joss sticks. On the top floor and the roof of that house of multiple joys a jumble of tightrope walkers slithered back and forth, and there were see-saws, Chinese checkers, mahjong, strings of fire crackers going off, lottery tickets, and marriage brokers.*[7]

The Majestic Gardens could cater for 2,500 dancers. With lawns and a boating lake, Rio Rita's was described in Mao Dun's *Midnight* as offering 'White Russian princesses, princes' daughters, imperial concubines and ladies-in-waiting to dance attendance on you.' As well as the 66-acre racecourse, there were three greyhound racing tracks, the largest holding 50,000 people. The French Club had Asia's best-sprung dance floor. The Canidrome Ballroom – the 'Rendezvous of Shanghai's Elite' – featured the American trumpeter, Buck Clayton, and his Harlem Gentlemen. The future Duchess of Windsor found Shanghai 'almost too good for a woman'. Tea dances were popular at top hotels though, as a historian of Shanghai, Stella Dong, notes, more whiskey than tea was served. Down the scale, dancing schools offered sex with the foxtrot, and Filipino bands ground out tunes in cheap dance halls while hostesses cracked melon seeds as they waited for men to hand over their 10-cent tickets.[8]

A survey found that almost 1 per cent of the female population was involved in selling sex. In 1920, the municipal council calculated that there were more than 70,000 prostitutes in the foreign concessions, among them 8,000 White Russians. Guide books listed the top hundred 'flowers': as a rule, the younger the better. Apart from sex, brothels were social gathering places where Chinese men smoked opium, enjoyed banquets and played mah-jong. Top courtesans received guests in brightly lit courtyard houses

---

* The Great World still stands, but is a shadow of its former self, with acrobatic displays by schoolchildren replacing the entertainment Sternberg witnessed.

with silk curtains, fine furniture, opium pipes, mirrors and chandeliers. 'Number Three' prostitutes, who charged $3 for a drink and the same for sex, operated in teahouses with suggestive names and carved blackwood furnishings. At the bottom of the rung were streetwalkers known as 'wild chicks' or 'pheasants'. The Salt-Water Sisters catered for sailors, and 'nailers' offered their services against alley walls.[9]

The greatest escape, for rich and poor, was in drugs. The legal import of opium had been integral to the Western presence from the mid-nineteenth century, bringing huge profits to the companies involved and to Chinese gangs which handled local distribution. International agreements provided for the elimination of the trade by 1917, but they were easily evaded in China where commonly used narcotics included morphine and heroin as well as opium, all of which were taken for medical and social purposes as well as to satisfy addiction.[10]

It was simply too lucrative a business to be eradicated by any but a determined and powerful government, something China signally lacked. The search for temporary relief from the harshness and pain of their lives turned the city's army of workers into a huge market for drug barons, while upmarket users headed for more select dens. The city's position at the mouth of the Yangtze made it a transit point both for opium from inland and for narcotics from India and the Middle East. The rough-and-ready state of public order in a city estimated to have 100,000 hoodlums meant importers, dealers and opium parlours were subject to attack by gangsters. So bigger bandits offered to safeguard the trade in return for protection money. And who better placed for this than the head of the Chinese detectives in the International Settlement who also led a gang called the Big Eight Mob?[11]

Such double roles were an extension of the comprador system. The foreigners, and the constabulary imported from their colonies, could not deal with the Chinese criminal world. So they appointed local figures who used their positions to enrich themselves by playing both sides of the street while making life as safe as possible for the expatriates. In 1923, the *North China Daily News* reported that protection ran at $1 per ounce – the mob's annual earnings were put at $30 million. The chief of the Chinese constabulary was also a member of the syndicate: after he was fatally shot leaving a bathhouse, his estate was found to include $4 million in cash.[12]

In 1924, a determined British police commissioner was appointed in the International Settlement. He set out to fight the Big Eight Mob, seizing large quantities of drugs. In contrast, the chief of police in the French Concession, Captain Fiori, favoured licensing narcotics to raise revenue. So the Green Gang bosses reached an agreement to open opium dens there in return for large payments. This gave a big boost to three gangsters who would play a key role in Chiang's ascension.

The first was the chief of Chinese detectives in the Concession, Huang Jinrong, known as Pockmarked Huang for the scar on his cheek from an attack of smallpox. Son of a policeman, he entered the service as a young man, but stormed out when told that his brocade robe was too grand for somebody of his low status. He went to the silk town of Suzhou,* where he met his formidable wife, a former brothel keeper known for her brains rather than her beauty who went on to run a lucrative monopoly of the Shanghai night soil business. Returning home, the squat, bullet-headed Huang rejoined the police and developed a network of connections and sworn brotherhoods. His status was enhanced when he helped to negotiate the release of the kidnap victims on the Blue Express in 1923. He owned a theatre and real estate, and acquired the Great World entertainment centre. For protection, he carried a tiny gold-plated revolver which folded in half and could be concealed in the palm of his hand. The epitome of an old-style gang boss, Huang lost ground in the 1920s to younger men who, in a similar pattern to the Mafia in the United States, exploited the huge potential of narcotics. His vulnerability was exposed when he was temporarily arrested after scuffling with a warlord's son who made disparaging remarks about a singer at his theatre. After that, he resigned from the detectives, returning later but only in an honorary position.[13]

The second member of the triumvirate, the suave and educated Zhang Xiaolin, acted as the go-between with the militarists controlling Chinese Shanghai and the region. But it was the third figure who was to be Chiang's most important ally. The orphan son of a poor rice shop owner, Du Yuesheng was known as 'Big-Eared Du' for the obvious reason. Fired for stealing from the till of a fruit shop where he worked, he moved into petty crime and drug dealing, developing a habit that gave his eyes a dead, blurred look as if they had no pupils. He became a protector of a sworn

* Known at the time as Soochow.

sisterhood of prostitutes, joined the Green Gang, and attracted the attention of Huang's wife, who gave him three tables to run at a gambling house.

Rising steadily through the underworld, Du set up his own gang, and by 1925 was eminent enough to play host at a dinner for the Dogmeat General for whom he provided a girl with each course. Thin and with a wide mouth, he took two fifteen-year-old virgins from Suzhou as concubines while his wife retreated into an opium haze: the three women lived on separate floors of his French Concession home. Opposite was a house where Du maintained high-class courtesans for hire. He also offered loans to influential figures which did not have to be repaid; some historians have seen this as proof of his generosity, but it also put them in his debt.

Though Du's wife bore no children, the concubines had six sons, who were protected by White Russian bodyguards. The boss was accompanied everywhere by four toughs. He was a complex character, cunning and ruthless but capable of great loyalty. Meeting him in the 1930s, W. H. Auden and Christopher Isherwood described his face as seemingly hewn from stone, like the Sphinx. 'Peculiarly and inexplicably terrifying were his feet, in their silk socks and smart pointed European boots, emerging from beneath the long silken gown,' the British writers added.[14]

In the French Concession, Du formed the Black Stuff Company to extort money from opium dens there, with a tax of 30 cents per pipe. The takeover of another drugs outfit meant the trio of gangsters controlled the trafficking of 40,000 chests a year through their Three Prosperities Company, whose name was taken as being self-referential. An agreement with the warlord, Sun Zhuanfang, helped to boost annual profits to an estimated $56 million. The enterprise was referred to simply as the 'Big Company'.

By 1927, as the historian of Shanghai's police, Frederic Wakeman, notes, very little illegal went on without the Green Gang's permission. Those who flouted it were likely to find themselves shot, kidnapped or having their tendons severed with a fruit knife. At Chinese festivals, Du invited leading drug merchants to a party, and told them what to pay for protection. Those who failed to cough up found a coffin delivered to their homes as a warning, sometimes accompanied by pall-bearers. In one murky incident, three French officials who had fallen into Du's disfavour died after a dinner he gave for them featuring mushrooms from the port of Ningbo. The gangster's hand was seen everywhere. Soon after the mushroom banquet, a ship carrying a report to Paris on the drug trade in the Concession caught fire and sank in the Indian Ocean. The report was lost, and, among those killed was a celebrated journalist, Albert Londres, who had boasted that he was taking a 'dynamite' story home. Naturally, the sinking was attributed to Du. Clearly he was a man with whom anybody who wished to control Shanghai would have to do business.[15]

On 18 March 1927, the Kuomintang troops pierced the defensive line south of Shanghai. Following negotiations with Chiang's agent, the garrison commander handed over military plans and cooperated with the attackers. Then, ignoring an offer of a post with the Nationalists, he fled. Stupidly, he went home to Shandong, where he was executed. His troops melted away. As the *North China Daily News* noted: 'It would be a mistake to say that the Northern resistance collapsed; none was ever offered.' 'Hardly a shot was fired in actual defence,' reported the American correspondent, Henry Misselwitz. 'The Northern troops, dispirited, virtually leaderless, fled in rout, deserting the city.' One rare act of resistance was by the Russian armoured train which moved along the track at walking pace firing at the southerners before its crew finally gave up.[16]

Refugees poured into foreign concessions which were surrounded by sandbags and barbed wire. Hundreds of northern troops tried to follow, and British infantrymen opened fire, killing dozens. Misselwitz called those eventually let in 'the most desolate, dispirited body of men I ever saw in my life. Their uniforms were ragged and torn, scores were wounded and poorly bandaged . . . disintegration seemed to possess the very souls of these men.'[17]

Still, it took the southerners under the Guangxi General, Bai Chongxi, four days to enter Shanghai. During that time, the General Labour Union brought the city to a standstill with a strike, raided police stations for arms and occupied the workers' district of Chapei where fighting killed an estimated 300 people and burned 3,000 dwellings. The strike was subsequently portrayed by the Communists as the proletarian action that delivered Shanghai to the Nationalists. While it did disorganise the defenders, the army would have taken Shanghai in any case. Rather than doing Chiang and Bai a good turn, the Communist leaders wanted to take control before the soldiers arrived, and to set up a Soviet. The fiercely anti-Communist Bai ordered an end to the strike, and instructed troops to put down disturbances. The unions were unbowed, executing 'running dog' employees of foreigners and keeping up armed street patrols.[18]

Anti-foreign feeling swelled, in Shanghai and up the Yangtze. In the French Concession, a mob stormed the gates on the Boulevard des Deux Républiques. Up the river, churches and missions were sacked. In Wuhan, unionists attacked the Japanese settlement, leading to a landing of marines who killed several of them. Less bloodily, the Jiujiang correspondent of the *North China Daily News* wrote of demonstrators insulting foreigners as 'turtle eggs', and small boys throwing stones at players on the foreign club tennis court.[19]

While Chiang wanted to wipe away the unequal treaties with the West and Japan, he was wary of confrontation with the foreigners, particularly after they moved military reinforcements into the settlements – though, according to the *Lancet*, the British had so little to do that their main health problem was venereal disease. Still, events in Nanking showed how explosive the situation was. As the southern Sixth Army had approached the city, the defending troops had left, looting, burning and raping as they went. The day after Shanghai was taken, the Nationalists moved into Nanking. Some northerners failed to get away and sporadic gunfights broke out, but there was no battle and the population welcomed the newcomers. Then the victors began to attack foreign houses and offices.[20]

One group headed for the British consulate. The port doctor was caught on the lawn outside and shot dead. The consul was badly wounded. The Harbour Master rushed round when he heard firing, grappled with two soldiers and was then riddled with bullets. Troops who broke into the home of Dr J. E. Williams, the American Vice-President of the University, shot him dead. A French and an Italian Catholic priest were also killed. The Japanese consulate was ransacked. The troops burned nine foreign-occupied buildings. One raiding party stole pianos and the billiard table from the Yangtze Hotel. Another prised open what it took for chests outside a missionary's home, only to flee from the bees buzzing from their hives. Foreigners donned Chinese gowns as disguise; dressed in coolie clothes, the manager of the Bridge Hotel and his wife hid in a muddy pigsty.[21]

At the American legation, the consul, John Davis, realised his Marine unit would not be sufficient defence. So two dozen women and children, accompanied by Marines, trekked 2 miles to a house owned by the

Standard Oil Company on a hill which they hoped would be safer. But Cantonese soldiers attacked. As the Marines shot back, the women and children took shelter in an upper-storey bathroom, lying on the floor. Then foreign ships moored in the Yangtze began to shell the city, and the soldiers broke off the attack to see what was going on. In the lull, the Americans used ropes, sheets, curtains and blankets to climb from the bathroom windows, ran to the city wall and forded a moat. Crossing fields under sniper fire, they reached the river where they boarded sampans for a British navy ship from which they were transferred to a boat to Shanghai.[22]

The Nanking Incident provoked an outcry from the foreigners, their missions in Shanghai and their governments. Chiang's supporters fingered the Communist head of the Sixth Army's political department for fomenting anti-foreigner activity to create difficulties for the general. Going ahead with the transfer of his headquarters to Nanking, the commander blamed it on 'bad characters', northerners in southern uniforms, and 'what might be called an anti-missionary movement'. Several dozen soldiers were executed. The Nationalists protested at the bombardment by foreign warships. For the foreigners, Nanking was a nightmare brought to life, with the Chinese turning on their small, privileged community. But the incident was only a sideshow to what was about to unfold in China's greatest city.[23]

CHAPTER 9

The Great Purge

POCKMARKED HUANG LIKED TO RISE at ten, take his breakfast, and then make his way to the Treasure Teahouse where, according to a historian of the city, he was 'besieged by callers, runners, supplicants, theatrical people, demi-mondaines, and finks'. In the afternoon, the Green Gang boss would play cards before meeting business associates, communing with his concubine or attending his theatre. On 26 March 1927 he varied his pattern to pay a visit to the commander of the victorious Nationalist forces.

Chiang had arrived in Shanghai earlier in the day on a gunboat. His position was weaker than the easy military victory suggested. He had only 3,000 troops in the city, including some former warlord soldiers whose reliability was uncertain. His allies on the Kuomintang right and in the business community could contribute no soldiers. Radical students in Shanghai demanded his removal, and workers waved banners declaring 'Overthrow Chiang Kai-shek'. His calls for calm towards foreigners at a mass rally at the West Gate were ignored by demonstrators who marched round the concessions denouncing imperialism.

Labour organisations held fortified positions in major buildings. A Communist committee authorised assassinations of opponents, and laid plans to take power after warlord troops left and before the Nationalists arrived. Armed union squads attacked strike-breakers, and searched passers-by for weapons. Zhou Enlai felt bold enough to visit military headquarters with an unsuccessful request to be given the password used to get through the curfew the army had imposed. A huge demonstration was planned for 12 April in honour of Wang Jingwei, who was returning from Europe to take up the leadership of the Kuomintang left. Yet the Communists were reluctant to take the final step. Chiang might have moved to the right, but he was still commander-in-chief of the Kuomintang, and Stalin was committed to the united front with both wings of the party Sun Yat-sen had founded. Reaching Shanghai, Wang Jingwei told Chiang he would do what he could to stop a full-scale rising. This gave the general a breathing space to consolidate a vital alliance.[1]

Huang had already made a trip up the Yangtze at the end of the previous year to meet the general whose links with the Green Gang stretched back more than a decade. Now he was Chiang's first civilian visitor in Shanghai. The deal was quite simple: the gangsters would throw their weight and men behind Chiang and, in return, would be assured of immunity, probably accompanied by an undertaking that they would enjoy a narcotics monopoly in the city.

After Huang had laid the groundwork, Big-Eared Du moved in, making the most of his contacts with the foreigners. He set up a militia under the name of the China Mutual Progress Association with the support of France's Consul General who called for 'the maintenance of public order and the struggle against the Soviet commune'. French police protected the Association's headquarters, and the diplomat arranged for the supply of 450 guns.[2]

Du also got the French police chief, Captain Fiori, to invite the American chairman of the International Settlement, Sterling Fessenden, to a meeting at Du's home in the Concession, where rifles and sub-machine guns were stacked in the hall. The short, plump, fifty-one-year-old American was later described by a State Department official as a 'feeble creature . . . who had gone to pieces in the Far East and was conspicuously unfit for his position'. Fiori spoke of the threat to the foreigners from the Communists, and Du said he was ready to attack the leftists provided the French would supply him with more guns and Fessenden would obtain permission for his men from the Mutual Progress Association to move with their arms through the International Settlement to the native areas.

Fessenden said he would agree, if the settlement's council approved, which it did.[3]

Having made his arrangements, Chiang travelled upriver to Nanking, leaving the Guangxi general, Bai, in military command in Shanghai. As usual, he preferred to stay away from the battlefield. On the night before the planned mass rally of the left, the Green Gang made its second contribution to his cause, with a dinner invitation by Du to the most powerful union leader in the city, Wang Shouhua.* Wang did not want to alienate the underworld, so, at 8 p.m. on 11 April, his chauffeur-driven car passed through the iron gates in front of Du's house.[4]

Inside, he was met by another of the Green Gang bosses, Zhang Xiaolin, who told him he should dissolve the pickets and change sides for his own good. When Wang refused, four gangsters beat him severely. At this point, according to one account, Du appeared at the top of the stairs, a vacant look on his face, his voice disembodied from opium. 'Not here! Not in my house!' he called out as a mobster known as Fiery Old Crow throttled Wang. Thinking he was dead, the hoodlums stuffed him into a hessian sack, and drove to waste ground outside the French Concession to bury the body there. As they finished digging a grave, they heard Wang moaning; so they interred him alive.

Eight hours later, 2,000 armed men in blue denim overalls from Du's militia moved onto the streets of the city. Their white armbands bore the character for 'worker'. As they made their way to working class districts in the pre-dawn darkness, they passed soldiers who had been posted in the streets during the night, some in civilian dress. At daybreak, a bugle call rang out from army headquarters and a siren sounded from a gunboat – the signal for the men in blue to attack union branches and labour strongholds.[5]

They were helped by troops who opened the way for the militia or themselves fired at left-wingers. Men were shot and beheaded in the streets. There was a report that captives were thrown alive into the furnaces of locomotives at the South Railway Station. A particularly fierce battle occurred at the employees' club in the big Commercial Press building, where pickets camped in the billiard room – among those who got away when it fell was Zhou Enlai. He was later arrested, but was allowed to

---

* Also known as He Songling.

escape, and fled with an $80,000 price on his head. It was said that Chiang had ordered him freed to repay the debt from an occasion when the Communist had saved him from violent leftists in Canton.

The police put the number killed on 12 April at 400, with 300 others arrested. But the death toll in the morning confrontation alone was probably double that while some of the prisoners taken to the military camp at Longhua were executed there. Green Gang men moved into the union headquarters to proclaim a new labour organisation. Sixty business groups sent a congratulatory telegram to Chiang and General Bai.

Though the unions and the Communists had been expecting an attack, they had failed to set up defences against the troops and Du's men. Now they acted with extraordinary naivety, as if believing that the forces arrayed against them could be won over by words. A young leftist who went to ask Zhou Enlai how he could help was told to distribute leaflets and put up posters. Demonstrators headed by women and children marched to army headquarters. Showing how little the power of the people counted, troops opened fire with machine guns; soldiers with fixed bayonets chased after fleeing demonstrators. In all, 300 were estimated to have died there. Writing much later, Chiang recorded simply that 'On April 12, to prevent Communist uprisings, the Revolutionary Forces in cooperation with local labour unions and chambers of commerce, disarmed the Red labour pickets and kept Communist saboteurs under surveillance. Only then was the situation in Shanghai brought under control.'[6]

Terror spread across the city as Du's men and the Nationalist soldiers killed indiscriminately, and more lorryloads of prisoners were taken to Longhua. Green Gang lieutenants staged attacks on five left-wing groups, arresting more than 1,000 people. Mass meetings and parades were banned. The journalist Edgar Snow, who was working in Shanghai at the time, estimated that between 5,000 and 10,000 in all perished in the purge. The author Han Suyin put the toll at 8,000, and added that 6,000 wives and daughters of workers were sold into brothels and factories. Later estimates put the number of people who died, Communist or not, at 34,000 with 40,000 hurt and 25,000 arrested. 'It was a bloodthirsty war to eliminate the enemy within,' Chiang's secretary, Chen Lifu, wrote. 'I must admit that many innocent people were killed.'[7]

The Communists retained strongholds in the middle Yangtze basin and in Hunan, where they pushed land reform, seized property, executed 'bad gentry' and organised peasant self-defence units. But the left had been given a clear warning of the repression awaiting it from the increasingly ruthless army. Sun Yat-sen's broad church was imploding.[8]

In Canton, real or suspected Communists were roped together, taken to the East Parade ground, and shot. As in Nanchang the previous year, women with bobbed hair were regarded as radicals who merited death. At Whampoa more than 350 cadets were executed. In Hangzhou, according to the American journalist Vincent Sheean, soldiers disembowelled a young woman for saying Chiang did not represent the Kuomintang or Sun Yat-sen's Three Principles. 'Her intestines were taken out and wrapped around her body whilst she was still alive,' he added. 'Girls and boys were beheaded for saying what they believed; men were hung up in wooden cages to die of hunger and thirst or were broken on the rack.'[9]

Hunan province, where the Nationalists had scored their first military successes in 1926, was the scene of particularly savage and prolonged conflict as the right sought to eradicate the rural radicalism engendered by the Communists. A peasant rising was savagely repressed. Mao Zedong, a Hunan native, told of 'gouging out eyes and ripping out tongues, disembowelling and decapitation, slashing with knives and grinding with sand, burning with kerosene and branding with red-hot irons. In the case of the women, they pierce their breasts . . . and parade them around naked in public, or simply hack them to pieces.' The bloodshed in the province would last for a decade, taking an estimated 300,000 lives.[10]

Shanghai's businessmen greeted the suppression of the left with pleasure, but soon found themselves becoming the second wave of victims of the new order. A firm believer that business should run for the benefit of his state, Chiang felt no sympathy with independent-minded capitalists. They were simply useful as a source of funds. A Financial Commission decided who was to pay what, and a former judge drove round in a large car telling companies and individuals the size of loans apportioned to them. The Green Gang and the security forces dealt with those who did not cooperate. More money was raised by kidnapping or direct extortion. 'Wealthy Chinese would be arrested in their homes or mysteriously disappeared from the streets; and those who reappeared came back as poorer men, but could in no case be induced to open their mouths to inform on their oppressors,' a contemporary author, Owen Chapman, wrote. 'Millionaires were arrested as "communists"!'[11]

Trying to placate the leaders of the new regime's shock troops, the Chinese General Chamber of Commerce gave a luncheon to honour the Green Gang bosses. It did no good. The three-year-old son of the Sincere department store tycoon was seized, and freed for $500,000. The ransom for the son of a cotton mill owner was set at $670,000. Assets reported to be valued at $7 million were grabbed from a flour magnate. When the conservative business leader Fu Xiaoan refused to raise a $10 million loan, he was made the target of an arrest warrant, reported to have been personally approved by Chiang. After Fu fled town, the authorities took over his shipping company, and the general appropriated one of his houses.

Chiang has been portrayed as being the creature of the Shanghai capitalists; events in the spring and summer of 1927 showed the reality of a relationship that would run through the following decades.[12]

For expatriates, life went on as usual behind the protection of barbed wire, sandbags and troops. Tanks patrolled the streets of the French Concession, and six two-winged Royal Air Force planes were parked in the grounds of the racecourse. On the day the purge began, ratepayers in the International Settlement approved a motion to keep Chinese out of the municipal parks and gardens, one speaker warning that relaxing the ban would risk seeing such places 'crowded with the scum of the city'. The French extended the drugs pact with Du and provided naval protection for boats carrying narcotics. In return for more cash, Captain Fiori agreed to let the gang boss open gambling houses in the Concession. Du made a lump sum payment to the authorities in the International Settlement, headed by the compliant Fessenden, to be allowed to sell narcotics there. Part of the proceeds found their way upriver to Chiang to help fund his confrontation with the left and complete his bid to conquer China.[13]

The Wuhan regime took five days to react to the attack in Shanghai. On 17 April, basing itself on its claim to be the legitimate expression of the Kuomintang, it expelled Chiang from the party, accusing him of 'massacre of the people'. A big rally denounced the 'counter-revolutionary chief', and $250,000 was reported to have been put on his head. Faced with the reality of the repression, Moscow began to shift position – the Comintern branded the Nationalist commander a traitor, and the newspaper *Izvestia* ran an open letter by his son, Ching-kuo, who was studying in Russia, saying: 'Revolution is the only thing I know, and I do not know you as my father any more.' Stalin managed to recall a signed photograph which he had dispatched to Chiang before the purge, and he now compared the general to a lemon which could be thrown away after being squeezed.[14]

In interviews with foreign correspondents, Borodin sounded an upbeat note. Wearing baggy grey flannel trousers and a white blouse, the Russian slapped his thigh with a thin riding crop as he told a reporter from the London *Daily Express* that Chiang had been the 'victim of a nice trick' by reactionaries and anarchists, and must go. But the position of the leftist regime was becoming steadily more fraught. Its finances were poor, aggravated by inflation and currency depreciation. The taking of a major customs post by Chiang's supporters cut its revenue from duties on the opium trade. Wuhan's workers were a law to themselves, and merchant supporters of the Kuomintang became increasingly alienated from the government. Thirty foreign warships lay in the mile-wide Yangtze as a reminder of the readiness of the great powers to intervene if their interests were attacked. A cholera outbreak killed thousands. In the former British Concession, the Reuter correspondent wrote of coolies 'using the formerly beautiful Bund front and the river foreshore as a public lavatory'.[15]

In Nanking, Chiang and his supporters formed a counter-government which was joined by Hu Hanmin, the Kuomintang ideologue who had been forced out of Canton in 1925 as a rightist. While lacking a populist base, it could claim to represent the middle class and the gentry who had always formed the core of the Kuomintang's financial support. As such, it could reach out to those in Wuhan worried about the move to the left there. At the same time, it represented a fresh step towards militarisation; as Hu later acknowledged, the use of the army to suppress the Communists meant the soldiers escaped from civilian control.

Meeting Chiang at the time, the journalist Vincent Sheean, who acknowledged his sympathy for the Wuhan left, detected a cruel look in his thin face, but found him 'sensitive and alert' and took him for ten years younger than his age of forty. 'I could discern the eager, ambitious nature of Chiang Kai-shek's mind, his anxiety to be well thought of, his desire to give his personal ambitions the protective coloration of a revolutionary doctrine and vocabulary,' Sheean wrote. 'It was impossible to avoid the conclusion that with this young man, in spite of his remarkable opportunities, the phrases of the movement had not sunk beyond the top layer of consciousness. He remained shrewd, ambitious, energetic . . . with his way to make in the world, and I fully believed that he would make it.'[16]

First, in the late spring of 1927, Chiang had to deal with the Dogmeat General's army advancing from Shandong on Nanking, coming close enough to bombard the city. At the same time, the KMT left faced a threat from the warlord's Manchurian ally under the twenty-six-year-old Young Marshal, Zhang Xueliang, who crossed the Yellow River to menace Wuhan from the north. The twin offensive showed the fragility of the Nationalists, and the need for Nanking and Wuhan to cooperate against their common adversaries. Even if they joined forces, they risked being outnumbered by the northern alliance. So they sought a new partner.

After having been beaten eighteen months earlier by the northerners, the Christian General had left his army to stage a dogged stand north of Peking while he took the train to Moscow, listening to gramophone records of Chinese opera to pass the time on the way. In the Soviet capital, he met high officials, and was instructed on revolutionary methods. For all his populism, Feng Yuxiang was never keen on anything like real Communism, but he knew how to get his hosts to provide supplies and money. Returning home, he rallied his army and, with the promise of Russian aid, saw his chance of getting his revenge. His troops, including his fast-moving cavalry, were based along the Yellow River in an area where the Nationalists had no support. By allying with them, Feng could hope to emerge as the key player in the fight against the northern warlords and to dominate the divided southerners. Always short of resources, he joined the Kuomintang and was promised money, though he complained of being short-changed.[17]

The three-pronged offensive started at the beginning of May, with the two Nationalist armies operating far apart. In the east, Chiang drove back the Dogmeat General's forces, and advanced into the warlord's home province, getting to within 60 miles of the major port city of Qingdao.* Fearing for the concessions it had acquired in Shandong after the First World War, Japan moved in soldiers to establish a garrison of 6,000 men. Tokyo's action provoked Chinese demonstrations and boycotts, and made Chiang a nationalist hero, though, setting a pattern for the next ten years, he avoided a fight with the better armed foreigners.[18]

Four hundred miles to the west, the 70,000-man Wuhan Army under

* Known at the time as Tsingtao.

the Buddhist General Tang crossed the mountains into Henan province. In mid-May, its crack 'Ironside' troops fought a series of tough battles for railway towns, emerging victorious but suffering heavy losses. The Young Marshal decided to fall back behind the wide Yellow River, establishing a strong defensive line with powerful artillery which stopped the Nationalists. Much later, he said that this was the time when he began to recoil from the idea of Chinese fighting one another. Be that as it may, it was on the Henan campaign that he contracted a serious drug habit. 'I smoked opium out of anger and the pressure of leading an army,' he said in a television interview in 1992. 'An army doctor tried to help me by using a dose of medicine to get rid of the addiction. In the end I got rid of the opium but became addicted to the medicine.' The medicine was morphine. Zhang became so addicted that there was said to be hardly a place on his back which had not been pricked.[19]

The Christian General took his time joining in the campaign. His men did not move until the bulk of the enemy had been engaged by the Ironsides. Then Feng's cavalry drove virtually unopposed along the Yellow River to the Manchurian rear, taking the key rail junction of Zhengzhou.* As a result of the delay, his men suffered only forty casualties compared to 14,000 for the Wuhan troops.

While the Ironsides were fighting their way up the railway line through Henan, Chiang showed how little the alliance between the two wings of the Kuomintang meant. In mid-May, he won over a general who had been allied with the left, but who now advanced on Wuhan. At the same time, the right attacked and took Changsha, the radical capital of Hunan, to the south. With the bulk of the army away at the war and its left-wing allies in Changsha defeated, Wuhan seemed doomed. But Borodin staged a rerun of his defence of Canton for Sun Yat-sen, organising a self-defence force under the Communist head of the Independent Regiment from the Northern Expedition which repulsed the defecting army, and saved the government.

Still, the situation remained precarious. Not only had Wuhan's military losses been heavy; officers were also alienated by news that their land had been expropriated by left-wing rural groups. Wang Jingwei and his colleagues decided it was time to cement relations with the Christian

* Known at the time as Chengchow.

General. In mid-June, a delegation, including Chinese Communists, travelled to Zhengzhou. To meet them, the hulking Feng arrived on the back of an army truck, wearing a simple soldier's uniform and munching a slice of bread; only later did it emerge that he had travelled to the outskirts of the city in a private train, and then transferred to the lorry. Knowing he was in a position to dominate, Feng laid down stiff terms. To win his favour, the Wuhan delegates agreed to withdraw their army from Henan, leaving the warlord master of its 65,000 square miles. He was also promised leadership of the campaign, and control of other provinces that might be conquered to the north, along with a handsome payment.

The Wuhan delegates were heartened by the warlord's description of Chiang as a 'wolf-hearted, dog-lunged, inhuman thing'. When they returned to Wuhan, the official newspaper there declared the Zhengzhou meeting as a victory for the united front. In fact, the very reverse was the case.

In talks the Communists were not told about, Feng had demanded that the Soviet advisers should be sent home, and the Chinese Communists ejected from positions of authority. Wang and his non-Communist colleagues were ready to go along with this. The growing disaffection of non-radical Kuomintang members and mounting economic problems were causing them to lose faith in the leftward slant of the revolution. The influence of Borodin and his protégés was increasingly resented. It was time to try to find common ground with Nanking – and having Feng as an ally would greatly strengthen Wuhan's hand in dealing with Chiang. But, in a rerun of the confrontation with the general in Canton in 1926, Wang soon found himself comprehensively outmanoeuvred, and had good reason to understand why Feng had a second nickname, the Betraying General.

Hearing of the Zhengzhou conference, Chiang arranged a meeting of his own with the warlord two weeks later at another key rail junction, Xuzhou,* on the line of his eastern advance. To proclaim his claim to be Sun Yat-sen's true heir, he travelled in a train drawn by a locomotive with a giant photograph of the doctor on its front. Along the way, Chiang, wearing a plain khaki uniform, stopped at stations to make speeches. 'His voice was clear and carried well, his features were strong and intelligent and he looked alert and full of energy,' a Danish journalist reported.

* Known at the time as Hsûchow.

Seeing the correspondent and two other foreigners looking out of the window of a train door on which 'Death to all Imperialists' was written, Chiang smiled and bowed. At the Garden Hotel in Xuzhou, he conferred with the Guangxi generals before going to meet Feng at the station. The Nationalist officers were in full dress uniforms, and Chiang had arranged for an army band to play on the platform. As the train drew in, the Guangxi chief, Li Zongren, recalled,

> We saw no general aboard, only a few uniformed waiters. Obviously knowing whom we were looking for, the waiters pointed towards the boxcars in the rear, which were usually used by the army to transport animals. Through the open door of one of the boxcars we saw a very tall, husky soldier, dressed in a shabby uniform, sitting on the train floor. As the train stopped, he stood up and walked out of the car. Chiang was the first to approach him, asking, 'Where is Commander-in-Chief Feng?'
>
> 'I am Feng Yuxiang,' the peasant-like soldier replied with a smile. It was quite a shock to all of us! Then the band started playing while Feng shook hands with each of us in the greeting party.

As in his show on the lorry for the Wuhan delegation, Feng had made most of the journey in the carriage with the waiters, moving to the boxcar as it approached Xuzhou.[20]

The unbuttoned warlord and the neat, aloof Chiang were very different characters, but they could see a common purpose. Whatever he had told the Wuhan delegation, Feng had given notice of his intentions by issuing orders for anti-Chiang posters to be removed in areas he controlled. The two men also had a personal link. Like Chiang's son, Feng's daughter was studying in Moscow, and the two teenagers began to live together. A further Moscow connection was provided by one of their classmates who returned to become an adviser in Feng's forces, a young Communist called Deng Xiaoping.[21]

In four days of talks, the warlord and the Nationalist commander reached agreement. The Christian General was promised $2 million a month, and control of Henan. Hitching a lift back to Nanking on Chiang's train, the correspondent Henry Misselwitz watched the general dictating to secretaries, and eating a meal of ham and eggs, toast and jam and coffee with Western knives, forks and spoons. During the journey, Chiang's

assistant read out a cable Feng had sent to Wuhan. The message built on
the secret anti-Communist agreement at Zhengzhou. Radical elements had
wormed their way into the party to try to control the Kuomintang, it
declared. The only solution was for Borodin to go home immediately and
for members of the Wuhan administration who wanted to leave to go
abroad 'for a rest'. General Tang should send troops to cooperate with
Feng. 'I make these suggestions sincerely and expect you to accept them,'
the telegram concluded.[22]

Having won over Feng, Chiang issued a warrant for the arrest of leading
leftists, including Borodin – sensing the changing wind, Deng Xiaoping left
the Christian General's camp for a Communist area. On the battlefield, the
Nanking troops advanced 'like lemonade through a straw', as the *North
China Daily News* put it. Their commander went to Shanghai to put a fresh
squeeze on the business community – rich locals were told they would be
denounced as pro-Japanese unless they paid up. In July, a ceremony in the
city decided to raise funds for a huge silver shield for Chiang bearing the
words 'Fame has been attained after great hardship'. The gang bosses who
had collaborated in the April purge were named as advisers with the
honorary rank of Major General. When Nanking established an opium
monopoly bureau which was meant to eradicate the drug over three years,
Zhang Xiaolin of the Green Gang was put in charge in return for payments
to the government.[23]

The general also entered into negotiations for an anti-Communist front
with the Old Marshal of Manchuria and the Model Governor of Shanxi,
Yan Xishan. But Zhang Zuolin broke off the talks, saying he doubted the
sincerity of Chiang's anti-Communism, while a new advance by the eastern
warlord, Sun Zhuanfang, forced Nanking back onto the defensive.[24]

As Chiang marshalled his troops to meet that threat, a crisis erupted in
Wuhan to match the 100-degree plus temperatures. Since the Communists
still did not know of Wang Jingwei's agreement with Feng to expel them –
Borodin insisted that 'Marshal Feng is our friend. He is *my* friend' – it was
farce played as tragedy. The detonator was a new Comintern
representative, Mahendranath Roy, a Brahmin described by Vincent
Sheean as having 'a beautiful, carved-oak head'. Instead of the united front
with the bourgeoisie pursued since 1923, the Indian saw rural revolution
as the way ahead. Peasants should be armed, and the revolution pursued
from below with its own army and rural self-government. Roy's message

showed that his master in the Kremlin had changed tack to counter criticism from Trotskyites who were preaching a more revolutionary gospel and pointing to the way Chiang had acted as proof of the bankruptcy of the united front.

A telegram from Moscow on 1 June 1927 said the agrarian revolution should be pursued, with an army of 20,000 Communists and 50,000 workers and peasants. Revolutionary tribunals should punish officers who supported Chiang. Communist influence in the Central Executive Committee of the Kuomintang should be increased. New blood should replace 'vacillating and compromising' veterans.

Chinese party chiefs read the cable with incredulity. One said they did not know whether to laugh or cry. The Communist leader Chen Duxiu, whose suggestions that the party should be armed and should ally with the Kuomintang left against Chiang had been repeatedly vetoed by Stalin, called it 'like taking a bath in shit'. After being tied to the united front for so long, they were suddenly being ordered to adopt policies that had previously been proscribed as Trotskyite – and at a time when they were suffering from massive repression. Even the loyal Borodin called the instructions ludicrous.[25]

Roy made things even worse by inviting Wang Jingwei to his home, and asking whether Borodin had shown him the message from the Kremlin. Evidently, he believed that the Chinese politician had been forewarned that something of the kind was coming when he paid a visit to Moscow on his way back to China from Europe in the spring. Wang said he had not seen the message. The Indian handed him the original and a Chinese translation.[26]

The following day, Wang called the telegram unacceptable, and said it changed the terms of the agreement reached between Sun Yat-sen and the Russians. The envoy replied that it was an ultimatum. 'If the Kuomintang will not collaborate,' he told a Politburo meeting, 'we must regard it as an enemy rather than an ally.'[27]

This was a desperate time for Borodin, who sought diversion in reading Sinclair Lewis's novel, *Elmer Gantry*. He had done his best to execute Stalin's policies to lay the basis for revolution in China through the united front. A keen chess player, he had planned his moves in advance and liked to speak of taking 'the long view' to make the most of often unpromising situations. Now, he faced the ruins of his schemes. Talking to a Swedish reporter, he spoke of having come to China to fight for an idea, 'but China itself, with its age old history, its countless millions, its great social problems, its infinite capacities, astounded and overwhelmed me.' Suffering from malaria and with a broken arm from a riding accident, he had other concerns. His American wife, Fanya, had been arrested by the northerners on a Russian steamer on the Yangtze. Accused of carrying propaganda leaflets, the formidable Mrs Borodin was taken to Peking, where the Old Marshal's men had shown their lack of scruple towards Communists by executing Chinese party members seized in a raid on the Russian embassy.[28]

Although Wang Jingwei had been ready to ditch the Communists in the secret talks with the Christian General, the Wuhan leadership took six weeks to decide how to react to the bombshell from Moscow. Sun Yat-sen's widow was among those who pleaded to continue the united front. Finally, on 15 July, the Political Council decided to expel the Chinese Communists and send the Russians packing. Most of the Communist leadership left Wuhan. Those who remained held a congress at which another new envoy from Moscow, Besso Lominadze, imposed Stalin's new line but insisted that the party still stay under the KMT flag. Since both wings of the Kuomintang had turned against the Communists, this added an element of unreality that even Stalin could not maintain – in September, Moscow finally ordered an end to the united front.[29]

Borodin delayed his departure until his wife was freed. According to various accounts, she owed her freedom to pressure from a visiting American senator or because Soviet diplomats bribed the judge who found, improbably, there was no suspicion of her being a Communist – and then promptly fled to Japan.[30]

On 27 July 1927, the Russian was seen off from Wuhan station by Wang Jingwei and other senior officials after a farewell ceremony with tea and fizzy drinks. Half a dozen Russians accompanied him, together with the sons of the Foreign Minister, Eugene Chen, and an American journalist, Anna Louise Strong. Rather than risking arrest in Shanghai, they made an exhausting overland trek to reach the rail line from Mongolia to Moscow. Ill and bad-tempered, Borodin reflected that, like all bourgeois parties, the Kuomintang was 'a toilet which, however often you flush it, still stinks'. He arrived home on 6 October, four years to the day from his first encounter with Sun Yat-sen.

Kept in limbo after his return, Borodin accepted partial blame for events in China, and was appointed director of an English-language newspaper in Moscow. For two decades he benefited from Stalin's protection, but then fell under suspicion of being in sympathy with independent-minded foreign communists. Arrested in the purges of 1949, he died in a Siberian prison camp in 1951.[31]

Four days after Borodin left Wuhan, the Communists staged a rising in the Jiangxi capital of Nanchang. Among those involved were Zhou Enlai and the future Red Army commander, Zhu De, who was the city's police chief. The plotters made their headquarters in the city's main hotel, a square concrete building where they stayed in spacious bedrooms with partitions decorated in coloured glass between the sleeping and sitting areas. There was heavy fighting, but the revolt was crushed in a week. The remnants of the rebels marched off to become the nucleus of the Red Army. Though ending in defeat, the Nanchang rising is celebrated in China today as marking the birth of Communist military power.

It was time for Galen to follow Borodin. Only a few officials saw him off from the station at Wuhan. 'He goes . . . unheralded and unsung,' Reuters reported. Still, the general felt able to travel via Shanghai where he bade farewell to the Chinese commander who owed him so much. Chiang recorded that the Russian was greatly depressed, but that he told him not to feel too badly about leaving. 'His reply was: "I hope, too, that this is not the last time we shall see each other. So, till we meet again!"' It was, Chiang added, 'one of the most moving partings in my life'.[32]

China had burnished Galen's military star, and, on his return to the Soviet Union, he was put in charge of a Far Eastern Army which fought off attacks by the Manchurians. Awarded the Order of Lenin, he joined the Central Committee of the Soviet Communist Party, and was promoted to the rank of Marshal. In 1937, he was listed as a member of the tribunal that tried leading generals as Stalin turned on the army – one report said he was forced to supervise the executions. This did not protect his own forces which were subjected to a massive purge. Galen himself was spared to lead a major battle against the Japanese in the Far East, which he won. Then he was called to Moscow and, on Stalin's orders, arrested with his schoolteacher wife and their children. The police chief, Lavrenti Beria, carried out the interrogation. When the Marshal refused to cooperate, he was tortured.[33]

Over the years, Chiang asked Stalin several times to send Galen back as an adviser. There was no reply. In 1939, he instructed an envoy to Moscow to renew the request. Stalin did not recognise the name of Galen. An aide murmured to him that it was Blyukher. The request could not be met, the Soviet dictator said, because the man in question had been shot for divulging secrets to a Japanese woman spy.[34]

Events in Wuhan and the alliance with the Christian General should have put Chiang on top of the world in the late summer of 1927. But, as so often in his career, apparent success was accompanied by deep threats. The expulsion of the Russian and the break with the Chinese Communists, whose leadership went underground under a new chief in Shanghai, removed the main bone of contention between the left and right of the Kuomintang, and thus undermined his position. The repression unleashed in April shocked many party members who now saw Chiang as the obstacle to re-unification. A new slogan was heard advocating 'Separating from the Communists and Opposing Chiang'. The Guangxi Clique opened secret talks with the Wuhan leaders. The Nanking commander's military status was also at issue after his troops were caught in a trap set by the warlord, Sun Zhuanfang. Though another general was blamed and executed, Chiang could not evade responsibility since he had been in overall charge, and had sworn to achieve victory.[35]

In mid-August, a proposal was put to the Military Council that he should move to the lesser post of commander of the eastern army. Chiang offered to resign altogether. 'For some minutes not a word was said by anyone present,' reported the journalist George Sokolsky. Then an unimportant member of the council rose to speak of the importance of union with Wuhan. Chiang got up, left the room and took a special train out of Nanking. After consultations with associates in Shanghai, he headed to his home village. His main political allies resigned, and the Green Gang leaders stopped funding the government to mark their displeasure.[36]

In Xikou, the general took up residence in a temple on the hill behind the village where fireflies glistened at night amid tall grass and bamboo stalks. Visiting him there, Misselwitz of the *New York Times* was woken by bells at 5 a.m. and brought a breakfast of Californian oranges, hot milk, cakes, bread and chocolate wafers. Sitting on a broad veranda, Chiang received his visitor in a silk suit buttoned up to the neck. 'He looked cool and rather less worn and drawn than when I had last seen him,' the journalist wrote. They drank green tea, and munched nuts and sweets as Chiang told the journalist that he was too much a part of the revolution, and it too much a part of him, for him to retire completely.[37]

Ten days after Chiang's departure, 30,000 of Sun Zhuanfang's troops crossed the Yangtze outside Nanking. The Guangxi leaders, who had formed a new government, drove them back in a six-day battle. The Wuhan forces tried to put up resistance to the new regime, but were beaten – their commander, Tang Shengzhi, took a boat for Japan. The Guangxi group also beat off a fresh attack by the northerners. But, for all its military successes, the Clique was isolated politically, and desperately short of funds. Chiang flexed his political muscle with a demonstration by supporters in Nanking during which security forces killed three people and wounded seventy-five. He also got in touch with Wang Jingwei, who had been excluded by the Guangxi group. On the principle of one's enemy's enemy being one's friend, Wang and Chiang met in Shanghai to plot strategy. Then things altered abruptly with a Communist uprising in Canton on 11 December, staged on Stalin's orders to prove his revolutionary credentials.[38]

'Reactionary' officers and merchants were shot out of hand. Police stations were attacked, and major buildings looted. A Soviet was established, promising workers food, clothing, housing and an eight-hour day. The counter-offensive by Cantonese troops was ferocious. The *North China Herald* spoke of 'the city of the dead' – the initial official death toll was 5,700. Executioners in fur caps and knee boots beheaded bound suspects in the streets. Bodies of children were piled up by the roadside. The *South China Morning Post* reported girls and women – 'mostly of the bob-haired type' – being shot in the street. The educator Earl Swisher watched seven boatloads of prisoners being pushed into the river, and shot.[39]

The Russian consulate, where the rising had been planned, was stormed; five diplomats were executed, their bodies left on the lawn. Nanking ordered the closure of all Soviet missions in its territory, and severed diplomatic relations with Moscow. As well as the violence in Canton, there were fierce clashes up the coast, with some reports speaking of the hearts of opponents being eaten and severed heads being pickled in brine. In Wuhan, Communist suspects were regularly shot in the streets, and the

Soviet consulate was looted – the consul reported seeing a soldier wearing his silk top hat and others in stolen women's clothes. A Communist organisation put the number of dead in the repression during the year at a very precise 37,981.[40]

Wang Jingwei had been in Canton before the rising, and this hurt him: either he knew something was about to happen or he had not realised an attempted coup was in the offing, which was almost as bad. Given the weakening of Wang's position and the shock of the Canton coup, Chiang no longer had to worry about rivalry from the left. At the same time, the fragmentation of the country meant the time had come for the return of the only man who could offer a broader hope for national unity. But, first, he had to seal an alliance with China's most influential family through a great personal betrayal.[41]

CHAPTER 10

Political Union

EARLY IN 1927, when he was beset by the opposition of Wuhan, Chiang received a well-connected visitor at his headquarters on the Yangtze. Ailing Soong was the most ruthless and cunning of the three daughters of the powerful Shanghai family. The first Chinese girl in the city to ride a bicycle, on which she made a scandal-raising trip in the International Settlement, she had been sent by her Methodist father, Charles Soong, to college in the United States. After a time as Sun Yat-sen's secretary, she married a rich banker from Shanxi, Kong Xiangxi, or H. H. Kung, who claimed to be a lineal descendant of Confucius. The couple settled in a house in Shanghai's French Concession where their four children were brought up. Kung, who had also studied in America and had developed a relationship with Standard Oil, shared his wife's obsession with getting even richer. Among his other activities, he acted as financial adviser to the Model Governor of Shanxi. Though appointed Industry Minister in the Wuhan government, he was no more left-wing than his brother-in-law, the Finance Minister, T. V. Soong. Both were naturally closer to Chiang's version of conservative revolution than to Borodin or the Communists, and each would come to play an important role in the general's future.

Short and plump, with carefully arranged hair, Ailing was an expert at pulling financial and political strings, preferably with the help of inside information. 'There was something about her anything but tall figure, something so authoritative, so personally powerful, so penetratingly keen that one would have been struck with her anywhere,' an American visitor recorded. 'Here was authority, conscious of itself, conscious of power. I suspected a mind that forgot nothing and forgave little.' An FBI source later described her as 'an evil and clever woman [who] sits in the background and directs the family'. The widow of the assassinated Kuomintang leader, Liao Zhongkai, warned Jennie Chiang: 'Steer clear of that woman, and don't let Kai-shek fall into her trap.'[1]

That warning had come after a dinner Ailing gave in Canton in 1922 at the home of the absent manager of Standard Oil. The guests were the Chiangs, the Foreign Minister, Eugene Chen, Mrs Liao and Ailing's youngest sister, Meiling, who was engaged at the time to a Kuomintang member. Kai-shek was highly excited by the invitation, telling his wife: 'I want the names of Sun, Soong and Chiang to be linked tightly together.' According to some accounts, he had set himself on marrying Meiling, and had asked Sun Yat-sen to help him. The doctor discussed the matter with his wife, the middle Soong sister. Qingling was extremely hostile to the idea, and the Nationalist leader advised Chiang to bide his time. His wish to enter the charmed circle was so strong that, according to Qingling, he proposed marriage to her after Sun's death, ignoring her lifelong detestation of him. She told the American journalist Edgar Snow that she declined as 'she thought it was politics, not love'. In all this, the general was clearly ready to ditch his second wife in pursuit of a power union. He was not the only member of the Canton leadership to be attracted to Meiling who had been educated in America and spoke flawless English. According to a story told by the writer Emily Hahn, Borodin was also smitten; a servant took to the Soongs a sheet of paper stolen from the Russian's bedroom on which he had written her name over and over with the addition of 'Darling'.[2]

Since Chiang was held up by work, Jennie had arrived first for Ailing's dinner in 1922. She was wearing her best white crêpe de Chine silk dress with white kid shoes, white-beaded handbag and sandalwood fan, trying to 'look fresh and smart so that Kai-shek would feel proud of me'. Ailing and Meiling wore brightly coloured Chinese gowns, their hair pulled into a bun at the back of their necks in the latest style. 'They looked as if they had stepped out of a Shanghai fashion book,' Jennie recalled in her memoirs, on which the following account is based.

It was hot and humid, so the party refreshed itself with iced drinks before Ailing deputed Eugene Chen to show Jennie round the house. As they walked back towards the drawing room, Chiang's wife heard the eldest Soong sister describe her as 'nothing more than a middle-class housewife'.

'How can she ever qualify to be the wife of a budding leader?' Mrs Kung asked. 'Something must be done about it.'

'That's true,' Meiling said. 'But I must say she has her good points. She makes a very good housewife for a Ningbo peasant.'

Mrs Liao jumped to Jennie's defence, but the talk stopped as Chiang's wife entered the room. When conversation resumed, the sisters pumped her for information about her husband. After Chiang arrived, they went to the dining table where he sat between Ailing and Meiling. The dinner began with jellied consommé, followed by pigeon breast served on toast with watercress and potato chips. Meiling said that 'pigeon eating is like eating mangoes. Both should be eaten with the fingers only, in the bathroom, without anyone looking on.' So, they must all keep their eyes on their plates until they had finished. Jennie marked the young lady down as a snob.

After the early victories of the Northern Expedition, Meiling sent Chiang a congratulatory letter. He suggested to Jennie that they ask the two sisters to come to his base at Jiujiang. She showed no enthusiasm, so he dropped the idea for the time being. But, early in 1927, he considered it time to try to activate the Soong connection. Responding to his invitation, Ailing travelled to the river port of Jiujiang on a steamer owned by the Bank of China which she did not leave during her twenty-four-hour stay.

Though her husband was a minister in the Wuhan government, she felt no loyalty to the regime up the Yangtze. According to Jennie's record of what Chiang told her immediately afterwards, Ailing warned that, unless he acted first, it would only be a matter of time before the left eliminated him. But Ailing could save him by getting her brother, T.V., to rally to his side and bring with him the Shanghai bankers and businessmen. Naturally, there was a price attached: Chiang would have to marry Meiling and become wedded to the Soongs – politically, economically and personally.[3]

Five years after his first attempt to pursue Meiling, the general was even more dazzled by the prospect of achieving a great ambition. While Jennie paints a generally idyllic picture of their marriage, she could not compete with the aura of the Soongs. It was also said that the general was irritated by some of her habits, notably her taste for spending their money which jarred with his frugal nature – given Meiling's resources, he could not object to what she paid out on her lifestyle. His arrogance was such that he told Jennie he was sure she would put his interests first. 'I am desperate,' his wife recorded him as saying. 'Ailing has struck a very hard bargain, but what she says is true. Her offer is the only way for me to achieve my plans to unite China. I now ask you to help me. I beg you not to say no. After all, true love is measured by the sacrifice one is willing to make.'

Though he insisted his decision depended on her, Jennie felt that a deal had already been struck. Despite the eternal love she says he had kept swearing, Chiang's mind was made up. He proposed she go to the United States on a five-year 'study trip'. He would wed Meiling in what she said he described as 'only a political marriage'. After that, they would resume life together.

Jennie's first instinct was to tell him to go to hell. But he upped the pressure by saying that, if she did not agree, the Northern Expedition would be doomed. 'If I can carry on, then China will be saved and I myself can live. Otherwise, I will die – die as a result of failure or disappointment. You don't want that, do you?' Jennie said she would think about it.

Chiang wrote letters to Ailing and Meiling, and left them with Jennie for her to send as he went off on the military campaign. Naturally, his wife read them. According to her memoirs, one asked Ailing to find out her younger sister's attitude towards him, while the other requested Meiling to send a photograph 'so that I can look at you constantly'. Jennie left for Shanghai where she had to put up with a stream of visitors praising Chiang and their 'wonderful' marriage. She blamed Ailing, 'that vile woman', rather than her husband. But she told her mother that her love for him was dead.

On 1 August, two weeks before his resignation in Nanking, Chiang called on his wife in Shanghai. Alone in the house, Jennie gave him a cool reception, but he continued to spin his idea of a reunion after she had spent five years abroad. She said the past was the past, and she would be content to stay with her mother, rather than travelling. But Chiang was insistent, admitting that her departure from China was one of Ailing's conditions. Clearly, the Soongs would not feel comfortable if his legal wife was in town when Chiang married Meiling. 'I looked at him contemptuously, but felt a deep pity in my heart,' Jennie wrote. 'He looked so very pale, tense and gaunt. His colour was bad and his expression was filled with desperation.'[4]

Chiang said he had tickets for Jennie and two of the daughters of his patron, Zhang Jingjiang, to travel to the United States on the liner, the *President Jackson*. After Jennie reminded him of broken promises in the past, the general stood in front of a Buddhist shrine to swear to resume marital relations within five years. 'Should I break my promise and fail to take her back, may the Great Buddha smite me and my Nanking government,' he declared. Then he handed over the tickets, saying the government would pay for Jennie's expenses while she was away.

A week after Chiang was forced out of Nanking, Jennie and the two Zhang daughters, Therese and Helen, left Shanghai for California. Their departure was reported as far away as London. In Hawaii, a Kuomintang rally greeted them with banners and flowers. By the time they got to San Francisco, rumours of Chiang's impending marriage to Meiling were current in Shanghai, so journalists wondered about his relationship to the woman who had travelled on the *President Jackson*.

The general told the *New York Times* he had divorced his first wife in 1921 and had set free his two concubines. 'I was surprised to learn that one of them went to America as my wife,' he added. Stepping up the hypocrisy, he claimed to have been 'courting Miss Soong all these many years without a thought of the political bearing of such a marriage and any suggestion in that direction is unfair to me and unjust to all the members of the Soong family.' He was, he said, 'free to marry in accordance with the most monogamous practices. Miss Soong would not consent to a marriage in any other circumstances and I should not dare to ask a lady of her character to marry me in any other circumstances.'[56]

Reading the stories in American newspapers, Jennie was shattered. She went to the Chinese consulate in New York where she was told that instructions had been received to have nothing to do with her. She was so worked up that she ran up and down her room on Riverside Drive during the night, tearing her hair, raving and shouting with such force that the janitor was called. Wandering the city, she was about to throw herself into the Hudson River when an old man restrained her and walked her home. Returning to Shanghai in 1933, she lived on funds from Chiang and earnings from language teaching. She moved to Hong Kong in the early 1960s to live in a house bought by Chiang and an associate, and died in 1971 after writing her memoirs to show 'our happy marriage and how an ordinary man may, with persistence and favourable opportunities, rise to become the undisputed leader of a nation'. The book contains what she says is an English translation of the text of a certificate dated 5 December 1921, recording the wedding at the Great Eastern Hotel with her name and Chiang's clearly stated. 'It is wished that the couple will live until their hair is grey and the union will be blessed with many children,' it reads. 'This certificate is proof of this marriage.'[7]

For a man who had become a dab hand at high-level political and military manipulation, disposing of Jennie must have seemed nothing special. She was powerless, and Chiang's word carried far more weight. For her part, Jennie readily acknowledged that she had stepped aside to assist him. 'But I did not know that in helping him, I had to pay and pay and pay again for the stigma he inflicted on me,' she concluded. 'All these bitter years I have never remarried. I live a life of embarrassment, concealment and repression . . . If I should be recognised in the street by those who know about my past, I am invariably stared at curiously and pointed out as the woman that Chiang Kai-shek discarded in order to marry Meiling Soong.'[8]

Having jettisoned Jennie, Chiang now had to surmount the hostility of his putative mother-in-law. Charlie Soong's widow had the traditional low view of soldiers, and disapproved of her daughter's suitor for not being a Christian. He had also been married before, kept concubines and was known to have lived a wild life during his twenties. Not an ideal son-in-law for the God-fearing matriarch, who was undergoing medical treatment in Japan.

Chiang crossed the East China Sea at the end of September, 1927. Mrs Soong had moved to a hot springs resort near Kobe. The general checked into a hotel there, and gained an appointment. He showed her his divorce papers from his first wife, and dismissed the allegations about Jennie. He said he would read the Bible, but could not guarantee becoming a Christian. That was enough for the engagement to be announced. As Qingling Soong remarked later: 'He would have agreed to be a Holy Roller to marry Meiling. He needed her to build a dynasty.' Sun's widow asked Eugene Chen to send her sister a letter telling her not to marry a 'Bluebeard'. Meiling took no notice.[9]

The wedding, on 1 December 1927, was according to the *Shanghai Times,* 'the outstanding Chinese marriage ceremony of recent years', bringing together military power, politics and finance as never before. Though Chiang had not yet converted, a Christian service was held at the Soong house, after which the bride and groom went to a Chinese ceremony in the ballroom of the Majestic Hotel where the walls were hung with white roses arranged in the shape of wedding bells. A crowd of 1,300 waited inside while 1,000 people gathered outside. Detectives swarmed. As well as leading local and national figures, the British, American, French and Japanese consuls were present.

There was applause as the forty-year-old groom entered the ballroom in formal, cut-away tail coat and striped trousers, carrying kid gloves. The thirty-year-old bride followed on the arm of her brother, T.V., to the strains of Mendelssohn's 'Wedding March' played by a Russian orchestra. Attended by four bridesmaids, two flower girls and two of her elder sister's children in black velvet suits, Meiling wore a gown of silver and white georgette, with a long lace veil, orange blossom spray and wreath of orange buds. Her shoes and stockings were silver. The bouquet was of pale pink carnations and fern fronds tied with white and silver ribbons.

While newsreel cameras spun, the couple bowed three times to a portrait of Sun Yat-sen set on the platform beside the Kuomintang flag. The altar was flanked by green and white foliage and huge shields of white flowers with the characters for long life and happiness worked in red geraniums. The marriage certificates were read out, and stamped. A singer intoned an uplifting hymn, 'O Promise Me'. Chiang and Meiling bowed to one another, and to the witnesses and guests before posing for photographs under a large bell of roses from which showers of petals fell on them when ribbons were pulled. Tea was served, and the couple went to the station to board the train for their honeymoon.

Chiang issued a statement that the wedding would enable the KMT cause to make greater progress 'because I can henceforth bear the tremendous responsibility of the revolution with peace of heart'. But he and his wife insisted theirs was not a political union. Meiling talked of moments in life when sentiment had to have the upper hand, and it was made known that he had learned to say 'Darling' in English, possibly at her insistence. In a letter which found its way into a newspaper, Chiang had written to Meiling: 'Thinking about the people I admire in this life, you, my lady, are the only one . . . Recalling the hundred battles fought on the front and my own type of heroism, I cannot but feel that so-called achievement is just an illusion or a dream. And yet, my lady, your talent, beauty and virtue are not things I can ever forget. The only question is: what does my lady think of this retired soldier who has been abandoned by the whole world.'[10]

Energetic and determined, the bride had studied at Wellesley College, outside Boston. Majoring in English literature, she obtained the highest academic distinction in her senior year. The college records recalled her as 'outgoing and popular, and according to a friend, there always seemed to be some nice Chinese boy or other on the doorstep.'[11]

After graduating in 1917, Meiling had returned to China where she became involved in social work, notably to alleviate child labour and encourage the YWCA. She also needed to brush up her Chinese – she always seemed more at home in the language of America. Her perfect English and connections to the United States made her a most useful ambassador with Westerners whom she invariably charmed. Acting as Chiang's interpreter and letter-writer, she became steadily more influential as an adviser. A saying had it that of the three Soong sisters, one (Meiling) loved power, one (Ailing) loved money, and one (Qingling) loved China.[12]

The couple spent their honeymoon at the mountain resort of Moganshan outside Shanghai with its Western-style houses, tennis courts, swimming pool, two churches and banks of dahlias. Chiang walked through the bamboo forest and gazed down from the peaks at the rice paddies below. Fifteen years later, Meiling informed the American publisher, Gardner Cowles, founder of *Look* magazine, that, on their wedding night, Chiang had told her that he did not believe in sexual relations except to produce children. 'And since he already had a son by previous marriage and was not interested in having any more children, there would be no sex between them,' Cowles wrote in his memoirs. He added that he was not sure whether he believed her.[13]

Returning from the honeymoon, Chiang issued a circular telegram calling for Kuomintang unity and attacking the Guangxi-led regime in Nanking. He was pushing at an open door. A stream of telegrams called for his return. As Nanking's crisis deepened, General He sent a cable from the front urging him to come back. The Shanghai branch of the Kuomintang petitioned him to resume office. A newspaper cartoon showed Chiang mounting a horse labelled 'Nationalism' held by a woman marked as 'Kuomintang'. The caption read 'Somewhat Restive'.[14]

The Nationalists might be coming into line, as expected. But somebody else who had helped in Chiang's ascent was ready to remind him he still needed to show proper deference. Soon after the marriage, according to a story current in Shanghai, a limousine called at the Chiang house and drove Meiling off to visit Ailing. When the general got home, he was concerned to find she had not reached her sister's house. Using his brother in law, T.V., as an intermediary, Chiang contacted Big-Eared Du to ask if he could help find her. The gang boss said Meiling had been found motoring with only a maid for company through the dangerous streets of Shanghai. For her own protection, she had been taken to a safe villa, though she was showing signs of annoyance and refusing to take food or drink. Du found it deplorable that Chiang did not look after his wife, but he would be happy to arrange for her return to her home after T.V. had completed the necessary 'formalities'. The gangster need say no more: the threat he could pose was crystal clear.[15]

On 1 January 1928 Nanking invited Chiang to come back with full powers. He rode into Nanking escorted by three armoured trains. Despite two reported attempts to derail the convoy, he arrived safely. Chiang's long-time Kuomintang associate, Tan Yankai, contrasted the 'gloom and despondency' at his departure in August with the rejoicing that accompanied his return. Once again, the general had used a temporary retreat to get his way. Now he had to complete the conquest of China.[16]

PART III

THE NANKING DECADE

Nanking, January 1928

———

Marco Polo Bridge, 7 July 1937

CHAPTER 11

Captain Chiang

ON 4 JANUARY 1928, a new government was sworn in at Nanking, firmly tilted to the right. Wang Jingwei, who had left for hospital treatment in Europe for his diabetes, was censured. Chiang became Chairman of the Political Council, and swiftly turned back to the Northern Expedition. The target now was Peking, where the Old Marshal of Manchuria, Zhang Zuolin, held sway. Emissaries went to canvass potential defectors, and the Christian General agreed to join the offensive. The Model Governor of Shanxi, Yan Xishan, came on board after Manchurian troops attacked his province.

This meant the expedition now had as many troops as the northerners, and there was at least a semblance of a philosophical thread between the commanders: Feng Yuxiang and one of Yan's leading lieutenants belonged to the Kuomintang. Crucially, Chiang kept control of the flow of money and supplies. To raise funds, he put fresh pressure on Shanghai banks and companies, raising $15 million. 'We are throwing money and men into the fight with almost heart-breaking extravagance because we want to make this a fight to the finish,' declared T. V. Soong, who had returned as Finance Minister.[1]

To replace Galen, Chiang turned to Germany. He first tried to engage the First World War commander Erich von Ludendorff but the Field

Marshal was not interested. Instead, Ludendorff recommended Colonel Max Bauer, who had advocated launching suicidal air raids in 1918 to reduce Paris to 'a glowing ash heap'. Bauer brought in other German officers from the far right, and contrasted 'the strength, dignity, soundness and goodwill' of the Chinese with the degeneration of white races 'under the impact of materialism, eroticism and nervous strain.' Chiang spent five hours with him at their first meeting in the Astor Hotel in Shanghai.[2]

The second stage of the Northern Expedition was formally proclaimed on 7 April 1928. The Nationalists mobilised a million men split into four armies – Feng's was the largest with 310,000 troops, Chiang had 290,000 soldiers under his command while the Guangxi Clique fielded 240,000 and the Model Governor of Shanxi 150,000. Chiang's First Army and the Christian General's cavalry mounted a two-pronged attack on Shandong province on the east coast. In the provincial capital of Jinan,* where he had just held a grand banquet to celebrate his new central heating system while 28,000 famine victims lived on a bowl of gruel a day, the Dogmeat General took the precaution of sending his mother and several concubines to safety in a northern port. On 1 May a vanguard of southerners secured a bridge across the Yellow River. The defenders fled in disarray, and the Dogmeat General headed for Peking to join his Manchurian ally. A Russian armoured train was captured; according to one report, its crew was paraded through the streets with 'stout rope pierced through their noses'.[3]

Chiang arrived in Jinan the next day. He ordered soldiers to maintain discipline, and promised to abolish excessive taxation. Reuters quoted an American missionary as saying the newcomers had moved in without trouble. But the scene was set for the general's first encounter with Japan, which had acquired the former German concession in Shandong in 1919 and had 1,800 civilians and 2,300 soldiers in Jinan. Chiang was anxious to avoid a fight with the well-equipped foreigners, and did not want any delay which might let his allies grab the initiative in reaching Peking. So he decided to move his troops out of Japanese-held areas of the city. Before this could be completed, shooting began in several places. Each side blamed the other.[4]

---

* Known at the time as Tsinan.

The Japanese marched into the office of the provincial Foreign Affairs Commissioner, alleging that shots had been directed at them from the building. After smashing up the offices and herding the staff into a room, they ordered the Commissioner to kneel and say who had fired. He refused. According to the account given by Chiang's Japanese biographer, Keiji Furaya, the soldiers then shot the sixteen staff one by one. An attacker knocked the Commissioner over with his rifle, broke his legs, cut off his tongue and killed him with a bullet in the head.[5]

The Japanese claimed 300 of their nationals had been killed by the Chinese, and that some bodies had been found with eyes gouged out and replaced by stones – they later cut the death toll to thirteen dead and twenty-eight missing. In a telegram to Nanking, Chiang reported that a thousand Chinese had died, presumably an order of magnitude rather than a precise count. It quickly became clear Tokyo would apply maximum force.

Facing a choice that was to dog him for a decade, Chiang sent a telegram to Nanking denouncing the 'malice and oppression beyond description' of the Japanese, and saying he could not 'bow to such bullying'. But he also urged 'a calm attitude' as the British and American consuls began to mediate. Chinese troops were told to quit the city, though some refused to go. Chiang himself came under attack when northern planes dropped two bombs in the courtyard of his headquarters; one landed 50 feet from his bedroom, killing two orderlies. On 6 May he left Jinan, advising Nanking to use diplomacy to solve the crisis. Anti-Japanese boycotts and demonstrations erupted in Shanghai, Canton and Wuhan. Despite his wary attitude, Chiang became a hero as the image spread of his troops standing up to the aggressor.[6]

On 8 May, the local Japanese commander, General Fukada, delivered a twenty-four-hour ultimatum for the remaining Chinese forces to withdraw. He also demanded the punishment of officers responsible for the fighting, the banning of anti-Japanese propaganda, and the disarmament of troops who had fought the Japanese. When the deadline expired, he launched artillery and bombing attacks on the square-mile old walled city. Most victims were civilians. The next day, Fukada let Chinese troops inside the old city leave, but the Japanese ambushed them and killed many.

Arriving on a train with Japanese reinforcements two days later, Hallett Abend of the *New York Times* found the streets deserted except for an occasional military patrol. Dead Chinese lay on the pavements and in the middle of the streets. 'Most of the corpses were already bloated and discoloured,' Abend wrote. 'And there were many dead horses, their legs sticking up stiffly at grotesque and pathetic angles . . . Nearly all the shops had been broken open, and showed disorder left by hasty looters.' An investigation gave the Chinese dead as 3,000; Abend put it at more than double that.[7]

Nanking called on the League of Nations to stop Japan, but Tokyo continued to demand an apology, compensation and punishment of Chinese officers involved. The major powers showed no interest: their own concessions in China led them to sympathise with Japan. Chiang issued a proclamation that: 'We should never let our vengeful feelings be known; otherwise we will never be able to fight against the enemy. Let us hide our desire for revenge, and never let it be seen. Let us store it in our minds, let us work together to avenge the insult, and let us attempt to lead the Chinese nation towards the goal of freedom and independence.'[8]

While Chiang was involved in Jinan, the war in the north had taken a favourable turn. The Shanxi troops and Feng's soldiers moved over the plain towards Peking from the west and the south. Remembering how the Christian General had grabbed the former imperial capital after betraying his warlord ally, Wu Peifu, in 1924, Chiang did not want him to get there first. So it was agreed that the capture of the city would be left to the Model Governor, Yan Xishan. Facing the two-pronged attack, the Manchurians decided to head home.

Peking's grey and white striped station, with its clock tower topped by a silver dome, was crowded with passengers going north. Before dawn on 3 June 1928, a convoy of twenty cars drove up, bringing the Old Marshal to start his journey back to his capital of Mukden* on an armoured train. As a military band played, Zhang Zuolin entered his cobalt blue private carriage – Reuters reported that he was smiling broadly. The Dogmeat General travelled with him for part of the way. At the request of foreign diplomatic missions, and with Nanking's agreement, a reliable Manchurian unit stayed behind to keep order until the Nationalists arrived.

* Now Shenyang.

At 5 a.m. the next day, the fifty-four-year-old Manchurian leader sat smoking a cigarette while the train entered the outskirts of Mukden. As his private carriage passed under a bridge, an explosion brought down a span of masonry. The area was controlled by the Japanese as part of their concession, but the guards were in their huts rather than watching the line.

Zhang was helped from the train by a Japanese adviser, bleeding heavily from his nose and from a wound in his left arm. A Ford motor car called from the Mukden Spinning and Weaving Works took twenty minutes to arrive. The Marshal was put inside, flooding the floor with his blood as he was driven to his residence. Carried inside on a stretcher, he vomited blood. A British doctor administered camphor injections. The Mukden Tiger was then taken to a Japanese hospital, where he died four hours after the blast.[9]

The assassination was the work of officers of Tokyo's increasingly independent force in Manchuria known as the Kwantung Army from the concession where they were originally stationed. They also arranged for bombs to be thrown at Japanese property in Mukden so that they could propose moving in soldiers for protection. Despite his past cooperation, they saw the Marshal as an obstacle to their expansionist schemes, and expected the morphine-addicted younger Zhang to prove a weak reed.

Things went somewhat awry when the Japanese Consul General, who was not in the plot, told Tokyo it was not necessary to take action to safeguard Japanese nationals. There was then another hiccup when Kwantung troops arrested three Chinese opium addicts, and accused them of setting off the explosion that had killed Zhang Zuolin. They were taken away to be executed, but one escaped and told the Young Marshal what had happened. Not that this made any difference. The Kwantung Army was firmly in the saddle. In Tokyo, the Prime Minister, Baron Tanaka, heard what had really taken place only a month later. When he called for those responsible to be court-martialled, the high command resisted, and Tanaka was told he had lost the confidence of the Emperor, who did not insist on serious punishment.

In Mukden, the Young Marshal came under heavy pressure from Japan to toe its line. After his father's funeral, the Japanese Minister to China told him Tokyo was determined to prevent any agreement between Manchuria and the 'internally unstable and pro-Communist government in Nanking', and would take whatever steps it felt were needed if the

Nationalist flag was raised in Manchuria. According to his own account, Zhang replied: 'You forget one thing – you forget that I am Chinese.' The conversation became so blunt that the interpreter said he could not go on.[10]

As the Old Marshal was travelling to his death, the vanguard of Nationalist troops had reached Peking. There was heavy fighting round the Summer Palace outside the capital, but no further opposition as tens of thousands of grey-coated soldiers caked with dust and grime marched in, moonlight glinting on their bayonets. In Nanking, Chiang went through the motion of submitting resignation from his military posts on the grounds that there was no further need for war. The offer was, naturally, refused. Accompanied by his wife, he set off on a victory trip, starting by travelling up the Yangtze to Wuhan where a huge banquet was held in his honour. He then went by train to Peking where a crowd of local notables waited all night at the station for him. Set on Nanking as the national capital, he showed his disdain for the imperial city by waving his hat, saying a couple of words and refusing to have his photograph taken.[11]

The trip was important as an expression of the government's national reach achieved by the 1,500-mile expedition launched two years earlier. Chiang's first business was to pay homage at Sun Yat-sen's coffin in the Western Hills; Meiling held a parasol over him as they walked from the temple, adorned with huge flags. At larger ceremonies two days later, Chiang broke down after reading a eulogy, throwing himself on the casket and sobbing. The Christian General took him by the arm to help him leave.[12]

There was a reminder of the kind of allies Chiang had collected when one of the Dogmeat General's subordinates who had switched sides looted Imperial tombs outside the city. In his haven in the Japanese Concession in Tianjin, the Last Emperor was roused to indignation. But Chiang took no action, and a rumour spread that pearls from a crown had been sent to Meiling who had put them on her shoes. One of the Christian General's officers created a bad scene by strutting round at Sun Yat-sen's tomb with an assertive bodyguard. But, for the most part, things went smoothly enough. The commander-in-chief and his wife moved into the best establishment in town, the Peking Hotel, and invited the Young Marshal, who was in town, round for tea. When Meiling called Zhang by a nickname, Chiang asked how she knew it. 'I met him before I met you,' she replied, recalling the time they had socialised in Shanghai in the mid-1920s.[13]

As well as enabling Chiang to meet the northern commanders, the stay in Peking gave him a chance to build bridges with the Western legations there. Relations with foreigners had improved since the end of the leftist regime in Wuhan – Nanking had reached an agreement on tariffs with Washington, which constituted de facto recognition. On 21 July, the Chiangs played host to the diplomatic corps. Then the British ambassador gave a dinner for the general. A month later, a Sino-British agreement on the Nanking Incident was announced by which the Chinese accepted responsibility, apologised, promised compensation – and blamed the Communists.[14]

The night after the embassy dinner, Chiang left by rail for Nanking. Armoured trains preceded and followed him. He was described as being in good spirits though looking tired and appearing thinner than when he travelled north a month earlier. From the capital, Chiang went to Shanghai for treatment of tooth abscesses which had been interrupted by the military campaign. The extraction led to a gum haemorrhage, forcing him to go to his home village to rest and recuperate. By the autumn he was back in Nanking, which was bursting with plans for a new China.[15]

The stream of proposals that flowed from the government would often prove to be beyond the regime's powers of implementation. But this was the time, more than any other until the 1980s, when China embraced modernisation. Recognition by foreign powers gave it international status. Only Japan refused to hand back the tariff autonomy China had lost under the unequal treaties. Though the foreign concessions remained, Chiang assured students: 'If, within three years, the foreign soldiers are not withdrawn from China and the unequal treaties are not abolished, I shall be the first man to offer to put himself to death for neglect of duty.' Nanking sent diplomats to Washington, Europe and Latin America. Military cadets went to train abroad. Meiling started to teach Chiang English; according to Emily Hahn's biography, this stopped after the general tried out his new skill on the British ambassador, Sir Miles Lampson – instead of saying 'Good morning, Lampson,' he told the envoy, 'Kiss me, Lampson.'[16]

Foreign advisers were appointed, including Henry Ford, who had not been asked in advance but accepted after it was stipulated that he would not need to visit China. An American city designer, Ernest Payne Goodrich, was engaged to re-plan Nanking and Canton. A Frenchman was taken on to help frame legislation, and a British colonial administrator, Sir Frederick Whyte, became a senior government adviser.[17]

T. V. Soong promised a proper national budget, with standardisation of taxes and currencies and the establishment of a Central Bank. A national system of weights and measures was drawn up. Salt tax revenue would be used to finance education. The abolition of tax farming and the *lijin* duty on movement of goods was announced for five provinces directly under Nanking's control. A register of land holdings was planned. Civil service salaries were to be raised to eliminate corruption. There were campaigns against foot-binding and cigarette smoking, and the lunar calendar was replaced by the solar one.

Programmes were elaborated to stop river flooding and develop mining and agriculture. Legislation was drafted to introduce an eight-hour working day, ban child labour, and provide for notice periods and profit-sharing. As Communications Minister, Sun Yat-sen's son, Sun Fo, followed his father's example with plans to build thousands of miles of rail track, along with highways and an air service. The military academy was expanded and moved to Nanking, though it still kept a mention of Whampoa in its name. Chiang told its first class, of 1,000 graduates: 'We must create a new environment; for otherwise we may fall victims to the former unhealthy environment.'[18]

The new capital, surrounded by the coiling dragon of the Yangtze and the crouching tiger of the Purple Mountain to the east, was to be a showplace for the new China with a network of 850 miles of modern roads. Ministry buildings merged modern concrete pillars and big glass windows with traditional curved roofs and archways. While pledging to preserve temples and old treasures, the American designer spoke of putting an elevated highway on the wall. Rich citizens had villas constructed in the surrounding hills. The city was so full of officials and office-seekers that not a hotel room was to be had.[19]

Some of the proposals were put into practice, particularly by T. V. Soong. A National Reconstruction Commission under Chiang's patron, Zhang Jingjiang, modernised power plants, improved transport and set up a network of radio stations. Industrial output, electricity generation and rail traffic grew by an average of almost 10 per cent a year. The state played an ever-increasing role in the economy. But these increases were from a very low base and concentrated in small areas of the country. Most of China remained backward, and poor.[20]

Half the provinces were ravaged by famine which brought up to 20 million people to the point of starvation and may have killed 6 million. There were plague outbreaks. Locusts ate crops: famished farmers caught and boiled them for food. A bitter winter claimed hundreds of thousands more lives. American charities raised $8 million for relief, but local officials stole and sold supplies. Defeated warlord troops swelled the ranks of bandits. Sick soldiers spread typhus and cholera. In the war zones, railway track had been torn up, bridges destroyed, and abandoned locomotives left to rust. Food and goods piled up at stations awaiting trains that never came. Canton was suffering a business depression. In Wuhan, 100,000 people were out of work. In Peking, renamed Peiping (Northern Peace) after Nanking became the national capital, a quarter of a million were said to be destitute.[21]

Chiang's indiscriminate collecting of allies meant the regime's umbrella covered militarists who flew the Nationalist flag but went on in their old ways. Despite prohibition decrees, opium remained a major source of income for soldiers, officials, local governments and outlaws. A visitor to Anhui province told of areas where no other crop could be seen. Reuters reported at the end of 1928 that nearly all the major military groups were involved in the traffic, and that enforcement of anti-opium laws might mean war. Despite denouncing the trade, the regime took much-needed cash from the Green Gang in Shanghai, and from taxing drug shipments on the Yangtze.[22]

The government was continually short of cash. Even if they paid lip service to Nanking, many provinces held back tax revenue – in 1929, T. V. Soong listed a dozen which hung on to money that should have been remitted to the central administration. Military spending and debt servicing consumed 80 per cent of the budget. To sell government bonds, the Finance Ministry had to pay a real interest rate of 20 per cent. At the same time, many officials proved incapable, or unready, to carry out the grand plans. Implementation was restricted by banditry and the obstruction of local militarists and gentry. The visiting British social analyst, R. H. Tawney, noted that 'nothing is being done, that no one is very hopeful that anything will be done, that there is little finance or administrative staff, that the last official concerned in the business was not wholly above suspicion in the matter of money, and that his successor cannot visit the areas which most need attention for fear of being kidnapped'.[23]

Chiang was well aware of the problem. 'I have observed that many of the staff members do not seem to know what they are supposed to do while others do not know how to work at all,' he told the State Council. 'That is why our organisation becomes worse and worse.' Though civil servants worked only a six-hour day, he added, 'I have often observed that many staff members just sit at their desks and gaze into space, others read newspapers and still others sleep.'[24]

Whatever the deficiencies of the administration, this was the moment when Chiang, still only forty-one, assumed his national mantle as China's Man of Destiny, seeing himself as the Confucian superior figure ordained to rule the nation. Nanking's authority might only stretch over five provinces, but he expected the deference due to a conqueror. When he entered the inner sanctum of the State Council building at the back of three heavily guarded courtyards, everybody stood bolt upright to attention. Meeting him, the Swedish explorer Sven Hedin was struck by his serious, unwavering expression – 'he created an immediate impression of a person of high authority, determination and character.' The visiting British historian, Arnold Toynbee, wrote of his 'cool-headedness and restrained vitality'.[25]

The general was caught between his desire to make China a modern nation which could hold its head up in the world, and his insistence on the supremacy of traditional precepts and modes of behaviour. His thinking was based on his reading of classical Chinese texts and the ideas of his old friend, Dai Jitao, who had helped to introduce Marxism to China but had then moved to Confucianism and bitter anti-Communism. A one-time secretary to Sun Yat-sen, Dai was an unstable figure who suffered nervous breakdowns and attempted suicide several times. The father of Chiang's adopted son, Wei-kuo, he proposed a state dictatorship representing all classes in which the Kuomintang should have free rein for its 'monopolistic, exclusive, unitary and dominative nature'. Picking up the baton, Chiang decreed that the party must exercise power for the people. Workers should not follow their selfish interests. Strikes and calls for a shorter working week would 'curb production, doom the labourers to perdition and bring the country endless harm.'[26]

When left-wingers set up a group called the Reorganisation Society to urge more democracy and a revival of revolutionary methods, mass movements and anti-imperialism, Chiang and his allies showed their muscle. For the Kuomintang congress of March 1929, only four of the thirty-eight party branches were allowed to elect delegates directly. When the meeting opened, it was ringed by soldiers, and the party's governing committees were packed with loyalists. To remove democracy from the agenda, the Central Executive Committee laid down that the party would exercise 'political tutelage' on behalf of the people until the end of 1935. Less publicly, a former Whampoa cadet called Dai Li, who boasted of having denounced seventy-five of his colleagues for execution in the 1927 purge, was laying the foundations for a secret police operation whose only loyalty was to the general – one of Dai's notions was said to have been the idea of injecting potential leftist turncoats with drugs to turn them into addicts who would do whatever he wanted.[27]

The anti-Communist repression continued unabated, helping to deepen the gulf between the regime and many of China's best young writers and thinkers that pointed to the intellectual sterility which would mark the Nationalist regime. Thousands more died in the crackdown in Hunan. At Shantou, political prisoners were thrown into the sea with weights attached to their bodies. Yet the Communists were far from beaten; after the failure of their rising in Nanchang, Red Army units moved south to join Mao Zedong in his haven in the mountains of Jiangxi while a big base area persisted north of the Yangtze. The success of the Nationalists was not going to halt the post-imperial pattern of Chinese constantly attacking one another. As the great allegorical novel of the time, Lao She's *Cat Country*, concluded, even if there were only two beings left alive, they would not stop fighting until they had bitten one another to death.

Still, to try to lay the basis for a modern state, a new political system was put in place, starting the period of political tutelage by the Kuomintang. Chiang became Chairman of the State Council, the senior political post. Five government branches – the *Yuan* – were established. The Executive Yuan, the equivalent of a prime minister's office, was in overall charge of ministries, economic affairs, and relations with provinces and local government. The Legislative Yuan debated and approved legislation, voting on foreign policy and budgets – the Kuomintang veteran, Hu Hanmin, took the chair and Meiling became a member. Other branches dealt with the appointment of civil servants and justice – though it was clear that the legal system would be subject to the interests of the Kuomintang. The fifth body, the Control Yuan, was to ensure ideological purity and discipline.

The Young Marshal joined the State Council. The Model Governor became Interior Minister. The Christian General, who appeared in Nanking wearing a pyjama-like white costume with infantry boots, an old straw hat and cotton shoes, was named Minister of War. True to form, he insisted on driving round in a freight truck instead of using the white Buick provided for him. Calling at ministries, he amazed sentries by presenting his card himself. Preaching frugality, he asked: 'At a time when so many millions are starving, why should we bedeck our ladies with diamonds, own numerous motor cars and houses and eat the luxuries of the earth?'[28]

Chiang, Hu Hanmin, Feng Yuxiang and other leading members of the regime gathered for a group photograph, Chiang as impeccably turned out as ever, Hu with a scarf wrapped tightly round his neck and the Christian General massive in greatcoat and puttees. Below the surface unity bred by the victory in the north, the regime was still deeply divided, and tension was increased by reports of assassination plots against Chiang. Like a medieval king surrounded by powerful barons, he knew that his army could be outnumbered by a combination of any two of his allies from the Northern Expedition. A conference of the major commanders agreed to halve the overall army strength of 1.6 million men, but the general then gave a speech making clear his centralising intentions – which was enough to lead the others to put disbandment into deep freeze.[29]

Feng, Yan Xishan, the Guangxi Clique and Zhang Xueliang were all intent on preserving their own regional authority, and resisting Chiang's desire to erect national military, tax and political structures. The Guangxi Clique was the first to go into open rebellion in the spring of 1929, with a bid to grab control of Wuhan from Nanking's administration. In response, Chiang fielded 100,000 men to his opponents' 60,000. Using bribery when necessary, he sewed up agreements with other militarists that kept them from allying with the rebels. Carrying umbrellas against the spring rain and marching to the Kuomintang anthem's tune of 'Frère Jacques', his troops advanced without opposition along the Yangtze, though, on the way, he lost his chief German adviser, Max Bauer, who died of smallpox.[30]

At Wuhan, 5,000 of the defenders were enticed to change sides, opening a gap in the line through which Nationalist troops poured. On 5 April 1929, greeted by artillery salvoes, Chiang arrived in the city by boat. Stamps were issued bearing his portrait set between laurels below an image of the sun, with the words 'To Commemorate Unification' in Chinese and English. The Guangxi leaders, Generals Li and Bai, launched a new offensive in Guangdong, dubbing their forces the 'Protect the Party, Save the Country Army'. But they were halted, and fled to Hong Kong, though they would be back.[31]

With a fresh victory under his belt, Chiang strengthened his forces by buying warplanes from Europe and America, field guns from Japan and 60,000 rifles from Britain. Another German adviser arrived – Colonel Hermann Kriebel, who had left armistice talks with the Allies in 1919 saying, 'See you again in twenty years,' and who then took part in the Nazi beer hall putsch in Munich in 1923 before sharing a cell with Hitler in the Landsberg fortress.

The pattern of virtually continuous conflict that marked Chiang's life soon asserted itself as the Christian General moved to take over positions in Shandong which the Japanese had occupied after the Jinan Incident the previous year but were now preparing to evacuate. Having no wish to see his unreliable ally grow more powerful, Chiang asked the Japanese to delay their departure while he dispatched troops of his own to the province. The warlord reacted by asking to be relieved of his post as War Minister, clearly signifying he was contemplating a fight. Falling back on his stock of silver bullets, Chiang bribed one of Feng's divisional commanders to defect and won over two Shandong militarists. Outmanoeuvred, the Christian General pulled back. Without any fighting, Chiang had won the first round.

That provided a breathing space for a major symbolic act. In mid-May 1929, a train brought the coffin containing Sun Yat-sen's remains from Peking to Nanking, which the doctor had wished to be his last resting place in memory of his brief time there as the first president of the Republic. His portrait hung on the front of the locomotive, with national and Kuomintang flags on either side. Straw-hatted propaganda workers expounded his doctrines through loudspeakers to crowds along the way. The body, which had originally been clothed in a Western suit, had been re-embalmed and dressed in a long blue satin gown, black silk jacket, white silk stockings, gloves and black satin boots. On arrival in Nanking, it was taken by boat to Kuomintang headquarters. During the river journey, Qingling Soong sat with her eyes fixed on the coffin, while Chiang stood to attention. At the party building, he put a wreath on the bier as three days of lying in state began.

This gathering of the Sun–Soong–Chiang clan was highly charged. Qingling, who had gone into exile in Russia after the fall of the Wuhan regime, was sharing the spotlight with a man she had denounced as a traitor to the revolution. Meiling had become a prominent figure in the administration her sister abhorred. Sun Fo had dodged across the political landscape. T. V. Soong held the key to Nanking's finances after serving both Wuhan and Canton. The master of ceremonies at the funeral was H. H. Kung, a man who had also shifted allegiance and whose wife, if Jennie Chiang was to be believed, had engineered Chiang's third marriage. And then there was the general who had come from nothing to assume the doctor's inheritance.

The cortège left the centre of Nanking at dawn on 1 June, preceded by four armoured cars. It was a warm day, with bright sunshine. As a 101-gun salute sounded, Qingling, the Chiangs, Sun Fo, and T. V. Soong travelled in the hearse up a broad avenue named after Sun to a huge white mausoleum in the foothills of the Purple and Gold Mountains east of the city. A large portrait of the doctor was fixed to the front of the vehicle. The national flag covered the casket. In a black cotton dress, black cotton stockings and black shoes, Qingling nervously fingered a white handkerchief and dabbed away tears. 'Her face showed that only by determination and a sublime attempt to keep calm did she manage to follow her husband's remains,' a journalist wrote.[32]

The line of soldiers, scouts, government workers, provincial representatives and students stretched for 2 miles. Crowds thronged the pavements. Most mourners wore plain white – the colour of mourning in China – though the principal officials were in black. The procession took six hours to cover the 10-mile route, moving so slowly that the *New York Times* correspondent was able to watch it depart, return to his hotel to file a story and then catch up by car. When the hearse reached the hill, only Sun's widow, his son, Chiang and T. V. Soong climbed behind the pall-bearers up the 400 broad granite steps to the mausoleum. Bands played dirges as the coffin was taken inside the classically proportioned, dimly lit building with blue tiled roof, blue, red and gold cornices, stained glass windows, wooden pillars and a mosaic of the Kuomintang flag on the ceiling. Orations were read. Planes circled overhead.

After the ceremony, Qingling left for the house on the Rue Molière in Shanghai which she had shared with Sun. From there, she issued a statement saying that nobody considered Nanking as representative of the Chinese people, and accusing Chiang of having betrayed her husband despite paying lip service to him each day. Such attacks were water off his back. It was time to turn his attention to the battlefield.[33]

An anti-Nanking coalition had been formed by Feng Yuxiang the Christian General, Xan Yishan the Model Governor of Shanxi, and Wang Jingwei, Chiang's Kuomintang rival who had returned from Europe. Chiang, whose 300,000 troops were outnumbered two-to-one, won over some of the Christian General's leading lieutenants with enormous bribes that led 100,000 soldiers to change sides. He also got the support of forces in Guangdong which cut the supply lines of Guangxi units that tried to advance into Hunan. But his opponents set up a separatist government in Peiping under the name of the Enlarged Conference of the Kuomintang – it had to be extremely large because it stretched from the militantly left-wing Reorganisationists to the traditional, right-wing Western Hills group. The only common motivation was enmity towards Chiang.[34]

The ensuing war saw some of the bloodiest battles of the time. Chiang put Nationalist deaths at 30,000 with twice that number wounded. He claimed 150,000 casualties for the northern forces. Other estimates spoke of total casualties of 250,000–300,000, 100,000 of them for the Kuomintang. The cost of the war increased Nanking's military spending by 50 per cent. Rail lines formed the axes of the campaign. Towns were ravaged. Farmers abandoned their fields. The northerners press-ganged masses of peasants, many of whom never returned. In places, troops dug trenches 20 feet deep, linked by tunnels: in one area, a relief official reported bodies stripped of flesh by dogs.[35]

With Chiang directing operations from an armoured train, his troops took Shandong in battles fought in heavy rain. At one point, the general was nearly captured. Moving into Henan province, his men occupied the strategic junction of Zhengzhou and the city of Kaifeng, where northern casualties were put at 20,000. They also experimented with poison gas, only for a change in the wind to blow it back on them. Journalists who met the commander-in-chief on the battlefield reported that he was very fit and distinctly cheerful. In August, his armies paused on the Yellow River. The crucial issue was what the Young Marshal of Manchuria would do – if he backed the rebels, Nanking looked doomed, and China would revert to the warlord era.[36]

Zhang Xueliang, who had taken on the Australian former journalist W. H. Donald as an adviser, remained a dandy, a keen ballroom dancer and golf player, a gambler, a drinker, and a drug addict. But he had introduced reforms and shown his mettle in confronting his father's chief of staff, who was believed to be ready to collude with the Japanese and was alleged to have built up a private stock of 20,000 rifles, and a fortune of $200 million. The Young Marshal invited the general and an associate to dinner and a game of mah-jong. The previous night, he had flipped a silver dollar to decide what to do with his guests. Acting on the way the coin had fallen, he got up from the table during mah-jong, put a handkerchief to his mouth, and said he was indisposed. This was taken as a sign that he needed a morphine injection, so the guests were not worried. As the Marshal went through the door, his bodyguards rushed in and shot the visitors dead. Zhang kept the silver dollar in his safe as a lucky charm.

While the fighting had raged between Nanking and the rebels in Peiping, the Marshal's attention had been on a conflict with the Russians over control of a railway in the north-east. His attempts to get the upper hand went badly wrong when Soviet troops, commanded by Galen, crossed the border and forced him to give way. That battle lost with substantial casualties, he could turn to China south of the Great Wall. According to Hallett Abend of the *New York Times*, Zhang saw Nationalist principles as the only hope for the country, but thought Nanking had betrayed China and was 'rotten to the core'. In truth, his prime aim was to retain his autonomy, and Chiang offered him the best prospect. If Feng and Yan won, further struggles on the old warlord pattern were inevitable. But Nanking would be content with Zhang coming into the Nationalist tent, and, in return, leave him free to rule Manchuria and dominate northern China.[37]

The rebels in Peiping came to Chiang's assistance by including Zhang Xueliang in their State Council without consulting him. His feathers seriously ruffled, the Marshal held a conference with his senior generals lasting till one in the morning which decided to back Nanking. Pinned between Chiang and the Manchurians, Yan and Feng gave up. At the age of thirty, Zhang Xueliang became deputy commander of Nationalist armies, and moved troops across the frontier into China proper as governor of the north.

After this latest victory, Chiang turned to religious matters, going to a ceremony at the Soong family house in Shanghai to adopt his wife's creed. Rather than invoking inspiration and wisdom from the scriptures, he told the pastor that his mind had been made up during a battle near Kaifeng when he was in danger of being cut off from his troops. He had prayed to God, pledging that he would become a convert if he was delivered from the threat. A snowstorm started, preventing the enemy from advancing and giving time for Nationalist reinforcements to arrive to clinch victory. Keeping his side of the bargain, Chiang donned a simple long gown for the occasion, and, with water sprinkled on his head, was welcomed into the Methodist church. The next day, Kai-shek and Meiling sailed to Ningbo and travelled on to his home village for ten days of rest. Having outplayed Feng and Yan, he needed to prepare for a very different showdown.[38]

His next opponent was the Kuomintang stalwart, Hu Hanmin, who wanted to make a reality of party control of government and army. Chiang counter-attacked by proposing the drawing up of a constitution which he would fashion to fit his ambitions. The politician insisted that Sun Yat-sen's teachings were enough to go by. At a dinner at his home, Chiang argued with Hu till the early hours about the advisability of a constitution. At 2 a.m., according to the official account, the politician accepted the general's 'invitation to stay the night'. The next day, in the euphemistic version put out in Nanking, Hu followed a suggestion that he should go to a nearby resort, where he was held under house arrest. Two days later, his resignation from all his posts was announced. Stories were circulated that he needed a rest after working too hard and sleeping for only three hours a night: he was said to have lost consciousness twice. When Chiang's aide, Chen Lifu, expressed doubts about arresting such an eminent figure, Chiang replied: 'It's already done. There is no way to pretend any further.'[39]

The treatment of Hu scandalised some party elders, and sparked off the formation of an opposition group based in his home province of Guangdong. Wang Jingwei travelled south to express his backing, declaring that everybody in the party and army wanted 'the suppression of General Chiang', apart from those who had private connections with him. Sun Fo added that, while his father was alive, the general had been 'a very insignificant man'. Given their relative lack of military strength, this challenge was no bar to Chiang's ambitions. He called a congress of supporters to approve a constitution, setting out the usual guarantees of citizens' rights and duties, but also providing for a president who would appoint the heads of the five Yuan branches. In June, he was named to this position, and also became Chairman of the Executive Yuan, or Prime Minister.[40]

In the four years since he had set out on the Northern Expedition, Chiang had got the better of half a dozen major warlords, the Wuhan regime, Wang Jingwei, Hu Hanmin, and the Guangxi Clique. The Communists had been pushed back into isolated base areas, and the Russian advisers were gone. He had established himself as the dominant figure in a government which laid claim to lead China into a new age. He was linked by marriage to the Soong dynasty, and allied with the Young Marshal. No wonder that a reporter who interviewed the general in the summer of 1930 found him in the best of spirits. Wearing a khaki tunic and trousers, and leather slippers, with a pen clipped into his breast pocket, 'his eyes almost lazily swept across the questioner and, yet, revealed a penetration and a power of assessment,' the journalist from the *North China Daily News* wrote.

Of middle height, his spare frame spoke of fitness and wariness . . . Accustomed to command, he showed no sign of uneasiness or any doubt in the capacity of his government to win through. The confidence did not suggest egotism but rather the happy reliance of a captain in his ability and co-operation of his team. Modest, unaffected and master of himself – that was the key note which lingered after he had shaken hands and, in dismissal, used the only English word in the whole of his part of the conversation: 'Goodbye'.[41]

CHAPTER 12

Two Chinas

THROUGHOUT HIS LIFE, Chiang Kai-shek showed an ability to work with yesterday's enemies. Opponents like the Christian General, the Model Governor, Wang Jingwei and the Guangxi Clique reappeared over the years in his camp, sometimes only to fall out again. Given the narrow base on which the central government and its army operated, such alliances were a necessary part of his realpolitik approach to power. But there was one foe with which he would not compromise, sensing that the Communists still constituted the greatest threat, offering the same breadth and depth of appeal as the Kuomintang had in its rise to power.

The city where the repression had started in 1927 remained a focal point for the crackdown. Police in the foreign areas of Shanghai handed over suspected leftists, making the concessions much less of a safe haven than in the past. In one raid, which attracted international attention, police in the International Settlement grabbed two dozen participants, including five writers, at a secret meeting in the hotel where Chiang and Jennie had been married. They were handed to the Chinese authorities, and taken to the detention camp at the Longhua barracks on the outskirts of the city. Manacled hand and foot, they were held in concrete huts for a month while a campaign was launched in the West for the release of the writers. Then they were led through a long, dark tunnel to the execution ground.

There were reports of political detainees being buried alive. Torture was used as a matter of course. The *North China Daily News* wrote that the police had acquired an electrical machine to speed up confessions. 'The KMT were very ingenious and could pump a mixture of kerosene and faeces up your nose so that you didn't drown but swallowed a lot,' wrote the American scholar John King Fairbank, who was in China at the time. Still, conditions at Longhua appear to have been better than at some of the other detention centres. The historian Frank Dikötter contrasts the rice and cabbage soup provided in Shanghai with 'the mixture of grit, gravel and coal dust' served at a jail in neighbouring Jiangsu province. One Communist recorded that, in the prison where he was held, nine tenths of inmates died of illness or other causes within a year in 'a form of execution which differed from the firing squad only in being slightly more drawn out'.[1]

Still, underground organisations continued to function in China's biggest metropolis, using shops, property companies and clinics as fronts to generate funds. Hit squads, known as 'dog-killers', operated under a Green Gang member called Gu Shunzhang, who had been trained by the Russian secret service in Vladivostok and was said to be able to strangle victims without leaving marks. The historian Frederic Wakeman describes him as a master of disguise and deception, eloquent, articulate and with the air of a playboy. As a sideline, he did magic tricks at the roof garden theatre of the Sincere department store, dressed as a foreigner with a large false nose and small moustache.[2]

In 1931, Gu was sent on an undercover mission which revealed how deeply the Communists had penetrated the Nanking regime. He joined an entertainment troupe that performed in cities where Chiang was preparing military action against Communist bases. His job was to infiltrate the Nationalists and discover their plans. There was also a report that he had been told to assassinate Chiang. After attracting attention by inviting left-wingers to his hotels, Gu was detained by security forces. Taken to Nanking, he was met by the security chief, Xu Enzeng, who gave him two hours to choose between Communism and the Kuomintang, between death and life. The assassin-magician decided to defect. Xu took him to see Chiang's lieutenant, Chen Lifu. They spoke the same language because of their common links with the Green Gang. Gu swore allegiance to the Nationalists.

16

16. Chiang and Chen Jieru
(Jennie) at Whampoa.

17. Chiang and Meiling at
their wedding in Shanghai.

17

18

18 & 19. Party challengers: Wang Jingwei (above) and Hu Hanmin (right). Both claimed Sun Yat-sen's political inheritance, and both were out-manoeuvred by Chiang.

1

20. Still friends: Chiang with the Young Marshal and their wives before the kidnapping in Xi'an.

21. Chiang and Meiling after his release.

22. Don and M'issimo: Australian adviser W. H. Donald and Meiling, whose life he saved in Shanghai.

23. Brothers-in-law: T. V. Soong, Finance Minister and Prime Minister, meets Roosevelt (and son James) while negotiating a loan agreement.

24. H. H. Kung, the banker who was also Finance Minister and Prime Minister.

25. War: Chiang announcing China's resistance to the Japanese in July 1937, from the balcony of his headquarters in Lushan.

26. A baby in Shanghai's bombed-out station in 1937 (there were allegations that the photographer, 'Newsreel Wong', posed the baby for the shot).

27. Spectators gaze at the smoke and flames after Japanese air raids.

28. Japanese use Chinese for live bayonet practice during the Rape of Nanking.

29. Chiang harangues a rally in Wuhan before the evacuation of the city.

30. Three sisters: Ailing, Meiling and Qingling Soong join forces in the new capital.

31. Vast cemetery: Chungking becomes the most heavily bombed city in history.

When he was arrested, Gu had told the police not to send a telegram announcing his detention to the secret service headquarters in Nanking. They took no notice. Gu had reckoned that, when the cable landed in Xu Enzeng's office, it would be seen by the security chief's secretary, Qian Zhongfei, a Communist mole. Having won the trust of his boss, Qian had been put in charge of a network of organisations set up to gather information about Communists. He named party members to run them, while his agents operated a clandestine radio transmitter. The cable announcing Gu's arrest landed in Nanking after Xu Enzeng had left his office to go to a tea dance. So it was handed to Qian who sent his son-in-law to Shanghai to warn party leaders there, including Zhou Enlai. They went into hiding, Zhou later leaving the city disguised as a priest. Qian slipped away, too.

While the revelation of Qian's activities was a nasty shock for the Nationalists, the fallout from Gu's defection was devastating for the Communists. He provided chapter and verse on the party's operations in major cities. By the Kuomintang count, thousands of cadres were arrested. Many were executed, while others changed sides. Much of the Communist urban infrastructure was destroyed, including communications links between the Shanghai leadership and rural base areas.[3]

Later in the year, one of the assassins who had worked for Gu defected, and took police and his former boss to several places in Shanghai where they found the decapitated, bound bodies of all Gu's family except for his younger son. Gu put an advertisement in Shanghai newspapers naming Zhou Enlai as the man behind the murders. He then went to live in Nanking, where he became a member of the Central Executive Committee of the Kuomintang, and a leading figure in hunting down Chiang's enemies. But he fell foul of the powerful Chen brothers, and was executed for supposedly having 'reverted to Communist ideas' – though rumours said this was a cover to enable him to engage in deep cover anti-Communist work.[4]

The continuing crackdown netted some big fish, including the Communist secretary general Xiang Zhongfa, 'China's Stalin', who was picked up in the French Concession, handed over, and executed at the killing ground at Longhua. The party's first leader, Chen Duxiu, was also arrested but, after a trial at which he was defended by fifteen lawyers and which aroused liberal public opinion on his behalf, he was sentenced to thirteen years in jail rather than death. A more obscure figure, the future Madame Mao Zedong, Jiang Qing, was said by her enemies to have bargained her way out of prison by agreeing to work for the Kuomintang: in later life, she assiduously destroyed evidence of her time as an actress in Shanghai in the early 1930s.

Other opponents of the regime – real or imagined – were also at risk. In one murky case, a potential Nationalist rival from Chiang's province of Zhejiang was shot on a bus, the two assassins escaping with suspicious ease. But most of those who died were from the left. Among them was Deng Yanda, the one-time dean of Whampoa who had called at Chiang's house during the gunboat incident in Canton in 1926, and now headed a 'Third Party' dedicated to following Sun Yat-sen's teachings independently of both Nanking and the Communists. Though the party was numerically small, Chiang had declared that, if it did not die, 'the nation will never be at peace'. Arrested at a clandestine meeting in the International Settlement, Deng was handed over to the Chinese police and taken to Nanking to be executed for treason. His arrest came soon after he had defeated a pro-Communist faction at a party congress; rumours swirled that internal opponents betrayed him.[5]

The blows suffered by the urban Communist apparatus and exponents of the third way increased the weight of the rural revolution, as the severing of wireless transmitters left the various arms of the party to follow their own paths in a long-term battle across the countryside of China. After facing death when captured in the rising in Hunan in 1928, Mao Zedong had escaped and made his way with a small band of comrades to a mountainous area on the border with Jiangxi where they reached an understanding with local bandits. When Nationalist forces closed in on them, Mao and his principal companion-in-arms, Zhu De, a former warlord soldier, moved through snowy peaks without paths, suffering extreme hardship – particularly Mao's female partner who was five months pregnant. They set up a new, larger Soviet in Jiangxi which was to be the future Helmsman's base for more than five years, building up enough strength to stage raids into the surrounding areas and into Hunan and Fujian.*

Though later history would focus on Mao's base, the Communists had other havens. A Red Army survived and sometimes prospered on the

---

* Known at the time as Fukien.

Hunan–Hubei border under the command of a former Kuomintang general and veteran of the Nanchang rising, He Long. Another sizeable Communist force operated north of the Yangtze between Nanking and Wuhan, led by a self-confident former Politburo leader called Zhang Guotao. In Shaanxi, in northern China, radicals formed a Soviet which hung on despite having been beaten back by the Christian General.

The possession of armies differentiated the Chinese Communists from radical left-wing movements in other countries, and ensured that the long struggle with the Nationalists would be military as well as political, with no room for quarter on either side. The Red Armies were pitiless with class enemies and anybody suspected of helping their opponents. A witch hunt in Jiangxi took the lives of tens of thousands accused of being counter-revolutionaries or 'rich peasants'. Overall, the process of bringing revolution to China was marked by ruthlessness at sharp odds with the folksy face Mao and his colleagues would adopt for Western visitors.[6]

On their side, the Nationalists devastated huge areas, and killed hundreds of thousands, if not millions. Farmers were herded into stockades, and forests burned down to deprive the enemy of cover. Women were sent off to be sold into prostitution. Some Nationalist units kept score by collecting the heads of those they killed: finding this constituted too heavy a burden, they took the ears instead – one division was said to have 700 pounds of them. The families of Communist leaders were executed. The last news Zhu De had of his wife and son was when he read a newspaper report of Chiang's troops raiding his home in Sichuan. After the Red Army took the Hunan capital of Changsha and held it for nine days, the returning Nationalists tracked down Mao's wife who lived in the city and beheaded her: she had declared her abiding loyalty to her husband though knowing he had left her for the younger woman who accompanied him to Jiangxi.

In October 1930, Chiang launched an 'encirclement campaign' by some 44,000 men against the Jiangxi Red Army. This flopped badly as the Nationalists were sucked into traps and the Communists applied their guerrilla tactic of avoiding frontal battles while concentrating strength against exposed or weak enemy formations. At the end of December, one Nanking division was, in the words of the *North China Daily News*, 'having a good time with the funds taken from the Communists' in a captured town when it was attacked. Caught by surprise, the division capitulated after five hours. Donning the uniforms of their captives, the Communists surprised and routed another vanguard division. The commander of the first unit was taken prisoner and tortured as he crawled round confessing his sins. His tongue was cut out, and his cheeks pierced before his head was cut off, wrapped in a red cloth, nailed to a board by the ears, and floated down the river towards the retreating forces.[7]

After that debacle, Chiang gave his long-time associate from Whampoa, General He Yingqin, responsibility for a second campaign with more than 100,000 troops. In mid-May 1931, as Mao watched from a Buddhist temple on a high peak, the Communists ambushed two Nationalist divisions, scoring total victory. In five battles in the following two weeks, Chiang's forces lost 30,000 men killed, wounded or captured, and 20,000 rifles. The area under Communist control tripled.[8]

It was time for the commander-in-chief to take personal command, declaring the third Jiangxi campaign a matter of 'Victory or Death'. Accompanied by his German advisers, Chiang moved into a compound by the lake in the middle of Nanchang which became, in effect, an alternative power centre to the government and party in Nanking. He established his headquarters in a school with a large map on which Communist positions were marked in red and government units in blue. He issued a manifesto deploring the 'cowardice and indifference' shown by some troops in previous campaigns, and promising 'glittering rewards' to soldiers who served with distinction. Before leaving for the front, Chiang invited leading generals to a dinner catered by the city's YMCA.[9]

The Communists had not expected a fresh attack until the autumn of 1931. Instead, Chiang launched a three-pronged offensive in July with around 130,000 men. Caught off-balance and with its forces dispersed, Red Army headquarters issued an emergency circular warning of an 'extremely cruel' campaign. But the Nationalist commander, who was carried about in a sedan chair, moved cautiously to avoid ambushes, and this allowed the Red Army to escape. Setting a pattern for the epic marches of the future, it swung in a 400-mile semicircular movement in the heavy summer heat, keeping away from the main routes and using rural tracks to evade surveillance. Moving into the abandoned base area, Chiang's troops suffered from peasant resistance, lack of food and dysentery from foul water. They reacted by burning villages, massacring the inhabitants and seizing crops.[10]

After a series of battles, two Nationalist armies pressed their 20,000-strong enemy back against a 3,000-foot mountain. Finally, Chiang seemed to have his foe trapped. But, during the night, the Communists climbed the heights behind them. It was an epic escape, and Chiang did not push the pursuit. Instead, he began to withdraw. That encouraged the Communists to stage a frontal assault which cost them 4,000 casualties. Still, they survived to pull back to their base and declare the Chinese Soviet Republic there. 'From now on,' Mao declared, 'there are two totally different states in the territory of China. One is the so-called Republic of China, which is a tool of imperialism . . . The other is the Chinese Soviet republic, the state of the broad masses of exploited and oppressed workers, peasants, soldiers and toilers.'[11]

Chiang's Jiangxi campaign had been weakened by the need to send troops to block Canton autonomists who were threatening to march on Nanking. In Nanchang, the commander-in-chief was shot at as he drove through a park: after the three gunmen were caught, it was announced that they had been working for the Cantonese. In Shanghai, men shouting 'Down with the Soong dynasty' opened fire on T. V. Soong as he stepped off a train at the North Station – the Finance Minister escaped unhurt but his secretary, who was beside him, was hit in the bladder, arms and hip and died later in hospital. The attack was, again, officially blamed on the Canton faction, but was widely seen as the result of a dispute between the drug barons of Shanghai and Soong, who had been deputed to deal with them but had not proved sufficiently pliable. The way in which the gunmen had not hit the portly Soong, who was easily identifiable in the crowd by his white sun hat, made it look like a warning shot to the regime. When the next opium suppression campaign was announced, Chiang put it under military control so that he could make sure his ally, Big-Eared Du, was not incommoded. For his part, T.V. had armed guards patrol the grounds behind the 12-foot wall of his Shanghai home.[12]

By coincidence, the minister's mother – known as 'the mother-in-law of the country' for her daughters' marriages – died four hours after the attack on her eldest son: Meiling was with her when she expired. Qingling returned from Europe for the funeral: neither of her sisters nor T.V. met her at the station. A hundred cars drove in the funeral procession. Walking mourners wore white gowns and hats. Soldiers lined the route. The three daughters sat in one car, the three sons in another – an armour-plated

Buick. T.V.'s bodyguards carried drawn revolvers. Chiang was protected by twenty-five Whampoa graduates, a dozen walking on each side of his car. Even at a matriarch's funeral, these were dangerous times.[13]

Not nearly as perilous, however, as life for the hundreds of millions living in the areas of the great floods that spread in the summer of 1931. In the Yangtze provinces, dykes gave way as winds whipped up the water; buildings collapsed; crops were devastated; business stopped; prisoners drowned when their cells were inundated. In Wuhan sampans navigated the flooded streets directed by traffic police perched on platforms as bodies floated past. White slavers moved in to buy the daughters of the 350,000 refugees round the city. The stench was unbearable; people lived in trees; disease spread. To the north-east, heavy rains caused the Grand Canal to spill over: a local official said that more than 200,000 people were killed. Then the Yellow River burst its banks. By the beginning of September, 180 million people were estimated to be affected. The famed American pilot, Colonel Lindbergh, flew over the area and said he was 'deeply moved', before having tea with Kai-shek and Meiling.[14]

In the middle of September, Chiang took a ship up the Yangtze for Jiangxi to renew the war against the Red Army. Halfway there, however, he was forced to head back to Nanking as demonstrators marched in the streets proclaiming 'Death before Surrender'. The Japanese had made a move in Manchuria. Though Chiang was intent on destroying the Communists before confronting the Japanese, this demanded his return to the capital, thus giving Mao and his colleagues a breathing space in the first episode of a triangular involvement between Chiang, the Communists and the Japanese which was to stretch over fourteen years.

Tension had been rising steadily in Manchuria during 1931, exacerbated by incidents involving Tokyo's Kwantung Army and by cross-border clashes between Chinese and Koreans. Having established his headquarters in Peiping and moved many of his troops across the border into northern China, the Young Marshal's eye had been off his homeland. After visiting Nanking in the late summer, Zhang Xueliang had flown to Peiping where reporters learned that his daughter might marry into the Soong clan to strengthen his links with the ruling group. On arrival, the northern commander, who cut a dashing figure with his thin moustache and swept-back hair, went to a hotel to watch the evening dancing, but was too tired to be interviewed. He then developed a high temperature, and was taken to hospital where he was diagnosed as having typhoid fever contracted from bad water in Nanking; rumours said he was really undergoing treatment for his drug addiction.

On his discharge on 18 September, the Marshal went to dinner at the British Legation, followed by a visit to a theatre. Returning to his residence, he received a message from Mukden which signalled the start of the Second World War in Asia, a full eight years before hostilities broke out in Europe, and a challenge to Chiang that would last until 1945.

For decades, Japan had seen Manchuria and northern China as the natural sphere for expansion. One leading politician, Prince Konoe, who had attended the Versailles peace conference and believed in supporting the spirit of the League of Nations, still thought Japan 'was perfectly entitled to aggrandize [its] Chinese territory to meet the needs of its own exploding surplus population . . . It was only natural for China to sacrifice itself for the sake of Japan's social and industrial needs.'

Feeling they were being treated as inferiors by the West, and suffering from American and European racism, the Japanese concluded that they had to make their own place in the world, using force to pursue the manifest destiny of the 'imperial way'. Though China had been seen as a source of their culture, and some prominent Japanese encouraged co-operation, many soldiers regarded the Chinese with contempt – there was a saying that they were akin to pigs, except that pigs had the advantage of being edible. A military specialist, Ikezaki Tadakata, thought three or four divisions and a few gunboats 'would be quite enough to handle the Chinese bandits'. Adopting Social Darwinism to justify crushing weaker powers, Japan argued that China was not a true nation, and needed to be guided to a better existence as its vassal.[15]

Adjoining Tokyo's colony of Korea, Manchuria was the natural first target with its large Japanese investments, natural resources and industry. The Young Marshal was proving less accommodating than Japan had expected, and reforms he was introducing to modernise the three north-eastern provinces threatened to strengthen his position. A Kwantung Army hawk, Lieutenant Colonel Ishiwara Kanji, proposed 'a fabricated pretext for military action' to overthrow him. 'It is Japan's divine mission to assist the Chinese people,' added Ishiwara, who wanted to engage the Chinese in an anti-Western crusade. 'The four races of Japan, China,

Korea and Manchuria will share a common prosperity through a division of responsibility: Japanese, political leadership and large industry; Chinese, labour and small industry; Koreans, rice; and Manchurians, animal husbandry.' 'It is futile to protect our interests in Manchuria and Mongolia through diplomatic channels and by peaceful means,' the leading Japanese newspaper in the region declared. 'There is only one way to do this. It is the way of armed might.' Even more sinisterly, a Japanese scientist with an imposing manner, Shiro Ishii, had gained permission to launch a programme of secret biological warfare research in Manchuria known as Unit 713 that would expose thousands of prisoners to anthrax and other deadly diseases and produce weapons which would kill an estimated one million people when used by Japan's army in China.[16]

Despite the high tide of nationalism in Tokyo, the Cabinet there was anxious to keep the Kwantung Army under control. So it sent the chief of the General Staff intelligence section, General Tatekawa Yoshitsugu, with a letter warning the army against provoking an incident. After landing in the evening of 18 September, Tatekawa went to a restaurant and geisha house where he drank too much, and fell asleep without having delivered the letter. Since he was said to be in sympathy with the Kwantung officers, this may have been no oversight.[17]

While Tatekawa slept, an army unit placed explosives on the South Manchurian Railway track north of Mukden; it did so little damage that a train was able to pass by soon afterwards. But it was enough for the Japanese to blame the Chinese, and deliver their ultimatum in the name of self-protection. If they did not get satisfaction, the city would be taken over – to protect Japanese nationals and interests. The switchboard in Mukden passed the threat to the Young Marshal in Peiping. He had no idea how to react, and did nothing.

By dawn, the Japanese had seized his capital's airfield and radio station. The Japanese commander in Manchuria, General Honjo, warned that he was 'in duty bound to take drastic action without the slightest hesitation'. When the Consul General urged negotiations, a major drew his sword threateningly, and said there would be no interference with the army's prerogatives. Eleven hours after the ultimatum, the Mukden switchboard operator told the Marshal in Peiping: 'I can talk no more. The Japanese have entered my office.'

Official buildings were occupied, and local troops disarmed. Reinforcements arrived from Korea. Learning of the events, the Japanese Prime Minister said: 'The units have already moved, so what can be done?' As his forces bombed defenceless towns and trains, it was noted that Emperor Hirohito regarded this as 'only natural in view of conditions at the time' – his semi-divine status made his benediction particularly important. Officials involved were decorated or promoted. The Kwantung commander became a baron.[18]

The Mukden Incident set off a wave of protest in China. Students seized a train and drove it along the line to Nanking calling for action against the Japanese. In Shanghai, 50,000 demonstrators demanded death for anybody who traded with the enemy. There were riots in Tianjin. Nanking students invaded the Foreign Ministry, breaking windows and assaulting the minister. Six thousand young people, including 300 young women dressed as nurses, staged a rally in the capital demanding to be sent north to fight. The Communists accused the Nationalists of betraying the masses with a 'weak-kneed and vacillating policy'. The *China Times* published a song urging: 'Kill the enemy! Kill the enemy! Hurry up and kill the enemy!'[19]

The Young Marshal flew to Nanking to confer with Chiang: apart from the loss of territory, he had a $100 million family fortune at stake in Mukden, a third of it in gold bars. Chiang declared that an hour of unprecedented gravity had struck for the Chinese nation, and called for an end to internal dissension. He invited foreign missionaries to give him spiritual guidance; after devotional services and dinner, they told him they were asking God to move the League of Nations to settle the crisis. Following a military review in Nanking to mark the anniversary of the 1911 revolution, at which nine Junkers planes bought from Germany performed stunts, a manifesto warned that the aggression was a prelude to the complete subjection of China.

Still, as over the attack on Jinan in 1928, Chiang decided Japan was too strong to be resisted. This would be seen as his first great failure to stand up for national interests against the enemy from across the sea, setting a pattern for the following years. Militarily, he could have tried to use the vastly more numerous Chinese troops to swamp the better equipped and trained Kwantung Army, counting on civilian politicians in Tokyo to rein in the expansionists. It is impossible to tell what the outcome would have been. But Chiang was also subject to constraints other than fear of Japanese military prowess – war in Manchuria would free regional barons to re-establish themselves elsewhere in China while his troops were in the north-east; the Kuomintang was divided; there was the impact of the Yangtze floods; and the Communists had not been beaten.

Chiang also counted on Japan eventually becoming embroiled in separate wars with a US-British alliance and with Russia. Rather than fighting on its own in 1931, he believed, Nanking should develop its defences and strengthen itself by liquidating its domestic foe. Then, when a Second World War broke out, China would emerge reinforced and with greater political independence than ever. In the short term, he also hoped for help from the West. But, though there could be no doubt about the rights and wrongs of the case, the League of Nations shied away from intervention in the first big test of its credibility. None of its leading members had the will or the means to take action. Instead, it was decided to send a mission under a British peer, Lord Lytton, to inquire into what had taken place.

In Manchuria, the Kwantung Army mined rail-tracks, took over communications companies and banks, removed the Marshal's picture from official buildings. The Japanese justified their action by accusing Zhang Xueliang of adopting an 'insincere attitude', and sent him his personal effects and furniture – but not his money – in 417 packing cases. Bombers attacked the industrial city of Jinzhou,* where the Japanese declared the very presence of Manchurian troops to be detrimental to peace and order. On 29 December 1931, pursuing a policy agreed with Chiang, Zhang ordered the soldiers there to withdraw. Though local commanders who did not espouse non-resistance staged guerrilla warfare elsewhere, Jinzhou was evacuated on the morning of 1 January – the American Minister in China reported that the station 'resembles a beehive, every possible car being pressed into service and loaded with troops, animals, baggage, to the last inch of space'.[20]

The shock of the Mukden Incident meant Chiang needed to promote national unity. He released Hu Hanmin, and met him with Wang Jingwei and Sun Fo in Shanghai – it was the first time the four of them had sat down together for six years. They agreed to work for the reconstruction of China, and to hold a party reconciliation conference. As always, Chiang

---

* Known at the time as Chinchow.

could depend on his rivals to be divided. A congress held by the southerners to pick their delegates turned into a shambles, with fighting on the floor. Wang Jingwei held a selection session of his own at the Great World amusement centre in Shanghai, courtesy of its owner, Pockmarked Huang Jinrong of the Green Gang. It was time for another coup by Chiang to destabilise his opponents.[21]

On 15 December 1931, the general went to a Kuomintang meeting in Nanking. After ninety minutes, he left, submitting his resignation in the interests of national unity and the fight against the Japanese – and to leave the way open for 'more competent men'. He attended the opening session of the reunification conference before heading for the familiar destination of his native village. The Young Marshal was flying to Nanking when he heard the news on the aircraft radio. He turned round to return to Peiping, and resigned as deputy commander-in-chief. He then flew to Shanghai in his three-motor Ford aircraft, with fourteen bodyguards and Meiling, who had been visiting the north. There was no doubt where his loyalties lay.

While fighting this latest political battle, Chiang was confronted with a very different decision. Acting on Moscow's behalf, Qingling Soong sent him a suggestion that his son, Ching-kuo, should return from Russia in exchange for the freeing of a Polish Communist arrested in Shanghai. Ching-kuo, then twenty-one, was dedicated to the Soviet system, excelling at the Red Army academy in Leningrad though suffering from diabetes and developing a taste for vodka. It had been made plain that he could not leave voluntarily. Meiling thought the deal should be accepted, though there is no indication that her stepson wanted to return home.

In the six years they had been apart, Chiang's feelings towards his son had softened, and he indulged in a bout of self-flagellation as a father who has not lived up to his obligations. 'I miss Ching-kuo very much. I am bad because I am not taking good care of him,' he wrote in his diary. Later, he reflected: 'I do not know how to be kind to my children. I regret that.' Still, he decided that he would rather let Ching-kuo stay in the Soviet Union than exchange a Communist agent for him since 'it is not worth it to sacrifice the interests of the country for the sake of my son'. Turning the issue to himself in typical fashion, Chiang reflected that a person would be remembered for moral integrity and achievements, 'not because he has an heir'.[22]

As this family drama played out, the situation in Nanking grew increasingly chaotic. Anti-Japanese students attacked Kuomintang headquarters, led by a girl and a boy whose faces were pitted by smallpox. Troops with bamboo clubs dispersed the demonstrators, and put them on trains out of the city. The reunification conference was a play without the main actors: Wang stayed in Shanghai, and Hu sheltered in Canton, wary of risking his safety in Nanking. The delegates split 42 per cent for Chiang, 39 per cent for Canton and 15 per cent for Wang, with others uncommitted. The plenum accepted a Cabinet headed by Sun Fo, but Chiang, Hu and Wang were elected to a nine-man Standing Committee which included three other members of the general's faction.[23]

Sun Yat-sen's stout offspring was described by the British journalist, Arthur Ransome, as being 'like many sons of famous fathers, an undistinguished personality'. His government was in immediate financial trouble as Chiang's friends in Shanghai turned off the money tap. T. V. Soong left with Chiang. Provincial leaders acted ever more independently. In desperation, Sun named the absent Chiang, Hu and Wang to a committee to deal with national emergencies. 'He was practically begging the three leaders to share the responsibilities of government,' as a historian of Kuomintang factionalism noted.[24]

Chiang was already negotiating with Wang, each man setting aside their enmity of the previous five years. In mid-January, they met in Hangzhou, and then called in Sun Fo to tell him that Wang was ready to become head of the government while Chiang resumed military command. The general and Meiling flew to Nanking in their new Sikorski seaplane, fitted with a couch and armchair in the cabin. Wang preferred to take the train. Arriving in the capital, the two returnees went to the Sun Yat-sen memorial. Wang, who was ill again, was carried in a sedan chair. On the way to the tomb, he wept so profusely that a halt was called.[25]

Taking tea and sandwiches with Kai-shek and Meiling, the journalist Hallett Abend found the commander had 'gained immensely in confidence and poise'. He had every reason to do so. He had now got the Kuomintang's most charismatic politician inside his tent, and isolated Hu Hanmin. T. V. Soong returned to run the regime's finances. Chiang's ideological guide, Dai Jitao, headed the Yuan that appointed officials. Other supporters ran the bodies which trained civil servants. The 'CC Clique' of the Chen brothers, whom Chiang had first met during his revolutionary days in Shanghai, was a key source of political and administrative support, as well as having its own secret police apparatus. As Chen Lifu, remarked, Sun Yat-sen's insistence that the Kuomintang party should be above the military was only a formality. To buttress his position further, Chiang attended the inaugural meeting of a group of dedicated supporters, mainly Whampoa veterans, known as the Lixingshe, who would form a loyal secret society devoted to the man they called 'our saviour'. Despite all this, however, he was to know no more peace in the next eighteen years than in the previous six.[26]

CHAPTER 13

Heart and Skin

AS CHIANG KAI-SHEK and Wang Jingwei were sealing their return to power in January 1932, an unpleasant incident took place in Shanghai. Five Buddhist monks from Japan were leaving the International Settlement when they were set upon by a group of Chinese. Two of the monks were badly injured; one subsequently died. Japan's consulate issued a graphic account of their suffering which was relayed home by correspondents. Feeling was already high, fuelled by the boycott of Japanese goods which had been intensified after the attack on Mukden the previous September. There had also been Japanese outrage when a semi-official Kuomintang newspaper ran a story about an attempt on Hirohito's life with a headline reading, 'UNFORTUNATELY BULLET MISSED: ASSASSIN ESCAPED'.[1]

After clashes at two towel factories in which Japanese killed two Chinese policemen, 2,000 Japanese residents marched through the streets of Shanghai, smashing up shops, attacking pedestrians, and trashing buses and trams. Wu Tiesheng, the one-time Canton police chief who had been rehabilitated as mayor of Shanghai, went to Nanking with the adviser W. H. Donald for consultations. On his return, he acceded to most of the Japanese demands for apologies and compensation. But that was not going to stop a plan hatched by the Kwantung Army in Manchuria. Having staged the Mukden Incident, it wanted to expand further there, and to distract attention with a diversion in Shanghai. For this, it conspired with Japan's military attaché in the city, Major Tanaka Ryukichi, a great intriguer who had a Manchurian princess as his mistress. Given $20,000 to foment trouble, he had engaged Chinese thugs to attack the Buddhist monks before organising the rally that ended in street violence.[2]

The Japanese navy, which had marines on ships moored in the river at Shanghai, was anxious to show that it could be as aggressive as the army had been in Mukden. Receiving the *New York Times* correspondent, Hallett Abend, for cocktails aboard his flagship on 28 January, its commander in Shanghai, Admiral Shiozawa, said that, despite the mayor's concessions, his marines would go ashore at eleven that night to protect 'helpless' Japanese civilians. Abend informed T. V. Soong and the US Consul General, who refused to believe him. At 11.05 p.m., firing began. In his room at the Astor House hotel, W. H. Donald telephoned the mayor, opened the window, and held the mouthpiece outside to pick up the sound of the shots.[3]

As usual, each side blamed the other for starting the shooting, but there was no doubt which was the aggressor. The heavily populated Chapei district was the main target as Japanese marines on motorcycles mounted with machine guns roared through the streets, firing at random while Chinese snipers shot back. Westerners in evening dress took taxis to watch the fighting. Abend recalled that they 'stood around the sloppy streets, smoking cigarettes, occasionally drinking liquor from bottles and enjoying sandwiches and hot coffee procured from nearby cafés'. Their view was simple: Japan was teaching the 'cocky Chinese' a lesson they deserved.[4]

At 7 a.m., Japanese planes circled in the grey sky over the city. As the light of day grew stronger, each plane dropped two small pointed cylinders which fell slowly in parallel lines below the roof line. 'The earth seemed to jar and shake,' Abend recalled, 'and then came a feeling of the concussion, and the blast of sound'. This was the world's first air raid on an unprotected civilian target the size of Shanghai, setting the precedent for Guernica and the Second World War. Meeting Abend on his flagship four days later, Admiral Shiozawa noted that American newspapers called him the 'Baby-Killer'; he added that he should be given credit for having used 30-pound bombs instead of 500-pounders.[5]

The Japanese onslaught was unrelenting. Waves of aircraft bombed from 300 feet above the rooftops, the crews leaning over the sides to observe their targets. Shipboard guns blasted targets on land. White-putteed marines raked the streets with machine-gun fire. *Ronin* gangsters brought in from Japan killed hundreds of civilians. A low-flying plane strafed a clearly marked Red Cross refugee camp.

But the Chinese stood their ground. The main defence was by the strongly anti-Japanese Cantonese Nineteenth Route Army which Sun Fo had moved from fighting the Communists in the south-east to act as his military shield on the Yangtze. Fierce combats raged round the North Station which blazed like a beacon in the wind. The Commercial Press building, home of China's biggest publisher and scene of violent clashes in the 1927 purge, was devastated. A priceless collection of ancient books was destroyed when the National Oriental Library burned. There was a stampede for the safety of the foreign settlements before they closed their gates. Up the Yangtze, Japanese ships shelled Nanking, and bombers cut the railway line between the capital and Shanghai – bus operators doubled the price of tickets for the twelve-hour trip. As fears rose of a general Japanese offensive, government leaders moved northwards to Wu Peifu's one-time stronghold of Luoyang.

On 28 January the Japanese used their privileged position in the International Settlement to send marines from there to attack nearby Chinese areas, and to land reinforcements in the concession. That drew a protest from the Mayor, but Brigadier General E. B. MacNaghten, Chairman of the Municipal Council, responded that the action was in order under the agreement between the nations represented in the Settlement, and that his organisation had no powers to intervene in any case. Other Japanese units advanced against a line of forts at Wusong* outside the city, and heavy fighting developed there. On 4 February, shells hit the Chapei district at the rate of one a minute. The next day, the *North China Daily News* reported: 'Larger buildings, with few exceptions, last night were bare and gaunt walls, their interiors a seething mass of glowing embers reflecting against the night sky. Homes by the hundreds are a wreck and ruin.' But, while the attackers had planes and big guns, their armoured vehicles could not manoeuvre through the narrow streets, and their infantry tactics relied on frontal assault, which laid them open to ambushes.[6]

Following plans drawn up by German advisers, the defenders dug deep trenches behind moats and barbed wire barricades, sheltering from

---

* Known at the time as Woosung.

artillery and air barrages and then emerging to mow down enemy troops trying to advance over the obstacles in their path. Green Gang members joined in as snipers. Local inhabitants donated millions. Financial aid flowed in from Overseas Chinese. The three Soong sisters raised money for a thousand-bed field hospital. The largest Chinese newspaper, *Shen Pao*, acted as the mouthpiece for resistance, backed by the Shanghai Local Peace Preservation Association whose members included Big-Eared Du. Chiang's patron, Zhang Jingjiang, heard of the Japanese attack while eating a meal: thinking of a saying about the strong making meat of the weak, he became a vegetarian.[7]

At last, Chinese troops were standing up to the Japanese, and doing well. But, according to the conventional wisdom, one man stood aside – Chiang Kai-shek, driven by his desire to avoid a clash with Japan and his fear that the Nineteenth Route Army, with its roots in the wayward southern province of Guangdong, would become a threat to him. That version of events was subsequently bolstered by the desire of the Communists to contrast Chiang's appeasement with their own patriotism, however little they actually fought. The Route Army's leaders, who had their own publicity department, massaged their fame by hosting press parties at which pâté de foie gras and Martel cognac were served. The operational commander, thirty-nine-year-old Cai Tingkai, became a media star, photographed in martial poses and vowing never to give up a foot of Chinese soil.

When the fighting started, Chiang did not have an official position in Nanking; it was only at the end of January that he joined the Military Council, as the Christian General, the Model Governor and the Young Marshal all rallied to the government in the name of national solidarity. Certainly, Chiang would have preferred to have avoided a battle at Shanghai: he and Wang Jingwei had told the Nineteenth Route Army not to give the Japanese any pretext for aggression. Once the battle began, he was keen to keep it confined, pressing for a negotiated settlement and worried that a major clash would force him to move troops from the fight with the Red Armies which remained his top priority.

Still, a mixture of motives propelled him to take a far more active position than has been generally acknowledged. Pressure for military action was strong in his elite, German-trained Fifth Army. His political enemies could use inaction to undermine him. Then there was the danger that, if Chiang did not have loyal forces of his own in the city, the Peace Preservation Association, which contained a number of his opponents, might become a force to challenge his mastery of Shanghai. Patriotic feelings were running high. T. V. Soong favoured action; thousands of his well-armed treasury agents took part in the defence. In an interview with an American journalist, the Finance Minister asked: 'Can you be surprised that China would turn to Communism or Sovietism, if that were to unite the country, rather than submit to foreign military domination?'[8]

After a meeting between Chiang and his closest military aide, General He Yingqin, in mid-February, the United Press agency reported that 'definite plans have been made to send important Chinese reinforcements to the Shanghai area'. Chiang kept back his central government units until the Nineteenth Route Army had suffered three weeks of combat; by then, it was clear that the Japanese were not interested in a quick truce. When he did send his men in, he put them under the command of the Nineteenth Route Army. This was partly recognition of the role the southerners had played since the battle began, but there was another reason – the Cantonese were not part of Nanking's core forces, so the fight between them and the Japanese could be put outside the category of a war between two nations. Had more been made of the presence of Chiang's Fifth Army, China might have been dragged into full-scale conflict. So the minimisation of his role was, in part, the product of his own desire to avoid an all-out confrontation with Japan until he had beaten the Communists.[9]

On 17 February the *North China Herald* ran eyewitness accounts of new troops with cavalry units moving into Shanghai. Their Western-style helmets distinguished them as Nanking troops, different from the southerners in their bamboo hats. T. V. Soong referred to 'Chiang Kai-shek troops' who were 'cheerfully ready to die side by side with their comrades of the gallant Nineteenth Route'. A statement at the end of February by the Nineteenth Route Army paid tribute to a Fifth Army division which 'has been fighting with courage and fortitude'. A letter to the *North China Daily News* from a hospital visitor who had seen wounded men from the division attested to their 'excessive bravery' in advancing and suffering 'rather high casualties'. An authoritative account of the battle by the historian Donald Jordan, published in 2001, contains a wealth of evidence to disprove the accepted version of the commander-in-chief standing to one side while the Route Army did all the fighting. As Chiang put it in a later interview: 'Who sent the Fifth Army, the 87th and 88th Divisions and the Revenue Guards to Shanghai to assist the Nineteenth Route Army who had no heavy artillery but only rifles and machine guns? Where did the Chinese heavy guns come from?'

When the assault began, the US Secretary of State, Henry Stimson, had suggested joint action with Britain to prevent further Japanese expansion. But London was cool, and the League of Nations showed blinkered even-handedness, reprimanding Japan for the attack and China for the assault on the monks, as if the two were comparable – even if the second had not been a Japanese provocation. There were flurries of concern in the West when shells landed on foreign concessions or threatened ships. But, as in Manchuria, nobody would take practical steps to hold back Japan even when its army landed at the end of February and marched in to bolster the lacklustre marines.

The Chinese counter-attacked and advanced in places. Japanese tanks were useless in fighting in the fields round the city where the narrow paths were easy to defend. In fierce battles for villages, the defenders set up 4 yards of barbed wire in front of their trenches, and a Chinese brigade staged five charges within an hour, losing a quarter of its officers. A division reported having 2,700 men put out of action in a single day. Tokyo's 200 planes widened their bombing range – one raid on the air force centre of Hangzhou damaged the wings of Chiang's aircraft parked there.

As the weight of the attack forced the defenders to fall back on a new line, General Cai of the Nineteenth Route Army received a visit from a Manchu princess known as Eastern Jewel, who had inveigled Sun Fo into giving her an introduction to the dashing soldier. She passed on secret information that the Japanese were going to throw another division into the Chapei–Wusong front. Accordingly, the Route Army concentrated there, disregarding a warning from Chiang of a possible flanking movement from the sea. The Japanese justified his prediction, landing thousands of troops at dawn under air protection, and then sweeping round behind the Chinese. According to the conspiratorial Major Tanaka, the Jewel had been sent to lure Nineteenth Army troops into the wrong place. In his diary, Chiang Kai-shek referred to her stories as the reason why the defenders had not followed his advice.[10]

The Chinese now abandoned Shanghai. Though keeping up their air raids, the attackers let them go to avoid a final stand, but arrested, abused and killed civilians at will. The *North China Daily News* described Chapei as a 'blazing bonfire' throwing up a glare so strong that a reporter could read his newspaper by its light half a mile away. More than 200,000 people sheltered in seventy makeshift camps. The Japanese set up a puppet administration in Chapei which encouraged opium dens and brothels to move in from the French Concession. As the historian Christian Henriot records, the troops 'flung themselves into systematic destruction in the zones they were occupying. Whatever had not been razed by bombardment and fire was either mined or dismantled and loaded onto Japanese ships.'[11]

Chinese forces involved in the fighting are reckoned to have totalled 63,000, though this may be an overstatement given the depleted condition of some divisions. Japan said it sent in 47,000 men; the Chinese put their numbers at 77,000. Estimates of Chinese dead ran from 4,600 to 6,080 with up to 10,000 missing, though Hallett Abend wrote of an overall toll of 35,000. The Japanese consulate put deaths on its side at a ludicrously low 385, with more than 2,000 wounded. A census report suggested half a million people fled. The city government reckoned damage of $1.5 billion. Twelve thousand dwellings were destroyed or damaged, along with 4,000 shops, 600 factories, 200 schools and five colleges. Hundreds of thousands were out of work. Farm land was chewed up. Railways were cut. The slowdown of trade badly affected tax and customs revenues.[12]

After a ceasefire on 3 March that enabled the government to return to Nanking from Luoyang, British and American diplomats joined peace talks, at which the Japanese pressed for demilitarisation of the Chinese city and the surrounding zone. This would have meant China withdrawing its troops while the treaty arrangements would allow Japan to retain forces in the settlement and on the river. Chiang told the British that this would be too great an insult, while Tokyo was keen to reach an agreement so that it could concentrate on Manchuria where the Kwantung Army had created the puppet state of Manchukuo* (Country of the Manchus) with the last Manchu emperor as nominal chief executive. Japan's focus on the north meant that there was surprisingly little reaction when a Korean émigré threw a bomb concealed in a water bottle during a ceremony in a Shanghai park to celebrate Hirohito's birthday. The head of the Japanese residents'

* Manchuguo in Pinyin.

association was killed on the spot. The military commander in Shanghai died a month later of wounds. The Minister to China lost a leg, and was sent an artificial limb by the Emperor. At other times, this would have been the spark for a fresh attack, but peace talks continued. Opposition to them came, rather, from Chinese hawks who pelted Nanking's negotiator with coins in the face to symbolise the 'sale of the nation'.[13]

In the end, a compromise saved face on both sides – the Japanese agreed to withdraw from Chinese areas within four weeks, and, while its troops were barred from the city, Nanking was allowed to send in national police. The document had to be taken to hospitals to be signed by the chief Chinese negotiator, who was receiving attention for his facial wounds, and the Japanese Minister, who was awaiting treatment for his leg.[14]

Much to its discontent, Chiang sent the Nineteenth Route Army back to rejoin the fight against the Communists. The Route Army's original commander, Chen Mingshu, who held senior posts in Nanking, stepped down in June, and left for Europe. He wanted a stiffer policy towards Japan, but he had other reasons for walking out. He had regional political ambitions, and, as he travelled to Paris, his deputy headed for Hong Kong with $700,000 in government money. Even more dramatically, T. V. Soong also chose this moment to resign. The Finance Minister favoured a tougher line against the Japanese, too, but, like Chen, had other motives. Though he had managed to balance the books for four months, the financial outlook was dire, exacerbated by the drop in revenue from Shanghai and Manchuria. The bond market, the main source of funds, had suffered a major collapse. But Chiang wanted to spend another $5 million on a fresh anti-Communist campaign in Jiangxi. Soong denounced the 'vicious cycle of debt' and called for economies and internal reforms. 'Have not banditry and communism thrived on political military and economic maladjustments, and will they not respond better to a systematic, if unspectacular, combination of politico-military-economic treatment?' he asked.[15]

Following Chiang's example, T.V. was using resignation as a weapon to get his own way. He kept in touch with Wang Jingwei, and was back in office after a month with an agreement that halved the increase in army expenditure. Despite his return to government, Soong maintained close links with the financiers critical of Chiang for his military spending. He kept up good relations with his middle sister, Qingling, who could be a conduit to the left. He had identified himself as an advocate of resisting Japan. A fresh trial of strength between the two men could only be a matter of time. On top of this, there were stories of a family falling-out between the Finance Minister and his eldest sister after she objected to his love affair with a friend of hers. Given the way Ailing influenced her younger sister, this created personal friction with the Chiangs to add to the policy discords.[16]

Chiang's position was buttressed when the government gave him the title of Generalissimo, to mark his primacy as its military leader which, given the weight of the army in the regime, also signified his overall supremacy. The head of the inquiry commission on Manchuria sent by the League of Nations, Lord Lytton, told a dinner in Nanking that, while the outside world might have difficulty with Chinese names, one 'is familiar all over the world – Chiang Kai-shek. All the world knows General Chiang Kai-shek as a great soldier.'

The commission produced a report that was generally favourable to the Nationalists. Though conceding some rights to Japan, it pronounced Manchuria an integral part of China, said the Mukden Incident could not be regarded as legitimate self-defence, and described Manchukuo as a Japanese creation, not an independent state. Tokyo, it found, had violated the Covenant of the League. When the report was debated at the League's headquarters in Geneva, Japan cast the only negative vote, and quit the international body. It knew that, whatever the Lytton team had decided, neither China nor the League was going to take action. A Japanese report even had Chiang remarking: 'If Japan will be satisfied with Manchuria, well, we aren't happy about it but we can pretend they aren't there.'[17]

It was not all plain sailing for the Japanese in the north-east, however. A Manchurian commander, General Ma, who had joined the puppet administration, raided the treasury, and rode off to set up a resistance force of 3,500 men. One guerrilla attack got as far as the Manchukuo capital of Changchun. Another stole six Japanese planes from an airfield. When the Kwantung Army announced finding Ma's corpse, dressed in a general's uniform and lying beside a Mongolian pony, it turned out to have been a decoy body – Ma slipped over the Soviet border, and got back to China via Europe.[18]

Manchuria's outlaws staged unremitting attacks on towns and travellers: after one raid on a train, they held 350 Japanese and Koreans for two weeks. In another kidnapping, bandits grabbed the eighteen-year-old English wife of an American oil company executive and the son of a British general at a racecourse, and kept them for seven weeks in a mud hut hidden in reeds. 'They are going to cut off our ears and I rather want to keep mine,' Muriel Pawley wrote in a message sent with the $1.2 million ransom demand. 'Am filthy and long for a bath. The chow is awful.' In a letter to her father, she begged to be got out of 'this Hell incarnate', and asked for a powder puff and lipstick. Eventually, a militia unit freed them.

Despite such local difficulties, the Kwantung Army was sabre-rattling on the frontier between Manchuria and the mountainous province of Jehol beyond the Great Wall.* There was also a threat from the Dogmeat General of Shandong, who had failed in one attempt to retake his province, but now made another comeback bid – however, he was shot dead in a train station by the nephew of a general he had killed years earlier. His concubines divided up what they could grab from the estate, one getting a locksmith to open the warlord's safe and filching the jewels inside.[19]

Wang Jingwei, as head of the Executive Yuan, blamed the Young Marshal for his ineffectiveness in the north which he contrasted with the 'gallant resistance' of the defence of Shanghai. 'This was admittedly an extraordinary feat and is therefore hardly one which may reasonably be expected of you,' he added in a telegram to Zhang. 'Although nearly a year has elapsed [since the Mukden Incident], there has been absolutely no achievement to your credit.' Wang then played the resignation gambit. Saying he could not meet Zhang's financial requests, he felt that he, himself, had to step down, and hoped the Marshal would do the same, which would be 'an inestimable blessing to China south of the Great Wall'. The younger man responded that organising resistance took time, but did submit his resignation. Meeting reporters in a Manchu palace in Peiping, he said he would go to study at Oxford or Cambridge, visit Italy, Turkey and Germany, and then settle in France.[20]

After the whole government resigned, Chiang stepped in, becoming Chairman of the Military Council for North China – the *North China Daily News* wrote that 'General Chiang Kai-shek yesterday became the Government of China'. Wang left for diabetes treatment in Hamburg, and

---

* Jehol, also known as Rehe, no longer exists as an independent province, being split between Hebei and Liaoning.

was succeeded by T. V. Soong as the cabinet withdrew its resignation. The Marshal, who still had the support of northern generals, continued as a member of the military council in Peiping, but his authority had been sapped. With the political crisis settled to his advantage, Chiang could turn to his main priority, for which he received the backing of an American visitor on an inspection tour of missionary work. The future Secretary of State, John Foster Dulles, said it would be ridiculous to resist Japan before the Communist issue was settled. As the governor of Jiangxi put it, invoking an old Chinese saying about adversaries, the Japanese were a skin wound; the Communists were a disease of the heart.[21]

The campaigns Chiang launched against the Red Armies in 1932 in the hope of liquidating them before having to deal with the Japanese involved a huge commitment of troops in four provinces. A major assault, accompanied by an economic blockade, was directed at the base area north of the Yangtze known as Oyuwan.* The Communists there won several victories, but the pressure forced them to move west on a long march to Sichuan, where they established a base area of 35,000 square miles with a well-supplied army of 80,000, including a 2,000-strong regiment of women. In Oyuwan, Chiang tried a strategy used in the defeat of the Taiping rebels in the nineteenth century. He ordered the establishment of civilian volunteer units in villages, their leaders trained and equipped by the government. Villages were to come to one another's aid, using roads built between them. Four army divisions per province would handle major threats.

The policy depended on villagers being ready to volunteer and work together against the Communists. But the regime lacked the political message to enthuse rural people, and came to count on the local elite to dragoon the population while soldiers implemented ruthless repression. As Chiang put it, 'in the emancipated territories, a thorough house-cleaning is being carried out'. Confirmed Communists were shot out of hand while those ready to turn over a new leaf were put to work as labourers.[22]

Next, Chiang turned south for a fourth campaign in Jiangxi, applying the village militia strategy to back up the army, and trying to bring local

---

* Also E-Yu-Wan. The name was an acronym of the classical names of the provinces at whose junction it lay.

administration under tighter control. He stationed 140,000 troops as blocking forces on the province's eastern and southern borders, and sent 100,000 men to confront the 65,000-strong Red Army. His campaign began well when the Communists suffered heavy casualties after launching an attack out of their mountainous stronghold. Nationalist planes helped to repulse an attempted foray into Guangdong. Then the main Communist force won a string of encounters, showing exceptional mobility as it wheeled round Nationalist units.

The expansion of Chiang's forces had meant a steady deterioration in their quality. Visiting the front, the British writer Peter Fleming found soldiers stealing food and turning to banditry when defeated. Their military abilities, discipline and equipment were poor. Officers thought only of defence. As for the local people, 'press gangs, conscript labour, extra taxes, and many forms of indignity and extortion have made their lives a burden to them, and in return they have received only the most inadequate protection. If anything is calculated to make the Chinese peasant turn spontaneously to Communism ... it is having troops permanently billeted on him.'[23]

The government established some welfare centres to try to win over the peasants. But they had little success. A League of Nations expert who visited one in a Jiangxi district of 18,000 inhabitants reported that just sixty people were receiving medical care at the hospital, which had twenty beds. Only 10 per cent of people joined the centre's co-operative farms. Elsewhere in Jiangxi, an agricultural economist reported, the war meant that 'weeds are growing rank in the rice fields, homes lie in ruins, bleak and forlorn, village upon village is totally depopulated, here and there a family huddles together in a shack, facing the winter's cold and gradual starvation.'[24]

At Christmas, Chiang broke off from the Jiangxi campaign and went with Meiling and the Kungs to spend the holiday at Xikou. They made part of the journey in a bus: seeing some soldiers behaving badly by the roadside, the Generalissimo stopped the vehicle and ordered their arrest. In his home village, he stayed in the family house, visited ancestral tombs and his mother's grave, and took walks in the crisp air. On 1 January, the Japanese made their next move.[25]

The scene was a coastal border town, Shanhaiguan, the gateway from Manchuria to China proper between mountains and sea at the start of the Great Wall. Japan had the right to station a small garrison there under the

Boxer Treaty. After provocative night manoeuvres, its soldiers announced the discovery of two bombs in their quarters. The town was bombed and shelled. Tanks and an armoured train joined the attack. On the third day, engulfed in smoke and flames, Shanhaiguan fell. The death toll among the defenders was put at nearly 600, with 300 Japanese killed or wounded. 'Are we going back to a state of savagery and barbarism?' the Young Marshal asked.[26]

In Tokyo, the Foreign Minister said that the province of Jehol was part of Manchukuo which needed to be defended against the Chinese. The governor there was a former bandit and sidekick of the Old Marshal called Tang Yulin, who ordered his wives to practise horse-riding each morning and was known for his cruelty and corruption. He had a drug factory in the grounds of his palace, and sold off plundered Manchu relics in foreign treaty ports. His 20,000-man army was a ragtag force.[27]

Travelling to Peiping, T. V. Soong called the region a powder keg. He arranged for imperial treasures to be moved to Nanking to protect them from the Japanese and from officials who were selling them to antique dealers. Zhang Xueliang and W. H. Donald drove through blizzards to the Jehol capital of Chengde where the only troops they saw were those guarding the opium factory. Governor Tang listened to the visitors urging him to resist, and did nothing. The steep mountains of his province should have provided excellent defensive terrain, but the Japanese brought planes and artillery to bear, slaughtering the local troops in bare, narrow valleys which offered no shelter, and where their camels, donkeys and bullock carts were sitting ducks for air attacks. Nanking declined to provide money or supplies, and so-called volunteers sent in were badly armed and untrained.[28]

The Japanese advance through snowstorms and biting winds was spearheaded by free-ranging columns of cavalry, trucks and armoured cars. Dogs carried communications between units. Defections weakened the Chinese further. Incendiary bombs burned down forests where their troops were hiding. The province's inhabitants believed the newcomers could be no worse than the old regime.

Governor Tang commanded lorries to take his belongings to safety, depriving the defenders of transport. When the trucks arrived at a Great Wall pass, Nationalist troops seized the freight and sent them back to Chengde. The Young Marshal ordered Tang's arrest, but he had fled on horseback with 200 bodyguards. After a heavy air attack, the city was taken by a brigade of the Kwantung Army, followed by lorries carrying Korean girls for the troops. The Japanese pursued the retreating Chinese to the Great Wall. From there, they could look down on the plain towards Peiping where martial law was declared.[29]

The most trenchant analysis of the disaster came from T. V. Soong. He contrasted Japan's preparations, mechanisation and equipment, and the Chinese army with 'no staff work, with the generals staying hundreds of miles behind, with no transport except of the most primitive sort, which took several weeks for supplies to reach the front, no liaison between different commands, no anti-aircraft guns and trenching materials or artillery, and soldiers trained only in drill ground requirements'. He blasted Chinese generals, who 'strut about in field-grey uniforms with Sam Browne belts', for their old-fashioned mindset and their *sauve qui peut* mentality. The greatest blame lay in 'the system which permits the existence of vast armies of ill-fed, ill-armed and ill-trained soldiery which in time of crisis degenerates into helpless mobs'.[30]

While this fresh disaster was unfolding in the north, Chiang had returned to the campaign in Jiangxi where there were some successes – the Nanking news agency told of one battle in a forest where the corpses bled 'black blood into the red sand' as the Red Army was forced to retreat, leaving behind shoes, belts, puttees, broken umbrellas, papers, books and red-starred caps. But the Communists ambushed two Nationalist divisions and inflicted heavy losses – one commander committed suicide. The Generalissimo decided to call an end to the campaign, and to find a culprit for the debacle in Jehol.[31]

On 8 March 1933, he and T. V. Soong arrived by rail in the town of Baoding south of Peiping. Waiting there was the Young Marshal, aboard his personal train. Zhang was called to a cool, five-minute meeting at which his resignation was accepted. Chiang compared the situation to an unstable boat that had to be righted by dropping one of those on board. The Marshal would be replaced by the Generalissimo's associate, He Yingqin.[32]

Two days later, Zhang addressed his troops outside Peiping. 'We came into China proper to effect national unification,' he told them. 'But the result is that we are now homeless.' He urged them to obey Chiang's orders. If they remembered their duty to the nation, the objective of returning to Manchuria could be attained, he added. Then he flew out in his Ford aircraft with two wives, four bodyguards, and W. H. Donald. A brass band played when they landed at Shanghai. Wearing a dark coat of silk and fur, the Young Marshal looked tired as he drove to T. V. Soong's house to meet officials. He invited local journalists to a press conference, but they boycotted it when guards frisked them for weapons. Somebody put up a scroll at the front door reading, 'Do you remember that you have lost Manchuria? And now, through you, Jehol is lost to China.'[33]

Zhang moved to a house on the Avenue Foch, and Donald arranged for treatment by an American drug specialist who put him and his equally addicted wives to sleep with anaesthetics, and then injected their arms with fluid drawn from blisters induced on their stomachs. They were unconscious for several days. 'If he dies, so will you,' a Manchurian aide warned the doctor. But the Marshal and his wives came round. Cured of his habit, he set out with Donald on an ocean voyage to Europe. At sea, he flirted with Mussolini's daughter whose husband, Count Ciano, was returning from a diplomatic posting in China. When the Marshal went to Rome in May, she took him to meet her father. By then, he had put on so much weight that he had to buy new clothes. In Britain, he called on the Prime Minister, Ramsay MacDonald, at his official country residence at Chequers, met eminent figures at the Dorchester Hotel in London, and rented a house behind the seafront in Brighton where he held black-tie poker parties that began after dinner and continued behind drawn curtains till the following afternoon.[34]

In the Marshal's old domain, Japan's troops ran into stiff opposition on the Great Wall from snipers and sword-wielding defenders. Returning from Europe to resume his chairmanship of the Executive Yuan, Wang Jingwei recorded a speech for the Star Motion Picture Company in Shanghai urging resistance to Japan. But, after its first reverses, the Kwantung Army advanced on Peiping. At a meeting with Nationalist officials that lasted till 4.30 a.m., the Japanese demanded demilitarisation of an area of 115,800 square miles with a population of 6 million. Otherwise, the old capital would be attacked. The Chinese agreed, and a date for signing the accord was set for 31 May in the walled coastal town of Tangku.*[35]

The Chinese delegation arrived in a long train of Wagons-Lits carriages which parked on a siding. Two Japanese destroyers were moored at battle

* Tanggu in Pinyin.

stations in a river estuary opposite them. 'Presently from the curtained coaches there descended nearly a score of high Chinese officials,' Hallett Abend of the *New York Times* wrote. 'No automobiles or carriages had been provided. They had to walk down the narrow, dusty little Tangku streets which had no sidewalks. At the gate of the Japanese Consulate, sentries brusquely challenged the Chinese, and kept them standing in the hot sun for nearly ten minutes. When they were finally admitted, they were received by Japanese officials who had been carefully selected from ranks below those of the Chinese delegates.'[36]

The Japanese presented a written document to be signed within an hour. The head of the Chinese team insisted this was a purely military accord without political ramifications. The Japanese cut him off, saying he either had to agree or not – that was all. He signed. Champagne was served. Then the Chinese walked back through the dust and heat to their train.

The Nationalist soldiers left Peiping quietly: an observer described them as going 'in small groups sauntering along rather dejectedly, and seemingly quite at random with rickshaws and carts loaded with every conceivable kind of household article'. Jehol, where a new governor arrived from Manchukuo with 3,000 cavalry, was incorporated into the puppet domain. Demilitarisation was a sham as far as the Japanese were concerned since the protocols imposed on China after the Boxer revolt gave them the right to station troops in the area; so they were free to build up their garrisons there. The zone Japan dominated included nearly all Hebei province north of Peiping, and the big port of Tianjin. Its officers tried to foment autonomist movements elsewhere in the north, offering $300,000 to one petty warlord who was, however, assassinated in his hotel bathroom in Tianjin. The Chinese commanders left in the region operated with virtual autonomy of Nanking, making deals with the Japanese and manoeuvring for survival.[37]

The appeasement provoked a fresh wave of demonstrations, particularly by students in Peiping, providing another rift between educated youth and the regime. Chiang's southern opponents accused him of having given the Japanese a free hand to interfere in China's internal affairs with the Tangku Truce. Qingling Soong organised an international conference in Shanghai where eighty participants met secretly by candlelight to denounce 'the base betrayal by the Chinese ruling classes and the Kuomintang'. T. V. Soong showed his colours by targeting tariff increases against imports from Japan – Tokyo revenged itself by sabotaging his plan for a committee of foreign advisers to stimulate investment in China, persuading American and European bankers not to join for fear of losing Japanese business. In the far north, the Christian General formed an anti-Japanese army which defeated Manchukuo troops but was then cornered between the Kwantung Army and Nationalist forces moved up by Chiang, who had no desire to see Feng reassert himself. Faced with this double threat, the Christian General handed over to two subordinates – one was arrested by the Nationalists after being shot and wounded in Tianjin; he was sent to Nanking and executed. Feng himself retreated to a mountain temple, rising at 4 a.m. to write poetry and sixty sheets of Chinese characters a day. One poem spoke of the nation getting weaker by the day:

> It is unbearable to think about! Unbearable to see!
> Let men of spirit arise and act!
> Recover our lost lands![38]

Wang Jingwei compared China to a man whose life was in grave danger. Describing Japan as a mad dog, Chiang wrote in his diary that asking it to be reasonable would be like asking a tiger to give up its fur. 'So long as there is any breath of life in me, I will not cease fighting the enemy,' he pledged. The truce, he added, provided a breathing space. The international situation might improve. 'At a time of national humiliation we should "lie in faggots and taste gall" and should never be discouraged or relax our vigilance,' he wrote to himself. 'We must draw up a plan for national reconstruction and carry it out with dispatch and effectiveness in ten years!'[39]

CHAPTER 14

~~~~

Follow the Leader

IN CHIANG'S IDEAL WORLD, China would have been the traditional family on which the country's society was based. The 480 million children would look up unquestioningly to their father figure, following his dictates and showing endless fortitude as they eliminated the noxious influence of the wayward Communist son and repaired the damage done by the aggressive Japanese neighbour. The paterfamilias did not need to be liked, but he had to be respected as the embodiment of national salvation. Were the people's devotion to that aim as wholehearted as his mother's had been to raising her children, he said, China would gain its place among the great powers.

'If his children behave well, the father feels they reflect honour upon him; if badly, they disgrace him,' Chiang noted. 'In a narrow sense, the family means simply a household. In a broader sense, however, it includes all civic and Government organs, including the Revolutionary Party, and the schools.' Army units directly under Chiang's command were regarded as 'family troops' and his close advisers, the Chen brothers, were 'adopted sons'. 'There exists not much difference in the management of the family and that of troops,' the leader said. 'I have often compared the army to a family wherein I look upon the soldiers under me as a father regards his children.'[1]

The national family needed to be told what to do rather than having a voice in its own affairs. Its thought had to be unified, so that it would not be tempted to seek different ways of thinking and create disorder. At the start of the Nationalist revolution in Canton, Chiang's guide Dai Jitao had compared China to a sheet of blank paper that could be coloured as its rulers chose. The Generalissimo told officials to treat ordinary people as if they were three-year-olds, and spoke of initiating a control system that would mobilise millions within hours in a 'strict, huge and healthy organisation'. 'I believe that unless everyone has absolute trust in one man, we cannot reconstruct the nation and we cannot complete the revolution,' he added.[2]

Like the Emperors before him and the Communist leader Deng Xiaoping after him, Chiang stressed the need for stability and order, and opposed political diversity. Democracy was ruled out as 'absolutely impossible for the entire nation' – instead, a carefully selected national congress would meet every three years to rubber-stamp legislation. As one loyalist put it, foreign aggression and the persistence of feudalism meant that the country needed a 'Chinese-style dictatorship'.

The Lixingshe movement set up by dedicated supporters from Whampoa in 1932 to ensure authoritarian allegiance to the leader grew to number half a million members, with offshoots such as the political shock troops known as the Blue Shirts. But the notion of a continuous mass movement remained deeply suspect to the militarised bureaucracy in Nanking – a major difference between Chiang's regime and Mussolini's Italy or Hitler's Germany. It presented an authoritarian view of Chinese tradition as a historic justification for dictatorship with a conservative cultural policy to buttress the supremacy of the state and its chief. Intellectuals were told to sacrifice their individual liberty for the sake of the nation. If the regime had fascist tendencies, it was 'Confucian Fascism', as the historian Frederic Wakeman has dubbed it.[3]

What became known as the Nanking decade was the moment to implement reform, modernisation and unity for the national family. While the years from 1927 to 1937 were marked by recurrent fighting, large areas were not affected, and the government could claim a national role not seen since the fall of the Manchus. After the upheaval of the warlord era, it was now up to Nanking to shape post-imperial China.[4]

With strong economic growth in the major cities and the development of some agricultural areas after land purchases by commercially oriented capitalists, the era produced material progress building on the plans drawn up after the initial victory of the Northern Expedition. A national currency was launched to replace provincial notes and coins. Income tax was introduced. Joint ventures were established with German firms to build trucks and aircraft. Big new buildings went up in major cities where the infrastructure was improved. Chiang's brother-in-law, H. H. Kung, proposed harnessing the power of the Yangtze for electric power. New crop strains were investigated, and a model farm was opened outside the capital. Prison reform was proclaimed, with a programme to build model jails in which inmates would be reformed. Pharmacy colleges were set up in Shanghai and Nanking. The Academia Sinica University researched everything from astronomy to agriculture. A simplified textual language, restricted to 800 characters, was evolved as an aid to literacy.[5]

Airlines were set up as joint ventures with American and German companies. Foreign countries used part of the indemnities they had received after the Boxer Rebellion to finance infrastructure projects, so long as the equipment was bought from them. During the 1930s, 3,000 miles of railways were constructed, and the completion of the link between Wuhan and Canton meant it was possible to travel between Peiping and Guangdong by train. Hundreds of locomotives and freight wagons were imported. China's first trucks and locomotives were assembled from foreign parts, along with a plane able to fly at 100 mph. By 1936, 15,000 miles of roads had been built, bringing the national total to 68,000 miles. An impressed American mission in 1934 reported a 'vast change' coming over China.

Despite the attempts of the Chen brothers to impose conformity, intellectual enquiry and cultural development sprouted among intellectuals, students and enlightened bourgeoisie. Leading writers, most of whom veered to the left, saw literature as playing a role in promoting social progress. Shanghai's film industry boomed. China engaged with the world to a degree not known before, both in its own presence abroad and in the inroads of foreign influences. Its modern-minded diplomats made their presence felt at the League of Nations and in international conferences. The country regained control over tariffs, maritime customs, and the salt monopoly, as well as steadily increasing its authority over foreign concessions. Despite all its problems, and the loss of Manchuria and Jehol, Nanking kept alive the notion of territorial integrity, leading the historian William Kirby to write of a record of 'stunning accomplishments from a position of unenviable weakness'.[6]

But most of the progress was still confined to small urban areas on the coast and to a tiny fraction of the population.* While Nanking sought to lay the foundations of a modern state and set up the requisite institutions, its reformist members were hobbled by lack of resources, the government's limited authority over large parts of the country, the conservatism of the rural elite, entrenched traditions, and a system that concentrated real power at the apex, in particular in the person of the Generalissimo who represented the state. Modernisation was viewed largely as a matter of economics and technology, not political evolution. Excessive privilege was invested in those favoured by the regime, and the stability and administrative framework needed for change was absent. As the historian Prasenjit Duara has put it, China was 'characterised by a weak state and a strong statist ideology'.[7]

Despite announcements of civil service reforms, many of the same functionaries stayed in place, and recruits came mainly either from the ranks of old warlord officials or the relatives of well-placed Kuomintang members. T. V. Soong still had to struggle to obtain funds from provincial governments. The business levy was not applied to farmers or small local merchants. Revenue collection from bigger fish was marked by corruption. Virtually the only people to pay income tax were civil servants since they were the only ones whose earnings the state could verify. Property taxes were hobbled by lack of information about who owned what – in some provinces, half the land was not mentioned on the registers. Japanese control of the four north-eastern provinces choked off revenue from there, and smuggling reduced the take from customs duties.[8]

Much of road and rail building was concentrated in areas where the army was fighting the Communists, rather than where it was needed for economic development. Immense regions had no rail connections – the track from the Yunnan capital of Kunming to the border with Vietnam was the only one in the whole south-west. A line to Xi'an was the sole spur westward from the main north–south connection, and there were no tracks

* Recent historical work on Republican China has emphasised advances made in the Nanking decade after earlier accounts had stressed its problems. Both schools can claim correctness, but on a different scale. Reappraising Republican China, Wakeman and Edmonds (eds) gives the latest 'revisionist' view.

to the south-eastern ports between Ningbo and Canton. Only a quarter of new roads had hard surfaces; a motorcyclist wrote that, after a day's rain, the highway south of Shanghai became a death trap at over 12 mph while a traveller on a bus from Hangzhou described how the vehicle 'jumped from hole to hole, and simply ploughed itself through mud and mire' in 'a tortuous quagmire not worthy to be classed with the dignity of a road'. Chiang, the Soongs and the elite took a quantum travel leap by using aircraft, but three quarters of China's transport was by unmechanised methods. On one campaign, the Generalissimo flew in two hours from Guizhou to Sichuan; others making the journey by foot or in sedan chairs took seventeen days.[9]

The capital was, in its way, symbolic of the gulf between the thin crust of modernity and the unchanging mass below. Nanking boasted smart new government and party buildings, the broad avenue leading to the Sun Yat-sen mausoleum, tall broadcasting masts and seaplanes flying up and down the Yangtze. Behind the bold front, the city was a mass of alleys, huts and low tenements. In 1933, a visitor noticed that the big sports stadium was covered with weeds, and the swimming bath had been cracked by the sun.[10]

Chiang's army contained some well-trained and well-equipped forces which gave the regime its military sheen. German advisers schooled elite units – Chiang sent his adopted son, Wei-kuo, to join the German army where he would participate in the annexation of Austria. An Italian mission arrived to train China's air force but proved less effective: most cadets at its centre in Luoyang came from prominent families and all those who were not killed in crashes were automatically given graduation certificates. Only when the Americans moved in with their training school at Hangzhou did a more effective group of pilots emerge.[11]

Still, many Nationalist units consisted of warlord troops who showed no improvement from the 1920s. Though Chiang's own circle was made up mainly of Whampoa graduates, other commanders from militarist forces were inexperienced in modern warfare. Promotions were more likely to be for political reasons than to recognise ability. With the army assuming unprecedented importance, this produced a central weakness. Generals ran most of China's provinces. The centre of power was the Military Council, and wherever Chiang happened to be. The army replaced the imperial mandarinate as the ladder for upwardly mobile young men from modest backgrounds following in the footsteps of the supreme leader. The regime was run on military lines, and its leader's concept of the state was rooted in his regimented view of life.[12]

Chiang's intolerance of dissent was mirrored in the system below him. As a result, there was no development of a political structure or an innovative administrative staff that could deal with China's diversity and the scale of its problems – on the contrary, power was concentrated on one man and the cliques surrounding him. The apparatus of repression grew steadily. Anti-subversion laws were draconian, and applied indiscriminately in the absence of a proper legal system, with free use of summary executions, arbitrary detention and torture. Terror squads disposed of critics. The editor of the leading Shanghai daily, who threatened to become a rallying point for the city's bourgeoisie as chairman of the civic association, was assassinated by Nationalist agents when he stopped to stretch his legs while driving back from holiday with his family – Big-Eared Du took control of the paper. The leader of the League for the Defence of Civil Rights was shot in Shanghai as he got into his car with his fifteen-year-old son – his friend, the noted left-wing novelist Ding Ling, was more fortunate; she was kept under arrest for three years, but allowed to be with her lover and provided with sheets, food and books before being released and slipping off to join the Communists.[13]

The factionalism which the Kuomintang had shown from its earliest days – fuelled by its leader's divide-and-rule tactics – meant there were fissures even among those who proclaimed their desire to eliminate opposition and solidify the regime. One such running battle opposed the secret police chief, Dai Li, and the Chen brothers, Lifu and Guofu, nephews of Chiang's Shanghai mentor, Chen Qimei.

Dai, a former Whampoa cadet and native of Chiang's province of Zhejiang, ran the innocently named Military Bureau of Statistics (Juntong), along with more clandestine outfits. His agents carried out intelligence, assassination and sabotage of political enemies and Japanese, and infiltrated the police to manipulate and control them. A Communist saying had it that, out of every 100,000 people, 3,000 were Nationalist spies. Dai used men from his home area as his communications staff because he could speak to them in an impenetrable local dialect that avoided the need for code. Already close to Chiang because of their shared provincial origin, Dai forged an even stronger bond by travelling to Xi'an to be with his boss in the kidnapping drama of 1936. Dai's critics said they could see the cruelty in his smile, his gold-capped teeth glinting. But he was also a subtle politician with qualities of personal leadership lacking in many of the other Nationalist kingpins. Above all, he was ready to do anything to defend the Generalissimo, telling his agents that a chief like Chiang required 'ears and eyes' everywhere who did not need to adhere too closely to the law.

The Chen brothers ran the Organisation Department of the Kuomintang, which supervised the party, and, from that power base, built up a following among officials. Their group, the CC Clique, became one of the regime's most significant political outfits, drawing support from rightist party factions. By 1931, the Clique accounted for 15 per cent of members of the Central Executive Committee. It trained loyalists at the Central Political Academy who went to infiltrate provincial governments as agents for Chiang. Drawing finance from government-backed banks, they branched out into publishing and propaganda, and ran their own intelligence and security arm. Referring to Dai Li's rival operation, Lifu told his group: 'Chiang needs two sets of eyes and cars.'[14]

The Chens were also bitterly opposed to the ultra-loyalist Lixingshe movement and the Blue Shirt Society set up in 1932 on a basis of veneration for the state, extreme nationalism including anti-Japanese terror, complete dedication to Chiang, and a belief that all opponents should be eliminated. The Blue Shirts urged that 'negative elements' in society should be killed with 'extreme measures, causing the masses to become so frightened that they . . . will not again transgress the laws'. Chinese classical tradition and its heroes were melded with devotion to the national leader as the path to salvation. Dai Li headed the group's security squads which carried out assassinations and intimidation.[15]

Chiang passed the Presidency of the Republic to a man who was no threat to his supremacy. Lin Sen, who had served as President of the Senate after the 1911 revolution, was the model of a Kuomintang elder with his round spectacles, goatee beard and reputation for wise counsel, except that nobody asked him for it very often. His official status made no difference to the Generalissimo's supremacy. At the head of the Executive Yuan and the Military Committee, Chiang controlled both arms of the regime. At one point, he held twenty-five different posts.[16]

He worked immensely hard, often exhausting himself. His inability to delegate meant that he got involved in fields where he was unqualified to make decisions – he even decided which fingerprinting system the police should adopt. His long speeches, delivered in a high-pitched voice marked by his provincial accent, were schoolmasterish admonitions in which he often equated himself with the nation. His audience was expected to go away and do as it was told. When the leader took a reality check, the results could be shocking. Early in 1930, for example, he paid a surprise visit to government departments to see how far they were following instructions to work harder, and were observing the abolition of the Lunar New Year holiday under a decree adopting the Western calendar. Only at the Interior Ministry did he find anybody at their desks. 'This points to one important fact – that the Chinese people have no respect for laws,' he told the government council. 'Inertia is our most powerful enemy . . . In all the Government offices, there is no noticeable activity. Everybody is sitting about and doing nothing. Indeed, it is difficult to tell whether the offices are still functioning.'[17]

'The revolution is in danger of failing, and the entire nation has gradually lost trust in the party,' he warned at the end of 1931. By the following year, he considered that 'the Chinese revolution has failed'. Government activity, he complained, consisted almost solely of passing round documents. 'With regard to practical work, Chinese either do not know how, or – if they know – they are slow in the extreme.' Party members had not paid enough attention to individual moral training, and had 'spent too much time putting up posters, shouting slogans and issuing manifestos rather than getting down to actual work . . . We must regulate our minds and be sincere in our aims, dispel dangerous ideas, sink personal differences, and act according to the dictates of conscience.' To illustrate how officials fell short of proper standards of behaviour, he cited party members going to Kuomintang headquarters in carpet slippers.[18]

Chiang should also have focused more closely on the wider problems affecting the country. Health, welfare and social services were notable by their absence. Disease was rife. Nearly half the children died before they were five. The Director of Health in Nanking blamed 50 per cent of the country's deaths on bad sanitation. There were 30,000 hospital beds, 5,000 registered doctors and 1,700 nurses for 450 million people. If Chiang had a dental clinic established in Nanking, with a Western adviser, his interest was essentially personal given his continual problem with his teeth.[19]

Education was in almost as poor a state. The government's target of free schooling for all would have required annual expenditure of $260 million: the budget allocation never went above $42 million, and was frequently half that figure. Schools of even the most rudimentary kind were few and far between in the countryside. Modern textbooks were more expensive and less available than the traditional brush, ink and paper. As in so many areas, the Nationalists were starting from an extremely low base. The number of secondary schools was almost trebled between 1926 and 1935 but still only reached 3,000, with 500,000 students. Even in Shanghai, only 2 per cent of the population had been to high school – in Western China, the figure dropped to 0.004 per cent. A League of Nations mission put the university population at 30,000.

A movement for 'plain speech' to replace classic literary Chinese did produce major changes in teaching, but its impact was mainly in urban centres. There were interesting initiatives such as a rural education movement and 'work-study units' developed by the reformer Tao Xingzhi, but these were only a drop in the bucket of need and ran into political opposition from those who preferred peasants to remain uneducated. Private schools for the middle classes in cities often taught a foreign curriculum. The real prize of education abroad further widened the divide: the Commercial Press in Shanghai paid American college graduates four times as much as those who had studied in China, and guaranteed them a custom-made desk, book shelf, crystal ink stand and rattan chair. In a country where literary accomplishment and learning had traditionally been venerated, the educational shortcomings of the Nanking decade were symptomatic of a regime in which military force was pre-eminent, and intellectuals were pressed to serve the corporatist state.[20]

The Kuomintang elite came mainly from the cities, or felt most at home there; in this respect, Chiang was atypical with his village roots and his frequent returns to Xikou – though his wife was a symbol of the urban, foreign-educated upper class. But, in the 1930s, only fifteen cities had more than 200,000 inhabitants and the population of urban centres with over 100,000 inhabitants accounted for only 4.5 per cent of the Chinese. In 1934, an economist, Yao Xinning, put the working rural population at

360 million, compared to 1.4 million industrial workers and 2.2 million soldiers.[21]

The village remained the fundamental social unit, far removed from the modernity of the coastal cities. It would usually consist of mud or adobe huts, sometimes strengthened with wood. Many contained only a dozen or fewer houses where the peasants lived with their animals. There was no power or sanitation. These were self-sufficient communities, illiterate, self-perpetuating, deeply traditional and inward looking, their horizons limited by lack of communications. Authority lay with the landlords or their agents; the national government was an abstraction. The regime made gestures – Chiang included agriculture in a programme of economic reforms he promulgated in 1935; new strains of rice and wheat were introduced on a small scale; there were talks about setting up a fertiliser factory. But the regime's engagement with the countryside was strictly limited, and frequently oppressive as it was conducted through the sieve of local power-holders.

A co-operative movement established 15,000 local societies, half of them offering cheap credit; but they were often used as a new milch cow by those running them, usually the local gentry – in some provinces, it was said that only half the available money actually went to the farmers. Serious change would have included the establishment of a national register of property ownership, redistribution of land and rent reform, plus a reduction in interest rates. But, when a Farmers' Bank was opened, its main object was to enable Chiang to draw more revenue for his military campaigns from the opium trade by offering drug producers and merchants financial services. It had no audits. When one was suggested, Chiang flew into a rage.[22]

Most of China's 58 million farms were uneconomically small, and tilled by humans, not animals or machines. Forty per cent of land was rented, often at rates that were high compared to the cash value of what was produced. In Chiang's home province of Zhejiang, 3.3 per cent of the population owned 53 per cent of the land; in Guangdong, the same proportion of land belonged to 2 per cent of the inhabitants. The handful of experts trained abroad in modern techniques often preferred to live in towns rather than where their knowledge could have been put to practical effect. Human waste, much used as fertiliser, spread disease. By one estimate, a quarter of deaths in China were attributed to parasites carried in faeces. Chemicals could have made the night soil safe, but they were not available. Imported fertilisers were subject to duties as high as 50 per cent.[23]

Research by the economic historian Loren Brandt suggests that agriculture grew more rapidly than the population, but average per capita annual income in the countryside was still only around $26. Fifty per cent of the revenue of farmers went to landlords. Moneylenders charged up to 6 per cent a month – in silk zones of Jiangsu and Zhejiang, the rate went to 100 per cent for forty days. Only a quarter of farmers could live without going into debt; a bad harvest, flooding or drought was a disaster. With no bargaining power, they were subject to the vagaries of markets. 'Rural China,' the economist Yao Xinning concluded, 'is now bankrupt.' The British social scientist R. H. Tawney compared Chinese farmers to 'a man standing permanently up to his neck in water so that even a ripple is sufficient to drown him'. In rural towns, the most prosperous commercial enterprise was often the pawnshop.[24]

Some of the Blue Shirts believed in nationalising land or limiting holdings to under 10 acres, but this was a subject of which the Kuomintang had been fighting shy throughout its existence. The party had thrown its lot in with the landlords and rural elite, which meant that, while he made speeches about the revolution, Chiang was committed to perpetuating the rural status quo. But this world was, in fact, changing. The traditional power of the local gentry and community leaders was sapped by the purchase of land by officials and army officers who often acted as absentee landlords, delegating to local agents so long as they received satisfactory rent remittances. This undermined the cohesion of village life, which was further affected by the move of younger members of the gentry to the cities and by the regime's 'anti-superstition' drives on religious cults that had provided social glue. At the same time, traditional notables in the countryside were suspicious of the centralised bureaucracy Nanking wanted to impose. The outcome was that, in many parts of China, the elite on which Chiang depended either found itself weakened or was leery of being bossed about by Nanking, further sapping the government's ability to make its authority felt.[25]

In the cities, the advent of the Kuomintang to power had been welcomed by the merchants and chambers of commerce. But they were soon disillusioned as the new regime brought them to heel. Nanking inherited from Sun Yat-sen a belief in a centrally planned economy in which the state would promote industry while China regained its rights from foreigners. This led the government to draw up plans to develop big plants, rather than encouraging smaller-scale private enterprises. A series of national economic programmes unveiled ambitious projects designed to contribute to China's security against external threats – Japan's development was an obvious model. Merchants were classified as profiteers who were foreign to an ideal Confucian system, and were to be squeezed for taxes rather than regarded as the basis for a modern trading economy. Like everybody else, the capitalists of the big cities were to be co-opted into the family, by force if necessary. Any sign of independence was cause for suppression. As for the workers, Nationalist cadres developed what the historian Elizabeth Perry describes as 'patron–client' relations in which underworld organisers were given privileged positions in return for delivering support from the 'yellow' unions they ran. 'Racketeers replaced radicals,' she observed.[26]

At the start of the great slump of the 1930s, the decline in the world price of silver, which constituted China's currency reserve, helped the economy by acting as an effective devaluation that boosted exports and attracted foreign investment. Fuelled by the expansion in coastal cities, annual growth reached 6 per cent. But the silver advantage disappeared after Japan and Britain left the gold standard in 1931, and America decided to purchase the metal, raising prices. Reserves flowed out; interest rates rose; deflation set in; manufacturing declined, with big lay-offs of workers. The world depression hit exports of tea, silk and tobacco. Rural income dropped – in 1934, the overall ratio of farm prices to the amounts farmers spent was half the 1926 level.[27]

The government's revenue base was too thin to pay for military spending and high debt interest. To raise funds, T. V. Soong visited Europe and the United States in 1933. He met President Roosevelt at the White House, and returned with a loan that would give China cotton and wheat worth $50 million which the government could sell on the domestic market. When he landed in Shanghai, the Finance Minister was treated as a hero. At the beginning of September, he travelled for talks on how to use the loan held in the mountain resort of Lushan above the Yangtze. The main issue was whether it should be employed to boost the economy, or to finance more military expenditure.

Soong's standing made him into a potential rival to the Generalissimo. On top of his strong links with Shanghai bankers and businessmen, his patriotic credentials had been burnished by his attempts to develop the national economy and by the introduction of tariffs that hit the Japanese. His opposition to increased military spending was well known. He had residual contacts with the non-Communist left from his time in Wuhan, and had seen the Young Marshal while in Europe. Even more than Chiang, he could draw on the Soong–Sun nexus. He also had 30,000 tax agents who might be used as a paramilitary force in a coup. But the Finance Minister also had his weaknesses, including a timidity that contrasted with Chiang's ruthlessness. Critics pointed out that the huge discounts Soong used to sell Nanking's securities meant the regime saw only half the face value. His target of a balanced budget seemed a pipe dream at a time when the deficit was $10 million a month. In his absence abroad, Nanking had contracted $60 million in fresh debts.[28]

As was his habit, Chiang appeared to give ground before striking. The Lushan meeting ended with a statement saying the American loan would be used for 'productive enterprises', and T.V. got the Shanghai banks to advance another $75 million. But then the Generalissimo called for more money for a new offensive against the Red Army. On 25 October 1933, Soong resigned. According to Chiang's opponent, Hu Hanmin, he remarked that 'being minister of finance is no different from being Chiang Kai-shek's dog. From now on, I am going to be a man not a dog.' Though Nanking put out the usual explanation that he had gone for health reasons, Soong said that, on the contrary, he was in excellent shape, and was stepping down because 'I was unequal to my task' – a polite way of saying he would not meet the Generalissimo's demands.[29]

Chiang attended a meeting of the Central Executive Committee at which it was decided to keep the Finance Ministry in the family by giving the job to T.V.'s brother-in-law, H. H. Kung. The new minister was experienced in Chinese banking, but the *North China Daily News* commented that 'the new shoes are a size larger than those which he comfortably and usually fits.' To reassure the businessmen of Shanghai, Kung went there immediately in a private carriage hooked on to the night train. Though he spoke of reining in expenditure, the stocky, amiable descendant of Confucius did all he could to ensure that the Generalissimo had the funds he wanted for the army. In doing so, he determined the eventually disastrous course of financial policy while developing an economic system which merged public and private interests in a way that further undermined the regime's claims to stand for the nation, but made him and his wife among the wealthiest people in the country.[30]

Kung's first moves were far from impressive. He increased taxes, which further depressed the economy, lowered duties on Japanese goods and increased those on imports from elsewhere. This exposed Chinese manufacturers to sharper competition from across the sea, and boosted the cost of primary products from other countries. To get money for Chiang, Kung offered even higher rates of return, but the financiers were becoming increasingly unwilling to invest in the government. So the regime simply took over the main finance houses, giving it control of almost three quarters of the nation's banking assets. Despite his row with Chiang, T. V. Soong became chairman of the biggest institution, the Bank of China, and a director of other leading outfits taken over by the state, alongside his brother, T. L. Soong. When the big Commercial Bank tried to resist the government, Kung enlisted Big-Eared Du to use his muscle to get it to cede. For his part, the outgoing head of the Bank of China recorded that he had been intimidated by Chiang's secret police and had been warned by the gang boss that he should not raise any opposition 'for the sake of my health'.[31]

The Kung connection was a godsend for the minister's acquisitive wife, Ailing Soong, who would pick up tips when her husband discussed policy at home, and make a killing through her various investment vehicles, including one in which Du was a partner. Not that things always went entirely smoothly. Before the introduction of the national currency known as *fabi* (legal tender) in Sichuan, Ailing gave the gang boss insider information which he used for a big speculative punt on the province's dollar. Unfortunately, there had been a misunderstanding, which left him with a heavy loss. Du demanded reimbursement. The Finance Minister refused. 'That evening,' a British adviser, Sir Frederick Leith-Ross recalled, 'a No. 1 style coffin was deposited on Dr Kung's doorstep by half a dozen funeral attendants.' The next day, a meeting of the Central Bank agreed to reimburse a 'patriotic citizen' who had suffered exchange losses.[32]

The national currency was an important step forward in rationalising China's financial system. But Kung accompanied it with a circular process by which Nanking issued bonds that were deposited in government banks which then used them as security for notes. In effect, Kung was printing money to finance government spending. This fuelled inflation. To begin with, that was no bad thing since it boosted purchasing power and pulled China out of its depression – by the end of 1936, industrial output was rising. But, in the longer term, Kung's policies undermined the credibility of government finances, and created a growing gulf between the vast mass of the Chinese people and a small group of urban and party insiders, personified by the Soong clan.

As well as running the Finance Ministry and chairing the Bank of China, H.H. and T.V., between them, headed an array of companies that invested a mixture of government and private money in factories, marketing and trading operations. As the historian of the Shanghai capitalists, Parks Coble, put it: 'H. H. Kung, as minister of finance, borrowed money from government banks he controlled by going through the medium of a private corporation of which he was the chairman of the board and a leading stock holder.' He gave family firms contracts for administrative jobs, as if the government did not have enough underemployed officials to do the work. A month after T.V. took a majority stake in the biggest domestic cigarette company, the Finance Ministry changed the tax structure to penalise its foreign competitors. In all this, the family could count on protection from on high. When a report by the Industry Ministry into speculation on the Shanghai Cotton Exchange mentioned 'certain influential persons' who had manipulated the market, Chiang packed the minister who had ordered the investigation off to a provincial governorship. The 'influential people' included Ailing, and the report criticised Du, who was the government representative on the exchange's supervisory board. Both were regarded as being beyond criticism.[33]

The political–business circles of the Nanking decade had a positive side in encouraging new industrial and commercial projects. But the system was fundamentally inefficient in spawning state-protected monopolies at which unqualified friends and relatives were given jobs. Personal enrichment and corruption were nothing new, but could only further deaden the promise of reform once proffered by the Kuomintang. With salaries kept low, 'for officials to benefit from their position was normal and ethical, as long as they didn't carry it to extremes', an American adviser, Arthur Young, remarked.

Chiang made things worse by his habit of handing out posts for political reasons or as rewards for loyalty, rather than as a recognition of ability. The Examination Yuan was meant to appoint officials, but, by 1938, only 4 per cent had achieved their jobs through it. The chopping and changing of senior posts created instability – between 1930 and 1937, Hubei had five different governors and Anhui six. Senior figures from Chiang down amassed more positions than they could possibly perform – one survey showed members of the Central Executive Committee and the Political Council with an average of five jobs apiece. Generals were paid the wages of their troops in lump sums for which they, alone, were accountable; they padded their rolls with dead or non-existent soldiers to inflate the money they claimed. Between 1931 and 1937, the Control Yuan, which was meant to fight sleaze, was presented with reports on 69,500 functionaries. Of these, 268 were found guilty, and thirteen lost their jobs. Chiang knew what was going on. 'The revolutionaries have become degenerate,' he said, pointing to the way party members thought only of power and profit. But, once again, his lament was not followed by action.[34]

The same was true with the major cash cow of narcotics, including morphine and heroin as well as opium. Despite repeated assertions by Chinese representatives to the anti-drugs bureau of the League of Nations that drugs were being suppressed, they were simply too important a source of revenue to be eliminated. Chiang could see the harm being caused, and launched campaigns to reduce consumption. But he also used these as a political weapon, targeting troops to interrupt the traffic through the territories of rebellious provincial barons.

In 1935, the Generalissimo became head of the Central Opium Suppression Commission which proclaimed the target of phasing out drugs under a six-year programme. Addicts were to be registered and supplied while they were reformed. Anti-opium centres treated a million addicts in three years, mainly poor people and vagrants. Many of them undoubtedly went back onto drugs after being discharged, and narcotics were still widely seen as a remedy for complaints from plague to malaria. Nanking won credit for honesty; Madame Tussaud's Waxworks in London was persuaded to remove a display of an opium den after China's embassy argued, against all the evidence, that such things no longer existed. But past experience could only induce doubt about how hard eradication would be pursued, given the revenue it spawned and the juicy prospects opened up for officials and military officers. Some reached lucrative agreements with the growers to leave the poppies unscathed or imposed high penalties on the crop. A revolt erupted in northern Anhui after local authorities increased the tax three-fold and slapped fees on everything from the rope to measure fields to the paper and ink they used; 20,000 farmers took part in the uprising in which more than fifty people died.[35]

The crowning irony was the appointment of Du as director of the Opium Suppression Bureau in Shanghai. The gang boss had suffered a setback in 1932 when a clean-up in the French Concession obliged him to move his narcotics operations to the Chinese city. But, having overcome that hiccup, his activities grew and prospered as he moved into legitimate business. He set up the Zhong Wai Bank in a fine five-storey building designed by French architects on the Avenue Edouard VII, and became chairman of the municipal council and a director of the Bank of China, the Shanghai stock exchange, the Bankers' Association and the Chamber of Commerce. The *China Yearbook* described Du as 'a well known public welfare worker', and an English-language Who's Who called him 'one of the leading financiers, bankers and industrial leaders of China', noting his 'long and honorable record of important achievements in public and civic service'. He was deputy director of the Chinese Red Cross, attended Sunday morning prayers at H. H. Kung's house, funded eight orphanages, contributed to flood relief and supported a rural centre emblazoned with anti-opium slogans.

But there was no doubt about the roots of his power. 'One hundred thousand men in Shanghai obey his orders,' Kung remarked. 'He could create a disturbance at any moment.' Du's control of the postal union meant he could open mail at will, and he remained the drug kingpin. Meeting the Godfather in his bank office in 1936, an anti-narcotics envoy from the League of Nations, Ilona Ralf Sues, described him as 'a gaunt, shoulderless figure with long, aimlessly swinging arms, clad in a soiled, spotted blue cotton gown; flat feet shod in untidy old slippers; a long egg-shaped head, short-cropped hair, receding forehead, no chin, huge, bat-like ears, cold, cruel lips uncovering big, yellow decayed teeth, the sickly complexion of an addict . . . He came shuffling along, listlessly turning his head right and left to look whether anyone was following him . . . I have never seen such eyes before. Eyes so dark that they seemed to have no pupils, blurred and dull – dead impenetrable eyes.' When they shook hands, Du's was cold and limp, 'a huge, bony hand with two-inches long, brown, opium-stained claws'.[36]

Taking tea from a small golden pot – its lid held tight by a golden chain and its neck so narrow and curved that nothing could be inserted, as protection against poisoning – Du admitted to being the head of China's opium merchants. But he insisted he made no more than $20 million a year from drugs, and that other merchants controlled the trade, passing a slice of the revenue to the suppression bureau. When Sues mentioned two barrels of confiscated drugs which she had seen at a customs warehouse and had been told were earmarked for him, Du's eyes blazed with anger – 'intelligent, passionate, cruel'. But he brought out the stock reply that all narcotics were burned. After Sues said she knew this was untrue, the gangster crashed his fist on the table, and bellowed, 'I protest. This is a lie! Everything is being destroyed except a small part, which the Government keeps for emergency stocks.'

Such was the man on whom Chiang leaned for control of China's richest city, and for whom he sent a congratulatory scroll when the gangster inaugurated his ancestral temple. Big-Eared Du and his associates, the Kung–Soong business nexus, lazy and corrupt officials, factionalism, feuding security services, an antiquated rural world, woefully inadequate education and health facilities – no wonder that the Generalissimo lamented the state of the revolution, and that those who had seen the start of the Nanking Decade as a new dawn for China grew progressively disillusioned while the regime, having laid the foundations for a modern state, lost its claim to legitimacy.

China was too big and too diverse for a government as weak as Nanking to impose its will. Sichuan province, alone, had 52.9 million people, Shandong 38 million, and Jiangsu, Henan and Guangdong 100 million between them. Shanghai housed 3.4 million, Tianjin 1.3 million and Nanking a million. Apart from the Communist base areas, thirteen of the eighteen provinces were, in effect, outside the orbit of the central government at one point or other in the Nanking Decade. Some were completely lost. The Japanese controlled Manchuria and Jehol and, by the mid-1930s, were expanding out of the demilitarised zone round Peiping.

In March 1934, the Last Emperor, Pu Yi, was enthroned in Manchukuo. In a blue and gold gown with dark red sleeves and a large red fur-trimmed hat with tassels and a pearl, he was given a 101-gun salute as he was driven to the ceremony in a bullet-proof Lincoln limousine followed by nine new Packards. Scrolls were read and sacred wine drunk round a brazier to inaugurate his 'Reign of Tranquillity and Virtue'. The situation in the north, Wang Jingwei said, was 'critical but not hopeless'.[37]

In Shanxi, the Model Governor returned to run his long-standing fief after temporary exile following his defeat by Chiang in 1930, encouraging industry, building railways, modernising education, and using his police to suppress any threat to his dictatorship. Sichuan was, as usual, immersed in civil wars, with almost a million men in various armies and militias. The huge Muslim territory of Xinjiang in the far north-west was out of Nanking's control as it drew close to the Soviet Union.[38]

The Dogmeat General's old stamping ground of Shandong on the north-east coast was under the sway of General Han Fuju, who served under the Christian General but then defected to Nanking in 1930. On bad terms with Chiang, the square, bull-like Han set out to establish the province as an autonomous fief, ordering the execution of Kuomintang officials, reaching secret agreements with the Japanese and suppressing Communists.[39]

In central China, Hunan withheld money from the central government to expand its own military forces. To its west, largely autonomous warlords ran Guizhou, where 80 per cent of the population was reckoned to use opium. In the wild far south-west, on the border with Indo-China, Yunnan was a law to itself. In neighbouring Guangxi, hostility towards anything that smacked of centralisation remained high as the Clique leaders, Li Zongren and Bai Chongxi, returned from their defeat by Chiang to run the province on the 'three selfs' policy of self-government, self-sufficiency and self-defence, with a large militia, village government and co-operative economic schemes. Next door, the one-time cradle of the Nationalist Revolution, Guangdong, was ruled by General Chen Jitang, known for his avarice, deceit and superstition. He instituted a ceremony at which officers swore to oppose the Generalissimo; they were given a wooden sword to strike a leather dummy with 'Chiang Kai-shek' written across it.[40]

The biggest challenge came in Fujian province on the south-east coast, where the Nineteenth Route Army had been sent to help the anti-Communist campaign after its feats in Shanghai. Used to glory and alienated from Chiang, its commanders became increasingly bad-tempered. Their egos inflated by publicity, including three films based on the combat with the Japanese, they resented being shunted into a backwater, and felt they had not received sufficient material rewards. Calling for stiffer resistance to Japan, the Army came under the influence of reform-minded, anti-Chiang politicians who had drawn on the legacy of Wuhan to form the 'Third Party' between the Kuomintang and the Communists.

Left-wingers, Social Democrats, Trotskyites and others, including the former Foreign Minister, Eugene Chen, flooded into the provincial capital of Fuzhou.* Measures were promulgated to better the lot of the peasants, improve communications and lift political oppression. In May 1933, the former Guangdong governor and founder of the Route Army, Chen Mingshu, who had gone to Europe after resigning from the Nanking government, returned to Hong Kong, financing the Third Party and setting up Chiang's southern political foe, Hu Hanmin, in a big house in the British colony.[41]

On the morning of 20 November 1933, a mass rally in a public gymnasium in Fuzhou called for a 'government of the producing people, and the overthrow of Chiang Kai-shek'. But the revolt failed to attract other opposition figures, and the Route Army was not as popular as it had supposed. Bereft of support, the soldiers signed an 'anti-Japanese and anti-Chiang agreement' with the Red Army which it was meant to be fighting. This afforded little practical help since Mao and his colleagues did not want to see a rival anti-regime force just over the border from their base while Moscow still saw Chiang as the best leader for China. So the Communists held back, and portrayed the rebels as counter-revolutionary reformists. Later, Mao acknowledged this to have been an important mistake.[42]

Nanking's troops moved fast along improved road communications while their planes caused panic with air raids. Chiang sent in a team to bribe leading rebels to defect. The Route Army's assistant chief of staff acted as a secret agent, passing the Nationalists information over a radio transmitter hidden in his house. Rebel commanders surrendered, some won over by Meiling who flew in to negotiate. The Fujian navy changed

* Known at the time as Foochow.

sides. Outnumbered more than two-to-one, the revolt collapsed. Two turncoat generals were each given $50,000 to travel abroad. Some of the Route Army soldiers stayed on in Fujian; 1,500 others trekked to Hong Kong where a do-gooder gave them a dollar apiece, and helped them return to their homes across the border in Guangdong. Chen Mingshu left for Europe. Though Cai Tingkai, the commander in the battle of Shanghai, went to the United States and was greeted as a hero by Overseas Chinese, Chiang had won again.[43]

Meeting the Nationalist commander at the time, the British writer Peter Fleming found him 'a man with a presence, with that something incalculable about him to which the herd instinctively defers. He was strong and silent by nature, not by artifice . . . He may not be a great statesman or a very great soldier . . . but, at any rate, Chiang Kai-shek has something to him. He is not only not a mediocrity or a wind-bag, but he could never look like one. That, I think entitles him to a certain singularity among modern political leaders.' The visitor found the Generalissimo's eyes the most remarkable thing about him – 'They were large, handsome, and very keen – almost aggressive. His glances had a thrusting and compelling quality.' As Fleming and his interpreter left, Chiang gave them 'one of those formidable glances, of the kind which prompts an involuntary self-accusation of some grave sartorial omission. We trooped down the garden path feeling very small.'[44]

Now free to turn his attention back to the anti-Communist campaign, Chiang felt the need for an ideology of his own to set against Mao's brand of Marxism. Two of Sun Yat-sen's three principles – democracy and the people's livelihood – had been put on the shelf by the evolution of the regime. That left nationalism. Chiang was ready to accept foreign military counsellors, retain a German, Walter Stennes, as his bodyguard, and see the regime guided by Western advisers. But he rejected the influence of modern foreign ideas epitomised by the 4 May movement of 1919. His nationalism remained resolutely Sino-centric, and rooted in a classical image of China. He warned that the iconoclasm and liberty preached by the 4 May reformers and by advocates of a New China risked the 'destruction of all discipline and the wanton quest for individual freedom'. At the same time, he inveighed against his compatriots as dejected, barbaric, and devoid of reason. 'Their clothes and homes were in utter disarray; they spat and urinated wherever they pleased,' he said. 'Having no principles, they smoked, gambled and whored their lives away. When they talked, they looked half-dead with a demeanour reminiscent of zombies.'[45]

The answer lay in getting the Chinese to subject themselves to moral regeneration which would assert traditional values as defined by the Generalissimo. A sense of rigour was to be injected into the nation. Apart from its regenerative effect, the obedience which would be propagated would make it easier to guard against Communism. The idea, Chiang said, came to him as he drove through the Jiangxi capital of Nanchang, and saw a student with a cigarette in his mouth behaving badly in the street. A new creed was needed to make such people shape up. At a mass meeting in the city in March 1934, he walked down from the flower-lined platform to confront an untidily dressed press photographer who had pushed his way to the front of the crowd. This man, he told the audience, was typical of those who did not respect the need for orderliness, cleanliness, simplicity, diligence, promptness and precision. To promote such virtues, Chiang and his wife launched the New Life movement, based on the four Confucian principles of *Li* (propriety), *Yi* (right conduct) *Lian* (honesty) and *Qi* (integrity and honour).

If properly applied, Meiling explained, *Li* would bring recognition of 'the sterling native qualities of our fellow men'; *Yi* would induce 'the obligation not to hold wealth and enjoy it wastefully while our fellow countrymen may be on the verge of starvation or suffering from sickness or other evils'; *Lian* would make officials recognise the rights of the people, and not try to benefit at their expense; *Qi* would mean that 'no one would become shameless or stoop to anything mean or underhand'. Alongside its Confucian elements, the movement contained a dash of the religion to which Meiling had converted her husband. 'There's Methodism in this madness,' ran one quip; *Time* magazine wrote that the Chiangs had decided to give China 'a big dose of the Castor oil of Puritanism'.[46]

A long list of rules was issued – one published in Nanking in 1935 contained eighty-six instructions. Simplicity, frugality and good behaviour were the watchwords. A lantern parade in Nanchang promulgated slogans such as 'Be prompt', 'Don't spit', 'Be neat', 'Kill flies and rats: they breed disease', 'Avoid wine, women and gambling'. With 'citizen detectives' to bring transgressors into line, the movement sought to touch all areas of life.

The Chinese were told to replace ornate marriages and funerals with simple ceremonies. Some local authorities banned mixed bathing and decreed that men and women should not walk arm-in-arm in the street.[47]

Following Chiang's instruction that 'lascivious or fantastic fashions' for women must be suppressed, the Jiangxi authorities ordained that women's gowns must be ankle-length; the distance between collar and cheek should be not less than an inch and a half; sleeves ought to reach at least to the elbow; slits in sides of skirts should be no higher than the knee; women must avoid tight clothes, and comb their hair backwards, not letting it fall below their necks. The Generalissimo later added curled hair to the list of prohibitions. All women working in government offices were to wear short blue jackets, black skirts, black stockings and black shoes. In Shanghai, woollen coats without buttons were banned. In Wuhan, a zealot poured nitric acid over a woman in what he considered revealing clothes.[48]

Boy Scouts and Girl Guides were encouraged as harbingers of the new morality; Kai-shek and Meiling presided at their parades, including one of 3,366 in Nanking. Superstitions were to be abolished. Censorship would protect peace and order. People were urged to buy Chinese goods, not imports. Foreign films reflecting badly on China were banned. Native productions were encouraged to 'promote good morals and demonstrate the spirit of fortitude, endurance, peace and the uprightness of the people'. Chiang's aide, Chen Lifu, told cinema directors their work should be 70 per cent educational and 30 per cent entertaining. In the Sichuan city of Chungking,* a magistrate ordered two fat pigs spotted eating sugar cane pulp in a park to be shot as an offence to public decency.[49]

To accompany the New Life movement, Chiang declared a national economic reconstruction movement to aid industry and commerce, regulate labour and capital, promote agriculture, build roads, develop communications, adjust finance, eliminate excessive taxes and reduce tariffs. It was to work on a five-year plan and spend $270 million on industrialisation, with powers to confiscate private enterprises. Since this was Chiang's project, much of the development was to be in areas of military importance. But it soon petered out for want of funds.[50]

Many New Life rules were eminently sensible, such as those advocating healthy living, cleanliness, vaccination, and the killing of flies

---

* Now known as Chongqing.

and mosquitoes. Compared to attempts to re-educate and dragoon the Chinese people by Chiang's Communist successor, the movement was positively benign. But, in a country with problems on the scale of those faced by China, the initiative was like the admonitions of a frustrated father wagging his finger at his unruly children. The message never reached the bulk of illiterate peasants, who were, in any case, more concerned with survival than with wearing their hats straight. Being told to eat in silence and go to bed early could only make the modern-minded urban elite regard the regime as a bunch of petty busybodies.

Streets would be swept and houses painted when the Generalissimo and his wife visited a city, but, behind the Potemkin Village front, nothing really changed. Old festivals and beliefs persisted: a few miles from government headquarters in Nanking, there was a stampede to grab fragments when the head fell off a statue of a sacred tortoise. To get round limits placed on the number of dishes that should be ordered, restaurants served several at the same time on large plates, with alcohol brought to the table in teapots.[51]

The hypocrisy was blatant. At New Life dinners, the Chiangs ate only soup and three courses instead of the usual banquet of a dozen or more dishes, but officials in Nanking and elsewhere lived as well as they could. While people were told not to smoke, Meiling puffed in private on imported cigarettes. The rule ordering 'Do not smoke opium' could hardly be reconciled with the regime's links with the likes of Big-Eared Du and provincial governors who lived off narcotics. The *North China Daily News* observed that 'the New Life Movement would have its best chance of success if, like charity, it could begin at home'. By 1936, the adviser, W. H. Donald, decided it was time to deliver some home truths.[52]

At a dinner with the Chiangs, he said that the regime had shown itself incapable of reform. 'You people sit in your *yamen* [headquarters], and your horizon is your window sill,' he went on. 'You are ignorant because no one dares to correct you. You might lose face and, what's more, some one might lose his head. You've retreated into your intellectual rat holes, having exposed only a posterior of vanity. Goddamn it, sir, you've all become insufferably stupid!' The Australian denounced graft, the opium trade, the lack of measures against disease and floods, the backwardness of transport, industry and the administration. 'China should be ashamed,' he concluded. 'There is the staleness, the obeseness of wealth on one hand –

the hog wallow of poverty on the other. The ricksha man and the wharf coolie are worse off than the horse and camel in many another land.'[53]

Though his lamentations in his diary showed he was aware of the truth of at least part of what Donald said, Chiang could not admit his own incapacity to put right what was wrong with the country. 'I am the Generalissimo; I do not err; I am China; and China cannot do well without me,' he declared. The truth was that Chiang, and many of those around him, were poor administrators, possessing neither the skills nor the application to put their plans into practice. Despite repeated revolts, the sanctions which would have shown that Nanking meant business were rare. The Generalissimo generally preferred to co-opt his enemies rather than punish them. He thundered on about morality, but allowed the regime to be undermined by corruption and profiteering. He spoke endlessly of the need for national unity, but used divisive tactics and allied himself with a shifting coalition of remnant warlords. All that may be regarded as par for the course at the time, but it meant that Chiang condemned himself to be the prisoner of his context instead of rising above it.

Change would mean opening up society and the power structure, renouncing paternalism, running an efficient economy, shaking up the civil service, clamping down on graft, reforming agriculture and land ownership, permitting debate, accepting that the army was not the supreme arbiter of power. All of which would put the leader's own position at risk, and encourage revolt by defenders of the status quo. Cautious and conservative, Chiang was not one to take the gamble. He preferred a system which had no fresh ambition to offer the nation. His inner circle consisted of generals, a few trusted aides and those in the Soong–Kung clan who worked with him. For the mass of Chinese people, he remained a distant figure riding a white horse or haranguing a crowd from a platform.

He was expert at operating in very different boxes, reading the Bible with missionaries but dealing with Big-Eared Du, proclaiming the importance of loyalty but manipulating the cliques around him, extolling national unity but allying with warlords, assuming the Olympian calm of the superior man but flying into the wild rages that had marked him since his early days in Shanghai. He concentrated all authority on himself, keeping control of money and supplies, but never fully mastering the provincial barons. He constructed an extensive network of personal relationships, but trusted very few of those around him. He ignored inconvenient facts, and erected a make-believe world epitomised by the New Life movement. He chose, as Zhou Enlai put it, to use all the contradictions in the country to his own ends. However, he never lost sight of his prime objective – to rid China of its disease of the heart, and the man who symbolised that ailment. Given the later tide of history, it is striking how near he came to achieving his goal.[54]

CHAPTER 15

The Long Chase

BETWEEN THEM, CHIANG KAI-SHEK and Mao Zedong dominated China for half a century. They were born six years apart, the Generalissimo in 1887, the Great Helmsman in 1893. Both came from country villages, from families that rose above the rural rut; the Chiangs owned the salt shop and claimed noble antecedents while Mao's father acquired 3 acres, sold grain and lent money. Each had a deep love for his mother, though Chiang's cool relationship with his father was far outdone by the hatred Mao expressed for his. Both had a Confucian childhood, studying the classic texts, whose top-down principles would remain with them through their lives. As teenagers they had been put into arranged marriages with older women, whom they soon repudiated, Mao saying he never slept with his first wife while Chiang's mother had to pressure him into having a child by his. Each abandoned a subsequent spouse, and ended married to politically ambitious much younger women. Both retained the accent of their home provinces – and both suffered from constipation.

The two men left home as teenagers, living erratic lives for several years, espousing nationalism, and then participating in the united front between the Kuomintang and the Communists in Canton in the mid-1920s. Neither was familiar with the outside world. After his time in Japan as a military cadet, Chiang did not go abroad for a quarter of a century, and then only in a setting of war; Mao's first foreign trip, to Moscow, did not come till 1949. Both had simple tastes, and little regard for money. Each saw himself as a teacher for the nation, the embodiment of what China should be, fighting his way to the top against political opponents of greater seniority, pursuing an often lonely path but convinced of his own rightness. Each stood at the top of an organisation structured on military lines in which party, state and army came together under his command. Deeply Sino-centric, they both believed in the power of the will, and saw armed force as the way to power. Neither recoiled from a huge expenditure of human life in pursuit of his goals. Both were consummate and ruthless political power players, who knew how to recover from a temporary reverse. Each represented the 'Do or Die' approach, unready to compromise, determined to destroy opponents and rule supreme.

'He was as stubborn as a mule and a steel rod of pride and determination ran through his nature,' an American wrote of one of them. 'I had the impression that he would wait and watch for years but eventually have his way . . . I had the impression that there was a door to his being that had never been opened to anyone . . . [his spirit] dwelt within itself, isolating him.' An English writer added: 'His personality inspired loyalty, not affection. He combined a fierce temper and infinite patience; vision, and almost pedantic attention to details; an inflexible will, and extreme subtlety; public charisma, and private intrigue.' Both were descriptions of Mao. Much of what they contained applied equally to Chiang.[1]

A Soviet adviser with the Communists wrote of hearing a Japanese radio calling the Nationalist 'persistent, merciless and highly ambitious' and wondering 'isn't this characteristic of Mao Zedong?' The Communist chief, he added, would not permit criticism in a system where 'party principles are replaced by self-seeking, undisguised toadyism and self-humiliation' – which might have been said of Chiang's court. Neither leader had true friends, courting those he needed, and then dropping them – or squashing them if they became a threat. Each was profoundly, chauvinistically nationalistic, and emotionally hostile to his principal foreign ally. Power was the sole dream and ambition.

Still, quite apart from the separate ideologies, their differences were equally evident, personally as well as politically. Though, like Chiang, he insisted on keeping his surroundings neat, Mao was famous for his lack of grooming and his peasant ways; Chiang, as one visitor remarked, had 'the air of fastidious distinction'. The Great Helmsman wore baggy blue peasant clothes and a Red Army cap; the Generalissimo neat suits, silk robes, uniforms hung with medals and a velvet Western trilby. Chiang was slim, erect, precise, his lips thin, his head shaven; Mao grew increasingly bear-like, his hair shaggy, his face round, his walk shuffling and rolling. Except when he flew into one of his fits of temper, Chiang exuded self-control; whatever his inner calculations, Mao behaved expansively to visitors, appearing to take them into confidence, even if this was to seduce them into his ideological embrace. Chiang delivered his speeches like military orders; Mao knew how to carry his audience with him, throwing in folksy asides, jokes, rural references before getting to the ideological core.

After the purge of 1927, Mao was an outsider, a political rebel, a guerrilla fighter while Chiang was ensconced in the palaces of power. The Communist leader lived close to the ground with his comrades; the Nationalist chief soared above in planes with American pilots. Early on, Mao identified China's small farmers and peasants as the seedbed of revolution; the Generalissimo held back from rural reform. Mao's ideology was unrelenting, and adapted to China's situation; the nearest Chiang came to expounding a creed was in a meld of Confucian classicism and Methodism that had little relevance to the real problems facing the nation. Chiang assured his soldiers that they were part of his great family, but he was a distant figure on a platform whereas Mao could establish a real human bond. While the Communist leader headed an ever-growing nationalist guerrilla movement, Chiang's distrust of mass organisations stood in the way of creating a great popular resistance to the Japanese. In the cocoon he wove around himself, the Generalissimo could not understand the popular appeal of the Communists, seeing them simply as a rival force to be eliminated. Hearts and minds were not his concern.[2]

From the autumn of 1934, the revolutionary and the organiser of the biggest armed force China had seen were pitched directly against one another in a confrontation that would stretch for fifteen years. One concentrated on the basic issue of survival, refusing to give up whatever the odds. The other was at the helm of a complex military and political campaign that could never achieve its final goal. Then, and later, it was as if, for all the forces at his command, Chiang was doomed to be on the losing side of history.

Such a possibility cannot have entered his mind as he travelled at the end of 1933 to the Lushan Mountains above the Yangtze in northern Jiangxi province. The wooded peaks, rising to 5,000 feet and often wreathed in mist and cloud, had inspired Chinese poets for centuries, and were the site of a 1,400-year-old temple. At the end of the nineteenth century, a black-bearded English missionary from Dorset called Edward Selby Little identified Lushan as an ideal escape for expatriates from the summer heat and humidity of the river valley below. In a pun on its main attraction, he used the name of one peak to give his resort the name Kuling.

Little, who later became the Far Eastern manager for a British chemicals company, bought land and handed it over to a self-regulating council. He had a 12-mile track built up the steep slope through the tea plantations along which coolies carried residents and their guests in sedan chairs – small children went in baskets at the end of poles. Five hundred houses were put up, many of thick stone. A British family ran a general store and the Fairy Glen Hotel – the bluff son of a London banker opened the Journey's End Inn down the slope, where bedrooms were provided with Bibles and volumes of French pornography.[3]

In the 1920s, wealthy and prominent Chinese began to move in. During his struggle with the leftists in Wuhan, Chiang held a meeting of his supporters at the Fairy Glen. In 1933, Meiling acquired a two-storey stone house in a garden by the stream that ran through the middle of the settlement. A missionary who lived in Kuling recalled watching Chiang, wearing a Chinese gown and felt hat, walking up the last lap of the mountain track one evening, preceded by bodyguards in grey suits with pistols at their hips. 'His forehead was broad, his brown eyes clear and steady, and his chin firm,' the watcher wrote. 'In repose, his face is austere but can light up round the eyes with a kindly smile.' Meiling, in a silver silk dress, was beside him, her face 'intelligent and beautiful', her 'animated and clear voice' cutting through the stillness as she spoke in English to Donald who walked just behind the couple. Further back came coolies carrying sedan chairs, and more bodyguards, their eyes searching the undergrowth for danger.

Chiang had his quarters on the first floor of the villa, with a bedchamber and a sitting room – his secretary and doctor slept down the corridor. Meiling had a separate ground-floor room, with a double bed from Britain, brown leather armchairs, a chaise longue, wooden desk and dressing table. The bathroom was fitted with imported green tub, basin, bidet and lavatory.

The Chiangs liked to sit on the large first-floor terrace, and to walk in the surrounding hills, sometimes taking a picnic with them. Meiling played an upright piano, painted landscapes, and read a collection of books in English, including a set of the *Encyclopaedia Britannica* and works by H. G. Wells, Strindberg, Dorothy Sayers's *Omnibus of Crime* and Robert Graves's *I, Claudius*. The Generalissimo brought cuttings from his native province to create a small bamboo plot beside the stone house which was known as the Meilu Villa. He appreciated the *feng shui* of the house, with slopes on either side, a mountain behind and the water from the brook in front.[4]

Chiang turned Kuling into a summer capital for the Nanking government. Wang Jingwei had a house looking down at the lake below the resort. The Young Marshal owned a residence in the trees with a red cupola over the entrance. Chiang ordered a large conference hall built on the outskirts of the settlement, flanked by military buildings with curved tile roofs and special quarters for his generals.* There, at the end of 1933, he planned what was intended to be his final campaign against Mao's Red Army. Facing his commanders and staff arrayed on twenty-five rows of seats in the stone conference centre, the Generalissimo traced his military plans with a long pointer on a series of maps. Twenty thousand elite troops underwent training in the Lushan Mountains, exercising in close-contact combat and climbing the peaks in preparations for those in the Communist base.[5]

An economic blockade had been thrown round the Soviet area, making food there scarce. To evade the embargo on salt, Communists smuggled it in hidden in bamboo – or, in one case, in a doll which a woman carried on her back as if it were a baby. Politically, splits had opened up between Mao and the party leadership in Shanghai which insisted on moving from guerrilla warfare to direct attacks on the superior Nationalist forces. Pressure increased with the construction of 700 miles of roads to enable Chiang's troops to advance more quickly. At the end of 1933, a visiting

---

* Mao would hold a key meeting in the hall to purge critics in 1959.

reporter saw columns of big military trucks, mules, coolies, ambulances and marching soldiers, including Salt Revenue Guards in steel helmets. In their cloth shoes or straw boots, the troops passed by with 'just a rustle, without noise'.[6]

Chiang's legions were of varying quality, ranging from Whampoa veterans and elite units trained by the Germans to former warlord irregulars, but they were well supplied and their towns stocked with food. They were backed by a force of 150 planes, and a short wave radio network which relayed information from aerial reconnaissance. The provincial capital of Nanchang was turned into a fortress behind deep moats, trenches, barbed wire emplacements, walls and turreted watchtowers with overlapping fields of fire which a Polish journalist described as giving 'an impression of the defensive constructions of the Middle Ages'.[7]

Government planes dropped leaflets offering rewards of $100,000 for the capture of Mao and the Red Army commander, Zhu De, but less if only their heads were brought in. A force of 24,000 special agents carried out underground police work, organised propaganda and enforced the economic blockade of the Red base. A campaign was launched to get Red Army troops to defect, with $20 offered for each rifle they handed over. Leniency was promised for those who had been coerced into joining the Communists, but had not done any important jobs for them. Such people, Chiang said, included men who had 'unwittingly succumbed to the wiles of women Communists'. Reformatories were set up for those who surrendered; photographs of one showed inmates lining up to receive textbooks, attending a sewing class, making stockings and sandals, and receiving a graduation diploma. Propaganda campaigns in conquered areas featured parades, stage shows, lectures, posters, cartoons and films – the first the country people had seen. But the Generalissimo made clear his rejection of rural reform by declaring that the gentry system should be restored in areas recaptured from the Communists. In return, landlords would provide coolies and forced labour to build roads and blockhouses.[8]

At the end of 1933, Chiang broke off from the campaign to travel to Hangzhou to meet the Young Marshal who had just returned from Europe, leaving his family in England where his sons were enrolled at a preparatory school. Described as fit and happy, Zhang Xueliang had been much impressed by the example of Mussolini and Hitler, and decried the divided state of his native land. 'Europe doesn't think much of either you or China,' he told Chiang.[9]

Over dinner with the Chiangs in a private room of a restaurant beside the scenic West Lake, Zhang and W. H. Donald kept up the attack with abrasive views of China. Though her husband did not react, Meiling was impressed, and asked Donald to join their staff. He replied that he did not work for women, but was struck when the Marshal told him she had translated everything he said, 'including the goddamns'. The next day, Zhang was appointed Deputy Commander-in-Chief of Bandit Suppression troops, the bandits in question being the Red Armies. Based in Wuhan, he also pressed a campaign of social reform at Donald's urging, including a drive against corruption which the Australian thought could only be expunged by high-level executions.

Chiang's mind was more focused on his fifth drive against the Jiangxi Communists in early 1934. He had a new adviser, General Hans von Seeckt, who had rebuilt Germany's armed forces after the defeat of 1918 and who suggested using lines of blockhouses to force the Communists back and withstand counter-attacks. Three thousand 'turtle shell' forts were built, linked by roads and bridges. Scorched earth tactics burned rings of open country round their positions. The terrain was difficult, with steep mountains, narrow stone paths, thick woods, and enemy machine-gun positions commanding valleys. But, with a numerical advantage of up to five-to-one, the Nationalists were finally forcing the Red Army to fight a static war. In the past, Chiang had used mainly regional troops against the Communists. Now, seventeen divisions put into the field were from his own central army, some of them trained by German advisers and with modern equipment.

In the Communist base, Mao had been elbowed aside by political opponents backed by the party leadership in Shanghai. Command was exercised by men who had returned from indoctrination in Moscow, and by an authoritarian German Communist adviser, Otto Braun. At his urging, the Red Army attacked the blockhouses, and suffered heavy casualties. 'We milled around between the enemy's main forces and his blockhouses and were reduced to complete passivity,' the admittedly partial but accurate Mao wrote.[10]

For once, Chiang had the initiative. Contemporary press accounts reporting little except Nationalist victories reek of propaganda. Still, there was no doubt that the Communists were undergoing defeats as never before. They tried an offensive into Fujian but were beaten back. Desertions soared. Paranoia set in. Beheading squads went to battlefields to drive on the Communist troops. Thousands of 'counter-revolutionaries' were killed. Mao was put under virtual house arrest.

In June 1934, a Red Army unit left the base area under the banner of the 'Anti-Japanese Advance Detachment'. But it was overwhelmed. Its leader was caught and executed, his head being taken round in a bamboo cage. Two other break-outs in the summer had more success: one reached Shaanxi in the north, the other linked up with Communists in the wild frontier region linking Hunan, Hubei, Sichuan and Guizhou. In Jiangxi the Nationalists moved inexorably forward, taking towns and defensive lines as they forced the Red Army to retreat.[11]

With the campaign going well, Chiang had time to turn to other issues. Diplomatic relations were re-established with Moscow. A ragged revolt by one of the Christian General's associates was put down in the far north. As the summer heat along the Yangtze climbed to over 100 degrees, there was both drought and flooding, affecting tens of millions. An official report put crop losses at $500 million. To try to stem the massive outflow of silver, the government slapped a duty on the export of the metal. The budget showed no signs of improvement, with customs revenue falling sharply, and military spending and debt servicing taking 70 per cent of revenue.[12]

There were several flare-ups with the Japanese in Shanghai, and the Kwantung Army issued protests at alleged Chinese infringements in the demilitarised zone round Peiping. In June, fears of a fresh incident rose after Japan's vice-consul in Nanking disappeared, but matters were resolved when he was found asleep in mountains outside the city, and he explained that he had gone missing because of family affairs and disappointment over slow promotion. There was tacit recognition of Manchukuo when rail links with the puppet state were restored. A bomb went off on the first train from Peiping to Mukden, killing four people, but the Japanese did not take this as a pretext for action, and their new Minister to China had a friendly half-hour meeting with Chiang at the end of June.[13]

At the beginning of October 1934, the Generalissimo and Meiling travelled to Wuhan to confer with the Young Marshal about the anti-Communist drive on the Yangtze. The three of them and Donald then took an old imperial train to the military centre of Luoyang. On the first morning of the three-day journey, the Australian was sitting in his carriage when Meiling staggered in with an armful of letters and documents which she put on a desk. 'It's too much for me,' she said, according to his recollection for his biographer. Through his acquaintance with her father, the Australian had known her since she was a girl. Now, he found her 'frail and delicate, intelligent and pretty, an elf with a dynamo'. To ease her tension, he told stories of his early days in China. That afternoon, she came back to his compartment with another load of documents, and asked him to help her. Donald said this might be a problem since he was employed by Zhang.

'There's nothing in China that's closed to you,' Meiling replied.

'Nothing?' Donald asked. Smiling, she pushed a pile of papers towards him, and he went to work.

When they had finished the visit to Luoyang, the Australian proposed that the four of them continue by train to Xi'an, one of the cradles of Chinese civilisation which the Generalissimo had never visited. Chiang nodded agreement when Meiling translated the suggestion.

In Xi'an, they drove into the city in bright sunshine to take tea with the local commander, General Yang Hucheng, who would suggest the kidnapping two years later. The visitors went to the hot springs to bathe. A New Life meeting was held, and Meiling spoke in 'perfect and beautiful English' with local missionaries. The Chiangs visited an orphanage where they ordered a feast for the children. Meiling announced plans for a rehabilitation home for women opium addicts. All 400 motor vehicles in the city were commandeered for use during the visit; yet a letter from a foreign resident spoke of the couple as 'unassuming, agreeable and capable', in contrast to the usual pomp of official visitors.[14]

A correspondent who interviewed the Generalissimo at the time was struck by how he had grown thinner and his closely cropped hair had become greyer – attributed to his sixteen-hour working days. Asked about rumours in Shanghai that he and Meiling were discussing divorce, Chiang said that was ridiculous, and both he and his wife laughed. He then mentioned another rumour that an office-seeker had offered him a dozen beautiful women – which he denied, too. Rather, the reporter noted, the couple 'acted like newly-weds'.[15]

Donald and Meiling hatched the idea of continuing the northern trip by air to give Chiang a taste of places no national leader had ever visited.

In backward Gansu, he went to woollen mills, launched a local New Life movement and attacked opium and foot-binding. In neighbouring Ningxia, where Chiang was impressed by the huge, barren spaces, he was greeted by a military band playing 'When Johnny Comes Marching Home'. Meiling suffered from airsickness and took along an oxygen tank for the high altitudes. The party then headed for Peiping where the Chiangs and Donald all received hospital treatment for stomach ailments. A medical bulletin said the Generalissimo was suffering from nervous indigestion caused by hard work, and possibly also by the absorption of poisons from abscesses in his teeth.[16]

Next, they set off for Mongolia, and for Shanxi where they stayed in H. H. Kung's mansion in the provincial capital. On their travels, the Chiangs were provided with the finest linen, silk eiderdowns and perfumed pillows. Streets were cleaned and houses painted for their arrival. They put on weight as they ate local delicacies. Flying through the cold winter over deserted, loess 'Yellow Earth' country, the party wrapped itself in thick furs. At stops along the way, the Generalissimo delivered rousing speeches, and Meiling busied herself with good works. There was only one alarm, when a bomb was thrown at their train, but the news was hushed up and responsibility for the attack was not established.

Returning to Peiping, Chiang had dental work, and was prescribed new spectacles to cope with compound myopic astigmatism. At a New Life dinner in the city, he had his first meeting with Wu Peifu – the absence of alcohol may not have charmed the wine-bibbing old warlord. Then the Chiangs and Donald headed for Nanking where the Australian moved into the Generalissimo's bungalow, and worked on papers Meiling passed him. During their travels, the Australian had paid her the highest compliment he could imagine – 'You think like a man'. When Zhang Xueliang next visited the capital, he went to see them both. Like nightclub pianists, Donald and Meiling sat at either end of a table, each busy on a typewriter. Tea was served while the two Chinese discussed the Australian in their language which he did not understand. The Marshal got up, and walked over to slap Donald on the back.

'It looks as if I've lost you,' Zhang said.

'Yes, I damn well think you have,' the adviser replied.

'I'll miss you,' the Marshal said.

'Tommyrot,' Donald responded, as they grasped hands.

The change of patrons enabled the blunt and active Australian to feed his ideas to Chiang through Meiling. But it did nothing to lessen his cussedness. Though he often ate with his employers, Donald still refused to touch Chinese food. As if to stress his linguistic incapacity, he reduced 'Generalissimo' to 'G'issmo', and called Meiling 'M'issimo'.[17]

The trip to the far north may have given Chiang only an airbrushed picture of the region, as local authorities spruced up their towns and pampered the visiting couple. But, to judge by Donald's recollections, it awakened the Generalissimo to realities he had not glimpsed before, and also brought out a less aloof side to him. The adviser sensed a change day by day – 'the Generalissimo's face grew more relaxed and, if only infinitesimally, more animated'. But the trip meant he was more than 1,000 miles away while his forces in the south drove into the heart of the Soviet base area in Jiangxi to devastating effect.[18]

As the Generalissimo arrived in Gansu province in mid-October, Mao Zedong, in grey cloth uniform and a military cap, walked to the bank of the foaming Gan River where Red Army units and support forces had been assembling in secrecy. While Chiang and his wife slept under silk eiderdowns in the north, Mao crossed the water, carrying two blankets, a cotton sheet, an oilcloth, a coat, a broken umbrella and a bundle of books, abandoning his two-year-old son whom he would never see again. Leaving behind rearguard elements to defend the Jiangxi base as best they could, the Red Army headed through a gap in the line of blockhouses, beginning the Long March which was to become one of the great exploits of the Chinese century.[19]

With the eventual victors setting the template, accounts of the march are cast in a heroic mode, making it the furnace in which the new China was forged, with survivors recalling superhuman triumphs born from comradely selflessness. It became, in the words of the French writer and politician Alain Peyrefitte, an 'epic poem' to Communism. In reality, the Long March was a drawn-out acknowledgement of major defeat. The endurance shown was, indeed, extraordinary. The Red Army's skill at manoeuvring, misleading the enemy and covering huge distances over forbidding terrain made it an icon for guerrillas, though it also had a great secret advantage in its Russian-trained decoders who were able to read Nationalist wireless messages and change tactics accordingly. Still, for all these achievements, the Communists lost their base in Jiangxi, failed to establish themselves elsewhere along their route, and were continually harried into making new retreats. Of the original force of 80,000–100,000 men, and 2,000 women, only some 5,000 were still marching when the expedition ended a year later, and were open to annihilation. If the Long March was any kind of victory, it was a victory of sheer survival.

This is not say that the Nationalists deserve praise. Chiang had immensely superior numbers at his disposal, and an air force. But he was beset by chronic lack of coordination bred by the desire of provincial governors to avoid seeing him station troops on their territories. Their fears were well founded – as always, Chiang was operating from a cocktail of motives in which the extension of his own authority over autonomous provinces was a major ingredient. The Nationalist troops and their allies often behaved terribly, and Chiang's tactics were, by turns, too cautious or overconfident. Nanking's soldiers failed to show the same determination and discipline as their foe. Subsequent accounts of the march say little about the impact on civilians along the way, but it is clear that their suffering was considerable. The Communists killed or punished class enemies, particularly landlords who had not managed to flee; the Nationalists were ruthless with anybody they thought likely to aid their enemy, using scorched earth policies to deprive the Red Army of succour.

Conducted in great secrecy, the start of the march attracted little attention. The Nationalists did not appear aware of what was going on as the Red Army moved across the border from Jiangxi and along the Guangdong frontier. The provincial governor, Chen Jitang, who wanted to keep the Nationalists out of his domain, reached a non-aggression agreement with Zhou Enlai, including exchange of information and provision of medical supplies, which ensured that the Communists moved on as speedily as possible and gave Chiang no excuse to intervene. The Red Army turned north to head for a Soviet base in neighbouring Hunan. Its baggage train stretched for 50 miles carrying everything from weapons to printing presses and an X-ray machine. As Mao said, it was more like moving a house than an army.[20]

Informed at last of what was going on, Chiang ordered fifteen divisions to encircle the Red Army in front of the Xiang River on the border between Guangxi and Hunan provinces. His own troops marched along one bank of the 300-foot wide waterway while the enemy advanced along the other; a second Nationalist army formed a blocking force. Despite their autonomist sentiments, Chiang counted on the strongly anti-Communist rulers of Guangxi to join in. But, by the time the Red Army vanguard crossed the river, the Guangxi army of Bai Chongxi had moved away to protect the city of Guilin. This let half the Communist force follow across the waterway. But the baggage train lagged behind and the Nationalists caught up: as one Communist veteran admitted, 'We were too slow and the enemy too quick.'[21]

Bai Chongxi now decided to participate after all as the Red Army was split on either side of the wide river. Before dawn on 1 December, its commander, Zhu De, sent a message to the forward units stressing the decisive nature of the battle. Nationalists with fixed bayonets swarmed up hillsides to attack defensive positions, and planes swooped on bombing and strafing runs. The fighting lasted for a week. It was the biggest single setback the Communists suffered during the whole of the Long March. Some accounts reported that their strength was halved, with only 30,000 men managing to get away. Much equipment was lost as the rearguard baggage train struggled across the river.

Chiang was far from the battlefield, having his bad teeth treated in Peiping. But he laid another trap for the Communist survivors, ordering a large plain in their path to be cleared of people, the crops destroyed, and food removed. That was where he planned to wipe out the remainder of the Red Army with the help of aircraft and artillery. Realising the danger, the Communists changed their course. At a meeting in mid-December in the market town of Tongdao on the borders of Hunan, Guangxi and Guizhou provinces, they decided to abandon the route to north Hunan since that would mean being caught in the Nationalist killing field. Instead, they would head for the wild interior of Guizhou, a province where Nanking's writ hardly ran. As was to happen many times in the coming decade, the Communists saved themselves by avoiding their adversary.

Chiang flew back to Nanking for a series of meetings on the military and political situation – one decided to send parcels of Christmas food to troops in the field, though a newspaper story noted that the supplies were more in the nature of necessities than treats. He and Meiling went to spend New Year at Xikou and Hangzhou, and travelled on to their large, European-style house in Shanghai with its pebble-dash walls and red tile roof. There, they received the Kungs, T. V. Soong, Big-Eared Du and Zhang Jingjiang, and visited the grave of Meiling's mother.[22]

Reaching northern Guizhou, the Communists held a conference in the confiscated home of a merchant in the town of Zunyi. The failure of their Moscow-backed leaders and the German adviser, Braun, had become evident. It was time for Mao to emerge from his semi-eclipse, gaining the upper hand as the Red Army committed itself to his guerrilla vision of warfare. The one-time warlord soldier, Zhu De, became operational commander of the march, and the supple Zhou Enlai rallied to the new strategy. Avoiding four separate armies converging on Zunyi, the Communists moved to the border with Sichuan, aiming to get to a Soviet base in that province. Among the places they temporarily occupied was the town of Maotai, home of the celebrated Chinese rice wine of the same name. One story went that, taking the white liquid for water, the soldiers used it to wash their feet; they soon realised what it was, however, and, when they left, not a drop of the 'foot water' remained.[23]

Picking up the chase, Chiang flew to Sichuan to organise defences and stiffen local forces for a counter-attack. The two great foes of twentieth-century China were now only some 150 miles apart. As the Communists moved back into Guizhou, Mao's partner, who was carried on a litter, gave birth to a baby girl who was left forever with a peasant family without having been given a name. Her father had other preoccupations, personally directing a battle in the mountains after the Red Army seriously underestimated the size and strength of forces pursuing it and had to retreat for its life. Still, it retook Zunyi, and its leaders were able to pause to consider their next move.

Establishing his headquarters in the Sichuan city of Chungking, situated on cliffs above the Yangtze, Chiang went into a whirl of activity. He made frequent speeches, some lasting for hours, and supervised financial reforms to try to bring order to the chaotic local finances. Visiting the city, the Swedish explorer Sven Hedin was particularly struck by Meiling who wore a dark high-necked dress with short sleeves. 'A gaily colored pattern of bamboo leaves formed a sort of wreath around her neck and also adorned the sleeves. She seemed refined and at ease,' he wrote in another instance of a Westerner being bowled over by the youngest Soong sister. 'She is intelligent, clever, gifted, and stands at the peak of Chinese as well as occidental culture . . . No doubt Madame CKS is the most remarkable woman of our time . . . Long after the thunder of war has been silenced she will remain a blessed mother among her people, and her name will be mentioned with reverence and admiration.'[24]

At the front, the main pursuer of the Red Army was a former Whampoa instructor and Northern Expedition veteran, General Xue Yue, who had headed Sun Yat-sen's bodyguard at the time of the attack on him in Canton in 1922, and had helped to put down the Communist rising there five years later. Xue had taken part in the encirclement campaigns in Jiangxi before chasing the Red Army through Hunan, Guizhou and Sichuan where he helped to reorganise the local forces. The improvement in the fighting quality of the Sichuan troops paid swift dividends when they forced the abandonment of the Soviet base in the province with which Mao had been hoping to link up.

While the pressure built up on the Long Marchers, the Generalissimo and his wife took a break with a cruise on the Yangtze, carried to and from the river at their ports of call in sedan chairs or on the shoulders of coolies. Opium dens were closed down temporarily in towns they visited. Wearing his trilby hat, Chiang was photographed grinning broadly. In a long coat with a fur wrap, Meiling snapped the passing sights, and donned baggy trousers to scale a steep slope on all fours. On 24 March, the Chiangs flew to Guizhou to resume the campaign.[25]

The province was poor and backward. In its capital of Guiyang, the electrical supply ran only from seven to twelve each night. Food was meagre, and officials did not turn up for work till the afternoon. Kai-shek established his headquarters in a new building by the river, and he and Meiling stayed in a house formerly occupied by a warlord. Nine-foot high partitions divided the interior into cubicles. The windows did not fit, nor did the sliding doors close. To keep out the winter wind, the couple slept in a tent of heavy blue cloth erected inside the building. When a fire was lit with the local coal, the room was filled with choking smoke that stained everything black. Chiang called local dignitaries together to denounce the use of opium and order them to wipe it out. When he stopped speaking, there was dead silence, broken only by the unsuccessful attempt of a Boy Scout band to play a tune. The Generalissimo strode off, and the audience slunk away.[26]

In early April, the Nationalists won a battle north of the provincial capital, but suffered substantial casualties. The *North China Herald* reported that many of the captured Communists were said to have been beheaded.

The application of the blockhouse strategy enabled Chiang to report to Nanking in mid-April that the backbone of the Communists had been broken. Though rain and heavy cloud prevented widespread use of the air force, one strafing attack wounded Mao's partner in fourteen places – one piece of shrapnel in her head could not be removed, and she was in a coma near to death for weeks before recovering.[27]

The Red Army's zigzag marching thoroughly confused the Nationalists. But Chiang could see that the only escape route for his adversary lay westwards into Yunnan. So he flew to confer with the ruler of the province that had always been far from the national mainstream on the border with Burma and Indochina. Though the small, delicate, ruthless governor, Long Yun, had rallied to the Kuomintang cause in name, his revenues from opium and slave-labour tin mines made him anything but a model ally for the national revolution. Conforming to the warlord pattern, he had invited a rebellious general with whom he had reached a peace agreement to a luncheon banquet in a tent – at the end of the meal, a swordsman behind the guest chopped off his head which was then hung from a telegraph pole at the entry to the capital of Kunming.[28]

On the flight south, Chiang sat up front in the cockpit to gaze down at the ground where the enemy lay – and at the poppy fields below. In Kunming, he and his wife were greeted with champagne toasts at the airport. They drove into the city along a road lined with cheering students in white and blue uniforms, Meiling noting the national flags flying from every house, the cleanliness of the streets and the orderly nature of the traffic. A French banker recorded a 'furtive view' of her white silk bloomers when the wind blew up her skirt at an open-air reception.[29]

Given Mao's strategy, it was highly unlikely that he would engage in a battle for the provincial capital. Still, the inhabitants of Kunming built walls of bricks made with soil and dug trenches. Long Yun ordered troops he had sent to confront a warlord in Guizhou over a quarrel about the opium trade to return as fast as they could. The French banker moved 20 tons of gold, which was sitting in his vaults after an arms deal, to the station to be taken by train to Hanoi – he was then warned that Long's men would seize it en route, so he decided to hold on to it.

Despite feints towards the city, the Red Army kept away from Kunming, which meant Chiang could return to Guizhou, where he ordered the land tax not to be collected for a year and local soldiers to stop taking tribute in grain. He gave the local warlord a choice between remaining governor or holding on to his military command. The militarist chose the second, but the Generalissimo stirred up sufficient disaffection among his subordinates to be able to replace him with his own nominee. The Chiangs pressed the merits of the New Life movement, though its effect on employment in the opium trade hardly made it popular. In a newspaper interview, the visitor called for a radical move to improve the standard of living of the people, and give them security of life and property, though he provided no indication how this was to be achieved. He and his wife made unprecedented – if highly staged – visits to the local Miao tribespeople, he in a long gown and trilby, she in dungarees and a big sun hat. Chiang faced another threat to his life when a man with a pistol was caught by the wall outside his residence.[30]

By then, the Red Army had escaped once more as the very different strategies of the two leaders played itself out across south-west China. Chiang wanted to trap the Communists in a set-piece battle like the one on the Xiang River where he could bring overwhelming force to bear. Mao was the apostle of constant movement, counting on his men being able to outmarch the enemy. 'The ability to run away is precisely one of the characteristics of the guerrillas,' he wrote. 'Running away is the chief means of escaping the passive state and regaining the initiative.' In that, he was greatly aided by the desire of autonomy-minded rulers like Long Yun to see the back of the Red Army as quickly as possible so as not to give Chiang a reason to bring in troops to take control, as he had done in Guizhou.[31]

With Long Yun offering minimum resistance, the Communists headed for the turbulent upper Yangtze to cross into Sichuan. Chiang ordered all the boats at the few crossing points to be secured or destroyed. That would catch the Red Army up against the river where they could be wiped out. The Nationalists' confidence was boosted by a false report from prisoners that the Communist commander Zhu De had died of wounds, and that his body was being carried along, wrapped in red silk.

Again spotting the trap laid for them, the Communist altered their line of march, heading for a different stretch of the river and moving mainly at night to avoid aerial surveillance. One battalion was reported to have covered 85 miles in twenty-hour hours. It then put on captured Nationalist uniforms, and took a ferry town without opposition. Others beat back an attack by Nationalist troops from Sichuan. One group of 18,000 men crossed the waterway in four days at the first great sweeping bend in the Yangtze where Chinese had beaten back an invasion from Tibet four centuries earlier.

On their way into the high plateau of southern Sichuan, the Communists had to deal with the Yi mountain people with whom a truce was agreed after negotiations sealed by the drinking of a cup of chicken's blood, though this did not stop the locals from robbing the passers-through when they could. Emerging from that trial, the Red Army headed for the wild Dadu River, a place of high historical significance as the scene of the slaughter of the last 40,000 troops of the Taiping revolution seventy years earlier. Surging between high cliffs, the waterway can be crossed at only a few spots by boat or over isolated bridges made of chains and ropes. Here, once more, Chiang seemed to have the Communists cornered, and be on the brink of sending the Red Army the way of the rebels of the previous century.

Waiting for the showdown on the Dadu, Chiang flew again to Yunnan to bolster his position there. A big parade by school children was held in his honour, the boys dressed in blue, the girls in white. They carried lanterns in the shape of frogs, crayfish, cabbages, rabbits, guns, ships, birds and butterflies – their lights described as looking like a many-coloured 'colony of glow worms crawling sinuously upwards'. They sang the Kuomintang song, and saluted as they climbed the steps to where the Generalissimo stood. 'Gently,' he murmured as they passed.[32]

To survey the battlefield, he made an aerial inspection in a Junkers plane, sitting in the cockpit and staring down at the mountain country with its soil of ochre, red, orange, sepia, magenta and purple. The first green of the rice plants was showing on paddy fields set on terraces in the highlands. At one point, the aircraft swooped down on a village on a sharp ridge with drops of thousands of feet on either side; the inhabitants must have wondered what wondrous metal bird was coming from the heavens. Flying over the Red Army's route, Chiang saw burned farms and stones arranged in a field to form two characters begging for quick salvation. Back in Sichuan, the Generalissimo pressed ahead with building blockhouses, and strengthening local defences. He issued decrees against opium and 'local bullies and bad gentry', lamenting that Sichuan was 'a house divided into disorder and confusion'. As he did so, the Red Army was staging its greatest escape of all, 120 miles to the west.[33]

The Taipings had been caught on the Dadu at the ferry town of Anshunchang as they paused there to celebrate the birth of a son to their leader. Mao, Zhu De and their troops were not going to stop. A vanguard unit was sent ahead to Anshunchang, covering 50 miles of extremely rugged terrain in a day, the thick forest hiding it from aerial surveillance. A couple of miles from the town, the soldiers lay down to rest, but were ordered to stage an immediate attack. Chiang's generals had assumed that the Communists would take longer, and had not yet sent in reinforcements for a small detachment of Sichuan troops camped across the river from the Communists. All three of the local ferries had been moored on the far side. But the regimental commander was married to a local woman whose family lived on the near bank, and he had crossed the river for dinner with his relatives just as the Communists arrived. The Red Army soldiers grabbed his boat, and used it to capture the town, while others staged a diversion to draw off enemy forces in the area.[34]

It took three days to ferry a division of soldiers over the rough river, swollen by the spring thaw. Planes began bombing, and Chiang's troops were moving up. So another crossing had to be found if the bulk of the Red Army was to escape. On the morning of 23 May a regiment which had crossed the river was ordered to march towards the town of Luding, 100 miles upstream, where there was an old chain bridge. The regimental political commissar later described the route: 'The road twisted like a sheep's gut along the side of the mountain, rising sharply vertical, as if cut by a knife straight up unto the clouds . . . To the right, dozens of yards below, were the white-capped waves of the rushing river. One mis-step and you were a goner.'

Fighting skirmishes with Nationalist troops along the way, the regiment reached Luding on 25 May, to find that some of the planks on the 120-yard bridge had been removed. In a feat much celebrated in Communist China, a twenty-two man advance party climbed across the chains, followed by comrades who laid planks to restore the bridge. The defenders started a fire at the town gate to block the attack but, within two hours, Luding was taken, and Nationalist troops fled as the Red Army poured over the bridge.

Avoiding Sichuan's main population centres and enemy concentrations, the Communists headed across the formidable barrier of the Great Snowy Mountain range, rising to 14,000 feet. The journey was an ordeal of precipitous climbs, typhus, dysentery, air attacks and ambushes by fanatically anti-Chinese Tibetans – the queen of one tribe threatened to boil alive anybody who helped the Red Army. Those who stopped to urinate froze to death, a marcher recalled.[35]

On 12 June 1935 the advance guard emerged from the mountains, and saw what it thought were enemy soldiers. Shots were exchanged before Mao's men realised that the others were comrades who had made their own long march from the base above the Yangtze. Hearing of the meeting of the two Communist forces, the Nationalists consoled themselves with the thought that it would be easier to attack a single army than to fight two. Chiang wrote in his diary of the way the Communists had been driven back, 'yet as long as they continue to exist, they remain a source of trouble for China'. 'I must blame myself for lack of necessary knowledge and foresight,' he added, but he told officers that their long pursuit was 'a feat of valour unparalleled in the annals of Chinese history'.[36]

Despite parades and banquets to celebrate the meeting of the two Communist armies, their leaders, Mao and former Politburo member Zhang Guotao, were uneasy bedfellows. Neither had any intention of giving way to the other. With four times as many men as Mao, and a longer pedigree in the party leadership, Zhang wanted to take the driving seat. He had been in Sichuan for some time, and had collected local support, whereas the southerners were in unfamiliar surroundings, worn out by months of exhausting marches and battles. But Mao had gained the upper hand in the Politburo, as he showed at a three-day meeting held in a Buddhist monastery lit by yak butter lamps. This appointed Zhu De as chairman of the military commission, with Zhang as his deputy. Mao also won the day for a march towards a new base area on the northern border of Sichuan instead of adopting Zhang's proposal to head for the expanses of the Far West where they would be out of Chiang's reach. To placate him, Zhang was made General Political Commissar, and joint head of the combined Red Armies with Zhu. The force was split into two columns, which moved forward 50 miles apart. Zhang headed the larger group, which contained the headquarters unit, including Zhu De.

The compromise did nothing to sink the differences between the two rivals. A Central Committee session held in Zhang's absence adopted a resolution that branded his idea of marching west 'flightist' and 'right opportunism'. For his part, Zhang tried to change the line of march, and to get Zhu De to abandon Mao. Ahead of both columns lay a huge icy swamp of black muck, water many feet deep and high grass on the border with Tibet. While Zhang's column held back, Mao's troops embarked on a week-long crossing. Men froze to death or were sucked into the swamps; foul drinking water provoked typhus and dysentery; the few local inhabitants set ambushes; soldiers hunted down rats for food; the only grain to be found was unmilled – famished men took undigested kernels from the bloody faeces of the dead, washed them and tried to eat them.[37]

Chiang dispatched a strong force to pursue Mao's depleted column as it emerged from the swamp. The Communists won one battle, but then faced a formidable fortress commanding a narrow pass on their route. In another feat of daring and physical skill, twenty commandos climbed the peak behind the fort and captured it in a surprise attack. On 21 September the remnants of the Red Army that had set out from Jiangxi eleven months earlier reached Gansu in the far north of China, and Mao learned from a newspaper of a Soviet base area 600 miles away in Shaanxi province. He decided that this would be the place where he would stop running away.

Escape was made all the easier because Chiang paused in his pursuit of Mao's army at this point. Given the way history was later written to focus on the Great Helmsman, this may seem strange. But the truth was that the Generalissimo was more concerned about Zhang Guotao's larger column than the remnants from Jiangxi. Zhang had given up the attempt to cross the grasslands when faced by a flooded river. Instead, he headed towards the Sichuan capital of Chengdu. After an initial defeat, Chiang's forces based round the city won two significant victories, making Zhang retreat. His numbers were, however, augmented by a link-up with two other local Communist forces, ensuring that he remained the major threat. So, rather than pursuing the fleeing Mao, Chiang sent his troops to fight Zhang's Red Army on the upper Yellow River, where they scored another victory and forced him to march to the Far West where Muslim cavalry further mauled his army.

The desolation caused by the campaign was reflected in a report by a French missionary after a journey near Chengdu. All the villages he passed through on the first day had been more or less burned down: 'the few houses that had been spared were left without doors, windows, frontage, or partitions. All faces expressed sadness and anxiety. When I inquired who the authors of this destruction were, I was told, "On the right bank, it was the government troops who burned the houses; on the left bank, the

Reds.'" He estimated that 300,000 people had died or disappeared in three districts he visited.

> The arrival of the Red troops was greeted joyfully by the common people, who had suffered so much from the government soldiery. Little by little, however, massive executions of the wealthy, and then of the proletarians suspected of being lukewarm towards the new regime, damped people's enthusiasm. The initial joy was succeeded by a general uneasiness. Finally, the population greeted the departure of the Red Army with the same feeling of relief as it had welcomed its arrival. Even though the Red Army is gone, however, the communist doctrine has left deep imprints on people's minds. It opened new horizons to the proletarian class, which is now endeavouring to preserve the newly won advantages. The farmers refused to pay their annual rent to the landowners, tenants reject the idea of paying their rent, debtors no longer acknowledge their debt.[38]

Arriving in its new home in the north of Shaanxi, Mao's Red Army declared its march at an end on 22 October 1935, 369 days after setting out. A charade of unity was organised the following year when Zhang Guotao's vastly depleted army made its way to Shaanxi, and he was named one of Mao's deputies. The reality was that Zhang was no longer in a position to challenge Mao. The Long March had marked out the man who would contest the leadership of China with Chiang. As for the Generalissimo, he had failed in his primary object of destroying the Red Army, but Communist strength was far less than it had been, and its main force had been pushed into a poor, barren corner of northern China. Though Nanking's authority remained tenuous, the Generalissimo had established a presence in western provinces where the government had previously had no sway. The long campaign further buttressed the preponderance of the military in the regime, and, more than ever, made its leader the dominant figure – sure that the elimination of the Red Army could only be a matter of time.

CHAPTER 16

End of Endurance

AS THE RED ARMY was marching towards its new base in northern Shaanxi, Chiang's other opponent was on the move again. The Kwantung Army staged threatening troop manoeuvres round Peiping, and its planes made warning flights over the city. The Japanese demanded the removal of the governor of Chahar province, west of Jehol, and the replacement of government officials in north China by 'friendly' figures. The Young Marshal's successor, General He Yingqin, reached an understanding with the Japanese commander in Tianjin, General Umeza, by which Nanking gave up control of a wide belt in the north along with the cities of Peiping and Tianjin. The secret pact, which formally outlawed the nationalistic Blue Shirts, had Chiang's approval. He was still set on playing for time with the Japanese until he finally crushed the Communists.

An autonomous administration was established under a puppet ruler over 29,000 square miles of Hebei province. The Nationalists pulled out of half of Chahar. In all, 180,000 Chinese troops withdrew from areas where they might clash with the Japanese, some going to Xi'an for an anti-Communist build-up there. Lopsided customs duties fostered trade within territories under the control of the Japanese who sought figureheads for their satellite areas. Among those mentioned was the former eastern warlord Sun Zhuanfang, who was living in Tianjin; but that came to nothing when he was shot dead while praying in a Buddhist temple by a woman to revenge his execution of her father eleven years earlier – she was pardoned after a nationwide appeal for clemency.[1]

As well as military pressure, the Japanese attacked China's economy and the health of its people. Smugglers, including *ronin* gangsters, moved large quantities of goods into areas under the sway of the Kwantung Army to be sold locally or taken on to central China – some got as far as Nanking. This undercut Chinese manufacturers, and deprived the government of much-needed tax revenue. Loss of customs income, put at $8 million a month in Hebei alone, jeopardised state loans based on it. Emboldened, the Japanese spread the smuggling to Fujian across the strait from the island of Taiwan, which they controlled. Chinese customs boats were made to remove their guns and stay 12 miles offshore; otherwise they would be treated as pirates and fired at on sight by Japanese ships.

At the same time, the occupiers encouraged narcotics, both to raise revenue and to sap the health of the Chinese. Three hundred drug dens and 100 shops were authorised in Peiping while Japanese navy ships moved opiates to Shanghai and the Yangtze. Visiting a town of 15,000 people in the demilitarised zone round the former capital, a British social worker, Muriel Lester, counted thirty outlets run by dealers who claimed extraterritorial status. 'When people bring their articles to the pawnshop,' she wrote, 'it is often suggested to them that they take heroin or morphine instead of money. If an injection is desired, a syringe is rented to the customer.'[2]

At the beginning of November 1935, Chiang joined other Kuomintang leaders for a meeting of the party's Central Executive Committee. After the opening session, a group photograph was taken outside the hall. Wang Jingwei, the Young Marshal and the Model Governor were among those standing in the five rows of dignitaries, but Chiang preferred to go to talk to delegates in the auditorium. As the group broke up after the photograph, a young man stepped forward and shot Wang three times with a Spanish pistol. One bullet hit him in the left lung, another in the left cheek, the third in the left arm. Blood poured from his mouth. Chiang hurried to the scene and helped to carry him to a car. Wang's wife, looking cool and calm, covered her husband with a blanket, and he was rushed to hospital. The Young Marshal and a Kuomintang official overpowered the gunman.[3]

The would-be assassin, Sun Fengmin, had gained entry to the building with a pass from a news agency whose other staff had left town. It was reported that Sun had been a sergeant in the Nineteenth Route Army. Under questioning, he insisted he had operated on his own. After complaining of a severe headache, he was given a stimulant, but died the next morning. Police said they found opium in his pockets. They added that Chiang had also been trailed by 'suspicious characters'.[4]

Wang was operated on, and then moved to Shanghai, resigning his government positions. He went on to Paris for another operation before going to a German spa. There was sporadic speculation that Chiang might have been behind the shooting: the politician's wife asked why the Generalissimo had not been at the photographic session, and the death of the assassin in custody could have been a way of silencing him. But Wang was no threat. It seemed more likely that the assassin had acted from patriotic motives in protest at the appeasement of Japan – or, as Chen Lifu stated, because he was a follower angry at not having been promoted.[5]

Chiang's pre-eminence was underlined when he received 495 of 515 votes in the election of the Central Executive and Supervisory Committees: his aides, the Chen brothers, jointly took second place. In December, the list of a new government was published. The wispy-bearded Lin Sen remained President. As head of the Executive Yuan, with the trusted H. H. Kung as his deputy, Chiang ruled supreme. Wang Jingwei was named as chairman of the Kuomintang's Central Political Committee, but said he was too ill to accept, so his seat was taken by his deputy – Chiang.

Still, the Generalissimo was under growing criticism for his avoidance of confrontation with the Japanese. A Shanghai-based body, the National Salvation Association, became a focal point for the desire for action against the invaders. Students staged demonstrations and hunger strikes in big cities. In Shanghai, they occupied the North Station and the Chapei police headquarters while unidentified gunmen assassinated the pro-Japanese former deputy foreign minister. Chiang received student leaders, but all he would offer was not to sign unequal treaties, as if the He–Umezu and Tangku pacts did not qualify for that description.

The death of Hu Hanmin in the summer of 1936 – from a heart attack in Canton – set off fresh patriotic demonstrations, and encouraged the southern warlords to raise yet another revolt in the name of standing up to the invaders. Given their strong anti-Japanese sentiments, the Guangxi Clique had genuine nationalist motives. That could not be said for the corrupt Guangdong ruler, Chen Jitang, who was out to increase his own power. Both had another reason to act – half a million Nationalist troops had taken up positions during the anti-Communist campaign in a huge arc stretching through Hunan, Yunnan and Guizhou north of their provinces. Chiang had also used his military presence in the south to block the opium trail to the north which provided most of the Guangxi tax revenue, forcing the generals there to seek an alternative outlet through Guangdong.[6]

The Canton warlord sent his brother to Nanking to sound out the Generalissimo on his intentions. According to the account given subsequently by the Guangxi ruler, Li Zongren, Chiang played a typical divide-and-rule game, telling his visitor he planned to eliminate the Guangxi leaders, but would leave Guangdong alone. The warlord's brother was a great believer in the occult. On his return to Canton, he reported that, from studying his host's face, he had divined that he would not survive the year. The brothers consulted oracles which predicted defections and the clipping of wings. This, they decided, applied to the Generalissimo and meant he was doomed.

On 1 June 1936, the Guangdong–Guangxi Anti-Japanese National Salvation Army advanced into Hunan. Back from his international tour, General Cai, formerly of the Nineteenth Route Army, joined it. Chiang avoided battle, though his forces did wipe out one of their own units which had deserted. Payments he had made over the past five years to southern commanders reaped dividends. The desertions and clipping of wings predicted by the soothsayers applied to Chen, not to the Generalissimo. The Canton air force chief flew with dozens of planes to side with the Nationalists; a leading general declared his loyalty to Nanking; and the Chief of Staff went to Hong Kong pleading ill-health. Just before midnight on 17 July, Chen invited Li Zongren to his home to say he was leaving, and hand over a note for $200,000 as a 'disbandment allowance'. Then he headed for Hong Kong, where he had stashed anything from $7 million to $50 million. Like so many others, he would be back, joining Chiang in 1939 after donating $12 million to the national treasury.[7]

To keep them quiet for the time being, Chiang named Li Zongren and his colleague, Bai Chongxi, as 'Pacification Commanders'. A defecting general was put in charge in Canton, and T. L. Soong was sent to introduce economic reforms. Once his authority had been asserted in Sun Yat-sen's one-time base, Chiang tried to get the Guangxi leaders out of their homeland by appointing Li to the National Defence Council in Nanking, and making Bai governor of Zhejiang province. They resisted that, and fresh fighting broke out, with the Guangxi leaders mobilising their formidable provincial militia.

On 11 August 1936 Chiang flew to Canton on his first visit since he set out on the Northern Expedition ten years earlier. Greeted by decorative arches over the streets, he stayed at Whampoa, accompanied by Meiling and W. H. Donald. He gave the Guangxi leaders three days to quit. Nationalist planes flew over their province dropping leaflets – and then ten bombs after being fired at. Confronted with the force of Chiang's army and an economic blockade, Li and Bai made peace; for his part, the Nationalist leader was keen not to get sucked into a war with the 100,000 Guangxi troops on their home ground. He gave his adversaries generous terms to placate them, and provide 'face'. Li was allowed to stay in his province, and Nanking undertook to pay Guangxi $2 million a month.

As Chiang tidied up loose ends in the south, Meiling and Donald flew to Nanking. The Australian and Madame Chiang had grown increasingly close. When Donald fell ill with a fever during the campaign against the Communists, Meiling had gone to his bedside. The adviser, whose Australian wife had left him twenty years earlier telling him he was married more to China than to her, was deeply attached to the youngest of the Soong sisters. He called a yacht he was building in Hong Kong the *Mei Hua*, or 'beautiful flower', incorporating the first part of her name.

In the plane from Canton, they spoke of the new psychology they were trying to bring to China. As the Australian talked, Chiang's wife watched him with searching eyes. Taking a piece of paper from his pocket, he drew squares for a game of noughts and crosses. Meiling won two games, Donald one. The Australian turned the paper over and, as the plane headed across hills green with rice paddies, wrote a poem – he was a dab hand at doggerel. It mocked the importance of 'face' to the Chinese. He said it was for Meiling, and added, 'Not for you – but for those who should be like you.'[8]

In late September, the Generalissimo left Canton with a farewell invocation to 'never complain of hardships or too much work'. A front-page cartoon in the *North China Herald* showed him on top of a pagoda, each storey of which bore the name of a province he had brought into the Nationalist fold. He was placing a dome labelled 'Guangxi' on the top; the caption read 'China's architect'. On the twenty-fifth anniversary of the revolution on 10 October, Chiang declared that China was no longer disunited, and that the Communists were 'no more a real menace' as 10,000 Scouts marched past his reviewing stand bearing model tanks, planes, battleships and forts.[9]

Two weeks later, the Generalissimo celebrated his fiftieth birthday – by the Chinese calculation which has a person one year old at birth. For the occasion, national subscriptions financed the purchase of fifty-five military planes for the regime. Among those handed over at Shanghai airfield was one paid for by Big-Eared Du, which was named for the opium suppression campaign. Chiang received 5,000 birthday telegrams. In Nanking, a fleet of planes flew over a crowd of 200,000 gathered for the occasion, drowning out a speech by President Lin Sen.

The Generalissimo was not present; he had chosen to go to Luoyang for the day. The Young Marshal joined him there to attend a celebratory lunch, with music provided by the orchestra of the Officers' Moral Endeavour Association. Chiang blew out the candles on two large cakes, and watched an hour-long parade in his honour. Wearing a long coat with a velvet collar and carrying a trilby hat, he sat for a photograph surrounded by officers, with a fur-coated Meiling by his side and the Young Marshal beside her, his gloved fists set firmly on his thighs. 'For so long as we have not recovered our lost sovereign rights and restored our territorial integrity, we will never be free as a people nor independent as a nation,' Chiang said in a speech. But his top priority remained elsewhere.[10]

To press the campaign against the Red Army, he flew to the Shaanxi capital of Xi'an to confer with the Young Marshal, who had been moved there to fight what was intended to be the final campaign against the Communists. Meiling accompanied her husband, and they were photographed sitting on a giant carving of a fish at an imperial tomb. Zhang Xueliang's troops, who still caressed hopes of returning to Manchuria one day, had lost two battles, but had been instructed to build forts and roads to press the offensive. The Marshal inspected his territory from the air, sometimes piloting his 'Flying Palace' plane himself, dropping messages to troops to which they replied either with characters written on cloth panels or by taking formations to create the characters themselves.

At one point, an air raid on the Red Army in which Zhang participated was shot at by Communist troops – in retaliation he ordered a mortar attack in which Zhou Enlai was nearly killed.[11]

On the surface, everything seemed in order. But Zhang had made his doubts about the civil war known to his chief. His visit to Europe had led him to attribute the success of the Italian and German Fascists to their restoration of national rights. On the other hand, he added, Nanking risked losing popular support and perishing if it 'recovered territory inch by inch in a civil war, while it lost its territory to the foreign aggressors province by province'. The Communist victories over his army meant he could not disparage the enemy's fighting strength, so, he said later, 'the thought of using "peaceful" means to solve the Communist issue was kindled in my heart'.[12]

Messages from Mao Zedong urged a united front against the aggressors who had killed Zhang's father and taken Manchuria from him. At a meeting with a Communist emissary, Zhang agreed to take a 'passive' position in the civil war, though he refused to oppose Chiang openly or to join an attack on the government. Mao reported that a verbal accord for a ceasefire had been reached. In April 1936, Zhang travelled to a meeting close to the Communist headquarters. The Nationalist and Communist flags had been placed outside a Christian church, a classic building with two towers that could have been picked up from Spain and plunked down beneath a high rocky outcrop in northern China. Inside, the Manchurian had all-night talks with Zhou Enlai whom he would describe as 'something else'. They agreed on the need for a united government and army. The Communists set up a base in Xi'an, in a courtyard labyrinth of one-storey buildings linked by circular moon doors, with wireless transmission facilities. The entrance was through a barber's shop run by a German sympathiser.[13]

The thirty-four-year-old Marshal did not hide his feelings about the Red Army from his senior officers. 'Who could lead an army like they did?' he asked. He told Chiang it was impossible to wipe out the Communists because of their popular support. He sent food to the forces he was meant to be fighting and claimed, fifty years on, to have saved the life of the later Communist leader, Deng Xiaoping, who had typhoid fever, by dispatching canned milk to him. In an interview late in his life, he said he even applied for Communist party membership, but was rejected by the Comintern.[14]

His feelings were only part of the growing revulsion against the Japanese aggression and Chiang's failure to offer resistance. National enthusiasm rose when Nationalist troops in Suiyuan province in Inner Mongolia moved outside the demilitarised zone agreed with the Japanese to beat separatists backed by the Kwantung Army. In Shanghai, there were riots at Japanese-owned mills, and a Japanese clerk was shot in the back and killed in Chapei. When a group of Japanese marines came ashore, one of its members was killed as he walked in the street. In the Sichuan capital of Chengdu, a mob grabbed Japanese visitors staying at an inn, paraded them through the streets and killed two, reportedly mutilating the bodies and gouging out the eyes. In a Guangdong port, where remnants of the Nineteenth Route Army had taken shelter, the sole Japanese resident was dragged from his pharmacy and stabbed to death. The chairman of the provincial government of Hubei was assassinated by a man who said he acted because his victim was 'attached to diplomacy rather than aggression' towards Japan.[15]

Zhang was not the only prominent northern figure to wonder whether it might be better to reach an accommodation with the Communists. In September 1937, Governor Yan of Shanxi announced the formation of a League for National Salvation Through Sacrifice to protect his province against both the Japanese and the centralising threat from Nanking which he could clearly see behind Chiang's new drive against the Red Army. 'There is some risk in a united front,' the Model Governor acknowledged. 'But if we don't collaborate with the Communists, what else can we do? . . . Otherwise we cannot hold off the Japanese and Chiang Kai-shek.'[16]

In fact, Chiang was preparing to fight the Japanese to a greater extent than realised by those who saw him as no more than an appeaser obsessed with the Red Army to the detriment of his nation. As early as 1932, he had set up a secret council to plan for dealing with the invaders. Now, he authorised his lieutenant, Chen Lifu, to open talks with Zhou Enlai about joining forces against the Japanese; according to Chen, the Nationalist conditions were that the Communists should observe Sun Yat-sen's Three Principles, follow Chiang's orders and abolish the Red Army, in return for which they would be allowed to maintain an autonomous government in northern Shaanxi. The secret talks broke down in mutual recrimination, but had, at least, provided the first face-to-face contact.

Internationally, experience since the Mukden Incident had shown how little assistance the West was ready to offer China against Japanese expansion. The failure of the League of Nations to do anything effective in the face of Italy's attack on Abyssinia in 1935 underlined the emptiness of talk of standing up to aggression. Having given up hope of help from powers which professed to be committed to his country's territorial integrity, the Generalissimo sent an adviser to Europe to study modern military methods – on his return, he stressed the importance of air power, economic mobilisation and propaganda. With the backing of the Young Marshal, who had been bowled over by Mussolini, a consignment of planes was ordered from Italy; unfortunately they turned out to be antiquated models, and the crates of spare parts that accompanied them contained junk.

More fruitfully, Nanking hired Claire Chennault, an American enthusiast for air power who had recently retired from the US Army Air Corps after his ideas had been rejected. The Texan-born Chennault, who used his southern charm on Meiling in her capacity as a director of the national aeronautics board, was entrusted with building up the regime's aviation strength, hiring mercenary pilots, training fliers and supervising the assembling of planes from American parts. At the same time, Germany agreed to provide weapons worth $100 million in return for supplies of minerals. A contract for delivery of submarines was also signed.[17]

South of the Yellow River, fortifications were built along major railway lines. 'Great dugouts of cement and reinforced steel have been completed at strategic cities in this area – some as places of refuge for the civilian population, and some as storage for grain, munitions, fuel oil and gasoline,' Hallett Abend of the *New York Times* wrote in a memo to his publisher. Chiang 'has been buying naval mines from abroad, and has secretly converted many of his ships into mine-layers', he added. At the beginning of 1937, the Chief of Staff, General He, reported on a wide range of industrial projects that would help the war effort – a further sign of the militarisation of the country. Fortifications were to be strengthened at key points, with three lines of defences between Shanghai and Nanking, pillboxes on railway lines and improved communication links. Army reform was pursued with the aim of developing an elite force of well trained officers and troops with local loyalties.[18]

The Generalissimo was keen to keep such developments secret for two reasons. Though Nanking told Tokyo it wanted to abrogate the Tangku Truce that had given the invaders a virtually free hand in the north, Chiang did not want to give the Japanese a pretext to advance further, or to alarm regional warlords by being seen to be building up the strength of the central army. Nor was he to be shifted from his insistence on finishing off the Red Army first. If that meant getting rid of the Young Marshal for a second time because he was becoming unreliable, so be it. On a visit to the north in November, Chiang appears to have told Zhang he was going to be replaced by a more gung-ho general for the final push in Shaanxi. This meant the prospect of the Manchurian ever leading his troops home would disappear for good. That, and the realisation by local commanders that the coming of the central army would inhibit their authority and weaken their 'irregular armies', could only buttress their resistance to Chiang's crusade.

However, everything appeared under control as the Nationalist chief got the usual New Life reception on his arrival in Xi'an at the beginning of December, 1936, to put the final touches to the sixth anti-Communist campaign. The streets were cleaned, and the dogs were chased away. Soldiers with drawn bayonets guarded his route. A large detachment of Blue Shirts arrived to weed out Communists.

But, by now, Zhang's mind was set. As he told Chiang, he did not like the idea of suppressing the Communists with whom he had reached an agreement to 'resist Japan and save the nation'. 'It wasn't that I was sympathetic with them,' he recalled fifty years later. 'But they were Chinese so why fight each other? We could talk with them. Later negotiating became my idea. It wasn't impossible to negotiate. We could talk with them. Mr Chiang became very unhappy with me in this matter.' He saw that the Generalissimo could play a double game by sending the local troops to fight the Communists, causing both to suffer heavy casualties, while the central government army conserved its strength and took control. 'I did my best to follow orders,' the Marshal insisted. 'But the soldiers were not stupid. They knew that, if they lost men or ammunition, they would not be replaced so they were unwilling to fight.'

Behind such reasoning lurked the possibility of an anti-Chiang alliance in the north west linking the Young Marshal, the Model Governor, the Communists and other regional figures. Chiang's response was to insist on obedience, threatening to move Zhang's troops to far-away Fujian province if they did not fight the Red Army. The Marshal, he wrote in his diary, lacked 'the resolve of the last five minutes'. Against this background of such mixed motives, the Marshal launched the kidnapping of Chiang, and the fate of China tilted.[19]

As the reaction to the kidnapping at Xi'an showed, for all his faults and weaknesses, the Generalissimo was the only possible embodiment of the nation. Even those who opposed his dictatorial ambitions gave him 'grudging support because they generally recognised no man in China equalled him in ability to command adherence,' wrote the American ambassador, Nelson Johnson. Xi'an, he added, 'suddenly made of Chiang Kai-shek a symbol of all that the Chinese people wanted most, namely, unity.' Still, the leader went through the motions of submitting his resignation three times, saying he was guilty of not having foreseen the December rebellion. These hollow offers, which were naturally rejected, only underlined his irreplaceability. In an Easter message, he looked back to his captivity, saying he had thought of Christ's forty days and nights in the wilderness, and remembered the injunction to forgive those who have sinned against you. So, he had let the rebels 'start life anew'.[20]

In Xi'an, the Marshal's supporters were not ready to give up their struggle. The city was in a rebellious mood. A hundred thousand soldiers and civilians staged a rally for the recovery of Manchuria. But their generals preferred to open peace talks with the Nationalists, leading the young radicals to stage an uprising in which Chiang's kidnapper, Colonel Sun, played a prominent role. As they shot several senior officers, the Young Marshal's companion-in-arms, General Yang Hucheng, turned against them, and the leaders of the uprising fled after sacking the army treasury. Then a Nationalist column entered the city, and Zhang Xueliang's army began to move out for the new home dictated for them by Chiang in the far north. Yang went too, leaving China for a tour of Europe; when he returned in 1938, he was arrested and held as a prisoner for seven years.[21]

Other legacies of the incident lived on in the top levels at Nanking. Chiang developed a trusting relationship with General Chen Cheng, a veteran of the Northern Expedition and the anti-Communist campaigns who had gone to Xi'an with him, and had also been held prisoner. On his return to Nanking, the Generalissimo designated the general as his successor – he was to tell the Model Governor that he could not get along without Chen's services for even a day. Such favour could only antagonise the War Minister, General He Yingqin, who saw himself as the second ranking military figure. This set in motion a lifelong feud between the two men which Chiang did nothing to moderate since it made sure that both would vie for his support.[22]

He's eagerness to bomb Xi'an, putting the leader's life at risk, was an obvious black mark against him. Newspaper stories, apparently inspired by Chiang supporters, spoke of a 'certain clique' in the capital, including military men, who had seen the kidnapping as a chance to dispose of the Generalissimo, and impose a dictatorship of their own. It became known that He and some of his colleagues had wanted Wang Jingwei to form an administration that would be more pliant towards the Japanese. Once the Generalissimo had regained the capital, the newspapers added, the plotters had become super-supportive, seeing the degree of popularity he enjoyed. It was plain that Chiang's confidence in figures like General He had been shaken, making him even more self-sufficient and unwilling to delegate real power.[23]

Needing rest, the Generalissimo lengthened his stay in Xikou to three months. His home village was what might be expected from the birthplace of the pioneer of the New Life movement. A visitor described it as being as clean as a new pin – 'no unemployment, no beggars, no prostitutes, and no sing-song girls'. There were public lavatories, a dry-cleaning shop, two Christian missions, barbers with tilting chairs, and dentists with drills propelled by belts powered by the feet of boys. The population had reached 2,000, half of whom claimed kinship with the Generalissimo. The salt shop where Chiang had been born was empty, but in good condition. His main home had been extended. His first wife, Mao, occupied a room on a balcony with a Buddhist shrine outside. Meiling had a room at the end of the balcony, with a low wooden bed, marble-topped dressing table and mirrored wardrobe. Mao gave her successor local food specialities. Meiling reciprocated with clothes and ginseng.

As well as this home and the residence on the ridge behind the village, Chiang had another house on the riverfront, the Wenchang Pavilion, which had been renovated for him. From the big double bed with a mirrored headboard, there was a fine view out to the hills across the water. Beside it, a modern house was built for Chiang's son, who had come back under his father's wing following his return from the Soviet Union with his

Russian wife. Across the road was a school where the Generalissimo was honorary headmaster. He and Meiling lectured the pupils on good behaviour in the cavernous assembly hall, and used the upstairs offices for meetings. The 700 students followed courses in agriculture; Chiang gave the director regular instructions on acquiring more land and planting trees – nothing, the Generalissimo told him, 'has more dignity than a tree'.

On arrival after the Xi'an Incident, Chiang went for a walk, and paid his last respects to a half-brother who had just died. The funeral drew the Christian General, in peasant garb, Wang Jingwei, who had returned from Europe, Big-Eared Du, and Ailing, Meiling and T. V. Soong. Some of the visitors took a trip up the hill behind the village to visit the Young Marshal, who was reported to be tanned and fit in his detention. At the monastery beside his new home, they shared with him a vegetarian meal of imitation duck, pork and ham. Chiang and Meiling were carried past in sedan chairs to their house on the peak. A visitor noted two beds there. One, for the daughter of the Soong clan, was big and soft; the other, for the self-made soldier with back trouble after his experience in Xi'an, was hard. At the back was a small room with a large porcelain bath.[24]

From Xikou, Chiang authorised meetings with the Communists to lay the groundwork for a united front; Zhou Enlai acted as the main point of contact. The survivors of the Long March used the breathing space that followed the kidnapping to expand their base area in the border areas of Shaanxi, Gansu and Ningxia provinces. After all their anti-Japanese rhetoric, cooperation with the Nationalist government against the invaders could not be rejected. A close and 'sincere' relationship with Nanking was advocated by Wang Ming, a leading party figure who had returned from Moscow, and by Mao's rival Red Army leader, Zhang Guotao. The Communists also adopted a more moderate land reform policy by which rich landlords were fined rather than being killed. As a sign of the new attitude, the Red Army gave a banquet for local military and civilian officials, north of Xi'an, to which an Italian priest and Protestant missionaries were invited.[25]

Each side was still determined to eliminate the other in the long term, but the context of 1937 meant neither could be seen to be putting its interests ahead of those of the nation. So a broad agreement was reached, with Nanking agreeing to pay money to 'reintegrated' territories and armies. The Red Army in Shaanxi, built up to number 30,000 men, became the Eighth Army of the united front, operating in the north under the burly, pug-nosed Long March commander, Zhu De. Nanking approved the creation of a second Communist force in central China, the 12,000-man New Fourth Army which included guerrillas left behind at the start of the Long March. Both armies expanded rapidly, reaching a combined strength of some 92,000 during 1937, and doubling the following year.

The Generalissimo ordered defensive positions to be established in the Shanghai–Nanking–Hangzhou triangle, and pushed the training of elite forces by the German advisers. On paper, he had 2 million troops to throw into battle, but the regime's real strength was well short of appearances. Central army commanders lacked experience in handling large units. Half the officers promoted from the ranks were reckoned to be illiterate. Provincial militarists retained control over substantial armies which they would use for their own ends. In his study of the Chinese army, Michael Gibson has calculated that seventy-nine of the 165 divisions reported to Nanking. Of the remaining eighty-six 'irregular' or warlord divisions, seventeen were of good fighting quality. Another historian of the Sino-Japanese war, Ch'i Hsi-Sheng, counts only thirty-one divisions as answering to Chiang. Many Chinese units were seriously under strength. Even elite forces lacked heavy weapons. Though Japan's strength was much less, with seventeen divisions in the country, its units were properly manned and equipped with artillery, logistical backing and air support. Chiang reckoned that it took three fully staffed Chinese divisions of 14,000 troops each to match one Japanese division.[26]

Still, the merits of taking a more aggressive approach were being pressed on Chiang by his chief German adviser, Alexander von Falkenhausen, a First World War veteran with a vulture-like head and pince-nez. 'China must resist in two ways: morally and materially,' Von Falkenhausen wrote. 'The will morally to resist requires a government that provides firm leadership.' He admitted that the Chinese army was not fit to face a modern war, but, meeting W. H. Donald, tapped him with his swagger stick and said, 'My friend, if Japan attacks, she would be defeated.'

As summer arrived, Chiang and his subordinates moved to the cool of Kuling in the Lushan Mountains where government conferences were held, with officials lodged at the Fairy Glen Hotel. In a letter to his son in June, the Generalissimo noted that the Japanese were 'again causing disturbance, a great annoyance indeed, but we will certainly be able to subdue them'. Half a million copies of his account of the kidnapping were sold. Meiling was awarded honorary degrees by two colleges in the United States.[27]

Elsewhere, the disasters which were such a feature of Chinese life continued unabated. Thirty million people were affected by famine in Sichuan, Shaanxi and Henan, where inhabitants ate mud, baked clay in leaves, hunted ants and devoured tree roots. There were outbreaks of smallpox and bubonic plague in several provinces. In Canton, soldiers shot 350 lepers out of hand at a sanatorium as health risks. A journalist reported seeing 1,500 horse loads of opium from Yunnan on their way through Guizhou. In a speech to mark the tenth anniversary of Nanking's becoming the national capital, President Lin Sen said the regime was 'far behind what we had hoped for'.[28]

The recent appointment of a new Japanese prime minister, Prince Konoe, had been widely seen in the West as a sign that the militarists were losing ground in Tokyo. But Chiang received a different story from one of his visitors at Kuling, Hallett Abend. The *New York Times* journalist had just returned from a tour of Korea, Manchukuo and northern China where he saw big troop concentrations. After the American ambassador pooh-poohed his fears of a new move by Tokyo, Abend went to see Chiang. The Generalissimo, Abend recalled, showed a 'grim determination' not to yield to the Japanese. He would have liked to have had more time to prepare, particularly in developing the air force. But he was well aware that he would lose popular support if he did not resist the next provocation.[29]

That came in the midsummer of 1937. In the afternoon of 7 July, a 100-strong company of Japanese soldiers marched by a stone bridge spanning the Yongding River 10 miles south-west of Peiping. Lined with columns topped by carvings of the heads of lions, the Lukouchiao Bridge* was known to foreigners as the Marco Polo Bridge because the Venetian traveller had visited it. South-east lay the town of Wanping, with some 2,000 inhabitants. To the north was a temple. Beside it was an open area with gravel pits where the Japanese were to carry out a night manoeuvre.[30]

On their arrival, the Japanese found 200 Chinese soldiers digging trenches and repairing pillboxes. To avoid a clash, the Japanese shifted the site of their exercise closer to Wanping, sending off soldiers with machine

---

* Now known as Lugouqiao.

guns to play the role of the enemy. When the first stage of the manoeuvre ended at 10.30 p.m., messengers were dispatched to tell the soldiers playing the adversaries to bed down till dawn. Shortly afterwards, machine-gun fire with blanks sounded from the 'enemy' position. This was followed by a dozen rifle shots from the area where the Chinese soldiers had been working. The Japanese company captain, who suspected that the machine-gunners might have taken the messengers for Chinese scouts, ordered a bugle call to summon his men to muster. When they gathered, it was found that one messenger was missing. The captain sent a dispatch rider to his superior officer to ask for instructions while telling his men to march away from the source of the rifle shots.

The Japanese regimental commander called in reinforcements, but also arranged a midnight meeting with the Chinese guarding Wanping and the bridge. According to recollections by Japanese at the scene, the captain and six men set out in the dark in an attempt to discover what had happened to the missing messenger. They ran into Chinese soldiers, and asked if their man had come that way. When the Chinese said they had seen nobody, the captain abandoned his mission for fear of being made prisoner. By then, the messenger had returned unharmed. His temporary disappearance was put down either to his getting lost in the moonless night after stopping to urinate, having been taken prisoner by the Chinese, having sneaked off to a brothel, or having fallen in a gravel pit and passed out.

The rifle shots from the Chinese were probably a reaction to the machine-gun blanks and the bugle call, rather than an offensive move. But, at the midnight meeting, the Japanese made much of the 'unlawful firing' and called for an investigation. The Chinese understood that they were demanding entry into Wanping for their troops to search the town and possibly to occupy it. When there was fresh Chinese rifle fire before dawn, the Japanese decided to advance, though only as far as the temple.[31]

Unlike earlier incidents exploited by the Japanese, the clash does not appear to have been cooked up to create a pretext for aggression on a wider scale. The local officers signed a provisional ceasefire. In Tokyo, those who wanted Japan to conserve its strength for a confrontation with the Soviet Union initially won the day against those who advocated using the episode to launch a major campaign in northern China. But then incidents multiplied round Peiping, and Emperor Hirohito gave his backing to the expansionists, ordering reinforcements of five divisions to be sent to China.

On the afternoon of 26 July, the Japanese issued an ultimatum for the remaining two Chinese divisions at Peiping to withdraw by noon the next day. In the morning, they began to attack the area round the Summer Palace and the airport outside the former capital. Travelling on the road to the airfield, the French military attaché saw hundreds of corpses of Chinese soldiers killed by fire from armoured vehicles and strafing from the air.[32]

The town of Wanping was heavily bombed before the Japanese blew their way through the gate in its crenellated walls. When the French attaché, Jacques Guillermaz, got there, he found that all the shops were showing Rising Sun flags. Lines of Chinese prisoners, chained round the waist and legs, carried munitions for the victors. Others sat, bound hand and foot, awaiting their fate. An old woman prostrated herself in the dust begging somebody to look after her wounded son – a French doctor took him to hospital and saved his life.[33]

In another walled town, Dongzhou, collaborationist Chinese militiamen changed sides after the Japanese garrison went to join the fighting. They massacred most of the Japanese and Korean civilians in the town, provoking an attack by Kwantung Army soldiers who killed everybody they could find.

The Japanese occupied Peiping and took the railway line to the port of Tianjin which was hit by waves of bombers that set off huge fires – the university was a particular target because, the Japanese explained, it harboured a nest of hostile students. North of the old capital, the Imperial Army pushed through the strategic Nankou Pass on the Great Wall, where the Nationalists had blown up locomotives in the railway tunnel to impede the offensive. The invaders used fast-moving armoured vehicles to outflank the defenders, broke through the Wall and pushed on into Inner Mongolia where they backed a separatist government led by a descendant of Genghis Khan.[34]

In his summer retreat, Chiang referred to the Japanese in his diary by a familiar term of abuse as 'dwarf bandits', and asked whether they were 'attempting to subdue us by taking advantage of the present situation when we have not yet completed our preparations'. It was, he added, 'high time that we decide to respond to the fire'. Central army units were ordered to move north. The Generalissimo insisted that any ceasefire had to be negotiated by Nanking, not by local commanders whom he rightly suspected of being too pliant. Appearing in field uniform on the balcony of military headquarters in Kuling, his chest thrust out, his face stern, he declared that 'the limits of endurance had been reached'.[35]

In an interview at the end of July, Chiang took responsibility for what had happened in the north, but said it marked only the start of the war. He conferred with Governor Yan Xishan of Shanxi; General Han Fuju, the largely autonomous Shandong warlord; General Bai, the Muslim member of the Guangxi Clique; and the governors of Sichuan and Yunnan. T. V. Soong was called in to advise on financing the conflict. As a sign of the new climate, a conference of 400 national leaders was held in Kuling, including representatives of non-partisan professional groups and non-Kuomintang political parties. Zhou Enlai attended to pledge support, asking, in return, for his party's activities to be legalised.[36]

Yan and the Christian General, Feng Yuxiang, were each given command of a northern war zone. The Communist Eighth Army was to be deployed in Shaanxi while the Fourth Army would operate in Jiangsu, above Shanghai. Bai was allocated a central role, and his Guangxi colleague, Li Zongren, was put in charge of the biggest war area reaching in from the central east coast. Chiang kept direct control of Nationalists in the north, though his ability to influence events there was limited by the strength of the Japanese and their collaborators. But he and Meiling showed their resolve by flying to inspect troops on a northern railway line.

In a message to the Communist military commission, Mao said a moment of truth had been reached at which it was imperative to enforce 'the policy of total resistance by the whole nation'. From his side, Chiang declared: 'No territory must be lost and no sovereign rights impaired.' In Tokyo, where the Emperor pressed for a 'war-ending' battle, Hirohito's brother, Prince Takamatsu, summed up the military mood as: 'We're really going to smash China so that it will be ten years before they can stand straight again.' A message to Berlin, from von Falkenhausen reported: 'This is . . . total war.'[37]

Six years after the Mukden Incident, the long-awaited war between Japan and China had begun. It came several years too soon for Chiang whose development and defence plans were far from fruition. But a failure to fight and the abandonment of northern China would have posed a potentially fatal threat to the Generalissimo. For their part, the Japanese expected a short war which could be confined to the north and would give them mastery there. Instead, the conflict would drag on for eight years, reaching across all China and reaping a death toll so immense that it will never be known for certain. Chiang put the 'sacrifices' at 10 million. Official accounts say 3.3 million soldiers and more than 8.4 million civilians were killed, not including others who perished from disease, starvation and forced labour. Chiang's adopted son said 20 million civilians died as Japanese troops made themselves notorious for their brutality and sadistic disregard for human life.

China's great cities were occupied and large tracts of the most fertile land devastated. The war put paid to the attempt of the government to establish a centralised regime, and halted modernisation schemes. The administration became even more militarised and repressive – and grew steadily weaker. The Communists used the war to develop their bases and military force, with Mao asserting his dictatorship.

The need to fight the Japanese before finishing off the Red Army had been forced on Chiang by events beyond his control. His eventual defeat might have happened in any case, but it was greatly facilitated by events after the incident by the Marco Polo Bridge. China would suffer its greatest ordeal since the Taiping Rebellion, and its leader would face his ultimate test. As an opening gambit, he decided to start the fight-back where the enemy did not expect it, provoking a huge urban battle in the city where he had cut his revolutionary teeth two decades earlier.

PART IV

BROKEN JADE

Shanghai, August 1937

———

Chungking, October 1944

CHAPTER 17

The Most Dreadful Nightmare

ON SATURDAY, 14 AUGUST 1937, as a typhoon blew through Shanghai picking up people bodily, five American-made planes from the Chinese air force flew in a tight V formation towards Japanese navy ships moored off the Bund. They had been meant to conduct a high-altitude bombing mission, but the bad weather made this impossible, so they swooped low in a shallow dive 1,500 feet above the water. This boosted their speed, but they failed to adjust their sights. Missing the Japanese ships completely, two of their bombs skimmed above the *North China Daily News* building on the Bund, falling towards the main shopping street of Nanking Road by the Cathay and Palace hotels.[1]

An Australian journalist from the paper, Rhodes Farmer, ran down to the street to see what had happened there. 'On the corner a decapitated Sikh policeman lay with his arms outstretched as though against oncoming traffic,' he wrote.

Yellow high-explosive fumes exposed a terror scene in Nanking Road. Flames from blazing cars were incinerating the bodies of their riddled occupants. In grotesque heaps where they had been huddling in doorways and annexes of the Cathay and Palace hotels were heaps of refugees whose blue coolie clothes were turning red. Heads, arms, legs lay far from mangled trunks . . . Across the tramlines was a tall European. His suit of white flannel was unspotted so cleanly had his skull been sliced off.[2]

Fallen masonry and shattered glass covered the road. The clock on the front of the Cathay was stopped at 4.27. Inside, bits of flesh lay among valuables on show in the hotel's display windows. Behind the bar, two Chinese stewards served brandy. A White Russian picked up a thumb from the floor, and asked the people in the bar, 'Any of you lose this?' The official death toll was 728.

There was even worse carnage in the French Concession. Two shrapnel bombs jettisoned by another Chinese plane landed in the crowded streets outside the New World entertainment centre. A hundred cars caught fire, burning the trapped occupants to death. The pavements ran with blood. More than 1,000 people died and as many were injured. Walking home that night, Farmer passed through an alley where he saw hundreds of people apparently asleep. Then he realised that they were unburied bodies.

The bombings came at the start of a three-month battle which Chiang provoked in Shanghai to open a second front in the war with Japan. He had sent troops into the city in defiance of the demilitarisation agreement that ended the battle of 1932. The Japanese riposted with an artillery bombardment of the edge of the workers' district of Chapei, and of the university area. As refugees crowded into the International Settlement and the French Concession, Emperor Hirohito pronounced the situation in Shanghai 'critical'. It was certainly not what the Japanese wanted. Their strategy was to consolidate in the north. To prevent that and to live up to the nationalistic hopes fanned after the Xi'an Incident, the Generalissimo decided on a dramatic gesture. There could be no better place to do this than China's biggest and richest city, making the metropolis that symbolised the drive for modernity into an icon for a new readiness to fight the invaders under the gaze of foreign diplomats, businessmen and correspondents.

Instead of confronting the enemy on the northern plains where it would be able to exploit its air, armoured and artillery superiority, the Generalissimo decided to suck Japan into a close quarters urban battle he hoped would arouse the nation psychologically to compensate for reversals in the north. The Shanghai–Nanking–Hangzhou triangle was the most fortified part of the country. Rail and road communications were good. The strength of the Green Gang would be used – Big-Eared Du had tipped his cap to the anti-Japanese struggle by visiting the 'seven gentlemen' imprisoned in Shanghai for patriotic activities whose trial had been abandoned when the war began. The city's businesses could be counted on to come up with funds. The Americans, British and French in their concessions might be caught up in the fighting, provoking foreign intervention. There was also the potent memory of the defence of the city in 1932, and the hope that, if they finally met resistance, the Japanese would lose heart while their home front recoiled from high casualties.

Chiang's policy certainly diverted the Japanese, preventing them from simply consolidating in northern China and dividing the country along the line of the Yellow River. The expansion of the war to the Yangtze and then further south meant that, so long as the Nationalists held out politically, Tokyo faced a challenge it would be unable to master, given the size of the nation and the inaccessibility of much of the interior. But Chiang's grand strategy came at an awful price. Japan was not going to allow itself to be driven into the sea at Shanghai. It controlled the lanes to the mouth of the Yangtze, so could bring in as many troops as it wished, and had no scruples about using air raids and artillery against urban areas. As for Western intervention, Washington, London and Paris had shown every desire to avoid a military clash – even if they intervened, Nanking could, at best, only expect a return to the status quo.

There was also a wider danger. Once they had become engaged in Shanghai, the Japanese were likely to press on up the river towards Nanking. If they took the capital, they could then advance further west to Wuhan. Chiang's second front also amounted to recognition that the central government was helpless in northern China. That may have been reality, but it meant he abandoned resistance there to the Communists who were able to draw on peasants, students and patriotic youth movements. The Generalissimo was acting on psychological-political grounds, rather than according to strict military calculations. As he ordered every unit to fight to the last man, what counted was to show that the enemy could no longer enjoy military walkovers whenever it chose. As a Japanese spokesman put it, 'the Chinese idea of a victory is very different from ours. When they do not retreat, they regard it as a victory.'

The main Japanese offensive began in mid-September and lasted for a month on a battle line that stretched for forty miles. There was heavy fighting in the surrounding countryside which rain turned into what one observer called 'a great wet rice field' while the urban front reached through the districts of Chapei, Hongkew and Yangtzepo. Hidden Chinese artillery fired across the river. Civilians helped construct defences and assisted medical and relief work – Du gave his bullet-proof limousine to the army. Cabarets turned into relief centres for wounded soldiers whom the sing-song girls comforted with sweet words, flowers and manicures.[3]

At the height of the battle, the Nationalists had committed half a million men, led by some of their best generals. Tokyo staged six troop mobilisations to raise its strength to 200,000 under the command of the slight, tubercular General Matsui Iwane, a devoted Buddhist from a scholarly family. His soldiers pushed forward slowly but steadily from the coast through heavy downpours. Japanese air operations were helped when Italian advisers who had been working for the Nationalists changed sides and handed over plans of the region.

The ten-storey concrete administration building of the North Station, rebuilt after the battle of 1932, became a centre of fighting once again. Ringed by vast craters, one end of the structure was holed and blackened by shells and bombs, but a Chinese unit held out inside, emerging at night on attack missions. Many prisoners in the city's main jail were killed when they were caught in crossfire. A foreign hospital treated 14,599 outpatients during August alone. In the Hongkew district, Rhodes Farmer saw streets lined with bodies of local people shot by the Japanese. Whole blocks of buildings had been burned to smoke out snipers; shops had been looted; the freebooting *ronin* gangsters did as they wished.[4]

Spectators lined the rooftops of the Bund to watch enemy warships firing shells from the river in the middle of the city; it was as if German cruisers had been anchored off Westminster in 1940 or Japanese naval craft in the Hudson in 1942. The foreigners went on with their lawn bowls, polo and cricket while an operatic troupe performed in the ballroom of the greyhound racing stadium; the Rotary Club heard a talk on world politics; a Japanese parliamentary delegation arrived to enquire into what was going on. At one bar, Hungarian gypsies played till dawn. At another, a broken-down Russian singer crooned 'Parlez-moi d'amour'.

Although Japan dominated the battle in the air, Chinese pilots directed by Claire Chennault, the American officer recruited at Meiling's instigation, made regular sorties. One particular target was the cruiser moored off the Bund, the *Idzumo*, which the planes had been aiming for in the early disastrous raid. Two unsuccessful attempts were also made to blow it up with torpedoes, but the antiquated boat remained invulnerable. In a second accident of war on Nanking Road, the Sincere department store was hit by a bomb dropped by a Chinese pilot who lightened his load while evading Japanese fighters. The blast sent shrapnel and debris flying into the Wing On shop opposite. The death toll was put at around 200, with 550 injured. Counter attendants and customers lay dead on top of one another. One heap of bodies was covered with toys. Water from burst mains washed blood down the gutters. A Boy Scout climbed to a lift caught between floors at Sincere; when he opened the door, the blood of the dead streamed out, and he handed down a pith helmet with a decapitated head still in it.*[5]

Chiang orchestrated the battle from his headquarters in the silk town of Suzhou,† north-west of Shanghai. He drew up detailed written orders which often bore little relation to the fluctuating realities of the battleground, and were out of date by the time they reached the front. His insistence that units must not retreat meant many of his best troops fell in protracted battles for villages outside Shanghai. German advisers went to the front line, including von Falkenhausen who subsisted on boiled eggs and cognac, and earned a decoration from the Nanking government for his work. A visiting correspondent, Hessell Tiltman, was greatly impressed by the quality of Chinese troops, but he noted the lack of medical facilities and the heavy losses – on one dark night he sat on what he thought was a heap of sacks but discovered he was resting on a pile of bodies. The Chinese, he concluded, 'are facing incredible hardships with a courage which deserves the most flattering tribute a pen can write'. The defenders suffered from bad co-ordination and poor intelligence. In places, they were in single trenches without barbed wire.[6]

At the height of the battle, Meiling drove from Nanking to visit refugees and emergency hospitals. W. H. Donald accompanied her. The

---

* The attack has sometimes been blamed on the Japanese but Hallett Abend watched the Chinese plane dropping two Italian-made bombs, and also recorded that they had been logged as imports to the Nationalists at the customs (Abend, *My Life*, p. 264).

† Known at the time as Soochow.

road was pitted with shell craters and under surveillance from Japanese planes – they had just attacked a car carrying the British ambassador, Sir Hughe Knatchbull-Hugessen, wounding him in the spine, despite a Union Jack marking on the roof of his vehicle. Meiling, wearing blue slacks and shirt, was chatting with Donald when their car hit a pothole. After the rear tyre punctured, the vehicle went out of control, shooting off the highway and turning over. Thrown out, Donald saw Chiang's wife flying over his head. She landed in a ditch 20 feet away, unconscious, her face caked with mud.

Thinking she was dead, Donald picked up Meiling, and carried her to a farmhouse. There, he felt her breathing as she stirred. Parodying the Chinese custom of shouting to frighten away life-claiming devils, the Australian sang in a booming voice, 'She flies through the air with the greatest of ease, this daring young girl who fights Japanese.' When Meiling opened her eyes, as Donald recalled a decade later, he told her, 'You can never say that I didn't pick you up from the gutter.'[7]

The youngest Soong washed her face, and put on make-up. Looking pale and weak, she said her side hurt; she held Donald's arm tightly as the car was put back on the road and they drove to the city. She had a broken rib, but went ahead with visits to army hospitals where she was photographed tending to the wounded in a nurse's uniform.

A Japanese landing at Hangzhou Bay to the south sealed the outcome as the attackers enveloped the Chinese forces with 30,000 men to their rear. Though the commanders at the front urged Chiang to order a general retreat, he held on for five days, losing many more of his best men in the process. A naval spokesman in Tokyo reported that 850 planes had dropped 2,526 bombs in two days. Huge blazes broke out, with acres of blackened ruins, charred timber and heaps of bricks.[8]

In Songjiang on the Japanese route to Shanghai, hardly a building was not gutted by fire. Once the town had housed 100,000 people; now only five remained, sheltered in a former French Catholic mission. The dogs had grown unnaturally fat after feasting on corpses.[9]

Finally, Chiang ordered withdrawal from Shanghai on 8 November. To cover the retreat, the Chinese set fire to Chapei. Despite rain, the blaze stretched for more than 5 miles and was still burning in places two weeks later. Across the creek from the International Settlement, an elite battalion stayed behind in a warehouse to provide a last outpost of resistance, choosing its position so that the Japanese would be inhibited from using their artillery for fear of shells overshooting and hitting the foreigners. A fourteen-year-old Chinese Girl Guide swam the creek bearing a national flag which was raised over the building. The colonel in charge asked to be sent supplies of sugar, salt and biscuits for a long stand. But, once it had made its gesture, Chiang ordered the battalion to evacuate. Leaving 100 bodies behind, the soldiers crossed the bridge into the Anglo-American area. Some carried umbrellas of oiled paper; one had a canary in a cage; many walked hand-in-hand. At the back of the column were six uniformed girls who had been with the battalion through the siege. Behind them, Japanese soldiers raised their flag on the warehouse roof to the cry of 'Banzai!'[10]

Estimates of Nationalist losses in the ninety-day battle range from 180,000 to 300,000, including many of the best German-trained units. The Japanese were reckoned to have lost 70,000 men. More than 100,000 refugees crowded into camps in the foreign areas run by a white-bearded French Jesuit with a wooden arm. Another 350,000 people fled the city during or after the fighting. By any rational calculation, it had been a disaster for the Chinese. If Chiang had been able to hold the line in Shanghai, it might have been argued that the resulting upsurge in national morale would have justified the heavy casualties. But that was far from being the case as the retreat turned into a chaotic race for survival by soldiers and civilians.

The enemy repeatedly outflanked Chinese defensive lines amid the rivers, lakes and canals of the area, laying waste everything in their path, clearing men from their homes and raping the women left inside, carrying off loot, food and livestock on stolen horses, donkeys and buffaloes. 'The farming area between Shanghai and Nanking, once the most populous area on earth, was the graveyard of almost a million Chinese,' Rhodes Farmer reported. Roads were clogged with fleeing soldiers and civilians, some in carts, rickshaws and boats but most on foot, targets for repeated bombing and strafing by enemy planes. A Japanese battalion was told simply: 'All law-abiding people have retreated within the walls of towns and cities. Treat everyone found outside the walls as anti-Japanese and destroy them.'[11]

As the Generalissimo moved back to Nanking, von Falkenhausen laid out plans to hold the Japanese at Suzhou for three months. He had reckoned without the effect of heavy air raids which, as one eyewitness wrote, sent 'tons of explosives hurtling down from the skies, exploding in a cascade of bits of human flesh, dirt, stone and mortar . . . The most dreadful nightmare could not compare with it . . . The death and destruction we witnessed defies all description.' After the raids, Japanese soldiers wearing hoods walked in through the gates of the town – it was said that the guards took them for Buddhist monks. Once inside, they drew their weapons and began to shoot, setting off fires and opening the gates to let in the main body of troops. Those who could escape fled; by the time the Japanese were finished, only 500 people were said to remain inside the walls.[12]

The bombing of civilian centres was condemned by the League of Nations and the United States. Britain offered to mediate between the combatants. A nine-power conference on China, backed by London and Washington, convened in Brussels. But Japan stayed away and asserted its will to fight to the bitter end until China 'reconsidered its attitude'. The China Incident became a sacred struggle, a holy war to extend the Emperor's 'benevolent rule' to a backward people across the sea. The Japanese commander said the Chinese should realise his troops were their real friends, ready to sacrifice themselves to rescue them.[13]

After the decades in which foreign powers had fed off China while professing concern for its integrity, Chiang could only draw bitter conclusions from the lack of help. Despite foreign Fascist and Communist involvement, the simultaneous war in Spain was primarily between Spaniards. In contrast, the Chinese were facing undisguised, unprovoked aggression from another country of the kind which the United States and Europe had vowed to prevent in the post-1918 world order. As Chiang said in an interview: 'The simple truth is that Japan took action with the object of crushing China and establishing for herself a Continental Empire' . . . The West appeared to feel that 'incident-making' should be allowed as a pretext to annex parts of another country.[14]

In line with that process, the Chinese areas of Shanghai came under a puppet administration supervised by the Japanese while the invaders worked to extend their influence in the foreign concessions. Chiang had not got the Westerners involved, and his hopes that Japan would start to suffer from war weariness were contradicted by an even more belligerent attitude in Tokyo. He had forfeited China's major city, with all its financial, tax, commercial and manufacturing resources – and drawn the enemy into the central government's base area. But, in keeping with the psychology he had adopted, the second battle of Shanghai was declared a glorious moment in Nationalist history. In a hagiography forty years later, the Generalissimo's adopted son would call the opening of the second front in central China 'the most brilliant, successful, difficult and representative of all the war directions that have been recorded in the history of war, both in China and across the world'.[15]

While attention was focused on Shanghai in the autumn and early winter of 1937, the Japanese had been pressing forward in the north where a puppet government was installed in Peiping in December. Widening their field of operations, they staged air raids on railway lines and major cities across much of the country. As they advanced, they displayed the brutality which was to mark their conduct during the war, killing at random, raping and looting. For fires in the bitterly cold north, they tore the frames out of houses, leaving the inhabitants without shelter. China also alleged that they used poison gas.

Units of the Communist Eighth Army under the Long March veteran Lin Biao scored the one notable Chinese victory in the north. After a marathon march, soldiers in blue-grey cotton uniforms ambushed a Japanese column moving through a narrow valley pass at Bingxingguan in the loess country of north-east Shanxi. Buoyed by previous victories, the invaders had not bothered to send out scouts. The Communists riddled them with gunfire and hurled down hand grenades, killing 3,000 men for some 400 casualties of their own. Bingxingguan went down in Communist history as a triumph for Mao's guerrilla tactics, but was hardly mentioned by the Nationalists.[16]

The ambush was an isolated victory, and the Japanese took the Shanxi capital of Taiyuan after a siege. In Tokyo, the Imperial General Headquarters was activated to enable Hirohito to meet regularly with his military chiefs and ministers. Japan still called the conflict an 'incident' in order not to risk vital imports from the United States being halted by neutrality regulations against supplying countries at war – on one occasion, its spokesman in Peiping told a questioner, 'You know, this is a special undeclared war.' But the activation of the imperial headquarters signified that the scale of the fighting required coordination at the very highest level. Tokyo changed its terminology from the 'North China Incident' to the 'China Incident'.[17]

Responding to the aggression, Meiling emerged as the regime's most effective spokesperson to the English-speaking world, in particular to America. In a radio broadcast to the United States, she said that the Chinese had laboured for years under the stigma of being labelled as cowards. Now, they would do their best. 'We will try to fight until we win or are really beaten to our broken knees, even if our good earth, with all its history, and its cares is steeped with blood and swept by fire and destroyed,' she went on. 'Japan is acting on a preconceived plan to conquer China. Curiously, no other nation seems to care. She seems to have secured their spell-bound silence, uttering the simple magical formula, "This is not war but merely an incident." All treaties and structures to outlaw war and to regularise the conduct of war appear to have crumbled, and we have a reversion to the day of savages.' Was Western silence 'a sign of the triumph of civilisation', she wondered, or 'the death-knell of the supposed moral superiority of the Occident'?[18]

With German help reduced by Berlin's increasingly pro-Japanese policy, Chiang turned to Moscow. Stalin saw every interest in strengthening China to divert Tokyo from attacking the Soviet Far East. As always each man calculated according to what he considered to be his strategic needs, without consideration of ideology. Moscow and Nanking signed a non-aggression pact, and arms and pilots began to arrive from Russia. But this renewed relationship could do nothing to save the situation on the Yangtze as the Japanese advanced on a 24-mile front towards Nanking.

The government decided to move to the Wuhan tri-cities of Wuchang, Hankou and Hanyang – and then, if necessary, beyond the Yangtze Gorges to Chungking in Sichuan. A vast operation had begun during the battle of Shanghai to dismantle factories and move around 150 of them to the deep interior. That was now stepped up; 15,000 cases of art treasures from Nanking were to go, too.[19]

For the time being, Chiang stayed in the capital where the German ambassador, Oscar Trautmann, passed on a feeler from Tokyo which may well have been an empty ploy to try to present Japan in the guise of peace-seeker. It got short shrift – the Generalissimo said talks were impossible so long as his country was being attacked. Demonstrating what was meant by their proposals of economic cooperation, Japanese companies announced a huge exploitative development scheme in coal, iron, communications and electricity in northern China.[20]

Chiang now had to decide whether to stage a second major urban battle at Nanking. A strong proponent of resistance was the Hunanese general, Tang Shengzhi, the Kuomintang's early ally on the Northern Expedition in 1926 who had subsequently led a revolt and fled to Japan before returning to rally to the cause once more. The 'Buddhist General' argued that holding the Japanese at Nanking would provide a breathing space for other armies to reorganise themselves. 'Either I stay or you stay,' Chiang told him.

The Nationalists, numbering some 90,000, set up machine-gun positions on the 20-mile city wall, dug trenches, strung barbed wire across streets and barricaded the gates with concrete, sandbags and iron. A mile-wide ring of open land was cleared by fire. At the end of November, Tang gave a press conference pledging to live or die with the capital. That earned him applause from the reporters; but some noted that the general, who had just recovered from a bad illness and had a record as an opium smoker, appeared dazed, if not doped, and sweated profusely. In the evening of 7 December, W. H. Donald suggested to Chiang that he had better have his aeroplane standing by. Nodding, the Generalissimo replied, 'We leave at dawn.' Before they went, his wife wrote to the *Atlantic Monthly* magazine in the United States asking for her subscription copy to be sent to a new address.[21]

Heading south-west at daybreak with Meiling and Donald in his Sikorski seaplane, Kai-shek could be heard reciting poetry to himself – sounding as if he were humming. As his taciturnity increased, so did his soft chanting of classical verses. The flying boat landed on the huge Poyang Lake in Jiangxi where Chiang and Galen had defeated warlord troops in the first phase of the Northern Expedition ten years earlier. The three passengers were carried up to a mountain haven to spend a week walking through the peaks when Chiang was not issuing instructions to his generals. By coincidence, on the day Chiang flew out of Nanking, the Japanese commander, General Matsui Iwane, suffered a relapse of his tuberculosis, and took to his bed. Hirohito promoted him to a non-operational post in charge of the overall campaign. The attack on the city was entrusted to the Emperor's uncle, Prince Asaka Yasuhiko.[22]

Whatever General Tang had vowed, the Chinese were in poor shape to resist. The defenders came from different units, and lacked a cohesive command. Many of the best officers had died in Shanghai. The departure of leading officials, including Chiang, sapped morale. Chinese planes had been pulled back further inland, and there was no air cover. Some defenders were boys of twelve or thirteen. And, despite his brave words, Tang was soon seeking an agreement with the Japanese to hand over the city provided his men were allowed to leave peacefully. The proposal was sent to Chiang in a radio message from an American gunboat, the *Panay*, moored in the Yangtze. The Generalissimo rejected it. Public accommodation with the enemy did not fit his strategy.[23]

On 10 December, Japanese planes bombed the city while artillery launched a huge wave of shelling. Civilians crowded into a Safety Zone set up by foreigners. Fierce fighting raged, often hand-to-hand. At 5 p.m., the attackers ran up their flag on major buildings. 'Our casualties are naturally heavy and we are fighting against metal with merely flesh and blood,' General Tang said in a message to Nationalist headquarters.

Once the defenders had made their stand, Chiang's attitude changed diametrically, and he sent an order to Tang to retreat across the Yangtze. His aim now was to save as many soldiers as possible. But, as was often the case, the orders the Generalissimo issued far from the battlefield were unrealistic. Tang told him that the battle situation made retreat impossible – his men were fighting in isolated pockets and could not stage a general move. The Japanese controlled the main escape route, the river. Tang himself managed to make his way out on a small launch, heading for his home province of Hunan and bearing the blame for the loss of the city. Behind him, Nanking descended into murderous chaos.*[24]

Thousands died trying to cross the Yangtze, some in Japanese air attacks, others as overloaded junks sank. Huge fires and exploding ammunition dumps killed many more. Three thousand wounded soldiers lay on the concrete platform of the main station, their moaning sounding 'like the wind in a pine forest', according to an American who fed them gruel. Chinese soldiers fled from the wall on ropes made from belts and puttees. Troops took off their uniforms, and tried to blend in with the civilians.

* A practised survivor, he would resurface in Communist China as a member of the National People's Congress.

Under orders to take no prisoners, the Japanese inspected palms to tell rough soldiers from townspeople, and shot those without smooth skin. Fine modern buildings erected during the past decade as symbols of China's modernisation were set on fire. Banks, shops, businesses and homes were looted. Half the city's million-strong population fled. Some of those who stayed hung out Rising Sun flags to appease their new masters.[25]

Amid the confusion, Japanese planes caused a diplomatic incident by sinking the *Panay*. Survivors were machine-gunned as they swam to safety. British gunboats were also targets. But both Washington and London were content with apologies from Tokyo. Chiang's hope that the Western powers would intervene proved illusory once more. In any case, the attacks on their boats were a tiny sideshow compared to what was unfolding in the city.

The Rape of Nanking was unique as an urban atrocity not only for the number of people who died but also for the way the Japanese went about their killing, the wanton individual cruelty, the reduction of the city's inhabitants to the status of subhumans who could be murdered, tortured, and raped at will in an outburst of the basest instincts let loose in six weeks of terror and death.* The death toll was put at 300,000 – some accounts set it even higher, though one source for the former figure, Harold Timperley of the *Manchester Guardian*, used it to refer to deaths in the Yangtze Valley as a whole.[26]

On the first day, a Japanese division killed more than 24,000 prisoners of war and fleeing soldiers. On the wharves by the river, coolies threw 20,000 bodies into the Yangtze before being killed themselves. Behind its white flags and Red Cross symbols, the foreign Safety Zone proved weak protection: indeed, by concentrating refugees there, it inadvertently provided a big target for the killers; the 'good Nazi of Nanking', the German John Rabe could only roam the streets trying to rescue individuals in his path.[27]

There were no imperial orders, as such, for the Rape of Nanking, and General Matsui gave senior officers a scathing rebuke after he entered the city for the victory parade on 17 December. But the general left for

---

* Japanese nationalists continue to deny the scale and nature of what took place, and have kept details of it from textbooks. But the evidence is overwhelming. Iris Chang's 1997 book provides a devastating chronicle of the horror, and of Japan's refusal to accept responsibility. Masahiro Yamamoto argues strongly in his account against the idea that the massacre was planned to intimidate Chinese elsewhere.

Shanghai two days later and, though he insisted there that misconduct must be severely punished, his words had no discernible effect. Any Chinese was liable to be a target. People were roped together and machine-gunned, doused with kerosene and set on fire. Thousands were buried alive – or put in holes up to their necks and then savaged by army dogs. Others were frozen to death after being thrown into icy ponds. Japanese soldiers used Chinese for bayonet practice. Civilians were nailed to boards and run over by vehicles. Mutilation, disembowelling and eye gouging took place before executions. People were sprayed with acid, or hung up by their tongues. Medical experiments were conducted in a former hospital where Chinese, known as 'logs', were injected with germs and poisons. Women, young and old, pregnant and ill, were raped in enormous numbers, and then killed, some with sticks rammed into their vaginas. Foetuses were ripped from the bodies of expectant mothers. Other women were taken to so-called 'comfort houses' set up for the soldiers, who called the inmates 'public toilets'.[28]

Japanese newspapers recorded a competition between two lieutenants to behead 100 Chinese with their swords. When they both passed the mark, it was not clear who had got there first, so the contest was extended to 150. One of the lieutenants described the competition as 'fun', though Japanese newspapers noted that he had damaged his blade on the helmet of a Chinese he cut in half. Revelling in their savagery, Japanese soldiers took photographs of the massacres and sent them to Shanghai to be developed; Chinese staff in the photographic shops passed copies to Rhodes Farmer who forwarded them to *Look* magazine in America in evidence of the horror.[29]

As the Nationalist capital, Nanking was obviously an important target where the Japanese wanted to achieve maximum humiliation of their adversary. But the sustained mass bestiality can better be explained – if it can be rationally explained at all – by the tensions that had built up in the army since the Shanghai battle erupted, by the knowledge of the Japanese troops that they were heavily outnumbered by the Chinese in the city, by the callousness bred in the previous four months – and, above all, by the dehumanisation of the Chinese which had become part of the psyche of the Imperial Army. The invaders saw the people around them as lower than animals, targets for a bloodlust which many, if not all, their commanders felt could only spur their men on to fight better. In his diary, one soldier described the Chinese as 'ants crawling on the ground . . . a herd of ignorant sheep'. Another recorded that while raping a woman, his colleagues might consider her as human, but, when they killed her, 'we just thought of her as something like a pig'.[30]

It seems certain that the Emperor in Tokyo knew at least the outline of what was going on. His uncle was in command, and Japanese newspapers reported the execution contests among officers as if they were sporting events. Hirohito still hoped that China could be defeated with one big blow, which Nanking might provide. Japan's terms for a settlement were toughened to include indefinite stationing of troops in China and reparations as well as recognition of Manchukuo and cooperation against the Communists. 'We must strengthen our resolve to fight through to the end with China,' the Foreign Minister told a meeting of the Imperial Conference. Tokyo withdrew recognition of the Nationalist government which, it said, was to be 'eradicated'.[31]

Moving to Wuhan, Chiang proclaimed that his strategy was one of trading space for time – the Japanese would be ceded territory but the Chinese would win time to strengthen their resistance. He announced that he was going to increase his focus on military affairs, handing over the chairmanship of the Executive Yuan to his brother-in-law, H. H. Kung. But there was no doubt as to his continued dominance. The organisation at the top was complex and simple – complex in the overlapping jobs held by generals and senior officials; simple in the pre-eminence of one man. 'The whole civil organisation of the Chinese Government has practically faded away, and is replaced by a military organisation which has developed out of General Chiang Kai-shek's headquarters,' Reuters reported. 'The various yuan and ministries exist in name only.' The staff at the Foreign Ministry had shrunk from 400 to fifty; the Legislative Yuan had seven officials.[32]

The unoccupied area of the country was divided into five war zones, with Chiang as overall boss. Area commands were held by the Guangxi leader, Li Zongren, Governor Yan of Shanxi, and Whampoa veterans. The man the Generalissimo had designated as his successor, Chen Cheng, was responsible for the defence of Wuhan. The losses along the Yangtze were put at half a million troops, with considerably higher civilian casualties. Official sources acknowledged that the lack of medical facilities 'resulted in colossal proportion of deaths among the wounded'. The officer corps had been severely mauled – one general reported losing eleven of his twelve battalion commanders as well as 70 per cent of his men in the space of ten days. The loss of northern China, where a pro-Japanese, anti-Kuomintang administration had been formed, was officially blamed on old-style warlord commanders who had flirted with the enemy. But Chiang could blame nobody else for the Shanghai–Nanking campaign, so justification had to be found in the idea that suffering acted as a path to redemption.[33]

In his memoir on his fiftieth birthday the previous year, Chiang had recalled how his family had been solitary and without influence, the target of ill-treatment – the same might be said of China in the late 1930s. He had written of the apathy of relatives and kinsmen when his family suffered injustice – again this could apply to the way no other country had stood by China after the Japanese invasion. Salvation lay in the discipline, grit and hard work epitomised by the Generalissimo's mother, backed by puritanism and the New Life movement – in December 1937, Chiang threatened execution for officials found dancing in Wuhan cabarets, and 'drastic punishment' for members of the administration discovered gambling or in the company of sing-song girls.[34]

Reality and logic had little place in his reasoning. 'I can only go forward,' he declared as he told General Tang to withdraw from Nanking. 'Let us all go forward; let us never retreat.' In a broadcast after the fall of the city, the Generalissimo proclaimed: 'We must not surrender but march onwards. To capitulate is to court sure national disaster.' The situation, he added, was 'definitely favourable' because the further the Japanese moved into the interior, the greater their problems would be as they 'swallowed like a whale', taking great areas of territory they would be unable to digest. 'The time must come when Japan's military strength will be completely exhausted, thus giving us ultimate victory,' he argued. Naming Chiang and Meiling as International Man and Wife of the Year at the start of 1938, *Time* magazine noted that China's prospects were 'for the long pull', but added that, if its leader could achieve his aims, he might emerge as Asia's Man of the Century.[35]

Anybody else would have buckled, thought W. H. Donald, who was often with the Chiangs during this period. But this was a man who had taught his son the parable of the tortoise and the hare as a lesson for life, and who would take whatever time he needed, retreating into himself and depending on nobody else. 'Days with him were like the silence of a lonely

Arctic night,' the Australian recalled. 'When he did speak, there were only single-syllable questions.' On his walks with the Chiangs, Donald would discuss the war with the bilingual Meiling for an hour or so while Chiang said nothing, just reciting poetry to himself. When the Australian clapped his hands to jar the Generalissimo into life, Chiang would incline his head slightly to his wife and ask slowly what the adviser wanted. Sometimes, Donald recalled, he would ask Meiling if she knew what her husband was thinking. She would give a helpless look, and the Australian thought, 'Good God! Doesn't he even talk in his sleep?'[36]

CHAPTER 18

I Am the State

'OLD WOMEN, CHILDREN, all sorts of soldiers, carts, wheelbarrows, rickshaws simply filled the steaming wet highway where the morning's heat had given place to a cold north-east wind,' the journalist Edgar Mowrer reported from central China.

> Dainty Chinese girls in silken semi-modern dress and slippers, older women hobbling on surprisingly quickly on their bound feet with the aid of long poles on which they balanced; occasional old men; rich wives of merchants in rickshaws; peasant girls plodding stolidly; tiny children wet to the skin but impassive in the long-suffering Chinese way; whole families in heavy ox carts with solid wooden wheels, drawn by inconceivable combinations of domestic animals, their small household goods all mixed up with the equipment of soldiers trotting beside them; babies in boxes on tiny wheels or strapped to the back of tottering older children, occasional sturdy farmers lifting the handles of gigantic loaded wheel barrows, their remaining donkey or wife or children pulling in front; these were inextricably mixed with the retreating Chinese army. There were almost no motor vehicles, and the few were piled to the sky with women and goods and attempts to purchase transportation were sternly refused.[1]

The Japanese advance turned millions of Chinese civilians into refugees as the Nationalist regime demonstrated its incapacity to offer its people even the most basic measure of security and protection. Travelling to Wuhan, the writer Han Suyin noted 'cattle trucks filled to overflowing with human salvage. Miserable, with drawn faces, in rags, dirty and thin, clutching their pathetic possessions tied in bundles. Children, old and wizened with fatigue, long past whimpering, rubbing at their trachoma-eaten eyes with their dirty hands, with the rags of their garments.' From the mountains by the Yellow River, Theodore (Teddy) White of *Time* wrote of

village after village completely destroyed. Houses shattered and burnt . . . Bridges torn up . . . The Japanese looted indiscriminately and efficiently. Everything of value was stripped and taken away. Telephones, wires, clocks, soap, bedding, collected for transfer to their own supply department. On their own, the soldiers went in for simpler forms of looting. Clothes and food were what they wanted, and they were not very discriminate in their tastes; women's silk garments, peasant cotton trousers, shoes, underwear were all stripped off the backs of their possessors.[2]

In some villages White visited, the Japanese had raped every woman – those who tried to hide in fields were forced out by cavalry riding through the wheat and barley.

Male villagers were stripped naked, lashed to carts and driven forward by the Imperial Army as beasts of burden. Japanese horses and mules were beaten to death in the mud; and on any road and all the hills of the valley, one can see the carcasses of their animals rotting, and the bones of their horses whitening in the sun. The Chinese peasants who were impressed to take their places were driven forward with the same pitiless fury until they collapsed, died, or were driven mad.

Reuters reported from a 'neat little town' where every building had been burned down in Japanese assaults. A magistrate said the enemy had killed 600 people in the first attack; when they returned, the inhabitants fought back and chased them into the hills, using swords made from the chassis of a captured lorry. Bodies lay in a gully, the skulls and bones bleaching in the sun. The locals destroyed the road, forcing the Japanese to abandon 200 lorries. The motors were taken out and used for power. Blacksmiths turned steel from the vehicles into guns – firing a single-shot pistol, the journalist found it had a 'tremendous recoil'. Local officials said the Japanese would attack again, 'but we will . . . take them by surprise and cut their communications till they are obliged to retreat'. The villagers would be defended by themselves, not by the far-away government.[3]

As for the Chinese army, Mowrer reported a retreat in 1938 in which

there was hardly a coat in the long defile. Steel helmets were the exception. Bayonets were anything but universal. On the other hand, umbrellas were plentiful. I saw a few machine-guns, one small thing that looked like a trench mortar, one anti-aircraft gun. In the course of two days on the road with the troops, I hardly noticed more than half a dozen batteries of field guns. During a week, not a single Chinese airplane flew over us while Jap planes were everywhere.[4]

On the Henan–Shandong border, Rhodes Farmer watched railway wagons filled with badly injured soldiers lying on mats of plaited bamboo. 'Gangrene was everywhere: maggots writhed in the wounds,' the Australian journalist wrote. 'They suffered silently and died silently. A 0.5 machine-gun bullet had smashed through one kid's crotch . . . He had been hit a week ago. I offered him a pack of cigarettes. He smiled wanly and fluttered his right hand: the sign of courteous refusal.'[5]

The Japanese seized cities and towns, main roads and railways, and launched regular, murderous expeditions to grab crops and to try to pacify the countryside where guerrillas operated. For all their armed strength, however, their forces were badly overextended, and their demands for munitions outstripped supplies. One metaphor used was of China as a net with the strings and knots representing Japanese positions around the much larger Chinese holes. The parallels with the war in Vietnam are evident, underlined by the reflections of the Red Army commander Zhu De to the journalist James Bertram. Japanese reliance on mechanised support units could be turned to the Chinese advantage, Zhu said. 'They cannot use animal transport, or human labor as our armies can. They cannot take advantage of the hill country, but must follow the easiest and most level route . . . so we always fight in the hills, not in open country.'[6]

In a further similarity with the Americans in Indochina three decades later, the invaders were subject to repeated terrorist attacks in cities, and their isolation was accentuated by Chinese destruction of highways to create areas where they could not use their vehicles. Later, some Japanese, lamenting the way their forces had been sucked into the quagmire of China, would argue that the Imperial Army should have stopped after taking the big Yangtze cities, and focused its attention on the north, confronting the Soviet Union on its Far Eastern frontier with Manchuria. But there was no way they could have done this without leaving much of China south of the Yellow River to the Nationalists. To that extent, Chiang's space for time strategy did work, though the cost to his people, and to his own authority, was huge.[7]

The Generalissimo linked the defence of the nation in the war of resistance to the preservation of the race; since the Japanese were out to destroy the Chinese wherever they lived, people must stick together behind him. Shellac records were made of his speeches, but which of China's multitude of villages had gramophones, and how many of them could the regime's propaganda teams reach? The search for survival under local forces was paramount. As the historian Zhijia Shen has written in a study of wartime Shandong province: 'Local people were much more influenced by pragmatic calculation than by the ideal of nationalism . . . When national and local interests clashed, they did not hesitate to compromise national interests.' Though later orthodoxy would present a picture of unified control from Yan'an, the same often applied in Communist areas which evolved their own models and sets of loyalties. Peasant nationalism took a fragmented form far from the distant figures of Chiang or Mao.

Behind the lines, Chinese administration continued. A *North China Herald* correspondent reported on places in the lower Yangtze basin where both the Chinese and the Japanese tried to collect taxes, and killed petty officials working for the other. Guerrilla-bandits kidnapped rich locals, and accused them of being traitors to the nation. Showing how little had changed since the warlord era, the victims might be tortured to make them tell where their money was hidden. 'In some districts,' the newspaper went on, 'it has been customary to roast the victims in big kettles, without water, until the flesh falls from the bone.'[8]

The 2,000-mile frontier between Japanese and Chinese could not be effectively patrolled. Trade soon began across the lines. Smuggling proliferated. Consumer goods, fuel, medicine and even military supplies were shipped in while minerals went out for the enemy's war machine. Profit was more important than patriotism. Steamers travelling through Japanese-held ports adopted European names and sailed under captains from nations allied with Tokyo. From his base in Hong Kong, the gang boss, Du Yuesheng, used his connections to get a big load of cotton to Chungking from occupied China. In 1939, the government began to issue licences for trade with the enemy, opening the way to corruption by officers and officials responsible for them on border areas.[9]

On the east coast, Rhodes Farmer reported, local people were getting on with life, using patience as a weapon. 'The rank and file Chinese appeared to have dourly accepted the rigors of war as just another calamity,' he wrote, comparing the Japanese effort to 'tunneling into sand without benefit of pit props'. After going through unoccupied China, the poet W. H. Auden found that 'looking for war in China is like a novel by Kafka'. Not that anywhere was safe from Japanese attack from the sky. One air raid hit Chiang's home village in 1939. His first wife, who was in the kitchen, ran outside to see what was happening, and was crushed to death by a wall brought down by the bombing. Travelling from the military command he had taken after returning from Moscow, her son erected a stone tablet with an inscription vowing vengeance.[10]

Some unoccupied areas, particularly in the south-west, maintained life as usual. In the 150,000-square-mile province of Yunnan, roads and railways were built, the capital of Kunming prospered, and the autonomy-minded governor welcomed dissident politicians and intellectuals so long as they did not challenge his authority. Yunnan had a special importance since it lay at the entrance to China of the overland route by which supplies were brought through neighbouring Burma. Businessmen flew in to make the most of the opportunities; everything from champagne and silk stockings to guns and petrol was on sale. Fighting seemed far away.

For the walled town of Taierzhuang on the border of Shandong and Jiangsu provinces, war could not have been closer at the beginning of 1938 as the Japanese launched a two-pronged offensive on their next target, Wuhan. Taierzhuang lay in the Fifth War Zone commanded by the Guangxi general, Li Zongren. Its stone houses backed onto the Grand

Canal at the end of a railway spur from the major junction of Xuzhou, where Chiang had won over the Christian General ten years earlier. If they triumphed there, the Japanese would be able to encircle Wuhan from the north and east. This made the struggle for Xuzhou the most important clash since the loss of Nanking, and Taierzhuang's position gave it an importance out of proportion to its size.

Chiang ordered in reinforcements, including German-trained soldiers under General Tang Enbo who had fought against the Red Army in Jiangxi. A series of counter-thrusts temporarily destabilised the Japanese advance. But they replied with air attacks. A raid on another major rail junction, Zhengzhou, blasted a row of hotels called the Abode of Heavenly Peace which housed the families of officers at the front. Casualties were put at up to 1,000. Other sorties hit the city of Kaifeng, where Edgar Mowrer saw nearly a hundred women and children killed or wounded by the East Gate – headless bodies of children lay on the ground, and 'a woman sat speechless beside the prostrate body of her dead husband, in her arms a baby missing from the waist down'.[11]

As the enemy moved on the Xuzhou area from three sides through snowy winter conditions, Chiang flew from Wuhan to confer with Li and his fellow Guangxi general, Bai Chonqxi. When his plane came in to land, Chinese gunners opened fire, taking it for a Japanese attacker. In a rage, Chiang wanted to execute those responsible, but Bai saved the situation by complimenting the airfield commander on his excellent welcome salute, and the Generalissimo subsided – he was to face another aerial threat later in the trip when only the speed of his plane enabled it to escape from an attack by Japanese fighters.[12]

Xuzhou still seemed fairly normal, with families strolling up its main hill to a pagoda among the peach trees. But air-raid shelters had been dug into the soft red earth, and walls were covered with messages put up by fleeing civilians who had lost touch with their families. Young volunteers were leading a campaign to teach resistance, civil defence and first aid. At the hospital, the matron told of a visit by a beautifully dressed Chinese woman who talked to the wounded soldiers: Meiling.[13]

Given their two rebellions, Chiang did not trust the Guangxi leaders – a female secret agent was infiltrated into their headquarters to keep watch in case they used visits from other generals to plot a revolt. Nor did Li, described by the writer Christopher Isherwood as 'a very polite, nut-brown man, with an enormous mouth and deeply intelligent eyes', have much time for the Generalissimo, telling the Nationalist leader he did not want to receive the usual detailed instructions dictated from his far-away headquarters. In his memoirs, Li says Chiang kept to their agreement, only telephoning him twice – on non-operational matters. Each time, Li told the commander-in-chief that his accent made him hard to understand over the wire.[14]

But the sternly anti-Japanese soldiers from Guangxi knew there could only be one leader for China at that juncture, while the Generalissimo required their military skills and leadership. So he put on a show of solidarity, spending the night in Li's headquarters in a small temple. Chiang took the general's bed, while his host slept on a door taken off its hinges. Li had a mosquito net to put over him; the visitor did not. Chiang called repeatedly to aides to drive the insects away. But 'the more they worked, the more the insects came', Li wrote. 'That night, neither of us got any sleep.'[15]

A trap was set for the Japanese who had been held at a town called Linyi. The Chinese troops there would retreat into Taierzhuang, drawing the enemy after them in the narrow streets between the fortress-like stone houses. Other Chinese units, including Tang Enbo's army, would shut off the Japanese rear. 'We [will] have them like fish in a pond,' said Li. Two lines of trenches were built below the Grand Canal. Artillery was positioned. Spies were executed – riding on a horse to the front, Isherwood saw a dog gnawing on the arm of one who had been buried in too shallow a grave. Bai took the train to Taierzhuang for a scouting trip. He cut an impressive figure, with his domed forehead, amber, darting eyes, high-bridged nose and prominent chin. Wearing a plain uniform with three-star, three-bar gold collar badges, he stopped the train to get down and walk in a wheat field talking to another general while bombs fell nearby.[16]

In its far smaller way, Taierzhuang was to be China's Stalingrad. Following the Linyi defenders as they fell back, the Japanese fought for three days to get to the Grand Canal. Reaching Taierzhuang, several hundred soldiers got inside by digging a tunnel under its wall. They were beaten back in fierce hand-to-hand combat. The Chinese sprayed kerosene on walls and set them on fire – the town was described as a 'burning hell' where the front line followed a crazy pattern between the houses.[17]

Despite heavy losses, the defenders hung on, and Li ordered a unit to attack the Japanese flank. When the commander dallied, he was threatened with execution. On 26 March Tang Enbo cut off the attackers from the rear. Most of the supplies dropped by Japanese planes fell behind Chinese lines. Still, by early April, the attackers had taken two thirds of the town – but the Chinese still held the South Gate. At one point, the soldiers there asked to be allowed to fall back. Li refused. The defenders pledged to 'obey absolutely and . . . fight till the whole army is annihilated'. Any soldier who tried to retreat over the canal was to be executed, the Guangxi general ordered.

The Chinese had modern weapons at their disposal, including thirty planes, tanks and flame throwing vehicles. They also co-ordinated well, making their numerical superiority tell. The Japanese, on the other hand, were over-extended and over-confident. The defenders organised 'Dare to Die' corps, some armed with long swords. Taking the enemy by surprise, they regained most of the town as Chinese reinforcements moved in. Li rode up on horseback to direct operations. 'Battle cries shook the skies,' he wrote in his memoirs. 'After grimly fighting for some ten days, the enemy troops had spent their energy and were running out of munitions and gasoline. Many of their motor vehicles had been destroyed, and those that remained had no fuel. The whole army broke and fled in disorder. Faced with this sudden victory, the morale of our men soared and they rushed after the enemy like a storm sweeping fallen leaves. There was no stopping them. Enemy corpses lay all over the plain, and vehicles, arms, and horses were strewn about.'

Two thousand Japanese fought their way out, leaving 8,000 dead behind; some committed hara kiri as the battle was lost. Though no reliable figure was given, Chinese casualties were higher. Li called the battle 'the first happy occasion since the war of resistance had started'. A Chinese reporter described the ruins of the bombed-out station as standing like a warrior protecting China. In the devastated town, the owner of one of the few houses still standing complained because a chair had been destroyed.[18]

If the immediate victory belonged to the generals and their men at the front, it had been Chiang who had made the key commitments of troops and agreed to the overall plan. For once, the Chinese had been able to put into effect a coordinated strategy executed over several weeks on a settled front. The battle, the Generalissimo said, was 'a concrete manifestation' of

China's spirit. But he did not follow up the victory, and, as a result, lost Xuzhou as the enemy regrouped – a reporter flying over the area saw endless columns of Japanese tanks, cavalry and soldiers pursuing the retreating Chinese through dozens of burning towns though a bid to trap Li's army failed when the Chinese escaped under cover of dust storms. On the Yangtze, the invaders landed from boats in thick fog to capture the Anhui city of Anqing, increasing the threat to Wuhan. The only consolation was that, on the day the Chinese abandoned Xuzhou, two Chinese planes flew over the Japanese archipelago. Instead of bombs, they dropped leaflets urging the Japanese to stop their militarists seeking to conquer China. The raid, Chiang wrote, should 'disabuse the arrogant Japanese of their long-cherished illusion that their island country is sacred and impregnable'. But it had no effect on domestic morale or the Imperial Army.[19]

Two weeks after Xuzhou fell, the Japanese took Kaifeng by the Yellow River in a night battle in the rain. This exposed the railway centre of Zhengzhou, and increased the danger of the Japanese moving in force down the line to Wuhan where the Hanyang arsenal was hit by an air raid that was reported to have killed 500 people. Isherwood saw bodies 'tattooed . . . with gravel and sand. Beside one corpse was a brand-new, undamaged straw hat. All the bodies looked very small, very poor, and very dead, but, as we stood beside one old woman, whose brains were soaking obscenely through a little towel, we saw the blood-caked mouth open and shut, and the hand beneath the sack-covering clench and unclench.'[20]

To stop the enemy advance on Wuhan from the north, the Generalissimo summoned up liquid force. The Yellow River, known as 'China's Sorrow' for its frequent flooding, ran through an artificial course behind high dykes. Chiang ordered these to be blown, unleashing millions of gallons of water in what a Japanese news agency described as 'a sea of swirling water . . . submerging roads, countryside and whole villages'. The biggest breach was 400 yards across. Dykes were also breached on the Grand Canal to increase the effect. In places, the floods were 9 feet deep and 20 miles wide. As many as 6 million people were reported to have been affected, and many thousands killed as a result of the river reverting to its natural course and sweeping over the plain to the south. This forced the Japanese to halt. When they tried to repair the breaches, they were fired on by Chinese from pillboxes. The Generalissimo had no qualms about what he had done, though his action would fuel hatred towards the regime in the affected areas and play a role in a subsequent famine.[21]

Seeing himself as the embodiment of the nation, Chiang arranged his elevation by the Kuomintang National Congress to the status of *Zongcai*, or General Director of the party, the supreme title Sun Yat-sen had held. This was the consecration he had been aiming at since the doctor's death. 'I have struggled thirty years for the party and the nation,' he said, 'and only today have I received recognition from the entire party.'

As well as heading the Military Committee, he became Chairman of the National Kuomintang Congress and the Central Executive Committee. He got the right to ask the congress to reconsider its decisions, plus the final say in its resolutions.

'General Chiang Dictator,' read the headline in the *North China Herald*. In an Easter radio broadcast, he compared Jews under the Romans to Chinese under the Manchus, describing Jesus as the self-sacrificing leader of a national, social and religious revolution. 'Let us march together towards the Cross, for the regeneration of our nation and for the realisation of everlasting peace on earth,' he added. It would have been sacrilege to have gone further, but the parallel was not hard to draw.[22]

Keeping to his policy of no surrender, he refused to receive the German ambassador who wanted to deliver another hard-line Japanese peace proposal. Instead, the envoy went to read the proposal to Meiling, H. H. Kung and W. H. Donald, saying he had been told to convey it without comment. 'I should think so,' Meiling replied, changing the subject to enquire after Herr Trautmann's son and daughter. The ambassador, according to Donald, 'bowed like an automaton, and retreated'.[23]

The German connection was unravelling fast, though Chiang congratulated Hitler on the Anschluss with Austria.* With the Foreign Ministry now headed by the strongly pro-Japanese von Ribbentrop, Berlin recognised Manchukuo, and cancelled military exports to China. The Nazi propaganda chief, Joseph Goebbels, described the breaching of the Yellow River dykes as worse than the German bombing of Guernica in Spain.

---

* China's Consul General in Vienna, He Gengshan, showed a different attitude by giving visas to an estimated 4,000 Jews to escape the Nazis, subsequently earning the description of 'China's Schindler'.

Trautmann and the military advisers were ordered to go home. When von Falkenhausen sought to stay, Berlin issued a veiled threat that the families of the advisers in Germany would suffer if they did not leave. On 27 June 1938, Chiang held a farewell dinner, and laid on a train to take them to Hong Kong.[24]

By then, Soviet aid was flowing in under a US$250 million agreement paid for in Chinese raw materials. During the first year of the war, Moscow sent 900 planes, 82 tanks, 2,000 artillery pieces, nearly 10,000 machine guns, 50,000 rifles and 2,000 vehicles as well as 2,000 airmen and 3,000 advisers who included the future Red Army commander, Georgy Zhukov. The north-western city of Lanzhou, which was the terminal for the supply chain, was described as 'bursting at the seams with Russians'. On the border with Manchukuo, the Soviet Army, under the command of Galen, fought a big battle with the Japanese which Chiang hoped might be a major drain on the enemy. But, despite gaining the upper hand, Galen did not advance – Stalin did not want a wider war with Japan. So Tokyo was able to hold its position in the north while Hirohito authorised the final offensive against Wuhan, using chemical weapons as well as conventional arms.[25]

The tri-cities had become the symbol of the united front. Chiang's authoritarianism was limited by the balancing effect of the Guangxi generals, Feng Yuxiang and other regional militarists – and the presence of the Communists under Mao's main rival, Moscow-trained Wang Ming. The regime had shown its patriotic claws by making an example of the Shandong warlord who had retreated from the Japanese with the provincial treasury loaded onto his personal train and who was in subversive contact with a Sichuan militarist. He was summoned for a meeting, and persuaded to leave his train on the way with a false story of Japanese planes being about to attack. After he had been separated from his bodyguards by being ushered to a shelter reserved for senior officers, he was arrested and moved to Wuhan. There, he was tried by a court martial under General He Yingqin, and shot in the back of the head while his Sichuan associate, who was in hospital in Wuhan, was taken violently ill after a visit from General He, and died soon afterwards. According to his official biographer, Chiang had nine other unreliable generals executed, and thirty dismissed.

After their revolutionary past in 1911 and 1926–7, Hankou, Hanyang and Wuchang were fertile ground for a national revival. A free press flourished, as did the arts and literature transplanted from Shanghai. The secret police was restricted to tracking down Japanese collaborators, rather than going after the regime's rivals. In the words of the historian, Stephen MacKinnon, 'democracy reached a twentieth-century zenith'. Foreign documentary film directors and the photographer, Robert Capa, arrived to record the defence of the city.[26]

'Everything through the united front,' Wang Ming proclaimed. It was, he said, 'no time to engage in a power struggle'. A People's Political Council met in Hankou in July 1938 with Chiang linking the war to national redemption in his main speech. The Communists and smaller groups, such as the Young China Party and the Socialist Democratic Party, occupied fifty of the 200 seats; independents took seventy. The National Salvation Association, whose members had been imprisoned before 1937, attended, as did vocational and educational organisations. This meant that, though the biggest group, the Kuomintang was in a minority. The council's powers were limited; it could propose and criticise, but not enforce decisions. Non-KMT delegates agitated for greater authority, and made apparent the potential challenge that even this small exercise in democracy could present.[27]

Chiang resisted giving any more ground. He could see how the Kuomintang's weakness increased the danger from rival political movements. In a stinging critique, he accused party members of lax living, lack of enthusiasm, lackadaisical work and the pursuit of power and pleasure. They had 'almost become a special class', he added, 'and the masses ... are not only cool towards the party but even become antagonistic toward it'. Once again he saw what was wrong, but did not do anything about it.[28]

For all Wang Ming's lyricism, the united front lacked roots on both sides. The Kuomintang could only take a dim view of the call for Wuhan to be defended as Madrid was being against Franco's forces – it sounded too like the mass leftist campaigns of the 1920s. Nor did the Communist delegate have backing from Yan'an, which had just been brought to world attention by visits from sympathetic foreign journalists. Mao was determined to retain his autonomy and to develop a brand of Marxism adapted to Chinese circumstances rather than becoming submerged in a Moscow-dictated common front led by his principal party rival and by his foe of the past decade.

The defence of Wuhan was entrusted to the brisk, diminutive and dapper General Chen Cheng, the Xi'an Incident loyalist who had also commanded troops at Shanghai. On paper, he had 450,000 men, while another 340,000 were drafted in from the Fifth War Zone to the east – though, as always, the number of men on the ground was less than the official count. The Chinese tactics were purely defensive. The critical Russian adviser, Cherepanov, who had returned to China, recalled strategy meetings at which a Whampoa officer unveiled maps marked with great arrows, but no troops ever moved along them. Bottlenecks were set up to try to hold up the Japanese on the Yangtze, and booms were laid to halt the enemy's ships. But the invaders resumed the advance from the north, and rode over the booms as flood waters from a tributary swelled the river.[29]

At the end of July, 45,000 Chinese troops fled from the town of Jiujiang, in the face of a force only a quarter their size – the victors promptly indulged in murders and rapes on the pattern of Nanking. In August, government offices began to leave Wuhan for Chungking up the Yangtze, and Chiang ordered half a million people to be evacuated. Among the few people moving in the opposite direction was a woman missionary from Scotland who had walked with a companion from the Yangtze down to the Jiangxi capital of Nanchang, where she got a ride to Wuhan on a military truck, moving through the lines in pitch dark. 'We enjoyed every minute of the trip,' said Miss F. H. E. Bartlett of Irvine in Ayrshire. 'We will do it all over again if we have to.'[30]

Air raids set off big fires in Wuhan, and hit a theatre being used as a shelter where the death toll was put at up to 1,000. The planes flew so low that their pilots could be seen from the ground in their open cockpits – in one raid, a Japanese ace died when a Chinese aircraft he had shot up from underneath fell on top of him. Four Japanese fighters attacked a clearly marked civilian plane, forcing it to land on a stretch of water. Fourteen passengers were killed by strafing as they tried to swim to safety. The Japanese said the pilot had been 'behaving suspiciously'.[31]

The Generalissimo seemed impervious to danger. When his office came under air attack in September, he was in the courtyard, and did not take shelter. His bodyguards hurried him into a dugout, returning to their posts outside – five of them were killed. During a dinner for the Red Cross director, Bob McLure of Canada, the Chiangs took no notice of an air raid alarm, and strolled out into the garden to look up at the planes. McLure watched them use stopwatches to time how long it took for the searchlights to find the bombers. Chiang, he recalled, 'was a little annoyed because the searchlight boys had picked out the bombers about half a minute earlier the night before'.[32]

The Chiangs lived in the army headquarters compound, behind a stone gateway flanked by stone lions and a large lawn. Taken by W. H. Donald to visit Meiling with his companion, Auden, Christopher Isherwood described the sitting room as sham walnut, like an English roadhouse. 'In the corner stood a cabinet full of cutlery and dusty champagne-glasses,' he recorded. Chiang worked in a plain, bare office, the huge desk piled high with papers. There were a few bowls of flowers, and a small porcelain clock.

The Generalissimo maintained a working day of twelve hours or more, rising before dawn, doing his exercises, praying and splashing his face with cold water whatever the temperature. According to his information chief, Hollington Tong, he took a light breakfast at 6.30 a.m. and worked through till lunch at 1. After a rest, he resumed work. He and Meiling went for a walk at 6 p.m. 'Immediately on his return home, he calls in the Mayor for reprimand if he has observed litter in the streets or inattention to their duties by police,' Tong added. Dinner was at 7.30, attended by officers and officials. Then Chiang read documents, telegrams and books, or practised calligraphy, before going to bed at 11 p.m. His specially made diary formed part of the daily routine. Apart from recording his thoughts day by day, it contained a page for personal analysis at the end of each week, followed by another page setting out his intentions for the following seven days. At the end of each month, a further page was set aside for a review of behaviour. From time to time, Chiang gave similar volumes to his generals in the hope that they would follow his example. The tone of his reflections is of high morality and self-regard, with suitably phrased lamentations about shortcomings balanced by exhortations to do better and misgivings about the sincerity of others. They seem written to be read – by the author and those who were meant to marvel at his high standards and ethical superiority.[33]

Each Monday, the Generalissimo affirmed his claim to be the successor of Sun Yat-sen by reading out the doctor's will at a morning meeting of ministers and department heads, which began with those present bowing three times to the portrait of the Kuomintang founder. He then delivered a lecture of up to two hours on whatever subject was uppermost in his mind. Speaking in his fast, falsetto Ningbo accent, he propounded new slogans, and criticised those who had fallen. 'He never praised,' recalled Rhodes Farmer, who had gone to work for the government information service. 'He scolded. He perpetually called for greater sacrifices and longer hours of work for the cause of national salvation'. His audience had to stand to attention, not wearing coats even when the temperature fell to zero. When finished, Chiang would grunt '*Wan le*' ('that's all'), and march out.

He employed a succession of speech writers who also ghosted his various books. His speeches made frequent use of proverbs, and, according to a detailed analysis by David Wu Chi-wei, blended traditional values and modern language, using a clear and straightforward vocabulary and sentence structure. Adapting his dress to the occasion, he wore a Chinese gown for national celebrations, a Sun Yat-sen suit for government and party gatherings, and uniform for military parades. His admonitions to frugality were reckoned to be having some effect when H. H. Kung was seen using a public rickshaw instead of his limousine. The story spread that the Generalissimo liked his officers to shave their heads, and to have craniums as smooth as eggs. He was also said to prefer his generals to be bronzed as if they had come from the battlefield. As a result, ambitious young men ran the razor over their skulls and exposed their faces to the sun.[34]

According to Rhodes Farmer's observations at the time, the Generalissimo acted like 'a man with a hundred pairs of hands and eyes . . . How his whip cord body generated such energy was a mystery . . . I do know however that there was the devil to pay at the Generalissimo's headquarters when an incoming plane failed to bring a consignment of a famous American tonic.' Visiting him one morning at his headquarters, Farmer found twenty men sitting in the antechamber, including a tailor with two apprentices and rolls of khaki cloth on their knees. The others were military men, and they had 'the looks of schoolboys waiting for a difficult meeting with the head'.

As Farmer entered his office, the Generalissimo – in a pale mauve suit, mauve silk socks and black slippers – stood up rigidly, and grasped his visitor's hand with a steely grip. He kept his back stiff as he sat down again, his hands on his knees. Farmer felt Chiang's eyes boring into him like gimlets, but found him affable, debonair, infectiously buoyant, and brimming over with vitality. 'Wherever I go is the Government and the centre of resistance,' Chiang declared. 'I am the State.' The outcome of the war would be determined by how the leader directed the people's resistance, he added. Then 'the expression of smiling courtesy left [his] face. He looked the tough autocrat. He stood up. The interview was at an end.'[35]

His wife was, meanwhile, playing an ever more prominent role, pushing the development of the air force, particularly the purchase of planes from America. She launched a scheme to get Chinese women to sew 2 million winter uniforms for the troops, and visited wounded soldiers in hospital. Han Suyin described her as 'a slim, youthful-looking woman, dressed in slacks and a woollen sweater. Her dark shining hair was caught in a knot at the nape of her neck. Her pale, smooth skin was untouched by make-up. Her black eyes were, I think, the most beautiful I have ever seen, and alight with keen vitality . . . all the traditions of Chinese womanhood meet in her . . . she is not only modern; that is the lesser part. She is Chinese.'[36]

Foreigners were particularly impressed. The writer, Edgar Mowrer, was bowled over by her 'gift of permanent elegance. Sex appeal. Quick feminine intelligence.' Christopher Isherwood judged that she knew how to deal with any conceivable type of visitor:

> She can become at will the cultivated, westernised woman with a knowledge of literature and art; the technical expert, discussing aeroplane-engines and machine-guns; the inspector of hospitals; the president of a mothers' union; or the simple, affectionate, clinging Chinese wife. She could be terrible, she could be gracious, she could be businesslike, she could be ruthless; it is said that she sometimes signs death-warrants in her own hand. She speaks excellent English, with an intonation which faintly recalls her American college-training. Strangely enough, I have never heard anybody comment on her perfume. It is the most delicious either of us has ever smelt.[37]

When Isherwood and Auden visited her, she appeared 'exquisitely dressed, vivacious rather than pretty, and possessed of an almost terrifying charm and poise'. But, behind her mask, she looked 'tired and far from well'. She asked Auden if poets ate cake. When he said yes, she trilled, 'I am glad to hear it. I thought perhaps they preferred only spiritual food.' Chiang joined them briefly, displaying 'the fragile impassivity of a spectre'.

His wife led him onto the balcony to pose arm-in-arm for a photograph. 'Under the camera's eye,' recorded the writer, 'he stiffened visibly, like a schoolboy who is warned to hold himself upright.'[38]

At this time of maximum peril for Wuhan, the youngest Soong sister decided to publish a collection of her English-language writings and speeches in book form. She had special paper brought in from Hong Kong, and handed Rhodes Farmer the job of executing the project. The Australian tracked down a Bible printer who had suitable printing equipment. However, the linotype operators did not know English, and he had to make endless corrections to the proofs. Meiling ordered extensive revisions which meant pulping the first print run. Eventually 10,000 copies of *Madame Chiang's Messages in War and Peace* were produced, bound in blue silk. The books were crated up and sent to Hong Kong by train for international distribution. Meiling upbraided Farmer for the remaining printing errors.[39]

The Chiang–Meiling partnership was unique, though Chinese women often enjoyed more influence than their public demeanour showed. Chiang liked his wife to walk behind him on ceremonial occasions, and his outlook was male-centred, as was his army world. But, like her two sisters, Meiling was extraordinarily liberated by the standards of the country and the time. The way she often appeared in public in slacks marked her out as a modernist. Even the left-wing American writer Agnes Smedley was impressed, finding her 'cultivated, tremendously clever, and possessed of charm and exquisite taste'. With coaching from W. H. Donald, she became the human face of the government, particularly for the outside world, and constantly travelled at her husband's side, pressing the New Life crusade and urging Chinese women to rally to the war effort. Still, the Americanised influence which she and her brother represented had its limits. The American correspondent Teddy White compared it to the lights winking on an electronic control panel, 'but the wires in back led nowhere, the switchboard did not connect to the operation system'. When it came to waging war and ensuring survival, Chiang was as solitary as ever while he confronted the bad news from the front in the autumn of 1938.[40]

In the south, the Japanese took Fuzhou and Shantou, and landed unopposed on the bay beside Hong Kong. Canton fell with little resistance, leading to rumours of money changing hands. 'It looks like dirty work somewhere,' a British diplomat said, while Reuters wrote of an 'inside job'. The withdrawal may, rather, have been a decision by Chiang to pull troops back to safety in the mountains of northern Guangdong that he had crossed at the start of the Northern Expedition.[41]

The loss of Canton meant supplies could no longer be brought in by sea in the south, so Wuhan lost its importance as the railhead from Guangdong. In any case, its time as the Nationalist capital was fast drawing to a close. The determined Cantonese general Xue Yue the great pursuer of the Red Army on the Long March, held the line in the mountains of Jiangxi province, south of the Yangtze where the Japanese were badly affected by dysentery from bad water. But, though short of ammunition, the invaders were still well equipped compared with their opponents and they advanced steadily along the river, which provided an excellent channel for their naval ships to act as floating artillery.

As the enemy took a key fortress in a deep gorge 90 miles from Wuhan, restaurants in the city closed while a patriotic play entitled *Keep Wuhan!* was put on. Only one cinema was still open; the film studios packed up to move out. Malaria spread among the soldiers. Street barricades were erected, and big war posters covered the walls; at his headquarters, a huge mural showed the Generalissimo on horseback urging troops forward. Official reports said that the sing-song girls had given up permanent waves for more Chinese hairdos as they danced into the night with clients beside the clock course at the Wee Golf Restaurant.[42]

While the Japanese moved ever closer, W. H. Donald, who had been in Indo-China recovering from a bad bout of fever, returned to his large, ramshackle flat on the Bund at Wuhan. Waiting for him was a letter from the Young Marshal saying he hoped 'you people do your best to help poor China', and adding, 'I never droop. Please do not worry too much for me.' Going to the Generalissimo's house, Donald found Chiang and Meiling in the garden. 'I am not disturbed by the loss of cities,' the Generalissimo said. 'If we lose too many, we shall build some more.'[43]

The National Day parade on 10 October 1938 included a 12-foot effigy of the Generalissimo. At that time, Han Suyin was in central Wuhan with her soldier husband. One moonlit night, she saw a car draw up in front of the Bank of China building. Out stepped a lean, uniformed figure who mounted the steps and turned for a moment, looking out over the crowd, unnoticed. 'A severely simple uniform without decorations, a face serene in the moonlight and torchlight, a face to be marked, with its characteristic long clean-cut jaw, high, unlined forehead and deep-set eyes,' she wrote.

> Chiang Kai-shek stood on the steps. As the crowd became aware of him, there was a murmur, then silence, then a roar, spontaneous as the roar of a forest when a wind goes over it. *Wei Yuan Chang! Wei Yuan Chang! Linghsiu wan sui!* – Generalissimo! Ten thousand years! The man they hailed stood at the salute, acknowledging their cheers, a small, grave smile playing about his lips; then bowed and passed from our sight into the building.[44]

Two weeks later, Chiang and Meiling drove slowly along the Bund by the Yangtze in an open car, reviewing troops drawn up there. That evening, they had a meal with Hollington Tong, the deferential head of the information service. The Japanese were 20 miles away. Meiling suggested leaving. Chiang went to a desk, got out his brush and ink pad and wrote a message explaining the loss of the city. At 9.30 p.m., the Chiangs and Donald went to the airfield with a couple of bags of personal possessions. Tong was left behind to put out the statement to the press, and find his way to safety as best he could.

The Generalissimo's American pilot, Royal Leonard, flew the trio out of the city, but the navigation equipment was broken and they found that they were going the wrong way. So they instructed Leonard to return to Hankou, only to be informed that the airfield had been mined. Chiang told the pilot to head there all the same. They landed safely, changed planes and went south to Hunan.[45]

Behind them, under arc lights and the yellow glow of kerosene lamps on the docks, the city's better-off inhabitants raced in rickshaws and cars to grab a place on boats leaving up the Yangtze. 'Officers in uniforms and gentlemen in suits of European style or long Chinese gowns [were] herding their families aboard or looking to the bestowal of their hastily assembled baggage,' Han Suyin recalled.

> Ladies, slender and elegant in their silk shan, their eyebrows pencilled delicately and their lips painted full and red. Raucous-voiced servant-women. Children, heavy with sleep. Crying babies and their imperturbable wet-nurses, with bovine calm unbuttoning their loose

blouses to give suck. Carriers staggering under mountainous loads . . . a woman with tiny bound feet had stumbled and fallen into the water and was being rescued with great outcry to the entertainment of many watchers.[46]

Japanese newspapers reported a desperate last defensive move by the Chinese – 5,000 orang-utans would be unleashed after having been trained to throw grenades, seize machine guns and attack company commanders whom they had been schooled to identify. The apes never put in an appearance, but the defenders left Wuhan as the attack moved in from three sides supported by twenty-six ships. Despite Meiling's programme for winter uniforms, the Chinese troops were still in their summer shorts, tunics and cotton puttees. Camouflaged straw hats the size of dustbin lids hung on their backs: when they wore them they looked like giant toadstools, but were hard to identify from the air. They moved, Rhodes Farmer recalled, 'as softly as ghosts. Even the cooks and their boy apprentices jog-trotting along with the pots, pans and rice sacks swaying from shoulder poles, had learnt the art of absolute noiselessness.'[47]

Buildings in Wuhan had been mined, and some were blown up, including the former Japanese consulate. But many property owners stayed behind to remove the explosives before the enemy arrived. Japanese troops showed discipline this time; though looting was reported, there was no repeat of Nanking. A combination of the blowing of the Yellow River dykes and the defensive fighting along the Yangtze had delayed the fall of the city for six months. Chinese casualties to date were put at up to a million. On the other side, Japanese losses in the undeclared war in China, mostly in the Yangtze region, were reported at 62,000 killed and 6,667 wounded – 12,600 of the dead perished from illness. The large ratio of dead to wounded may have stemmed from the creed that death in battle was glorious. Another reason was given by Bob McLure of the Red Cross, who recounted that, at a Japanese field hospital, he had seen only very lightly wounded men, none wearing even splints. Nearby was a burial ground. 'There wasn't a shadow of doubt that the Japanese were doing away with their badly wounded men,' he added. 'Crippled men back in Japan would have spoiled the picture of easy conquest the High Command was painting.'[48]

Despite the loss of yet another major city, Chiang maintained his poise.

It was 'better to be a broken jade than a whole tile', he declared. The enemy had only 'scorched earth and dead cities' to show for the offensive. 'Already the Japanese are deep in the mire,' he added, 'and, from now on, they will tread on thornier ground . . . in revolutionary war, there is no end till the final victory is won.' It might have been Mao speaking.[49]

Chiang stopped in the Hunan capital of Changsha, where he met the British ambassador, Sir Archibald Clark-Kerr.* A photograph shows the diplomat looking grave while the Generalissimo seems almost jaunty. Changsha had just been the target of a Japanese air raid – one bomb narrowly missed a British warship, hitting a crowded junk nearby. Sir Archibald and Meiling became godparents to a girl rescued from the water who was given the name of Water Fairy.

Leaving Changsha, Chiang set up his new headquarters on the sacred mountain of Nanyue, a small settlement with 4,000 years of history, where tall trees and glens surround a great temple of golden tiles with seventy-two columns. The single street was of blocks of stone, flanked by one-storey wooden houses. A traditional poem described the mountain in azure blue with cloud below and snow blowing off the peaks. One poem, apposite to Chiang's situation, told of a bird looking down from the heights

> Bitter at heart as it watches
> Birds caught in nets below
> Down to even the tiniest golden ones.[50]

Nanyue provided the first encounter between old and new China induced by war. Before a road was blasted up the mountain, coolies carried furniture for the new arrivals over a 2,000-foot climb. Slung between two of their poles was a gleaming porcelain lavatory – the foreman called to install it had to be told what it was for. The recently constructed Grand Nanyue Hotel had no glass in its windows and no plumbing; its central courtyard was always muddy from water basins emptied by clients from their rooms. The General Staff established itself in a school. Dispatch carriers took messages from there up steep pilgrim paths to Chiang's residence in a temple. The Christian General arrived, bronzed and unshaven in his infantryman's uniform and black cloth shoes. A captured

---

* Later Lord Inverchapel and ambassador in Washington.

Japanese spy, suffering from malaria and beriberi, was exhibited in a cage; local people walked miles to see this novelty, and threw him oranges.[51]

Calling his principal commanders to a conference in Nanyue in November 1938, Chiang told them that, after sixteen months of war, the first phase was over. Instead of defending each position, they should adopt 'mobile front resistance' using guerrilla tactics to trap the adversary and hit its weak points. General Chen Cheng said the key to the future lay in 'whether we can seize the initiative and conduct mobile warfare throughout the entire country, in order to harass and disperse enemy forces, thereby leading to their attrition and total destruction'.[52]

To strengthen the armies after their enormous losses, conscription was decreed, along with a training programme for officers and men. Chiang stressed the importance of political education and propaganda. A guerrilla training school was set up, with Communists as advisers. 'There must be no peace in the rear for the Japanese,' its manifesto proclaimed. They 'must live the lives of condemned men, with every man, woman and child their foe'. Tokyo's commander-in-chief in the south declared that the Chinese strategy 'invites only contempt and is not in keeping with a soldier's honour'. On the contrary, said the Guangxi General Bai, 'Japan's adventure in China will meet with a similar fate to that of Napoleon at Moscow'. By then, Chiang had found a new home in a mist-shrouded city where he would stay for six and a half years.[53]

CHAPTER 19

In the Clouds

CHIANG SAID THE IDEA HAD come to him when he was pursuing the Long Marchers. China's largest province of Sichuan, together with its southern neighbours of Yunnan and Guizhou, would be 'the fundamental base for the reconstruction of the nation' and the centre for protracted resistance against the Japanese. At the time, this might have seemed perverse. The country's future appeared to lie in the coastal cities, Nanking and Wuhan, but Chiang's planning implied that he expected them to fall. 'I dare say that, even if we lost fifteen provinces out of the eighteen,' he declared, 'if only we could keep our Sichuan, Yunnan and Guizhou we could defeat any enemy, recover the lost land, restore our country, and accomplish our revolution.'[1]

Far up the Yangtze behind the river's great gorges, ringed by protective mountains, Sichuan was known as 'the Heavenly-endowed province', covering territory slightly bigger than France. Everything except cotton grew there, and mineral resources included coal, salt, silver and copper. There were huge forests, and the hydroelectric potential of the Yangtze Gorges. Still, the province was a backward place sunk in warlordism, epitomising the inland realities of China. Secret societies were powerful. Family clans held sway. The largest landlord owned 1,500 shops and twenty-eight homes. Opium-smoking was rife; the drug accounted for almost a sixth of the province's output, seven times as much as its industrial production. Tuberculosis, dysentery, cholera and smallpox were common. Transport was rudimentary over rough terrain.[2]

For his new base, Chiang chose not the provincial capital of Chengdu, where independent local militarists were powerful, but Chungking in the south-east of the province which he had used as a base against Mao's marchers in 1935. Perched on cliffs at the junction of the Yangtze and Jialing rivers, the city suited his psychology of war perfectly. An imperial city in 340 BC, it had become a place where emperors and warlords retired to lick their wounds. The fog, cloud and mists were such that it was said 'when the sun shines, even the dogs bark in fear'. The American scholar John King Fairbank saw the city as resembling 'a junk heap of old boxes piled together . . . There is no color. Nothing grows out of the rock, the stone is all gray and slightly mossed; people, houses, pathways all blend into gray, with the gray river swirling between.'[3]

Chungking was one of China's dirtiest cities. The rats were as big as cats. A maze of dingy alleyways led from the hundreds of steep, slippery steps up from the river. Beggar children and dogs burrowed into rubbish dumps on the slopes. Lepers wandered in the streets. Crowded tenements hung from the cliffs like birds' nests. Night soil was taken down to the Yangtze and poured into 'honey barges' to be stirred by naked men before being shipped off to be sold as fertiliser. Illness was endemic – a survey of 5,000 students in 1938 showed only ninety-six to be completely healthy. Hundreds of bodies were found in the streets each month.[4]

The coming of the government confronted this provincial centre with the modern, cosmopolitan ways of the newcomers in a clash of old and new. Sewage ran in open ditches while neon signs flashed from the heights above the river. Though the 2,000-foot air strip was kept busy on a sandbank on the north shore of the Yangtze, most people in the city moved about on foot or in rickshaws and sedan chairs. The post office found itself handling 200,000 messages a month, but most of the locals remained illiterate. Young refugees from different regions lived together while local husbands and wives met for the first time at the weddings arranged by their parents. Thoroughfares were renamed the Road of the National Republic or the Street of the People's Livelihood, but rickshaw pullers still called them the slope of the Seven Stars or White Elephant Street. Processions through the streets invoked the aid of the gods while chorus girls from

Shanghai danced, six cinemas opened, and *Mourning Becomes Electra* starred an actress who had studied drama in London. American-trained dentists advertised their services alongside soothsayers. While rich officials flew in French wine and American liquor, drinking water for most inhabitants came from the river where 500 tons of sewage flowed each day.[5]

Factories which had been dismantled and brought from the Lower Yangtze region were erected to give the city a taste of modern industry – in all, nearly 2,000 enterprises were moved up the river, dragged through the gorges on ropes hauled by coolies walking along paths cut into the sheer rock face. The Shanghai Machine Works was the first to make the journey, followed by a steel mill and the Wuhan power plant which was towed through the rapids on special pontoons. A rotary press was brought in to enable newspapers from Shanghai to resume publication. Sichuan women were trained to operate spindles in textile plants. Propaganda units were sent out into the countryside with health caravans. Universities, with nationalistic students, shifted to the interior where they were exempted from military service – perhaps as a result, their numbers doubled between 1936 and 1944.[6]

The city's population soared from 300,000 to a million. Rhodes Farmer recalled the mix of people from all parts of the country:

> A Peiping scholar's fur hat marched along beside the pith helmet of a businessman from Hong Kong (just up by aeroplane), the felt hat of a Nanking civil servant, the wide bamboo sun-hat of a refugee artisan from sub-tropical Canton, or an old-fashioned . . . skull cap. An east coast banker's smart Western suit rubbed shoulders with the red surplice of a lama from Tibet, or a sheep-coated trader from Sinkiang where China borders Russia. The fashionable gown of a Chinese film star from Shanghai (now doing wartime propaganda films) swished past the blue, multi-kilted skirt of a barefoot, silver-earringed Lolo tribes girl from the mountains and the . . . eye of both expressed amazed interest.

There was a Nanking Hat Shop, a Hankou Dry-Cleaners and a Shanghai Garage and Motor Repair Works. An influx of cooks brought dishes from all over China. However, verbal communication could be tricky, as Cantonese and Mandarin speakers failed to understand one another and both were defeated by the Shanghai dialect and the local patois.[7]

The journalist Teddy White, who arrived to take over from Rhodes Farmer at the government information service before joining *Time* magazine, found the officials who had piled into Chungking from more advanced parts of China 'historically romantic' as they ate in communal messes, while their children were drilled in air-raid precautions and their wives hung laundry from dormitory buildings where families slept in one room heated by a charcoal brazier in the winter. Still, a shock awaited many from the developed coastal regions as they returned to China's past. The climate was terrible, hot and humid in the summer, cold and clammy in the winter. The crush of refugees meant food and supplies were scarce – driving to the province's other main city of Chengdu in 1938, an American academic, Oliver Caldwell, saw roadside ditches full of people dead or dying from starvation.[8]

Geographical isolation had made Chungking's inhabitants 'arrogant and self-sufficient', wrote a foreign doctor. 'To any authority outside its boundaries, they were openly and vociferously antagonistic.' The beggars were famed for their persistence, and the rickshaw men for setting their rates at the end of the journey. Arriving in 1939, the writer Han Suyin recalled people turning to stare and mutter, 'Outsiders. Down-river people.' Taking up residence four years later, John King Fairbank recorded that 'every local person seems to have a surly temper'. As middle-class émigrés used their positions to take good jobs, requisition buildings and grab perks, they came to be even more resented by the locals. While officers and officials bought, or seized, land, the old residents gouged newcomers for rent and food.[9]

In case the newcomers made life too jolly, Chiang forbade 'harmful amusement' while encouraging 'proper amusements like sports, music and reading'. He ordered the closure of ice cream and fizzy drink parlours which did a roaring trade in the 80-degree summer heat. They were, he declared, unsuitable frivolities in wartime; bribery soon got them back in business, disguised as restaurants with ice cream and lemonade served in soup plates. The government told police to tear down crude portraits of the leader put up by admirers in the streets since they could 'give the populace a wrong impression of the likeness of the Generalissimo, impairing [his] dignity'. But Chiang could relax on occasions. At a dinner for foreign journalists, he sat rocking his head, smiling and murmuring, '*Hao hao hao*' ('Good, good, good', in Mandarin, but in Chiang's provincial dialect closer to 'I see, I see, I see') while his wife, in gay spirits, acted as translator. To put the guests at ease, knives and forks were used instead of chopsticks, and despite the New Life ban on smoking, Meiling gave the game away on her own habit by accepting a 6-inch Russian cigarette from the head of the Soviet Tass news agency.[10]

For all the changes war brought to Chungking, the Nationalist base was weak from the start. Though the transfer of factories brought modern industry to the interior, it was far less than what was needed. The provinces Chiang still controlled were, for the most part, poor and backward – they produced only 5 per cent of China's cloth, mined hardly any iron ore and contained little in the way of modern transport. Many Shanghai businessmen had preferred to stay put and chance their luck with the Japanese. Showing the limits of patriotism, money which might have been sent to Chungking found its way to Hong Kong or the United States.[11]

As well as depriving Chiang of China's manufacturing and commercial centres and putting a brake on industrial development, the Japanese also occupied big food producing areas. To make up for the shortfall, compulsory grain purchase and taxation programmes to feed the army and officials were imposed on peasants in Nationalist areas, giving rise to widespread oppression and corruption. Implementation was in the hands of the local authorities without effective control from the centre. Quotas were raised at will, and farmers cheated by rigged scales. Military storehouses bulged with food while local people lived on the brink of starvation. Officers and venal officials sold off the surplus, sometimes back to the very peasants from whom it had been taken. Not surprisingly, there were rural revolts – one, in Sichuan itself, would involve 50,000 armed men. Told of abuses, Chiang refused to credit them. When presented with the evidence, he would fly into a rage and punish those responsible, sometimes beating the culprits with his stick. Then he would fall back into his faith in the power of orders, despite all the proof to the contrary.[12]

No sooner had the Chiangs got to Chungking than Meiling was off on flying visits to Changsha, Nanchang and the Guangdong–Hunan border region during which she declared Japan to be the enemy of all women, whom it subjected to 'unbelievable oppression and slavery'. The survival of the nation depended on Chinese women not being afraid to die, she said. They must be ready to forsake vanity and luxuries, added the Soong sister who radiated the first and had lived in the lap of the second all her life. She saw in 1939 at a New Life dinner which raised $16,000 to buy necessities for troops. Patriotic songs were sung, along with a Chinese version of 'Auld Lang Syne'. There was a big torchlight parade through streets hung with national flags, and thousands of firecrackers went off at midnight.[13]

Meiling and the Generalissimo had two homes – a squat villa in his headquarters on the heights in the city, and a residence on the other side of the river, where she had marmalade made from the citrus fruits in the garden. Guards in German-style helmets and khaki uniforms with pink collar badges stood at the gates. Crossing the water one day, the academic and writer Robert Payne recalled seeing a streamlined blue motor boat sweep past taking Chiang back from his second home. Showing that he, too, could deviate from New Life injunctions, the Generalissimo reclined in the back, 'smoking a cigarette, wearing a trilby hat and a military overcoat'. On such trips, it was said, he sometimes sang duets with Meiling.[14]

T. V. Soong, who became Foreign Minister, and H. H. Kung, who deputised for Chiang at the head of the Executive Yuan as well as running the government's finances, had substantial homes in the city. Qingling arrived and was photographed with the Generalissimo though she later went to Hong Kong where her elder sister was in residence. Early in 1940, Meiling joined them for treatment for her sinus complaint which had been aggravated by the Chungking climate. On 1 April, they flew together to the Nationalist capital, Ailing taking a supply of oxygen with her for the flight. Sun Yat-sen's widow, whose house was watched by police, made no secret of her left-wing views and held regular evening salons at which, according to the American information officer, Graham Peck, she expressed her opinion of her family indirectly, popping out her eyes when the subject of her brother-in-law came up and rolling out his title 'Generrra*liii*ssimo'. One evening, slapping a mosquito on her leg, she said laughingly, 'No stockings you see . . . I can't get nylons from America the way my little sister the *Em*press does.' Her pension as the widow of the Father of the Nation had not been increased to keep pace with inflation, but T.V. provided her with a car.[15]

Dai Li set up a secret police headquarters in town, and developed a training camp spread over three mountain valleys 12 miles from Chungking where dissidents were brainwashed and torture was practised.

Du Yuesheng came in from Hong Kong, putting his gangland connections in occupied territories at the regime's disposal, and maintaining a healthy personal cash flow by gambling with local generals. The Christian General lived on a nearby mountain, rising at dawn and writing poetry. Zhang Guotao, former Politburo member and leader of one of the other Red Armies of the mid-1930s, moved to Chungking after losing a power struggle with Mao and defecting to the Nationalists, the highest-ranking Communist to change sides. Some of the veterans of the 4 May nationalist movement rallied to the regime, becoming awkward partners in a National Spiritual Mobilisation launched by Chiang as a rallying point in 1939. An intriguing Chinese woman, known as Iris, flitted in and out on complex secret missions, including the formation of a group of child assassins to kill collaborators in occupied territory. After ill-advisedly returning from his trip to Europe, the instigator of the Xi'an kidnapping, General Yang Hucheng, was held as a prisoner – his wife staged a hunger strike and died of what was described as 'mental illness'; Yang carried her ashes around with him in a box.*[16]

The Communists had one office in Red Rock village overlooking the Jialing River, and another in the city in a shabby building at the fiftieth house on an alley running along the edge of a cliff. The street outside the second was deep in mud for much of the year. There were two courtyards. Kuomintang secret police occupied one, the Communists the other, with an exit through a trapdoor. The Communists printed their own newspaper and pinned maps of the Chinese and Russian fronts on the walls. The chairs and sofa in their reception room had broken springs, and were covered in coarse blue cloth.

Heading the Communist team, Zhou Enlai was a popular and respected figure among diplomats and foreign journalists. Chiang told an American adviser that he regarded him as reliable while the Communist said that the Generalissimo was indispensable for the war against the Japanese. According to Teddy White, an added attraction of Zhou's headquarters was the presence of the guerrilla daughter of a minor warlord whom the *Time* correspondent described as 'the most beautiful Chinese woman I ever

---

* One who did not join the exodus to Chungking was Chiang's patron from Shanghai, the businessman and Kuomintang veteran, Zhang Jingjiang, who went to Europe and then to the United States where he stayed as his paralysis got worse before dying in 1950.

encountered'. There were also Communist moles, including a seven-person ring headed by another attractive young woman that would operate for three years within the Nationalist intelligence service before being uncovered.[17]

A Living Buddha moved into Chungking after being smuggled out of Mongolia. A Canadian missionary made Chiang a new set of dentures. Among later visitors would be the Indian Congress leader, Jawaharlal Nehru, who impressed his hosts by talking non-stop throughout a Japanese air raid. Stafford Cripps, the prominent British Labour politician, spent time in the city at the start of 1940, and found the Chiangs 'perfect dears, so kind and simple and natural'. Bowled over like so many Westerners by Meiling, he wrote of her as 'extraordinarily intelligent and superbly kind to everyone and full of courage and initiative often in the most difficult circumstances'. The Generalissimo offered him a job, but W. H. Donald advised the future Chancellor of the Exchequer not to accept given the 'heartbreak' other advisers had suffered.[18]

Two successive American ambassadors were old China hands. The first, roly-poly, orange-haired Nelson T. Johnson, who had been his country's senior diplomat in China since 1929, hung a Daoist saying on his office wall, 'Through not doing, all things are done.' His successor, Clarence Gauss, a dour chain-smoker of cigars, had spent thirty years in the country and was well-informed and shrewd. But the Nationalists were unhappy with him on two counts. Having worked his way up the diplomatic tree through the consular service, he was regarded as insufficiently grand: China felt it merited a more imposing figure. Also, Gauss knew the country too well for the government's liking, and was not taken in by its window dressing. In one dispatch, he called China 'a minor asset' which could become 'a major liability'. In another, he dismissed as 'rot' the idea that Chiang was a great leader directing the war with energy.[19]

Among other diplomats, the pipe-smoking British ambassador, Sir Archibald Clark-Kerr, whose blonde Chilean wife enlivened the social scene, said Chungking reminded him of his native Scotland. The erudite, gouty Australian Minister held a salon in his large stucco house on a cliff edge, with a blue-carpeted drawing room filled with Chinese paintings. The chargé d'affaires of the Netherlands, who had witnessed the Rape of Nanking, had a country house in the pine trees across the Yangtze where he handed out cigars from his homeland as he listened to the BBC news.[20] After the defeat of France in 1940, General Zinovi Pechkoff, a one-armed

Russian and adopted son of Maxim Gorki, came to town to represent the Free French.

Texas-bred Claire Chennault, with what an American diplomat described as 'a face of cold lava', built up the Nationalist air force, and told Chiang victory could be won from the air rather than by slogging it out on the ground. His Volunteer Group of fliers set up bases across south-west China, becoming known as the Flying Tigers from the insignia of the jaws of tiger sharks painted on the noses of their advanced P-40 planes. During Japanese raids, Teddy White reported, Chennault stood in the open watching the planes 'as a football coach studies a team he expects to meet soon on the field'.[21]

The Nationalists hired an American code breaker, Herbert Yardley, whose 'black chamber' operation had been closed down by Washington on the grounds that 'Gentlemen do not read each other's mail'. A heavy drinker and womaniser, he used the pseudonym of 'Osborne', and pretended to be a dealer in leather and hides. During air raids, he would get a drink, lie down on a couch and put pillows on his eyes and groin to protect his vital organs. John McCausland, a Cambridge graduate from Dublin, broadcast on the Nationalist radio in English. Adopting a Chinese name, he wore a gown and skullcap, but kept Western shoes, and swore not to have his hair cut until the war was won. Six feet tall, with a 4-inch wisp of hair hanging from his lower lip as a sign of scholarship, McCausland knew 15,000 Chinese characters. In 1941, he was given Chinese citizenship.[22]

An American information officer, Graham Peck, also remembered a Bulgarian doctor, an Armenian guerrilla, an Indian novelist, a ballet dancer from Trinidad, and a Siberian Yakut who later became the Metro-Goldwyn-Mayer representative in Xi'an. The foreigners set up the Chungking Club along the lines of their social establishment in the treaty ports. An American former marine produced the only ice in town safe to put in drinks. Two Germans who styled themselves as barons made a gin they called 'Mountain Dew'. When China and Germany declared war after Pearl Harbor, an internment camp was set up by the government, but the only inmate was a German Jew who had married a Chinese woman and was living in poverty in a nearby village. The camp was modern, with new plumbing, and the prisoner was given a generous food allowance. When word spread, two other poor German Jews asked to be detained. Since they had taken out Chinese nationality, they were disbarred.[23]

At the end of 1938, one of the leading figures in the Kuomintang decided that he had had enough. Doubtful of the chances of victory and driven by his own ambition and his marginalisation by Chiang, Wang Jingwei slipped out of town, travelling by plane to the Yunnan capital of Kunming and then going on to Hanoi. There, he called for peace talks with Tokyo. The Generalissimo brushed this aside, and the one-time head of the Canton government was the target of an assassination attempt in the Vietnamese capital, apparently organised by the Nationalist secret police chief. It misfired when the killers went into the best room in the house and machine-gunned Wang's confidential secretary – his boss had chosen a simpler room. Wang said he had planned to go abroad from Hanoi, but that the killing so shocked him that he changed his mind and returned to occupied China, to set out on a path of active collaboration. He and his associates would claim that they were simply seeking peace and were thus acting in the nation's best interests as a counterweight to Chiang's war of resistance.[24]

He could draw on Sun Yat-sen's partiality for Japan – 'without Japan, there is no China; without China, there is no Japan,' the doctor had said. But Chiang made sure that he was expelled from the KMT, charged with desertion and defiance of government policy. Two of Wang's associates, whose defection to Hong Kong was arranged by Big-Eared Du with Chiang's approval, further discredited him when they leaked accounts of his earlier contacts with occupation authorities.

Setting up in Nanking, Wang embarked on negotiations to unite the puppet 'reformed' government there and pro-Japanese administrations in the north, with himself as the overall collaborationist boss. This fitted in with Tokyo's desire to add a political dimension to its military superiority. The new Japanese Prime Minister, Baron Kiichiro Hirauma, made his country's ambitions plain in a statement in which he said the final goal in China 'does not lie simply in the achievement of military victories but in the establishment of a new order in East Asia on a foundation of China's rebirth and mutual co-operation among Japan, Manchukuo and China. As long as this goal is not attained, there will be no end to the conflict.' Such warnings, however, took no account of the resolution of an opponent described by a missionary in Chungking as having 'a personality tempered to bright steel'.[25]

After the outbreak of war, Chiang had been given dictatorial 'emergency powers'. He was free to act as he wished in military, party and political matters, and to issue decrees as he chose. Chronically incapable of delegating or of letting any organisation escape from his grasp, he amassed jobs on a ridiculous and inefficient scale – at one point he was said to hold eighty-two posts ranging from chief of the government, the army and the party to the presidencies of the Boy Scouts, the National Glider Association and the School for Descendants of Revolutionary Martyrs. But his position was much weaker than it appeared, and he was anxious to rebuild his armies rather than fight fresh battles.

In his detailed survey of Chiang's forces the historian Michael Gibson concluded that 'by the end of 1938, the Central Army had all but ceased to exist as an effective fighting force'. Most divisions had lost at least one third of their manpower. As Chiang acknowledged, the general staff was weak and badly trained – some members could not read maps. Only a quarter of middle-rank and junior officers had received a regular education. Many regional commanders had a doubtful record of loyalty – in his account of National China at war, Ch'i Hsi-sheng calculated that 39 per cent of the top thirty-six generals had rebelled against Nanking before 1937 and only a third could be counted on totally. Regional militarists regained the autonomy which the Generalissimo had threatened in the mid-1930s. At the local level, commanders dominated administration and commerce. Senior generals were either provincial governors, or outranked the holders of those posts, drawing additional influence from their status in the Kuomintang.[26]

Redevelopment of the army was slow, equipment poor, desertion rates high. Conscription diminished the quality of troops who were badly fed and subject to disease: in Sichuan, in 1942, only a third of recruits met the official health standards. Those who could afford it escaped by bribery or by paying deserters to serve another spell under the flag in their place. Local militarists took their pick of the new men, and sometimes demanded more. To meet quotas, officials would press-gang peasants from the fields or grab passing travellers. For fear that they would desert, recruits were often marched to camps hundreds of miles away tied together with ropes round their necks, and stripped naked at night to prevent them running away. Many died on the way. Those who escaped the draft might be rounded up with their wives and children for forced labour.[27]

An indication of the scale of deaths, desertions and evasion of the draft was given by the way in which the overall strength of China's armies remained at 4 million although the government had ordered the conscription of 1.5 million men annually from 1938. As Galen had preached a dozen years earlier, China would have been much better off with a smaller, better trained army, but the faith in sheer numbers lived on from the warlord era.[28]

The Generalissimo did not help military cohesion by his habit of issuing far-off armies with orders that ignored battlefield realities – on one occasion, the able Cantonese commander, Xue Yue, remarked that he had taken his troops to a distant area of Jiangxi to ensure he was out of telephone contact. Explaining how he handled his generals, Chiang said: 'I have to lie awake at night, thinking what fool things they may do. Then I write and tell them not to do these things. But they are so dumb, they will do a lot of foolishness unless you anticipate them. This is the secret of handling them – you must imagine everything that they can do that would be wrong, and warn them against it. That is why I have to write so many letters.'[29]

He bypassed the military structure to deal directly with regimental commanders and frequently changed his mind. He kept troops out of battle so that they could be used for other purposes at a later date, or stationed them to check potential domestic rivals. He was surrounded by yes-men. His generals did not dare to stand up to him, knowing, in the words of Li Zongren of Guangxi, that he put obedience above ability. 'What Chiang liked,' said the hostile Li, 'were men . . . who would obey absolutely but who had no talents of their own.' When Meiling mentioned to him that one particularly incompetent general did not seem able to exercise his command, Chiang was said to have replied: 'But where do you find a man who is so obedient?' All of which heightened his belief in his own infallibility, and his unwillingness to engage in discussion, pursuing divide-and-rule tactics that were reflected in the factions below him.[30]

One was headed by the short, plump General He Yingqin who ran the military supply and administrative web. With his round face and circular spectacles, he looked benign – Teddy White described him as appearing 'almost schoolmasterish'. But anybody who had been Chief of Staff since 1927 and War Minister for almost as long, had to have become a master at manipulation. General He had extensive connections through the ranks of the Whampoa graduates, and he and his associates at the rambling, grey Military Council building in Chungking made fortunes for themselves from their positions. He also became one of the wealthiest landlords in his native Guizhou by annexing land, particularly from the minority populations there. China's most powerful Roman Catholic layman, the general was closely connected to the church's reactionary establishment. He advocated major campaigns to liquidate the Communists, and did all he could to block army reforms. Though Chiang did not trust him, He was too powerful to be ousted.

He's group was often at loggerheads with younger generals who were less desk-bound, had stronger regional roots and were anxious to build up their own power bases. The War Minister was particularly at odds with the more reform-minded Shanghai and Wuhan defender, Chen Cheng, who married one of Chiang's wards. Even shorter than his rival but much slimmer, Chen was the regime's main conduit to semi-autonomous forces outside the Central Army, and enjoyed good relations with commanders like the successful Cantonese Xue Yue whom Chiang regarded with suspicion. Known to be disgusted by the corruption and apathy of the regime, Chen pushed reform in his base of southern Hubei province, associated himself with the liberal Third Party and had a working relationship with Communist representatives in Chungking. This all made it inevitable that, as well as his rivalry with He, he became a *bête noire* for the repressive CC Clique of the Chen brothers.[31]

The general who had fought in the victory at Taierzhuang, Tang Enbo, established himself as the dominant Nationalist force in the key province of Henan, covering 65,000 square miles between northern and central China. Another ambitious Whampoa graduate and veteran of the war against the Red Army and the Japanese, Hu Zongnan, 'the Eagle of the North-West', commanded forces posted on the edge of the main Communist area in the north. Hu, who was said not to smoke, drink or chase women, was on particularly bad terms with He and dealt directly with Chiang. Lower down the ranks, fragmentation often ruled. In the central coastal area of eastern China, for instance, a dozen generals, plus politicians, secret police groups, Green Gang leaders, pirates and local dignitaries jockeyed for influence in Jiangsu and Anhui provinces – facilitating the expansion of the Communist army there.

As the glow of the united front era in Wuhan was destroyed by war, repression and censorship increased. Universities were purged. Textbooks were edited to make sure they toed the official line. The leading newspaper, *Ta Kung Pao*, was suspended for three days until the publisher apologised for writing that 'there is a halo of sanctity and silence around the Generalissimo'. The divorce widened with intellectuals and those who thought seriously about China's future. Minority groups on the Political Council were hounded after they set up a Federation of Democratic Parties with offices in Yunnan, Guangxi and Chengdu.

Despite this, Nationalist China was not a closed society like Nazi Germany or Soviet Russia. But Chiang showed how hollow the talk of democracy had been by reorganising the Council to drop the dissidents. In the absence of political debate, the regime's thinking became increasingly stultified. Chiang emphasised the importance of action; 'the only failure is in failing to act', he declared. The revolution needed a strong driving force based on wisdom, love and courage. Action should be based on 'true knowledge', to create 'an all-pervading moral attitude to life such as is rationally comfortable to man's true nature and [which] brings into full play the deep funds of humanity and benevolence in our own people'.[32]

His thoughts, expressed in lengthy speeches, hardly breathed life into the Kuomintang. In 1939, its membership was a third of the pre-war level; while the total rose to 2.5 million by the end of 1944, most recruits were attracted by the perks the party offered rather than by ideology or proselytising zeal. Thirty per cent of members came from three provinces – Sichuan, Zhejiang and Guangdong. The Central Executive Committee was a rubber stamp, with formal status but little influence.[33]

Internal rivalries round Chiang remained strong, and he fostered them on the divide-and-rule principle to get the most out of his subordinates. In particular, the Chen brothers who headed the CC Clique fought a bitter battle with the police chief, Dai Li. One of the Chen brothers, the grey-haired, ultra-energetic – and ultra-conservative – Lifu, became Education Minister and led the attempted brainwashing of students and intellectuals. His tubercular sibling, Chen Guofu, handled the flow of paper in Chiang's office, and decided who got to see the Generalissimo. An American adviser described their philosophy as 'a combination of Confucianism and European authoritarianism modelled on Italian and German fascism, with a dash of the YMCA type of Christianity'.[34]

During the war, their opponent Dai Li rose to become in many ways the second most powerful figure in the regime at the head of the secret police. Dubbed 'Chiang's Himmler' by critics, he was said to be the only person allowed to carry a gun in Chiang's presence. Slender and handsome, with tiny hands, Dai walked in long strides with a ramrod-straight back. He had piercing eyes, a taste for cashew nuts, and a lively distrust of the British, who once detained him for a night in Hong Kong. He always carried a small pistol presented to him by an American naval officer. His personal communications staff spoke the impenetrable dialect of his home area to communicate with one another by telephone so that anybody bugging their conversations could not understand what they were saying.

Universally feared, Dai had deepened the trust of his fellow Zhejiang native, the Generalissimo, by going to join him in Xi'an in December 1936. He had close links with secret societies and underworld gangs, including Big-Eared Du and the Shanghai mobs. After the He-Umeza secret pact outlawed the Blue Shirts, they welded into Dai's Juntong organisation and conducted terror missions for him. Overseeing a wave of terror attacks on collaborators in Shanghai, he preached 'saving the nation in devious ways' which became code for maintaining ambiguous links with collaborators. Chiang gave him control of the salt monopoly, which helped to finance his police whose numbers were put by some in the millions. His agents were posted to military and police units to check their reliability, and given responsibility for fighting hoarding, black marketeering and profiteering as the economy spun out of control.[35]

The war had been bound to face Chiang with a major financial problem, but his response made it far worse and accentuated disenchantment with his regime. Loss of China's richest cities severely cut the tax take – in 1937–39, expenditure rose by a third, mainly on military spending, while revenue fell by two thirds. Washington extended loans worth a total of US$145 million, and Britain granted a £500,000 credit, but these were not enough to meet Chiang's requirements. Some funds were raised by sending the stocks of the opium monopoly for sale through Hong Kong and the Portuguese colony of Macau in an operation run by Big-Eared Du and Dai Li. Longer-term, the Generalissimo and H. H. Kung decided to pay the bills by printing money at a rate never seen before.[36]

This caused a national disaster. The value of the currency plunged.

Inflation soared. Even more money had to be found; so the presses were set to work even more – it was, in the words of a Chinese proverb, a case of 'drinking poison to kill thirst'. But the man in charge of the country's finances waved aside any criticism. 'Inflation, inflation!' Kung told a questioner. 'There is no inflation in China! If people want to pay twenty five dollars for a fountain pen, that's their business, it's not inflation. They're crazy, that's all. They shouldn't pay it.'[37]

Three quarters of wartime spending was financed by notes from the main state-controlled banks. The annual issue rose from 1.45 billion yuan in 1937 to 15 billion in the early 1940s, hitting even more stratospheric levels in the following years. By the second half of 1941, prices were doubling on an annual basis, boosted by poor harvests and scarcities of manufactured goods. In 1940–41, food prices in Chungking increased by 1,400 per cent.[38]

The soaring cost of living was accompanied by an upsurge in graft that became a hallmark of the regime, particularly when the government tried to lessen the inflationary spiral by holding down the salaries of officials and soldiers. A widely read book of the time compared corruption to a banyan tree under which the Chinese sought shelter. Virtually everybody made what they could on the side, from avarice or necessity. Those with access to food or goods hoarded and profiteered. 'To get rich quickly, to have a beautiful mistress . . . to be able to give dinners at which shark's fin, already almost unobtainable, will be served as a delicacy, to ride in motor-cars and be able to say that your income can be measured in millions are the hallmarks of the most exquisite taste,' the academic Robert Payne wrote in his Chungking diary. 'There is no sign of the greatness of China here.'[39]

Corruption had long been a prime concern for W. H. Donald who had never reconciled himself to the prevalence of 'squeeze'. In the past, he had urged Chiang to execute high-profile miscreants. Now, his unhappiness crystallised round an incident he had seen before the fall of Wuhan. An ambulance bought with American donations had stopped in front of a bank where an official had a lot of money deposited. The cash was taken out of the bank, loaded into the ambulance and driven away in a centuries-old pattern of the wealthy fleeing with their possessions and leaving the ordinary people to their fate. Later that day, Donald had gone to the Chiangs' house, and led Meiling into the garden. Something must be done about the high-level sleaze, he insisted; his biography says he cited the wife of an official who is not named, but who was clearly the eldest of her sisters, Ailing Kung. Meiling turned on the Australian in a blaze of anger, and said, 'You may criticise the government or anything in China, but there are some persons even you cannot criticise.' Donald stood silent for a moment, and then walked away quickly as the blood leaped to his cheeks.[40]

In Chungking, he continued his work, promoting Chiang's wife as a Chinese icon to the West and flying with her to Hong Kong to talk about arms procurement. But he was taking stock of his position, and of the regime he was serving. Eventually, he decided to quit at the end of three decades in China. After saying goodbye to Meiling, he flew to Hong Kong. There, he boarded his yacht called, in part, after her. On the boat was a collection of gifts she had given him over the years including a compass, a wireless and silverware. The Australian put a sheet of paper in his typewriter and, as he later told his biographer, wrote, 'Dear Madame Chiang: once I told you there were all sorts of roads out of China and that you need only say the word and I would kick up a dust so fast it would be as a locust cloud in retreat. Well, at last I am on a road, a big highway.' He pulled the paper out of the machine, and tore it up.

The following summer, Donald set sail for the Solomon Islands with the eighteen-year-old daughter of a Chinese merchant friend in Hong Kong who was to act as his secretary while he wrote his memoirs – which he did not do. Meiling would urge him to return, and, terminally ill with lung disease, he eventually flew back to China seven years later saying he wanted 'to go home to die'. He and the woman he had carried from the car crash in Shanghai never met again, but Meiling, wearing black, attended his funeral at the end of 1946, and a cross of yellow and white chrysanthemums was placed on top of the coffin as it was taken to the city's International Cemetery.[41]

On 3 May 1939, Japanese navy planes swooped on Chungking like a whirlwind. During the winter and early spring, the cloud and fog had acted as a protective blanket. Now, the sky had cleared. It was a sultry day, and the streets were crowded as the planes started bombing. There was an eclipse of the moon that night; priests beat bronze gongs to scare off the Dog of Heaven which was trying to swallow the moon. Town criers walked the streets ringing bells warning that, along with bombs, the Japanese had dropped poisoned cigarettes. The planes returned the following day and, that night, Reuters reported:

Chungking presented a strange picture. One half of the city was in total darkness. There was no electric light, no telephone service, and thousands of homeless persons slept on the pavements. Lighted candles burned at the doors of houses, this telling that at least one of the inmates had been killed. Some bodies rested in coffins inside houses while others lay on the pavements, covered with mats. Meanwhile the other half of the city is full of bright lights, and life is going on there as usual.

In the bombed areas, corpses were everywhere. 'Loose limbs are scattered about amid smouldering heaps of furniture and beams,' a French missionary wrote. 'I ask myself whether such horrors are possible, or whether I am the victim of ghastly hallucinations . . . Chungking has become one vast cemetery.' The municipal hospital had room for only 250 patients. The main water tower was hit, so fire-fighting was difficult. Doors were pulled off houses to serve as stretchers. One group of Chinese sought refuge in the British consulate. The ambassador ordered the gates to be opened, and they settled on the tennis court which was then hit by a bomb that dug a 24-foot crater and killed twenty-five of them.

Below the German embassy, several hundred Chinese were trapped against the city wall. Some of their bodies were charred black by flames; others died of the heat so gradually that their clothes were not even scorched. The flesh was missing from the top joints of their fingers, ripped away as they tried to climb to safety. Children and babies lay under them. Asked why they had not helped the Chinese to escape, a German diplomat replied: 'There were too many of them. Besides they were only coolies.'[42]

The main streets were filled with craters and wrecked buildings. Amid the raging fires, the city was a sea of fleeing people. Old women hobbled on bound feet; the blind were dragged along by relatives; children howled for their parents; mothers shrieked for their children; trucks and cars drove headlong into the mob; the crackling, rushing sound of the flames came from all sides. Going back to where her home had stood, Han Suyin found the whole district 'a wilderness of dust and debris, oven-hot'. Red Cross men and Boy Scouts were pulling out bodies, charred to bones or shrunk to half their normal size by the heat.[43]

Many of those caught in the raids could, literally, have had no idea of what had hit them. They might have seen a plane flying overhead, but they had no concept of aerial warfare. To the traditionally minded inhabitants of Chungking, it was as if mythological monsters were raining death and destruction on them from the sky. Bombs hit refugees sheltering in a park in the middle of the city. 'One small girl was sitting against a wall as if sleeping but a trickle of blood flowing down her neck revealed that she was dead,' a Reuters correspondent wrote.

A Chinese mother was holding the hand of her dead boy, who was about six years of age, crying uncontrollably. Further on lay another woman, still alive but unconscious, awaiting removal while beside her lay her small girl in a pretty print frock – dead. An almost headless soldier had slumped at the foot of a cut-down tree, and beyond him two young girls, their bodies almost unmutilated, sprawled against a wall. What was once a children's playground was littered with bodies, bomb craters, and uprooted trees.[44]

One raid caught a general at his wedding party; the couple and their guests went into a big shelter, but a bomb landed on a fuel dump nearby and they were all killed when burning oil ran into the dugout. A group of 250 well-off people sought safety in the basement of a ten-storey building being put up for the Bank of China, but were crushed to death when it was hit. Three hundred died by bombs that landed on a home for opium addicts. Chicken Street, home of the sing-song girls, was wrecked. Creeping into an abandoned mansion, Rhodes Farmer slept on silk pillows and brocade bedspreads, and breakfasted on chicken and champagne from the fridge.[45]

There was no effective anti-aircraft defence, and, at the first alarm, the remnants of the Nationalist navy – high-funnelled torpedo boats and small gunships moored on the Yangtze – weighed anchor to head for shelter under the rock faces downstream. The death toll from the raids in early May was put at between 6,000 and 8,000. Up to a quarter of the city was gutted by fire. As buses and lorries evacuated civilians, Chiang's bullet-proof limousine was pressed into service – an old woman threw herself into the dust and kowtowed before she was carried into it. In the cellar of the French religious mission, the Bishop served up noodles, cold boiled cherries and his last bottle of red wine. The British ambassador came walking up the street in old flannels swinging his stick viciously. 'On no other man's face have I seen such a mixture of hate and horror,' Rhodes Farmer recalled.[46]

By mid-September, there had been thirty attacks, and the network of shelters was said to be able to house 200,000 people, ranging from damp, mosquito-infested tunnels to concrete-lined private shelters with battery lighting, and fan ventilation. The bunker under the Soviet embassy was particularly well-appointed, with telephones, a bar, bedrooms, and a kitchen; the Germans preferred one-person shelters dug into the lawn of their embassy. The atmosphere mixed fear, disregard for human life and a search for pleasure, with an undercurrent of pride at not being crushed. Shops offered 'Fresh eggs direct from Tokyo' with a drawing of a plane dropping bombs. The morning after a big attack on the business district, the banks were opened as usual, though their floors were littered with glass and debris. Restaurants served 'after-the-raid meals', and queues formed outside cinemas in one street while relief teams recovered bodies in the next. When electric light was restored after an attack, Chungking, wrote Han Suyin, stood 'proudly above the rivers, like a ship majestic with all its lights ablaze, riding the ocean'.[47]

In its vulnerability and resistance, the gaunt, grey city smelling of ashes and death reflected the man who had made his haven there. 'The enemy is cruel, inhuman and barbarous beyond belief,' Chiang wrote in his diary. 'This is the most horrible scene I have witnessed in my life.' Still, Japanese planes could not destroy the will to resist, he declared.[48]

The initial alarms were sounded after Nationalist agents down the Yangtze had sighted the planes. At that, the Generalissimo went to a first shelter where he could go on working until the Japanese were almost overhead. Then he moved to an inner shelter where senior generals awaited him. 'Here, the Minister of War, in tightly buttoned uniform and very shiny boots, paces up and down restlessly,' Han Suyin wrote.

Other generals converse in low tones or look over papers. The Generalissimo sits erect and stiff on a hard wooden chair, his arms folded, his back six inches from the back of the chair. He is resting. He is never seen to relax, to slouch or cross his legs; not a muscle moves. Overhead, bombs crash. Others in the shelter start, glance upward. They open their mouths and some stop their ears. Not Chiang Kai-shek. His face wears an expression of curbed annoyance, as though he was trying not to listen to a boring speech. Staring straight before him, he sits motionless – resting.[49]

CHAPTER 20

Magnetic Warfare

AS CHUNGKING BECAME the most heavily bombed city on earth, the Japanese troops staged a series of advances. They finally occupied Chiang's summer capital in the mountain resort of Kuling, the defenders leaving an hour before they arrived. North-west of Wuhan, a fresh attempt to encircle twenty divisions under Li Zongren and Tang Enbo failed when the Chinese melted away into the mountains, re-appearing later to harass the enemy's communications lines. To the south, seven columns backed by planes and tanks advanced along the road and rail line on the Jiangxi capital of Nanchang, from where Chiang had organised his campaigns against the Red Army – the attackers were temporarily blocked on the far bank of the wide river beside the city, but then grabbed a flotilla of passing junks to complete the offensive after which they then advanced on a string of fortified towns, including one where the only defender left was a twelve-year-old cadet. The invaders then drove westwards into Hunan. By September 1939, they were moving on its capital of Changsha where the Chinese stocked inflammable materials to meet the attackers with fire if the defences were breached.

Lulled into overconfidence, the Japanese advanced without their usual heavy equipment and vehicles. Springing their trap, the Nationalists attacked on the flanks from surrounding hills. The Japanese were forced to retreat. The victory set off firecracker celebrations in Chungking. But it was accompanied by tragedy. The Hunan authorities had reacted to news that enemy cavalry was within 20 miles of the city by ordering the fire trap to be lit. Changsha burned for five days, killing many thousands. Chiang flew in to order the court martial of the garrison commander, another general and the police chief. All were shot.[1]

In the south, the Japanese took Hainan Island, and staged a landing in Guangxi, but met resistance from General Bai, and pulled out in the autumn. The odds against which the Chinese fought were reflected in an account by Bai's colleague, Li Zongren, of a battle against a Japanese advance in central China. 'Our troops who had fought for a long time and received no adequate replacements, were worn out and lacked anti-tank guns,' he recalled. 'They simply could not resist the onslaught . . . they fought from their trenches and some climbed onto tanks and threw grenades inside, but where the enemy tanks passed, our ditches were leveled and the defenders either crushed to death or buried alive.' Falling back into mountains, they held out for ten days, waiting for the Whampoa veteran, General Tang Enbo, to stage an encircling movement. But Tang preferred to stay out of the battle to conserve his forces.[2]

On the terrorist front, Shanghai was riddled with attacks on collaborators by Dai Li's men, sometimes in association with the Green Gang which received $500,000 a month from Chungking. They were estimated to have carried out more than 150 political murders in the four years after the start of the battle for the city in August 1937. The banking and shipping tycoon Fu Xiaoan, whom Chiang had had detained in 1927 and who had become mayor of Shanghai, was cut to death with a meat chopper as he slept by his cook who had been recruited by the Nationalist secret service. The chief secretary of the collaborationist police force was shot dead in the alley behind his home, and the foreign minister of the puppet administration was killed in his house in front of his family by assassins who unrolled pro-Chiang scrolls before they fled the blood-stained room. Another victim was Big-Eared Du's Green Gang associate Zhang Xiaolin, who had thrown his lot in with the Japanese. Bombs were thrown in public places and an unsuccessful plan was laid to eliminate Wang Jingwei. An attempt was made to stage a mass poisoning of the 'reformed' government and Japanese dignitaries at a banquet – they were saved by prompt medical attention. Chinese guerrillas blew up a train from Shanghai to Nanking carrying officials to the signing of a treaty between Japan and the puppet regime, killing seventy-four and injuring a hundred.

There were frequent reprisals by a collaborationist secret service which had its headquarters in a house in the Huxi 'badlands' district outside the International Settlement. Headed by two ex-Communists who had worked in Dai Li's police, it assassinated pro-Chungking Chinese, arrested citizens at will, kidnapped businessmen for large ransoms and attacked judges, banks and newspapers while running protection rackets for casinos, opium dens and brothels. One of its leaders defected to the Nationalists after surviving a murder attempt by his teenage mistress – before leaving, he poisoned his main associate in the collaborationist police, the former chauffeur of the International Settlement chairman who had agreed to let Big-Eared Du's men through to attack the Communists in April 1927.[3]

The military success at Changsha emboldened Chiang to launch a wholesale offensive. He was also encouraged by events abroad. Washington said it would not recognise Japan's new order in East Asia and would let its trade treaty with Tokyo lapse. Chiang's hopes that a war between Japan and the Soviet Union in the far north-east would draw enemy troops from China had appeared to have some substance when fighting along the Manchurian–Mongolian railway culminated in the major battle of Nomonhan in August 1939. Zhukov's victory over the Kwantung Army's 23rd Division led the Japanese to plan a bigger offensive, but, following the Nazi–Soviet Pact, Tokyo opted for a ceasefire with Moscow instead.

That left Chiang, once again, to fight on his own. Soviet aid declined, with the number of planes delivered to China dropping by 60 per cent in 1940 at a time when the Japanese increased their air force in China to 800 machines, including much-feared Zero fighters. Showing their ability to strike wherever they wished, the invaders staged a large landing on the Guangxi coast in the south and drove on to the provincial capital of Nanning. Still the Generalissimo hankered after a decisive battle to enable him to affirm his position as the national leader against regional militarists and the challenge from Wang Jingwei who accused him of being 'an aspirant dictator' lacking 'even the minimum moral and ethical qualifications of the normal human being'.[4]

On 19 November 1939, after a series of late-night meetings, Chiang issued a mobilisation order for a Winter Offensive involving half his armies. Casting aside the gradualist strategy, he decreed frontal attacks, and spoke of retaking Nanking. But his troops were still weak after the losses on the Yangtze, and woefully equipped while the diversion of forces to oppose the attack in Guangxi cut the numbers available elsewhere. Only one in three soldiers had a rifle; the armies possessed just 2,600 artillery pieces, and 1,500 vehicles. Some commanders dragged their feet or ignored orders to advance. Still, the Chinese staged 2,300 attacks between 12 December and 20 January, managing to break briefly into Kaifeng and the Wuhan area. But, overall, the campaign was a considerable failure. By April 1940 it was all over.[5]

As a result, the Generalissimo and those around him reverted to their belief in a long-term struggle dependent on the United States' eventually going to war and defeating Tokyo. The failure of his last big offensive also further decreased Chiang's authority over the regional power barons, including the Communists. To try to counteract this, he increasingly deployed central army troops to keep regional forces in check and assert Chungking's presence, rather than putting them where they would best fight the Japanese.

Events abroad now turned against China. France fell to the Germans, and the Vichy regime cut off the rail link to Yunnan from Hanoi as the Japanese moved into Indo-China. Standing alone against the Nazis, Britain felt obliged to yield to Japanese pressure and to close the Burma Road supply route for three months. The following year, Tokyo and Moscow signed a neutrality agreement while the German attack on the Soviet Union meant Stalin had less aid to offer. At home, Wang Jingwei's Reorganised Government took office in Nanking. It proclaimed its agreement with Tokyo's vision of a new order in Asia which included the overthrow of Chiang, but also spoke of protecting China's independence and sovereignty. Though Wang was the main collaborator, separate puppet administrations continued in the north.

The Generalissimo unveiled a new strategy: 'magnetic warfare', to draw the enemy into losing positions. He also issued a list of behavioural instructions to officials and officers: No smoking, no drinking; Sleep early, rise early; Thrifty life; Absolutely no gambling; Absolute obedience to superiors; All uniforms to be made of cotton; No office stationery to be used for private correspondence; No badges of office to be worn in places of amusement; No public banquets unless absolutely necessary.[6]

None of this did anything to save his forces from further heavy losses, put at 200,000 men, when the Japanese launched attacks in Hubei, Henan, Anhui and Shanxi. Over Chiang's home province of Zhejiang, planes dropped fleas carrying plague germs which had been tested on Chinese prisoners at Japan's secret biological warfare unit in Manchuria. This caused an outbreak of disease in Ningbo. In another campaign in the province, the Japanese spread anthrax, plague, typhoid and cholera, but suffered over 10,000 casualties among soldiers who had not been warned of the contamination.[7]

The invaders captured the strategic Yangtze city of Yichang,* where goods were transferred from big boats to smaller craft to make the journey up through the river gorges to Chungking. This further restricted supplies to the Nationalist capital, particularly of food. Air raids on Chungking continued unabated, setting off fresh fires, hitting the university, destroying the British legation, and covering the street with greenish-yellow sulphur dust. Meiling visited street kitchens for air-raid victims while Chiang ordered a relief grant of $1 million. In April 1940, the Soong sisters made a joint broadcast to the people of the United States. Qingling began by saying that the Chinese 'instead of becoming the helots of an all-conquering slave empire have taken up arms for their own freedom as well as for yours'. Ailing declared that China's fighting strength was greater than ever and noted how her country's women had 'escaped from their cloistered lives and are working everywhere'. Meiling called for China to be 'given the justice that is her right, the justice she has earned by almost three long years of unparalleled bloodshed and suffering'.

There were occasional displays of resistance, such as the performance of General Zhang Zizhong, a former warlord officer and veteran of the Taierzhuang battle, who became a national hero after refusing to retreat or surrender when his unit was surrounded and fighting on until he died from seven separate wounds.† Changsha was defended successfully for a

* Known at the time as Ichang.
† He was the highest-ranking Allied general to die in combat in the Second World War, and is regarded as a patriotic hero by the Communist regime. See Arthur Waldron's account of his posthumous treatment in *Modern Asian Studies*, Vol. 30.4, Oct. 1996.

second time after the Japanese were lured into an ambush. But a review of the army pointed to lack of initiative, coordination and equipment, and poor staff work, intelligence, logistics and discipline. Chiang criticised his generals for arrogance, inexperience, corruption and low interest in training their men. The Japanese estimated that Chinese combat effectiveness had fallen by up to a third since 1939.[8]

Despite his declarations of unyielding resistance, the Generalissimo took steps to open a channel to the enemy, using one of Dai Li's agents who bore a striking resemblance to his brother-in-law, T. L. Soong. The lookalike went to Hong Kong where he arranged for a reporter to introduce him as T.L. to a colonel in one of Tokyo's intelligence services who was visiting the colony. Though not sure whether the man was who he said he was, the Japanese decided to build on the contact.

Secret night-time meetings were held in the British colony, attended by delegates from Chungking. Japanese surveillance showed that, however late the sessions lasted, the Chinese followed them with a long discussion of their own, after which a man went to the airport to fly to the capital. At one point, the Chinese delegates brought with them credentials signed by the Generalissimo. An agreement was reached for a meeting between Chiang, Wang Jingwei and the Chief of Staff of the Japanese forces in China. Before this could take place, the negotiations collapsed on the issue of Manchukuo. Tokyo insisted on recognition, but Chiang knew he could not grant this without being branded a traitor. The Japanese command decided that China was 'not sincere in her desire for peace' and downgraded the Hong Kong operation to a simple intelligence-gathering channel.[9]

This did not stop fresh secret contacts between Chiang and the enemy, who were not enamoured of the Reorganised Government in Nanking – one Imperial Privy Councillor contrasted Wang's 'lack of integrity' with the Generalissimo's 'heroic life'. Tokyo offered to remove troops sent to China since the Marco Polo Bridge Incident within six months, and to ensure that China's need for resources was met. In return, they wanted demilitarisation of the Yangtze Valley, recognition of Manchukuo, autonomy for the five northern provinces under Japanese economic control and Japanese concessions in all ports. Those conditions were unacceptable even as the basis for opening talks. In his diary, Chiang concluded that the only viable policy was to fight Japan, while remaining neutral between the Berlin–Rome Axis and the Anglo-American block until Moscow had clarified its position. His contacts with the Japanese were probing missions to see if there was any relaxation in their position. Any serious concession would fatally weaken him against domestic opponents, including the Communists. On the other hand, by letting Washington know about these contacts he sent a signal that he might change policy if he did not receive the aid he wanted.[10]

In pursuit of that, T. V. Soong flew incognito to Washington, and negotiated a US$25 million loan after a sandwich lunch with the President at the White House. Roosevelt then announced a US$50 million currency stabilisation agreement, a loan and a credit to buy raw materials from China. This brought total US aid to Chungking to US$245 million, but raised an immediate question reflecting the fragmentation of Nationalist China. Was Chiang going to share the aid with other forces fighting the Japanese or keep it all for himself? If he did the first, he would buttress the independence of regionalists like the Guangxi Clique, not to mention the Communists. If he did the second, he would risk alienating generals whose support he needed, pushing them into revolt or non-cooperation, or to join Wang Jingwei. He chose the second path, but it was a question which was to become more acute as the volume of American aid grew, and would cause a running battle with the country he counted on to win the war for him.

Another piece of good news came from Britain which agreed to a £10 million loan and, even more important, reopened the highway from Burma into Yunnan on 17 October 1940. Five hundred trucks left on the first day, carrying 1,500 tons of supplies. Tunnels provided shelters against Japanese planes as the highway crossed 8,000-foot mountains; one section climbed round twenty-two hairpin loops. Lorries wended their way past trains of ponies laden with freight and carts with 1,000-pound loads pulled by three men who could average 20 miles a day. Driving up one steep stretch, Rhodes Farmer's vehicle was outpaced by coolies carrying 180-pound loads of rock salt. On the way through Guizhou, he noted heavy bombing along the road, and saw locals walking round in frock coats, Western waistcoats and fancy trousers which had been sent by mistake by the Red Cross from London.[11]

At the end of 1940, Chiang invited Zhou Enlai to a Christmas dinner in Chungking, four years after their encounter in Xi'an. The two men discussed the longer-term relationship between their movements. Zhou said the Communists must be treated as a political party, not a warlord army. When he said the government was undemocratic, Chiang replied, 'You mean to call *me* undemocratic?'[12]

By then, the united front was under severe strain. Chiang had never lost sight of his aim of eradicating his Red disease of the heart, while, from the caves of Yan'an, Mao was equally set on winning national power however long it took. The Communist Eighth Route Army was enlarging and deepening its presence in the north, and the New Fourth Army was expanding in the coastal region north of Shanghai. The hawks in Chungking were agitating for action. General He and Chen Lifu wanted a full-blooded anti-Communist campaign. The Kuomintang Secretary General objected to the fact that the Red Army 'has not actually participated in any great battles'.[13]

To disprove that increasingly common criticism, the Communists launched a major campaign against the Japanese in central-northern China in the late summer of 1940, known as the Hundred Regiments Offensive, though many of the units were smaller formations. This abandoned Mao's doctrine of only engaging when sufficient force could be concentrated on the enemy's weak points to ensure a knockout blow – and then withdrawing. The Red Army now felt confident enough to launch frontal attacks and show it was willing to fight on a broad front. There were other motives at work as well. The Japanese were using a blockhouse strategy similar to that employed by Chiang six years earlier, and the Communists wanted to burst the cage being erected around them. They also feared that Chungking might be about to reach an agreement with the invaders to attack them. After their early moves met with success in cutting railway lines, Eighth Route Army commanders launched frontal attacks which the Japanese repulsed without difficulty. Most of the damaged railways were soon back in service, and the offensive fell well short of the achievements proclaimed by the Communists. Though it had petered out by the end of 1940, Mao sent a cable to the commander at the front pointing out that the publicity it had generated was needed as a weapon against Chiang.[14]

But it was the 100,000-strong Communist New Fourth Army in the east which most irked the Generalissimo as it expanded its core zone north and south of the lower Yangtze. Though Maoist history would play down its role compared to troops commanded from Yan'an, the New Fourth Army was a formidable force, based on guerrillas left behind by the Long March, plus workers and intellectuals from the Lower Yangtze region, including political prisoners freed under the united front agreement.* Applying the 'united front from above' policy, it established working relationships with gentry leaders whose local power was threatened by the Nationalists. As recognition of his position as China's commander-in-chief, Chiang had been given the power to decide who should be its military leader. He had to choose a Communist, and his decision harked back to the Canton days as he gave the job to the highly regarded Ye Ting, who had fought in the vanguard of the Northern Expedition at the head of the Independent Regiment of the original Fourth Army. But Yan'an named the political boss, Xiang Ying, who had led the guerrillas in eight southern provinces since 1934.

In the autumn of 1940, the tension between the New Fourth Army and the local Nationalists round the Lower Yangtze spilled over into a major battle which the Communists won decisively. That presented a special threat to Chiang since, once the Japanese were beaten, he intended to re-establish himself there with Nanking as his capital and Shanghai as his financial centre. So he had to eject the Communists from his past and future power base, and get them to move up to the Yellow River, where there was a good chance that they would come under attack from the Japanese. There was also a question of authority – if the Generalissimo could make the New Fourth Army withdraw, that would send a message to other semi-autonomous forces; if he could not, he would be seen to be powerless. His Green Gang allies were anxious that the Communists should not interfere with the drug trade; the senior Nationalist commander in the area had a particular interest as the brother of the man running the Shanghai underworld in the absence of Big-Eared Du.[15]

The New Fourth Army's presence on the Yangtze was not provided for in the united front agreement. So Chiang was on firm ground in insisting that it pull back from its base at Yunling, south of the river in Anhui province. Two groups did depart in the first ten days of December. That left

---

* Its proper place has been established for English-language readers by Gregor Benton's magisterial study on which I have based much of the detail in this section.

the headquarters unit of more than 4,000 soldiers and 6,000 non-combatants. Chiang fixed a deadline of 31 December for them to start moving out. He assured Zhou Enlai that they would enjoy safe passage.[16]

The situation on the ground made this increasingly unlikely. The Guangxi general, Bai, said force was needed. The Generalissimo told the local Nationalist commander that, if the 31 December deadline was not met, he should 'finish it off at once [and] stop being lenient'. In late December, Nationalist troops moved into position; their officers were told that a decision had been taken to 'mop up the bandits'. At midnight on 4 January 1941 the Communist headquarters units, grouped into three columns, began to move on the southerly route from their base. Snow and rain bucketed down through icy winds. The lighting the Communists carried in the night made it easy for the Nationalists to track their progress. The direction they took heightened suspicions that they were heading for their old guerrilla strongholds in Jiangxi province rather than keeping to the agreement to go north across the Yangtze.[17]

As the columns moved through the mountains, one was fired on by a Nationalist patrol. By 9 January the Communists were under heavy pressure from their much more numerous and better equipped foes. Told what was happening, Zhou Enlai went to see the Generalissimo who dismissed the reports from the battlefield; he had agreed to a safe passage for the New Fourth Army, he recalled, so it could not have been attacked. As the tired, hungry Communists concentrated in a village called Shijing, their commander Ye Ting wrote a message to Chiang asking him to stop the attack and adding that he was ready to receive punishment. 'Though I do not fear death, I do fear your radio message,' he added, 'I await your order.' Ye sent the message to the Communist base in Yan'an to be passed on. It was not forwarded to Chungking.[18]

On 12 January the Nationalists unleashed an intense artillery and bombing attack. Two days later, Mao sent a message saying that Chiang had agreed to a ceasefire. By then, the battle was over. Estimates of Communist dead ranged from 2,000 to 10,000; Mao said at the time that 7,000 had been 'finished off'. Survivors told of women being raped, and captives being marched 400 miles to a camp – 'when they sickened, they were beaten; some were shot, and others were buried alive'. Ye Ting was among those taken prisoner. Held for five years, he died in a plane crash on his way to Yan'an in 1945. His fellow commander, Xiang Ying, escaped, but was killed by a companion who made off with the gold he kept in a pouch.[19]

Zhou Enlai told Teddy White he was sure Chiang had not commanded the generals to attack, but had led them to believe he would not mind if they did so. Was Chiang lying? White asked. 'No,' said Zhou. 'Someone was lying to the Generalissimo but the G'issimo lies to a certain extent, too.' For his part, Chiang told a meeting of senior officers that the New Fourth Army had been guilty of disregarding orders, mutiny and sabotage. 'It was purely a matter of the assertion of military law,' he added in an implicit warning to other independent-minded generals.[20]

Where did this leave the united front? Zhou Enlai said he considered cooperation with Chungking to be over. From Yan'an, Mao warned that 'those who play with fire ought to be very careful . . . Fire is not a very good game. Be careful about your skull.' The Communists boycotted the nearest thing China had to a united assembly, the People's Political Council. But Stalin was anxious not to dismantle the front, and Mao soon moderated his tone, speaking of some time elapsing between the start and the completion of a split with the Kuomintang. The bitter medicine contributed to his negative feelings about Moscow which continued to be Chungking's main source of arms.

Chiang increased the pressure on the Red Army by cutting off supplies, and blockading Yan'an. Cavalry attacked a New Fourth Army detachment in northern Henan, inflicting 4,000 casualties. Communist activities were banned in Nationalist areas. Dai Li's police stepped up arrests of real or suspected dissidents, taking in liberals and opponents of Chiang, critics of corruption and anybody who appeared to be a potential threat.

The Generalissimo had another cause for satisfaction when the Japanese were again beaten back from Changsha, forced to retreat after their sense of superiority led them to neglect flank and rear defence. Visiting the 'gray, bomb-spattered, fire-gutted, grim stone island' of Chungking, Ernest Hemingway found the Chinese officers he met 'extraordinarily frank, straight-talking, intelligent and articulate' and summed up Chiang as a military leader who was 'going through the motions of being a statesman'. Another eminent American visitor, Henry Luce, boss of the *Time-Life* magazine empire, flew into the Nationalist capital, and revelled in the sense of optimism spread out for him. The son of a Presbyterian missionary in Shandong, Luce was in the process of becoming the regime's most devoted powerful foreign friend. Kai-shek and Meiling appeared to him to epitomise his dream of 'Christianising and Americanising China'. Lodged in H. H. Kung's mansion in Chungking, the publisher saw only the positive aspects which the regime laid out for him. As proof of how the Nationalists were fighting, he was taken to the Yellow River front to witness a shelling barrage. After ten days in China, he wrote that the Generalissimo was the greatest ruler Asia had seen for 250 years, and threw all his resources to sway public and political opinion behind Chungking, putting Chiang on the cover of half a dozen issues of *Time*.[21]

The truth was that it was an awful time for Chiang. There had been rare successes such as the defence of Changsha and a battle at the town of Shanggao in Jiangxi where the Japanese were surrounded and lost nearly half their men. But the Winter Offensive had flopped, and the enemy had scored victories in Guangxi, along the Yangtze and on the plains of north Hubei. Wang's regime was posing a political threat, and the Model Governor had reached an armistice with the invaders. An oral message from Franklin Roosevelt, delivered by his emissary Lauchlin Currie, boded badly for the showdown with the Red Army which Chiang still planned after the war – the President said the Communists were 'what in our country we would call Socialists. We like their attitude towards the peasants, towards women and towards Japan.' The New Fourth Army incident had broken the united front; in one engagement north of the Yellow River, Communist troops were seen attacking Nationalists fleeing from the Japanese. Not that Mao and his colleagues were immune from assault. The Japanese launched a campaign against the main base area known as the 'Three Alls' – kill all, burn all, destroy all. By the time it ended, the base population was reduced from 40 million to an estimated 25 million, and the party was plunged into its worst period since the Long March.[22]

Abroad, Stalin added to Chiang's woes by signing a non-aggression pact with Tokyo, including recognition of Manchukuo, which removed the military pressure from Japanese troops in the north. Two months later, Hitler attacked the Soviet Union. Fascist aggression seemed unbeatable. Chiang became concerned at the possibility of an accord between Washington and Tokyo to head off the looming conflict between them – one condition would have been for the United States to have press-ganged China into recognising Manchukuo and the Imperial positions in the north. But then, at the start of December 1941, Tokyo finally did what Chiang had been hoping for after standing alone since 1937. By attacking Pearl Harbor, Japan finally melded China's struggle with that of the most powerful nation on earth.

CHAPTER 21

Peanut and Vinegar

HAVING SHOWN HIS JOY at the news of Pearl Harbor by playing a gramophone recording of 'Ave Maria', Chiang proposed to Washington that control of the whole Far Eastern war effort should be concentrated in Chungking. Japan should be isolated by a blockade and pummelled by air attacks while its forces were destroyed in China. He did not specify how this was to be achieved, and an American diplomat observed that the plan was 'uncluttered by considerations of supply, command or what should be done about the inconvenient war with Germany'. All the Generalissimo got from President Roosevelt was a message advocating that 'immediate steps be taken to prepare the way for common action against our common enemy', with a handwritten note at the end of the typescript: 'I am working hard on continuing our contribution to your supplies and am trying to increase it. I send you my very warm personal regards.' At the end of December, a further message from the White House scaled down Chiang's command to China, Thailand and Indo-China. Still, in one of his broadcast fireside chats to the American people, the President insisted that it was essential to help China 'in her magnificent defense and in her inevitable counter-offensive – for that is one important element in the ultimate defeat of Japan'.[1]

The Chinese began the new phase of the war with another successful defence of the Hunan capital of Changsha, under the command of the

Cantonese Xue Yue. The defenders staged eleven sorties against the 100,000 enemy; in one sector, a burial mound on which the Japanese had tried to set up an artillery piece changed hands five times. Visiting the city, the writer Robert Payne watched young, blue-helmeted Chinese soldiers walking round 'with an unexpected swagger, their bayonets gleaming . . . Farmers' lads, mostly, with faces like ripe apples.' The Japanese had burned down the Yale-in-China hospital, where Chiang had had his teeth fixed in the first stage of the Northern Expedition, throwing their dead into the flames and killing patients before they retreated. By the East Gate, where corpses lay stripped and turning green, Payne picked up a photograph of a Japanese girl sitting in front of flowering cherry trees.[2]

Despite this victory, the American military staff in Chungking had few illusions, setting a pattern by which the men on the spot took a jaundiced view of the regime's record while politicians on the other side of the world built castles in the air about China's capabilities, egged on by optimistic briefings by Chungking's diplomats and by T. V. Soong, who had gone to Washington to solicit help in 1940. A military team sent by the War Department to China in late 1941 had attributed reports of Nationalist successes to 'clever deception' while the American mission in the wartime capital warned that the condition of Chinese troops and the state of the economy were both so poor that Chiang might be undermined by those who favoured making peace. This, it added, could give 'the Japs free access to the resources of China and the manpower of China, thus fully developing the long predicted "Yellow Peril"'.[3]

In contrast to such realism, Franklin Roosevelt proceeded on a mixture of romanticism, a determination to keep Chungking in the war, and a desire to treat China as the great power of Asia with which Washington would work to establish a new world order. He saw the country's east coast as a base for a counter-offensive against Japan, but did not want to commit troops, regarding Europe as the top priority. Nor would the US give Chungking control of the distribution of its military aid. For his part, Chiang's main concern was to ensure American political backing and supplies. To cement the relationship, he suggested the appointment of an American as his Chief of Staff. To Washington, that seemed a good way of getting a handle on the Chinese war effort, and pushing through a modernisation of the Nationalist forces that would make them an effective opponent for the Japanese. So the Chief of Staff, George Marshall, nominated a colleague he greatly appreciated – Lieutenant-General Joseph Stilwell, who was working at the time on a planned invasion of French North Africa.[4]

On the eve of his fifty-ninth birthday, Stilwell knew China well from his years there with the US detachment in the concession at Tianjin and as a military attaché. He read and spoke the language. He had travelled widely through the country. His experience made him an ideal candidate in Marshall's eyes, but the appointment was to spark off an epic battle which would pit 'Vinegar Joe' against Chiang for two and a half years. A foretaste of the trouble ahead came when T. V. Soong, who had become Foreign Minister, expressed concern that Stilwell saw China through the lens of the warlord years, which was rubbish since the general had been back as military attaché during the Nanking Decade. Soong's real worry was that he would be hard to spoon-feed with the official view of events. For his part, Stilwell made no bones about his opinions when he met Teddy White of *Time* as he started his mission. 'The trouble in China is simple,' he told the journalist. 'We are allied to an ignorant, illiterate, superstitious, peasant son of a bitch.' Soon the American was referring to Chiang in his diary as 'Peanut' – later it became 'the rattlesnake'.[5]

The idea that the tough, abrasive Yankee could work with the Generalissimo to develop a more effective Nationalist army was, at best, a sad commentary on Washington's knowledge of China and its leader. Well intentioned as the appointment was, it also reflected a naively arrogant assumption that a military approach formed in a Western democratic context could be transferred to a country with a completely different tradition and system. Historically, the Stilwell mission was a major step for both sides. Chiang had used Russian and German advisers but this was the first time a foreigner had been given the title of Chief of Staff. For the Americans, it represented a formal involvement in the internal affairs of an Asian nation that would set a pattern stretching to the present day. But, as Stilwell set out to fly to the Far East, neither party realised quite what it had embarked on.

The general and the Generalissimo were about as different as it was possible to be. Stilwell wanted to build a modern, professional army; Chiang saw military units as chess pieces to be manipulated for his benefit. The Generalissimo was a distant commander on a white horse; the American made a fetish of comradeship with infantrymen, marching with them and sharing their rations rather than the food cooked by his chef, a former employee of New York's Stork Club. In a broadcast from Chungking, evoking China's long war, Stilwell paid tribute to 'the man who has carried the burden and gone through the test of battle' [who] 'asks for little, and always stands ready to give all . . . the Chinese soldier'. It was not a tribute ever heard from Chiang.[6]

The Nationalist leader believed in conserving forces, and put loyalty above competence; his new Chief of Staff longed for a big, decisive battle with the deployment of maximum force, and advocated sacking – or shooting – generals who did not do their jobs properly. Chiang was secretive, manipulative and insistent on receiving due deference; Stilwell was too open and direct for his own good, ultra-critical of those he regarded as hypocrites or shirkers, a man who hid his sophistication behind a mask of simplicity that could become ostentatious – when he went to Allied headquarters in South-east Asia as the senior officer present, he refused to use the Cadillac sent to meet him and insisted on a jeep being called.

The contrast extended to their clothes and appearance. Chiang was always immaculately turned out, with silk socks and a well-brushed trilby. Stilwell liked to dress in simple field uniform, sometimes wearing shorts – when the strap on his battered scout hat broke, he replaced it with a shoelace. The Generalissimo's head was smooth, unlined, and close-shaven; Stilwell's craggy face had deep folds and a great beak of a nose topped by a soaring cockscomb of hair. Even their Chinese was different; Chiang kept the accent and dialect of his native Zhejiang while Stilwell spoke Mandarin. The one thing they did share was utter belief in their own rightness – Chiang convinced that he, alone, held the key to China's future, and Vinegar Joe, in the words of the writer Emily Hahn, 'incapable – surely to an abnormal degree? – of appreciating that there are more points of view than one's own, and that the world is considerably larger than America'.[7]

Though subject to a cat's cradle of overlapping Allied commands in the Far East, the American's powers were unprecedented – on paper, at least. He was both to be Chiang's Chief of Staff and to command all US forces in the China–Burma–India sector (CBI). He also controlled supplies sent in under the Lend-Lease agreements by which Washington delivered aid to its allies. He would represent the United States on war committees, and act as liaison between the Generalissimo and the British. Despite such authority, there was no way he could win against the Nationalist leader who would continue his practice of dealing directly with field commanders, using his ability to play on the loyalties of generals Stilwell was meant to be in charge of. The only way for Vinegar Joe to have his way would have been for the United States to have taken over the government of China. Since it was not going to do that, Chiang just had to hang on, and to ensure that no American protégés emerged powerful enough to challenge him. Repeatedly, in the eight years after Pearl Harbor, he showed how a weak client state can run rings round a powerful ally by a combination of cunning, obstruction and single-mindedness. Again, it presaged the future, though the wrong lessons would be drawn by critics who counted Stilwell among those who 'lost' China.

Despite the doubts expressed by Soong, the appointment created a warm glow in Washington, and T.V. was able to negotiate a new US$500 million loan, doubling American aid. It would be used, the Foreign Minister explained, when Chiang saw fit. The money was to be exchanged with Chinese dollars at the official rate of 1:20. By 1942, inflation had made that rate wildly unrealistic, with a single American dollar worth hundreds of Chinese dollars on the black market. So the government in Chungking, and its officials, made enormous profits on handling the US funds, and, at the same time, hugely overcharged the Americans for local supplies.

Anxious though he was to ensure American backing, Chiang was hostile towards Britain, which he regarded as a power that would always put its imperial interests ahead of those of China. A Nationalist mission to Hong Kong, headed by a one-legged admiral, helped briefly to rally resistance to the Japanese, but an army unit Chiang sent to assist the defence of the colony did not arrive before its fall at the end of 1941. He also accepted a British-run programme to train guerrillas, but ordered it terminated after a year though some instructors stayed on in the south. On a visit to India, which was meant to signify Allied solidarity, the Generalissimo made clear his preference for the nationalist leaders over his colonial hosts. Gandhi warned him that the West would never accept him as an equal ally, and Meiling read a broadcast message from Chiang calling for the granting of political freedom to India – she also wrote an article for the *New York Times*, saying the British could achieve nothing fundamental without 'a radical and drastic change in their present-day Indian policy and its application to the Indian people'. The Chiangs shared a convivial picnic with Nehru during which he suddenly took off his jacket and began to turn somersaults, at which one of the Chinese delegation joined in the fun by rolling on the grass.[8]

Chiang's low opinion of Britain's military capabilities was deepened as the Japanese swept forward to overrun the colonies of Malaya, Singapore and Hong Kong – the day after Pearl Harbor, they had also occupied the foreign concessions in Shanghai. On his return from India, the Generalissimo sent a message to the embassy in London asking that Churchill be told how shocked he was by the military and political situation he had found there. He copied the cable to T. V. Soong to be passed to Roosevelt. London needed to take urgent action, he wrote; otherwise, Japan would be virtually unopposed. If, on the other hand, the British gave the Indians real power, they would rally to the Empire. 'As for military preparations,' he added, 'the present Indian preparedness is very much behind even that the British had in Malaya.' After visiting Burma in the spring of 1942, he wrote to Churchill that he had never seen anything 'to compare with the deplorable and unprepared state, confusion and degradation of the war area'.[9]

The dislike was reciprocal. Just before Pearl Harbor, a mission from London had concluded that the government in Chungking was incapable of dealing with its problems, and that Chiang 'did not have an intelligent grasp of the situation'. Churchill could see the psychological downside of having to call on Chinese troops to help defend the colonies of India, Burma and Hong Kong, and had no desire for China to undermine the re-imposition of the Empire in the East. He consistently expressed surprise at the importance America placed on China, which he dismissed to Roosevelt as 'four hundred and twenty five million pigtails'. As his personal representative in Chungking, the Prime Minister sent General Adrian Carton de Wiart, a valiant, one-eyed, one-handed First World War veteran who said he expected to find China 'full of whimsical little people with quaint customs who carved lovely jade ornaments and worshipped their grandmothers'.[10]

Still, the Japanese pressure on Burma forced the British to change their mind, and to accept Chinese troops. Despite his feelings about the country which had pioneered the imperialist penetration of his country, the

Generalissimo sent 25,000 men, and flew with Meiling to Lashio in northern Burma to supervise their deployment, making a speech to his officers from the balcony of a missionary centre. While he took his after-lunch nap, the telephone rang to warn that Japanese planes were on their way. But none of Chiang's English-speaking aides were around, and nobody at the other end of the line spoke Chinese. So the message did not get through, and the raiding aircraft were almost overhead when the Nationalist leader scrambled into a car to be driven to a safe shelter. Less dramatically, the visit gave him a chance for a brief meeting with Stilwell who had flown in after a stop-over in India on his way to Chunking. Playing her accustomed role, Meiling took over from the 'nervous and sweating' interpreter. The American recorded that Chiang 'seems willing to fight and is fed up with the British retreat and lethargy. Also extremely suspicious of their motives and intentions.'[11]

After arriving in the Chinese capital, Stilwell was invited to dinner with the Chiangs; the Guangxi generals, Li and Bai, were present, but kept quiet. After the meal, the Generalissimo delivered a lengthy lecture on the importance of holding the Burmese city of Mandalay, where he had sent troops under one of his most capable generals, Sun Liren. He also insisted that Stilwell must be in charge in Burma, whatever London wanted; otherwise, he would pull out his forces. He later changed tack, and agreed to the British commander, Field Marshal Harold Alexander, taking overall control – the American was informed by a letter from Meiling. In the following months, he would become well accustomed to Chiang's mind swings that made coherent strategy hard to pursue.[12]

The two men had three more meetings, some attended by the Chinese general Shang Zhen, a polo-playing, English-speaking northerner who acted as liaison with foreign forces and would become one of the American's closest contacts in the Chinese military. Then Vinegar Joe flew to take charge of two Chinese armies which had been stationed on the 300-mile Rangoon–Mandalay railway in the middle of the country, while the British held positions to the east and west towards the borders with Thailand and India. Stilwell found the Fifth Army, under General Du Yuming, 'solid on tactics. Ready to fight' and the Sixth Army, commanded by General Gan Lichu, 'OK'. He was less taken with his supply chief, a relative of Chiang, 'a damn glutton, a fat man' who was stealing Lend-Lease supplies.[13]

As the Japanese advanced towards a town called Toungoo, Stilwell saw the chance of a classic flanking attack by Chinese and British units. But Du refused to move. When Field Marshal Alexander asked him where his field guns were, the Chinese general said they had been moved to safety. What use were they if they would not be used in battle, the British commander asked. Du explained that his army was China's best because of its field guns – 'If I lose them the Fifth Army will no longer be the best.' Stilwell sent a message to Chiang asking him to order Du to join the attack. When he got no response, he flew to Chungking.[14]

The reason for Du's attitude soon became evident. Following his usual practice, Chiang was in direct touch with him, bypassing Stilwell and advising caution. Under pressure from Stilwell, the Generalissimo said one division could advance, but, when the American got back to Burma, he found Du wavering between depression and a gung-ho stance. At one point, the Chinese general went into his room and refused to come out. Chiang was still showering his subordinates with messages advising caution. He even gave individual instructions to the few Chinese tanks in Burma.[15]

His plan undone by Chiang's interference, Stilwell asked in his diary for 1 April whether he was the April fool. 'Chiang Kai-shek . . . can't keep his hands off: 1,600 miles from the front, he writes endless instructions to do this and that, based on fragmentary information and a cockeyed conception of tactics. He . . . thinks he knows everything, and he wobbles this way and that, changing his mind at every change in the action.'[16]

Returning to Chungking, the American told Chiang he wanted to be relieved of his command. The Generalissimo lied that the divisional commanders had been acting against orders, and would be shot. Stilwell was not fooled. The Nationalist leader, he decided, had 'been boss so long and has so many yes-men around him that he has the idea he is infallible on any subject . . . He is not mentally stable, and he will say many things to your face that he doesn't mean fully or exactly.' But he also judged that Chiang was 'determined and forceful, and wants to get on with the war'.[17]

One outcome of the confrontation was that Chiang appointed a Cantonese general in his forties, Luo Zhuoying, as Stilwell's executive officer – a senior figure who was meant to do as the American instructed.

Stilwell called Luo, who had fought in the defence of Changsha, 'snappy, energetic, forceful'. He believed Chiang had come round to his idea of fighting a big battle to halt the Japanese. The Generalissimo had reason to be on his best behaviour since Claire Booth Luce, the wife of his important supporter Henry Luce, had flown in to write an article for *Life*. The soft-soaping continued when Meiling sent Stilwell a pot of marmalade made from the fruit in the garden of her home across the river. An accompanying note told him: 'You have a man's job ahead of you but you are a man, and shall I add – what a man!'[18]

After lunching with Mrs Luce, Chiang flew for two days of conferences in Burma, where he was greeted by a Gurkha guard of honour complete with a bagpipe and drum band. During the visit, he and Meiling were caught in the open by a Japanese air raid – a bomb fell 50 yards from them but did not explode. On their way back to China, according to the authorised biography by Hollington Tong, 18 enemy planes searched the sky for their plane, but did not find it.

Despite the Generalissimo's anti-British sentiments, Stilwell sent Chinese troops to the unsuccessful aid of British units; the front which the Allies had tried to draw across the middle of Burma was undone when Japanese forces moved in from the Thai border to the east, turned the line and raced up the railway to block the highway to China, greeted as liberators by the anti-colonial inhabitants. The American's irritation with the Generalissimo exploded when Chiang sent him a message saying that Chinese soldiers liked watermelons, and telling him to arrange a supply of them for the troops. His angry reaction became known in Chungking, and created further bad blood with the Generalissimo. The incident would be cited by Stilwell's champions as an example of the Nationalist leader's pettiness. But Chiang had a deeper reason for his growing alienation – the way Stilwell had used up good Chinese troops in his abortive bid to help the British. The air force commander Claire Chennault, who was close to the Chiangs and loathed Stilwell, recorded that the Generalissimo regarded this as 'the sheerest sentimentality and incredible military callowness', adding that, 'If Stilwell had been a Chinese general there seems little doubt that his performance would have ended with the firing squad.'[19]

As the Japanese advanced northwards, Chinese commanders again refused to follow Stilwell's orders. The American went to the front, and personally directed an infantry attack. He wanted to throw another Chinese division into the battle, but its commander refused to send trucks to transport it – he wanted the lorries to move supplies to be sold in China.[20]

Some Chinese did hold off the Japanese for a few days in a couple of encounters. But the retreat quickly turned into a rout with some Chinese units heading west to India. Stilwell's Executive Officer, General Luo, got his men to seize a train so that he could head for safety up the single-track railway north of Mandalay: the locomotive collided with an oncoming train, putting the line out of service for two days. As the enemy surged forward, more good troops were lost. Chinese planes were destroyed on the ground. Throngs of refugees headed for the Yunnan frontier on the deep Salween Gorge.

Stilwell was nowhere to be found. On 1 May, Chennault had sent him a message advising that air force headquarters were being transferred back across the border, and suggesting that he fly out, too. 'Am staying at the front,' the general replied. The next day, he disappeared.

The Japanese advance had cut China's land supply route through Burma. Worse, it threatened south-western China. The Imperial Army had been temporarily halted by the destruction of the bridge across the Salween Gorge, but would clearly soon find a way of rebuilding it. Then the province of Yunnan would be at its mercy. From there, it could strike northwards to Sichuan and Chungking. Stilwell's absence meant there was nobody on the spot to organise resistance.

Chennault was only too ready to step into the breach, asking Chiang for authorisation to bomb the enemy on the far side of the gorge – though this would mean killing civilian refugees as well. He got the go-ahead, and launched concentrated dive-bombing and strafing attacks that devastated the Japanese vanguard and destroyed scores of trucks moving up reinforcements. The result was a stand-off across the gorge which held for two years.[21]

As the Japanese halted their advance, Stilwell reappeared – in India. The day after refusing to fly out of Burma, he had left his headquarters to walk 140 miles westwards through the jungle with a party of twenty-six Americans, sixteen Chinese, thirteen British plus some forty medical personnel from a Quaker hospital, Indian cooks and mechanics, twenty mules and a dog. They started their trek in vehicles, then took river boats, scaled 75-degree gradients and wended their way through snake-infested jungles. All survived.

The media hailed a heroic achievement, something to be proud of amid the debacle in Burma. The legend of Vinegar Joe was born. But it is hard not to see the walkout as, at best, an aberration bred by the frustrations he had encountered and, at worst, a grave dereliction of duty by a commander who, whatever the frustrations of dealing with the Chinese, should have stayed at his post to organise the retreat. Stilwell explained that, rather than flying to safety, he needed to set an example by staying with his group, small as it was. He did not explain what good that did when China faced the very real threat of an invasion of Yunnan. Even his supportive political officer, John Paton Davies, called it a case of 'questionable command judgment'.[22]

His selfish irresponsibility was underlined by his failure to inform Chiang of what he was doing. He had found time to keep in touch with his patron, George Marshall, in Washington, but did not tell his superior officer that he was abandoning his troops to their fate. In a grave loss of face, the Generalissimo only learned what was happening from a message Stilwell sent to the American military mission in Chungking saying the Chinese had disintegrated, and that it was useless to try to exercise command over them. 'Stilwell deserted our troops,' Chiang commented. 'I doubt that he knows the importance of military discipline.' Vinegar Joe had good reason to resent the way the Chinese leader had behaved, but his own conduct greatly deepened the distrust between them while heightening his messianic view of his mission.[23]

Stilwell arrived in India suffering from dysentery and jaundice – the result of a bad yellow fever serum he had been administered. Writing to his wife, he described himself as looking like 'the guy in the medical books with his skin off, showing the next layer of what you have'. He told a press conference: 'We got a hell of a beating. We got run out of Burma and it is humiliating as hell. I think we ought to find out what caused it, go back and retake it.' By the end of May, the Japanese not only held most of Burma with its rice, oil, minerals and 16 million inhabitants, but had also isolated China by land as well as sea.[24]

After a dinner with journalists in Delhi, Stilwell wrote a memorandum for Chiang with his proposals to reorganise the Chinese army. He handed it to Chiang in Chungking at the beginning of June. It was characteristically blunt; in letter to his wife, Stilwell called it 'like kicking an old lady in the stomach'. After looking at the paper, Meiling said, 'Why, that's what the German advisers told him.'[25]

The memorandum began by saying that the army was too big. It could not be fully supplied with American weapons; better to have 'a few dependable, well-equipped, well-supported divisions' than mass forces. Units should be merged to bring them up to their paper strength. Inefficient junior and middle rank officers should be dropped. Rewards for gallantry should be made swiftly, medical services improved and punishment be 'prompt and ruthless no matter what the rank of the offender'.[26]

'Division and Army commanders are a great problem,' Stilwell went on in an explosive passage.

> Very few of them are efficient. They seldom get up to the front and they very rarely supervise the execution of their orders . . . Reports from the front are accepted without check, and very often prove exaggerated or are commonly ignored, often with fatal consequences . . . Many of the officers are personally brave, but most of them lack moral courage . . . I recommend a rigid purge of inefficient commanders . . . without a clearing out of the inefficient, the Army will continue to go down hill, no matter how much material is supplied to it.[27]

The memorandum mentioned Chiang's messages to the field, and said a new command system was needed, with an overall chief who would control supplies, transport and communications as well as fighting forces. Chiang must give this commander a directive, and then let him get on with the job without interference. With such reforms, Stilwell reckoned that the Chinese would be able to hold off the Japanese until Allied force was brought to bear – the fightback in the Pacific had just begun with the American naval victory in the Midway.

The implications of Stilwell's proposals went well beyond strictly military considerations, threatening the system in which generals were as much political barons as military figures. Merging understrength divisions would reduce the money received by commanders for men who existed only on paper. The appointment of an omnipotent commander would shift power from the regional potentates. If an efficient army of thirty divisions saw the light of day under a single commander, it would inevitably pose a major threat to the Generalissimo. To attack senior figures as Stilwell did was to shake the pillars of the temple. 'The head cannot be lopped off, otherwise nothing would be left,' Meiling commented.[28]

There was another fundamental issue involved. Chiang was a nationalist, and would not take dictation from foreigners. He was all too ready to accept American help, but he had no intention of finding himself obliged to follow a reform path laid down by Washington. As he would show repeatedly, he regarded maintaining his independence as an essential element in his authority. The more the United States pushed, the more resistant he became, the more anti-American, the more determined to go his own way.

Stilwell should have been aware of all this, though his diary contains no mention of it. He was behaving as if he were in a stable democracy, where a professional army is answerable to an elected government, fenced off from interference in politics. But, in Chiang's China, as in future Asian quagmires, there was no fence; the whole structure rested on the supremacy of the military. If he did not grasp this, Stilwell was extraordinarily obtuse for a man in his position and with his experience of China. If he did know the implications of what he was doing, he was equally misguided since he was, in effect, declaring a political war which he had no means of winning, ensuring that his laudable aim would be damned in Chiang's mind as a fundamental threat that had to be blocked.

To cap it all, Chiang was annoyed at what he viewed as a lack of material support from Washington, and held Stilwell responsible – he regarded the Chief of Staff as a quartermaster whose job was to ensure a never-ending flow of supplies. To make his discontent known, he sent a message to T. V. Soong in Washington talking of 'demoralising doubts' among his officers at how their country was being treated. Forwarding this to Roosevelt, the Foreign Minister added a note saying that the 'Generalissimo feels himself entirely out of touch with the main decisions of strategy which profoundly affect China's future . . . in vital questions, his role is that of an onlooker'. It was hardly an observation which T.V. would have made off his own bat. To mollify Chiang, the President agreed to let a Nationalist representative sit on the munitions board that decided arms supplies. But, for security reasons, Marshall refused to allow China to join the conferences of Allied Chiefs of Staff – his caution was justified since the Japanese were breaking

Chinese codes and could read everything transmitted to and from Chungking.[29]

Yet another cause for discord arose from Stilwell's burning desire to reverse the rout of April 1942. Reopening the Burma Road was, obviously, greatly in China's interests since supplies now had to be flown over the Himalayas on the route known as the 'Hump' which could handle far less tonnage than the highway. But the Generalissimo did not share the American's fixation with making up for the humiliating defeat of his first major field command. Having been at war for five years, Chiang saw no need to hurry. For him, keeping the military balance was much more important than recapturing a colony for the British.

But Stilwell's quest for revenge was unstoppable, and was justified by a plan that, though initially sensible, broadened out into a wider strategy which took leave of reality. The American proposed to train two Chinese armies, one made up of men who had reached India, the other based in Yunnan. The first was to be known as X Force, the second as Y Force. With the British landing from the sea in the south of Burma, X and Y would pierce the Japanese defences from west and east, take the country and reopen the highway to China. So far, so good – so long as Churchill lifted his eyes from Europe and agreed to commit men and landing craft to the Far East.

But Stilwell then envisaged his two armies sweeping into China to join a newly trained third force, called Z, which would push the Japanese back to the ocean where American ships would land GIs to achieve a great final victory. A few elite units might be formed, but the scope of the plan demanded a mass mobilisation that took no account of the military performance of the Chinese since 1937, Chiang's reservations about modernisation, the fragile state of China, the strength of regional autonomists in the south – or Japanese strength.

Chiang went along with the part of the plan which presented no threat to him. The Chinese units in India were far away, so nothing was lost by agreeing to that part of the proposal. He could also do with good troops being trained for the central army. But, when it came to agreeing to send them to Burma, he dragged his feet – he preferred to hold them in reserve against the independent-minded Governor Long Yun of Yunnan.

He and Meiling were being wooed by Stilwell's American rival, the air

force adviser, Claire Chennault. The Texan, who had managed to reduce
the number of Japanese air raids on Chungking, had been authorised by
Washington to recruit American military fliers who were given an
honourable discharge and went to China on one-year contracts, receiving
US$500 for each plane they brought down. Chennault believed as deeply
in the power of planes as Stilwell did in that of infantrymen. He held that
Japan could be strangled by air raids on its ships launched from China,
while his fighters and bombers held back enemy troops on the ground.
The prospect of winning the war from the air and not having to commit
large forces appealed to the Chiangs as much as it did to Roosevelt – and
to future presidents. The Americans had just made their first bombing
attack on Tokyo, known as the Doolittle raid from the name of its
commander. Launched from aircraft carriers, it appeared to show the
potency of the air approach, but it also demonstrated the consequences
that could follow.

After dropping their bombs, the Doolittle planes headed towards an
airstrip in Chiang's home province of Zhejiang on the East China coast.
Foreseeing the danger of sparking off a Japanese reprisal there, the
Generalissimo had insisted that the aircraft fly to a safer area inland. But
the American pilots disregarded this, and headed for Zhejiang. None of
the planes reached the airfield, crash-landing or being scuttled as they
approached, the pilots parachuting to safety. As Chiang had feared, the
Japanese swept in to stop coastal airfields being used for future raids, using
biological weapons that included bombs carrying birds infected with
anthrax – in one country alone the death toll from the germs developed
by Japan's scientists in Manchuria was put at 50,000. The Generalissimo
directed the defence operations from Chungking on the other side of
China, with chaotic results that led to heavy casualties. A report by an
American colonel who visited the battlefield said the Chinese had poor
equipment, and no medical facilities or transport. Most of the conscripts
arrived tied to one another. The regional commander spent the campaign
in a villa 50 miles behind the front.[30]

Unabashed, Chennault demanded that more of the capacity on the
Hump run should be used to bring in aviation fuel and supplies. 'My
stomach is getting nervous,' he told Teddy White on one occasion. 'I used
40,000 gallons this past ten days, and I got only 17,000 gallons in.' To drop
one ton of bombs, he needed eighteen tons of supplies. The transport

planes burned as much fuel flying over the Hump as they brought in their holds. Bulldozers, trucks and other equipment Chennault needed to build airfields had to be diverted from the army.[31]

Naturally, this brought him into mounting conflict with Stilwell who wanted as large a volume of supplies as possible. The two men were chalk and cheese – a Confederate versus a Yankee, a Good Ole Boy who recognised human foibles against a puritan who prized moral courage. All they shared was an intense self-belief, and physical afflictions – Chennault was very hard of hearing while Stilwell had hardly any sight in his left eye as a result of an explosion of an ammunition dump in the First World War and needed a thick lens on his right eye. Meeting the two of them later, Britain's Chief of Staff, Alan Brooke,* described Stilwell as 'a hopeless crank with no vision', and Chennault as 'a very gallant airman with limited brain'.[32]

One of the lesser, but characteristic, clashes between the two Americans followed Chennault's decision to open a brothel for his pilots. One of his officers was sent to recruit prostitutes who had fled to Guilin from Hong Kong. The establishment was officially devoted only to dancing, but there were plenty of dark corners and a garden from which the girls inevitably returned with grass stains on their dresses. The place also became a centre for organising diversion of Lend-Lease supplies to the black market. When the Lieutenant General learned about it, he had the place shut down.[33]

In the competition for Chiang's favours, Chennault was the clear winner, aided by Meiling, who had always been interested in aviation and who called the Flying Tiger pilots her 'boys'. At a dinner she and her husband gave for them in February 1942, one of the fliers recalled, Meiling 'lectured us in a motherly sort of way about our behaviour, bragged about us, and told us she was very proud of us and honored to be our honorary Commander-in-Chief'. She revelled in their success in downing Japanese aircraft – though their critics accused them of exaggeration, they reported 299 confirmed 'kills' and perhaps twice that number of aircraft destroyed in the air or on the ground. While Chennault's hopes of winning the war from the air were not to be borne out, his unit, which was renamed as the Fourteenth Air Force in March 1943, did a lot of damage to enemy

* Later Lord Alanbrooke.

shipping, reduced the bombing of Chungking, and assisted Chinese armies in key battles.[34]

Chiang's concern about where China stood in the Allied scale of priorities deepened in the summer of 1942. When German victories in North Africa gravely threatened the British position there, Washington decided to move China Theatre planes based in India to Egypt and to divert other aircraft intended for the Nationalists there. The Generalissimo pointed out that the planes in India came under Stilwell's mandate – so he could not understand why the general had let them go. The situation in Egypt might be serious, he added, but so was the position in Zhejiang, which had been provoked by an American action and the refusal of the pilots to follow his instructions about where they should land.[35]

The truth was that Stilwell had been told of the decision to move the aircraft from India after it had been made, and was also unhappy that his forces had been weakened. But Chiang was not to be stopped. At a meeting with Stilwell attended by Meiling, he produced what became known as the Three Demands – three US divisions to be sent to Burma to open the road to Yunnan, 500 planes to be dispatched to China and 5,000 tons of supplies to be flown over the Hump each month. Adopting her role as spokeswoman for her husband and China, Meiling pulled no punches. If the demands were not met, she warned, the other Allies could 'wash out the China Theater'. Since each British defeat led to the removal of equipment, 'there is no need for China to continue the war'. Why did Britain 'always have to have someone else to pull her chestnuts out the fire', she asked. Chiang wondered why London did not send its 'thousands of planes' to Egypt. In case anybody missed the point, Meiling noted that 'the pro-Japanese element is very active'. According to American minutes, she added: 'The Generalissimo wants a yes or no answer to whether the Allies consider this theater necessary and will support it.' The Chinese account has her saying: 'The question was whether or not the United States wants China to make peace.'[36]

Stilwell told Washington of the demands and complaints. He also sent his deputy to Washington to discuss the issue. But, given the war situation in Europe and North Africa, there was no way Chiang's requirements could be met – and his threats were obviously hollow. Making peace with Tokyo would undermine his nationalist claims, and getting even limited US supplies was better than receiving nothing. For all his irritation, good progress was being made at the training camp at Ramgarh in northern India where the 66,000 Chinese soldiers of X Force were being drilled by Americans with arms flown in from the United States.

Stilwell commuted the 2,000 miles between Chungking and Ramgarh over the Himalayas in a battered DC-3 cargo plane equipped with a few chairs and a camp bed. Several times the plane lost its course, but it was never attacked by Japanese fighters. For the first time, Chinese soldiers at Ramgarh were paid their wages directly, instead of receiving what was left after their officers had skimmed off their take. They had health care and were properly fed, gaining an average of 20 pounds. General Sun Liren, who had fought well in Burma, and the short, stocky, General Liao Yaoxiang showed themselves capable commanders while Stilwell impressed the soldiers by talking to them in Chinese.

But he was under attack in Washington, as well as in Chungking. Chiang had a direct channel to the White House that ran from an American academic, Owen Lattimore, whom Roosevelt had sent to him as a personal adviser, to a member of the President's staff, Lauchlin Currie. After a visit to China, Currie recommended getting rid of Stilwell, along with Ambassador Gauss. George Marshall quickly moved to defend his protégé. But it was a warning signal that Stilwell was not everybody's cup of tea back home. The pressure was not only political. After one stormy meeting with the Chinese, Vinegar Joe developed stomach trouble, and vomited five times during the night. The next day, a blood test showed he had worms. Over the next thirty-six hours, he took eight different medicines, and then recorded: 'Feeling better!' In his diary, he called Chiang a prejudiced, conceited despot. 'The Chinese government,' he wrote, 'is a structure based on fear and favor, in the hands of an ignorant, arbitrary, stubborn man.'[37]

Chiang was equally critical of the American. In a cable to T. V. Soong and the ambassador in Washington, he complained: 'The China Theatre has no organisation, or preparation for it . . . It seems that victory or defeat and the life or death of the China Theatre has nothing to do with Stilwell. This man does not place much value on organisation, concrete planning, and overall implementation.' The Burma campaign still rankled, Chiang complaining that the American 'did not ask for my instructions beforehand, nor did he make any direct report to me. His undertakings were devoid of human feeling and reason.' These were two men who were meant to be working together to fight Japan. But there was also another player who would extend her operations from Chungking to Washington and Hollywood as the rivalry within Chiang's family-in-law intersected with the Generalissimo's grip on power and his relationship with Vinegar Joe.[38]

CHAPTER 22

Snow White, Madame Empress

IN 1942 AND 1943, Meiling Soong was the most powerful woman in the world. Her influence might depend on her husband, and be limited largely to dealing with foreigners. But the American entry into the war had made her a key figure in handling China's most important ally. She attended top-level conferences, and held the code book for messages between her husband's American adviser, Owen Lattimore, and the White House. Dubbing her 'Madame Empress', Stilwell described her in his diary as:

> Quick, intelligent. Wants to get things done. Wishes she was a man. Doesn't think deeply, but catches on in a hurry. Very frank and open . . . Impulsive to point of precipitation . . . A clever, brainy woman . . . Direct, forceful, energetic, loves power, eats up publicity and flattery, pretty weak on her history. No concession to the Western viewpoint in all China's foreign relations. The Chinese were always right; the foreigners were always wrong.[1]

In her mid-forties, Meiling showed her growing authority by summoning Stilwell, Chennault and the two heads of the Chinese air force to a meeting on 1 July 1942. She asked the Chinese what they required. Two hundred planes, they replied. And Chennault? Three hundred, he said. That made the magic figure of 500 contained in Chiang's Three Demands. So, Meiling said, all that needed to be done was for Stilwell to 'get busy and tell' Washington. When the others had left the room, she added, 'We are going to see that you are made a full general!' 'The hell they are!' Stilwell recorded in his diary.[2]

Keeping up the pressure, she called for Vinegar Joe's report to Washington, and upbraided him on the telephone when she found he had not put in recommendations of his own to back the Chinese demands. Then she summoned him for a meeting, kept him waiting and called in her secretary to take everything down. 'Obviously mad as hell,' the general recorded in his diary. 'She had snapped the whip and the stooge had not come across, and she'd reported to Chiang Kai-shek that I had.' But the Chiangs' persistence earned a reward when Roosevelt told the Generalissimo he could expect 5,000 tons of supplies a month from the beginning of the following year, plus 265 combat aircraft. Three airfields were developed at Kunming, Dali and Lijiang in Yunnan to handle the traffic. How the cargo would be split between Stilwell and Chennault was a matter for bitter dispute between the two men, but Chiang had got part of what he wanted – and his wife could share the credit.[3]

Meiling was firmly established as the caring face of the regime, making well-publicised visits to hospitals, urging women to join the war effort, writing articles for foreign publications and recording broadcasts for the United States. One Christmas, she staged a nativity play for the foreigners, which ended with her husband handing the guests red silk ties with his monogram. She tried her hand at warlord politics with a mission to the huge and largely autonomous north-western region of Xinjiang, where she won the support of the Governor, a man so afraid of assassination that he examined melons to check that they had not been injected with poison. She also visited Chinese troops in India, and came home with an enthusiastic report on progress there. An American correspondent asked if she did not grow tired of having to appear as a great heroic figure. 'If you ever publish this, I'll have your head off,' she replied. 'But, yes, I do get tired of it.' Though her health was suffering, she showed no sign of letting up as Chungking received its highest-ranking American visitor in October 1942.[4]

Defeated by Roosevelt in the presidential election of 1940, the Republican, Wendell Willkie, had been sent on a world tour by the White

House in an act of wartime bipartisanship. His trip came after America had scored big naval victories in the Pacific, and after the landing at Guadalcanal in the Solomons at the start of the advance through the Pacific islands to the Japanese homeland. In Chungking, a lavish programme of visits, banquets, military displays and meetings awaited Willkie. Shacks were pulled down; poor-looking shops were ordered to close; peddlers and beggars were cleared from the streets. The big, exuberant politician, with his mop of hair and charismatic style, was important not only as Roosevelt's envoy. He might run again for the presidency, and, in the meantime, could put pressure on Washington to replace Stilwell with somebody more pliant.

There was a slight hitch when Willkie flew in aboard a converted bomber. The welcoming party led by H. H. Kung marched down the runway carrying big bouquets of flowers as an army band played 'America the Beautiful'. But the plane had not yet taxied to a stop, and it turned and moved forward. 'There were squeals and a great dropping of bouquets and band instruments as the greeters scattered,' Graham Peck of the US information service recalled. By the time the plane halted and the visitor came down the steps, the welcoming party had re-formed, and the band was playing the Kuomintang anthem.[5]

From the start, Willkie fell for the show the Chiangs put on for him. He described the ranks of carefully drilled children waving flags along the road from the airport as 'an impressive show of the simple strength in people and emotions which is China's greatest resource.' He decided to stay in a government guest house rather than with the well-informed Ambassador Gauss, who muttered that he would vote for the Socialist candidate at the next presidential election. He was impressed by an enormous military parade held in his honour, and got a carefully prepared glimpse of the war on a trip aboard a luxurious train to the Yellow River.

Chiang's adopted son, who acted as escort on that trip, presented the visitor with Japanese swords and French wine which he said had just been captured by Chinese soldiers who had made night sorties across the river – Peck reported that the supposed booty was on sale locally. The only Japanese Willkie saw, through a telescope, was a soldier sitting in his undershirt at the mouth of a tunnel on the other side of the waterway. But, when he was told that enemy planes had dropped bombs nearby, he called the reporters accompanying him and said: 'Well, boys, I guess they were after us all right.' Going on to Xi'an, he was greeted by more crowds of flag-waving children, and returned to Nanking declaring that 'Military China is united. Its leaders are trained and able generals; its armies are tough fighting organisations of men who know both what they are fighting for and how to fight for it.'[6]

The regime had the good sense to fix a meeting between Willkie and Zhou Enlai to show its open-mindedness, but, otherwise, it kept control of the visitor. Stilwell was sidelined; when he did meet Willkie, the politician did not ask him for his views. Chiang stressed the importance of air power, and Chennault presented a memorandum claiming that he could achieve the downfall of Japan with a force of 147 planes. Stilwell noted in his diary that the visitor had been 'immersed in soft soap, adulation and flattery'. But an independent-minded American Foreign Service officer, John Carter Vincent, depicted Willkie as a man who smelled of raw beef to the Chinese – Chiang was said to have ordered the windows of his office opened when he left, to 'let the smell of the foreigner out'.[7]

The Generalissimo had added to his titles by becoming President of the Chinese Republic on the death of the venerable Lin Sen, and there was even what looked like political progress to show the American that the regime was not as dictatorial as its critics said. A coalition of six non-Kuomintang parties had formed the Democratic Federation the previous year as a third force between the regime and the Communists. The group had offices in Kunming, Chengdu and Guilin, and published two newspapers. Its members were harried by the secret police, but Chiang had the People's Political Council, on which it was represented, reorganised to give an appearance of democracy. The number of appointed delegates from various parties and organisations was cut, and the elected representatives raised to 70 per cent. This was, in fact, the opposite of what it seemed since the Kuomintang controlled the elections, and could ensure that most of those who voted would back its candidates. By reducing the number of appointed seats guaranteed to small parties and professional groups, the move actually increased the regime's control. The Communists and the Democrats reacted with a boycott that made the Council even more of a fig leaf for Chiang. But nobody could accuse him of not having tried.

The Willkie trip was a perfect occasion for Meiling. Described by the American military attaché, David Barrett, as 'exuding charm at every pore', she found Willkie an easy conquest. Appearing at a tea party with the cloak of an air marshal thrown dashingly over her shoulders, she told the politician in her American-accented English that he was a very 'disturbing influence', a confession which visibly gratified him.[8]

Their relationship progressed one evening when Chiang presided over a huge reception for the visitor. The Generalissimo, his wife and Willkie formed a receiving line. Among the guests was one of the politician's principal backers, Gardner Cowles, publisher of *Look* magazine, who was accompanying Willkie on the world tour. As the evening went on, the politician asked Cowles to take his place in the receiving line because he and Meiling were going to leave the room.[9]

The publisher stepped in, and, when Chiang left about an hour later, Cowles went back to one of T. V. Soong's houses where he and Willkie were staying. There was no sign of the other man. Cowles sat drinking Scotch which Meiling had sent him when he said he could not take Chinese rice wine. Soon after 9 p.m., as the publisher recorded in his privately published memoirs, 'there was a great clatter in the courtyard. The Generalissimo marched in, visibly furious. He was accompanied by three bodyguards, each carrying a little Tommy gun. Trying to restrain his rage, the Generalissimo bowed coldly, and I returned the bow.'

Chiang asked where Willkie was. Cowles said he did not know.* He then offered Chiang tea. After they had drunk this in silence, the Generalissimo repeated his question, and Cowles repeated that he had no answer. At that, Chiang stormed through the house followed by his bodyguards. He searched every room, peered under the beds and opened cupboards. Not finding what he was looking for, he left without saying anything.

Cowles sat up drinking more Scotch. At 4 a.m., he recorded, 'a very buoyant Willkie appeared, cocky as a young college student after a successful night with a girl. After giving me a play by play account of what had happened between him and Madame, he concluded that he had invited Madame to return to Washington with us.'

'Wendell, you're just a goddam fool!' Cowles exclaimed. He acknowledged that Meiling was 'one of the most beautiful, intelligent, and sexy women either of us had ever met', and he could understand the tremendous attraction between her and Willkie. But the politician had to

---

* Cowles does not mention an interpreter but there must have been one.

be discreet. There was already gossip among correspondents in Chungking about the two of them. Mrs Willkie would probably be waiting to meet him at the airport in Washington. If he wanted to run against Roosevelt again, arriving with Madame Chiang would be a considerable embarrassment.

Willkie stomped off to bed, but was up a couple of hours later for breakfast. He had a speech to make, and asked Cowles to go to see Meiling to tell her she could not fly to the United States with him. The publisher inquired where he could find her. Willkie suggested an apartment which she kept on the top floor of a hospital for women and children. With her own private guards protecting them, that was where they had gone the previous night.

When Cowles delivered the message, Meiling asked who was preventing her making the trip. Cowles took the responsibility on himself, explaining that it would be unwise politically for Willkie. Before he knew what was happening, she scratched her long fingernails down both his cheeks so deeply that the marks remained for a week.

'It is interesting the influence which enforced celibacy has on judgment – and the course of political events,' noted an American diplomat in Chungking. Though he followed Cowles's advice, Willkie ended the visit by suggesting that Meiling should visit the United States to win support for China with her 'brains, persuasiveness, and moral force . . . with wit and charm, a generous and understanding heart, a gracious and a beautiful manner and appearance, and a burning conviction'. There was a suggestion that the idea had come from her.[10]

The Sino-American relationship warmed further when, immediately after Willkie's departure, Chiang announced in his National Day speech that the United States – and Britain – had agreed to waive all territorial rights in China, abandoning their concessions. This had become inevitable in the context of the wartime alliance, though it had no immediate practical effect since the Japanese had taken over the settlements in Shanghai and other occupied cities. Showing his feelings for the British, the Generalissimo congratulated them on having won a moral victory over themselves.

Meanwhile, the relationship with Stilwell veered dramatically. One lunchtime, the Nationalist leader and Meiling summoned the US naval attaché, and criticised the general, knowing their views would be passed on to Washington. But, then, in early November 1942, Chiang suddenly told Vinegar Joe that he could issue orders to anybody in the Chinese headquarters, and promised fifteen divisions for a Chinese-British-US offensive in Burma which Stilwell hoped to launch in the spring. Chiang's designated successor, General Chen Cheng, who got on well with the American, was appointed to command the Y Force which was to attack Burma from south-west China. But Roosevelt and Churchill then decided to delay the start of the offensive until the end of 1943. Transport of supplies to China was ranked last in Allied planning at their summit in Casablanca. Stilwell's only compensation was the award of the American Distinguished Service Cross for his combat performance. Chiang gave a celebratory dinner, followed by a film provided by the Americans. 'There was a lot of kissing and swapping of wives,' Stilwell wrote in his diary of what appeared on screen. 'What crude barbarians we must still appear to them.'[11]

Meiling was not at the dinner. She had flown to New York at the end of 1942, suffering from a combination of ailments, including a bad back, sinus trouble aggravated by her smoking, skin rashes, insomnia, exhaustion, dental problems and damage to her ribs suffered in her accident in Shanghai in 1937. On top of which, Chiang suspected she had stomach cancer, and wanted her to take tests not available in China. His wife was carried into the Stratoliner plane leased from TWA, accompanied by two nurses and her niece, Jeannette Kung, who liked to dress as a man and wore her hair in masculine style. Arriving at a military airfield outside New York, Meiling was met by Roosevelt's close aide, Harry Hopkins.

On the way to the Harkness Pavillion medical centre, where a whole floor was reserved for her under a false name, she began by telling Hopkins that she had come only for medical treatment. But then she went on to talk at length about relations between the United States and China, to say the best way of winning the world war was to concentrate on beating Japan, to attack Stilwell for losing Chinese troops in Burma, to criticise Britain, and to praise Chennault. Eleanor Roosevelt visited her three times in hospital – the President's wife owed her a personal debt since Meiling had made sure her son, James, had received a proper diet when he visited China as a marine after undergoing an operation for a gastric ulcer. 'She seemed to me quite nervous and suffering a great deal; she could hardly bear to have anything touch any part of her body,' Mrs Roosevelt recalled in her memoirs. 'Madame Chiang seemed so petite and delicate . . . that I had a desire to help her and take care of her as I would have if she had been my own daughter.'[12]

Something appears to have gone wrong in January 1943, when Meiling called on T. V. Soong to go to New York to help her. Stilwell noted rumours in Chungking that her mission had bogged down. But, once her treatment was completed and she had rested for two weeks at Roosevelt's house at Hyde Park in New York State, she regained her usual drive, and was ready to take up Wendell Willkie's suggestion to barnstorm America, heavily promoted by Henry Luce. Her aim was to raise funds for Chungking and put China on the map in the minds of the people of its most important ally. In the process, she would make herself even more famous. As a US army public relations officer, Don Knight, put it, for most of Americans, China at the time of Pearl Harbor meant Marco Polo, Pearl Buck's novel and film *The Good Earth*, Fu Manchu and Charlie Chan (who was American). After her visit, he added a fifth entry – 'the billions contributed to that pretty Mrs Chiang'.[13]

The tour began in mid-February 1943. Staying at the White House, Meiling brought her own silk sheets which had to be changed every day – more often if she took a siesta. Usually, the President sat beside visitors on a sofa, but, to avoid being 'vamped', as he put it, he had a card table set up with a chair for her on the other side. Roosevelt found the visitor 'hard as steel'; when he asked her at dinner how strikers would be dealt with in China, she drew a nail across her throat. In conversations with senior administration figures, she pressed for more military aid, getting agreement to deliver most of the supplies to Chennault and to send in a new model transport plane which, however, proved unsuitable for conditions over the Hump. She told the Secretary for War he had beautiful hands, and invited everybody to go back to China with her. Criticising Stilwell, she recounted the watermelon incident in Burma as an example of his 'bitter and contemptuous attitude'.[14]

The first woman, and the first Chinese, to address both houses of Congress, Meiling got a four-minute standing ovation before she began speaking to the Senate. She started modestly, pretending she had only realised just before she arrived that she would be asked to say more than 'How do you do? I am so very glad to see you.' She launched into a hymn to Sino-American friendship and the importance of the Far East in the war. Assuming that her audience would not be familiar with Chiang's strategy, she declared that it was better 'not to accept failure ignominiously but to risk it gloriously'. 'I feel that it is necessary for us not only to have ideals and to proclaim that we have them; it is necessary that we act to implement them,' she concluded.[15]

Meiling – called 'Snow White' in the State Department code – scored another success at a banquet in her honour attended by Vice-President Henry Wallace and Mrs Roosevelt. She charmed 172 reporters at a press conference with the President in the Oval Office of the White House, for which she wore a dress decorated with the wings of the Chinese air force. Her impact was such that American military planners worried about congressional and public opinion shifting in favour of a greater emphasis on China to the detriment of the campaign in Europe. Back in New York, she addressed a rally of 20,000 people at Madison Square Gardens where Willkie described her as 'an avenging angel'. Luce put her on the cover of *Time*, and she was written up by American papers as the spirit of an indomitable China fighting Fascist aggression for democracy. American heartstrings were tugged, and missionary links drawn upon to the full.*

In New York Meiling took the whole of the forty-second floor of the Waldorf-Astoria Towers for herself. Security men kept watch outside her rooms, and cleared the corridors and a lift when she left. She brought her own staff, and, one night, invited the Willkie backer, Gardner Cowles, to dinner. The invitation specified a black-tie occasion, but they were alone except for the four servants who, she assured her guest, did not understand English – so they could speak freely.[16]

Then she told the publisher that her union with Chiang was a marriage of political convenience, and recounted the story of his having said on their wedding night that they would not have sex – a tale which, as Cowles recorded, he was not sure he believed. Next, she moved into the reason for inviting him. She was sure Willkie could get the Republican presidential nomination, and urged Cowles to do all he could to achieve this. 'I was to spend whatever amount of money I thought was necessary,' he wrote in his

---

* Missionary enthusiasm was reflected in the title of a book published in America in 1943 – *Generalissimo and Madame Chiang Kai-shek, Christian Liberators of China*. It called them 'divine instruments for altering the fate of the sleeping giant which is China'.

memoirs. 'She would reimburse me for all expenditures.' Funding to buy the presidency for Willkie would, presumably, have come, in part at least, from the residue of US loans to China sitting in the American bank accounts of the Chungking regime. 'If Wendell could be elected, then he and I would rule the world,' she told Cowles. 'I would rule the Orient and Wendell would rule the Western world.' It was, as Cowles noted, a totally mad proposal, 'but I was so mesmerized by clearly one of the most formidable women of the time that this evening I would not have dismissed anything she said'.[17]

From New York, Meiling went to Boston, Chicago and California. The United China Relief fund collected large sums as she spoke to rallies across the country. At her alma mater of Wellesley College, she strolled across the campus in slacks, which were not accepted garb there at the time. 'Anyone who can look as smart as Madame Chiang in slacks may wear them,' the college president remarked. In Hollywood, stars including Rita Hayworth, Ginger Rogers, Ingrid Bergman, Shirley Temple and Mary Pickford joined the welcoming committee, and she met Spencer Tracy and Henry Fonda. On 31 March a big banquet was followed by a night in aid of China at the Hollywood Bowl, attended by 30,000 people, during which the Los Angeles Philharmonic played 'The Madame Chiang Kai-shek March'. Actors Edward G. Robinson and Walter Houston read a narrative on China, and Meiling told of the Rape of Nanking. The producer was David O. Selznick, of *Gone With the Wind* fame.[18]

Along the way, Meiling developed distinct diva tendencies. She objected to an American officer who called her 'M'am' rather than 'Madame' until he pointed out that the former term was the way the British Queen was addressed, at which point she grew radiant. The historian Jerome Chen records that she refused to give an interview to a reporter because he was black. When she met the adviser Owen Lattimore, who had returned to the United States at the end of his mission, she cut him dead at a reception in San Francisco – presumably because he was of no further use. During her stay at the White House, her way of clapping her hands to summon servants, rather than ringing the bell, went down badly. There was consternation when she insisted on a shipment of English cigarettes being fetched from bond in New York and flown to Washington. The Treasury Secretary, Henry Morgenthau, whose men went to get the cigarettes, told his staff Roosevelt was 'just crazy to get her out of the country'.[19]

Before the Madison Square Garden rally, she declined to come down from her hotel suite to a dinner organised by Luce and attended by 270 prominent people, including nine state governors: she was, she said, conserving her energy for her speech. While she was in New York, Churchill visited Washington, and she invited him to come to see her. To save the Prime Minister the trip, Roosevelt laid on a lunch at the White House for Meiling and the British leader, but she refused to make the trip with what Churchill described as 'some hauteur'.* As it headed across the country, her train stopped in the early morning in a small town in Utah where the whole population lined up on the platform to greet her. Meiling preferred to stay in her berth, and sent one of her maids out onto the platform where she was greeted by the locals as the real thing.[20]

Back in New York, she received Joseph Kennedy, ambassador to London and father of the future president. His diary recorded that he had been told by the British newspaper baron and minister, Lord Beaverbrook, that Meiling was a lesbian who was being accompanied by her girlfriend – a reference to the mannish Jeannette Kung. When he met her, Kennedy found her 'a most interesting and attractive woman'. He told her that she was both managerial and had sex appeal. 'You mean like Gypsy Rose Lee?' she replied. She smoked incessantly, and Kennedy noted that she told him the tests showed she did not have stomach cancer. She spoke of editing a newspaper, or of being paid vast sums for her writing. Then she showed him two of her stories; one, he recorded, was 'a bit naughty'. After that, she sent out to Schrafft's drug store for strawberry sodas, saying she did not care if they upset her stomach, which they did not.[21]

While Meiling was grandstanding from coast to coast, news of floods, crop failures and a plague of locusts in central China began to reach Chungking. Worst hit was Henan province where no rain had fallen in 1942. The diversion of the Yellow River by Chiang's blowing of the dykes had deprived large areas of irrigation. The troops of the Nationalist general, Tang Enbo, had imposed grain taxes running from 30 to 50 per cent – sometimes they might take all a peasant's crop. Grain was moved out of the province to be sold elsewhere, but army warehouses still bulged with

---

* Churchill wrote that FDR was 'somewhat vexed', but, 'in the regretted absence of dame Chiang Kai-shek, the president and I lunched alone in his room and made the best of things'. (Davies, p. 267)

food as up to 30 million peasants faced starvation. 'If the people die,' an officer said, 'the land will still be Chinese. But if the soldiers starve, the Japanese will take the land.'[22]

When a Chungking newspaper ran a story on the famine, it was suspended for three days. Teddy White, whose boss at *Time* magazine was boosting Meiling's American trip, decided to go to investigate. He observed endless streams of people walking in the cold along the railway tracks, falling and dying where they lay. At stations, refugees 'swarmed over the [rail] cars like ants on a dead worm, clinging on wherever they could find a foothold or handhold,' wrote the American information officer, Graham Peck. 'For hundreds of miles the railroad was littered with the corpses of those who had been too weak to hang on.' In the rail junction of Zhengzhou, the surviving inhabitants were 'like scarecrows, whining and crying or stumbling in silence'. In the city of Luoyang, reported another correspondent, people were packed into wagons like lumber, so close together that they could not move. Outside the city, dogs dug bodies out of piles of sand. Families sold their children; white slavers bought girls; speculators arrived to snap up land at low prices. Mothers were said to exchange babies, saying, 'You eat mine; I'll eat yours.' A woman was found boiling her two-year-old child as food; a father was charged with strangling his two boys to eat them; the bones of a boy were discovered in a big pot in a village which had been told to take in destitute children.[23]

'Half the villages were deserted; some simply abandoned, others already looted,' White's report went on. 'Spring compost rested in heaps, untended. To hear a sound or see a person in such a village was startling: an old man tottering through the street all by himself; or in another village two women shrieking at each other with no one else in sight . . . what were they arguing about in death? One saw, as one travelled, people chipping bark from trees, with knives, scythes and meat cleavers. They were stripping bark from all the elms . . . because you could grind the bark and eat it.' An orphanage he visited 'stank worse than anything I have ever smelled. Even the escorting officer could not stand the odor and, holding his handkerchief to his nose, asked to be excused. These were abandoned babies. They were inserted four to a crib. Those who could not fit in cribs were simply laid on the straw. I forget what they were fed. But they smelled of baby vomit and baby shit, and when they were dead, they were cleared out.'[24]

White reckoned the death toll at 2 million. As many more faced death. Another 2 million had fled the province. A group of peasants came to see him one night with a petition they asked him to take to Chiang. In their county, two thirds of the 150,000 people had nothing to eat; 700 were dying each day. Chungking had ordered taxes to be remitted, but they had already been collected so it was too late. The government also earmarked $200 million for relief, but only $80 million was actually sent.

On his return to Chungking, White got an audience with the Generalissimo who 'received me in his dark office, standing erect and slim, taut, holding out a stiff hand of greeting, then he sat in his high-backed chair, listening to me with visible distaste'. Chiang denied that the peasants were being taxed: had he not ordered that taxes be remitted in distressed areas? 'They see a foreigner and tell him anything,' he said to one of his aides. In China, cannibalism was impossible, he added. When the correspondent said he had seen dogs eating corpses, Chiang replied that this, too, was impossible.

To prove his points, White produced photographs by another journalist who had accompanied him. Chiang's knee began to jiggle slightly as he asked where the pictures had been taken. When White told him, he took out a little pad and brush pen to make notes. 'He asked for names of officials,' the American recalled. 'He wanted more names; he wanted us to make a full report to him leaving out no names. In a flat manner, as if restating a fact to himself, he said that he had *told* the army to share its grain with the people. Then he thanked us; told me that I was a better investigator than "any of the investigators I have sent on my own". And I was ushered out twenty minutes after entering.' Sanctions were taken, grain was rushed in, relief kitchens were opened and the army gave back some of its food.[25]

White had filed an epic story on his way back to Chungking. By chance, it got through an inattentive censor. Meiling heard about it – not the kind of news she wanted America to read while she was busy raising support and funds. She asked Luce to fire White. The publisher refused, but his magazine ran only 750 words of the far longer report, excising all mentions of failures by officials, corruption and peasant anger.

White's story was not the only sand in the relationship Meiling was trying to nurture with America. A fresh Roosevelt–Churchill conference at the White House, known as Trident, led to a decision to scale down the much-delayed Burma operation. At the meeting with Stilwell and Chennault, Roosevelt asked the general what he thought of Chiang. 'He's a vacillating, tricky, undependable old scoundrel who never keeps his word,' Vinegar Joe growled, according to Chennault's memoirs. Roosevelt cut in to ask the air force commander for his opinion. 'Sir,' Chennault replied, 'I think the Generalissimo is one of the two or three greatest military and political leaders in the world today. He has never broken a commitment or promise made to me.' When word of Stilwell's remark got back to him, Chiang sent his wife a message complaining: 'Not only does he abuse us and humiliate us, he thinks nothing of threatening us and of making false accusations against us. This is indeed too bitter a pill to swallow. For the sake of the future and for the successful prosecution of the war, I hope that President Roosevelt will understand the difficulties of my present position.'[26]

There was also cause for concern about Chiang's literary activities. As Meiling had begun her tour of the United States, he had a book published in China. Priced at only 10 cents to encourage sales, *China's Destiny* had been largely ghosted for the Generalissimo by a man who had initially joined Wang Jingwei when he left Chungking, but who subsequently returned to the regime and was lodging with Chiang's secretary. The 213-page work became a must-buy for anybody who wanted to be in with the regime. Sales soared through the hundreds of thousands, some said up to a million. The book insisted on the supremacy of traditional Chinese ways and blamed foreigners for all the country's ills. A subsequent volume on economic theory, not generally regarded as Chiang's strong point, claimed that the country's sages had 'understood all the principles of economic development'. Both books were highly conservative and paternalistic, stressing the need for order and discipline, and subordination of individuals to the state. Chinese intellectuals gave it a dusty reception. The American scholar John King Fairbank, in Kunming at the time, said the academics there thought it was 'twaddle' and an affront.[27]

Chiang's highly reactionary message could have alienated the public of China's main ally; so an English language version was shelved, and then issued in a version which cut out objectionable passages. Meiling was widely believed to have been behind the decision. The Chungking censors deleted references to the book in copy from correspondents. The State

Department classified its copy of the Chinese original as 'top secret'. Washington was about to award the Generalissimo the Legion of Merit, the highest award that could be given to a foreigner; it would hardly do for the recipient to be known as an opponent of everything the Allies were meant to be fighting for.*[28]

At the beginning of July, Meiling flew back to Asia with her niece in a converted Liberator bomber. When the plane landed for a stop-over at Assam in north India, her clothes were wrinkled and her hair untidy. A GI took a photograph of her as she left the aircraft. Meiling hurried back inside and sat glaring out of the window, insisting that the soldier be ordered to destroy the film. The two women had amassed such a treasure trove of American goods to take home that some had to be brought in on another aircraft. At Assam, one of the crates was dropped and broke open. The US army grapevine had it that inside were ermine brassieres, which was probably not true; but there was certainly a lot of cosmetics, groceries and lingerie, wrote Graham Peck. Angered, the American soldiers dropped other crates, kicked the contents around and then threw them into the Liberator.[29]

Meiling had been expected to land at the airfield being developed for American bombers at Chengdu, but the pilot decided to head for Chungking instead. Unaware of this change of plan, Chiang flew to Chengdu – by one report, his plane almost colliding with his wife's on the way. The Americans at Chungking, who had not been warned of its arrival, suspected that Meiling's aircraft might be a Japanese decoy. So they drove up in a jeep to check it out on the runway. This time, Madame Chiang had made sure she was ready to meet the reception committee she expected. As she walked down the steps, her hair done and her face made up, she realised there was no party to greet her return home. So she stood alone, tapping her foot bad-temperedly. Jeannette Kung, in masculine clothes and with her hair cut short, ordered the American pilot of their plane to pipe fuel into some empty drums so that she could take it for her own use. The pilot refused. Jeannette commandeered a station wagon being driven past by two Chinese officers. As she did so, an American sergeant asked her, 'Sure you know your way into town, bud?' The two angry women left in a

---

* The full version later appeared in an unauthorised edition critically annotated by an American Communist sympathiser, Philip Jaffe (see bibliography).

great grinding of gears. Behind them, members of their party grabbed food and cushions from the plane.

A secret report by the American adviser, Arthur Young, recounted that, when Chiang flew back to Chungking from Chengdu, his pilot tried to save time by touching down without circling the airstrip as was customary. At the same time, another Chinese plane, carrying Chiang's son, flew in to land in the opposite direction. Its pilot managed to lift it to avoid a head-on collision. Already in a bad temper because of the mix-up over Meiling, Chiang called for the head of the airfield administration, and threatened to have him shot, though the near accident was nothing to do with him or his staff. After Meiling, Ailing and H. H. Kung intervened on the official's behalf, his punishment was reduced to being given a 'great demerit' before being forced to retire.[30]

To welcome Meiling back, the Kungs held a reception for foreigners in the garden of their large house. A throne-like chair was set up on a dais in front of an ornamental screen. Meiling was to sit there and greet the guests. Then Chiang decided to come, too. That caused a protocol problem – the dais was not large enough for two thrones. So a couple of wicker chairs were set on the lawn, but the Chiangs received the guests standing up. Photographs of Meiling meeting Hollywood stars were shown. Graham Peck recalled that, looking beautiful but rather annoyed and wearing lace gloves, she stood in front with her husband behind her muttering, '*Hao, hao, hao*'.[31]

The rumour mill said Chiang had scolded Meiling for her behaviour in the United States which he considered inappropriate at a time of such suffering in China. It is also quite likely that one of the various intelligence services working for him had followed the Meiling–Willkie relationship – the Generalissimo's furious behaviour when he went to the American's villa on the night of the Chungking reception demonstrated his suspicions. Chiang was widely reported to have taken a mistress. The stories were so prevalent that the critical American diplomat John Service reported them to the State Department: 'There is so much smoke, it would seem that there must be some fire,' he wrote. The main rumour focused on a young nurse on his staff. Various other women were mentioned, including Chiang's early concubine from Shanghai, Yao. There was even speculation that he might have seen Jennie again though her memoirs say she did not meet him after he banished her in 1927.

Service's report said Meiling took to referring to her husband as 'that man' and complained that the only time he put in his false teeth was when he went to see his mistress. One day, the American added, Meiling had found a pair of high-heeled shoes under Chiang's bed, and had flung them out of the window, hitting a guard on the head. On another occasion, she was reported to have thrown a vase at her husband, and so injured him that he did not receive callers for four days. A woman visitor said that, every time she went into Meiling's bedroom, she saw the same pair of carefully pressed trousers 'draped so ostentatiously across the foot of the other twin bed that she was quite sure the Generalissimo was no longer using them'. In a conversation with Stilwell, she 'let out that she has a hell of a life with the Peanut', the general wrote in his diary. 'No one else will tell him the truth so she is constantly at him with the disagreeable news. It can't be easy to live with the crabbed little bastard and see everything balled up.'[32]

Only power could hold the internalised traditionalist and the Westernised woman together. For all the smiling photographs of them together, the couple had always been deeply different. Chiang dealt in harangues and homilies; his wife was far more sophisticated. Despite the New Life proclamations, she smoked heavily and took luxury for granted while he was happy with simple food and military conditions. At their home on the peak above Xikou, her bed was large and soft, his small and hard; at the villa in Kuling, the bathroom had a Western toilet and a traditional Chinese squatting hole for each of them. Meiling's visit to the United States introduced another element – she now saw herself as a world figure, and intended to establish her power, even if it meant provoking a take-no-prisoners family feud.

The little sister's success threw down a gauntlet to her brother, threatening T. V. Soong's position as Chungking's point man in Washington. Stilwell wrote that Meiling had 'put it over like a tent' on Roosevelt. She bragged that the President had promised her to send two divisions to the China theatre. Hump supplies rose to 8,000 tons after her return. T. V. knew that he was the person best equipped to run the Nationalist regime, with his administrative ability, his understanding of finance, his contacts and his modern grasp of the world. He could see the danger of collapse if reforms were not brought in. He was reported to be so contemptuous of H. H. Kung that he could barely speak civilly of his brother-in-law. His ally, General Chen Cheng, was known for his disgust at the corruption and inefficiency in the army. Another military associate, Xue Yue, had repeatedly shown himself to be one of the very few effective field commanders.

The conditions were ripe for a power bid by the portly, owl-spectacled Soong, who was given the improbable code name of 'Rhumba' by the Americans. He had another reason to act – his position in Washington enabled him to ensure that companies run by him and his brother, T.L., were able to profit hugely from the American aid chain. The amount of money that went through their various enterprises during the war years was estimated at US$3.5 billion, and some of it stuck to the Soongs, partly from a transport company of theirs which handled distribution of supplies in south-east China. That was something to be protected from his sister's growing influence.[33]

Any move by T.V. would threaten his oldest and youngest sister, and their spouses. If he became prime minister, Chiang's wings would inevitably be clipped, and Meiling's ambitions would be dashed. But if she got anywhere near to realising her worldwide plans, he would be relegated to the back seat. Each sibling needed to act to check the other, and, as is customary in such battles, the conflict was played out over an apparently extraneous issue – Joseph Stilwell.

T.V. drafted a plan for a new command structure that would eject the American general and replace him with a Chinese who might well be Soong's ally, Chen Cheng. Knowing Chiang's very different feeling for Vinegar Joe and Chen, he could calculate that this would win the support of the Generalissimo. Meeting Roosevelt, Soong said there was 'cause for concern about Sino-American cooperation' if Stilwell was not replaced. His telegram to Chiang reported that the President was concerned.

On 13 September 1943 Meiling began her offensive by calling Stilwell to the Chiangs' residence. Waiting with her was Ailing. Short, dumpy and with tiny hands, the eldest Soong sister was the epitome of what Vinegar Joe detested in China. She was said to control a bank through which she bought American dollars at the ridiculously low official rate, just before a fresh splurge of printing of banknotes sent the Chinese currency plunging even further. One frequently told story had it that, when a special plane was sent from Chungking to collect her from her home in Hong Kong after Pearl Harbor, she insisted on taking her dachshund with her to China. The pilot said this would make the aircraft overweight. Ailing was adamant. So a security man was left behind, and subsequently killed by the Japanese. Given the difference between the weight of a small dog and that of a man, the story made no sense; but it said much about the way she was regarded.

Chiang's American adviser, Owen Lattimore, recorded that Meiling was much under her sister's influence, and that the Generalissimo had more confidence in her than in the wife whose marriage to him she had set up. For her part, Ailing had good reason to line up with Meiling against their brother. If T.V. increased his power in Chungking, it could only be at the expense of her husband, both as head of the government and in the Finance Ministry. If, on the other hand, Soong's grip on Lend-Lease was diminished by his being humbled, that would open up a very tasty cornucopia for the Kungs.[34]

The sisters – Stilwell referred to Meiling in his diary as May, and to Ailing as Ella or Sis – told him they were worried about China's military forces, and wanted to do something about it. He gave them 'the low-down on conditions in the Army', and said they were appalled. In fact, it was what they wanted to hear. Apart from jousting with her brother, Meiling was out for the scalp of General He Yingqin, the War Minister with whom she had first crossed swords at the time of the Xi'an Incident. According to Stilwell, she called He 'the unmentionable' and 'that goddam old fool'. The generals round Chiang were, she said, 'like a lot of ostriches with their heads in the sand and their bottoms sticking out. How I would like to take a big club and go after them.' Stilwell was an ideal ally; he despised He as 'a terribly conceited little monkey', a feeling increased when the minister sent him a letter complaining that a bottle of iodine had been broken in transit by the Americans. The meeting at the Chiang residence came up with the revolutionary idea that Meiling should become War Minister. 'May craves action,' Stilwell noted. 'We signed an offensive and defensive alliance.'[35]

Vinegar Joe had no idea what was really going on. His diary shows him to have been an innocent caught in the middle of a feud which he read the wrong way, assuming that the sisters had been told by T. V. Soong at the urging of George Marshall to 'get behind me and co-operate'. He might have recalled an incident the previous year when Soong had failed to pass on to Chungking a letter from Roosevelt laying out Stilwell's remit in clear terms, including his decision-making authority over Lend-Lease supplies. He might have also pondered the way in which General Chen Cheng, the

T.V. ally and commander of Y Force at the training centre in Yunnan, had told the Generalissimo that the American had called one of Chiang's relatives a bandit.[36]

The struggle intensified in the following weeks. The sisters told Stilwell they had argued the case for army reform so strongly that Chiang had walked out of the room. But T.V., who had flown into Chungking, attacked the American for his arrogance. The family battle reached a climax over two days in the Chiangs' home. Chennault's aide, Joseph Alsop, who was close to Soong as well as being related to Roosevelt, recalled the Foreign Minister returning from the argument in a state of complete exhaustion. Chiang certainly would have preferred a more emollient replacement for Stilwell. But he did not feel comfortable with T.V., preferring the more biddable Kung. On one occasion, he had told Owen Lattimore, 'T. V. Soong has been so long in the United States that he thinks like an American – to my mind a not very intelligent American.'[37]

On 17 October 1943, the overall Allied commander in the India–China theatre, Lord Louis Mountbatten, flew to Chungking for talks, ingratiating himself with Chiang by saying that he wanted to draw on his vast experience, and presenting Meiling with a vanity case from Cartier with her initials set in diamonds – the Chiangs reciprocated with gifts of jade seals. Mountbatten aided the sisters by saying he had no wish to have to find a replacement for Stilwell to head the Chinese in the Allied forces. Accompanying him, an American general in charge of military aid also argued Stilwell's case. Ailing and Meiling urged Vinegar Joe to tell the Generalissimo his only aim was the good of China, say he was ready to cooperate fully, and blame any mistakes on misunderstandings.

After considerable hesitation, Stilwell went to see Chiang, who delivered a lecture on the proper relationship between a commander-in-chief and his chief of staff, and warned him not to fall victim to a superiority complex. 'I listened politely and Peanut said that under those conditions we could go on working harmoniously again,' he wrote. Chiang recorded in his diary: 'Stilwell has expressed his regrets and I am glad to retain his services and once again to put my confidence in him. This represents a turning point in Sino-American relations.'[38]

The sisters had, Ailing remarked, been 'down to the last trench' and had put the family jewels on Stilwell. Later, she added that she had been obliged to choose between her own flesh and blood and the good of China – which was one way of putting it. As for himself, the American wrote: 'All through this mess I have felt as free as air – no regrets and no self-blame. A grand and glorious feeling.' The Generalissimo noted in his diary that he was 'ready to let bygones be bygones' and show 'magnanimity'.[39]

The eldest Soong's ambitions were dashed, for all to see. 'T.V. got a good swat,' Stilwell noted as he began to piece together what had been happening around him. Chen Cheng lost his command of Y Force. Though He Yingqin survived, Chiang raked him over the coals for the slow pace of troop replacements. A family meeting held in December ended with another row over T.V.'s suggestion that all China's economic agencies should be unified under his control – Chiang was said to have thrown a teacup at him. To protect themselves, Soong got his brother to move the headquarters of their transport company handling Lend-Lease supplies to New York.[40]

The strain of having bested her brother made itself felt on Meiling. She was suffering from dysentery and influenza; John King Fairbank found her tired and 'her head shook a bit as old men's do' though she was trying hard to be a great lady. 'Conversation too cosmic to be real,' Fairbank wrote after their meeting.

An actress, with a lot of admirable qualities, great charm, quick intuition, intelligence; but underneath, emotions that are unhappy . . . bitterness about something, a penchant for acting a part which produces falsity . . . Occasionally a real laugh, with a round and relaxed face and higher-pitched voice, which seemed natural and at ease and made all the rest seem forced and tragic.[41]

She told Fairbank that everybody was an actor in a great experiment whose denouement they did not know. But, with Wendell Willkie waiting for her in the USA, American acclaim, her brother sidelined, her protégé, Stilwell, in the ascendant, Meiling had every reason to see herself as Madame Empress. As for her husband, he had allowed the family contenders to fight it out, and had emerged with his own power unscathed. Now he was ready to meet his international peers.

CHAPTER 23

'All Asia Is at Stake'

THE ALLIED SUMMIT held in Cairo at the end of November 1943 consecrated China as one of the big four powers which were to shape the post-war world. A month earlier, it had been included in the Four Power Joint Declaration on the pursuit of the war with the United States, the Soviet Union and Britain. As well as the plenary sessions, Chiang and Meiling had private meetings with Roosevelt and Churchill in their villas by the pyramids. But Stalin, who had a non-aggression pact with Japan, chose not to attend, insisting on a separate subsequent meeting with the President and Prime Minister in Teheran. That underlined the way in which, however much the American President boosted its claims to great power status, the Nationalist regime was very much the junior partner of the four.

The contrast between the Generalissimo's attendance at Cairo and the state of his country was striking. The Japanese were still on the attack. Despite American supplies, the Nationalist armies remained weak. More than half a million troops, mainly from mercenary armies, had switched to the collaborationist regimes in Nanking and the north. Inflation roared ahead at 243 per cent in 1943 as the volume of banknotes printed doubled by the year, and the Japanese added to the economic chaos by flooding southern China with $100 billion in counterfeit money.

Corruption and speculation soared. Military spending took 60 per cent of the budget. Taxes covered only an eighth of government revenue. Across the Nationalist areas, a quarter of the inhabitants were estimated to be refugees or homeless. Drought hit the south, killing more than a million people; yet troops sold food to the Japanese as starving people perished around them.[1]

The Cairo summit was held at the heavily guarded Mena House Hotel which was turned into a miniature fortress with anti-aircraft guns and massed searchlights. Kai-shek and Meiling were the first participants to arrive, after a four-day air journey from Chungking with a twenty-strong delegation from which T. V. Soong was conspicuously absent. The Generalissimo kept to his routine, rising at 5 a.m., meditating, and working till 6 p.m. when he and his wife took a walk in the garden of their villa. The British general, Sir Alan Brooke, wrote in his diary that Chiang reminded him of 'a cross between a pine marten and a ferret. Evidently with no grasp of war in its larger aspect and determined to get the best of the bargain . . . a shrewd but small man . . . very successful at leading the Americans down the garden path.'[2]

Meiling accompanied her husband into the conference, and made her presence very much felt. Churchill found her 'most remarkable and charming'. Meeting her for the first time, he said he supposed she regarded him as a scoundrel and imperialist out to grab more colonies; to which she replied smoothly: 'Why are you so sure what I think of you?' For Brooke, she was 'a study in herself, a queer character in which sex and politics seemed to predominate, both being used indiscriminately, individually or unitedly to achieve her ends'.[3]

For the opening session, Meiling wore a black satin dress with a yellow chrysanthemum pattern, slit up the side, a neat black jacket, big black tulle bows at the back of her head, a black veil over her face, light stockings and black shoes with large brass nails. At one point, she shifted position, showing what Brooke called 'one of the most shapely of legs' through the slit in her dress. 'This caused a rustle among those attending the conference and I even thought I heard a suppressed neigh coming from a group of some of the younger members,' the general added. Far away from the New Life provisions against cigarettes, she chain-smoked, using a long holder. Because of eye trouble, she wore what the future Prime Minister Harold Macmillan described as 'some very strange kind of glasses' – she took the opportunity to visit a medical centre set up by the Americans and to see Churchill's doctor who told her she would only get better when the strain of her life relaxed.[4]

Chiang's inability to speak English gave the bilingual Meiling her opportunity. Repeatedly, she butted into the discussions to correct the translators, leading to confusion as to who was talking for China. When the interpreter relayed points to Chiang, she interrupted to recast them to her husband. When he replied, she again broke in to say she needed to convey the full meaning of the Generalissimo's thoughts. Brooke felt she was 'the leading spirit of the two'.[5]

She also joined a group photograph taken in the garden with her husband, Roosevelt and Churchill, thus giving China two of the four places in the record books. Madame sat on the left of the white-suited Prime Minister, smiling at him while he appeared to be chuckling at what she had just said. At the other end, Roosevelt seemed to be making a point to which Chiang smiled, despite his lack of English. The picture was widely circulated in China as a sign of the eminence of the Generalissimo and his wife.

The main issue at Cairo was to confirm the common front against Japan and discuss the launching of an offensive in Burma, though the Chinese took the opportunity to ask Roosevelt for more money and supplies. Chiang kept changing his mind, even about whether to attend sessions. Mountbatten wrote in his diary that the others had been 'driven absolutely mad' by his behaviour. Chinese generals were unable to reply to questions about their own forces. When they tried to insist on control over the use of American planes and supplies, George Marshall told them: 'Now let me get this straight. You are talking about your "rights" in this matter. I thought these were *American* planes, and *American* personnel, and *American* matériel. Don't understand what you mean by saying we can't do thus and so.'[6]

Finally, agreement was reached to launch a Burma offensive in the spring of 1944, with the British staging a sea landing using American landing craft. The summit ended with a declaration that, after the defeat of Japan, China would regain Manchuria and the island of Taiwan, known in the West by the name of Formosa given to it by the Portuguese in the sixteenth century. Roosevelt offered Chiang a vague undertaking that America would train and equip ninety Chinese divisions, but without any timescale. Chiang disagreed with the President and Prime Minister about dismantling Japan's imperial system after the war. He advocated a softer approach, reflecting both his antagonism to Westerners telling Asians how to organise themselves, and his realisation that he might have to cut some deals with Tokyo if the war went badly for him.

Roosevelt and Churchill then left to meet Stalin in Teheran, while Chiang and his wife flew back to Chungking, leaving Stilwell and the political adviser, John Paton Davies, behind to be briefed by Roosevelt on his return from the talks with the Soviet dictator. The good news was that Stalin agreed to declare war on Japan after Germany had been defeated. The bad news for China was that the Teheran meeting decided on a cross-Channel invasion of France plus landings from the Mediterranean. This meant all available landing craft would have to go to Europe. So the Burma operation would be postponed again. On the way back to their quarters, Davies recalled, Stilwell held his head in his hands. In his diary, the general noted that 'a brief experience with international politics confirms me in my preference for driving a garbage truck'.[7]

In a broadcast fireside chat after getting back to Washington, Roosevelt lauded Chiang as an 'unconquerable man . . . of great vision [and] great courage'. The United States and China, he added, were closer together than ever before in deep friendship and unity of purpose. But the evolution of American strategy in the Pacific had major implications for the Generalissimo, as the focus switched from fighting Japan in, and from, China to an island-hopping advance that left his country on one side. With US forces unlikely to land in large numbers in China, the Americans began to ask themselves pertinent questions.[8]

Why was Chiang keeping 200,000 troops tied down in northern China to watch the Red Armies which had some 50,000 men on the other side of the line? Why had the united front been allowed to wither after the New Fourth Army Incident three years earlier? Why were the US advisers in China not allowed to meet the Communists – had not Zhou Enlai remarked to John Paton Davies, half-jokingly, half-seriously, that he was ready to take Red Army troops to fight in Burma under Stilwell? American writers who went to the base of Yan'an generally painted a favourable picture, depicting Mao and his colleagues as agrarian reformers whose dedication, patriotism and honesty contrasted with the unreliability and venality in Nationalist ranks. Launching a debate which was to run through the following six years, the question arose of what attitude Washington should take if civil war broke out, and whether it could deal with Mao while remaining allied with Chiang.[9]

Chinese suspicions of American intentions rose after a plot was discovered by the secret police chief, Dai Li, around the time of the Cairo summit. Several hundred younger officers were said to be involved. Motivated by anger at the corruption and inefficiency of the government and army, they would have kept Chiang as the ultimate leader, but would have got rid of General He, H. H. Kung, the Chen brothers and Dai Li. The rebels asked an American general involved in training troops for help. The reply was negative, but the Office of Strategic Services (OSS), forerunner of the CIA, took an interest. Returning from Cairo, Chiang ordered the plotters to be rounded up, and had sixteen executed.[10]

He would have been even more concerned had he known of a conversation initiated by Roosevelt with Stilwell in Cairo. The President had asked how long Chiang could last. The general said a fresh Japanese offensive might topple him. In that case, FDR suggested, they should look for 'some other man or group of men to carry on'. On his return to China, Stilwell told his deputy that Roosevelt was 'fed up with Chiang and his tantrums and said so. In fact he told me in that Olympian manner of his: "If you can't get along with Chiang and can't replace him, get rid of him once and for all. You know what I mean. Put in someone you can manage."' Another version had Roosevelt ordering contingency plans for the Chinese leader's assassination.

The Generalissimo's constant demands for money did not help matters, particularly since Chungking insisted on all transactions being done at the ludicrous old rate of 20 Chinese dollars to one unit of American currency – the black market level was many times that. Though his government still had nearly US$500 million in funds in the USA, Chiang called for a loan twice that size. When this was refused, he insisted that Washington cough up US$100 million in gold for the big airfield being built at Chengdu to house US Stratofortress bombers that were to attack Japan. Otherwise, he warned, China would be unable to offer any more assistance with the project in the form of hundreds of thousands of labourers who had been drafted in to build it. A compromise was reached after H. H. Kung had dropped remarks about Japan making 'some very good offers'. But the regime was getting a nasty reputation for financial blackmail, earning its leader the nickname of 'Cash My Cheque'.[11]

Still, for all the exasperation he would feel towards the Generalissimo, Roosevelt always ended up by regarding him as the figure round whom China might coalesce one day. To help the regime, he approved the establishment of a clandestine American outfit in China, independent of the OSS and of Stilwell. It was led by a naval officer, Milton Miles – known as 'Mary Miles' after a pre-war Broadway star. Under the innocent title of the Sino-American Cooperation Organisation (SACO), the group worked with Dai Li's secret police, supplying them with training and equipment which was meant to be used against the Japanese but was often directed against Chiang's domestic enemies. The operation would become a cause for controversy in later years, with Miles insisting that it was in the best patriotic interests of China and critics saying it supplied arms to a Gestapo. SACO operated from Dai Li's headquarters outside Chungking which also housed men from the OSS. Relations between the two American outfits deteriorated as the OSS became disenchanted with the Chinese police chief, seeing him as a hostile figure whose agents failed to carry out planned operations, spied on American officers, physically attacked them on occasion, used aid for their own purposes, and might even be passing information to the Japanese as the basis for post-war cooperation.[12]

The tension between Dai Li and the OSS was symptomatic of increasingly frayed relations between Americans and Chinese. Chiang himself did not much like his ally, and distrusted American motives. His feelings went wider than the irritating Joseph Stilwell. They were exacerbated by what was meant to be a goodwill mission in the summer of 1944 by a Marine general who, however, got drunk at a banquet given by Dai Li and laid out home truths about China, including criticism of Meiling, that would have been relayed to the Generalissimo.[13]

At the grassroots level, there was racism on both sides. Far away from the creature comforts of home, the Americans often saw the Chinese 'slopeys' as unwilling to fight and shot through with corruption – though the amounts of fuel that went missing from Chennault's bases made it clear that the local inhabitants were not the only ones diverting supplies to the black market.* Americans were shocked by the extent of the trading with the enemy which saw Japanese-made cars running on the streets of

---

* Barbara Tuchman, in her book on Stilwell, cites an estimated take of US$4 million by American personnel on the black market up to the end of 1944.

Chungking and medical aid sold by Nationalists to Japan. On the other hand, the drunkenness and demands for sex of Americans offended the Chinese. The US embassy reported that the 'better class of people' was taken aback by the rowdiness of the Westerners and the boorish manners and disreputable appearance of American fliers. Respectable Chinese women who walked in the streets of Chengdu with Americans found themselves being called prostitutes. An American officer and China expert, Oliver Caldwell, who had been born in the country and spoke the language fluently, wrote that he had never seen such racial prejudice from the Chinese as during the war, adding that it was frequently earned. After his experience in the OSS, Caldwell came to believe that the friction was being exploited and exacerbated by Nationalist figures like Dai Li who were anti-American and wanted to keep US influence to a minimum.[14]

Having been rebuffed over Burma after Cairo, Chiang decided to go ahead on his own, as if to shame his Western allies. He put Stilwell in charge of the Chinese troops trained in India, with power to order them to take the offensive. Vinegar Joe wasted no time. On 21 December 1943, he led his 50,000 men into the north of Burma, armed with the vermilion seal of command given to him by Chiang.

Apart from reversing the defeat of 1942, Stilwell was intent on showing that properly trained, supplied and led Chinese troops could perform as well as anybody. The US enjoyed air superiority by now, and food and ammunition were dropped to the troops as they advanced. American commandos, known as Merrill's Marauders from the name of their leader, Frank Merrill, harassed the Japanese on the flanks.[15]

The aim was to cross 200 miles of jungle, swamps and 6,000-foot mountains to take two strategic towns that would open the north-eastern route to China. The Y Force troops based in Yunnan would then move forward from the west to form a link. Leading the march over the terrible terrain, Stilwell slept in bamboo huts, tents and dugouts, washed with water in his helmet, ate C-rations from a mess kit and handed cigarettes to soldiers. For his sixty-first birthday in the jungle, Stilwell was presented with a cake inscribed 'Uncle Joe'.

On 7 March 1944, the first big objective was taken, a town called Maingkwan in a strategically important valley. Labour gangs and engineers moved in to work on a road and pipeline between India and China. But

Chiang did not want to risk the Y Force, under its new commander, 'Hundred Victories' Wei Lihuang, a veteran of the Northern Expedition who had scored one of the rare Nationalist successes against the Communists in Jiangxi a dozen years earlier. Rather than seeing these troops go into the jungle in Burma, the Generalissimo preferred to keep them in China where they could contain the autonomist ambitions of the Yunnanese governor, Long Yun. Roosevelt sent a cable saying he found it 'inconceivable' that Y Force had not gone into action – Stilwell's deputy handed it to Meiling and she may not have passed it her husband since she said he might react badly. Vinegar Joe flew to Chungking to press the case for Wei's army to be unleashed, and his deputy, General Hearn, warned He Yingqin that, unless it moved, its supplies would be stopped. The order was given – though the War Minister, naturally, insisted that the decision was an entirely Chinese matter.[16]

General Wei's men – with one of Stilwell's most trusted officers, Frank Dorn, as senior adviser – moved through precipitous river country in western Yunnan, aiming to push out Japanese who had occupied the area since 1942. Their target was the 5,000-foot deep Salween Gorge on the Burmese border, described by the Rockefeller Foundation as one of the three worst malaria areas in the world. Dorn reported that the officers were keen to fight. But they got bogged down in frontal battles and only advanced 20 miles in a month against fanatical resistance; in some cases, isolated Japanese units ate the bodies of their dead comrades. 'Generalship was atrocious, manpower was squandered. Ammunition wasted, and weapons misused and neglected,' the political officer, John Paton Davies, wrote later. The limits of Stilwell's training programme were cruelly exposed.[17]

In Burma, meanwhile, the X Force advanced on its next objective, a town called Myitkyina on the narrow gauge railway north from Mandalay. Vinegar Joe was feeling his age. After one climb, he wrote of himself: 'All out of shape. No wind, no legs. Swore off smoking then and there. Felt like an old man when I staggered in.' He dreamed of breakfast at his home in California, and the 'fancy eats' he would enjoy when the war was over.[18]

Frank Merrill had a heart attack, and his commandos suffered badly from disease and casualties. But Stilwell ordered them to press on through the jungle towards the target, observing radio silence. On 17 May 1944, the attack on Myitkyina began with the seizure of the airfield. Then there was a bad setback when two Chinese units mistook one another for the enemy and opened fire, causing heavy losses. Merrill's men were in rebellious mood after all they had undergone, and developed a deep hatred for the unrelenting Stilwell. The Japanese swiftly reorganised the defence under the general who had taken Singapore from the British. 'Rain, rain, rain, mud, mud, mud, typhus, malaria, dysentery, exhaustion, rotting feet, body sores,' Stilwell wrote. 'A knockdown and drag-out affair.' Despite his superior numbers and control of the air, the battle lasted for two months.

When Myitkyina finally fell, Stilwell was in Ceylon,* at the regional Allied headquarters where he had been summoned to fill in during Mountbatten's absence. He was promoted to be a four-star general, a rank he shared with only four other American officers. His view of Chiang was as harsh as ever. 'I believe the Peanut is going to pay dearly for being stupid and stubborn,' he wrote to his wife. 'The jackass had salvation offered to him free, and wouldn't take it. Now it's too late and he's screaming.' But the taking of Myitkyina and the progress of the Y Force, slow as it was, enabled the Chinese to link up as planned, and reopen the road for supplies to Yunnan.

By then, however, the Generalissimo had every reason to scream. In the spring of 1944, the Japanese launched their biggest single offensive of the war, Operation Ichigo. This was provoked primarily by the desire to choke off American bombing attacks on Japan from bases in eastern China – as Stilwell had foreseen, success in the air brought retaliation on the ground. But both he and Washington were taken completely by surprise, despite a warning from Chiang that Tokyo might try to exploit America's focus on Europe to 'liquidate the China affair'. Driving down to southern China, Ichigo had the second objective of creating a Japanese-controlled belt stretching from the north of Manchukuo to the border with Indo-China, and linking with the Imperial Army troops in Canton. Before the campaign began, the Japanese launched a propaganda blitz with pamphlets declaring that its enemy was not the Chinese but 'the white-faced demons'. Soldiers were told to stop ill-treating local people, and taught a marching song that proclaimed the kindness of their hearts.[19]

Reaching its height as the Allies were staging the D-Day landings in Normandy, Ichigo involved half a million men, with anywhere from 70,000

* Now Sri Lanka.

to 100,000 horses, 800 tanks and 12,000–15,000 vehicles. It began by sweeping across the Yellow River and into Henan province where Tang Enbo's troops crumbled – their commander was away at the time and his headquarters staff was surprised by the enemy while playing basketball. In three weeks, Chinese armies of 300,000 men were routed, with a kill ratio of forty Chinese to one Japanese. Three airbases and the key railway lines were soon taken. Chinese units fought one another for the spoils to be taken away. Peasants with crude weapons attacked the fleeing soldiers in revenge for their past exactions, in some cases burying them alive. Chiang refused to move troops blockading the Red Eighth Army to try to stop the enemy's advance. Typically, Chungking described the huge defeat in Henan as a 'defensive offensive'.[20]

Ichigo next rolled south from Wuhan into Hunan, crossing the Miluo River where Chiang's Revolutionary Army had fought Wu Peifu eighteen years earlier. The Generalissimo called on the troops in the province, under the Cantonese Xue Yue, to fight to the death. The battleground was described by Teddy White and his colleague, Annalee Jacoby, as 'the most ravaged of all the belts of no man's land in all the country'. Chennault's planes flew non-stop attack missions. The Chinese had beaten off three attacks on the provincial capital of Changsha since 1938, but the Generalissimo refused to send arms to Xue, whom he suspected of being in league with southern autonomists. The spirit behind the previous victories evaporated. By advancing on a 120-mile front, the Japanese sheltered their central force from flanking movements that had vanquished them in the past.

Raging arguments between Stilwell and Chennault disrupted the counter-offensive. The air force commander insisted that, with a little more supplies, his planes could halt the offensive. But Stilwell showed no interest in checking Ichigo which he viewed as proof of the fallacy of Chennault's theory that wars could be won in the air. His eyes were concentrated on Burma, not China. Relations between the two Americans plunged even further as Chennault came to believe that Vinegar Joe was taking a positive pleasure in seeing his predictions of doom come true. The airman wrote later that Stilwell's aides told him the general was deliberately scuttling positions in southern China as a gambit to force Chiang to grant him command of the Nationalist armies.

While the Japanese moved south through areas that had provided the

Nationalists with both grain supplies and army recruits, Chennault proposed throwing almost all the available planes into a massive attack on Wuhan to cut them off from their main base. According to Chennault's account, Stilwell stuffed the plan into his pocket and flew off to Burma from where he sent no response – the 'pocket veto' was one of his favourite ways of scuppering proposals he did not like.

However, the general's overall strategy in China was being undermined by his patron in Washington. When he sent a message to Washington re-stating his belief that, to achieve ultimate victory, the Imperial Army would have to be engaged in a great battle in China, George Marshall replied that, if possible, Japan should be beaten without such a confrontation. In June, new B-29 Superfortress bombers flew from the huge base at Chengdu to stage their first raid on Japan. They were not part of Chennault's command, but the strategic tilt was clearly in the direction he had always backed, and diametrically opposed to Vinegar Joe's dream of a campaign headed by Chinese infantrymen. With Washington demonstrating its faith in air power and focusing on the advance across the Pacific, China was pushed into the wings of the war as far as the United States was concerned.

This may not have been immediately apparent when Roosevelt dispatched the most eminent American to visit China during the war. Vice-President Henry Wallace travelled first to the Soviet Union, and then flew to Chungking for a four-day stay. Having been much impressed by what he saw in Russia, he pushed Chiang to work with the Chinese Communists. In reply, the Generalissimo insisted that they were far from being 'agrarian democrats' as the Americans imagined, and asked Washington to display 'aloofness' to them. Why, he wondered, did the United States keep pressing him to come to terms with the Communists, rather than pressing them to come to terms with the Nationalists? But he did agree to let American military observers go to Mao's headquarters in Yan'an so long as they travelled under government auspices.

Known as the Dixie Mission, since it was operating in rebel territory like a Unionist delegation in Confederate lands, the initial party consisted of eight military members, plus John Service from Stilwell's political staff. As soon as he arrived, Service began to file glowing reports, saying that Mao had no intention of creating a Soviet state, favoured real democracy and wanted an alliance with Kuomintang liberals and other parties to bring about reform of the central government. A press party which followed was equally impressed. Missing from all these reports was any mention of the four-year Rectification Campaign which the fifty-year-old Communist leader had launched to ensure that he and his doctrine, alone, dominated – complete with confession of their errors by leading figures and a purge of 'enemy agents', many of them innocent of anything worse than having relatives who belonged to the Kuomintang.

Seeing Wallace off on 24 June 1944, Chiang repeated his criticism of the Communists as untrustworthy, but said he would move towards democratic government if they fell into line with him. The left-leaning Vice-President, who had amazed his hosts at one point by insisting on pulling a rickshaw, did not believe him. Reporting to Roosevelt, he called the Generalissimo a 'short-term investment'. 'It is not believed that he has the intelligence or political strength to run post-war China,' Wallace added.

Militarily, China's performance was showing all its old weaknesses. As Operation Ichigo bore down on Changsha, troops under Xue Yue pulled out of the Hunan capital, hoping to be able to pummel the enemy from artillery positions in surrounding hills and attack them from the sides. But their guns were old and few. Unit commanders bickered. Collaborators moved easily through the hills to spy out Chinese positions, and carry out sabotage. Suspicious of Xue as a possible ally of opponents working to form a coalition to replace him, Chiang kept troops directly under his own control out of the fray, leaving the forces under the Cantonese general to bear the brunt of the fighting. Crossed wires and arguments with Chungking led to one army being trapped and destroyed. Chiang ordered the execution of several commanders. Then he told Xue to move west, towards Sichuan; instead, preferring to keep his independence, Xue headed south, and sent his crack Tenth Army to hold the city of Hengyang whose position made it the key to halting the enemy's advance.

At the end of June, the Japanese took the airbase at Hengyang, and enveloped the city. Elsewhere, the Nationalists would have melted away, but what Chennault called 'one of the truly great epics of the Sino-Japanese war' was about to unfold. As the air force commander could not refrain from remarking, Stilwell was far away conducting his campaign in Burma while the fate of southern China hung in the balance.

Ten thousand troops of the Tenth Army under the immediate command of a veteran of Taierzhuang barricaded themselves in pillboxes and in the grey brick houses of Hengyang. The Japanese vanguard was weakened by bombing and strafing raids, tiredness, food shortages and lack of ammunition as the American pilots of the Fourteenth Air Force halted their supply columns. Chennault put enemy losses at 210 planes, ninety of them caught on the ground in one raid. By coincidence, the cabinet in Tokyo fell, and the Imperial Army was being pushed off the strategic Pacific island of Saipan. According to Chennault, who had an obvious interest in picturing the summer of 1944 as a potential turning point, post-war interrogation of Japanese commanders showed that they were weighing the prospect of abandoning some positions in China to move forces to resist the US advance across the Pacific. However much truth there is in that, the battle of Hengyang stands as an indictment of the feuding and indecision that marked the war at the top – this time among the Americans as well as the Chinese.

The Japanese pulled back slightly in mid-July, setting off celebrations in Nationalist areas. Chiang still refused to send in supplies, but he did finally dispatch reinforcements to join forces preparing a flanking attack. The Chinese now had four times as many men as the Japanese in the Hengyang area. Though many suffered from malaria and subsisted on two bowls of rice a day, their spirit was 'absolutely amazing', an American intelligence officer reported. But, as so often, they were badly equipped, with, at best, bolt-operating rifles and few machine guns or heavy weapons. What Xue needed was weapons, not more sick men. 'It's not easy to fight with the guns I've got,' he remarked.[21]

Accompanying one unit to the front, Teddy White reported that only a third of the soldiers had a rifle. There were no vehicles, and just two antique French First World War artillery pieces. The soldiers were wiry, their yellow and brown uniforms threadbare, straw sandals on their feet and leaves on their heads for shade and camouflage. Before dawn one morning, they stormed the dug-in Japanese, but got nowhere. 'All that flesh and blood could do the Chinese soldiers were doing,' White wrote. 'They were walking up hills and dying in the sun but they had no support, no guns, no direction. They were doomed.'[22]

Despite issuing his usual constant instructions from Chungking, the Generalissimo never organised a major attack as the enemy sent in reinforcement with tanks, and set fire to the outskirts of the city. The air force was running short of fuel – at one point it was grounded for three days and was only saved from Japanese aerial attack by bad weather.

Desperately short of food and supplies, the defenders sent urgent radio messages for help. But, when pressed by Chennault and his own deputy in Chungking, Vinegar Joe replied that to drop supplies would 'set a precedent for further demands that could not be met'. It was, he added, all a matter for Chiang. Receiving a request from Xue for 1,000 tons of supplies, he was reported to have replied: 'Let them stew.' Chennault's American lieutenants took the initiative by dropping some rice, medical supplies and ammunition from planes that swooped down to 300 feet over the flaming city. But it was nothing like what the Tenth Army required. A final request by Chennault for 500 tons of weapons to be parachuted to other Chinese troops to make an attack to relieve the city was turned down by Stilwell's headquarters as a 'waste of effort'.[23]

On 7 August, the Tenth Army commander sent a radio message saying that the Japanese had entered the city. 'We are now in the midst of street fighting. Our men are all but wiped out,' it went on. 'This is my last message.' Hengyang fell the following day, after holding out for seven weeks. Three hundred of the defenders fought their way to join forces positioned only 2 miles east of the city. By then, Ichigo had destroyed half the good Central Army divisions engaged in Hunan. Stilwell may have been right in concluding that the Chinese would crumble sooner or later, but it is hard not to see Hengyang as a major missed opportunity.[24]

Xue was one of the best Nationalist generals; the Tenth Army fought with great determination; the Japanese were exposed to encirclement and flanking attacks. If Stilwell had wanted to force a key battle, he could have put together his control of supplies and the air superiority of Chennault's planes to equip the troops in the city and those poised to attack the Japanese from the side and the rear. The Fourteenth Air Force could then have attacked the enemy's line stretching back to Wuhan. Instead, Vinegar Joe chose to focus on the campaign in Burma, and to do nothing to aid the Chinese soldiers for whom he expressed such undying admiration. Hengyang would probably have been lost in the end in any case: the Japanese could have brought overwhelming force to bear. But protracted resistance would have held them up, weakened them elsewhere by sucking in troops from other parts of China, given more time to prepare the defence of airbases further south and put a question mark over the whole Ichigo campaign at a time when Japan badly needed the men tied down in China to meet the expected American assault on its homeland.

After a month's rest, the enemy resumed its southerly advance. Chiang ordered commanders who retreated without orders to be shot, but that did no good. The demoralisation of the previous years had eaten away at the fibre of his forces. The Nationalists had been so hard hit that he could put only 60,000–70,000 men into the field as the Japanese entered Guangxi province, housing the big American airbase and military training centre at Guilin. Chaos and panic spread, with the familiar hordes of refugees clinging to trains or fleeing on foot. Railway stations closed their ticket windows, and operated a black market at the back for those who could pay over the odds. Several hundred people were killed in Guilin station when a locomotive ploughed into a crowd on the tracks. Freight cars were fitted with several layers of steel to provide floors so that they could carry more paying passengers. Soldiers would charge steep prices to let people board trains which would steam a few miles; then they would stop; the passengers would be forced off at gunpoint, and the trains would go back for another load.[25]

The Imperial Army's advance took place against the backdrop of political and military in-fighting in Chungking that brought the Generalissimo's running conflict with Joseph Stilwell to a head. On the one hand, the two men were confronted with the severing of China by the belt the Japanese established from the far north to the far south – and their inability to do anything to prevent it. On the other, they were engaged in a bitter, and unique, struggle for power. At the heart of their contest was the simple question of whether Chiang Kai-shek would continue to rule Nationalist China, or whether the country would follow the path laid out by Stilwell, Marshall and the War Department in Washington.

One key figure from the intrigues that had swirled round Stilwell the previous year was missing. The strains in the Generalissimo's relations with his wife had reached crisis point. Her behaviour on her American trip and then at Cairo had offended his notions of a wife's proper place. For all her social status and ability to charm English-speaking notables, it was he, not she, who was the ruler. His American adviser, Owen Lattimore, had observed what he termed 'a lack of total confidence between Chiang and Madame Chiang', and noted how the Generalissimo kept discussion of serious matters until after she had gone to bed.[26]

The marriage was put under increased stress by her ambitions for the relationship with Wendell Willkie and by continuing rumours about

Chiang conducting affairs – one official told Lattimore that his job was to supply young ladies to the Generalissimo. In the summer of 1944, an extraordinary tea party was held at the Chiang residence for foreigners, particularly journalists. 'Of late rumours about my private life have been in circulation,' the Nationalist leader told the guests. 'One says that I have secretly kept a woman last year. Another says that there has been an illicit relationship between myself and a nurse and the latter has given birth to a child.' He denied it all, and said the rumours jeopardised the future of the revolution given the importance of his moral example. Getting up from her chair, Meiling added: 'I wish to state that never for a moment did I stoop or demean myself to entertain doubts of his uprightness.'

The text of Chiang's statement was made generally available by the government information office. Naturally, the fact that he felt the need to speak publicly only fuelled the rumours. Meiling's illnesses were also causing her a major problem – she pulled down her stockings to show one American visitor the marks of a skin disease on her legs.[27]

It was time for her to make another trip to the Western hemisphere. She hoped to score another triumph in the United States, but went first with her eldest sister to Brazil. There she rested while, according to a US National Security Agency document obtained by the author Sterling Seagrave for his book on the Soong Dynasty, Ailing had business talks with the Brazilian ruler about investing part of the family fortune in a safer place than China. Meiling then travelled to New York to be treated for nervous exhaustion for a month in the Harkness Pavillion. After that, she moved to the Kungs' house in Riverdale, outside the city.

Her reception in the US was a far cry from that of the previous year. Hopes of a geopolitical partnership with Wendell Willkie collapsed when the Republican failed to gain the nomination to face Roosevelt, and then died suddenly in October 1944. Though Chungking still had its fervent supporters in the United States, its failure to live up to the bright vision she had painted on her first trip dulled her appeal. And the trip meant she was far from Chungking as Chiang and Stilwell came to grips.

While Ichigo pushed forward, Roosevelt urged the Generalissimo to give Stilwell full responsibility and authority for coordination and direction of operations against the Japanese. 'I feel that the case of China is so desperate that if radical and properly applied remedies are not immediatcly effected, our common cause will suffer a serious setback,' the

President had added. 'The future of all Asia is at stake along with the tremendous effort which America has expended in that region.'[28]

To follow up that message, Roosevelt sent two emissaries to China – Patrick Hurley, a former Republican Secretary for War, and a businessman, Donald Nelson. While Nelson was to look at China's economic prospects, Hurley's brief was to get Chiang to commit himself to expanding Stilwell's authority, and to bring the Communists under the American's command with Lend-Lease supplies going to Yan'an. Stilwell had a visit from two Communist emissaries who said their forces would fight for him, but not under Chiang. Vinegar Joe replied that he hoped to visit Yan'an. Egged on by Marshall, Roosevelt said in one message to Chiang that it seemed 'unsound to refuse the aid of anyone who will kill Japanese'. When Stilwell wrote of moving troops from the north to fight Ichigo, he appears to have been thinking not only of the Nationalists blockading the Red Army there, but also of using the Communists.

Chiang had himself put on a show of reasonableness the previous spring by authorising talks with the Communists which lasted for all of four days, and made the gulf between the two sides evident. The Kuomintang team did no more than to re-state Chiang's position that the base areas and the Red Army must be put under his control. The Communists insisted on being recognised as a legal party, and on a 'democratic form of government' being introduced. The KMT said both would have to wait until the war ended. The Communists wanted to be authorised sixteen divisions – the Nationalists offered to let them keep ten. The Generalissimo saw no reason to give ground. The blockade of the main Red base area was proving quite effective, and the Japanese Three Alls campaign had hurt the Communists badly.

Though he was concerned by Stilwell's desire to work with the Red Army and by Wallace's enthusiasm for the united front, it was over strategy in south-western China and then over Burma that Chiang found himself at loggerheads with the Americans in the early autumn of 1944. The Generalissimo wanted Guilin to be defended to the last. Flying south for an on-the-spot inspection, Stilwell concluded that it would be 'another rat trap'. Commenting on the calls for arms and supplies to be sent in, Vinegar Joe had another solution, writing in his diary: 'What they ought to do is to shoot the G-mo and Ho [He Yingqin] and the rest of the gang.' He ordered the Americans to pull out of Guilin – as they went, the prostitutes hung out signs: 'So long, buddies, and good luck.' Then Stilwell drew up what was called a 'flexible, manoeuvring strategy' for the Chinese defenders – in practice what this meant was abandoning the city. After some resistance, Chiang accepted this. But he recorded how affected he was by the loss.[29]

When Stilwell got back to Chungking, the Generalissimo told him that he wanted the US-trained Y Force to return from Burma to defend Yunnan and its capital of Kunming. This threw the American into a fury; in his diary, he referred to Chiang as 'the crazy little bastard [with] that hickory nut he uses for a head . . . Usual cockeyed reasons and idiotic tactical and strategic conceptions. He is impossible.'

Stilwell promptly informed his boss, George Marshall, who was at an Anglo-American summit in Quebec and passed the news to Roosevelt and Churchill. From the Generalissimo's viewpoint, defending Kunming was much more important than linking up with Stilwell's troops in Burma. But, for the Allies, his attitude could only be a fresh irritation. The main point of the Burma operation had been to open up China's land supply line, and the Americans had trained Y Force for that purpose; now Chiang was proposing to withdraw them. Given the success of Operation Ichigo, they might be lost in Yunnan, and the Japanese would then be able to counter-attack into Burma from China. The war was going well for the Allies in both Europe and the Pacific; only China and its ruler stood out as losers who went on causing complications.

In that context, Marshall had no trouble getting Roosevelt to put his name to a message to Chiang which must be unique as a communication from one Allied president to another. 'I have urged time and again in recent months that you take drastic action to resist the disaster which has been moving closer to China and to you,' it read. 'Now, when you have not yet placed General Stilwell in command of all forces in China, we are faced with the loss of a critical area . . . with possible catastrophic consequences.' Noting that the fall of the Guilin base threatened the Hump airborne supply route, Roosevelt called for 'drastic and immediate action' to avoid military disaster, and – contrary to Chiang's desire – for Y Force to be reinforced in Burma. Stilwell must be given 'unrestricted command of all your forces', the message stipulated, adding a none-too-subtle reference to American aid.

The deeply antagonistic Claire Chennault later charged that Stilwell had been working since the summer for a final showdown, and had withheld supplies to engineer a situation where Chiang would have to cede command of his armies. In his memoirs, the airman wrote that, when he asked for help for the defenders at Hengyang, he had been told by the general's staff that Stilwell was working on a piece of 'real face losing' – presumably for the Generalissimo – and that help should be refused 'until things precipitate a bit more'.

An entry in the general's diary suggests that such thoughts were not far from his mind at the time. If the crisis in China was 'just sufficient to get rid of the Peanut without entirely wrecking the ship,' he wrote, 'it would be worth it.' He contrasted the Nationalist 'cesspool' and its 'corruption, neglect, chaos . . . hoarding, black market, trading with enemy' with 'Communist program . . . Reduce taxes, rents, interest. Raise production, and standard of living. Participate in government. Practice what they preach.' To reform Chiang's system, it must be 'torn to bits' and the Generalissimo had to go.[30]

Stilwell's frame of mind ran counter to Patrick Hurley's attempt to craft an agreement that Chiang could accept. Later, as he swung to the far right and denounced Americans who had 'lost' China, Hurley maintained that he had been making good progress in talks with T. V. Soong. When Stilwell showed him the message from Roosevelt, he said he feared that the tough language would so annoy the Generalissimo that he would veto any accord. According to Claire Chennault, Stilwell agreed to delay pending the outcome of talks at Chiang's home which he did not attend. But, as these discussions were going on, the general arrived, and asked Hurley to step outside where he said he felt he could not hold back Roosevelt's message.[31]

The two men went back inside. Stilwell accepted a cup of tea, and waited for a few minutes, savouring what was to follow. Then he announced that he had come to deliver a message from his President. Hurley interrupted to ask if there was a Chinese translation that Chiang would be able to read, rather than hearing its contents from an interpreter while Stilwell watched his reaction. The general said he did have a Chinese version.

'I handed this bundle of paprika to the Peanut and then sank back with a sigh,' Stilwell recorded in his diary. 'The harpoon hit the little bugger right in the solar plexus, and went right through him. It was a clean hit, but beyond turning green and losing the power of speech, he did not bat an eye.' When he had finished reading, Chiang said simply, 'I understand,' and sat in silence, jiggling one foot. Then he put the lid on his cup. 'That gesture still means, I presume, that the party is over,' Stilwell said. After he had left, the Generalissimo exploded.

Going back across the river that night, the American noted the 'pretty sight . . . Lights all on in Chungking'. The next day, he wrote in his diary, 'The dope is that after I left the screaming began and lasted into the night.' In a letter to his wife, he wrote a few doggerel verses:

> I've waited long for vengeance –
> At last I've had my chance.
> I've looked the Peanut in the eye
> And kicked him in the pants . . .
> The little bastard shivered,
> And lost the power of speech.
> His face turned green and quivered
> As he struggled not to screech . . .
> I know I've still to suffer,
> And run a weary race,
> But oh! the blessed pleasure!
> I've wrecked the Peanut's face.

Roosevelt's message may have seemed the right thing to the straight-ahead Marshall, but it lacked the essential political follow-through. The Americans had no alternative to the Nationalist chief. They had rebuffed approaches from the anti-Chiang coalition formed by southern generals and the Democratic League. For all their interest in Yan'an, they were not ready to ally with the Communists and ditch the Nationalists. Unless the President was ready for America to take over effective control of China, or halt Lend-Lease supplies and abandon the KMT to its fate, his stern words merely amounted to bluff. In her biography of Stilwell, Barbara Tuchman suggests that the seriously ill Roosevelt was past caring about Chiang's dignity 'or else signed Marshall's message with little attention, which amounts to the same thing'. Defeating Germany, dealing with Stalin and beating Japan were what mattered – not a deeply irritating game in a fog-shrouded city few Americans had heard of. For all his doggerel jubilation, the President's message would seal Stilwell's fate.[32]

Calling the letter 'the greatest humiliation I have been subjected to in my life', Chiang noted that it was 'all too obvious that the United States intends to intervene in China's internal affairs'. Drawing a careful distinction between Vinegar Joe and the broader question of Sino-American cooperation, he told Hurley that the Chinese were 'tired of the insults which Stilwell has seen fit to heap upon them'. In his response to Roosevelt he said that, while he would accept an American as commander-in-chief, the general was unfitted. 'Almost from the moment of his arrival in China, he showed his disregard for the mutual confidence and respect which are essential to the successful collaboration of allied forces,' the Generalissimo added.[33]

At the beginning of October, Chiang was emboldened by a message from H. H. Kung in Washington who quoted Roosevelt's close aide, Harry Hopkins as having said that the President would agree to replace Stilwell if the Generalissimo insisted. Hopkins later claimed he had been misquoted, but Stilwell wrote in his diary, 'FDR proceeds to cut my throat and throw me out'. At a meeting of the Central Executive Committee of the Kuomintang, Chiang pounded the table as he called for the general's dismissal. To agree to Roosevelt's proposal, he added, would be to accept a new form of imperialism, making him no better than Wang Jingwei and the collaborationists in Nanking. If the Americans withdrew support, the regime could survive in the four western provinces. News of his speech was leaked so that the American embassy could relay it to Washington as a sign of his intent.[34]

On the night of 12 October, Hurley could not get to sleep, knowing he had to make a decision. At 2 a.m., he called his secretary and dictated the draft of a message to Roosevelt recommending Stilwell's recall. The general was 'a fine man', he said, 'but was incapable of understanding or co-operating with Chiang Kai-shek'. If he stayed, China might be lost. Before sending the cable in the morning, Hurley showed it to Stilwell who likened it to 'cutting my throat with a dull knife'. Suffering from a cold and sore throat, he still hoped that Marshall would prevail with the President.[35]

But Roosevelt refused to send another sharp message drafted by the US Chief of Staff. Instead, he told Stilwell to ask Chiang for the names of three American generals he would accept as replacements. Knowing he was winning, the Generalissimo sent a cable to Washington saying that, as head of state and supreme commander, there could be no question of his right to demand the recall of an officer in whom he did not have confidence – enlarging the issue to one of his prerogatives as President and of China's sovereignty which Roosevelt could hardly gainsay. On 19 October the

AXE FELL, as Stilwell put it in capital letters in his diary. Marshall sent a radio message recalling him. Albert Wedemeyer, a smooth operator who had spent time at the German staff college and then become a skilful desk general, would go to Chungking as the Generalissimo's Chief of Staff and commander of US forces. He was one of the generals Chiang had asked for.

A minor Chinese official arrived at Stilwell's office with an offer from Chiang of a high Chinese decoration, the Special Cordon of the Blue Sky and White Sun. The American sent back an officer of equivalent rank with his refusal. He saw Qingling, who cried. At a last meeting, the Generalissimo insisted on how much he regretted what had happened, and put it down to their different make-ups. As Chiang accompanied him to the door, Stilwell quoted the Chinese motto, *Zuihou Shengli* (Ultimate Victory). He wrote to his wife of 'hanging up my shovel and bidding farewell to as merry a nest of gangsters as you'll meet in a long day's march'. Chiang blamed the whole affair on Communist manipulation; eleven years later, he wrote that his heart still ached over his failure to have confided his knowledge of their schemes to the American.[36]

One of the last Americans to see Vinegar Joe in Chungking recalled him saying: 'God help my successor.' Accompanied by Hurley and T. V. Soong, he went to the airstrip on the sandbank in the Yangtze. At the last moment, General He drove up and stepped onto the tarmac to salute. Stilwell returned the gesture, and then asked, 'What are we waiting for?' His desire to leave and his self-absorption were so strong that he could not stay in Chungking for just one day to brief Wedemeyer. Instead, he flew to Kunming, where he had dinner and attended an American touring variety show. Then he went to Karachi – 'felt like hell', he recorded. The next day he set off for the United States, where he was told to say nothing about what had happened; 'Not a word – this is dynamite,' Marshall advised. But the story came out through the *New York Times* whose correspondent Stilwell had called in before flying home.[37]

When the road to China from India through Burma was opened the following year, Chiang decided to name it the 'Stilwell Road' but Vinegar Joe was not invited back for the occasion.* Instead, he was named to

---

* The road was abandoned in October 1945. In 2002, north Indian states pressed for it to be reopened to boost trade, but the government rejected the idea on security grounds. (*Mizzima News*, Dec. 5, 2002)

command the US Tenth Army in Okinawa – the Japanese surrender came before he could see action. When he wanted to visit friends in northern China, the Generalissimo refused to give authorisation. Owen Lattimore, who called on him in Washington, recorded Stilwell as saying that he would be proud to shoulder a rifle in the Red Army. He died in his sleep on 12 October 1946; stomach cancer had affected his liver. The Generalissimo attended a memorial service in Nanking, and extended posthumous honours.[38]

For Chiang loyalists and the right-wing China Lobby in the United States, Stilwell helped to open the door to Communism. The more generally accepted view portrayed him as an authentic American hero, a fearless soldier whose drive to introduce vitally needed reforms had been baulked by a reactionary, corrupt regime. Both verdicts are flawed. Had he been able to achieve what he wanted, Vinegar Joe would have left the Nationalists in far better shape to fight the impending civil war. While he was in Chungking, Yan'an got no American supplies. Their rise to power had nothing to do with him.

As to his heroic status, there is no denying his courage and awareness of what was wrong in China. The American media and government adroitly spun the Stilwell story after his return – Roosevelt personally authorised the publication of the account the general had given to the *New York Times* which heaped all the blame on Chiang and served an obvious political purpose for the President in his 1944 re-election campaign. Teddy White of *Time* then engineered the canonisation of Vinegar Joe with the publication of his diaries in a process that culminated in Barbara Tuchman's Pulitzer Prize-winning biography published in 1970. But Stilwell's record in the field hardly marked him out as a great commander while, in military politics, he failed to do the job he had been sent to perform, and could not push through the wider changes he proposed to Chiang. His insistence on being at the jungle front in 1944 can be seen as a massive displacement exercise to escape from his main task, just as walking out from Burma to India in 1942 was an attempt to prove himself through individual effort, regardless of the consequences for the army he was meant to be leading. He exhausted his President's patience, and his honesty and principles too often appeared as priggish self-satisfaction. In his alliance with Ailing and Meiling, he blocked the best hopes of reform in China in 1943, strengthening, albeit inadvertently, forces he wished to overturn. He then failed to appreciate the impact of Operation Ichigo, and refused to help the Chinese when they needed it most.

Fundamentally, what Stilwell wanted to achieve and the way he wanted to achieve it were impossible, requiring the ditching of Chiang's regime and the imposition of a neocolonialism that would have made a mockery of the declared American commitment to democracy and national freedom. Vinegar Joe was the wrong man at the wrong time, and his Peanut emerged once more as the immediate winner, ensuring that America was tied even more closely to his cause, but with an accumulated backlog of bad feeling which could only colour post-war relations.

While the last act of the Stilwell drama was being played out, Operation Ichigo rolled on, taking the Guangxi capital of Nanning. But provincial forces under General Bai put up a good enough defence to dissuade the Japanese from going any further, and they abandoned the city after setting it on fire. Other enemy units turned north towards Sichuan and Chungking, moving to a mountain town called Dushan where they halted. As if forewarned, the defenders did not bother to dig into a stockpile of 50,000 tons of military supplies there. Instead, Americans moved in to blow it up to prevent it falling into enemy hands.

There were good reasons for the Japanese to stop. Ahead were the heights of Sichuan. Their lines were much extended. They did not have winter uniforms. The aim of Ichigo had been to strike to the south-west, not to become involved in a war in the mountains. But it was intriguing that Dushan had been mentioned six months earlier in a rumour that Chiang had reached a secret agreement with the enemy. This was said to provide for a rectangular safe zone round Chungking; Dushan lay on its southern limit. In return for the line not being crossed, it was said, the Generalissimo would wind down resistance elsewhere, and promised to protect Japanese and collaborators after the war. When an American raised the matter with him, the Generalissimo neither denied nor confirmed it – 'his spontaneous reaction was a dry cackle', his visitor recorded.[39]

Chiang had indulged in several flirtations with the enemy in the past, and the lines of communication with both Tokyo and the collaborationist regime in Nanking had never been closed down. Some Americans suspected that Dai Li was passing information to the enemy in return for an assurance of their help in handing over occupied areas to the

Nationalists when the war ended; on the only occasion the police chief's agents were allowed to attend a briefing before a bombing raid on Japan, fighters were waiting to meet the US planes. A former Kuomintang official who had gone to work with the collaborationists in Nanking tried to produce an agreement in 1944–45, with some backing from Tokyo. This came to nothing – given the American advance in the Pacific, Chiang had no interest in a formal pact. But his stance on post-war arrangements in Japan at the Cairo conference certainly indicated that he was ready to be understanding towards the enemy of the skin. By conserving his remaining forces and their American supplies, he would be in a stronger position for the coming confrontation with Mao. Chinese collaborators would be useful allies in that struggle – in all but the most flagrant cases, their past behaviour could be overlooked in the interests of bolstering the Nationalist position in occupied areas. A later Communist historian even claimed that Chiang had ordered Nationalist troops to defect to puppet administrations so that they could be preserved to fight later against the Red Army.[40]

The Generalissimo certainly needed to conserve strength for the future. Alone of the Allies, Nationalist China was ending the Second World War weaker militarily than ever. Hundreds of thousands of soldiers had been lost to Ichigo. The regime's already thin industrial base was weakened when the enemy overran areas to which factories had moved in the late 1930s. Tax revenue fell even further. National morale and the attachment felt by civilians to the government had plummeted.

To try to put new life into the administration, President Chiang called in the brother-in-law he had banished the previous year. Like a defeated warlord, T. V. Soong could now be brought back into the tent, his loss of face and his anxiety to ingratiate himself acting as a brake on the threat he posed. While T.V. cut an impressive figure in Washington and London, his position in China was much weaker than it appeared to those impressed by his Westernised mind and brainpower. He might be the man best equipped to run the country, but his support came from a thin layer of businessmen and officials. His lack of army experience meant he was incapable of leading an essentially military state. He had no power base in the KMT party. He was, in the words of the diplomat, John Paton Davies, against whom he intrigued, 'acute rather than wise, tricky rather than deft, arrogant rather than poised, alien rather than persuasively different'. The only way he could regain his previous political eminence was through the exercise of his brother-in-law's favour.[41]

Unlike the family struggle of the previous year, T.V. did not have to worry about his sisters. Far away in the United States, Meiling was unable to intervene, and the Kungs' status had been dented by a series of allegations of graft, diverting American loan funds and taking commissions on the purchase of planes. Their reputation sank further when reports spread of the crash-landing of an aircraft carrying the trousseau for the New York wedding of their elder daughter, Rosamund – the finery had been sewn by the Women's Work Department set up by Meiling to make clothes for soldiers. The Kungs' profiteering was common knowledge; after more than seven years of war and privation, they had become the unacceptable face of the regime. Despite censorship, a newspaper was able to comment that the cost of flying Rosamund's trousseau to America would have fed thousands of refugees, and that the labour at the Women's Work Department could have made uniforms for a regiment. As for the price of the wedding, that would have endowed a university.[42]

Appointed Acting President of the Executive Yuan – prime minister to Chiang's president – T.V. immediately shook things up. Though suffering from recurrent stomach trouble, he worked late into the night, insisting on fast and more effective decision-taking. H. H. Kung was replaced as Finance Minister by a former Mayor of Shanghai reputed to be efficient and honest. The reform-minded Chen Cheng became War Minister, though Chiang kept General He as Chinese Chief of Staff. The new American commander, Wedemeyer, set to work to improve the army, using diplomacy to achieve results – though fans of Stilwell would dismiss him as a general more adept at playing politics than at fighting.

In the face of a massive Japanese offensive, military, political and economic weakness, and a presidential-level battle with the United States, Chiang had survived once again. But, as always since his rise to power in Canton two decades earlier, survival was never more than a temporary achievement. As the Imperial Army started to wind down Operation Ichigo and the Americans advanced across the Philippine Sea towards Japan, it was time to focus on the post-war shape of the country the Generalissimo aspired finally to unite under his rule as one of the Big Four powers of the world.

PART V

THE LONG GOODBYE

Yan'an, Shaanxi Province, November 1944

———

Sun Moon Lake, Taiwan, December 1949

CHAPTER 24

Red Leaves

THREE WEEKS AFTER Joseph Stilwell was recalled, the man who had drawn the blunt knife across his throat flew over the seemingly endless hills of Shaanxi province towards a settlement built into the caves of the loess soil. Normally, the weekly US plane to the Dixie Mission at Communist headquarters in Yan'an carried only its crew and supplies. On 7 November 1944, it bore an improbable figure bent on bringing unity to China.

Tall, with a curling moustache and a carefully combed mane of white hair, Patrick Hurley had been born in a log cabin in Oklahoma. He followed a classic rags-to-riches career, working in coal mines and as a cowboy before making money and connections as a lawyer. In the army in the First World War, he put members of the Choctaw tribe at either end of telephone lines to baffle German code-breakers. As a politician, he rose to be Secretary of War under President Herbert Hoover, acquiring the rank of general, a title by which he liked to be addressed. He wore banks of medals when he put on his uniform, and used the royal 'we'. 'His handsome aquiline head suggested a Roman bust capriciously pasted up with butterflies of a huge bow tie, pinch-nose glasses, curly white moustache and coiffure,' the American information officer, Graham Peck, wrote.[1]

Roosevelt had enrolled Hurley as a tame Republican. Since he had nothing to do, the President sent him on the mission to back up Stilwell which ended up with the envoy taking the opposite tack. On the way to Chungking, Hurley had called at Moscow for a visit during which the Foreign Minister, Molotov, assured him that Mao and his comrades were not real Communists, and that the Soviet government was not associated with them – similarly, Stalin told the US ambassador in Moscow that Mao and his colleagues were just 'margarine Communists'. Flattered by information from such a high source, Hurley took it as his guiding light, alongside his belief that Chiang could be committed to introducing democracy.

When the crotchety career diplomat Clarence Gauss retired in the autumn of 1944, Hurley was appointed to succeed him as American ambassador to China. He ordered a new Cadillac, and had the ambassadorial residence redecorated. He believed that, in return for the removal of Stilwell, Chiang had agreed to try to reach an agreement with the Communists, and he saw a chance for glory in bringing together the Generalissimo and Mao.[2]

American policy towards China was in a mess, backing Chiang but also trying to get him to collaborate with his domestic enemy in the cause of national unity. Washington blew hot and cold, pressing the Generalissimo to make reforms but recalling Stilwell. As Germany's defeat loomed, attention was focused on Europe, and the advance towards Japan dominated thinking about the Pacific. Formulation of political policy in China was left much to Patrick Hurley, who was manifestly as far out of his depth as he was convinced of his ability to work miracles. He knew nothing of the country, pronounced Mao Zedong's name as Moose Dung, and called Chiang 'Mr Shek'. The American adviser, Arthur Young, saw 'a senile old man who couldn't keep his mind on any subject'. An American journalist who visited the ambassador for lunch recalled that they spent three hours drinking before sitting down to eat. When he invited the American information officer, Graham Peck, to dinner, Hurley forgot who his guest was. At a banquet for prominent Chinese figures, he toasted the journalist, Annalee Jacoby, as 'the most important person in the world, my tall, blonde goddess of a bride', rambling on about their children, the joy she had given him and their wedding night. Far from being a blonde goddess, Jacoby was a short brunette – and was certainly not Mrs Hurley.[3]

The ambassador had an unquenchable belief in his own abilities which helped the Generalissimo to play him like a fish, letting out enough line to encourage him to get the hook ever more deeply embedded in his jaws as he sought his rendezvous with history. Authorising Hurley's trip to Yan'an was a risk since it implied a degree of recognition, but, having got rid of Stilwell, Chiang was ready to show a conciliatory face. The Generalissimo could calculate that the Good Ole Boy from Oklahoma would end up by falling out with the Communist ideologues. To keep his finger on the pulse of the mission, however, he ensured that he conferred with Hurley before the envoy set out, so that the proposals the ambassador took with him expressed Chiang's views.

Zhou Enlai and the Dixie Mission chief, Colonel David Barrett, a stout China veteran, were at the airfield waiting for the supply plane. When the elegantly uniformed ambassador walked down the steps, Zhou hurried off to summon Mao. The Communist leader raced to the airfield in a Chevrolet ambulance he used for transport – it had been donated by the New York Chinese Laundrymen's National Salvation Association, as a sign on its side proclaimed. As Mao, Zhou and the army commander, Zhu De, came from their vehicle to meet him, Hurley yelled his favourite greeting, an American Indian war cry of 'Yahoo!' He and Barrett got into the ambulance to ride back to Yan'an with Mao, rattling over the potholes and bumps in the road in a cloud of dust.[4]

With the colonel, a fluent Chinese speaker, acting as interpreter, the ambassador from Oklahoma and the revolutionary from Hunan exchanged stories about their rural boyhoods. Barrett recalled that interpretation was not easy 'due to the saltiness of the General's remarks, and the unusual language in which he expressed himself. His discourse, in addition, was by no means connected by any readily discernible pattern of thought'. That night, Hurley attended a huge banquet for the anniversary of the Russian revolution, disrupting the proceedings with yells of 'Yahoo!'[5]

The main Communist base region had evolved from the original haven round Yan'an into an area of some 135,000 square miles which was run without reference to the Nationalists. Its two main military units – the Eighth Route Army and the reconstituted Fourth Army – numbered half a million men plus auxiliaries: a massive recruiting drive would double the size of the armies by the following spring. In addition, the Communist militias were 2 million strong. Chiang was as much the enemy as the Japanese. Slogans denouncing the Kuomintang decorated walls while Mao tightened his grip on power and prepared for the post-war struggle, hoping the Americans would need the Communists to fight the Japanese and would provide weapons and political support in return.

Like the Long March, the cave town of Yan'an, with a pagoda as its main landmark, became a sacred reference point as the place where the ideology and practices of Maoism were finally forged. Since history belongs to the winners, the Communists were depicted as the only true resisters to the Japanese as they rallied China's peasants to a nationalist revival and met the rigours of wartime by a self-denying production campaign. Under the quasi-divine leadership of the Great Helmsman, the eventual victory of the revolution was seen as an inevitable process which, whatever obstacles it encountered, could be subject to no second-guessing while it drew on the legacy of resistance as a badge of legitimacy.

The Communist hosts had gone out of their way to make a favourable impression on the Dixie Mission. The Americans were offered political discussions, reports of resistance to the Japanese and tours of model rural developments. The dedicated, clean-living Communists appeared eminently reasonable, removing anti-Kuomintang slogans in areas the visitors toured so as to avoid raising doubts about their allegiance to the united front. Puffing on Camel cigarettes in his armchair, Mao showed his emollient face; if agreement could be reached, he declared, Chiang would 'naturally' continue as President, and the Communists would not overthrow the Kuomintang or confiscate land. There were dances and long nights fuelled by Haig & Haig and Johnny Walker flown in by the Americans.[6]

The political adviser, John Service, compared the progressive ways of Yan'an with the 'enthronement of reaction' in Chungking, and called for an end to Washington's unilateral support for the Generalissimo. In talks with the political officer, John Paton Davies, Mao undertook to collaborate fully if US forces landed in eastern China, provided the force was big enough and brought the Communists supplies. Davies forecast that 'Chiang's feudal China cannot long coexist alongside a modern dynamic popular government in north China'.[7]

The reality which the Americans missed was noted by the contemporary diaries of a Soviet emissary, Petr Parfenovich Vladimirov. Unlike Western sympathisers whose writings dominate non-Chinese accounts of the time, Vladimirov was an unquestioning Communist, though, as a patriot, he was alienated by what he saw as Mao's 'organic dislike' of the Soviet Union. This colours his broader ideological verdicts, but, as reportage of what was going on in Yan'an, his diaries leave no doubt about the need for serious revision of the picture propagated after the Communist victory. This cannot be taken as a vindication of Chiang's regime vis-à-vis his major foe, but it does show that, as so often during the Generalissimo's life, the black-and-white picture of events which became conventional wisdom after his defeat in 1949 should be shaded in grey.*

In 1940–41, the failure of the Hundred Regiments Offensive and the attack on the New Fourth Army had cost the Communists dear. The Japanese Three Alls campaign had dealt a substantial blow to the base. As a result, Vladimirov noted in 1942, the Red Armies 'have long been abstaining from both active and passive action against the aggressors'. Another Russian returning from a visit along several hundred miles of the front line reported seeing no Communist troops – when he asked about this, he was told they were hidden by camouflage. In January 1943, Vladimirov wrote that the Communist armies had been 'strictly ordered not to undertake any vigorous operations or actions against the Japanese . . . down to retreating under an attack and seeking, if possible, a truce'. Soldiers in one unit of the Eighth Route Army told him they had been instructed not to touch the enemy for fear of Japanese reinforcements being brought in. Like Chiang's space for time strategy, and knowing he could not liquidate the invaders, Mao was ready to cede ground to preserve the size of his forces for the reckoning to come.

An American mission that went to Hebei province, south of Beijing, in the spring of 1945 bore this out, reporting that the amount of fighting done by the Eighth Route Army there had been 'grossly exaggerated'. Vladimirov reckoned that 'the years of inactivity have had a degrading influence on the armed forces of the CCP. Discipline is slack and cases of desertion have become more frequent. The men neglect their weapons. Training in the units and in staffs is not organised. Cooperation between the units is not organised.'[8]

In some areas, an American team noted, Communists had non-aggression understandings with collaborationist forces, which they

---

* Vladimirov, whose diaries have rarely been quoted, later served as Consul General in Shanghai and became ambassador to Burma before dying in 1953.

infiltrated with the aim of winning them over when the war ended.
Vladimirov saw a telegram from a Communist army making it 'absolutely
clear that there is a permanent contact between the Communist Party
leadership and the Supreme Command of the Japanese Expeditionary
Force'. This contact 'had been established long ago under great secrecy'.
A liaison officer appointed by Mao was attached to the Japanese general
staff in Nanking, moving freely between the enemy command and the
Fourth Route Army. Other sources make plain that there were also contacts
in Shanghai between leaders of the Communist underground and the
collaborationist authorities. In some of the areas where the Red Armies
faced Nationalists or Japanese troops, trade went across the lines with the
Communists buying arms and supplies from their enemies in return for
exports of salt, wool and cattle.[9]

The long-accepted account of the economic survival of the base area
puts this down to a huge productive effort fuelled by devotion and self-
sacrifice. The areas under Communist control were mostly poor and short
of natural resources. On one trip out of Yan'an, Vladimirov was astounded
by the poverty of peasants who offered their sisters or daughters for a tiny
portion of rice. Disease was rife. Local commanders imposed their own
taxes.[10]

In the hard era of 1942–43, food prices rose steeply and quotas of
produce which peasants were required to deliver to the Communists were
increased. Inflation rose. Following the example of H. H. Kung, the
printing presses were used to provide the regime with more cash, which
devalued the base area currency. A talk with a member of the leadership
left Vladimirov in no doubt about the critical nature of the economic and
financial situation. The campaign to boost production and impose frugality
was not enough. Another means of finance was needed to sustain the
regime economically and give it funds to buy military equipment.[11]

During the Long March, the Communists had seized opium and
repressed drug consumption. Seven years later, to cope with the severe
economic pressure, the Politburo decided to get into the narcotics trade
while outlawing its use in the base area. By 1942, according to research by
the historian Chen Yung-fa, opium had become the most important
financial resource. An official remarked to Vladimirov that selling salt
to Nationalist areas only produced 'an undernourished purse'. 'Now,' he
went on, 'we send along an undernourished bag of opium and bring

back a caravan loaded with money.'[12]

In September 1943, the Russian wrote that it was impossible to conceal the scale of opium production, though soldiers were sent to tear up poppies along roads used by American visitors. A Communist cadre explained to the Comintern agent that, while Mao realised that it was not good to be in the drug business, 'opium was to play a vanguard, revolutionary role and it would be erroneous to ignore it'.[13]

The records in Yan'an referred to narcotics as 'foreign trade', 'special product' and 'soap'. The enterprise was known as the 'Local Product Company'. The opium was bought by itinerant merchants or taken out by the Red Army. Chen Yung-fa's study shows that, in 1943, nearly a million boxes of opium were exported, raising $2 billion. By the following year, the revenue had gone up ten times, and profits accounted for up to 40 per cent of the administration's total revenue.[14]

As well as being unaware of the drug supply side of Yan'an, the Dixie Mission also remained ignorant of the way in which Mao was consolidating his dictatorship with a mixture of force, fear, manipulation and personal magnetism. He stamped on colleagues suspected of allegiances to the Soviet Union and the Comintern. He saw off his Moscow-trained one-time rival, Wang Ming, who was in any case seriously ill – there were reports that the political police chief had arranged to feed him poisonous medicine. In a rehearsal for future purges and mass mobilisations, campaigns were launched to ensure loyalty and to uncover Kuomintang spies. Hundreds of agents, real or supposed, paraded to admit their guilt. In the decade after the Long March, Yan'an developed into a hermetically sealed, paranoiac breeding ground for a ruler who harked back to the most authoritarian of emperors and cast aside the dreams of moderate progress which Nanking had spawned but had been unable to sustain.

At the opening day of talks with Hurley, Mao blamed China's problems on the Kuomintang. Unsurprisingly, the Communists rejected the proposals Chiang had agreed with the ambassador before he left Chungking; instead, they called for a coalition government, a joint military council, American supplies for their army, and the freeing of political prisoners, including the Young Marshal. Hurley, who was suffering from a cold, said this seemed fair, but asked to consider their proposals further. On his third day in Yan'an, he came back with a document that added promises of democracy and liberty to the Communist draft. 'The Chinese traditionally do not much show their feelings in their faces, but it was evident from their expressions that they were greatly pleased,' Colonel Barrett recalled. Mao and Hurley each signed a copy, the ambassador as 'Personal Representative of the President of the United States'.[15]

When he got back to Chungking, Hurley was told that Chiang was ill, and could not receive him. But T. V. Soong warned the ambassador he had been 'sold a bill of goods by the Communists', and said the government would never grant what Mao had asked for. Chiang took ten days to react. Then he issued hard-line proposals calling for Chungking to take control of Communist troops.

Mao dismissed this as 'tantamount to complete surrender'. To Hurley's observation that the Communists could get a foot in the door, he replied: 'A foot in the door means nothing if the hands are tied behind the back.' He also used the ultimately insulting Chinese epithet of 'a turtle's egg' for the Generalissimo, and raised the temperature by threatening to publish the document Hurley had signed and, in part, co-written. That would expose him as an envoy who had put his name to an agreement with the Communists on behalf of his President without even having shown it to America's ally in Chungking. When Barrett told him of Mao's threat, the ambassador seemed about to burst a blood vessel. 'The motherfucker, he tricked meh,' John Paton Davies records him as having said. Falling back on an old Oklahoma saying, Hurley added: 'Why do leaves turn red in the fall? Because they were so green in the spring.' After a message from the ambassador, the Communists relented, and agreed not to publish the document – for the time being.[16]

What Hurley did not grasp was the reluctance of either Chiang or Mao to enter into an agreement that would weaken them when their struggle for control of China resumed. The Communist leader must have known that the Generalissimo would reject the conditions he laid down to Hurley, let alone the ambassador's subsequent additions. In an eight-hour conversation with the Russian, Vladimirov, Mao described Chiang as 'a dictator, a butcher, and a half-wit' and made it plain that the Americans were naive in striving for concessions which neither side intended to make. But, equally, neither Mao nor Chiang wished to be seen by the Americans as responsible for the failure of the Hurley initiative. Both hankered too much after US supplies and support for that.

Unable to accept that he was trying an impossible squaring of the circle,

Hurley blamed T. V. Soong for turning Chiang against the proposals he had signed in Yan'an. His composure was further shaken when Chiang arranged a briefing for him at the start of 1945 by the secret police chief, Dai Li, and his American confederate, 'Mary' Miles, of the undercover SACO group. The subject was a mission to Yan'an by Lieutenant Colonel William Bird of the American OSS agency which Hurley had not been told about.

Bird, accompanied by David Barrett of the Dixie team, had laid out sensational plans for cooperation between the Americans and the Communists. Up to 5,000 US airborne troops would use the base area as the launching pad for sabotage against the Japanese while a division would be moved in from Europe to work with the Red Army, possibly leading to invasion of Japan from Shandong. The OSS would supply training teams, equip up to 25,000 guerrillas, and bring in at least 100,000 Woolworth one-shot pistols (one-shot so that they could not be kept and used against the Nationalists). In return, Communist troops and militia would be deployed when the Americans wanted. The OSS suggestions were evidently to the liking of the hosts – they presented Bird with a fine sword taken from a Japanese officer.[18]

Though they kept the ambassador in the dark, the American officers had outlined the proposals to the War Minister, Chen Cheng, and to T. V. Soong, asking them not to tell Chiang. They should have known that no Chinese official was going to keep such an explosive plan from the Generalissimo, who decided to block it by arranging the briefing, which was bound to enrage Hurley. Dai and Miles had a motivation of their own – they both wanted to do down the OSS which the police chief saw as an opponent and the American viewed as a rival. T.V. attended the meeting, and took the opportunity to stir the pot. The ambassador concluded that Barrett and Bird had offered the Communists recognition, undermining his own efforts. He sent Roosevelt a message to condemn those involved. The President sided with him, and considered apologising to Chiang. The OSS initiative died a swift death.[19]

The crisis produced a fissure in American ranks that could only strengthen Chiang's position. Hurley accused Stilwell's successor, Albert Wedemeyer, of harbouring staff who were conspiring against him. Relations were further strained by a Communist request for an American loan and a proposal from Mao and Zhou that they should go to Washington on an unofficial basis to explain the situation in China; they hoped to be invited to the White House. Both notions were channelled through Wedemeyer, not Hurley. When the general told the ambassador, he grew even more irate. (There was no official American reaction to the idea.)

The tension had domestic ramifications since Wedemeyer was staying in the envoy's house. Annalee Jacoby recalled that they had 'loud, noisy quarrels', and that the general told the War Department in Washington about the condition of the ambassador's mind. For several days, Hurley refused to talk to his lodger, which was particularly awkward at the meals they shared. Then, the ambassador came into the soldier's room one night while he was reading in bed. 'He sat on the edge on my bed, clasped my right hand in both of his and said that he was sorry for his behaviour towards me,' Wedemeyer recalled.[20]

Hurley brought in two press attachés to burnish his image while the Chungking censors excised any criticism of him from the dispatches of American correspondents. He ejected the political advisers, including John Paton Davies. Still, his remaining staff did not stint their criticism of the regime; when Hurley went on a visit to Washington, they sent a joint message to the State Department in his absence saying that unqualified support of the Generalissimo would accelerate the outbreak of civil war, and that the United States should cooperate directly with the Communists and other anti-Japanese parties.

Not surprisingly, Hurley exploded. In a complete reversal of his original stance, he now saw anybody who envisaged cooperation with Yan'an as his personal foe. He got Washington to agree to give a full endorsement of Chiang's regime – and had the offending diplomats recalled. In a supreme exercise of imagination, he blamed China's problems on 'the imperialist governments of France, Britain and the Netherlands'.

Thus, the Generalissimo emerged from this tragicomedy with even stronger backing, and the removal of diplomats who were ready to think of regime change. In America, the right and the emerging pro-Chiang China Lobby geared up for a witch hunt that began with the trial of the Foreign Service officer, John Service, and later flowed into McCarthyism.* Chiang was also comforted by the attitude of the emollient Wedemeyer, who pursued Stilwell's programme to train and equip elite units but

---

* Service was arraigned after he had left files at the office of the *Amerasia* magazine which had Communist sympathisers among its senior staff. He was acquitted.

avoided confrontation – he held a weekly planning conference with Chinese generals to signal a new era of cooperation. In a discussion of whether to move the capital to Yunnan, Wedemeyer said he would stand by Chiang come what may. 'Both Hurley and Wedemeyer have shown sympathy for and understanding of our problems,' the Nationalist leader wrote in his diary.[21]

In fact, the rangy, sharp-featured general, who could have stepped out of a Western movie, shared many of his predecessor's views – but he knew how counterproductive it would be to air them in Chungking. With Washington, however, he pulled no punches. In a series of messages to George Marshall, he stressed the incomprehensible degree of disorganisation, muddled planning, lack of training for modern war and the destructive effects of political intrigue, pride and mistrust – he also found it tragic that many high-ranking Chinese officials were asking him to arrange their evacuation to America. The Generalissimo, he wrote later, was 'very sensitive and almost as intuitive as a woman . . . It was my feeling that he was not too well equipped, either in training or experience, to cope with the multitude of problems confronting him.'[22]

Wedemeyer also enjoyed better relations than his predecessor with Claire Chennault, giving the air force commander more supplies and authority to organise an air attack on Wuhan which has hardly been mentioned in the history of the time. It began with a mass firebomb raid by seventy-seven Stratofortress bombers just before noon on 18 December 1944. Chennault's own planes from the Fourteenth Air Force kept up the assault. Fires burned for three days, gutting the docks and warehouses as well as destroying the Japanese air force facilities on the ground. The military effect was devastating; what the attacks did for the civilians of Wuhan can only be imagined. For Chennault, it was proof of the doctrine of air power he had always espoused, and he claimed that it inspired the firebombing of Japan which preceded the atomic bomb. However, in his moment of triumph, the Texan airman fell foul of a power play in the American military, and found himself squeezed out, leaving China in the early summer of 1945 after being decorated by Chiang – like so many figures in the Generalissimo's life, he would be back.

As Chennault's planes were attacking the city where he had once held sway, news came of the death of Wang Jingwei, who had suffered from diabetes and the effects of the wound from the assassination attempt in Wuhan. Taken to a hospital in Japan, Sun Yat-sen's original heir died in November 1944; his remains were put in a tomb at Nanking which was later blown up by the Nationalists with Chiang's approval. Wang's death further facilitated existing contacts with the collaborationist regime which had been maintained by the Nationalist secret police since 1941. Wang's successor was an old contact of Dai Li, and the two men ensured that clashes were kept to a minimum.

The winding-down of Operation Ichigo had reduced the military pressure. In one notable encounter, Nationalist troops put up stiff resistance to a Japanese attack on an airbase at Zhijiang in Hunan – within Chiang's alleged safe haven. American-trained troops flown in by Wedemeyer executed a series of adroit tactical moves while Chennault's fliers enjoyed air superiority. Supply and medical chains worked more effectively than usual, and the Chinese commanders co-operated. It was a highly significant performance that boded well for the future – though, as always, Chinese casualties were much greater than those of their foe, the Japanese were reckoned to have lost 6,500 men.

But the situation in the south remained dire. On a trip through the region in the spring of 1945, Graham Peck saw 'a land of numbing wretchedness' with burned-out towns and hordes of ragged refugees. Guangdong suffered its worst cholera outbreak since 1932. A visiting journalist reported that, in Canton, there were just ten syringes and forty-eight needles for inoculations; profiteers in Shanghai cornered the market in both and demanded high prices for them.[23]

At one railhead, however, Peck found that the station had been rebuilt and redecorated, complete with potted plants. A few hundred feet of track were being relaid, to accommodate some carriages and a locomotive. The reason for this activity was that Chiang was due to fly in and be photographed there as a sign that the Chinese were fighting back. One carriage was his personal one. While it was sitting on a siding, locals had ripped out its fittings for fire fuel. When Peck passed through, 'three or four scarecrow families of refugees were crouched under the monstrous deluxe coach, beating palm fiber against the track with rocks, softening it as new stuffing for the seats in the car'.[24]

The clearly approaching American defeat of Japan led Chiang's opponents to consider ways of ousting him before he extended his control over post-war China. The OSS officer, Oliver Caldwell, was approached by a Mr Chen who said he represented one of the big national sworn brotherhoods, and asked for a message to be passed to Washington that the secret societies were ready to cooperate with non-Chiang politicians to put the Guangxi general, Li Zongren, in power. Caldwell forwarded the proposal to Washington, where it gained considerable support when discussed by the Cabinet. But Admiral Leahy, the head of the navy which was running the secret SACO operation with Dai Li, spoke strongly for Chiang. When the President took a poll of the meeting, there was a narrow majority in favour of continuing to support the Generalissimo.[25]

In a linked initiative, regional potentates including Long Yun of Yunnan, the Model Governor of Shanxi and some of the Sichuan generals, were discussing the formation of a coalition to block Chiang's domination when hostilities ended. Long had made his capital of Kunming a haven for dissident politicians who planned to set up a Government of National Defence, linking independent elements of the Kuomintang, Communists, the Democratic League and other smaller parties. One idea was that the regional rulers would stop fighting the Japanese, expecting them to turn on Chiang and destroy him, thus leaving them free to take charge after the war. Like earlier anti-Chiang coalitions, this movement was shot through with its own contradictions – the US Consul in Kunming wrote that 'it would indeed be difficult to imagine a more heterogeneous group of feudal barons and radicals, idealists and practical politicians'. After an unsuccessful mission to Kunming by Meiling and T. V. Soong, the Generalissimo fired a 'silver bullet' by allocating Long Yun sufficient Lend-Lease aid for three divisions. The plot collapsed.[26]

The Red Army was also showing its intentions by making ground in east China, where it expected to link up with an American landing, as well as consolidating its main base in Shaanxi and its smaller areas round Kaifeng on the border between Shaanxi and Henan. South of the Yangtze, fighting broke out between Nationalists and Communists who were taking up positions round Shanghai in the expectation of a Japanese withdrawal. The Communists also advanced into Hunan, getting to within 50 miles of Changsha.

Still, despite the reservations he expressed to Washington, Wedemeyer was in a sufficiently optimistic mood to work on a plan for an offensive by

1.7 million men to retake Canton to provide ports for American landings he thought would be needed to defeat the Japanese. But the Generalissimo was in a grave frame of mind when he made his New Year diary entry for 1945. The only thing of which he felt proud, he wrote, was that he had not allowed his meditation and his morning and evening prayers to have been interrupted for a single day.[27]

Chiang soon had cause for concern on a broader front as Roosevelt, Stalin and Churchill met at Yalta on the Black Sea in February 1945. Once more, China's second-class status was made evident – not only was its leader not invited; he also had to wait four months to be told officially of what had been decided, though he appears to have got a good idea earlier from his own sources. In return for agreeing to back Chungking and confirming that it would enter the war against Japan after Germany surrendered, the Kremlin had been handed port and railway concessions in Manchuria, and the right to move troops there when Tokyo was beaten.

This raised the worrying prospect that the Soviets would impede the Nationalist return to the lands lost in 1931, and hand over territory to the Communists when they withdrew. 'I feel more than simply hurt and sad,' Chiang wrote in his diary. 'The Chinese people have . . . been placed in an unparalleled and dangerous predicament . . . Henceforth we have no choice but to take our own fate in our own hands and struggle for a place in the sun by the sweat of our own brow. There is no other way to break through the oppressive and enveloping darkness.' Roosevelt's death on 12 April 1945 caused Chiang further uncertainty. 'Roosevelt had at times shown a tendency to appease the Communists,' he noted. 'But he set a limit to that . . . After his death, I am afraid that the British will exert a greater influence on American policy. As to Sino-Soviet relations, we should all the more be vigilant.'[28]

Chiang's solution was extraordinarily ambitious, and would be pursued until the Cold War made it unfeasible. He resolved to exploit the growing rivalry between the two superpowers to his own advantage by playing on the desire of each to keep China out of the hands of the other. Ideology had nothing to do with it – he calculated, quite correctly, that Stalin would be motivated by realpolitik rather than solidarity with the Chinese Communists. This meant he could prepare to fight Mao when he judged the moment right while concluding a pact with the Soviet Union which was negotiated in Moscow by T. V. Soong.

Signed in June 1945, this handed Stalin inducements in Manchuria in the shape of joint operations of the main railway, Soviet use of Port Arthur* as a naval base, and the neighbouring city of Dairen† becoming a free port. The independence of Outer Mongolia was recognised, meaning that Moscow would be able to make its influence felt there. In return, Chiang got recognition of Manchuria as an integral part of China, an undertaking that Soviet troops would only stay in the former Manchukuo for three months and a pledge of non-interference in the north-western territory of Xinjiang. Most important, the treaty renewed Moscow's recognition of the Nationalists as the government of China, and Chiang could be further comforted by a decision at the American-Soviet-British summit at Potsdam affirming that Korea as well as Japan would fall into Washington's sphere at the end of the war, thus establishing a regional counterweight to the Soviet presence.

Stalin, who did not believe in the ability of the Chinese Communists to take power, had kept them in the dark about Yalta, and did not consult them before reaching the agreement with the Nationalists. As in the 1920s and at Xi'an, he put relations with Chiang ahead of those with his ideological allies, seeing China as an Asian buffer zone that would protect the Soviet Union against attack from the east. As one ruling dictator to another, he was more comfortable dealing with the Chinese President than the prickly, opinionated Mao. For his part, the Generalissimo had told his adviser, Owen Lattimore, that Stalin was a man whose word could be counted upon though, as an expert in the shifting sands of agreements, he would worry repeatedly about the Georgian playing a double game with Mao.[29]

Two months after the Sino-Soviet truce, the Generalissimo was dining with the new Mexican ambassador on a swelteringly hot evening in Chungking when Emperor Hirohito broadcast Japan's surrender on 15 August 1945. The dropping of the atom bombs on Hiroshima and Nagasaki had been a surprise to Chiang. His planning had been for a war that would drag on for at least another year, and its sudden end aborted Wedemeyer's scheme for a great offensive in southern China. Now, it was time to look to the future. In a radio address, the Generalissimo said the

---

* Now known as Dalian-Lûshan.
† Now Dalian.

enemy had been militarism, so there should be no revenge on the 'innocent people of Japan'. Calling an emergency military meeting, he worked for four days on his plans. In his diary he wrote: 'God be praised for wisdom He has revealed to me and for the blessings He has bestowed upon me . . . His guidance has enabled me to forge ahead with courage and in a spirit of humility.'[30]

In a diary entry on 2 September, when Japan's surrender document was signed with the Americans, Chiang gave the outcome of the war a personal touch by noting that 'fifty years of national humiliation as well as the indignities and insults that I have endured, are being washed away'. But he also noted that 'while old wrongs have now passed into history, we are in danger of being engulfed by new ones'. A week later, he sent General He Yingqin to accept the surrender document for China at a ceremony in Nanking at which the enemy delegates were allocated lower chairs than the Chinese. Chiang reflected that 'the crisis with which the nation is faced today is more serious than at any time since the Japanese invasion of Mukden on September 18th, 1931. If we are not careful, we will give Stalin and Mao Zedong the opportunity to do irreparable damage to our plans.'[31]

The most important thing, he decided, was to take over Manchuria where Soviet troops had moved in after Moscow launched its offensive on Japan a week before Tokyo surrendered.* This meant a massive movement of his armies which had been kept in southern China as part of the pre-atomic bomb strategy of recapturing Guangdong and linking up with American landings there. Wedemeyer warned against the dangers of a hugely extended military line from the south to the very north of China.† It has been argued that the dispatch of the best Nationalist troops to the north-east constituted a major blunder, and that Chiang would have done better to have established a strong defensive line on the Great Wall. But, if the Generalissimo was to live up to his claims to be the leader of the nation, he had to regain Manchuria, its significance heightened by its fourteen years under foreign rule. It was the most industrialised part of the

---

* Among their first acts was to detain the Last Emperor, and fly him to the Soviet Union from where he was returned to China five years later, to be 'remoulded' through labour and study.

† He also suggested putting Manchuria under a United Nations mandate. This would have been an affront to Chinese sovereignty – and would have been unacceptable to Moscow since the Nationalist permanent Security Council seat would give them veto power.

country, and a prize the Nationalists needed to improve their economic position. Ceding it to the Communists under Soviet auspices would have meant handing his adversary a major prize, giving them a huge area in which to establish their rule and build up their forces. Once they had done so, the likelihood must have been that they would have moved south sooner or later. A defensive line on the Wall would have required sustained and increased American support. So it was not surprising that Chiang decided to send his best troops to reclaim the north-east.[32]

The United States came to his aid by ordering Japanese troops to give up only to the Nationalists, and by landing Marines to occupy strategic points in Shandong and Hebei provinces. The US forces worked only with Chiang's troops, which naturally strengthened the Communist view that Washington was its enemy. Though Stalin advised seeking a modus vivendi with the Nationalists, the Red Army chief, Zhu De, instructed his men to occupy any cities they chose. Chiang denounced this as an 'abrupt and illegal action' which led Yan'an to brand him as a ruthless, Fascist chieftain who cared more for the Japanese than for his countrymen. Despite the vituperation, however, both sides needed to show an eagerness for national unity after the long conflict with Japan. The country was sick of war, and expected progress towards internal peace. So China's two great enemies of almost two decades met for the first time since Chiang's purge of 1927.[33]

Patrick Hurley was first out of the plane, a broad smile on his face as he waved his fedora hat in triumph. Behind him, in a rumpled blue cotton uniform, his hair long under a solar topi, pudgy and soft-faced, came the fifty-one-year-old Mao Zedong. In an arrival statement the Communist leader said political and military problems should be 'resolved in accordance with justice and reason, as well as on the basis of peace, democracy and unity [to] build a unified, independent, prosperous and strong new China.' Asked how he had found his first flight, Mao replied, 'Very efficient.' Then Hurley ushered him into his black Cadillac to drive into Chungking.[34]

The suggestion of meeting had come from Chiang, with three invitations starting the day before Japan surrendered. Mao, who had just presided over a party conference that buttressed his position, did not reply immediately. When he accepted, he asked the Russians to guarantee him a refuge at their military mission in Chungking if he needed it; as an additional precaution against his plane being shot down, he insisted that Hurley go to Yan'an to fly in with him. 'How comical this is!' Chiang noted in his diary. 'Never imagined that the Communists could be so chicken-hearted and shameless. Only three days ago, communist newspapers and radio denounced Hurley as a reactionary imperialist. This selfsame imperialist has become Mao's guarantor of safety.'[35]

His arrival in Chungking on 28 August 1945 was the first time the Communist leader had been outside the base area in Shaanxi since the end of the Long March ten years earlier. While he had established himself as the unquestioned leader of his party and chief of the Red Armies, his experience was limited to the world around him in Yan'an. His knowledge and judgement of international affairs, and their effect on the power struggle in China, was, in the words of the historian Odd Arne Westad, 'schematic and shallow . . . his analyses [built] on guesswork and castle-building'.[36]

On the night Mao came to town, Chiang held a dinner for him. The Generalissimo toasted the hope that 'we can now go back to the days of 1924'. Mao smoked between courses, and ate like a trencherman. 'I treated him with utmost sincerity,' the Generalissimo noted in his diary, using one of the words by which Chinese often judge one another. But things soon went wrong, and the Nationalist leader noted of Mao: 'His appetite seems insatiable . . . he does not hesitate to take advantage of my friendliness to make exorbitant demands.'[37]

The gulf between them was enormous. Chiang was intent on not giving up significant political or military power. In the spring, he had spoken of setting up a National Assembly, and forming a coalition administration – but he immediately added that there was no way the Kuomintang would 'abdicate to a loose combination of parties'. He proposed a significant cut in the size of the Red Army, and the extension of his regime's authority over all China. Mao wanted Communist governors in five northern provinces and the chairmanship of the Peiping military council, plus a substantial army.

The two leaders left the talks to negotiating teams, while controlling things from behind the scenes during more than a dozen sessions of discussions. The Reuters correspondent, Doon Campbell, wrote that Chiang showed the visitor off at social occasions as if to say, 'Look – isn't he a prize exhibit?' At a tea party, Mao shouted, 'Long live President

Chiang Kai-shek!', but the object of his tribute was not moved. On 4 September the Generalissimo recorded that he got up at dawn to pray God to show Mao the way to national peace and unity. Following one meeting, he noted in his diary: 'I promised him to resolve all our differences in a spirit of fairness and magnanimity. He asked for twenty-eight divisions.' After another talk and a photo-session with Mao and Hurley, the Chinese President recorded that Zhou Enlai had upped the Communist demand to forty-eight divisions. 'This shows how difficult it is to negotiate with the Communists,' Chiang complained. 'Such is their faithlessness and duplicity!'[38]

Three weeks into Mao's stay in Chungking, the two leaders announced what was described as a temporary agreement to avert civil war, including the formation of an all-party government. The Communist leader then agreed to answer questions put in writing by Doon Campbell, who was summoned to his house and was handed the answers by the Communist press chief, the soft-spoken daughter of a wealthy Shanghai family. Campbell's report, filed in lower case cablese, quoted Mao as saying 'eyem confident in outcome of present negotiations dash they cannot break down . . . what china needs presently is policy peaceful reconstruction dash no other policy stop therefore civil war in china must be determinedly averted.' The censor passed Campbell's cable without any alteration.[39]

Apart from the negotiations with the Nationalists, Mao found himself facing angry protests from General Wedemeyer after Communists in Shandong bayoneted to death the leader of an OSS unit – the dead man, Captain John Birch, would later be adopted as an icon by the far right-wing American movement named after him. Wedemeyer warned Mao and Zhou that news of the killing would have a 'very disturbing effect' in the United States. At the same time, Communists in Hebei province were holding captive another American intelligence mission. In both cases, part of the motive appears to have been to prevent the OSS men collecting evidence of Communist understandings with local puppet troops which would have sat uneasily with their patriotic image. When Mao and Zhou recalled their party's friendliness towards the Americans, Wedemeyer noted that this had changed in recent months. Zhou had the Hebei group freed – only for Communists in Shaanxi to seize an OSS party there.[40]

At the beginning of October, Mao, who had taken the opportunity to meet leaders of the liberal Democratic League and the Democratic

Socialist Party, decided it was time to prepare to return to Yan'an. On 8 October he was guest of honour at a dinner attended by 500 people at which he again shouted, 'Long live President Chiang,' to loud applause. Among the guests was Chiang's American champion, Henry Luce, who noted that, in their conversation, the Communist leaders greeted his comments with a 'polite grunt'.[41]

The next day, Mao called on his rival for an hour-long conversation. The Generalissimo wrote in his diary that, when he asked the Communist leader for his views on cooperation with the Kuomintang, 'he was evasive and did not give any clear-cut answer'. When he said the Communists should give up the idea of independent territory, Mao agreed – 'but was he really convinced? Was he moved by my sincerity?' It sounded as if the Communist leader was just anxious to get back to his safe haven. He had grown depressed during his time in Chungking, and must have longed for more familiar surroundings.[42]

On 10 October, China's National Day, the two men had two meetings, with Chiang insisting that Communist areas must be part of the national system if China was to be a unified country. When Mao left the next day, an agreement was announced to call a political consultation conference, guarantee civil liberties, recognise the legality of all political parties, and release political prisoners. But there was nothing on the strength of the armed forces or the distribution of provincial administration – or on how the proposed National Assembly was to be elected to usher in democracy. As Doon Campbell noted in a letter home, 'Neither side trusts the other and [neither] will make the first concession. Each side is out to prevent provincial bloc building by the other. Each wants territorial, military, civil, political control. Yet each side claps hands for democracy, unity, freedom, nationalisation of the armies.'

By then, both armies were on the move, the Communists occupying 200 towns and the Americans moving Nationalist troops to the north by air and sea. Chiang postponed the political conference until the following year because of the military situation. On 15 October he held a tea party for foreign correspondents to assure them that he was still in control. In a letter home the next day, Campbell noted his 'soft, delicate hands and enormous charm. He speaks no English but tries – "seet down".' Meiling, who had returned from New York, was also in attendance. The correspondent described her as 'quite dishy – it isn't fright that sends shivers down your spine when you shake hands with her. She is one of the most physically attractive forty-year-olds I have come across. Her poise and make-up are impeccable.'

On his return to Yan'an, Mao fell into what seemed like a trauma. According to his interpreter, he lay for days 'prostrated on his bed, his body trembling. His hands and legs twitched convulsively, and he was bathed in a cold sweat . . . He asked us for cold towels to put on his forehead, but it didn't help. The doctors could do nothing.' Mao's collapse may have been, in part at least, the result of his realisation of how little the dominance he had established in the enclosed world of his party counted for on the wider stage, and how resolute his opponent was. Having had his hopes raised by Hurley's initial mission to Yan'an, he returned from Chungking isolated, and facing a regime that enjoyed the backing of both Washington and Moscow and was ready to break any part of their agreement when and as it wished.[43]

Recovering, Mao reacted with characteristic obstinacy. The Chungking agreement was merely a scrap of paper, he told a meeting. As for Stalin's instruction to seek a modus vivendi with the Nationalists, he asked: 'Does this mean that we are going to hand over our guns to the Kuomintang?' His answer was firm as it was evident – 'The arms of the people, every gun and every bullet must all be kept, must not be handed over.'

Though it had ended the war on the winning side and was one of the Big Four with a permanent seat on the United Nations Security Council, China was in an extremely bad way. Major cities were devastated. The Japanese had stripped the countryside. The economy was crippled. The regime enjoyed little support outside the ranks of its members. The Red Army had grown in size; the Communists had extended their support among the peasants; and were now free of the pressure of the Japanese campaigns in the north. Still, the moment Chiang had been waiting for since 1937 had arrived. He set up a headquarters for Manchuria including his son, and appointed as regional commander General Du Yuming, who had caused Stilwell such aggravation in Burma. Du had just shown his loyalty and usefulness by carrying out a coup on Chiang's behalf to remove the troublesome Yunnan governor, Long Yun, who was held as a virtual prisoner in Chungking.

But the Soviet occupation forces were proving less than helpful. In places, they stopped the Americans landing Nationalist troops while allowing the Communists to expand and demanding that big industrial plants be put under joint Sino-Soviet control. In protest, Chiang withdrew a liaison mission he had sent to deal with the Russians in Manchuria, and invoked American help. This produced the desired effect on Stalin, who did not want a major clash with Washington and wished to maintain the relationship with Chungking. At the Kremlin's instruction, the Soviet commander, Marshal Malinovsky, changed tack to define his aim as being 'to assist the Chinese government [to] establish its political power in the north-east'. The head of the occupation force in the former Manchukuo capital of Changchun declared that it was 'not permissible to oppose the Nationalist government', and the city's Communist mayor was sacked.[44]

Stalin agreed to delay the withdrawal of Soviet troops until the Generalissimo had enough men in Manchuria to take over properly. Chiang sent troops and southerners to run major cities. He pointedly ignored local figures, and rejected out of hand a suggestion that the Young Marshal might be freed from captivity to help establish the Nationalists in his former domain – the Communists, on the other hand, used Zhang's brother to recruit Manchurian support. To strengthen the Nationalist position, the Central Army won a big battle against heavily outnumbered Communist troops on the route north of the Great Wall.

With Mao forced to accept the reality of his position and go along with Soviet policy, Chiang appeared to have his best prospect ever of establishing his authority from the South China Sea to the Manchurian-Soviet border, achieving a reach not enjoyed by any ruler since the fall of the Manchu Empire. Stalin went as far as to tell Washington that he would not object if the United States kept troops in China. In fact, as Wedemeyer warned Washington, Chiang lacked the means to occupy all Manchuria against Communist opposition. His apparent strength at the end of 1945 rested on the collusion of the Soviet Union, and his ability to retain backing from both Washington and Moscow.[45]

That was soon thrown into doubt by the development of the Cold War. Policy-makers in Washington grew increasingly concerned at the prospect of Stalin asserting himself in Manchuria. The ultimate nightmare was of Moscow taking control of China through a fatal combination of pressure from the Chinese Communists and a weak, overextended central government that had not recovered from the damage of the war with

Japan. Combined with its strength in Europe, this could make the Soviet Union the winner of the post-war confrontation.

The issue of what to do about China was pushed to the point of decision by the final implosion of Patrick Hurley. Visiting Washington at the end of 1945, the ambassador went to see President Truman to complain about the way he believed he was being undercut by the State Department. Two hours later, he announced his resignation, blaming diplomats who sympathised both with the Communists and with European imperialism. Ignoring the way in which the ambassador had courted Mao, right-wing Republicans in the United States tried to turn him into a martyr of Communist infiltration of American diplomacy, making the administration's China policy into a domestic political issue that would fester for years. Realising immediate action was necessary, Truman telephoned George Marshall, who had just retired from his wartime post of Chief of Staff, and asked him to go to China as his special envoy. The general said he would do whatever the President wanted, and hung up, anxious that his wife should not overhear. He wanted time to break the news to her that, instead of a rest, he would be heading to deal with a challenge which had defeated his country since Pearl Harbor.[46]

Marshall had the double task of stemming Soviet influence and of getting the Nationalists and Communists to cooperate to build a strong China. If there was anybody whom Truman and the American people trusted to work such a miracle, it was the man who had organised the Allied victory in the Second World War. Later, he would become Secretary of State and author of the plan to rebuild Europe that bore his name. Between lay China, and the deepest morass of his career as Chiang outplayed the greatest power on earth.

CHAPTER 25

Mission Impossible

THE EIGHT-YEAR WAR WITH JAPAN had been an extended body-blow for a regime already shot through with weaknesses. The length, scale and nature of the conflict had debilitated China and the Nationalists. In the words of the historian Hans Van de Ven, 'society itself had come unstuck'. A film director recalled that 'in the months after victory, we all felt defeated'. Later, Mao would tell a group of Japanese who apologised for their country's conduct that he owed Tokyo thanks for, without the war, he might still have been living in a cave in Yan'an. Political reform which could have rallied support for the Nationalists was derailed. T. V. Soong's attempt to make government more effective ran into two obstacles – Chiang above him and hundreds of thousands of ineffective officials below. The death of Dai Li in a plane crash, variously attributed to an accident, Communists or American sabotage or fall-out from a wartime Japanese intrigue, deprived Chiang of a trusted follower, but the repression the secret service chief had masterminded did not slacken. 'The Chinese masses are used to what you might call cruelty, they understand it, they have always understood it,' a police colonel told a foreigner. 'If we were to use kid glove methods we would be lost.' Many persecuted intellectuals and students decided to do what they were suspected of, and became Communists.[1]

General Chen Cheng, who was suffering from stomach ulcers, sought to make the army more efficient by disbanding bad regiments and melding units from different regional armies to curb their autonomy. But many either stayed where they were, living off looting and banditry, or joined the Communists. One group of officers was so indignant at the disbandment that it staged a 'crying demonstration' at the Sun Yat-sen memorial in Nanking. When the Guangxi leader, Li Zongren, pointed to the danger of supplying recruits for the Red Army, Chen replied: 'If they go over to the Communists, we shall cook them in the same pot with the Reds.' Li pointed out that the pre-war campaigns had not cooked the Reds; Chen responded, 'That was because our air force was not yet strong enough.'

Conditions in the ranks remained as bad as ever, despite a well-publicised episode in which Chiang used his stick to beat an officer at whose camp ill and starving recruits had died. The basic truth was that he had only half a dozen fully operational, properly trained and equipped divisions, each containing around 11,000 men. His army, as a whole, looked huge. But, after the devastation of the internal wars and the conflict with the Japanese, Chiang was extremely weak militarily – and this counted so much when he chose to decide the future by military means.

Had he wished to, he might have done more to exploit his position as the only man who stood for China. Had he gone along with American ideas for a coalition administration, he could have used his status to ensure he came out on top, with Washington tied more firmly to him as a result. But, despite occasional liberalisation gestures, he was as intent on destroying the Communists as he had been in the previous decade, and shied away from any flexibility that might be seen as weakness – on top of which, he distrusted the Americans. So, victory won, things went on as before. Though an expert survivor, the Generalissimo learned nothing because he could not see beyond his own limited horizons.[2]

Nationalist carpetbaggers moved into liberated areas, grabbing assets from people accused, rightly or wrongly, of having collaborated. Chiang accepted the help of former puppets and even Japanese officers, lending credence to the story that he had fixed up a mutual protection deal in the later stages of the war. 'Reconstruction' taxes were levied, and the state's agents seized buildings and factories, as the regime sank its claws ever deeper into the business world. Urban Manchuria became what the historian Edward Dreyer has described as a 'kleptocracy' under General Du

Yuming, Joseph Stilwell's *bête noire* in Burma who was considered unusually corrupt. A fresh famine swept through Henan.[3]

In the countryside, the rural masses were alienated by oppression, corruption and the policy of collecting land tax in grain. Nationalist troops brought back the old order with them. A report by the American journalist Jack Belden, from a county in Henan province where the Communists had implemented their programme of change during the war, gave a taste of what happened when government forces returned. Peasants who had taken part in land reform were publicly executed. Farmers who had campaigned for rent reductions were buried alive, sometimes together with their families – in one village, Belden saw two dozen bodies, including those of women and children, being dug out of a pit. In another, a landlord who returned after fleeing with the Japanese had members of twenty-four of the twenty-eight families in a village killed, some being thrown into a well. Militias extorted money, and bought rifles from troops.[4]

The Communists had used violence ruthlessly on their enemies in the countryside, but the repression that accompanied the return of the Nationalists added to the alienation from a regime which had nothing to offer in answer to Mao's doctrine of rural revolution. As a result, when the Red Armies withdrew under Nationalist pressure, local units continued to operate; they might not be truly Communist, but their experience could only make them support the cause, with at least tacit backing from the peasantry around them. As they revenged themselves for repression, killed landlords and threatened officials, such guerrilla outfits kept alive a spirit of revolt that would provide the Red Armies with a sea of support when the time came to make their move against Chiang.

The regime remained a tightly controlled oligarchy, personified by the 'Four families' – the Chiangs, T. V. Soong, the Kungs and the Chen brothers. The economy was the area that affected most people worst. 'On top of the lack of military protection, the broad mass of Chinese could not count on the government to run the economy in the national interest,' as the adviser, Arthur Young, noted. Inflation roared ahead, making money virtually worthless and increasing the value of an American dollar forty-fold.

Corruption was a way of life. There were scandals over government bonds and an American gold loan involving members of Chiang's inner circle, including Big-Eared Du. Supplies from the United Nations relief organisation, UNRRA, were diverted to the black market after being handed over to the Chinese for distribution. In one place Jack Belden visited in Central China, soldiers stopped supplies getting to an orphanage, selling them from their own warehouse while the children died of hunger. An American doctor who insisted on personally safeguarding a railway wagon of aid destined for a Communist-held area died from hunger and exposure after being shunted onto a siding in a lonely area with no heat or food.[5]

A tiny upper crust prospered, making fortunes on the black market and driving round big cities in imported limousines – meeting his officers in Shanghai, Dai Li had been moved to remark on the number of their cars blocking the road outside. American military personnel, who each cost 500 times as much to sustain as Chinese troops, sped through Chungking and Chengdu with their 'Jeep girls'; H. H. Kung complained that they ate so much meat that there would soon be no animals left. Meanwhile, millions starved. A satirical show in Shanghai called *How Officials Get Promoted*, which was set in olden times for safety's sake, featured a governor whose headaches could only be cured by application of gold bars.[6]

As George Marshall set out for China in December 1945, a cartoon in the *New York Times* showed him looking at a table covered with broken crockery labelled 'Our China Policy'. On arrival in Shanghai, he was given a downbeat assessment by General Wedemeyer of the chances of bringing Nationalists and Communists together. Agreement was impossible, the American commander explained, since the first were determined not to give up any of their power while the second wanted power for themselves. But the straight-ahead envoy refused to be put off. 'I am going to accomplish my mission and you are going to help me,' he told Wedemeyer. The Reuters correspondent, Doon Campbell, who saw him many times, recalled that, apart from an occasional 'wrath-of-God expression over some diabolical let-down', Marshall was patience personified. He needed to be, given the nature of his mission.

Truman said that American policy aimed to produce 'a strong, united and democratic China'. His envoy carried a stick in the form of a presidential warning to Chiang that 'China disunited and torn by civil strife could not be considered realistically as a proper place for American assistance'. But his claims to be an honest broker were undermined by US military supplies pouring in to the Nationalists, and the use of US ships and planes to move Chiang's soldiers to the north. Washington set itself the aim of keeping out of the internal Chinese conflict. But this was specious reasoning.

Apart from 60,000 men sent to hold ports, industrial centres and mines as the Japanese left, Truman was determined to hold back Soviet influence, and saw the Chinese Communists as part of a worldwide movement orchestrated from Moscow. He feared that Stalin was aiming to establish authority over Manchuria, and one of Marshall's main aims was to ensure that Nationalists were strong enough to check this. American aid to Chiang's regime was clearly one-sided, and produced growing alienation among the Communists. Though Mao and Zhou Enlai saw the advantages of working with the Marshall mission as they built up their strength, Jack Belden was struck by slogans daubed on walls on the northern plain proclaiming: 'Oppose Chiang Kai-shek's betrayal of China to America.'[7]

In fact, from the moment Marshall arrived in Chungking on 21 December 1945 – his sixty-sixth birthday – the Generalissimo entertained doubts about him. As Chiang had shown repeatedly, he put his own position first, and would do all he could to stall his main ally if that was threatened. He felt no fondness or debt towards Washington whose intervention nationalists could easily view as a quasi-imperialistic resumption of foreign interference in China. Incidents such as the rape of two Chinese girls by American marines in Peiping aroused popular feeling against the wartime ally, while the equation of progress with Westernisation espoused by modernisers in the first half of the century had lost much of its appeal for a regime that had survived on its own terms during the long years of war.

The American drive for a coalition government could only help the Communists, and the search for peace inhibit the re-conquest of Manchuria. While Chiang was anxious to fight his domestic enemy as quickly as possible, and on the widest scale, the Communists' interest lay in delay to gain time to build up military and political strength. So the American bid to negotiate a truce and engage in talks about a coalition could only be seen by the Generalissimo as helping his foe. Internationally, he was leery of alienating Stalin by appearing to be too close to Washington, and was anxious to keep as much room for manoeuvre as possible between the two superpowers. The powerful Kuomintang figure

Chen Lifu warned that 'anybody else coming here would be better than General Marshall' since his mission would expose the Americans to the Communist propaganda, and bring blame on the Nationalists if it ended in failure.

The envoy's tone went down badly – Chen recalled that he spoke like a colonial governor 'and severely lectured us'. There was also the background of Marshall's championing of Stilwell, and his authorship of some of the toughest messages sent over Roosevelt's signature during the war years. After hosting a banquet and then holding the first of sixty meetings with Marshall over the following year, Chiang confided to his diary that the emissary had no understanding of China's internal problems and the behaviour of the Communists – 'in the end, this will have a harmful influence on major events,' he added.[8]

Still, the mission got off to a promising start as a three-man committee of Marshall, Zhou Enlai and a Nationalist former Foreign Minister, Zhang Zhun, swiftly reached an agreement for a truce to take effect in mid-January, though it left the Nationalists free to continue moving troops into Manchuria. This was followed by an accord to cut government forces to a maximum of 700,000 and the Red Armies to 140,000 in eighteen months. Chiang would remain in supreme command, and the Communists would pull out of their southern base areas. Yan'an regarded the agreement as a success in that it was recognised as a negotiating partner, rather than a target for destruction.

Political reforms were also agreed in principle, including the calling of a consultative conference with non-Nationalist parties and the establishment of an interim state council which the Kuomintang would not dominate. Here, again, the Communists saw progress since they would be able to line up with smaller parties to challenge the KMT. The Americans pressed for disbandment of the secret police, and Marshall showed what he had thought of Dai Li by refusing to give the American undercover agent 'Mary' Miles permission to attend his funeral – Miles took leave and went anyway.[9]

Marshall appeared to have achieved yet another success when the Russians began withdrawing from Manchuria in mid-March, 1946, apparently as a conciliatory move towards an increasingly tough-minded West – six days before the withdrawal began, Churchill, with Truman beside him, had made his speech about the Iron Curtain. The Soviet troops stripped the territory of whole factories and anything else they wanted; an

American inquiry put the value of the loot at US$2 billion – the Soviet estimate was far lower. The presidential envoy made a six-day trip to the North during which he met Mao; in the evening they watched a film, stretched out on reclining chairs under thick rugs. Marshall appeared to have pulled off the impossible. When he paid a visit to Washington in mid-March, he was greeted as a hero. In fact, this was precisely the moment at which he was doomed to fail, and civil war to the death became inevitable.

Chiang had agreed to the truce in the expectation that a combination of backing from Washington and Moscow would enable him to build up overwhelming strength in Manchuria. He sent his son, Ching-kuo, to Moscow to sound out Stalin on a wider agreement. But, reversing his earlier stance, the Soviet leader launched a broadside against the presence of American troops in China. In the Cold War context, Chiang's attempt to avoid choosing between the USSR and the USA was becoming untenable. The belated publication of the Yalta agreement, together with Soviet conduct in Eastern Europe and the Balkans, deepened concern about the Kremlin's intentions. Intelligence reports from Manchuria told of collusion between the remaining occupation troops and Communists as Stalin steered an erratic course that could only threaten the Generalissimo. On 6 March 1946, the Chinese government issued a protest about Soviet behaviour in Manchuria, and called for the immediate withdrawal of the whole of the Red Army. Chiang had made his inevitable choice.

As Chiang saw his hopes of working with both Washington and Moscow dashed, the agreements brokered by Marshall were unravelling fast. The Soviet withdrawal freed the Communists to launch an offensive. The Russians left them a trove of captured Japanese weapons – Tass news agency later put the volume at 700,000 rifles, 14,000 heavy and light machine guns, artillery, mortars and 700 vehicles, including tanks.

Though Chen Cheng's reforms did cut the size of the Nationalist forces from 3 million in 1945 to 2.6 million by the middle of the following year, the troop reductions agreed by the Marshall committee remained a dead letter. Some cosmetic measures were introduced for the secret police, but repression continued as before. Strong elements in both the Nationalists and the Communists were none too keen on moving towards democracy. While Marshall regarded a coalition as a means of bringing peace, the Communists saw it as a step along the road to power, and, appreciating that in a way the Americans did not, Chiang was bound to avoid opening the

32. Chiang, Meiling and Joseph Stillwell are all smiles for this photograph despite their differences.

33. Vinegar Joe (centre, in profile) at the front in Burma.

34. The aerial prophet: Claire Chennault (right) and Albert Wedemeyer (left) with Yunnan warlord Long Yun.

35. Meiling addresses a rally in New York in 1943.

35

36

36. As guest of honour at a Hollywood dinner, with *Gone With the Wind* producer David O. Selznick.

37. Disturbing influence: Wendell Willkie.

37

38. Mao Zedong (left)
flies to Chungking
for talks with
Chiang. With him are
US Ambassador
Patrick Hurley and
Zhou Enlai.

39. Mao and Chiang
exchange toasts
at a banquet in
Chungking — Hurley
looks on from the
side.

38

40

40. Chiang inspects Yan'an after the Communist base was taken by the Nationalists in 1947.

41

41. Mao rides out before the government troops move in.

42. Broken China: the *New York Times'* view of George Marshall's mission.

43. Chiang and Meiling greet the American envoy.

44. Bank raid: a crowd seeks its money as the economy spirals out of control.

45. An army implodes: Nationalist soldiers waiting to be evacuated.

46. Resignation: Chiang leaving Nanking in January 1949 after resigning – but he continued to pull the strings.

47. New Life: the Generalissimo in Taiwan.

door to the enemy. He dismissed the idea of giving significant powers to a national assembly. Pressure from the right diluted the promised reforms, leading to a boycott of the consultative conference by the Communists and Democratic League, whose Chungking newspaper offices were attacked by organised mobs as hardliners staged big anti-Soviet demonstrations.

When Marshall returned to China in mid-April with a new aid package, civil war was in full swing in Manchuria where the Red Army had taken the city of Changchun. The Nationalists refused to continue the Marshall talks until they withdrew. The Communists were unyielding. So Chiang ordered a successful siege. By early summer, the Nationalists held all the major cities in the south and centre of Manchuria. Their advance infuriated Marshall, who could not accept the basic fact that Chiang was more interested in the victory he saw ahead than in a peace with the Communists which would lessen his own power.[10]

Meanwhile, the Generalissimo supervised the return of the capital to Nanking in May 1946, installing himself in an office suite in the building behind Sun Yat-sen's presidential quarters, or receiving visitors at the Officers' Moral Endeavour Association furnished with a glass-topped walnut desk, red leather chairs and a sofa. A portrait of Sun Yat-sen hung on the wall. The floor was covered with chequered linoleum. Among his visitors was a French general sent by de Gaulle to award him the grand cross of the Legion of Honour with a citation hailing him as 'First Fighter for Democracy'. Chiang then visited Peiping where he attended a huge rally held in his honour in front of the Forbidden City, before flying to Mukden to inspect operations in Manchuria.[11]

By now, he was accusing Marshall in his diary of acting aggressively, 'his face and voice . . . harsh . . . I tried to patiently endure this and ignore his behaviour towards me.' The American had some strong cards to play, threatening to end the use of US transport planes, advising Washington not to increase aid, and talking of calling off his mission if the Nationalist offensive continued. As a result, the Generalissimo agreed to a fresh truce, which he later called 'a most grievous mistake'. It enabled several Communist armies to evade pressure in China itself, but, most important, it meant that Nationalist troops in Manchuria stopped only 30 miles south of the big city of Harbin in the far northern province of Heilongjiang, which became a major base for the Communists, giving them time and space to develop their forces.[12]

As the climate got hotter and more humid, the Chiangs moved to the mountain resort of Kuling above the Yangtze, where Marshall and his wife occupied a villa across the stream in the middle of the village. Chiang worked as hard as ever – one official who had been appointed as a secretary recounted arriving on his first day at 6 a.m. only to find that the Generalissimo had already received two visitors. Still, there was time for evening meals in the mountains, to which he and Meiling invited Katherine Marshall while her husband was away mediating. They were carried up the slope in chairs with white-fringed awnings by blue-clad coolies. Waiting for them were wicker chairs and a hot supper. Twenty-five guards stood watch. Mrs Marshall, whose spelling was atrocious, described it as 'a scene out of Arabian Knights [sic]'. In a letter, she recorded that, on the last evening of his stay, Chiang said it had been his happiest summer. 'He had never had any fun before,' Katherine Marshall wrote to a friend. 'I guess not. Married at 14 to a woman 20 he did not like for nuts and War ever since.'[13]

Invited to the Chiangs' villa one evening, John Robinson Beal, an American who had been called in to advise on the regime's publicity, found the fire crackling in the hearth of the main room below a 'not very good' painting of the Nationalist leader. The Chiangs were playing draughts in one corner, he wearing a plain khaki uniform and she in a black dress with a tan, sweater-like top. Meiling said she had been taught the game five days earlier by Mrs Marshall, who also gave a croquet lesson.[14]

While Chiang was in Kuling, his troops moved across the Yellow River into southern Shaanxi, and took dozens of counties in Jiangsu and the Shandong–Henan–Shanxi region. In August, Nationalists planes bombed the Communist headquarters of Yan'an. Ignoring Marshall's opposition, Chiang ordered an offensive on the city of Kalgan* north-west of Peiping, which had become a major Red Army centre. The commander of that campaign, General Fu Zuoyi, who had gained his military education in the United States and was highly regarded by the Americans, was another of the accomplished commanders whom Chiang distrusted for his regional links – in this case with the Model Governor of Shanxi.

The Nationalist build-up in Manchuria meant that the Red Army, now renamed as the People's Liberation Army (PLA), was outnumbered

* Now known as Zhangjiakou.

three-to-one. Against such odds, it retreated from most of its urban centres into the countryside, only fighting when it was sure of winning, and then moving off swiftly after grabbing the enemy's weapons. In a final bid to check the Nationalist offensive which was sabotaging Marshall's mediation efforts, Washington slapped an embargo on military aid. Truman warned Chiang of his view that 'the selfish interest of extremist elements, equally in the Kuomintang as in the Communist party, are hindering the aspirations of the Chinese people'.

Unless there was convincing proof of genuine progress towards a peaceful settlement, the President added, 'it must be expected that American opinion will not continue in its generous attitude towards your nation.' The words had clearly been written by Marshall. The Generalissimo drew the conclusion that 'American policy towards China has worsened as the result of the failure of Marshall's mediation effort'. The envoy, he concluded, had done irreparable damage not only to China, but also to the United States.[15]

Still, Chiang expressed himself ready to show willing by agreeing to a pause in the fighting. But the Communists insisted that the Nationalists must fall back to their earlier positions. Since Chiang was clearly not going to agree to that, Marshall began to admit that his efforts might be futile. In a sign of his lack of success with the two main players, he looked to the small liberal groups to act as an intermediary, but that was never going to get anywhere. The Communists criticised the envoy as an imperialist who was too supportive of the Nationalists while Chiang accused him of not caring 'whether China survives or perishes'.[16]

The rejection of Marshall's suggestion of another truce spelled the end of the three-man committee, and led Zhou Enlai to fly back to join Mao in the north. Intent on pressing ahead militarily, Chiang summoned leading generals to a conference in Nanking which he did not grace with his presence, leaving the chairmanship to Chen Cheng. The War Minister read out an order from the Generalissimo that the railway line from Peiping to Wuhan should be taken within three weeks, a clearly impossible task. Li Zongren, the only one to protest at the idea, sent Chiang a message pointing out that the order could not be carried out. The leader's reply 'commended' Li's viewpoint, and the order was shelved in another example of the way he would set impossible targets, and then abruptly switch tack.[17]

Whatever their difference, Chiang maintained correct relations with the American envoy. He invited the Marshalls for a picnic on an island in the Yangtze for his birthday along with Henry Luce, who was on another visit. On another occasion, when Meiling was talking to Mrs Marshall on the telephone, her husband took the receiver and said, 'Hello; I see you tomorrow' in English, the first English sentence the envoy's wife had heard him utter.[18]

On Christmas Eve 1946, Marshall, whose wife had gone for medical treatment in Hawaii, was among the guests at a party at the Chiangs' home in Nanking. A lighted Christmas tree stood in one corner. There were cocktails, and when the Martinis ran out, Meiling mixed some more. Dinner consisted of tomato soup, gelatin salad, roast turkey with trimmings, raisin pie, brandied fruitcake and ice cream; then, the party moved back into the living room for sweet melon and coffee. Dressed in a Father Christmas outfit, one of Chiang's aides stepped from behind a screen to hand out presents. Marshall got a reading board to use in bed. Liqueurs were served to round off the occasion.[19]

By then, the American envoy was ready to pack his bags, leaving relations with the government to an academic and old China hand, John Leighton Stuart, who had been appointed ambassador. Born of missionary parents in Hangzhou and former head of an American-sponsored university in Peiping, the tall, dignified Stuart, who had just entered his seventies, was to become a tragic figure as he tried to cope with the disintegration around him. His first dispatch to the State Department reflected the deeply divergent aims he was trying to achieve, expressing his great desire to see Chiang survive, but also hoping for a revival of the old revolutionary aims and the installation of democracy.[20]

The slim chances of that happening were evident when the National Assembly met at the end of the year to draw up a new constitution. The Kuomintang had made plain its intention to dominate, and the Communists and the Democratic League boycotted the session. Loud applause broke out as a Kuomintang elder handed Chiang the new constitution at a session on Christmas Day. It came in a gold box with ribbon on the front, looking, noted John Robinson Beal, 'a bit like a five-pound box of chocolates'. Naturally, the document contained promises of freedom and progress, but it laid down a powerful presidential regime designed to the leader's specifications. To celebrate the occasion, Kai-shek and Meiling were hosts that evening at a Chinese opera performance starring the celebrated actor, Mei Lan-fang, who performed his female role 'as graceful and smooth in his movements as a seventeen-year-old girl'.

At their last substantive discussion, Marshall had warned Chiang that the Red Army was too strong to be defeated. The Generalissimo would have none of it. His foes had to be dealt with militarily, he insisted, forecasting victory within ten months. Though he did not say so, he was also sure that war would break out between the United States and the Soviet Union, and that China would benefit as both sides courted it.

On 7 January 1947, Marshall went home. Chiang, who was suffering from a cold that had led him to have an electric heater placed above his chair, drove to Nanking airport to see him off. The American attributed his failure to 'almost overwhelming suspicion' between the Nationalists and the Communists, aggravated by a 'group of reactionaries' in the Kuomintang and 'dyed-in-the-wool Communists'. True enough, but nobody in China had asked for Marshall to undertake his mission. His had been an American operation, well-meaning, certainly, yet fatally flawed. Washington's aid to Chiang disqualified its envoy as an impartial mediator – as Joseph Stilwell said, even George Marshall was not able to walk on water. He had not been able to cut the knot with the Generalissimo. But the two truces he had engineered had enabled the Communists to escape from the enormous Nationalist pressure in the spring and summer of 1946, and given them vital time to regroup. As his envoy returned, Truman declared support for the Nationalists, while saying Washington would not intervene in Chinese affairs, as if the US$2 billion Washington had sent in aid plus another US$1 billion worth of cut-price equipment did not constitute intervention.[22]

Whatever his personal qualities and abilities in other fields, Marshall had proved no more adept than his predecessors in China. His mission ignored a visceral struggle that stretched back two decades, and was now encompassed by the Cold War. As the Nationalist secret police arrested, tortured and killed anybody who looked liberal, a Communist song proclaimed 'Chiang is a murderer, butchering countless Chinese. His face is covered with the people's blood.' In such a context, well-meaning intervention in pursuit of a democratic coalition had no chance of getting anywhere. Chiang and Mao preferred the fight to the death that had shaped their lives.

With his troops victorious in the north, the Generalissimo added Marshall's scalp to that of others who had tried to get him to change his ways. But his victory meant he now stood alone as he confronted his greatest enemy. The moment of truth for him, and his country, had arrived.

CHAPTER 26

Dying Light

ON 7 AUGUST 1947, Chiang Kai-shek flew over the loess country of northern Shaanxi to the town where Mao had found his haven at the end of the Long March. The Generalissimo walked briskly through Yan'an, accompanied by a triumphant group of generals led by General Hu Zongnan, the 'Eagle of the North-West' who had ring-fenced the base area during the war with Japan.

After George Marshall's departure at the beginning of the year, Hu had launched the offensive from Xi'an that the Young Marshal had refused to lead eleven years earlier. Aided by Muslim cavalry, he had taken Yan'an without a fight – the Communist leadership had already trekked out. The place was of no importance in itself, and the bleak countryside of northern Shaanxi offered no benefits for the Nationalists. But that meant little beside the symbolism of having forced Mao and his colleagues to flee once more, the Communist leader on a horse while his troops marched round him. Chiang went to see Mao's house and the long tunnel connecting it to Zhu De's headquarters as Nationalist photographers took snaps of poppies and the 'Local Product Company' building to show that the Communists had been dealing in opium.[1]

A combination of huge forces, American supplies and transport, plus some good generalship in the north had put Chiang in what looked like an unassailable position in the first eighteen months after the end of the war with Japan. Mercenary armies came back under the Nationalist flag. He had the active support of the China Lobby in the United States, combining politicians in Washington, a network of businessmen round T. V. Soong and H. H. Kung, and the influence of the Luce magazines. The Republican, Thomas Dewey, seemed well placed to beat Truman in the 1948 presidential election – after a visit to America, Chen Lifu told a Shanghai newspaper that this would mean 'extraordinary measures' to send military aid to China. But, as so often, Chiang's position was more hollow than it appeared. By the time he walked through Yan'an, his military fortunes had peaked, and the disintegration of areas under Nationalist control was racing ahead.[2]

Hyperinflation was destroying the middle classes and honest officials; wholesale prices in Shanghai rose by 45 per cent in a single month. The mother of the author of *Wild Swans*, Jung Chang, had to hire a rickshaw to carry the huge pile of notes needed to pay her school fees in the Manchurian city of Jinzhou where beggars tried to sell their children for food. Labour unrest grew – there were 4,200 strikes in Shanghai in 1946–47. In some universities, police agents masquerading as students patrolled the campuses with guns under their gowns searching for subversives. In Peiping, troops fired on a protest by 3,000 students, killing several. In Kunming, five dissidents were shot by police, and more than 1,000 were held in a jail, pulled out of the cells at midnight to kneel in the gravel yard while soldiers waved bayonets at them and told them to confess to being Communists – the American journalist Jack Belden added that more than thirty were buried alive. The protests were encouraged by the Communists, but were, above all, a sign of war-weariness and alienation from a regime that had nothing more to offer.[3]

Not that support for the Communists was as widespread and automatic as subsequent propaganda would assert. The party demonstrated great skill in organising the peasantry, but its revolution was often imposed rather than being the result of spontaneous popular uprising. This was particularly true in Manchuria where the end of the Manchukuo system had left a power vacuum. Chiang had appointed trusted figures to run the region, but they were foreign to it, as were the troops he drafted in from the south. Moving into the gap, the Communists used the time given to them by the George Marshall truces to purge class enemies, introduce land reform, mobilise the peasants and build up a strong rural support mechanism for the People's Liberation Army. Harbin and other towns and cities in the far north served as political and economic centres. Communication links were rebuilt, administrative cadres formed, and resources channelled into strengthening Lin Biao's forces. The symbiosis between ideology, grassroots revolution, political organisation and military force reached a peak. As the historian Stephen Levine has put it, 'Without the revolution there could have been no military victory for the Communists, but without the Communists there would have been no revolution.'[4]

Chiang's lines were hugely extended while the size of the territory he sought to control depleted his reserves. His armies were largely confined to cities and dependent on rail links which could be sabotaged – between 1945 and 1947, the Communists destroyed 10,250 miles of track, and the Nationalists rebuilt only 3,700. Instead of pursuing the aggressive blockhouse strategy of the mid-1930s, government troops preferred safety, staying put behind urban walls, and leaving the countryside to their enemy. They were also weakened by a spy ring which recruited senior defectors and ran a secret wireless transmitter that kept Communist armies apprised of their plans.[5]

Nationalist generals feuded among themselves as much as ever, and Chiang went on appointing commanders for their perceived loyalty rather than their skill, as in his decision to send the incompetent, corrupt – but faithful – Du Yuming to Manchuria. Their inability to manage big forces led to bungling, confusion and inefficiency. Chiang issued instructions without consultation, or after meeting only a few close aides. Orders sent to the field following his 9 p.m. military conference in Nanking were often out of date when they arrived the next day. In one case, a Nationalist commander received conflicting instructions from his immediate superior, the Chief of Staff and the Generalissimo, all of which deprived him of an impending victory.[6]

The first Communist counter-attack came in Manchuria at the start of 1947 when the lean, phlegmatic Long March veteran, Lin Biao, staged three successful short-term PLA raids across frozen rivers in the bitter north-eastern winter – the Young Marshal recalled that it was so cold there that soldiers urinated on their rifles to free the frozen bolts. These victories were important not only for the Nationalists they destroyed but also for the arms seized. Success led to an overconfident frontal attack in the early summer that was beaten back. However, a fresh offensive in the autumn isolated government armies by surrounding the cities they held and cutting railway lines, yielding more weapons. As Mao issued an exhortation to 'try for complete annihilation', Chiang replaced Du Yuming as commander in Manchuria with Chen Cheng, and sent reinforcements north. He was getting more American arms after Truman decided the situation merited lifting the embargo imposed by Marshall the previous autumn.

There was also heavy fighting in Shandong where the Nationalists lost nearly 100,000 men in two battles. Communist forces crossed the Yellow River in the summer of 1947, marching to the old base area of Oyuwan above the Yangtze which they occupied the following spring. Chiang changed the path of the Yellow River for a second time, building dykes to return it to its artificial course to divide Communist forces on either side. The water rose above the barriers, causing flooding which affected 500 villages, as well as displacing 400,000 people who had settled in the river bed after the diversion of 1938, further increasing the regime's unpopularity in the region.[7]

But it was in Manchuria that the first decisive stage in the civil war unfolded. Both the Nationalists and the Communists fielded their best trained and best equipped armies. Divisions formed by the Americans faced units Lin Biao and his colleagues had prepared for a major conventional campaign. In the summer of 1948, the Communists launched 700,000 troops on a new offensive. Reduced by death, wounds and desertion, Chiang's men were outnumbered almost two-to-one. Lin Biao also had the support of a mass of peasants, well-drilled and motivated by land reform. In addition, he and his subordinates proved themselves masters of swift movement, feints that unbalanced the enemy and sheer fighting ability, using modern equipment taken from the Japanese and Nationalists.

Chiang recalled Chen Cheng, who was increasingly ill with stomach trouble, and sent 'Hundred Victories' Wei Lihuang, from the Salween Gorge campaign, to take command in Mukden. This brought no improvement. Three airlines – one run by the prophet of air power, Claire Chennault who had returned to China – flew in supplies, but they could not carry enough weapons and food. Though Chiang had command of the skies, poor maintenance and losses had reduced the number of usable planes in the air force from 1,000 planes in 1945 to a fifth of that number. For safety's sake, bombers tended to stay so high that their attacks lacked any precision.

The Nationalists held three major cities – the Manchurian capital of Mukden, the former Manchukuo capital of Changchun and the industrialised centre of Jinzhou on the corridor up from the Great Wall. The manner in which Chiang lost all three showed his faults as a tactician, and how he had lost the initiative which had been his after the Japanese surrender. The US Consul General remarked that government tactics would have resembled a comedy of errors if the results had not been so tragic.

When Lin Biao advanced towards Jinzhou, the Generalissimo flew to Mukden to order almost half the city's 230,000-strong garrison to march south-west to help save the other city. He then moved to Peiping to direct operations from there, without keeping the War Minister or the general staff informed of what he was doing. As the 100,000-strong column moved slowly down from Mukden, the PLA took Jinzhou after a siege and a heavy bombardment – a blockhouse defensive system planned for the city had been left incomplete as the contractor sold building materials on the black market. Chiang ordered the column to continue, only for it to be surrounded and badly defeated. That was a disaster for the defence of Mukden, which was cut off. Starvation spread; corpses lay in the gutters; people fought and bribed their way onto planes. After the garrison commander defected, the PLA entered the city as the cold wind whistled through empty avenues.[8]

Changchun, the most northerly Manchurian city held by the Nationalists, fell after a siege that deprived it of electricity, gas and water. 'Crowds of people were always rummaging in refuse dumps for anything that might serve as fuel,' the wife of the British consul recalled. Lack of food led to cannibalism – human flesh was on sale for the equivalent of US$1.20 per pound. In a civilian zone set up behind a barbed wire fence between the opposing armies, bodies lay so thickly in the street that there was no space to walk between them. After a Yunnanese unit in the garrison defected, the Communists captured the city. The death toll was estimated at anywhere from 120,000 to 300,000.[9]

Across the north-east, the Nationalists had suffered 400,000 casualties. General Du Yuming, who had been sent back to the region to replace the hapless Wei, withdrew at the head of 140,000 men. The Communists captured more than 2,000 trucks, 200 tanks and armoured vehicles, plus a large array of guns. They absorbed huge numbers of defecting Nationalist soldiers who had heard tales of the good treatment the Communists gave prisoners. In an interview at the end of October, Chiang reached back to the loss of Manchuria after 1931. 'History is repeating itself,' he said. If the Communists took the region, 'it would mean the virtual beginning of another world catastrophe'.[10]

By mid-November, the survivors of the Long March did, indeed, control all Manchuria with its rich mineral deposits, agriculture, and what industry was left behind after the Soviet looting. The one-time guerrillas from southern and central China had won a major conventional campaign in far-away territory which they had turned into a revolutionary heartland. They had scored an enormous victory in terms of morale, and shown that they understood the idea of total war, melding political and economic factors behind a tough, trained, well-equipped and united army which knew what it was fighting for, as Lin Biao and his colleagues demonstrated clarity of vision and consistency with a marked ability to manage very large bodies of troops in an effective manner. The Communist victories were also revolutionary in Chinese terms as battles of annihilation which aimed to wipe out the enemy as a fighting force, very different from the tradition of leaving the adversary with a means of escape. Singing a song that looked forward to 'driving Chiang the Thief to his doom', the PLA moved down towards Peiping and the major port of Tianjin, where refugees had swollen the population to nearly 2 million as a 15-mile moat was dug and municipal officials prepared to sue for peace.[11]

Other Communist armies had recaptured Yan'an, and were advancing on big cities in central China showing tight discipline under standing orders to respect property and civilian welfare. The Long March veteran Chen Yi launched a 400,000-man force on an offensive in Shandong which took the provincial capital of Jinan after heavy fighting. West of Peiping, the Nationalist general Fu Zuoyi tried to regain control of rail links, but his armies were surrounded and defeated. He pulled his remaining troops back inside the city wall as the Communists took the airport and the Summer Palace outside the city, along with the power plant.[12]

Chiang tried to rally political support by appointing a relatively liberal figure, Wang Wenhao, as Prime Minister, and calling a National Assembly in Nanking. The 2,700 delegates ranged from young businessmen to elderly scholars, and included a beautiful Manchu who was named Miss Assembly. Naturally, there was no place for the Communists and the Democratic League which had been outlawed for collaborating with them. Still, after an optimistic speech from the Generalissimo, the discontent in Kuomintang ranks became evident. A delegate from Henan criticised the leader's report as 'inadequate', and the Assembly decided to set up seven committees on a wide variety of issues. These produced hundreds of resolutions, including one calling for the liquidation of 'wealthy families'. But the Assembly still voted to give Chiang 'extraordinary powers' during the campaign against the Communists, and elected him President by 2,430 votes to 269.

However, things went off the rails in the first round of voting for the vice-presidency. Chiang's candidate, Sun Yat-sen's son, Sun Fo, finished second to the Guangxi general Li Zongren, who, however, lacked the necessary margin to win outright. Despite intimidation by Chiang loyalists, later rounds of voting elected Li. Given Chiang's supremacy, the position meant little, but the episode showed the strength of feeling in the party.

The Generalissimo was inaugurated into the presidency in a ceremony in the former imperial complex in Nanking where Sun Yat-sen had been sworn in as first President of the Republic in 1912. Afterwards, he and Li, with their wives, greeted dignitaries lined up to congratulate them. Wearing a simple gown and a single decoration, the Generalissimo posed with Meiling for a formal photograph; then they went outside for a group picture with members of the Assembly, Chiang's expression radiating confidence while his wife stared determinedly ahead.*

The Generalissimo worked in a three-room suite on the first floor of a 1930s brick building at the back of the complex, behind a courtyard with two pine trees. A long passageway led between the imperial pavilion where Sun Yat-sen had worked and Chiang's building. Midway along the passage

---

* Photographs of the occasion currently mounted outside the hall are set on a background of fallen leaves.

was the Unicorn Gate, with mythical creatures carved in stone on either side, which was only opened for the Generalissimo. In the main room of the brick block, he sat at a glass-topped desk or in a brown armchair to receive visitors. On the floor above, he presided at meetings in a conference room with rows of black leather armchairs draped with white antimacassars. A photograph of Sun Yat-sen stared down. On the wall of the adjoining Supreme State Conference Hall were characters for loyalty, filial piety, kind-heartedness, good faith and peace.

As Chiang was being voted into office by the National Assembly, one of his long-term sparring partners was setting out for home. In 1946, the Christian General had arranged to be sent to the United States on an unlikely mission to study irrigation and water conservation. Once in America, he spent his time meeting contacts, attacking Chiang, and calling for an end to the dispatch of American weapons which, as he pointed out, often ended up in the hands of Communists. Visiting him at an apartment he took on Riverside Drive in New York, Teddy White found Feng Yuxiang barricaded behind cases of groceries, coffee, tins of soup and canned meats as if living under siege. In 1948, the general decided to go back to China, and took a Russian ship to travel via the Mediterranean and the Black Sea. But, on 5 September, Soviet newspapers reported that the projector had caught fire during a film show on board, and that the warlord had died either of asphyxiation or a heart attack: there was immediate speculation that this was one of Chiang's dirty tricks, but no evidence of foul play was produced.[13]

Two months later, there was bad news for the Generalissimo from the United States. The pro-Chiang Republicans failed to win the presidential election of 1948, and the activities of the China Lobby on their behalf had deeply irritated Harry Truman. He refused to let Meiling stay at the White House when she made another mission to raise support and funds. 'I don't think she liked it very much, but I didn't care one way or the other about what she liked and what she didn't like,' Truman remarked later, adding that he guessed the 'grafters and crooks' in the Chinese government had stolen a billion dollars from loans. 'They're all thieves, every damn one of them,' he added. Estimates were to put T. V. Soong's wealth at anywhere from US$500 million to double that amount while Ailing and her husband were said to have had a billion between them.[14]

Nationalists reflected bitterly on the difference between Greece, where the Truman administration committed itself fully to a government victory in the civil war with Communists, and China, where it took a much cooler attitude. What they did not appreciate was how the playing field had tilted. George Marshall had got a close-up view of the regime and its leader that could not encourage any increase in support. Truman called the loss of the north-east 'a great blow' but the Soviet withdrawal from Manchuria lessened the fear that Stalin would use it as a springboard in the Far East. Halting Lin Biao's forces would involve the United States in sending troops of its own in huge numbers, which was not something the White House was ready to do. Chiang had had his chance, and his conduct in the six years since the arrival of Joseph Stilwell meant that he had run out of rope. He had squandered too many chances and disappointed too many hopes to be given another go.

Not that American policy was any more coherent than it had been since Pearl Harbor. A cable to the State Department on 29 November 1948 from the ambassador encapsulated the dilemma Washington could not resolve. Commenting on Meiling's trip to seek more aid, the aged John Leighton Stuart wrote:

> We are confronted with the choice of aiding a leader who has not only lost the support of his own people but has allowed the military situation to deteriorate to a point where Barr [Director of the US Military Advisory Group in China] is convinced it is too late to be retrieved even with immediate American advice and matériel, or of witnessing the establishment of a Communist-dominated coalition. If we hold out no hope to Madame Chiang of increased military assistance, Generalissimo will probably yield to the strong pressure from Kmt to delegate powers to others. But by same token, these others will then probably feel compelled to compromise with victorious Communists. On the other hand, should Madame Chiang be given assurances of increased and continuing military aid, we can expect a continuance of the Generalissimo in power, with his ineffective manner of handling affairs, and a rising tide of resentment against us for prolonging the war.[15]

In the circumstances, the best the State Department could come up with was a White Paper saying the USA had done all it could in China, and making plain that it would do no more. In Washington, Marshall called the situation 'critical'. But, when Chiang blamed the setbacks in the north on the Yalta agreement and said the United States must send help, all he got in return was an acknowledgement of his message from the White House. Sun Fo called for the appointment of an American supreme commander in China of the calibre of Douglas MacArthur, the viceroy of Japan, but Truman ruled that out. Though it ensured that the Nationalists retained their permanent seat on the Security Council of the new United Nations, the administration again suspended aid.

The choice was clear – the Cold War was to be fought in Europe, not in China. The decision not to commit to Chiang would provoke the search for The Men Who Lost China and McCarthyism, fuelling the rise of the Republican right, Barry Goldwater and Ronald Reagan. From Roosevelt's confused attempts to cast China as a major power whose leader belonged in the club of democratic nations to the debacle sweeping over the Nationalist regime, the inability of American policy-makers to rise above the tangle they set for themselves stands as a failure of attention and nerve, an example of how a preponderant power should not let itself behave.

The railway city of Xuzhou had been where Chiang had won the backing of the Christian General against the left-wingers in Wuhan in 1927. Nearby was the walled town of Taierzhuang where the Chinese had registered their victory in 1938. Sitting at the junction of north–south and east–west lines and with a population of 300,000, Xuzhou was the vital junction between north China and the rich Lower Yangtze. More than a year earlier, the Communists had told the American journalist Jack Belden that the war would be decided by the battle for the city. Echoing the metaphor about the Japanese and the Communists, a Nationalist minister said that, while Manchuria was a limb, central China was the heart.[16]

Two Communist armies totalling more than half a million men, with twice as many peasants as bearers and helpers, advanced towards Xuzhou in the late autumn of 1948, establishing themselves in a triangle between the Yangtze and Yellow rivers. The East China Field Army, led by Chen Yi, who had been with Mao in the original Soviet base in Jiangxi, fought its way through southern Shandong while the Central Plains Army advanced from the west under Liu Bocheng, 'the one-eyed dragon', who had lost an eye in a grenade explosion and had served as Chief of Staff on the Long March, drinking a libation of chicken's blood to seal a pact with the Yi people of Yunnan.

The Nationalists built up an equivalent force for what became known as the Huai-Hai battle because it took place between the Huai River and the parallel Longhai railway line. Chiang could have pulled back south of the natural defensive line of the river, but he chose to fight on the flat countryside outside Xuzhou rather than relinquishing the rail junction. One Nationalist army group was positioned to the west, one inside the city, and two to the east. Chiang's forces controlled the air and enjoyed supremacy in artillery, vehicles and tanks – his adopted son, Wei-kuo, commanded an armoured unit. But they had few planes left, and proved incompetent in using heavy guns and motorised equipment. Their generals were badly coordinated, and subject to the usual instructions from Chiang in the capital. After General He Yingqin had got one of his men appointed in overall field control, the Generalissimo made sure he had his own man on the spot by sending in his protégé, General Du Yuming, as deputy commander.

The PLA won a first victory when they took a town defended by 90,000 troops, only a few thousand of whom escaped. In contrast to the traditional image of Communist infantrymen and peasants storming the barricades of reaction, the victory was won with a final tank assault against a double defensive ring of walls and moats. Caught in a huge pincer movement, three Nationalist armies totalling 300,000 men were swiftly surrounded and subjected to intense bombardment. Their motorised units bogged down in the mud, while their pilots flew too high for accurate bombing. Their intelligence was poor compared to what the Communists learned from peasant supporters. Static defensive tactics left the government divisions as sitting ducks in face of the PLA's speed and manoeuvring skill in attacking weak spots one by one with massive force in pursuit of Mao's doctrine of annihilation.

One Kuomintang general was killed in action. Another shot himself after sending Chiang a farewell message following the defeat of his army. Cut off on the barren, wintry plain, some government units ran short of food. Defections soared. A photographer flying over the area in mid-November reported that every village for 30 miles was on fire. Xuzhou airfield was abandoned as the PLA formed a 20-mile arc north of the city. Soldiers and officials fought to board the last planes. Fuel dumps were blown up, sending smoke 8,000 feet into the air.[17]

The overall Nationalist commander, General Liu Chih, a rotund man with gold-capped teeth, had flown out to the safety of the town of Bengbu, standing on the Huai River and the railway line from Nanking. Armies which had withdrawn from the battle concentrated there with their American trucks and armoured vehicles. At the beginning of December, Liu sent two of these armies back to relieve a unit surrounded by the PLA. 'We are closing a trap,' he told a visiting correspondent. But the counter-attack failed under heavy Communist artillery fire, and a Nationalist division defected. On 16 December government tanks and trucks rattled across the Bengbu bridge, followed by long lines of infantry, to establish a new defensive line 30 miles closer to Nanking. As they did so, the Communists issued a list of forty 'war criminals' – Chiang headed it followed by T. V. Soong, H. H. Kung, Meiling and Nationalist generals, including the Peiping defender, Fu Zuoyi.[18]

The Xuzhou garrison of more than 100,000 men under General Du was cut off; the PLA radio bragged that they were 'encircled as tightly as in an iron barrel'. Abandoned American vehicles lay in fields, and long lines of Nationalists troops were marched off to prisoner-of-war camps. Landlords were purged, and land distributed to the peasants. Like the Kuomintang troops in 1926–27, the PLA impressed the villagers by behaving well, and paying for supplies. Local people turned into guerrilla fighters. A militia leader gave a simple explanation. 'These are our fields,' he told an American correspondent.[19]

The chain of military disasters was accompanied by the bursting of a brief economic bubble in coastal cities caused by the flow of civilian aid organised by the United Nations. The diversion of goods onto the black market had produced a sheen of prosperity in some places, particularly in Shanghai where even blood plasma donated by the American Red Cross was on sale in shops for US$25 a pint, and supplies were smuggled out to be sold to the Communists for gold bars. Then the remorseless pressure of inflation and depreciation of the currency took its toll. With military spending sky-rocketing, the volume of new banknotes printed by the government rose twenty-two times in a year. A single US dollar was worth millions of its Chinese counterpart. A mill was reported to have bought up banknotes to pulp into high quality paper which was more valuable. A well-known professor killed himself because he could not pay for his hospital bills. A major general jumped to his death from a ship saying he could not bear watching his family dying of hunger. In Shanghai, the issue of certificates that could be redeemed later for gold drew queues of 200,000 people who stood through a rainy night; seven were trampled to death.

As money became useless, shopkeepers were unwilling to sell because they knew prices would double within a few days. Farmers hoarded food, further boosting prices in urban areas. Businessmen moved operations to Hong Kong and other safe havens. China was proving the truth of Lenin's observation about the power of hyperinflation to undermine a regime.[20]

The government was reluctant to act both because it needed all the cash it could print to pay for the war, and because it feared that taking drastic measures would increase its unpopularity. Some steps were tried to control prices, wages, credit and production but they had little effect given the way in which the regime was pumping up inflation. As the economist Chang Kia-ngau pointed out, such measures were aimed at the symptoms of the economic disease, not its cause.[21]

A new currency, the gold yuan, was introduced. Each unit was to be worth 3 million of the old money. Individuals were to hand in gold and silver in return for the new notes. The scheme had to be aborted when word got out and sparked a storm of speculation – T. V. Soong was blamed for the leak, and sent off to become Governor of Guangdong, after which the Chen brothers launched an investigation of his affairs. In August 1948, a new attempt was made, and Chiang's thickset, crew-cut son, Ching-kuo, went to Shanghai to oversee implementation, launching a 'tiger hunt' against speculators. Using methods he had seen in the Soviet Union, he made a target of the middle class to try to raise popular support for what he called a social revolution, and forced shopkeepers to sell hoarded goods at low prices. This produced a buying stampede – a coolie who snapped up a bottle of penicillin was asked if he knew what it was; 'No, but I know it's worth more than money,' he replied.[22]

Many shopkeepers were ruined. Confidence in the new currency dropped sharply, and it plunged in value, wiping out the savings of those who entrusted their valuable metals to the government. There were runs on banks. Rioters raided food stores. Ching-kuo turned on the rich, confiscating their assets and detaining some. In a sign of the Godfather's loss of influence, the son of Big-Eared Du was among those pulled in – after a newspaper ran a photograph of him in handcuffs on its front page, the old man refused to go out or to receive guests for more than a month before decamping to Hong Kong. Ching-kuo's agents also raided the warehouses of the Yangtze Development Corporation, an enterprise controlled by the Kungs. One of their sons, David, was detained. In an echo of her reaction to W. H. Donald's criticism of her sister, Meiling flew to Shanghai to confront her stepson on behalf of her family. According to one account, she slapped him in the face for what he had done. The Kungs were said to have threatened to release embarrassing information about the Chiangs if their son was not freed. David made a settlement to the government, reportedly US$6 million, and left for Hong Kong and New York. Ching-kuo resigned, presumably having been told by his father he had gone too far.[23]

Chiang's New Year message for 1949 contained what was billed as a peace offer, but the terms were so unyielding that it was bound to be rejected by the Communists. After a lull at the turn of the year, fighting resumed at Xuzhou where bodies were thrown into open graves, cannibalism was reported and people wore winter coats made from the skins of dogs and cats they had eaten. Chiang halted supplies to try to force the garrison to break out, but they made no concerted move. On 7 January, a section of the defences was breached. Some Nationalist troops surrendered; others tried to get away. General Du fled disguised as an ordinary soldier, pretending to be the prisoner of his bodyguards who were dressed as Communists; but he was captured.* Another general did escape, shedding his uniform and being taken through the lines in a wheelbarrow. According to Chiang's son, Ching-kuo, the loss of the city meant that the Communists gained control of 'our chemical shells' and used them against the Nationalists.

On 15 January, after looting the shops, the last Nationalist crossed the Huai River, blowing up the main bridge and killing thirty civilians who were on it at the time. The campaign cost the Nationalists 200,000 casualties. Even more men surrendered or defected. Victory opened the road for the

---

* He was held as a war criminal until being pardoned in 1959 after expressing repentance for his misdeeds.

Communists to the Yangtze, Nanking and Shanghai. Officials and their families there joined an exodus to the south on 'dispersal trains'. So many members of the Legislative Yuan left the capital that the body lacked a quorum. In the north, the Communists took Tianjin, firing their rifles in the air as they marched past the great Western buildings in the former American and British Concessions.

Though he thought of trying to raise a new army in Yunnan, Chiang's eye was now on Taiwan, which had been returned to China after the surrender of Japan following a fifty-year occupation. He had sent Chen Cheng there as Governor to prepare the island as a new base – four of the Generalissimo's cars were taken over as a sign of his intentions. Refugees boarded boats from Shanghai to cross the Strait; more than 2,000 passengers died when one hit a Japanese mine and sank.[24]

The 14,000-square-mile island was an ideal base both because Chiang's navy would protect it, and because of the lack of Communist presence. The prospect of safe passage to the offshore bolt hole also induced Nationalist generals to stay loyal to the island's master. The coming of the mainlanders wreaked havoc in what had been a harshly ruled but relatively progressive Japanese colony. The island's currency depreciated and the black market flourished. There was a cholera outbreak. Education declined. Mainlanders used military support to grab local businesses and impose government monopolies. The islanders showed their resentment with a revolt on 28 February 1947 after police beat an old Taiwanese woman who resisted arrest for selling cigarettes in contravention of the monopoly. Troops fired on a protest rally, and the ensuing repression took anywhere from 5,000 to 20,000 lives. Taiwan was cowed, and Chiang could go ahead with the transfer of troops, along with the navy and air force. He also held on to two islands off the coast, Matsu and Quemoy, which the Communists failed to take in a rare Nationalist success.[25]

Political pressure to seek an end to the war rose when the Executive Yuan proposed an immediate unconditional ceasefire. But there was no way the Generalissimo could even start to talk about Mao's conditions – elimination of reactionaries from government, punishment of war criminals such as himself and his wife, confiscation of 'bureaucratic capital', land and army reform, an end to treaties with imperialists, and, less threatening, adoption of an Anno Domini calendar. The gall Chiang was tasting became even more bitter when it became clear that his northern commander, Fu Zuoyi, was negotiating to surrender Peiping. An appeal to Truman for a 'firm statement of American policy in support of the cause for which my Government is fighting' evoked no response. From his headquarters in Nanking, Chiang conducted tense late night conversations about military movements with his generals in the field, and then found it difficult to sleep. Pills did not help, so he took to drinking a cup and a half of whisky to help him nod off.[26]

On 21 January 1949 the Generalissimo rose at his usual early hour. He wrote a letter to Fu urging him to resist, and then prayed in church. After holding a lunch for the presidents of the five Yuans, Chiang went to a meeting of the Kuomintang Central Committee to announce that he was handing over to the Vice-President, Li Zongren, 'in the hope that the fighting will come to an end and that the suffering of the people can be lessened'. Some committee members broke into tears. Others tried to dissuade him. But it was time for a last tactical retreat.

Leaving the Central Committee, Chiang drove in his black Cadillac to visit the Sun Yat-sen memorial on the edge of the city. With the aid of a walking stick, he climbed the white steps he had ascended nineteen years earlier behind the coffin of the founder of the Kuomintang. Entering the great hall, the Generalissimo bowed three times before the marble statue of the doctor. When he came out into the sunshine, he spent a while looking out over his capital, then walked down the steps between thick ranks of guards, followed by a posse of generals. He drove to the airport and flew with his son to Hangzhou – Meiling was away in America. In the city he had led a revolutionary 'Dare to Die' unit in 1911, he stayed at the air force academy, and went out to dinner at a restaurant. Before going to bed, he told Ching-kuo: 'I feel most relieved after unburdening myself of such a heavy load.'

As soon as Chiang was gone, Li Zongren put out peace feelers to Mao Zedong. Two days later, Peiping was handed over to the Communists. In icy weather, an advance guard of 200–300 PLA men marched in, described by one observer as 'red-cheeked, healthy looking and seeming in high spirits'. Behind them came a column of students carrying portraits of Mao and Zhu De. Observers noted that most of their equipment was captured American matériel. Under the surrender deal, General Fu's name was taken off the list of war criminals, and his troops integrated into the PLA.[27]

Returning to his home village, Chiang decided that 'the fundamental cause of failure this time is that the old system had collapsed before the new one could be established'. The blame, he wrote, lay with the Kuomintang for having done nothing to reform society or promote the people's welfare. The sixty-two-year-old Generalissimo walked in the countryside, watching the birds and relishing the peace. His son cooked taro which he enjoyed. 'He often looked at his grandsons and smiled,' Ching-kuo recorded in his diary. At the Lunar New Year at the end of January, Chiang paid tribute to his ancestors at the family temple. In the evening, lantern parties with dragon dances were held in his honour.[28]

Despite the walks and smiles for his grandsons, Chiang was still intent on pulling the strings of what remained of the Nationalist administration, as he had done in earlier retreats to Xikou. His resignation had been ambiguous. His statement said that Li Zongren 'will act for me', leaving it unclear whether he was stepping down definitively or just taking a break. Pressed by reporters, officials in Nanking telephoned Xikou and came back to journalists with the formulation, 'I have decided to retire,' which left matters no clearer. Chiang was still the Generalissimo and Director of the Kuomintang. Keeping in touch with loyal commanders and officials, he issued orders that undercut Li Zongren, whose hopes of peace were dashed by stern Communist terms and opposition from his long-time Guangxi colleague, General Bai, who wanted to go on fighting.

Chen Lifu went to Xikou to confer with his old boss over the Lunar New Year. The Model Governor, who had pointed to a pile of cyanide pills on his desk when interviewed by *Life* magazine and said he would rather kill himself than surrender, also visited Chiang before decamping to Nanking with his province's gold reserves – his capital fell to the Communists in April after house-to-house fighting. The Generalissimo's lobbyists in Washington encouraged Republican congressmen to press Truman to help the Nationalists, and to introduce a Senate bill for aid totalling US$1.5 billion – it did not get through, but the China Lobby kept up the pressure, expanding its following in Congress with the backing of Henry Luce's publications.

From Xikou, Chiang telephoned senior generals to issue orders. Li Zongren recalled one evening when the Generalissimo called the army Chief of Staff three times during a dinner. He also had the faithful General Tang Enbo, who was in command of the Shanghai region, arrest the governor of his native province of Zhejiang for disloyalty without informing Nanking. On the other hand, when Li asked Chiang to agree to free the Young Marshal, he replied that, as a retired man, he could not act in matters of state.

As the victors of the Huai-Hai battle moved towards Nanking and Lin Biao's troops sliced southwards, a major disagreement arose over defending the Nationalist heartland. Li and his team wanted to use the Yangtze as a defensive moat, holding out on the southern bank. The participation of Tang Enbo's large army based in Shanghai was an essential part of the plan. But Tang refused to join in – for his own reasons, Chiang was telling him to remain where he was. At a conference organised by Li Zongren, the head of the Operations Department pointed out that this would weaken the attempt to stop the PLA crossing the river. Tang said he did not care; he had orders from Chiang, and they must be followed. Slamming the table and sweeping the papers in front of him onto the floor, he shouted threats to shoot the operations chief and stalked out – his threat was not treated lightly since Tang was known for his temper; he had once killed the owner of a ship on which he was travelling after it hit a pier. Li Zongren looked at General He Yingqin, who had by now become Prime Minister, and wondered what they should do. 'If the big boss does not agree, what can we do?' was He's reply. 'Let the situation go to blazes.'

Chiang wanted to hold on to Shanghai so that he could extract as much of its wealth as possible to be transferred to Taiwan. He also wanted to take trusted troops to the island rather than seeing them chewed up in fighting along the Yangtze. The city was subjected to brutal military misrule as Tang's troops looted shops and occupied homes, executing dissident students in the streets while crowds besieged banks trying to draw out their remaining deposits. Green Gang men loaded gold and notes from the Bank of China onto ships to be taken across the Strait. China's national collection of antiquities and art treasures which had followed Chiang round his various capitals also made the voyage. So did the Young Marshal, who was installed in a police post on the island.[29]

To try to straighten out the situation, Li attempted to get Chiang either to resume power or to leave the country. That was a waste of time – the Generalissimo's purpose was to leave Li dangling while he built up his new power base in Taiwan, where he could make a fresh start and would face no opposition. While he did that, he had no desire to make things easier for his successor; indeed, his interest lay in Li failing – a successful defence on the Yangtze would have spelled the end to his ambitions to re-emerge as the Nationalist leader when he saw the time as right.

His peace efforts blocked by tough Communist conditions, Li approached both Washington and Moscow. The notion of an American air and naval blockade along the Yangtze was floated, linked to Chiang's definitive retirement. This would have divided China in the way of Germany, Korea and Vietnam. Had Washington accepted the idea, the recent history of East Asia might have been very different, or Americans might have found themselves fighting the PLA at the height of the Cold War. But, predictably, Truman and Marshall were not interested.[30]

Nanking also sought Russian intervention. Stalin was tempted – the idea of a weak and divided China under Soviet influence had its attractions while he worried that a triumphant Mao would become an independent force like Tito in Yugoslavia. In 1948, he had sent an emissary to urge Mao not to seek total victory for fear of provoking US intervention. Now, Moscow advised the PLA to stop on the Yangtze rather than aiming to conquer the whole nation. Mao was in no mood to listen; fourteen years later, he would note that the Chinese revolution had succeeded against Stalin's will, and that the roots of the subsequent split with Moscow lay in the Kremlin's attempt to check him.

In a final bid to win Chiang's support, Li Zongren flew to Hangzhou for a meeting at the air force college there. According to Li's memoirs, the Generalissimo assured him of support, but, even at this drastic juncture, considerations of 'face' prevented the Guangxi general from insisting on specific undertakings. When Li got back to the capital, he found that the government had left for Canton. After a sleepless night, he took a jeep to the airfield, and flew to his native region in the south-west.[31]

The fall of Nanking was symptomatic of the collapse of the regime. Mobs rampaged through the streets; troops blew up the railway station; soldiers and police shed their uniforms. Looters stripped abandoned houses – the American journalist Seymour Topping watched an old woman in a ragged black tunic hobble away on bound feet with four elaborately embroidered cushions from one villa. At the huge Executive Yuan and the Ministry of Communications, everything that could be removed was stolen, including the window frames. The residences of General He Yingqin and Li Zongren were ransacked, in the latter case with the help of the housekeeper.

The Mayor tried to escape in a car with 300 million gold yuan, but was beaten up by his chauffeur and bodyguards who broke his legs and left him on the road after making off with the money. At the airport, crowds of civilians tried to force their way onto the few planes left. Senior officials and generals took piles of furniture and belongings, including, in one case, a grand piano. A dazed Kuomintang official was photographed standing in line grasping a tennis racket. A Peace Preservation Committee was formed to arrange the handover of the city, its chairman sitting alone in a dingy, pea-green room in the Cairo Hotel.[32]

The PLA crossed the Yangtze without opposition on 20 April 1949. The defenders melted away or defected, one unit turning its guns on the Nationalist boats in the river and protecting the Communist craft. Nanking was formally taken three days later by steel-helmeted troops in mustard-brown uniforms accompanied by tanks. Watching them, the French military attaché, Jacques Guillermaz, was struck by how tired they looked as they marched in, bags of rice slung over their shoulders.[33]

Though students staged a welcoming rally, most of the people in the streets regarded the newcomers silently. A dozen PLA soldiers burst into the bedroom of the American ambassador, pointed to the furniture and said, 'These will soon belong to the people.' There was a more serious incident when Communist forces fired at a British naval vessel, the Amethyst, which had been sent up the river to take supplies to the embassy. Three British ships tried to go to its aid, but were shelled in their turn. In all, forty-four sailors were killed and eighty injured, and the Amethyst remained trapped for 100 days as its captain refused to sign a confession of 'criminally invading Chinese territorial waters' – the ship eventually escaped under fire, using a passing boat as cover. In the past, foreign warships had sailed at will on the Yangtze; now they were unwelcome intruders.[34]

To the east, Hangzhou was taken, isolating Shanghai. To the west, Lin Biao's army surged to Wuhan, then marched south through the rain. Other Communist units drove into Jiangxi to take Nanchang. The Guangxi Muslim general, Bai Chongxi, tried to organise resistance in Hunan; still anxious to check independent-minded commanders, Chiang used his influence to deny him supplies.

On a last visit to Shanghai, where he stayed in the Moral Endeavour club, the Generalissimo issued instructions for the defence of the city that had contributed so much to his rise to power. 'Seeing the Republic of China on the verge of death, I am moving ahead with tears in my eyes,' he wrote in his diary on 7 May. 'There is only one road ahead, but it is torturous. Don't fear. The road has been blazed with blood by our revolutionary forefathers. We must move forward today – forward, never retreat. Around us is darkness; ahead of us are dangers. With a ray of hope and my allegiance to Dr Sun Yat-sen, I will continue my struggle without fail.' Others were less determined. In despair at the current of events, the Generalissimo's long-time ideological mentor, Dai Jitao, killed himself. So did one of Chiang's secretaries who left a note saying, 'The light is dying.'[35]

Tang Enbo swore to make Shanghai a second Stalingrad. He had coolies dig a large moat and build a 10-foot-high bamboo barrier – it was said that one of his relatives was in the wood business. The general imposed arbitrary taxes to raise funds, requisitioning houses, hotels and dance halls which his troops stripped of anything valuable. Censorship blocked out news of Nationalist defeats, but the city was awash with rumour and fear. Frantic crowds besieged banks as the value of the currency spiralled down even further and outgoing ships charged extortionate prices for berths. 'The city was filled with men, women and children rushing about in dilapidated trucks or pedicabs,' wrote the Filipino Consul-General. 'People with blank stares [were] running around aimlessly for places of safety.' Most of the defenders melted away as the warlord troops had done against the Nationalists twenty-two years earlier. The business community paid them to go quietly and made a placatory offer of funds and medicine to the PLA. Tang Enbo headed for Canton, awaiting further orders from his master. On 24 May 1949, the Communist vanguard marched up the Avenue Edouard VII in the old French Concession area. A few Nationalist soldiers tried to hold out, but then changed into black gowns and fled. A huge portrait of Mao was put up at the Great World entertainment centre. On the same day, Li Zongren asked the American ambassador to get him a statement of support from Washington. Leighton Stuart cabled the State Department that, despite all his sympathy for the acting President, he could not envisage any statement from the US which 'would be effective in changing the course of military events'.[36]

*

The political, economic and military situation grew even more chaotic for the Nationalists as their military defeats rolled on. Tang Enbo's concentration in Shanghai had left no troops to defend the region to the south, so the Communists moved swiftly down from the Yangtze. Chiang repeatedly intervened to undo defensive plans worked out by the Guangxi generals. Defections sapped the government's position; General Bai was forced to retreat from Hunan after the provincial governor switched sides. As the PLA advanced, General He stepped down as prime minister, telling Li that, if he did not do so, he would have only two alternatives – desertion or suicide. Chiang showed his political influence by getting the Chen brothers to block the appointment of Li's preferred candidate as his successor. Instead, the Model Governor took the job.[37]

While the Nationalists crumbled, there were indications that the Communists might not have finally set their face against an understanding with the United States. In June, a friend of the American ambassador who had been to the north told John Leighton Stuart that Mao and Zhou Enlai would welcome a visit from him. At the same time, an Australian journalist approached the former head of the Dixie Mission, Colonel David Barrett, who was in Peiping, with what he said was a message from Zhou that the Communists were split between a pro-Soviet faction and a liberal group headed by Zhou which wanted working relationships with foreign governments, notably America. The State Department was very cautious on both fronts, and, at the end of the month, Mao ruled out any rapprochement with a speech hailing Moscow as China's true friend – despite Stalin's attempts to halt the PLA – and saying he expected no help from the West.[38]

Having moved hundreds of thousands of troops, his bureaucracy and the gold and silver reserves to Taiwan, Chiang was now ready for his final act on the mainland. In July, he flew through bad weather to Canton and laid out plans for military operations. He also established a body called the Extraordinary Committee of the Central Executive Committee of the Kuomintang to control party affairs, with himself as chairman. Without consulting the Prime Minister in advance, he appointed Tang Enbo as Governor of Fujian, across the Strait from Taiwan. According to Li Zongren, some southern generals grew so angry that they proposed arresting Chiang: as Li pointed out, since he had the national treasury and the loyalty of many of the other commanders, a rerun of the Xi'an Incident would achieve nothing.[39]

Convinced that it was only a matter of time before a Third World War between the United States and Communism paved the way for his resumption of power on the mainland, Chiang paid visits to the right-wing governments in the Philippines and South Korea. Failure to come to his aid would cost the democracies dearly, he warned in an interview. 'If we cannot stop Communism in China, I am sure it will spread to the whole of Asia,' he added in an early exposition of the domino theory that would reach its apogee in Vietnam. But Washington made it plain there would be no eleventh-hour rescue mission.[40]

In the increasingly unreal atmosphere, Chiang returned to Canton, where he expressed outrage at the extent of gambling and drug smuggling. Meeting General Bai, he said that if they stuck together, all would not be lost. Moved, the Muslim soldier told his colleague, Li Zongren, that he thought the Generalissimo was sincere this time. So Li invited Chiang to dinner. His guest arrived with a heavy detachment of guards who ringed the building. Ching-kuo went to the kitchen to check each dish to make sure it did not contain poison.[41]

Following the dinner, Li requested an interview with Chiang and, according to the account in his memoirs, delivered an angry and lengthy attack, listing the Generalissimo's shortcomings and wrongdoings. To Li's surprise, Chiang reacted humbly, and accompanied him to the door, waving goodbye as he left. But it was too late for a recovery. The Eagle of the North-West, Hu Zongnan, was forced to retreat from Shaanxi to Sichuan. Gansu province and the city of Lanzhou were lost in the north-west. The huge territory of Xinjiang went over to the Communists. On 1 October, Mao Zedong proclaimed the People's Republic in the restored capital of Peking, declaring that 'the Chinese people have stood up'. At the end of the month, Canton fell, 'with scarcely more than a quiet sigh', as the *New York Times* reported. The Nationalists moved to the safest city they could identify, Chungking, though Chiang headed in the opposite direction, to Taiwan.[42]

'The past year has been the darkest and bleakest in my life,' Chiang noted in his diary on his birthday at the end of October, adding, however: 'I am confident that I shall receive the divine decree and can consummate my task.' He then set down a typical self-admonition mixing flagellation and self-regard: 'I have spent my past life in vain. I have suffered ignominy and defeat. However, I should not be worried, angry, nor should I be conceited. I have nothing to be ashamed of before God and man. How lucky I am to have the love of God. Danger and difficulty lie ahead. I must heighten my vigilance so that I can revive China and re-establish the republic.'[43]

On 11 November he received a letter from the Model Governor, writing as Prime Minister, which said that, without his presence in Chungking, collapse was almost inevitable. Three days later, the Generalissimo made a five-hour flight to the city where he had spent seven of the war years. His son, who accompanied him, recorded that Chungking was 'in the grip of panic, terror, and an atmosphere of deadly silence'. Chiang tried to get Li Zongren to join him. But, suffering from bleeding bowels, the general decided to go to hospital in Hong Kong before heading for New York where he checked in at the Presbyterian Hospital.[44]

Guizhou province fell after General Bai decided to conserve his troops across the border in his native Guangxi and a local general was executed for purloining money meant for his soldiers. By the end of November, the Communist forces led by the Sichuan native, Deng Xiaoping, were closing in on Chungking. On the 29th, Chiang held a military conference to give detailed orders for retreat. He had to walk back to his residence because the streets were blocked with fleeing people and cars. At 10 p.m. rifle fire broke out on the edge of the city, and there were frequent explosions. At dawn the next day, the Generalissimo decided to fly to the Sichuan capital of Chengdu. One story had it that, before getting in his car, he paid a last visit to military headquarters in Chungking but found it deserted. Seeing a map on the floor, he picked it up and burned it to prevent it falling into the hands of the enemy. Then, when his car stopped in the crush of fleeing traffic, he got out and walked to the other side of the jam to commandeer a jeep. As he went, according to the recollections of a police agent, 'he wanted to kill all the people he hated'. Most of the inmates of the secret police jail run with the Americans of the SACO programme were shot. Political prisoners held in a coal mine were executed. There was also one special life Chiang wanted taken.[45]

General Yang Hucheng, the man who had suggested the kidnapping in Xi'an, had been brought to Chungking and kept with his family under house arrest. As the Communists approached, secret police agents went round. First, they shot one of Yang's sons. Then the general was murdered, followed by his daughter, and six members of his staff and their families.

The bodies were doused in acid and buried, the general in a brick flower box. Another of Yang's sons later unearthed the bodies, and took his father's corpse for proper burial in the city where he and the Young Marshal had snatched the ruler of China thirteen years earlier.

Chungking fell on 1 December 1949. Deng Xiaoping became Mayor and political commissar. The Communists also took Guangxi, as Bai was forced to retreat. In Chengdu, Kuomintang members who remained called on Chiang to resume the presidency, and the north-western 'Eagle', Hu Zongnan, organised his troops to defend the city. Many of the inhabitants were trying to flee. Vehicles jammed the streets. Soldiers fired at random. Looters grabbed what they could of what was left. On 8 December, the Executive Yuan voted to remove the capital of China to Taiwan. On the 10th, thirteen years almost to the day after he had prepared what was meant to be the final elimination of the Communists from his headquarters in Xi'an, Chiang went to the airfield to fly to Taiwan. There were no radio stations to give guidance, and heavy cloud prevented the navigator working by reference to the land below. The DC-4 plane flew by the instinct of the pilot and his reckoning of the wind. At 9 p.m. a break in the cloud enabled him to see an island off the coast of Fujian. The course for Taiwan was set. The major on the flight deck went back to tell the Generalissimo. He just nodded.

After arriving, Chiang went with his son to a hotel at one of the island's beauty spots, Sun Moon Lake. There he received a message telling him of the loss of Yunnan. According to his biographer Hollington Tong, the sixty-two-year-old Nationalist leader sat quietly for an hour before telling Ching-kuo they should take a walk. They reached the edge of a forest where Chiang sat and meditated. Then he suggested a fishing expedition. Ching-kuo found an old man who had a boat and went back to the hotel to fetch money to pay for it. His father set off alone, casting a net. According to this story, he caught a fish that was five foot long – 'it was a good omen and Chiang felt the curtain of his black thoughts lifting'.[46]

The civil war had taken perhaps 5 million lives, on top of the 10 million or more who perished in the conflict with Japan and up to 3 million in Chiang's earlier campaigns. Small-scale fighting continued as Hu Zongnan's army conducted a rearguard action in the far west and General Bai held out on Hainan Island. Other Kuomintang troops stayed in the

Burmese border region, becoming big players in the opium trade of the Golden Triangle region. But, despite such last-ditch resistance, the regime that had ruled for two decades ended without any great final confrontation with its enemy. The crucial battles had been fought a year or more before. Since the loss of Manchuria and the north followed by the great defeat in the Huai-Hai campaign, Chiang had been preparing for his long-term future.[47]

In Taiwan, he developed a litany to explain the defeat, from which he fully expected to spring back with a triumphant return to the mainland. He had shown too much good faith in the face of Red treachery. The changes in American policy had been the result of the machinations of international Communism. But all was not lost. 'If I can continue my ambition and carry it out,' he wrote in his diary at Christmas 1949, 'I should become aware that the new undertaking and history should begin from today.'[48]

EPILOGUE

Next Year in Nanking

ON HIS RELEASE FROM XI'AN at the end of 1936, Chiang spoke of having been given a second life. Thirteen years later, his flight to Taiwan provided him with a third. For twenty-six years, he ruled as dictator of the Republic of China on the island 100 miles off the coast of the mainland. Most of his associates followed him across the Strait, though some, including Li Zongren and the Yunnan governor Long Yun, made their peace with the new regime in Peking. Others preferred to go to America, like the Kungs, or to Hong Kong, like Big-Eared Du.

Facing the bastion of Asian Communism, Chiang became a Cold War icon in the 1950s, assured of American protection as the Nationalists clung on to their Security Council seat in an increasingly bathetic echo of the era when Roosevelt had seen the Generalissimo as a pillar of the new world order. Around 1960, he proposed to invade the mainland after the chaos of Mao's Great Leap Forward, but Washington declined to back an offensive or provide him with the atomic warheads he wanted. In 1971, the United Nations finally admitted the People's Republic as the only legitimate representative of China, including Taiwan. The following year Richard Nixon visited Beijing and the United States signed the Shanghai communiqué which proclaimed 'there is but one China and Taiwan is part of China'. Full diplomatic relations followed in 1979. For all his claims to be sole legitimate ruler of his country, Chiang's life and career after 1949 were markedly different from the previous quarter of a century, which is why this book ends then.

After suffering from recurrent bouts of pneumonia, Chiang died of a heart attack on 5 April 1975, aged eighty-seven – seventeen months before Mao Zedong passed away in Beijing. Meiling, who had been spending more time in the United States, was back in Taiwan during her husband's last days, and secretly took the Young Marshal to see the corpse before it was laid out for official mourning. The Generalissimo's son, Ching-kuo, became President. Under him and his successor, Lee Teng-hui, the island turned into a great economic success story, and evolved into a fully fledged democracy, realising Nationalist ambitions and seeking to establish its own identity as it confronted reunification demands from Beijing.

Though a giant statue of the Generalissimo looks down in the monumental mausoleum erected to his memory in Taipei, his legacy has faded by the year as the island evolves a character distinct from the Nationalist past, electing a president and a legislature from the opposition. Having failed to impress herself on the post-Chiang Kuomintang leadership, Meiling retreated to a house on Long Island and then moved to an apartment in Manhattan where she died in 2003 at the age of 106. Chiang's face has been taken off some banknotes, and officials have been told that they can remove his portrait from their office walls if they wish to.

The Cold War made an objective assessment of Chiang almost impossible as the past was viewed through the lens of what followed. Either he was a faithful friend of the West who had been undone by Communist cunning, Western irresolution and treachery in the State Department; or he was a reactionary, cruel, incompetent dictator who was no better than the warlords, who betrayed the true interests of his nation by failing to stand up to the Japanese in time, and who perverted the sacred teachings of Sun Yat-sen. Verdicts on the Nanking regime range from revisionist historians who see it as an essential stage in the construction of modern China to those who condemn it as a corrupt, reactionary nest of self-seeking politicians, generals, gangsters and businessmen. Both views contain their degree of truth, but each fails to take the true measure of the man and his time, judging him by absolute standards which could not be expected to be applied to China in the first half of the 20th century.

Chiang was undoubtedly a reactionary authoritarian who set no great store by the lives of his compatriots and put the defeat of the Communists ahead of fighting the Japanese. There was no way he could conform to the American dream that resistance to Fascism and democracy should walk hand-in-hand. He was a bad administrator with no understanding of economics and deep suspicion of the mass movement needed to invigorate the country. While his overall strategic concept against Japan made eventual sense, it entailed huge losses of life and territory, with the attendant demoralisation and weakening of his regime. As a tactical commander, he had a poor record and owed his military status to politics and control of money and supplies, not battlefield prowess. He exploited factional divisions and prized loyalty above merit in making appointments. He tolerated corruption and amorality that would help to destroy his administration. His short-term battles against the Americans ended up by losing him the one ally who mattered. Worst of all for somebody engaged in a constant struggle for supremacy, he doomed himself to be the man who lost China.

But the purely negative verdict on Chiang which followed the Communist victory ignores the often vital nature of his role. Even if progress was patchy and the effects were felt in a relatively small portion of the country, his was a time of modernisation such as China had not seen before, until the outbreak of the war with Japan slammed on the brakes. The Nationalists established the institutions for a modern state, however imperfectly these functioned. The Northern Expedition gave China back its status as a nation, buttressed by the quest for strong central authority to replace the anarchy of the warlord era – a quest that continued up to the outbreak of the war with Japan in 1937 and resumed after 1945. The Nanking Decade saw the country engaging with the rest of the world. The foreign concessions were abolished, industry and finance began to develop, roads and railways were built, and air services began. Though often in opposition to the government, there was a flowering of thought, literature, art and the cinema – and, despite the horror of the purges unleashed in 1927, the repression used by the regime was nothing compared to what was to come under Communism.

The scale of Chiang's defeat masks the equivalent scope of his earlier success. At Sun's death in March 1925, he was not even a major contender to lead the Nationalists. By the following summer, he was the dominant figure in Canton and led the Nationalist forces on the triumphant campaign to the Yangtze. Nine months on, he was at the head of the Kuomintang right in Nanking, emerging on top against the leftist government in Wuhan. In June 1928, Peking was taken and, a year later, Chiang defeated his principal military and political rivals.

Despite that dazzling succession of victories, however, he lacked the political, administrative, ideological and economic bases on which to construct a new China in the face of almost constant warfare and huge natural disasters – one study puts the number of people who died from military violence or famine in China between 1916 and 1949 at 35 million. From the assumption of power in Canton in 1926 to the flight from Chengdu in 1949, everything happened too fast; he could not stop to consolidate. Instead, he had to confront recurrent military and political challenges from rivals, the Japanese and the Communists. Huge as the Nationalist forces were on paper, their effective strength was far smaller, and Chiang's central army was severely weakened in the fighting along the Yangtze in 1937–38. Nor was the regime very effective at totalitarianism – despite his lack of concern for human life, the Generalissimo did not bring to bear the degree of sustained ruthlessness shown by Mao or by the imperial suppression of the Taiping Rebellion. The only way he knew of operating was to go on as before, extending his authority little by little over recalcitrant provinces, playing clan politics, printing money and issuing orders that he often had no means of enforcing.[1]

His short-term political skills were of the highest order, but, for all the sweeping statements in his diary, he lacked a long-range vision that could give coherence to his actions. Obedience was all. The Chinese were to be treated like children, not offered any aspirations beyond the approval of their uniformed father figure. Chiang's manipulative, secretive, suspicious nature played a key part in his early successes, but then prevented him from developing a team to run China and sealed him in a hermetic status quo isolated from his country.

Profoundly conservative, walled off from reality, the Generalissimo was stuck mentally in the era in which he had grown up, making him incapable of offering anything new to a country that was crying out for progress. Obsessively, he pursued his set ideas to the bitter end. Brilliant at tactical retreats and at engineering temporary compromises, he was also deeply stubborn, convinced that he, and he alone, personified his country. His expressions of admiration for his mother enabled him to construct a selfless, dedicated, long-suffering image with which he could identify, a rock to cling to as he navigated the rapids of the 'inter-dynasty' period between the Manchus and the Red Emperor. Given all that, his greatest feat was to have survived for so long at the head of an increasingly united China, even if that unity would become the platform for his greatest adversary.

To establish more accurately Chiang's influence, for good or ill, consider what might have happened had he not been there. Without him, would the Nationalists ever have marched out of Guangdong in search of national unity under Wang Jingwei, Hu Hanmin or one of the regional generals who rallied to the Kuomintang flag? If they had staged a northern expedition, would any of the other potential leaders have been able to hold the movement together, let alone take it on to Peking and the key alliance with the Manchurians? Without Chiang, the odds would have been on a continuation of the warlord era, and the fragmentation of China into eternally conflicting fiefdoms.

If the Generalissimo had been killed in Xi'an in 1936, would the pro-Japanese elements in the administration have allied themselves with Tokyo? If so, a vast Chinese army trained by imperial officers could have joined Japan in an attack on the Soviet Union from the east while Hitler moved from the west, altering the whole history of the Second World War. If Chiang had been replaced at the head of the Nationalists after the outbreak of the war in 1937, would anybody else have been able to hold unoccupied China together for so long? However loose the coalition over which he presided, the Generalissimo alone came to personify his country, preventing the Japanese from achieving political success to accompany their military victories. And, then, what would have happened if Chiang had not been there to manoeuvre so effectively against Stilwell and Marshall? If a coalition government had emerged with a reformed army, Washington would have felt obliged to support it to the end, thus either heading off the final showdown of 1948–49 or turning China into another divided Cold War nation, split along the Yangtze.

Nor was defeat by the Communists as much a matter of historical inevitability as the post-1949 conventional wisdom holds. For two decades, Chiang held the advantage, shown vividly by the great retreat of the Long March. Had the Xi'an Incident not taken place, the Generalissimo might well have finally crushed the Red Army. Nine years later, the Communists had been seriously weakened by Japanese campaigns in the north, and, in 1946, the PLA was pushed back to the north of Manchuria. The protective sea of the peasantry was of little help in any of these cases. Rather than the inescapability of Communist victory, it was the weakness of the Nationalists, Chiang's failure as a military leader, and economic disintegration that sent the one-time man of destiny fleeing to Taiwan.

Year by year, the Generalissimo has become less of a taboo subject in Communist China. Archives in Nanking have been opened. Xikou has been renovated, and attracts crowds of tourists. The Chiangs' villa in the mountain resort of Kuling has been kept as it was when Kai-shek and Meiling left it for the last time. The military headquarters in Lushan from where the Generalissimo launched the campaign that forced the Red Army onto the Long March can be visited. His Shanghai house is a music school. The pavilion from which he fled outside Xi'an has been preserved, bullet holes and all. His wartime home in Chungking stands by the river. His residence in Beijing during the abortive defence of Manchuria against the Communists has become the headquarters of a property company, but the Kuomintang symbols are still inlaid into the floors and ceilings. Visitors to Sun Yat-sen's presidential palace in Nanking can walk down a passage to the brick building from which Chiang ruled and stand in the auditorium where he was elected as President.

There may be an undeclared motive underlying this tolerance of traces of the enemy of the people. Under Chiang, China had a one-party administration organised on Leninist lines with a repressive internal security apparatus and a refusal to permit democracy. There was growing involvement with the rest of the world. Shanghai was the icon of growth and modernity pursued by economic channels rather than through political progress. Coastal areas prospered while vast rural regions remained backward hinterlands. The army played a big political role, and the leader hung on to supreme command of the military even when obliged to step down from other posts. A middle class emerged, with an elite that drew its power and wealth from political connections – and sent its children to be educated in America. A wave of corruption sapped the ruling party. The banking system was run by the state, and was riddled with financial black holes. The government announced ambitious infrastructure plans, and foreign investors saw China as a new business frontier. There was an alliance with Washington against a common foe.

Each of those factors is at play again in the China of the early 21st century. So Chiang's era in power can be seen in many ways as a precursor of the post-Mao nation. After three decades of revolution pursued with religious zeal, China is returning to a more normal state which it had previously experienced under the Generalissimo.

In that context, Chiang and his era become less of the nightmare painted after the Communist victory, and more of a period of missed opportunities under a regime and a ruler who lacked the resources and strength to carry their mission to a conclusion. Following the route of the Long March in the south-west at the end of 2002, I asked my young guide what he thought of Chiang. He replied that, if the Nationalists had not been defeated in 1949, China would have been spared tens of millions of deaths, and would have ended up much as it is today. Walking by the river in Xikou, I put the same question to a thirty-year-old university graduate who was showing me round the Generalissimo's home village. 'Chiang was a major figure, who made major mistakes,' she answered, and then, after a pause, added, 'Like Chairman Mao.'

Waiting for the wheel to turn, the Generalissimo has not given up the cause, even in death. His body has not been buried. To have interred it on Taiwan would have admitted final defeat. So the corpse lies in a marble casket at his country home by a lake outside Taipei, awaiting its eventual return to the mainland Chiang always considered it his destiny to unite, but which, in a quarter of a century of endless struggle, he doomed himself to lose.

NOTES

CCK   Chiang Ching-kuo
CET   *China Express and Telegraph*
CKS   Chiang Kai-shek
CP   *Conference Proceedings on Chiang Kai-shek and Modern China* (Taipei, 1982)
CWR   *China Weekly Review*
MC   Madame Chiang (Soong Meiling)
NCH   *North China Herald*, Shanghai
NYT   *New York Times*
OH   Harry S. Truman Library for Oral Histories, Missouri
PRO   Public Records Office, London
SCMP   *South China Morning Post*
RTR   Reuters news agency
UP   United Press news agency

PROLOGUE: THIRTEEN DAYS IN XI'AN

1 This account is based on the author's visits to Xi'an, where the Young Marshal's headquarters and other sites are preserved, and Huaqing, where bullet holes can still be seen in CKS's pavilion, and on Bertram, pp. 124–38; Tien-wei Wu, particularly pp. 76–81; NCH for December 1927; Selle, Chapter 23; CKS and MC in *China at the Crossroads*; CKS's diary, written after the event, Tong, pp. 212–237; and the recollections of Zhang Xueliang in the four-part video recording, *A Century Walked Through*, made available by Kuo Kwan-ying.

2 Wu Tien-wei, p. 80; NCH, 20 January 1937.

3 Bertram, *First Act*, p. 134.
4 MC in CKS, *Crossroads*, pp. 93–5; Han-sheng Lin in Coox, p. 234.
5 The Communist side of the Xi'an story is well told in Short, pp. 347–52.
6 Borg, p. 225.
7 Gibson, p. 322; Selle, p. 323.
8 Auden and Isherwood, pp. 55–6.
9 NCH, 20 January 1937.
10 MC in CKS, *Crossroads*, pp. 84 et seq.
11 Selle, p. 326.
12 Hahn, *Chiang*, p. 209; see also photograph at Zhang compound in Xi'an.
13 Auden and Isherwood, p. 129.
14 CKS, *Crossroads*, pp. 215 et seq.; Young-tsu Wong in Barrett and Shyu, p. 17; Mao, *Selected Works*, p. 294.
15 MC, *Crisis in China*, p. 141.
16 Central News, 28 December 1936; Selle, p. 334.
17 Kuo Kwan-ying, *Century*, Part Three.
18 Chen Li-fu, p. 126; MC, *Crisis*, p. 83; CKS, *Crossroads*, p. 213.
19 *China Post*, 7 June 2002; SCMP, 18 October 2001.

1: COLD REALITIES

1 NCH, October 1887. Description of Xikou from author's visit, 2001.
2 Photo caption at CKS's birthplace.
3 Xikou villager Sheng Zheng-sheng, quoted in local records, 1984.
4 Chen Chieh-ju (Chen Jieru), pp. 231–5.
5 Ibid., p. 7; Loh, *Chiang*, p. 10; Furaya, p. 6.
6 Loh, ibid., p. 11.
7 Ibid., pp. 9–10, 120.
8 Chen Chieh-ju, p. 54.
9 Tong, p. vii.
10 Ibid., p. 12.
11 Taylor, pp. 6–7, 15.
12 Tong, pp. 13–14.
13 Furaya, p. 18; Tong, p. 15.
14 Furaya, pp. 16–18. The quotes are from lectures Chiang gave in 1944 and 1946.
15 Loh, *Chiang*, pp. 124–5, finds apocryphal nature of 1908 meeting 'generally acceptable'.
16 Hahn, *Chiang*, pp. 13–14; Furaya, p. 30.

2: SWORN BROTHERS

1 Jerome Chen, pp. 278–9. A more positive view is presented by Audrey Wells in her analysis of Sun's thought, which she calls 'a courageously unique synthesis of Eastern and Western ideas'. (p. 201)

2   Selle p. 110; Furaya, p. 40.
3   Sun on Lea, in an exhibition at presidential palace, Nanking.
4   Reinsch, p. 2.
5   Loh, *Chiang*, p. 42. Photographs of Zhang: Spence and Chin, pp. 53, 98–9.
6   CP, Vol. I, p. 297; Furaya, p.34.
7   Reinsch, pp. 1–3; Bergère, *Sun*, p. 229.
8   Martin, p. 80; NCH, 1 May 1913.
9   Friedman, p. 143.
10 Jerome Chen, p. 309; CP, Vol. II, pp. 11–12.
11 Bergère, *Sun*, p. 250; Friedman, p. 89.
12 Selle, pp. 133–8; Hahn, *Soong Sisters*, p. 51.
13 NCH, 13 November 1915.
14 CP, Vol. II, pp. 25–7.
15 Chen Chieh-ju, pp. 79 et seq.; CP, Vol. II, pp. 24–5.
16 CP, Vol. II, p. 29; Loh, *Chiang*, p. 131; Furaya, p. 57.
17 NCH, 27 May 1915; CP, Vol. II, p. 32; Chen Chieh-ju, p. 81.
18 CP, Vol. II, p. 34, pp. 37 et seq.
19 Chen Chieh-ju, p. 87.
20 Bergère, *Sun*, p. 274; Chien Tuan-sheng, pp. 86–7.

3: GOING TO EXTREMES

1   Loh's study, *Chiang*, gives a thorough examination of CKS's character which is drawn on here, including the warrant, pp. 132–3; Martin, pp. 81, 243 (note 9).
2   Loh, p. 32; Chen Chieh-ju, p. 49; Chen, Wang and Wang, p. 11.
3   Chen Chieh-ju, p. 7; Tang, p. 252; Chen, Wang and Wang, p. 10; Loh, *Chiang*, p. 32.
4   Chen Chieh-ju, p. 32.
5   Ibid., pp. 3–21.
6   This and the following is from Chen Chieh-ju, Chapter 2.
7   PRO, Alston/Curzon FO 405/236/219.845 of 24 March 1922.
8   Bergère, *Sun*, p. 302; Saich, *Origins*, p. 40.
9   CP, Vol. I, p. 278.
10 Sie, p. 131.
11 This account is from Chen Chieh-ju, pp. 21 et seq.
12 The wedding story is in Chen Chieh-ju, Chapter 4.
13 Chen Chieh-ju, pp. 53, 66–9.
14 Ibid., p. 73; Taylor, pp. 12–14.
15 Chen Chieh-ju, pp. 83–5.
16 SCMP, 3 October 1997.
17 Chen Chieh-ju, pp. 88, 91.
18 Ibid., pp. 91 et seq.
19 Bergère, *Sun*, pp. 200, 302; Chen Chieh-ju, pp. 97, 99.
20 Loh, *Chiang*, pp. 70 et seq.

21 Chen Chieh-ju, pp. 109 et seq.
22 Loh, p. 142.
23 Ibid., p. 72.
24 Consul letter on show at Musée Kahn, Paris, 2002; Wilbur, *Frustrated Patriot*, p. 128; Saich, *Origins*, p. 121.
25 Loh, *Chiang*, pp. 76–7, 80–1, mainly quoting CKS's diary.
26 Chen Chieh-ju, pp. 112–13.
27 Loh, *Chiang*, p. 87.

4: THE WILL OF HEAVEN

1 Chen Chieh-ju, pp. 119 et seq.
2 Lary, *Warlord Soldiers*, p. 72.
3 Francke, p. 266.
4 Tsin, p. 57 et seq.
5 Bonnard, pp. 295–6.
6 Chen Chieh-ju, pp. 130–4; CKS, *Soviet Russia in China*, p. 21; Chen Chieh-ju, pp. 131, 133–5.
7 Wilbur and How, pp. 88–9.
8 Furaya, p. 117.
9 Borodin's life and his time in China is well told in Jacobs's biography.
10 Bennett, p. 221; Abend, *Life*, p. 19.
11 Jacobs, pp. 115–16.
12 Friedman, p. 57; Bergère, *Sun*, pp. 319–20.
13 CKS, *Soviet Russia*, p. 24.
14 PRO, FO 371-12440/9156. FO 94/87/10; Wilbur and How, Document 3.
15 PRO, FO 371-12501/9132. F 6605/3241/10; Wilbur and How, p. 490.
16 Loh, pp. 94–5.
17 Ibid., p. 95.
18 Chen Chieh-ju, p. 155.
19 Jordan, *Northern Expedition*, p. 17.
20 Landis, in Chan and Etzold, p. 76; Martin, p. 81; Chen Li-fu, p. 64; Loh, *Chiang*, p. 98.
21 Chen Chieh-ju, p. xxiii.
22 Wang, p. 89; Chen Chieh-ju, pp. 142, 156.
23 Quotes in this and next paragraphs in Loh, *Chiang*, pp. 63–5; Chen Chieh-ju, p. 142.
24 CCK, *Calm*, p. 121.
25 Chen Chieh-ju, p. 175.
26 Ibid., pp. 155–6.
27 CWR, 12 June 1924, p. 82; Tsin, pp. 88 et seq.
28 Chen Chieh-ju, p. 148.
29 CET, 23 October 1924; Swisher, pp. 2–3; NCH, 15 November 1924; CET, 23 October 1924.
30 Swisher, p. 3.

31 NCH, 29 November and 9 December 1924.

32 Wilbur, *Patriot*, p. 290; RTR, 27 March and 2 April 1925.

33 CET, 19 March 1925.

5: THE RED PROTECTOR

1   NCH, 3 March 1937; Wilbur and How, p. 117.

2   Bennett, pp. 124–5; Wilbur and How, pp. 523 et seq.; Cherepanov, p. 104.

3   CKS, *Soviet Russia*, p. 51; F. F. Liu, p. 20.

4   Salisbury, p. 258; NCH, 4 April 1925.

5   Wilbur and How, p. 145; Swisher, p. 32.

6   F. F. Liu, p. 16; Wilbur and How, p. 485; NCH, 5 September 1925; Chen Chieh-ju, p. 158.

7   Short, p. 157; Chan and Etzold, p. 223; CET, 12 March 1925; RTR, 16 March 1925.

8   Wilbur and How, pp. 698, 219.

9   Wang Ke-wen, p. 27; Chen Chieh-ju, pp. 177–8.

10 Furaya, p. 153; Chen Chieh-ju, p. 168.

11 RTR, 4, 6 and 9 June 1925.

12 Swisher, p. 7.

13 Chen Chieh-ju, p. 168.

14 Wilbur and How, pp. 523 et seq.

15 NCH, June and July 1925; Abend, *Life*, p. 17.

16 T'ang, *Wang*, pp. 113–14; Wilbur and How, pp. 168 and 203 (note 89).

17 Cherepanov, p. 158; T'ang, *Wang*, p. 114.

18 Cherepanov, p. 158; T'ang, *Wang*, p. 115.

19 Chen Chieh-ju, p. 164; Wilbur and How, p. 480; Jacobs, p. 183.

20 Chen Chieh-ju, p. 164.

21 Ibid., pp. 161–2; Cherepanov, pp. 163–6.

22 NCH, 17 October 1925; Jordan, *Expedition*, p. 12.

23 Young, OH, p. 23; Abend, *Life*, p. 19.

24 Ch'i, pp. 174 et seq.; Botjer, p. 55; Jordan, *Expedition*, p. 18; Van de Ven, pp. 137–8.

25 Young, OH, pp. 22–3; Jordan, *Expedition*, pp. 15–17.

26 Jordan, *Expedition*, p. 304; Furuya, p. 165; NCH, 28 November 1925.

27 Wilbur and How, p. 698.

28 Chen Chieh-ju, p. 182.

29 Boorman, Vol. I, p. 206; Chen Li-fu, pp. 24–5.

30 Jerome Chen, p. 315.

31 Chen Li-fu, p. 26.

32 Chen Chieh-ju, pp. 181 et seq.

33 Chen Li-fu, p. 28.

34 Wilbur and How, p. 252.

35 Chen Li-fu, p. 29.

36 Cherepanov, p. 202; Van de Ven, pp. 146–157 includes latest Chinese research; NCH of 1 May 1926 has report dated 5 April.

37 *Min-kuo jih-pao* newspaper, quoted in Wilbur and How, p. 257.
38 NCH, 3 April, 1926, 29 May 1927.
39 Jordan, p. 60.
40 NCH, July 10 1926; Wilbur and How, pp. 705–6.
41 Report of 14 June 1926, French Foreign Ministry papers E-505-4-E22-LA, p. 160; Chen Chieh-ju, pp. 198–9.
42 French Foreign Ministry papers E-505-4-E22-LA, pp. 174, 152; Jordan, pp. 50 and 60.
43 Abend, *Life*, p. 19; Chen Li-fu, p. 37; Wilbur and How, p. 292; French Foreign Ministry papers, Chine 187 E50-51.

6: LORDS OF MISRULE

1 Tai Hsuanchih, p. 20; NCH, 27 September 1928; Abend, *Life*, p. 64; Pu Yi, pp. 185, 183.
2 Wu Peifu is the subject of Odoric Wou's biography; Powell, p. 84.
3 Kuo Kwan-ying, Part One.
4 Tong and Li, pp. 256–7; the Model Governor is the subject of Donald Gillin's biography.
5 Abend, *Life*, pp. 64–5; the Christian General is the subject of James Sheridan's biography.
6 Hewlett, pp. 125–7.
7 Eastman, *Family*, p. 233.
8 Tai Hsuanchih, p. 26.
9 Ibid., Chapter IV; Wilbur and How, p. 310; Friedman, Chapter 9.
10 Chien Tuan-sheng, p. 12.
11 Pelissier, p. 293.
12 NCH, 4 September 1926.
13 CET, 16 October 1924.
14 Tuchman, p. 109.
15 Spence, *Gate*, pp. 142–3.

7: TO THE NORTH

1 Anon., *Military Exploits*, p. 80, with slight grammatical corrections.
2 Chen Chieh-ju, p. 206.
3 Cherepanov, p. 226; Wilbur, *Revolution*, p. 51; Wilbur and How, Document 26; Botjer, p. 56; Abend, *Life*, p. 33; Van de Ven, pp. 137–8.
4 Jordan, *Expedition*, p. 24; Wilbur and How, Document 26.
5 Lary, *Region and Nation*, p. 7; overview of Guangxi, pp. 21–7.
6 Cherepanov, p. 236; Wilbur and How, Documents 49 and 66.
7 Jordan, *Expedition*, p. 71; Lary, *Region*, p. 67; Tong and Li, p. 164.
8 Jordan, *Expedition*, p. 277.
9 Abend, *Life*, p. 33; Jordan, *Expedition*, pp. 74–8, 278, 211.

10 Chen Chieh-ju, pp. 207–8.

11 NCH, 7 August 1926.

12 Ibid., 2 February 1929.

13 Cherepanov, p. 256; Fitzgerald, *Why China*, p. 90; NCH, 4 September 1926.

14 Wilbur and How, pp. 318–19.

15 NCH, 31 August and 11 September 1926; RTR, 27 August 1926; Powell, p. 85.

17 Cherepanov, pp. 241–2; Wilbur and How, Document 69.

18 NCH, 11 September 1926.

19 Chen Li-fu, p, 43.

20 Jordan, *Expedition*, p. 85.

21 Wilbur and How, p. 324, and Document 69.

22 NCH, 6 November 1926.

23 Wilbur and How, p. 324.

24 NCH, 31 December 1926.

25 Wilbur, *Revolution*, p. 62; RTR, 23 November 1926; Lary, *Region*, p. 218; Van de Ven, p. 192.

26 Chen Chieh-ju, p. 214; NCH, 31 December 1926.

27 Jordan, *Expedition*, pp. 212, 240–1.

28 Isaacs, p. 111; Jordan, *Expedition*, p. 201. Part Three of Jordan has detailed evidence.

29 Jordan, *Expedition*, p. 281; following para, MC, *Conversations*, pp. 7–9, 70.

30 NCH, 4 March 1927.

31 RTR, 12 December 1926; NCH, 18 December 1926; French Foreign Ministry papers Chine Vol. 188, Série E, carton 505, p. 194; Chesnaux, *Labour*, p. 331.

32 Misselwitz, p. 91.

33 Wilbur, *Revolution*, pp. 64–8; Short, p. 166; Isaacs, p. 117.

34 NCH, 18 and 26 December 1926.

35 Chen Chieh-ju, p. 210; Ransome, pp. 67–70.

36 Cherepanov, p. 266; Wilbur and How, Document 69.

37 French Foreign Ministry papers Chine 188 E-505; Isaacs, p. 126; NCH, 26 January 1927; Wilbur and How, Document 80.

38 NCH, 26 February 1927.

39 Chen Chieh-ju, pp. 218 and 236.

40 Ibid., Chapter 23.

41 Ibid., p. 224.

42 Ibid., pp. 226–7.

43 Jordan, *Expedition*, pp. 283–4.

44 NCH, 26 March 1927.

45 Jacobs, p. 240.

46 Chen Li-fu, p. 53.

8: LIGHT, HEAT, POWER

1 Leo Ou-fan Lee, pp. 6–7; Wen-hsin Yeh in Wakeman and Edmonds, pp. 132, 139.

2 Fewsmith, pp. 116, 118–19.

3 Pan, *Shanghai: A Century of Change*, p. 51; Johnston and Erh, *A Last Look: Western Architecture in Old Shanghai* shows mansions and offices that have survived.

4 Guillermaz, p. 17.

5 NCH, 25 November 1930; Perry, p. 170; Dong, pp. 154–6, 160–3; NCH, 13 March 1926.

6 Chesnaux et al., *China from the 1911 Revolution*, p. 183.

7 Sternberg, pp. 82–3.

8 Johnston and Erh, *Last Look*, p. 90; Dong, p. 97.

9 Dong, pp. 40–51; Pan, *Shanghai*, pp. 41–2. Studies of prostitution include Hershatter and Henriot. Wakeman's *Policing Shanghai* has an excellent shorter account and survey of crime in the city.

10 Martin, Chapters 2 and 3; on general role of narcotics, see Dikötter et al., *Narcotic Culture*.

11 Wakeman, p. 25.

12 NCH, 11 August 1923, 16 and 23 May 1925, 17 November 1925.

13 The pistol is on display at the Shanghai Museum of Public Security.

14 Pan, *Old Shanghai*, pp. 38 et seq.; study of Du in Y. C. Wang, *Journal of Asian Studies*, Vol. 26; Auden and Isherwood, p. 170.

15 Wakeman, pp. 25, 122, 202–5; Exhibition, Musée Albert Kahn, Paris, 2002.

16 Misselwitz, p. 25; NCH, 24 March 1927.

17 Misselwitz, p. 27.

18 Jordan, *Expedition*, pp. 115–17, 211–12.

19 Sergeant, p. 75; NCH, 25 March 1927.

20 Sergeant, p. 74.

21 NCH, 2 April 1927.

22 Ibid.

23 Ibid.

9: THE GREAT PURGE

1 NCH, 2, 9 and 16 April, 1927; Wilbur, *Revolution*, p. 108; Chen Li-fu, p. 55.

2 Martin, pp. 88–90, 113–15; French Foreign Ministry papers, Chine, Vol. 189, p. 15.

3 Powell, pp. 158–9; Pan, *Old Shanghai*, pp. 53–4.

4 This account of Wang's murder draws on Martin, pp. 91–3, 104–5; Chen Li-fu, pp. 60, 63; Pan, *Old Shanghai*, pp. 48–51. Relations between Communists and the Green Gang are explored in Frazier, *Republican China*, November 1994.

5 This account of the purge is based on editions of the NCH for April, 1927; Wu 'Chiang Kai-shek's April 12 Coup' in Chan and Etzold; Wilbur, *Revolution*, pp. 99–113; Seagrave, pp. 228–9; Fewsmith, Chapter 5.

6 Zheng Chaolin, pp. 103–4; CKS, *Soviet Russia*, p. 47.

7 Van de Ven, p. 181; Chen Li-fu, p. 62.

8 Wilbur, *Revolution*, p. 112; NCH, 23 April 1927; McDonald, p. 312.

9 CKS, *Soviet Russia*, p. 48; Dong, pp. 184–5; NCH, 30 April 1927; Wilbur, *Revolution*, pp. 110–11; NCH, 23 April 1927; Swisher diary, 24 April and 29 May 1927; Sheean, p. 227.

10 Short, p. 188; McDonald, p. 316.

11 Chapman, pp. 231–2.

12 Coble, *Capitalists*, pp. 33, 34–5, 40; NYT, 4 May 1927; NCH, 30 April, 21 May and 4 June 1927; Martin, p. 197.

13 NCH, 16 and 30 April 1927.

14 Trotsky, p. 384; Taylor, pp. 42–3; photograph in Academia Sinica library, Taipei.

15 *Daily Express* quoted in NCH, 14 May 1927; Misselwitz, p. 97; NCH, 14 and 21 May 1927; Jacobs, pp. 255–6; RTR, 14 April 1927.

16 Sheean, pp. 197–8.

17 Sheridan, *Warlord*, pp. 197–292, and Chapter 9.

18 Jordan, *Expedition*, p. 130.

19 Kuo Kwan-ying, Part Two.

20 Tong, p. 86; Tong and Li, pp. 216–17.

21 Taylor, pp. 32–3, 37–8.

22 Misselwitz, p. 118.

23 Coble, *Capitalists*, p. 38; Abend, *Tortured China*, pp. 176–7; NCH, 11 June 1927; Misselwitz, p. 123.

24 NCH, 25 June 1927.

25 North and Eudin, p. 107; Short, pp. 190–1.

26 North and Eudin, pp. 111, 127.

27 Ibid., p. 123 and Chapter 6; T'ang Leang-li, p. 155.

28 Misselwitz, p. 126; Sheean, p. 240; Jacobs, p. 279.

29 Zheng Chaolin's memoirs give a rank-and-file account of events, pp. 131–3.

30 Bennett, p. 301; Sheean, p. 256; NCH, 30 July 1927.

31 Sheean, p. 302.

32 RTR, NCH, 13 August 1927; CKS, *Soviet Russia*, pp. 51–2.

33 Wilbur and How, p. 427; Davies, p. 183.

34 CKS, *Soviet Russia*, p. 52.

35 Tong and Li, pp. 219–20, 222.

36 NCH, 20 August 1927.

37 Misselwitz, pp. 138–9.

38 NCH, 17–24 December, 1927; Wilbur, *Revolution*, pp. 164 et seq.

39 SCMP, 14 December 1927; NCH, 24 December 1927; photographs, Spence and Chin, pp. 90–2; Swisher, pp. 115, 91.

40 NCH, 14 December 1927, 10 November 1928.

41 NCH, 16 July 1927.

10: POLITICAL UNION

1 Mowrer, pp. 80–1; FBI Memorandum to the Director, 9 January 1943, quoted in Seagrave, p. 261: Chen Chieh-ju, p. 194.

2 Chen Chieh-ju, p. 187, dinner described in Chapter 19; Snow, *Journey*, p. 85; Hahn, *Chiang*, p. 86.
3 Chen Chieh-ju, Chapter 25.
4 Ibid. pp. 252–4.
5 NCH, 1 October 1927.
6 NYT, 24 September 1927; Chen Chieh-ju, p. 257; NCH, 1 October 1927.
7 Chen Chieh-ju, p. xxix.
8 Ibid., pp. 260–3.
9 Jung Chang, p. 66.
10 The letter was subsequently published by a newspaper, Crozier, p. 6.
11 Wellesley Person of the Week, 14 August 2000.
12 James Hsioung Lee, p. 41.
13 Cowles, p. 90.
14 NCH, 17 December 1927.
15 Sues, pp, 69–70.
16 Crozier, p. 123; Furaya p. 236.

11: CAPTAIN CHIANG

1 NCH, 7–14 April 1928.
2 Liang Hsi-huey, pp. 47–8; NCH, 27 October and 17 November 1928; F. F. Liu, pp. 61–2.
3 Abend, *Tortured China*, pp. 90–1; NCH, 5 May 1927; Van de Ven, pp. 137–8.
4 Kuo Min, 2 May 1928.
5 Furaya, pp. 244–5.
6 NCH, 12 May 1928; Botjer, p. 81.
7 Abend, *Life*, p. 78–80; RTR, 21 May 1928; Furaya, p. 247.
8 NCH, 12 May 1928; RTR, 7 May 1928; Kuo Min, 8 May 1926; *Toho*, 14–15 May 1928; CKS, *China's Destiny*, p. 123.
9 *Manchuria Daily News* in NCH, 7 July 1928.
10 Furaya, pp. 263–4; Kuo Kwan-ying, Part One.
11 Strand, p. 11.
12 Abend, *Tortured China*, pp. 259 et seq.
13 Pu Yi, p. 196; Kuo Kwan-ying, Part Two.
14 Abend, *Tortured China*, p. 251.
15 Kuo Min, 27 July 1928.
16 Hahn, *Chiang*, p. 138.
17 RTR, 13 December 1929.
18 RTR, 21 January 1929.
19 Charles Musgrave in Esherick, *City*, pp. 139 et seq.; RTR, 22 April 1929; NCH, 1–8 December 1928 and 4 May 1929; Kuo Min, 24 October and 1 December 1928.
20 Boorman, Vol. I, p. 76.
21 NCH, 2 February, 9 March, 6 April and 4 May 1929; Abend, *Tortured China*,

p. 256; NCH, 21–28 January 1930; NCH, 9 and 30 March 1929.

22 NCH, 28 December 1928; RTR, 2 December 1928; NCH, 25 February, 8 April and 20 May 1930; Martin, pp. 117, 137–9.

23 CWR, 20 June 1931.

24 Kuo Min, 4 December 1929.

25 Hedin, pp. 27–8; Mackerras, p. 122.

26 Wang Ke-wen, pp. 49 et seq.

27 NCH, 16 March 1929; Wang Ke-wen, pp. 250, 258; Kuo Min, 23 March 1929; Falgiot and Kauffer, p. 78; Chen Li-fu, p. 65; Eastman, *Abortive Revolution*, pp. 74–5.

28 Misselwitz, p. 161; Kuo Min, 3 August 1928.

29 NCH, 5 January 1929; Crozier p. 30; NCH, 5 January 1926; Kuo Min, 17 January 1929.

30 Liang Hsi-huey, p. 50; NCH, 14 April 1929.

31 RTR, 4 April 1929; NCH, 13 April 1929; Kuo Min, 9 April 1929.

32 NCH, 8 June 1929.

33 Abend, *Tortured China*, pp. 61–2.

34 NCH, 25 May 1929.

35 RTR, 13 October 1930; Sheridan, *Disintegration*, p. 186; Coble, *Capitalists*, p. 87.

36 NCH, 8 July 1930.

37 Abend, *Life*, p. 118; Chen Li-fu, p. 266; RTR, 11 April 1930.

38 NCH, 28 October 1930; Hahn, *Chiang*, p. 147.

39 Kuo Min, 19 November 1930; NCH, 3 December 1930; RTR, 3–4 March 1930; Central News, 5 March 1930; Chen Li-fu, pp. 104–5.

40 *Rengo*, 7 May 1930.

41 NCH, 9 June 1931.

12: TWO CHINAS

1 Short, pp. 281–2; NCH, 1 December 1931; Longhua, author's visit, 2001; Dikötter, *Crime*, pp. 292–3; Fairbank, *Chinabound*, p. 68.

2 Falgiot and Kauffer, pp. 36, 39, 41–2, 46–7, 63; Wakeman, pp. 138–41, 151–60.

3 Falgiot and Kauffer, pp. 67–8; Warren Kuo, Vol. II, pp. 313–19.

4 NCH, 1 December 1931; Falgiot and Kauffer, p. 79.

5 Eastman, *Abortive Revolution*, pp. 93–6.

6 Short, pp. 282–3, and Chapter 8 on Communist purge.

7 NCH, 27 January 1931; Dreyer, pp. 160–1; Short, pp. 256–7. Figures for the troops CKS put into the field in the five campaigns against the Communists vary considerably because of discrepancies between the strength of units on paper and their actual numbers: I have taken those in Ch'i, *Nationalist China*, p. 246.

8 Dreyer, pp. 163–4; Short, pp. 258–60.

9 Kuo Min, 3 July 1930.

10 NCH, 1 March 1932; Mao put the number at 300,000 (Short, pp. 286–7).

11 Short, p. 287.

12 Martin, p. 140: Seagrave, p. 333; NCH, 23 August 1933.
13 NCH, 23 July 1931; Abend, *Life*, p. 124.
14 NCH, 11 and 18 August, 1 and 8 September 1931.
15 Ienaga, pp. 6–11; Iris Chang, p. 218.
16 Bix, pp. 276, 176; Ienaga, pp. 6, 11–12; Furaya, p. 309; Amelia Hill, 'The Day the Earth Died', *Observer* Magazine, London, 2 March, 2003.
17 Furaya, p. 309.
18 Furaya, pp. 316–19; Selle, p. 268; Mitter, pp. 77–9; Bix, pp. 240, 236–9, 247.
19 NCH, 3 November 1931.
20 Mitter, pp. 85–7.
21 Photograph, Nanking Presidential Palace.
22 Taylor, p. 59, quoting diaries for 15–16 December 1931, and p. 60 for diary of 27 December 1931.
23 Wang Ke-wen, p. 306.
24 Ransome, pp. 65–6; Abend, *Tortured China*, pp. 267 et seq.; Wang Ke-wen, p. 311.
25 Kuo Kwan-ying, Part Three.
26 Abend, *Life*, p. 132; Wakeman in Wakeman and Edmonds, pp. 141 et seq., 151, 158.

13: HEART AND SKIN

1 NCH, 2 February 1931; Jordan, *Trial*, pp. 11–12; Furaya, pp. 350–1.
2 Furaya, pp. 348–51; Jordan, *Trial*, pp. 7, 11–12; Selle, pp. 270–2.
3 Selle, p. 273.
4 Abend, *Life*, pp. 186–91.
5 Ibid., p. 193.
6 Kwei, pp. 148–51; NCH, 9 February 1932.
7 Boorman, Vol. I, p. 77.
8 Fewsmith, p. 18; Soong interview with *New York American*, 2 May 1932.
9 For CKS's role in this and the following two paragraphs, UP, 14 February 1932; NCH, 23 February 1932; Jordan, *Trial*, pp. 103, 105, 121–2, 130, 138, 144, 155; CKS in NCH, 17 October 1934.
10 Jordan, *Trial*, pp. 146–8.
11 Ibid., p. 223; Henriot, *Shanghai*, pp. 92–3.
12 NCH, 22 March 1932; Henriot, *Shanghai*, pp. 94–5; Abend, *Life*, p. 193; Fogel, *Journal of Asian Studies*, Vol. 59/4; NCH, 22 March 1932.
13 Photographs in Han Suyin, *China, 1890–1938*, pp. 212–14.
14 Jordan, *Trial*, pp. 230–1.
15 Kuo Min, 10 June 1932.
16 Hahn, *Chiang*, p. 180.
17 Beasley, p. 261.
18 NCH, 3 December 1932.
19 NCH, 26 February 1929; RTR, 2 March 1929; UP, 12 March and 25 May 1929; RTR, Kuo Min, 27 March 1929; NCH, 1 February 1933; RTR, 4 September 1932; NCH, 7 and 14 September, 23 December 1932.

20 Kuo Min, 6 August 1932; RTR, 9 and 11 August 1932.
21 Lattimore, p. 48; Jordan, *Trial*, p. 103, credits the Jiangxi governor with first applying this old expression to the Japanese and Communists.
22 NCH, 19 October 1932; RTR 14 and 15 July 1932; Kuo Min, 19 December 1932.
23 Fleming, pp. 35–6.
24 NCH, 16 October 1935; NCH, 24 January 1934.
25 NCH, 11 November 1933, 14 December 1932.
26 NCH, 11 and 18 January 1933.
27 Fleming, p. 80.
28 RTR, 20 February 1933.
29 Selle, pp. 280–1; RTR, 4 March 1933; NCH, 1 and 8 March 1933; Fleming, p. 92.
30 NCH, 8 March 1933.
31 NCH, 15 January 1933; Kuo Min, 24 September 1933.
32 NCH, 22 March 1933; Selle, p. 281.
33 NCH, 22 March 1932.
34 RTR, 8 and 10 March 1933; Kuo Min, 12 March 1933; NCH, 15 March 1933; Selle, pp. 281–4; RTR, 5 May 1933; Kuo Kwan-ying, Part Two.
35 Stolley, pp. 22–3; Furaya, p. 408.
36 Abend, *Life*, p. 204.
37 NCH, 24 May 1933.
38 Ibid., 25 April 1934; Sheridan, *Warlord*, p. 274.
39 NCH, 20 September 1933; Furaya, pp. 417–18.

14: FOLLOW THE LEADER

1 CP, Vol. III, p. 151; White, *History*, p. 117; Wakeman in Wakeman and Edmonds, p. 168.
2 NCH, 4 November 1935, 15 January 1936; Ch'i, *Nationalist China*, p. 28; Chiang speech at Omei College, September 1935.
3 Wei and Liu, pp. 64–5, 68; Ch'i, *Nationalist China*, p. 32; Wakeman in Wakeman and Edmonds, particularly pp. 170 et seq.
4 Tien's *Government and Politics in Kuomintang China* gives an overview.
5 Kirby, *Republican China*, April 1987.
6 Kirby in Wakeman and Edmonds, p. 182.
7 Duara in Wakeman and Edmonds, p. 316; Dikötter, *Crime*, pp. 295 et seq.; Yeh, pp. 10–11.
8 Mann, Chapter 9; Botjer, p. 135.
9 NCH, 14 and 28 June 1933; Kuo Min, 12 September 1933; Sheridan, *Disintegration*, p. 223; CP, Vol. III, p. 648.
10 Fleming, pp. 159–62.
11 Chennault, p. 39.
12 The Sino-German relationship is dealt with in papers in CP, Vol. IV, by E. G. Mohr, Liang Hsi-huey and Hsin Ta-mo; Eastman, *Family*, pp. 205–6; Van de Ven in Wakeman and Edmonds, pp. 99 et seq.

13 Spence, *Gate*, pp. 288, 298 et seq.; Roux in Shanghai annés 30, p. 107.

14 Tien, p. 47–52.

15 Ibid., pp. 54–65; Eastman, *Abortive Revolution*, pp. 47, 78–9, 308–9; Wakeman in Wakeman and Edmonds, pp. 141 et seq.

16 UP, 16 July 1935; Tien, p. 23.

17 Dikötter, *Crime*, p. 212; NCH, 11 February 1930.

18 Eastman, *Abortive Revolution*, p. 35; CP, Vol. III, p. 173; Abend, *Tortured China*, p. 303; NCH, 7 January 1936.

19 CP, Vol. III, p. 648; NCH, 29 May 1934 and 2 September 1936; Cochran in Yeh, pp. 85–6.

20 Sheridan, *Disintegration*, p. 231–2; Eastman, *Family*, p. 202.

21 Zhang Kaimin in Wakeman and Edmonds, p. 61.

22 Pringle, p. 95; Brook and Wakabayashi, p. 277; Coble, *Capitalists*, p. 195; Young, OH, p. 47.

23 NCH, 24 January 1934; Eastman, *Family*, p. 70; NCH, 1 July 1936; Brodie, p. 120.

24 Wakeman and Edmonds, p. 53; NCH, 24 January 1934; Tawney, p. 77.

25 Ch'i, *Nationalist China*, pp. 147–9.

26 Coble, *Capitalists*, pp. 61–5; Perry, p. 106; Perry in Wakeman and Edmonds, p. 263.

27 Sheridan, *Disintegration*, p. 22.

28 Coble, *Capitalists*, pp. 86–90; Abend, *Life*, p. 215.

29 NCH, 1 November 1933.

30 Ibid.

31 This account is based on Coble, *Capitalists*, pp. 178 et seq., and McElderry (p. 59 for Bank of China).

32 Leith-Ross, pp. 207–8.

33 Coble, *Capitalists*, pp. 220, 231–5, 249–50.

34 Sheridan, *Disintegration*, p. 209; Young, OH, pp. 30–2; Tong and Li, p. 419; Li Pu-sheng in Tien, p. 23; Eastman, *Abortive Revolution*, pp. 18–19, 216.

35 Dikötter et al., *Narcotic Culture*, pp. 332–3; Wakeman, pp. 264–6; Brook and Wakabayashi, pp. 286–9 and 312.

36 Nellist, p. 110; Leith-Ross, pp. 207–8; Sues, pp. 88–90, 92–4.

37 RTR, 1 March and 18 April 1934.

38 This summary draws on Sheridan, *Disintegration*, pp. 187–203; Ch'i, *Nationalist China*, p. 19.

39 Wei and Liu, p. 78.

40 Tong and Li, p. 306.

41 RTR, 1 October 1933.

42 Warren Kuo, Vol. II, pp. 556–7; Eastman, *Abortive Revolution*, p. 125.

43 Abend, *Life*, p. 195; NCH, 26 December 1933.

44 Fleming, p. 177.

45 Schwarcz, pp. 214–15, 236–8, 246–7.

46 MC, *New Life*, pp. iii–v; *Time*, 3 January 1938.

47 Cheng and Lestz, pp. 298 et seq.

48 Schwarcz, p. 215; NCH, 21 March 1934; Central News, 12 December 1934; NCH, 5 May, 13 June 1934, 24 April 1936.
49 NCH, 4 January 1933; Kuo Min, 28 November 1932; NCH, 29 April 1936.
50 Coble, *Capitalists*, p. 236. The following passage draws on Chapter 8.
51 Crozier, p. 169.
52 NCH, 4 April 1935 and 19 February 1936.
53 Stelle, pp. 289–90.
54 White, *History*, p. 117.

15: THE LONG CHASE

1 Smedley, *Battle Hymn*, p. 121; Short, p. 2; next para, Vladimirov, pp. 140, 272.
2 Farmer, p. 169.
3 Auden and Isherwood, pp. 173 et seq.; missionary in next para, James, p. 19.
4 Based on author's visit to Kuling-Lushan, March 2002.
5 NCH, 29 November 1933.
6 RTR, 20 September 1933; Hedin, p. 59.
7 NCH, 20 December and 1 November 1933.
8 NCH, 20 and 29 November 1933; RTR, 15 October 1933; NCH, 7 April 1935; NCH, 6 December 1933.
9 Selle, pp. 289 et seq.
10 Kuo Min, 29 April 1934; Short, pp. 313; Mao, p. 231.
11 Wilson, *March*, pp. 55–7.
12 Kuo Min, 20 July, 19 and 24 September, 1934.
13 Kuo Min, 6 June 1934; NCH, 20 June 1934; RTR, 1 July 1934; NCH, 4 July 1934.
14 NCH, 24 October 1934.
15 RTR, 12 October 1934.
16 Hahn, *Chiang*, p. 183; RTR, 24 and 31 October, 2 November 1934.
17 This and preceding account from Selle, pp. 305–6.
18 Ibid., p. 304.
19 NCH, 24–31 October, 28 November 1934; RTR, 22 October 1934. The NCH reports read as if written by W. H. Donald.
20 Salisbury, pp. 62–3; Wilson, *March*, p. 74.
21 Salisbury, pp. 92–104; Short, p. 4; Wilson, *March*, pp. 77–9.
22 Wilson, *March*, pp. 137–43; Central News, 3 and 14 December 1934; NCH, 26 December 1934.
23 Wilson, *March*, p. 113.
24 Hedin, pp. 64–7.
25 NCH, 3 April 1935.
26 Ibid., 5 June 1935.
27 RTR, 6 April 1935; NCH, 10 and 17 April 1935.
28 Davies, p. 161; Lacam, p. 122 – the photograph of the head on a post is opposite p. 65.
29 Hall, p. 175; Lacam, p. 158.

30 NCH, 24 April 1935.

31 Mao, p. 128.

32 RTR, 19 May 1935; NCH, 5 June 1935.

33 NCH, 12 June 1935; RTR, 6 June 1935; NCH, 12 June 1935.

34 Wilson, *March*, Chapters XV and XVI for Dadu River; Snow, *Red Star*, pp. 224–9; Short, pp. 324–6.

35 Short, pp. 327–8.

36 Furaya, pp. 455–6.

37 Wilson, *March*, p. 204.

38 Pelissier, pp. 336–8.

16: END OF ENDURANCE

1 NCH, 20 November 1935; Central News, 14 October 1936.

2 PRO, FO paper F 10393/27/87, Clark-Kerr to Halifax, 31 August 1938; NCH, 13 May 1926; NCH, 2 February, 13 May and 3 June 1936; Abend, *Life*, pp. 207–10.

3 RTR, 1 November 1935.

4 Central News, 2 November 1935.

5 Chen Li-fu, pp. 115–16.

6 Levitch, pp. 243–4.

7 Central News, 9 June 1936; Tong and Li, p. 308; NCH, 2 and 9 September 1936; Abend, *Life*, p. 198.

8 Selle, pp. 313–14.

9 NCH, 2, 9 and 23 September 1936.

10 NCH, 11 and 4 November 1936.

11 Kuo Kwan-ying, Part Three.

12 Wu Tien-wei, pp. 24–5.

13 Kuo Kwan-ying, Part Three; Route Army office and church photograph from author's visit to Xi'an, 2002; NCH, 20 January 1937.

14 Kuo Kwan-ying, Part Three.

15 NCH, 2 and 16 September 1936.

16 Eastman et al., *Nationalist Era*, p. 206; this and next para draw on Van de Ven, pp. 231, 244.

17 Liang Hsi-huey, p. 112; Jason Pipes, Internet postings, 1996–2001.

18 Abend, *Life*, pp. 223–4; Van de Ven, pp. 247–9.

19 Kuo Kwan-ying, Part Three; Van de Ven, pp. 276, 286.

20 Borg, p. 225; NCH, 31 March 1937.

21 Wu Tien-wei, pp. 200–2; NCH, 10 February 1937.

22 Donald Gillin, 'Problems of Centralization in Republican China', *Journal of Asian Studies*, Vol. 27/4, pp. 839–41.

23 Ho-Wang, Han-sheng Lin, in Coox, p. 234.

24 Farmer, pp. 242 et seq., 263.

25 NCH, 27 January 1937.

26 Chang Jui-te on illiteracy in *Modern Asian Studies*, Vol. 30/4, p. 1049; Gibson, pp. 362–3; Ch'i, pp. 43–9, and, more generally, Chapter 2.

27 CCK, *Calm*, p. 123.

28 Kuo Min, 10 April 1937.

29 Abend, *Life*, pp. 240–5.

30 Details in Ikuhiko Hata's paper in CP, Vol. II, pp. 497–524.

31 Hata in CP, Vol. II, p. 515.

32 Guillermaz, p. 44.

33 Ibid., p. 45.

34 Ibid., p. 47.

35 Farmer, p. 14; CCK, p. 124; Hsu, p. 583; Spence, *Search*, p. 422.

36 Hata in CP, Vol. II, pp. 521–2.

37 Central News, 29 July 1937; Liang Hsi-huey, p. 126; Bix, pp. 321–2.

17: THE MOST DREADFUL NIGHTMARE

1 This account of why the bombs were dropped is from Chennault, p. 45. Contemporary accounts also speak of a plane climbing to avoid anti-aircraft fire, loosing bombs as it did so.

2 Farmer, pp. 46 et seq. for this and next two paragraphs.

3 This account is based on contemporary accounts, notably from the NCH and by Farmer, Abend, Timperley and Donald, plus histories of the city by Dong, Henriot, Lynn Pan, Sergeant and Wakeman, military studies by Dreyer and Ch'i, Van de Ven and Teitler and Radtke and Bix's biography of Hirohito.

4 Farmer, p. 78; Bix, pp. 324–5.

5 Farmer, p. 55.

6 NCH, 18 September 1937; Van de Ven, p. 321; Teitler and Radtke, p. 115.

7 This and next paragraph, Selle, pp. 339–40.

8 Farmer, p. 85; Timperley, p. 119.

9 Timperley, pp. 85–6.

10 Farmer, p. 85; NCH, 25 September 1937.

11 Farmer, p. 97; Bix, p. 333.

12 Pelissier, p. 382–3.

13 Bix, p. 326.

14 NCH, 8 September 1937.

15 Gibson, p. 385; Ch'i, p. 43; CP, Vol. II, pp. 627–9.

16 Smedley, *China Fights Back*, pp. 123–6.

17 Eastman et al., *Nationalist Era*, pp. 207–8; Guillermaz, p. 65.

18 NCH, 8 September 1937.

19 RTR, 27 November 1937.

20 NCH, 1 and 8 December 1937.

21 Iris Chang, p. 68 quoting Sun Zhawei, *Nanking Beige* (Taipei, 1995), pp. 31–3; the Atlantic Monthly Online.

22 Selle, pp. 341–2.

23 Iris Chang, pp. 72–3.

24 Ibid., pp. 74–6.

25 Caldwell, p. xiv.

26 *Guardian*, 4 October 2002.

27 This account draws on Iris Chang's account of the massacre, the NCH for December and January 1937–38, Powell, Bix, Timperley and Farmer.

28 Iris Chang, pp. 50, 53.

29 Cheng, Lestz, Spence, p. 330; Farmer, pp. 101–2.

30 Iris Chang, p. 44.

31 Bix, pp. 343–5.

32 RTR, 10 December 1937.

33 Gibson, p. 391; RTR, 10 December 1937.

34 RTR, 21 December 1937.

35 CKS, *Wartime Messages*, p. 49; NCH, 12 December 1937; *Time*, 3 January 1938.

36 Selle, pp. 343–4.

18: I AM THE STATE

1 Mowrer, p. 107.

2 Han Suyin, *Destination*, p. 58; White, *History*, pp. 90–91.

3 RTR, 30 March, 2 and 7 April 1939.

4 Mowrer, p. 109.

5 Farmer, pp. 136–7.

6 Bertram, *Unconquered*, pp. 163–4, 444.

7 Coox in Coox and Conroy, p. 303.

8 NCH, 28 February 1940.

9 Wang, *Journal of Asian Studies*, Vol. 26/3; Van de Ven, p. 423.

10 Auden and Isherwood, p. 234; Farmer, p. 289.

11 Farmer, p. 120; NCH, 2 February 1938; Mowrer, p. 94.

12 Farmer, p. 128.

13 Farmer, p. 146.

14 Auden and Isherwood, p. 102; Tong and Li, p. 356.

15 Tong and Li, pp. 372–3.

16 Auden and Isherwood, p. 102; Farmer, p. 150.

17 NCH, 29 March 1938.

18 Tong and Li, pp. 353–4, 417; Domei, 4 April 1937; Auden and Isherwood, p. 151; Teitler and Radtke, pp. 175 et seq.; Van de Ven, pp. 329–333.

19 NCH, 1 June 1938; Furaya, p. 603; Van de Ven, p. 336; Teitler and Radtke, pp. 190 et seq.

20 Auden and Isherwood, pp. 174–5.

21 Domei, 14 June 1938 ; RTR, 12 and 14 June 1938; Davies, p. 22.

22 CKS, *Selected Speeches*, p. 20; Jerome Chen, p. 109.

23 Selle, p. 342; Central News, 5 October 1937; Chen Li-fu, pp. 135–6.

24 Liang Hsi-huey, pp. 131, 140.

25 Bix, p. 348.

26 MacKinnon, *Modern Asian Studies*, Vol. 30/4, October 1969, pp. 933–5.

27 Kataoka, p. 69.

28 Eastman, *Seeds*, pp. 89–90.

29 Cherepanov, pp. 307–8; Dorn, p. 185.

30 NCH, 25 August 1938.

31 RTR, 25 August 1938.

32 Farmer, p. 130.

33 Auden and Isherwood, pp. 64–5; Tong, Vol. II, pp. 582–3; Hahn, *Chiang*, p. 210.

34 Wu Chi-wei, pp. 228–9, 245, 277, 279–80, 282.

35 Farmer, pp. 168–9.

36 Han Suyin, *Destination*, pp. 91–2.

37 Mowrer, pp. 78–80; Auden and Isherwood, pp. 64–5.

38 Auden and Isherwood, pp. 64–5.

39 Farmer, pp. 172–3.

40 White, *History*, pp. 74–5.

41 RTR, UP, 22 October 1938.

42 Autumn 1938 battles: Yangtze, RTR, 21 September, NCH, 28 September; Jiangxi, RTR, 10 October; Wuhan, RTR, 11–13 October, NCH, 29 September, Auden and Isherwood, p. 157.

43 Auden and Isherwood, p. 55; Selle, pp. 345–6.

44 Han Suyin, *Destination*, p. 64.

45 Farmer, p. 180.

46 Han Suyin, *Destination*, pp. 79–80.

47 Farmer, p. 184.

48 NCH, 5 October 1938; Dreyer, p. 233; Bix, p. 346.

49 RTR, 1 November 1938.

50 Alley, p. 14.

51 Farmer, p. 193 with poster opposite; Han Suyin, *Destination*, pp. 98–101.

52 CP, Vol. II, p. 668; Ch'i, *Nationalist China*, pp. 54–5; Farmer, pp. 186–91.

53 RTR, 17 December 1938; NCH, 21 December 1938.

19: IN THE CLOUDS

1 CP, Vol. III, p. 421; Vol. II, pp. 653–4.

2 Bramall, pp. 30, 23; *China Daily*, 7–8 April 2001; Farmer, pp. 192, 199.

3 Fairbank, *Chinabound*, p. 243.

4 Esherick, Chapter 11; Farmer, pp. 207–11; White, *History*, pp. 66–76; Han Suyin, *Destination*, p. 162; Peck, p. 143.

5 White, *History*, pp. 67–8; RTR, 29 December 1939; White and Jacoby, pp. 8–9; Esherick, Chapter 11.

6 White and Jacoby, pp. 56–7; Eastman et al., *Nationalist Era*, pp. 130–3.

7 Farmer, p. 210; White and Jacoby, p. 8.

8 White, *History*, p. 72; Caldwell, p. xvi.

9 Eastman et al., *Nationalist Era*, p. 131; Basil, p. 2; Han Suyin, *Destination*, p. 163; Fairbank, *Chinabound*, p. 243.

10 Peck, pp. 413–16; NCH, 21 December 1938; Farmer, p. 226.

11 CP, Vol. III, p. 649.

12 Ch'i, *War*, pp. 153–64.

13 NCH, 7 December 1938 and 4 January 1939.

14 Payne, *Diary*, pp. 111–12.

15 Peck, pp. 603–4.

16 Ibid., p. 606.

17 White, *History*, pp. 120; Lattimore, pp. 155–6; Yu Maochun, pp. 43–4.

18 Peter Clarke, *The Cripps Version* (London: Allen Lane/The Penguin Press, 2001), p. 152–6.

19 Davies, pp. 183–4, 233, 343; Tuchman, pp. 262; Crozier, p. 216.

20 Payne, *Diary*, pp. 130–3, 258, 393.

21 Davies, p. 192; White, *History*, p. 74.

22 Guillermaz, p. 87; White, *History*, pp. 75–6; Hart, pp. 27–8; Farmer, pp. 222–5.

23 Peck, pp. 419 and 481.

24 Lin Han-sheng in Coox and Conroy, pp. 211–41.

25 Boyle, pp. 228–31; CP, Vol. II, p. 665; RTR, 2 January 1939; Boyle, p. 231, 278–8; RTR, 5 April 1939; Homer, p. 75.

26 White and Jacoby, p. 124.

27 Farmer, p. 204; Eastman et al., *Nationalist Era*, p. 140.

28 White and Jacoby, p. 140.

29 White, *History*, p. 77; Bix, p. 346; Ch'i, *War*, Chapter 2; Stilwell, p. 117.

30 Tong and Li, pp. 426–8; Stilwell, p. 80.

31 Donald Gillin, 'Problems of Centralization in Republican China', *Journal of Asian Studies*, Vol. 29.

32 Linebarger, pp. 230–1, 373, 380.

33 Ch'i, *War*, pp. 187–9.

34 Lattimore, p. 147.

35 Caldwell, p. 73; Ch'i, *War*, p. 211.

36 Wang, *Journal of Asian Studies*, Vol. 26/3.

37 White, *History*, p. 163.

38 Eastman et al., *Nationalist Era*, pp. 152–3; Ch'i, *War*, pp. 166–76; Young, *Helping Hand*, pp. 300–4 and *Wartime Finance*, p. 304; Botjer, pp. 211–14.

39 Jerome Chen, p. 43; Payne, *Diary*, pp. 99–100.

40 Selle, pp. 348–9.

41 Ibid., pp. 350, 367; *Shen Pao*, Shanghai, 11 November 1946.

42 Farmer, pp. 233–4.

43 Han Suyin, *Destination*, pp. 220–1.

44 RTR, 25 May 1939.

45 This account is from Farmer, pp. 230–4; RTR, 4–5 May 1939; White, *History*, pp. 76, 80–83; NCH, 10 and 24 May 1939; Pelissier, p. 389.

46 Guillermaz, p. 81; Farmer, p. 233.
47 Han Suyin, *Destination*, pp. 236, 256, 270.
48 Furaya, p. 541; NCH, 24 May 1939.
49 Han Suyin, *Destination*, pp. 255–6.

20: MAGNETIC WARFARE

1 RTR, 18 and 21 November 1938.
2 Tong and Li, pp. 379–82; following para, Wakeman in Yeh, pp. 314–21.
3 Wasserstein, p. 20; Boyle, p. 278; NCH, 16 October 1940 and 19 February 1939; Domei, 11 June 1939; Boyle, pp. 281–5; Wakeman, *Badlands*, has first-rate account.
4 NCH, 16 August 1939; Domei, 10 October 1939.
5 Ch'i, *War*, pp. 590 et seq.; NCH, 3 January 1940.
6 Peck, pp. 277–8.
7 Williams and Wallace, pp. 65, 69–70.
8 NCH, 4 April 1940; RTR, 20 June 1940; Hahn, *Soong Sisters*, p. 276; Havas, 28 August 1940; Ch'i, *War*, pp. 62–3.
9 Boyle, pp. 289–93; Kataoka, p. 191.
10 NCH, 16 October 1940; Boyle, pp. 299–304; Furaya, p. 654.
11 UP, 17–18 October 1940; Farmer, pp. 238–40.
12 White, *History*, pp. 113–14.
13 Domei, 18 November 1939.
14 Van Slyke, *Modern Asian Studies*, Vol. 30/4, October 1996, pp. 979 et seq.
15 NCH, 16 June 1940.
16 Benton, *Fourth Army*, Appendix, gives exchanges between Mao and Yunling; Xiang agreement, p. 773.
17 Ibid, pp. 515–16, 545–6.
18 Ibid., pp. 563–4, 567.
19 White and Jacoby, p. 76; Benton, pp. 572–8.
20 White, *History*, pp. 115–17.
21 Bachrack, p. 17; Carlos Baker, *Ernest Hemingway* (New York: Scribners 1969).
22 Kataoka, p. 270; Tong, p. 287.

21: PEANUT AND VINEGAR

1 Davies, p. 223; Franklin D. Roosevelt Library, marist.edu/psf/box2/a15b02.
2 Furaya, p. 725; Payne, *Diary*, pp. 44–50.
3 Bachrack, p. 18, Koen, p. 27.
4 Franklin D. Roosevelt Library, marist.edu/psf/box2/a16b05.
5 Davies, p. 221; White, *History*, p. 134. Van de Ven (Introduction and Chapter 1) presents a closely argued critical analysis of Stilwell which revises the admiring portrait in Tuchman's Pulitzer Prize-winning biography.
6 White, *History*, p. 158.
7 Hahn, *Chiang*, p. 248.

8 CP, Vol. IV, pp. 224 et seq.; Tuchman, p. 235; Davies, p. 237; Hahn, *Chiang*, p. 245; Snow, pp. 61, 69, 73–5, 70–1.

9 Franklin D. Roosevelt Library, marist.edu/psf/box2/a15g03; Tuchman, p. 282.

10 Tuchman, p. 235; Davies, p. 280

11 Tong, p. 183; Stilwell, p. 50.

12 Stilwell, p. 50, 54–5.

13 Stilwell, p. 62; Romanus and Sunderland, p. 103.

14 Tuchman, pp. 285, 288–9.

15 Stilwell, p. 63.

16 Ibid., p. 77.

17 Ibid., pp. 77–8, 80.

18 Ibid., p. 81; Tuchman, p. 281; next para, Tong, p. 305.

19 Chennault, p. 159.

20 Stilwell, pp. 92–5.

21 Chennault, pp. 160 et seq.

22 Davies, p. 240; Van de Ven has detailed account, pp. 39–49.

23 Liang Hsi-huey, p. 41.

24 Stilwell, pp. 105–6.

25 Ibid., p. 113.

26 Romanus and Sunderland, p. 154; Liang Hsi-huey, pp. 66–7.

27 Romanus and Sunderland, p. 168.

28 Davies, p. 242.

29 Liang Hsi-huey, pp. 59–60.

30 Amelia Hill, *Observer* Magazine, London, 2 March, 2003; Franklin D. Roosevelt Library, marist.edu/psf/box2/a16001; Stilwell, p. 158 – the report was by Colonel David Dean Barrett, the military attaché. US air strategy, Van de Ven, pp. 53–4.

31 White, *History*, p. 142.

32 Alanbrooke, entry for 23 November 1943.

33 White, *History*, p. 140.

34 Robert Smith, p. 65.

35 Liang Hsi-huey, p. 55; Stilwell, p. 119.

36 Romanus and Sunderland, pp. 169–71; Liang Hsi-huey, pp. 70–72.

37 Stilwell, pp. 122–3, 126.

38 Liang Hsi-huey, pp. 43–4, Stilwell, p. 115.

22: SNOW WHITE, MADAME EMPRESS

1 Stilwell, p. 122.

2 Liang Hsi-huey, p. 158; Stilwell, pp. 120–1.

3 Stilwell, p. 122.

4 Guillermaz, pp. 89–90; MacKinnon and Friesen, p. 92.

5 Peck, p. 427–8.

6 Hart, p. 33, quoting Barrett; Tuchman, pp. 333–4.

7 Stilwell, p. 156–7; Chennault, pp. 212–16; Tuchman, p. 335.

8 Hart, p. 34; Davies, p. 255.

9 Cowles, pp. 88–9.

10 Davies, p. 255.

11 Stilwell, p. 194.

12 Robert Sherwood, *Roosevelt and Hopkins* (New York: Harper, 1948), pp. 660–1; Eleanor Roosevelt, *This I Remember* (New York: Harper, 1949), pp. 282–3.

13 MacKinnon and Friesen, p. 120.

14 Seagrave, p. 384.

15 Congressional Record, 1943, pp. 1080–1.

16 Cowles, p. 90.

17 Ibid.

18 Seagrave, pp. 389–90.

19 Lattimore, pp. 168–9; Jerome Chen, p. 79; Tuchman, pp. 352–3.

20 Seagrave, p. 389.

21 Amanda Smith, pp. 581–61.

22 Ch'i, *Nationalist China*, p. 160; White, *History*, p. 150; Belden, pp. 61–4.

23 White, *History*, pp. 146 et seq.; Peck, p. 393; Belden, p. 62.

24 White, *History*, pp. 147–8.

25 Ibid., p. 155.

26 Furaya, p. 761; Liang Hsi-huey, pp. 118, 122 – Chapter 6 has account of Casablanca and Trident from Chinese records.

27 Fairbank, *Chinabound*, pp. 252–3.

28 Tuchman, p. 369; Stilwell, pp. 203, 211–2, 215.

29 Peck, pp. 477–8, also for arrival in Chungking in next paragraph.

30 Young, OH, Appendix.

31 Peck, p. 477.

32 Service, pp. 92–6; Peck, p. 477; Stilwell, p. 229.

33 Seagrave, p. 411.

34 Lattimore, p. 142.

35 Stilwell, p. 229.

36 Quotes in following passage are from Stilwell, Chapter 7. Soong, Van de Ven, p. 59.

37 Feis, p. 78; Lattimore, p. 113.

38 Stilwell, pp. 232–3.

39 Liang Hsi-huey, pp. 145, 378–9; Furaya, p. 769; Stilwell, pp. 232–3.

40 Service, pp. 79–84; Seagrave, p. 410.

41 Fairbank, *Chinabound*, pp. 245–6, Furaya, p. 778.

23: 'ALL ASIA IS AT STAKE'

1 Boyle p. 323; Eastman in Akira Iriye, p. 284; Hsiang and Levine, p. 180; Peck, pp. 21–3; Potter and Potter, p. 31.

2 Churchill, p. 328; Alanbrooke, 23 November 1943. Cairo, Van de Ven, pp. 60–71.

3 Hahn, *Chiang*, p. 275; Alanbrooke, 23 November 1943.

4 Churchill, p. 329; Alanbrooke, 23 November 1943; Harold Macmillan, *War Diaries* (London: Macmillan, 1984), p. 304.

5 Alanbrooke, 23 November 1943.

6 Stilwell, p. 255; Davies, p. 278.

7 Stilwell, p. 252; Davies, p. 281.

8 Roosevelt 'fireside chat', 24 December 1943; Stilwell, p. 256.

9 Davies, p. 247.

10 Tuchman, p. 455; quoting Gauss/Service reports in USFRC 44, pp. 312, 319–26, 334–6. Following para, Stilwell, p. 252; Frederick Marks, *Wind Over Sand* (Athens: University of Georgia Press, 1988), p. 182.

11 Tuchman, p. 413.

12 Liang Hsi-huey, p. 233; Wilson, *Tigers*, pp. 221–2; Caldwell, pp. 54–60.

13 Caldwell, pp. 113–14.

14 Ibid., pp. 102–3, 207.

15 Stilwell, pp. 274 et seq.

16 Davies, p. 298.

17 Ibid., p. 299.

18 Stilwell, pp. 273 et seq.; Van de Ven, pp. 74–7 calls the operation 'a gamble that did not work'.

19 Toland, p. 618.

20 Ch'i, *Nationalist China*, pp. 9 et seq.; Dreyer, pp. 284 et seq.; White and Jacoby, Chapter 12; Peck, p. 560.

21 Chennault, p. 309.

22 Ibid., p. 302; White and Jacoby, p. 188.

23 Chennault, pp. 300–301; Tuchman, p. 472. Stilwell and Ichigo, Van de Ven, pp. 80–2.

24 Furaya, p. 793.

25 Peck, pp. 588, 590.

26 Lattimore, p. 139.

27 Ibid., p. 186.

28 Tuchman, p. 470.

29 Chen in Saich and Van de Ven, pp. 265 et seq.

30 Ibid., pp. 273–92.

31 Stilwell, pp. 329 et seq.; Tuchman, p. 489; CCK, *Calm*, p. 5; Stilwell, p. 327.

32 Chennault, p. 300; Stilwell, pp. 316–17.

33 Chennault, pp. 320–1.

34 Tuchman, p. 492.

35 Furaya, pp. 809, 804.

36 Tuchman, p. 498, quoting Ambassador's report to State Department.

37 Liang Hsi-huey, pp. 270–1; Stilwell, p. 343.

38 Davies, p. 337; Stilwell, p. 346; CKS, *Soviet Russia*, p. 118.

39 Tuchman, p. 504; Stilwell pp. 346–7.

40 Lattimore, p. 217; for closely argued revisionist view of Stilwell, see Van de Ven,

Introduction and Chapter One.

41 Davies, p. 383.

42· Caldwell, p. 90; Yiji Akashi in Coox and Conroy, p. 267; Eastman in Akira Iriye, p. 286.

43 Davies, p. 378.

44 Tuchman, p. 411; Snow, *Journey*, p. 217; Peck, p. 556.

24: RED LEAVES

1 Peck, p. 638.

2 Feis, pp. 208, 212–13; Davies, p. 368.

3 Al Ravenholt of UP in MacKinnon and Friesen, p. 144; Peck, p. 639; Jacoby in MacKinnon and Friesen, pp. 142–3.

4 Vladimirov, p. 261.

5 Barrett, p. 51.

6 Service, p. 1037; Vladimirov, pp. 211 et seq.

7 Exhibit 252, Institute of Pacific Relations Hearings, pp. 808–9; Davies, p. 363.

8 Vladimirov, p. 58; Maochun Yu, p. 222.

9 Dreyer, p. 293; Vladimirov, pp. 30, 35, 483–4, 83, 162. Van de Ven, pp. 87–8.

10 Vladimirov, pp. 55–60, 109, 111–13, 120.

11 Chen in Saich and Van de Ven, pp. 265 et seq.; Vladimirov, p. 123.

12 Vladimirov, pp. 83, 89.

13 Vladimirov, p. 134.

14 Chen in Saich and Van de Ven, pp. 273 et seq.

15 Barrett, p. 63.

16 Hart, pp. 49, 51–2; Davies, p. 382.

17 Vladimirov, p. 287.

18 Hart, pp. 59–60.

19 Ibid., p. 61.

20 Wedemeyer, p. 313; Jacoby in MacKinnon and Friesen, p. 143.

21 Chennault, pp. 329–30; Furaya, p. 818.

22 Wedemeyer, pp. 323–4.

23 Dreyer, pp. 304–5; I am indebted to Keith Stevens for pointing to the importance of the Zhijiang battle, and for providing a Chinese map of the encounter. Peck, p. 650; Moorad, pp. 221–2.

24 Peck, p. 650.

25 Caldwell, pp. 9, 26–7, 202.

26 Service, pp. 1418–23.

27 CCK, *Calm*, p. 52; Furaya, p. 824.

28 Furaya, p. 824.

29 Ibid., p. 821; Westad, pp. 31 et seq.

30 Furaya, p. xiii.

31 Ibid., pp. 831–2.

32 On Chiang and Manchuria, see exchange between Donald Gillin and Martin

Bernal, *New York Review of Books* (25 February 1971). Also Arthur Waldron's account of what might have happened if CKS had not tried to take Manchuria, in Robert Cowley, *What If?* (London: Macmillan, 2000).

33 Feis, p. 357.

34 Moorwood, pp. 5–7.

35 Vladimirov, p. 491; Furaya, p. liii.

36 Ibid.; Westad, pp. 167–8.

37 Westad, pp. 167–8.

38 Doon Campbell papers; Furaya, p. 853.

39 Campbell papers.

40 Yu Maochun, pp. 235–241.

41 Bland, p. 119; Campbell papers.

42 Furaya, p. 853.

43 Short, p. 403 and for following para.

44 For events in Manchuria, see, in particular, Steven Levine's account of the Communist victory and Odd Arne Westad's analysis of the effect of the start of the Cold War on China. This passage draws on Levine, pp. 49–51, and Westad, pp. 119 et seq.

45 Westad, p. 135.

46 Bachrack, pp. 27 et seq.; Koen, pp. 66–73.

25: MISSION IMPOSSIBLE

1 CP, Vol. II, pp. 732 et seq.; Yu Maochun, p. 256; Van de Ven, p. 443; Pickowicz in Yeh, pp. 395–6.

2 Tong and Li, p. 437.

3 Dreyer, p. 325.

4 Belden, pp. 224–6.

5 Ibid., pp. 6, 39.

6 Young, OH, pp. 76 et seq.; Beal, p. 138.

7 Belden, p. 20.

8 Westad, p. 136; Chen Li-fu, pp. 184–5; Bland, p. 153; Jung Chang, pp. 104–112.

9 Clubb, OH, p. 37.

10 Westad, pp. 163–4.

11 Guillermaz, p. 151.

12 Bland, 154; Stuart to Secretary of State, 21 July 1946 in Rea and Brewer, p. 2; Dreyer, p. 324; Levine, p. 240.

13 Beal, p. 40; Bland, pp. 580, 586, 589.

14 Beal, pp. 147–9.

15 Furaya, pp. 884, 885.

16 Ibid., p. 882.

17 Tong and Li, p. 447.

18 Bland, p. 569.

19 Beal, p. 333.

20 Stuart to State Dept, 21 July 1946, in Rea and Brewer, p. 3.
21 Ronning, p. 116.
22 Beal, p. 349.

26: DYING LIGHT

1   *Pictorial History*, Vol. II, pp. 265–8.
2   Koen, p. 34.
3   Jung Chang, p. 97; Belden, p. 404.
4   This passage draws on Chapter 4 of Levine.
5   CP, Vol. II, pp. 728 et seq.
6   Loh, *Débâcle*, p. 11.
7   Belden, pp. 354–7.
8   Loh, *Débâcle*, p. 12; Topping, p. 312.
9   *Japan Times*, Tokyo, 25 February 2002; Hutchings, p. 248; Levine, p. 124; *Time*, 1 April 1948.
10 Levine, p. 237.
11 Dreyer, pp. 350 et seq.
12 Pepper, p. 387 gives details of military discipline.
13 Sheridan, *Warlord*, pp. 277–81; White, *History*, p. 96.
14 Merle Miller, *Plain Speaking* (New York: Putnam, 1973), pp. 288–9; Seagrave, pp. 426–7.
15 Stuart to State Department, 29 November 1948, in Rea and Brewer, pp. 282–3.
16 Belden, p. 421; *Time*, 15 November 1948.
17 *The Times*, 2 and 4 December 1948.
18 Topping, pp. 32–3.
19 Ibid., pp. 35–42.
20 Belden, pp. 407, 410; Chang Kia-ngau in Loh, *Débâcle*, pp. 24–5.
21 Chang Kia-ngau in Loh, *Débâcle*, p. 24.
22 Belden, p. 408.
23 Taylor, pp. 154–61; Perry, p. 126; Dong, pp. 288–9; Taylor, pp. 153–4.
24 *The Times*, 20 January 1949.
25 Barnett, pp. 30–9; Belden, pp. 386–93.
26 Topping, p. 44; CCK, *Calm*, p. 146; Tong, p. 425.
27 CCK, *Calm*, p. 152; Topping, p. 52; Bodde, p. 100; *The Times*, 24 January 1949.
28 CCK, *Calm*, pp. 154 et seq.
29 Dong, pp. 291–2.
30 Guillermaz, pp. 191–2.
31 Tong and Li, pp. 515–16.
32 Topping, p. 64.
33 Guillermaz, p. 197; Topping, Chapter 4, describes Nanking's fall; Belden, p. 456.
34 Topping, p. 63.
35 Belden, p. 440; CCK, *Calm*, pp. 207, 214–15.

36 Stuart to Secretary of State, 24 May 1949, in Rea and Brewer, p. 326; Barber, p. 125.

37 Tong and Li, pp. 522–8, 526.

38 Hart, p. 76.

39 Ibid., pp. 534–5.

40 CCK, *Calm*, p. 239.

41 Tong and Li, pp. 536–7.

42 Ibid., p. 541.

43 CCK, *Calm*, pp. 276–7.

44 Ibid., p. 283; Taylor, p. 184.

45 Kuo Kwan-ying, Part Four – also for following paragraph.

46 Tong, pp. 476–7.

47 Rummel, p. 12.

48 CKS, *Soviet Russia*, pp. 211 et seq.; CCK, *Calm*, p. 297.

EPILOGUE: NEXT YEAR IN NANKING

1 Rummel, p. 12.

BIBLIOGRAPHY

NEWS SOURCES

North China Herald, Shanghai (NCH) (weekly edition of *North China Daily News*), *China Express and Telegraph* (CET), *China Weekly Review* (CWR), *South China Morning Post* (SCMP), Reuters, United Press, Kuo Min and Kuo Wen news agencies, Central News, Domei, *The Times* (London), *Guardian*, *New York Times*, *Time* magazine, Havas news agency

PERIODICALS

Republican China and *Twentieth Century China*, St John's University, New York; *China Yearbook*; *China Quarterly*; *Modern Asian Studies*; *Journal of Asian Studies*

ARCHIVES

Public Records Office, London; French Foreign Ministry, Paris; Kuomintang, Taipei; Academia Sinica, Taipei; Harry S. Truman Library for Oral Histories; Franklin D. Roosevelt Safe files; Doon Campbell private papers

BOOKS

Abend, Hallett, *Tortured China* (New York: Washburn, 1932)
——, *My Life in China* (New York: Harcourt Brace, 1943)
Alanbrooke, Field Marshal Lord (ed. Alex Danchev and Dan Todman), *War Diaries* (London: Weidenfeld & Nicolson, 2001)

Alley, Rewi, *Amongst Hills and Streams of Hunan* (Peking: New World Press, 1963)

Anon, *Suppressing Communist-Banditry in China* (Shanghai: China Today, 1934)

——, *President Chiang Kai-shek: His Life Story in Pictures* (Taipei: n.p., 1971)

——, *In Everlasting Memory of the Late President Chiang* (Taipei: n.p., 1977)

——, *Military Exploits of Generalissimo Chiang Kai-shek* (n.p., n.d.)

Auden, W. H., and Isherwood, Christopher, *Journey to a War* (London: Faber & Faber, 1938)

Batbayar, Bat-Erdene, *Twentieth Century Mongolia* (Cambridge, MA: White Horse Press, 1999)

Bachrack, Stanley, *The Committee of One Million* (New York: Columbia University Press, 1976)

Baker, Barbara, *Shanghai* (Oxford: OUP, 1998)

Barber, Noel, *The Fall of Shanghai* (New York: Coward McCann & Geoghegan, 1979)

Barrett, David, *Dixie Mission* (Berkeley: University of California Press, 1970)

Barrett, David, and Shyu, Lawrence N. (eds), *China in the Anti-Japanese War* (New York: Peter Lang, 2001)

Barnett, A. Doak, *China on the Eve of the Communist Takeover* (London: Thames & Hudson, 1963)

Basil, George, *Test Tubes and Dragon Scale* (Chicago: Winston, 1940)

Beal, John Robinson, *Marshall in China* (Toronto: Doubleday, 1970)

Beasley, W. G., *The Modern History of Japan* (Tokyo: Charles E. Tuttle, 1982)

Bedeski, Robert, *State-Building in Modern China* (Berkeley: University of California Press, 1981)

Belden, Jack, *China Shakes the World* (New York: Modern Reader Press, 1949)

Bennett, Milly, *On Her Own* (Armonk: M. E. Sharpe, 1993)

Benton, Gregor, *Mountain Fires* (Berkeley: University of California Press, 1992)

——, *New Fourth Army* (Richmond: Curzon, 1999)

Bergère, Marie-Claire, *L'age d'or de la bourgeoisie chinoise* (Paris: Flammarion, 1986)

——, *Sun Yat-sen* (Stanford: Stanford University Press, 1998)

Berkoff, Robert, *Strong Man of China* (Freeport: Books for Libraries Press, 1938)

Bertram, James, *First Act in China: The Story of the Sian Mutiny* (New York: Viking, 1938)

——, *Unconquered: A Journal of a Year's Adventure Among the Fighting Peasants of North China* (New York: John Day, 1939; reissue, New York: Da Capo Press, 1975)

Bianco, Lucien, *Origins of the Chinese Revolution* (Stanford: Stanford University Press, 1971)

Bix, Herbert, *Hirohito* (New York: HarperCollins, 2000)

Bland, Larry (ed.), *George C. Marshall's Mediation Mission to China* (Lexington: George C. Marshall Foundation, 1998)

Bodde, Derk, *Peking Diary* (New York: Octagon Books, 1976)

Booth, Martin, *Opium* (London: Simon & Schuster, 1996)

Bonnard, Abel, *In China* (London: Routledge, 1926)

Boorman, Howard (ed.), *Biographical Dictionary of Republican China* (New York: Columbia University Press, 1967–71)

Borg, Dorothy, *The United States and the Far Eastern Crisis of 1933–38* (Cambridge, MA: Harvard University Press, 1964)

Botjer, George, *A Short History of Nationalist China 1919–1949* (New York: G. P. Putnam's Sons, 1979)

Boyle, John Hunter, *China and Japan at War, 1937–45* (Stanford: Stanford University Press, 1972)

Bramall, Chris, *Living Standards in Sichuan, 1931–78* (London: SOAS, 1989)

Brandt, Conrad, *Stalin's Failure in China* (New York: W. W. Norton, 1958)

Brodie, Patrick, *Crescent Over Cathay* (Oxford: OUP, 1990)

Brook, Timothy, and Wakabayashi, Bob Tadashi (eds), *Opium Regimes* (Berkeley: University of California Press, 2000)

Caldwell, Oliver, *A Secret War* (Carbondale: Southern Illinois University Press, 1972)

Candlin, Enid Saunders, *The Breach in the Wall* (London: Cassell, 1973)

Chan, F. Gilbert (ed.), *China at the Crossroads* (Boulder: Westview, 1980)

Chan and Etzold (eds), *China in the 1920s* (New York: New Viewpoints, 1976)

Chang, Iris, *The Rape of Nanking* (London: Penguin, 1997)

Chang, Jung, *Madame Sun Yat-sen* (London: Penguin, 1986)

——, *Wild Swans* (London: HarperCollins, 1991)

Chang Kia-ngau, *The Inflationary Spiral: The Experience in China 1939–1950* (New York: John Wiley, 1958)

Chang, Maria Hsia, *The Chinese Blue Shirt Society* (Berkeley: University of California, 1985)

Chapman, H. Owen, *The Chinese Revolution, 1926–27* (London: Constable, 1928)

Chassin, L. M., *La Conquête de la Chine par Mao tse-tung* (Paris: Payot, 1952)

Chen Chieh-ju (Chen Jieru), *Chiang Kai-shek's Secret Past* (Boulder: Westview Press, 1993)

Chen, Jerome, *China and the West* (London: Hutchinson, 1979)

Chen, Leslie, 'Chen Jiongming and the Chinese Federalist Movement' (*Republican China*, November 1991)

Chen Li-fu, *The Storm Clouds Clear Over China* (Stanford: Stanford University Press, 1994)

Chen Tung-hsi, Wang An-tsiang and Wang I-ting, *General Chiang Kai shek: The Builder of New China* (Shanghai: Commercial Press, 1929)

Chen Yung-fa, 'The Blooming Poppy Under the Red Sun', in Saich and Van de Ven (q.v.)

——, Israel, John, and Klein, Donald, *Rebels and Bureaucrats* (Berkeley: University of California Press, 1976)

Cheng Pei-kai, and Lestz, Michael, with Spence, Jonathan, *The Search for Modern*

China: A Documentary Collection (New York: W. W. Norton, 1999)

Chennault, Claire, *Way of a Fighter* (New York: Putnam, 1949)

Cherepanov, A. I., *As Military Adviser in China* (Moscow: Progress Publishers, 1982)

Chesnaux, Jean, *The Chinese Labour Movement, 1919–27* (Stanford: Stanford University Press, 1968)

——, *Secret Societies in China* (London: Hutchinson, 1972)

——, Le Barbier, Françoise and Bergère, Marie-Claire, *China from the 1911 Revolution to Liberation* (Hassocks: Harvester Press, 1977)

Ch'i Hsi-sheng, *Warlord Politics in China* (Stanford: Stanford University Press, 1976)

——, *Nationalist China at War* (Ann Arbor: University of Michigan Press, 1982)

Chiang Ching-kuo, *My Father* (Taipei: Ming Hwa Publication, n.d.)

——, *Calm in the Eye of a Storm* (Taipei: Le Ming Cultural Enterprises, 1978)

Chiang Kai-shek, *China at the Crossroads* (London: Faber & Faber, 1937)

——, *Collected Wartime Messages of Generalissimo Chiang Kai-shek, 1937–45* (New York: John Day, 1945; two volumes)

——, *Soviet Russia in China* (New York: Farrar, Straus & Cudahy, 1965)

——, *President Chiang Kai-shek's Selected Speeches and Messages, 1937–45* (Taipei: China Cultural Service, n.d.)

——, *China's Destiny,* commentary by Philip Jaffe (London: Dennis Dobson, 1947)

Chiang Kai-shek, Madame, *Meiling Soong: New Life for Jiangxi* (Shanghai: n.p., 1935)

——, *May-ling Soong: War Messages and Other Selections* (Hankou: n.p., 1938)

——, *Conversations With Mikhail Borodin* (n.p., n.d.)

Chien Tuan-sheng, *The Government and Politics of China, 1912–49* (Stanford: Stanford University Press, 1950)

China Quarterly, 'Reappraising Republican China' (June 1997)

Chu Shao-jang, *On Chiang Kai-shek's position on Resisting Japan* (Thesis submitted to University of British Columbia, 1999)

Churchill, Winston, *Closing the Ring* (London: Cassell, 1950)

Clark, Carter Blue (ed.), *Chiang Kai-shek and the United States* (Long Beach: California State University, 1986)

Clubb, Edmund, *Twentieth Century China* (New York: Columbia University Press, 1964)

Coble, Parks, *The Shanghai Capitalists and the Nationalist Government, 1927–37* (Cambridge, MA: Harvard University Press, 1980)

——, *Facing Japan* (Cambridge, MA: Harvard University Press, 1991)

Colville, John, *The Fringes of Power* (New York: W. W. Norton, 1986)

Coox, Alvin, and Conroy, Hilary (eds), *China and Japan* (Santa Barbara: ABC-Clio, 1978)

Cornelius, Wanda, and Short, Thayne, *Ding Hao: America's Air War in China, 1937–45* (Gretna: Pelican, 1980)

Cowles, Gardner, *Mike Looks Back: The Memoirs of Gardner Cowles* (New York: Gardner Cowles, 1985)

Crowley, James, *Japan's Quest for Autonomy* (Princeton: Princeton University Press, 1966)

Crozier, Brian, *The Man Who Lost China* (London: Angus & Robertson, 1976)

Curtis, Richard, *Chiang Kai-shek* (New York: Hawthorn, 1969)

Davies, John Paton Jnr, *Dragon by the Tail* (London: Robson Books, 1974)

Dikötter, Frank, *Crime, Punishment and Prison in Modern China* (London: Hurst, 2002)

——, Laamann, Lars, and Zhou Xun, *Narcotic Culture* (Centre for Crime and Justice Studies, 2002)

Dolan, Sean, *Chiang Kai-shek* (New York: Chelsea House, 1988)

Dong, Stella, *Shanghai* (New York: William Morrow, 2000)

Dorn, Frank, *The Sino-Japanese War, 1937–41* (New York: Macmillan, 1974)

Drage, Charles, *The Life and Times of General Two-Gun Cohen* (New York: Funk & Wagnall, 1954)

——, *One Arm Sutton* (London: White Lion, 1973)

Dreyer, Edward L., *China at War* (London: Longman, 1995)

Dryburgh, Marjorie, *North China and Japanese Expansion* (London: Curzon, 2000)

Dubarbier, Georges, *La Chine contemporaine* (Paris: Librarie Orientaliste, 1926)

Eastman, Lloyd, *The Abortive Revolution* (Cambridge, MA: Harvard University Press, 1974)

——, *Seeds of Destruction: Nationalist China, 1937–49* (Stanford: Stanford University Press, 1984)

——, *Family, Fields and Ancestors* (Oxford: OUP, 1988)

——, 'China's Democratic Parties and the Temptation of Political Power' (*Republican China*, November 1991)

——, et al., *The Nationalist Era in China* (Cambridge, MA: Harvard University Press, 1991)

Epstein, Israel, *The People's War* (London: Gollancz, 1939)

——, *The Unfinished Revolution in China* (Boston: Little, Brown, 1947)

Esherick, Joseph, 'War and Revolution: Chinese Society During the 1940s' (*Twentieth Century China*, November 2001)

—— (ed.), *Last Chance in China: The World War II Despatches of John S. Service* (New York: Random House, 1974)

—— (ed.), *Remaking the Chinese City* (Honolulu: University of Hawaii Press, 2000)

Etzold, Thomas H., *Aspects of Sino-American Relations Since 1784* (New York: New Viewpoints, 1978)

Fairbank, John King, *Chinabound* (New York: Harper & Row, 1982)

——, *The Great Chinese Revolution, 1800–1985* (New York: Harper & Row, 1986)

——, *China: A New History* (Cambridge, MA: Harvard University Press, 1994)

—— and Feuerwerker, Alfred (eds), *Cambridge History of China, Vol. 13* (Cambridge: CUP, 1986)

Falgiot, Roger, and Kauffer, Rémi, *The Chinese Secret Service* (New York: William Morrow, 1987)

Farmer, Rhodes, *Shanghai Harvest* (London: Museum Press, 1945)

Feis, Herbert, *The China Tangle* (Princeton: Princeton University Press, 1953)

Feng Chongxi, and Goodman, David, *North China at War* (Lanham: Rowman & Littlefield, 2000)

Fewsmith, Joseph, *Party, State and Local Elites in Republican China* (Honolulu: University of Hawaii Press, 1984)

Fitzgerald, C. P., *The Birth of Communist China* (Harmondsworth: Penguin, 1964)

——, *Why China* (Melbourne: Melbourne University Press, 1985)

Fitzgerald, John (ed.), *The Nationalists and Chinese Society* (Melbourne: University of Melbourne Press, 1989)

——, *Awakening China* (Stanford: Stanford University Press, 1996)

Fleming, Peter, *One's Company* (London: Jonathan Cape, 1934)

Forman, Harrison, *Report from Red China* (London: Robert Hale, 1946)

Francke, Harry, *Roving Through Southern China* (New York: The Century Co., 1925)

Frazier, Martin W., 'Mobilizing a Movement: Cotton Mill Foremen in the Shanghai Strikes of 1925' (*Republican China*, November 1994)

Friedman, Edward, *Backwards Towards Revolution: The Chinese Revolutionary Party* (Berkeley: University of California Press, 1974)

Friedman, Edward, Pickowicz, Paul, Selden, Mark, *Chinese Village Socialist State* (New Haven: Yale University Press, 1991)

Fung, Edmund S. K., *In Search of Chinese Democracy* (Cambridge: CUP, 2000)

Furaya, Keiji, *Chiang Kai-shek* (New York: St John's University Press, 1981)

Geisert, Bradley, 'Toward a Pluralistic Model of KMT Rule' (*Chinese Republican Studies*, February 1982)

Gibson, Michael, *Chiang Kai-shek's Central Army, 1924–38* (Dissertation, George Washington University, 1985)

Gilbert, Rodney, *What's Wrong With China* (New York: Frederick A. Stokes, 1932)

Gillin, Donald, *Warlord: Yen Hsi-shen in Shansi Province, 1911–49* (Princeton: Princeton University Press, 1967)

——, 'The Case of Chen Cheng and the Kuomintang' (*Journal of Asian Studies*, August 1970)

——, *Falsifying China's History: The Case of Sterling Seagrave's 'The Soong Dynasty'* (Stanford: Stanford University Press, 1986)

——, and Myers, Ramon (eds), *Last Chance in Manchuria: The Diary of Chang Kia-ngau* (Hoover Archive, 1989)

Ginsbourg, Sam, *My First Sixty Years in China* (Beijing: New World Press, 1982)

Gittings, John, *The World and China, 1922–72* (London: Eyre Methuen, 1974)

Godley, Shirley, 'W. Cameron Forbes and the American Mission to China (1935)' (*Papers on China*, Vol. 14, 1960)

Gottschang, Thomas, 'Incomes in the Chinese Rural Economy, 1885–1945' (*Republican China*, November 1992)

Gray, Jack, *Rebellion and Revolution* (Oxford: OUP, 1990)

——, *Modern China's Search for a Political Forum* (London: OUP, 1969)

Guillermaz, J., *Une Vie pour la Chine* (Paris: Pluriel-Laffont, 1989)

Hahn Emily, *The Soong Sisters* (London: Robert Hale, 1942)

——, *Chiang Kai-shek* (New York: Doubleday, 1955)

Hall, J. C. S., *The Yunnan Provincial Faction, 1927–37* (Canberra: Australian National University, 1976)

Han Suyin, *Destination Chungking* (London: Jonathan Cape, 1943)

——, *A Mortal Flower* (London: Panther Books, 1972)

——, *China, 1890–1938* (Vaduz: Jeunesse Verlagsansalt, 1989)

Hart, John, *The Making of an Army Old China Hand* (Berkeley: Institute of East Asian Studies, 1985)

Hauser, Ernest, *Shanghai: City for Sale* (New York: Harcourt Brace, 1940)

Hedin, Sven, *Chiang Kai-shek: Marshal of China* (New York: John Day, 1940)

Henriot, Christian, *Shanghai, 1927–37* (Berkeley: University of California Press, 1993)

——, *Prostitution and Sexuality in Shanghai* (Cambridge: CUP, 2001)

Hershatter, Gail, *Dangerous Pleasures* (Berkeley: University of California Press, 1997)

Hewlett, Meyrick, *Forty Years in China* (London: Macmillan, 1943)

Holcombe, A. N., *The Chinese Revolution* (New York: Alfred A. Knopf, 1930)

Homer, Joy, *Dawn Watch in China* (London: Collins, 1941)

Hsiang, James, and Levine, Steve (eds), *China's Bitter Victory* (Armonk: East Gate, 1991)

Hsiung S., *The Life of Chiang Kai-shek* (London: Methuen, 1948)

Hsu, Immanuel C. Y., *The Rise of Modern China* (Oxford: OUP, 2000)

Huang, Philip, 'The Study of Rural China's Economic History' (*Republican China*, November 1992)

Hunt, Michael H., *The Genesis of Chinese Communist Foreign Policy* (New York: Columbia University Press, 1996)

Hutchings, Graham, *Modern China* (London: Penguin, 2000)

Ienaga, Saburo, *The Pacific War, 1931–45* (New York: Pantheon, 1978)

Iriye, Akira, *The Chinese and the Japanese* (Princeton: Princeton University Press, 1980)

Isaacs, Harold, *The Tragedy of the Chinese Revolution* (Stanford: Stanford University Press, 1938–61)

Israel, John, and Klein, Donald, *Rebels and Bureaucrats* (Berkeley: University of California Press, 1976)

Jacobs, Dan, *Borodin* (Cambridge, MA: Harvard University Press, 1981)

Jeans, Roger, 'Third Force' (*Republican China*, November 1993)

Johnson, Chalmers A., *Peasant Nationalism and Communist Power* (Stanford: Stanford University Press, 1963)

Johnston, Tess, and Erh, Deke, *A Last Look: Western Architecture in Old Shanghai* (Hong Kong: Old China Hand Press, 1993)

——, *Far from Home* (Hong Kong: Old China Hand Press, 1996)

Jones, F. W., *Changing China* (Kilmarnock: Christian Literature Publications, 1946)

Jordan, Donald, *The Northern Expedition* (Honolulu: University of Hawaii Press, 1978)

——, *Chinese Boycotts v Japanese Bombs* (Ann Arbor: University of Michigan Press, 1991)

——, *China's Trial by Fire* (Ann Arbor: University of Michigan Press, 2002)

Kapp, Robert, *Szechwan and the Chinese Republic, 1911–38* (New Haven: Yale University Press, 1973)

Kataoka, Tetsuya, *Resistance and Revolution in China* (Berkeley: University of California Press, 1974)

King, Frank H. H., *A Concise Economic History of Modern China* (London: Pall Mall, 1969)

Kirby, William, 'Joint Ventures: Technology Transfer and Technocratic Organization in Nationalist China' (*Republican China*, April 1987)

——, *State and Economy in Republican China* (Cambridge, MA: Harvard University Press, 2001)

——, *Engineering China: Birth of the Developmental State 1928–1937* in Yeh, *Becoming Chinese* (q.v.)

Koen, Ross, *China Lobby* (New York: Harper & Row, 1974)

Kou Chang-ming, *Labour and Empire: the Chinese Labour Movement in the Canton Delta, 1895–1927* (Doctoral Dissertation, Stanford University, 1975)

Kuo, Helena, *Westward to Chunking* (London: Hutchinson, 1943)

Kuo Kwan-ying, *A Century Walked Through* (four-part video documentary and interview with the Young Marshal) (Taipei, 1993)

Kuo, Warren, *Analytical History of the Chinese Communist Party* (Taipei: Institute of International Relations, 1969)

Kwei Chung-shu et al., *Japan's Undeclared War* (Shanghai: Chinese Chamber of Commerce, 1932)

Lacam, Guy, *Un Banquier au Yunnan dans les années 1930* (Paris: L'Harmattan, 1994)

Lary, Diana, *Region and Nation: The Kwangsi Clique* (Cambridge: CUP, 1974)

——, *Warlord Soldiers* (New York: Columbia University Press, 1985)

Lattimore, Owen, *China Memoirs* (Tokyo: University of Tokyo Press, 1990)

Laughlin, Charles, *Chinese Reportage* (Durham: Duke University Press, 2002)

Lee, James Hsioung, *A Half Century of Memories* (Hong Kong: South China Printing, undated)

Lee, Leo Ou-fan, *Shanghai Modern* (Cambridge, MA: Harvard University Press, 1999)

Leith-Ross, Sir Frederick, *Money Talks* (London: Hutchinson, 1968)

Leung, Edwin, *Historical Dictionary of Revolutionary China* (New York: Greenwood Press, 1992)

Levine, Stephen, *Anvil of Victory* (New York: Columbia University Press, 1987)

Levitch, Eugene William, *The Kwangsi Way in Kuomintang China* (Armonk: M. E. Sharpe, 1993)

Liang Chin-tung, *General Stilwell in China* (New York: St John's University, 1972)

Liang Hsi-huey, *The Sino-German Connection* (Amsterdam: Van Gorcum, 1977)

Lin Hua, *Chiang Kai-shek, De Gaulle contre Ho Chi Minh* (Paris: L'Harmattan, 1994)

Lin, Yu-tang, 'The Dogmeat General' in Edgar Snow (ed.), *Living China: Modern Chinese Short Stories* (New York: Reynal & Hitchcock, 1937)

Linebarger, Paul, *The China of Chiang Kai-shek* (Boston: World Peace Foundation, 1941)

Liu, F. F., *A Military History of Modern China* (Princeton: Princeton University Press, 1956)

Liu Po-cheng et al., *Recalling the Long March* (Peking: Foreign Language Press, 1978)

Loh, Pichon, *The Kuomintang Débâcle of 1949* (Boston: Heath, 1965)

——, *The Early Chiang Kai-shek* (New York: Columbia University Press, 1971)

Lou Ruiqing et al., *Zhou Enlai and the Xian Incident* (Beijing: n.p., 1963)

Lu Han-chao, *Beyond the Neon Lights* (Berkeley: University of California Press, 1999)

Lumley, F. A., *The Republic of China Under Chiang Kai-shek* (London: Barrie & Jenkins, 1976)

McCord, Edward A., 'Warlordism at Bay' (*Republican China*, November 1991)

——, *The Power of the Gun: The Emergence of Chinese Warlordism* (Berkeley: University of California Press, 1993)

McCormack, Gavan, *Chang Tso-lin in Northeast China* (Folkestone: Dawson, 1977)

McDonald, Angus, *Urban Origins of Rural Revolution* (Berkeley: University of California Press, 1978)

McElderry, Andrea, 'Robber Barons or National Capitalists: Shanghai Bankers in Republican China' (*Republican China*, November 1985)

MacFarquhar, Roderick, *The Whampoa Military Academy* (Cambridge, MA: Papers on China, Vol. 9, 1955)

Mackerras, Colin, *Sinophiles and Sinophobes* (Oxford: OUP, 2000)

MacKinnon, Stephen, and Friesen, Oris, *China Reporting* (Berkeley: University of California, 1987)

McLane, Charles, *The Soviet Union and the Chinese Communists, 1920–42* (New York: Columbia University Press, 1958)

MacNair, Harley Farnsworth, *China in Revolution: An Analysis of Politics and Militarism Under the Republic* (Chicago: University of Chicago Press, 1931)

Malraux, André, *La Condition humaine* (Paris: Gallimard, 1946)

Mann, Susan, *Local Merchants and the Chinese Bureaucracy* (Stanford: Stanford University Press, 1987)

Mao Zedong, *Selected Works* (Beijing: Foreign Languages Press, 1967)

Maochun Yu, *OSS in China* (New Haven: Yale University Press, 1996)

Marshall, George, *Marshall's Mission to China* (2 volumes) (Arlington: University Publications of America, 1970)

Martin, Brian, *The Shanghai Green Gang* (Berkeley: University of California Press, 1996)

Misselwitz, Henry Francis, *The Dragon Stirs* (New York: Harbinger Books, 1941; Ann Arbor: University Microfilms, 1978)

Mitter, Rana, *The Manchurian Myth* (Berkeley: University of California Press, 2000)

Moorad, George, *Lost Peace in China* (New York: Dutton, 1949)

Moorwood, William, *Duel for the Middle Kingdom* (New York: Everest House, 1980)

Mowrer, Edgar Ansel, *Mowrer in China* (Harmondsworth: Penguin, 1938)

Myers, Ramon, *The Chinese Peasant Economy* (Cambridge, MA: Harvard University Press, 1970)

Nellist, George, *Men of Shanghai and North China* (Shanghai: n.p., 1933)

North, Robert C., and Eudin, Zenia J., *N. M. Roy's Mission to China* (Berkeley: University of California Press, 1963)

Pan, Lynn, *In Search of Old Shanghai* (Hong Kong: Joint Publishing, 1982–91)

——, *Shanghai: A Century of Change in Photographs* (Hong Kong: Hai Feng, 1991)

——, *Old Shanghai: Gangsters in Paradise* (Singapore: Cultured Lotus Publishers, 1994)

Payne, Robert, *Chungking Diary* (London: Heinemann, 1945)

——, *Chinese Diaries* (New York: Weybridge & Talley, 1945, 1947, 1950)

——, *Chiang Kai-shek* (New York: Weybridge & Talley, 1969)

Peck, Graham, *Two Kinds of Time* (Boston: Houghton Mifflin, 1950)

Pelissier, Roger, *The Awakening of China* (London: Secker & Warburg, 1967)

Pepper, Suzanne, *Civil War in China* (Lanham: Rowman & Littlefield, 1999)

Perry, Elizabeth, *Shanghai on Strike* (Stanford: Stanford University Press, 1993)

Philips, Richard T., *China Since 1911* (London: Macmillan, 1996)

Pictorial History of the Republic of China (Taipei: Modern China Press, 1981; two volumes)

Potter, Sulamith Heins, and Potter, Jack M., *China's Peasants* (Cambridge: CUP, 1990)

Powell, John, *My Twenty-Five Years in China* (New York: Macmillan, 1945)

Pringle, J. M. D., *China Struggles for Unity* (Harmondsworth: Penguin, 1939)

Proceedings of Conference on Chiang Kai-shek and Modern China (five volumes) (Taipei, 1987)

Pu Yi, Aisin-Gioro, *From Emperor to Citizen* (Beijing: Foreign Languages Press, 1989)

Pye, Lucian W., *Warlord Politics* (New York: Praeger, 1971)

Rabe, John, *The Good Man of Nanking* (New York: Alfred A. Knopf, 1998)

Ranbir, Vohra, *China's Path to Modernization* (Englewood City: Prentice Hall, 1987)

Rand, Peter, *China Hands* (New York: Simon & Schuster, 1995)

Ransome, Arthur, *The China Puzzle* (London: Allen & Unwin, 1927)

Rawski, Thomas, *Economic Growth in Pre-war China* (Berkeley: University of California, 1989)

——, 'Ideas about Studying China's Rural Economy' (*Republican China*, November 1991)

Rea, Kenneth (ed.), *Canton in Revolution: The Collected Papers of Earl Swisher* (Boulder: Westview Press, 1977)

——, and Brewer, John (eds), *The Forgotten Ambassador: The Reports of John Leighton Stuart* (Boulder: Westview Press, 1981)

Reinsch, Paul, *An American Diplomat in China* (London: Allen & Unwin, 1922)

Reischauer, Edwin, and Craig, Albert, *Japan: Tradition and Transformation* (Tokyo: Tuttle, 1978)

'Republican China: Disintegration and Integration of Political Systems' (*Twentieth Century China*, April 1978)

Republican China, Symposium on Second Sino-Japanese War (April 1989)

Roberts, J. A. G., *Modern China* (Stroud: Sutton Publishing, 1998)

Romanus, Charles, and Sunderland, Riley, *Stilwell's Mission to China* (Washington: Department of the Army, 1953)

——, *Stilwell's Command Problems* (Washington: Department of the Army, 1956)

——, *Time Runs Out in the CBI* (Washington: Department of the Army, 1959)

Ronning, Chester, *A Memoir of China in Revolution* (New York: Pantheon Books, 1974)

Roy, N. M., *Revolution and Counter-revolution in China* (Calcutta: Renaissance, 1946)

Roux, Alain, *Le Shanghai ouvrier des années trente* (Paris: L'Harmattan, 1993)

——, *Grèves et politiques à Shanghai* (Paris: Editions de l'EHESS, 1995)

Rummel, R. J., *China's Bloody Century* (London: Transaction Publishers, 1991)

Saich, Tony, *The Rise to Power of the Chinese Communist Party* (New York: M. E. Sharpe, 1996)

——, and Van de Ven, Hans, *New Perspectives on the Chinese Communist Revolution* (New York: M. E. Sharpe, 1995)

——, *Origins of the First United Front in China* (Leiden: E. J. Brill, 1991)

Salisbury, Harrison, *The Long March* (London: Macmillan, 1985)

Schoppa, R. Keith, *Columbia Guide to Modern Chinese History* (New York: Columbia University Press, 2000)

Schram, Stuart, *Mao Tse-tung* (Harmondsworth: Penguin, 1967)

Schurman, Franz, and Schell, Orville (eds), *Republican China* (Harmondsworth: Penguin, 1967)

Schwarcz, Vera, *The Chinese Enlightenment* (Berkeley: University of California Press, 1986)

Schwartz, Benjamin, *Chinese Communism and the Rise of Mao* (Cambridge, MA: Harvard University Press, 1951)

Seagrave, Sterling, *The Soong Dynasty* (London: Sidgwick & Jackson, 1985)

Selden, Mark, *The Yenan Way of Revolutionary China* (Cambridge, MA: Harvard University Press, 1971)

——, *China in Revolution: The Yenan Way Revisited* (Armonk: M. E. Sharpe, 1995)

Selle, Earl Albert, *Donald of China* (New York: Harper, 1948)

Sergeant, Harriet, *Shanghai* (London: John Murray, 1991)

Service, John, *The Americasia Papers* (Berkeley: Center for Chinese Studies Research, 1971)

Sheean, Vincent, *Personal History* (New York: Garden City, 1937)

Sheridan, James, *Chinese Warlord* (Stanford: Stanford University Press, 1966)

——, *China in Disintegration* (New York: The Free Press, 1977)

Short, Philip, *Mao: A Life* (London: Hodder & Stoughton, 1999)

Sie Cheou-kang, *President Chiang Kai-shek: His Childhood and Youth* (Taipei: China Cultural Service, n.d.)

Sih, Paul (ed.), *Nationalist China During the Sino-Japanese War* (Hicksville: Exposition Press, 1977)

——, *The Strenuous Decade, 1927–37* (New York: St John's University, 1970)

Smedley, Agnes, *China Fights Back* (London: Gollancz, 1938)

——, *Battle Hymn of China* (London: Gollancz, 1944)

——, *Portraits of Chinese Women in Revolution* (New York: Feminist Press, 1976)

Smith, Amanda, *Hostage to Fortune: The Letters of Joseph P. Kennedy* (New York: Viking, 2001)

Smith, Robert, *With Chennault in China* (Blue Ridge Summit: Tab Books, 1984)

Smith, Sara, *The Manchurian Crisis, 1931–32* (New York: Columbia University Press, 1948)

Snow, Edgar, *Red Star over China* (London: Gollancz, 1937)

——, *Journey to the Beginning* (London: Gollancz, 1960)

Snow, Philip, *The Fall of Hong Kong* (New Haven: Yale University Press, 2003)

Spence, Jonathan, *The Gate of Heavenly Peace* (New York: Penguin, 1981)

——, *The Search for Modern China* (New York: W. W. Norton, 1999)

——, *Mao* (London: Weidenfeld & Nicolson, 1999)

——, and Chin, Annping, *The Chinese Century* (New York: Random House, 1996)

Stapleton, Kristin, *Civilizing Chengdu* (Cambridge, MA: Harvard University Press, 2000)

Sternberg, Josef von, *Fun in a Chinese Laundry* (New York: Mercury House, 1988)

Stilwell, Joseph, *The Stilwell Papers* (ed. Theodore White) (New York: Schocken Books, 1972)

Stolley, Richard (ed.), *Life: World War Two* (New York: Bullfinch Press, 1999)

Stone, Albert H., and Reed, Hammond, *Historic Lushan* (Hankou: Arthington Press, Religious Tract Society, 1921)

Strand, David, *Rickshaw Beijing* (Berkeley: University of California Press, 1989)

——, 'A High Place Is No Better Than a Low Place: The City in the Making of Modern China', in Yeh, *Becoming Chinese* (q.v.)

Strauss, Julia C., *Strong Institutions in Weak Politics* (Oxford: OUP, 1998)

Sues, Ilona, *Shark's Fin and Millet* (New York: Little, Brown, 1944)

Sun Tzu, *The Art of War* (Oxford: OUP, 1963)

Sutton, Donald, *Provincial Militarism and the Chinese Republic: The Yunnan Army, 1905–25* (Ann Arbor: University of Michigan Press, 1980)

Swisher, Earl, *Canton in Revolution, 1925–1928* (Boulder: Westview Press, 1977)

Tai Hsuanchih, *The Red Spears, 1916–49* (Ann Arbor: University of Michigan Press, 1985)

Tang, Peter S. H., *Russian and Soviet Policy in Manchuria* (Durham: Duke University Press, 1959)

T'ang Leang-li, *The Inner History of the Chinese Revolution* (London: Routledge, 1930)

——, *Wang Ching-wei* (Peiping: China United Press, 1931)

Tawney, R. H., *Land and Labour in China* (London: George Allen & Unwin, 1932)

Taylor, Jay, *The Generalissimo's Son* (Cambridge, MA: Harvard University Press, 2000)

The Opium Trade, Vol. 6 (Wilmington: Scholarly Resources, 1974)

Teitler, Ger, and Radtke, Kurt (eds), *A Dutch Spy in China* (Leiden: Brill, 1999)

Thomson, James C. Jnr, *Communist Policy and the United Front in China* (Cambridge, MA: *Papers on China*, Vol. 11, 1957)

Thornton, Richard, *China: The Struggle for Power, 1917–72* (Bloomington: Indiana University Press, 1973)

Tien Hung-mao, *Government and Politics in Kuomintang China* (Stanford: Stanford University Press, 1972)

Timperley, Harold, *What War Means* (London: Gollancz, 1938)

Toland, John, *The Rising Sun* (London: Cassell, 1970)

Tong Te-kong and Li Tsung-jen (Li Zongren), *The Memoirs of Li Tsung-jen* (Boulder: Westview Press, 1979)

Tong, Hollington, *Chiang Kai-shek* (London: Hurst & Blackett, 1938, two volumes; revised edition, Taipei, 1953)

Topping, Seymour, *Journey Between Two Chinas* (New York: Harper & Row, 1972)

Trotsky, Leon, *Problems of the Chinese Revolution* (New York: Pioneer Publishers, 1932)

Tsin, Michael, *Nation, Governance and Modernity in China: Canton, 1900–27* (Stanford: Stanford University Press, 1999)

Tuchman, Barbara, *Stilwell and the American Experience in China* (New York: Macmillan, 1970)

Twitchett, Denis, and Fairbank, John K., *The Cambridge History of China*, Vol. 12 (Cambridge: Cambridge University Press, 1983)

Van de Ven, Hans, *Nationalism in China, 1925–1945* (London: Routledge, 2003)

Van Slyke, Lyman, *The Chinese Communist Movement During the Sino-Japanese War* (*Cambridge History of China*, Vol. 13)

Vladimirov, Petr Parfenovic, *China's Special Area, 1942–1945* (Bombay: Allied Publishers, 1974)

Wakeman, Frederic, *Policing Shanghai* (Berkeley: University of California Press, 1995)

——, 'Hanjian (Traitor)! Collaboration and Retribution in Wartime Shanghai' in Yeh, *Becoming Chinese* (q.v.)

——, and Edmonds, Richard Louis (eds), *Reappraising Republican China* (Oxford: OUP, 2000)

——, *The Shanghai Badlands*, (Cambridge: Cambridge University Press, 1996)

Waldron, Arthur, *From War to Nationalism: China's Turning Point, 1924–25* (Cambridge: Cambridge University Press, 1995)

Wang Ke-wen, *After the United Front: Wang Jingwei and the Left Kuomintang* (Republican China, April 1993)

——, *The Kuomintang in Transition* (Dissertation, Stanford University, 1985)

Wasserstein, Bernard, *Secret Wars in Shanghai* (London: Profile Books, 1998)

Wasserstrom, Jeffrey (ed.), *Twentieth Century China* (London: Routledge, 2003)

Wedemeyer, Albert, *Wedemeyer Reports* (New York: Henry Holt, 1958)

Wei, C. X. George, and Liu, Xiaoyuan, *Chinese Nationalism in Perspective* (Westport: Greenwood Press, 2001)

Wells, Audrey, *The Political Thought of Sun Yat-sen* (Houndsmill: Palgrave Macmillan, 2001)

Westad, Odd Arne, *Cold War and Revolution* (New York: Columbia University Press, 1993)

White, Theodore, *In Search of History* (London: Jonathan Cape, 1978)

——, and Jacoby, Annalee, *Thunder Out of China* (New York: Da Capo Press, 1980)

Whitson, William, *The Chinese High Command* (London: Macmillan, 1973)

Who's Who in China (Shanghai, 1931)

Who's Who in China, 1918–50 (Hong Kong: Chinese Materials Centre, 1982)

Wilbur, C. Martin, *Sun Yat-sen: Frustrated Patriot* (New York: Columbia University Press, 1976)

——, *The Nationalist Revolution in China* (Cambridge: Cambridge University Press, 1983)

——, and How, Julie Lien-ying, *Missionaries of Revolution* (Cambridge, MA: Harvard University Press, 1989)

Williams, Peter, and Wallace, David, *Unit 731* (London: Hodder & Stoughton, 1989)

Wilson, Dick, *The Long March* (Harmondsworth: Penguin, 1971)

——, *When Tigers Fall Out* (London: Hutchinson, 1982)

Wilson, Sandra, *The Manchurian Crisis and Japanese Society* (London: Routledge, 2002)

Wong, R. Bin, 'Studying Republican China's Economy' (*Republican China*, November 1992)

Wong Young-tsu, *The Xi'an Incident and the Coming of the War of Resistance*, in Barrett and Shyu (q.v.)

Wou, Odoric, *Militarism in Modern China: Wu Peifu, 1916–39* (Canberra: Australian National University Press, 1978)

Wu Chi-wei, David, *A Historical Analysis of Selected Speeches by Generalissimo Chiang Kai-shek During the War of Resistance against Japanese Aggression, 1937–45* (Dissertation presented to Ohio University, 1986)

Wu Tien-wei, *The Sian Incident* (University of Michigan Papers in Chinese Studies, 1976)

Wylie, Raymond F., *The Emergence of Maoism* (Stanford: Stanford University Press, 1980)

Yamamoto, Masahiro, *Nanking: Anatomy of an Atrocity* (Westport; Praeger, 2000)

Yang Tianshi, 'The Hidden Story of the Zhongshan Gunboat Incident' (*Republican China*, April 1991)

Yeh Wen-hsui (ed.), *Becoming Chinese* (Berkeley: University of California Press, 2000)

Yongnian Zheng, *Discovering Chinese Nationalism in China* (Cambridge: CUP, 1999)

Young, Arthur, Oral History in Truman Library

——, *The Helping Hand, 1937–45* (Cambridge, MA: Harvard University Press, 1963)

——, *China's Wartime Finance and Inflation* (Cambridge, MA: Harvard University Press, 1965)

Young, Ernest P., *The Presidency of Yuan Shih-k'ai* (Ann Arbor: University of Michigan Press, 1977)

Yu Maochun, *OSS in China* (New Haven: Yale University Press, 1996)

Yu Min-ling, 'A Reassessment of Chiang Kai-shek and the Policy of Alliance with the Soviet Union' in Leutner (ed.), *The Chinese Revolution in the 1920s* (London: Curzon Press, 2002)

Zheng Chaolin, *An Oppositionist for Life* (trans. Gregor Benton) (Highlands, NJ: Humanities Press, 1997)

INDEX